Fred Sulok
210 Teri St.
South Bend, Ind. 46614
291-6006

D1450923

Law and the Changing Environment

THE HISTORY AND PROCESSES OF LAW

Law and the

Changing Environment

THE HISTORY AND PROCESSES OF LAW

Leland Hazard

CARNEGIE-MELLON UNIVERSITY

HOLDEN-DAY

San Francisco

First Printing June, 1971

Second Printing December, 1971

ISBN 0-8162-3706-9

Library of Congress Catalog Card No. 70-140784

Printed in the United States of America
34567890 MP 79876543

Foreword

Leland Hazard can truly be called a statesman of our society. He has had significant careers in law, in business, and in academia. It has been my personal pleasure to have been his colleague for the past twelve years at the Graduate School at Carnegie-Mellon University.

Professor Hazard's book gives the student of management the kind of broad law background he needs to successfully carry out his function as a citizen and as a manager. It is not designed to give the reader a series of rules to memorize in order to function as a lawyer-manager. Rather, it is a lively presentation, full of dramatic case examples, showing the evolution of the law as a dynamic force, changing — and being changed by — its environment. In addition to this broad view, the student is given enough technical understanding to enable him as a manager to deal effectively with professional lawyers. Further, he will be stimulated and equipped to explore particular aspects of the law not covered in this book.

With the growing complexity of organization and the increased interaction between the private and public sectors, the role of the law takes on expanded significance. A course built around the law is a vital requirement in the modern management curriculum. The student will find some aspects, such as labor-management issues, specifically relevant to his decision making. Other areas of the law, such as questions concerning civil rights, are crucial for him to understand if he is to deal effectively with his environment.

In today's world the legal aspects of many social questions, from pollution to privacy, are being aired in popular magazines. No longer is law seen to be the exclusive concern of the lawyers. It is so interwoven in everyday life that a broad understanding of its origins and evolution is essential to everyone. Clearly, *Law and the Changing Environment* is not only valid for the student of industrial management but also is important reading for any citizen of an industrial society.

Richard M. Cyert

Dean, Graduate School of Industrial Administration
Carnegie-Mellon University

Preface

If a little knowledge is dangerous, where is the man who has so much as to be out of danger? This question, proposed by Thomas Henry Huxley in 1877 in a treatise on *Elemental Instructions in Psychology,* is timeless. It has arisen in many forms, but perhaps one of the most poignant is that, since no one may have all knowledge, is any knowledge worthwhile? The practical answer to the need for all knowledge lies in the work of such men as Aristotle, Thomas Aquinas, the French Encyclopedists under Diderot, or in the efforts of the makers of any encyclopedia.

The counterparts of those who would produce compendia of all knowledge can be found in any branch of learning—medicine, law, engineering, or the natural and social sciences. Such efforts to encompass the universe of particular knowledge are as persistent as the efforts to produce distillations. After centuries of assuming that all but a few men must be ignorant, we burst into the twentieth century with the assumption that all men can be literate—and quickly realized that we must employ the outline, the synthesis, the extraction, and the interpretation to impart some portions of the accumulated wisdom of mankind.

Just as the quest for all knowledge is vain, so is the aphorism, "A little knowledge is a dangerous thing," false. A little knowledge is *not* as dangerous as exultation and pride in ignorance. A substantial number of people, particularly an increasing number of young men and women, are students—not only in the academic sense, but also in the sense of pursuing knowledge as the spice of life. In this pursuit law takes a high priority. Law touches people in daily life and is understandable by millions in a way that nuclear fission may never be. It was said that in the early twentieth century only 12 men in the world could comprehend Einstein's general or special theories of relativity. But there *is* no need for a general understanding of the theory that produced the atomic bomb as there *is* a need for the understanding of law. Indeed, an understanding of law is more likely to produce a consensus of what to do or what not to do with the atomic bomb than would an understanding of how the bomb was created.

The title of this book, *Law and the Changing Environment,* predicts its flavor. Law is an aspect of the environment. Law may make the environment, and equally important, the environment may make law. This is a book for readers who want to know what law is like because they want to know what modulates human activity. It is a book for students who do not intend to become lawyers but who do want a basic understanding of the law. The method of learning employed in this book is that of illustration through exposition. Precepts and propositions are clearly elucidated, but then we continue to say, "for example . . ." An example is always more lively than a precept. That truism is explicated in the cases.

This book is not about how to be one's own lawyer. If it were, it would, indeed, justify the cliche, "A little knowledge is a dangerous thing." It is not a book about how to make a will, how to deal with one's landlord, how to read an insurance policy, or how one may do-it-for-himself in any area of human involvement. This book is not a manual. There are books of that sort—very good ones—that may do some harm if they are taken too seriously. This book is not about how a business executive may run his business without a lawyer, nor is it about how a housewife may deal with a fraudulent seller of merchandise. This is not a book in which a reader will learn formulas that can be applied in the way that, for example, the mathematical formula for ascertaining the number of square feet in a circle can be applied. This is a book through which a business student or a concerned mother may better understand the role of law when the distemper of disturbance besets the times—thereby permitting a more equanimous understanding of the events of the day.

The book preserves a forward thrust, uninterrupted by educational methodology. On the other hand, the reader is not left without guidance with respect to the cases, that is, the examples. Some of the cases are introduced with prefatory notes; others are followed by expository commentaries. The author does not hesitate to predict where prediction seems appropriate. At the end of each chapter questions are posed that will be helpful to the teacher and of optional interest to the general reader.

Chapter 1 exemplifies the survey form of exposition about the origins and the continuum of law, called "the long thread;" Chapter 2 elucidates the limits of judging; Chapter 3 deals with the law's tenderness toward accused persons; Chapter 4 presents the law's concern for the keeping of promises; Chapter 5 details the law's preoccupation with consistency and the impact of economics and technology upon consistency; Chapter 6 concerns the *inadequacy* of a natural sense of justice; Chapter 7 describes the law and social conflict, particularly in labor; Chapter 8 encompasses the law and dissonant minorities; and Chapter 9 compares the law with fallible human beings and institutions. The teacher will look at these chapters as (1) legal history; (2) jurisdiction and justiciability; (3) criminal law; (4) contract law; (5) manufacturers' liability; (6) legal philosophy; (7) labor law; (8) the limits of dissent; and (9) authentic courtroom scenes.

Although this book moves sequentially from the beginnings of law to the climax of all law, the fair trial, it may be read or taught in chapters and combinations of chapters, each of which is self-sufficient for its subject. The content and arrangement are based upon the author's experience in teaching upperclassmen and graduate students at Carnegie-Mellon University, where the materials have been equally interesting to students of engineering, the physical or social sciences, drama, architecture, or the arts. Law cuts through every discipline. If the reader's interest is intellectual, the book will frequently satisfy a proper curiosity. If the reader's interest is practical, he had best consult a lawyer.

April, 1971   *Leland Hazard*

Acknowledgments

This book reflects, in substantial measure, the research assistance of Paul M. Singer. Fortunately, he was interested in devoting to this work a year of his life immediately after graduation from the University of Pittsburgh Law School. His experience as an editor of the Law Review of that school was of great value. Also of prime importance was his recent association with students in that period of the middle and late 1960s in which students were critically appraising course content and disciplinary norms. He bridged the generation gap for me—if there was a gap.

This book has been constructed with great deliberation. There have been innumerable "bull sessions," as the phrase goes among students, between Paul Singer and me. We have not always agreed, but in such cases I have assumed the responsibility. The text is all mine, but the research and the preliminary editing of the cases essential to implement my concepts have been the work of my respected and valued associate, Paul M. Singer.

In the final stages of manuscript preparation the cases were "Shephard-ized" by Leonard I. Wanetik, who also combined all sources for both case and legislative developments that would update the book to early September 1970.

For the final, severe editing of the cases—in order to produce a book of felicitous length—and for all closing additions to commentary treatment of developments just prior to press time, I am personally responsible.

Paul M. Singer, after his return from the Harvard Law School where he received the Master of Laws degree, supervised the conversion from manuscript to final printing.

I am indebted to Richard M. Cyert, Dean of the Graduate School of Industrial Administration, Carnegie-Mellon University, for encouraging me to make this book a product of my teaching in that school and for making available to me not only the services of Paul M. Singer but also those of my editorial assistant, Grace S. Couchman.

No book can be written without those Martha-like attentions which tell the author that an intelligent person is watching over his shoulder. The discovery of mistakes, the appreciation of niceties, the burdens of minutiae would have frustrated me except for the high competence and responsibility with which Mrs. Couchman attended the project.

I acknowledge the important assistance of Sharon Kulpa, the copy editor assigned to my book by Holden-Day, Inc. Happily, I could agree with the majority of her suggestions, effectively communicated at long range between San Francisco and Pittsburgh. She has often tightened my writing. Occasionally, I have disagreed with her and have insisted upon my more flamboyant style.

To my wife, Mary, I acknowledge the greatest debt of all because it is of the longest standing. In a quarter of a century of writings, none has ever been released which did not go through the fine sieve of her understanding of grammar, diction, and content. Much more than the usual genuflection to a wife's patience is due to her.

Permissions to Reprint
from Other Sources

Grateful acknowledgment is made to the following for permission to reprint copyright material:

Adler, Mortimer J., *A Syntopicon of Great Books of the Western World,* Encyclopedia Britannica, Inc., Chicago, 1952.

Andrae, Tor, *Mohammed: The Man and His Faith,* Harper & Row, Publishers, Inc., New York, 1960.

Berle, Adolf A., Jr., *The Twentieth Century Capitalist Revolution,* Harcourt Brace Jovanovich, Inc., New York, 1954.

Bowen, Catherine Drinker, *The Lion and The Throne,* Little, Brown and Company, Boston, 1957.

Brecht, Bertolt, "The Threepenny Opera," *From the Modern Repertoire,* Series One, edited by Eric Bentley, and translated by Desmond Vesey and Eric Bentley, Copyright © 1949 by Eric Bentley. Reprinted by permission of Indiana University Press.

Cozzens, James Gould, *The Just and the Unjust,* Harcourt Brace Jovanovich, Inc., New York, 1942, 1970.

Devlin, Sir Patrick, *Trial by Jury,* Stevens & Sons, Limited, London, 1956.

Fitts, Dudley and Robert Fitzgerald (eds.), *Sophocles: The Oedipus Cycle,* Harcourt Brace Jovanovich, Inc., New York, 1939, 1941, 1949.

Folsom, Victor C., "Toward a Rule of Reason in the Extraterritorial Application of the Antitrust Laws," *Problems and Solutions,* Matthew Bender & Company, Inc., New York, 1967.

Freud, Sigmund, *Civilization and Its Discontents,* Encyclopedia Britannica, Inc., Chicago, 1961.

Holmes, Oliver Wendell, Jr., *The Common Law,* Little, Brown and Company, Boston, 1909, 1923.

Joiner, Charles W., *Civil Justice and the Jury,* Prentice-Hall, Inc., Englewood Cliffs, 1962.

Klapper, Joseph T., "Effects of Mass Communication," *Public Opinion Quarterly XXI* (Winter 1957-58), Columbia University, New York.

Larson, John A., *Lying and Its Detection,* The University of Chicago Press, Chicago, 1932.

Lofton, John, *Justice and the Press,* Beacon Press, Inc., Boston, 1966.

Maine, Henry Sumner, *Ancient Law,* Everyman's Library Edition. Published by E. P. Dutton & Company, Inc., New York, 1917.

Mann, Thomas, *The Tables of the Law,* Armin L. Robinson and Alfred A. Knopf, Inc., New York, 1945.

Menninger, Karl, *The Crime of Punishment,* The Viking Press, New York, 1966.

Münsterberg, Hugo, *On the Witness Stand,* Doubleday Company, New York, 1923.

Niebuhr, Reinhold, *The Structure of Nations and Empire,* Charles Scribner's Sons, New York, 1959.

O'Connor, Harvey, *Steel Dictator,* The John Day Company, New York, 1935.

Pollock, Sir Frederick and Frederic William Maitland, *The History of English Law,* Cambridge University Press, New York, 1952.

Pound, Roscoe, *An Introduction to the Philosophy of Law,* Yale University Press, New Haven, 1954.

Wellman, Francis L., *The Art of Cross-Examination,* The Macmillan Company, New York, 1924.

Woodward, W. E., *A New American History,* Holt, Rinehart and Winston, Inc., New York, 1936.

Statement of Format

In each of the cases cited in this book the author has followed the official report, excerpting only the portions thereof deemed essential to the purposes for which the case was selected. Omissions from court opinions are indicated by a series of dots. The author's additions are enclosed in brackets.

The court's footnotes to the text of the cases, when included, are identified by consecutive capital letters within each section.

The author's footnotes are numbered sequentially within each section.

he author has where necessary excerpted portions of United States Constitution. However, it is advisa- at the reader have this document at hand to aid nderstanding of the text.

Table of Cases

References are to page numbers. References to principal cases are in italic type. References to cases cited or discussed are in Roman type. Criminal cases are indexed by the name of the defendant.

Abel v. United States, 94, 389
Ablett, Charles R., Co. v. Sencer, 157
Adamowski v. Curtiss-Wright Flying Service, Inc., 138
Adderly v. Florida, 369
Alexander v. Holmes County Board of Education, 62
Ash v. Childs Dining Hall Co., 200

Baker v. Carr
   Supreme Court of the United States, 31, *63,* 77, 78, 384
   District Court, Middle District of Tennessee, 69
Baldwin v. New York, 409
Balfour v Balfour, 141
Ballou v. Massachusetts, 111
Bennett v. Moon, 185
Board of Education of the City of New York v. Shanker I, 326
Board of Education of the City of New York v. Shanker II, 328
Bond v. Floyd, 358
Bonham's Case, 26, 398
Boys Markets, Inc. v. Retail Clerks Union, Local 770, 333
Bradshaw v. Millikin, 189
Brewington v. Lowe, 33, 37, 61
Britton v. Turner, 170
Brockington v. Rhodes, 49
Brown v. Board of Education I, 31, 58, 77, 384
Brown v. Board of Education II, 62
Bullock v. Harwick, 144
Bushell's Case, 399

Camara v. Municipal Court, 96
Campbell Soup Co. v. Wentz, 185
Chambers v. Moroney, 94
Charles R. Ablett Co. v. Sencer, 157
Chimel v. California, 87, 389
Cintrone v. Hertz Truck Leasing, 247
City of New York v. DeLury, 330
Clydebank Engineering and Shipbuilding Company, Limited, v. Don Jose Ramos Yzquierdo y Castaneda, 172
Cohen v. United States, 123
Coleman v. Alabama, 123
Congress of Industrial Organizations v. Dallas, 320
Cordle v. Renault, Inc., 247
Corkey v. Edwards, 58
Cotnam v. Wisdom, 192
Cowen v. Pressprich, 262
Cox v. Louisiana, 369
Culkin; People ex rel. Karlin v., 422

Dellinger; United States v., 435
Davis v. Mississippi, 124
Devlin v. Smith, 212
Doe v. Scott, 58
Donaldson; State v., 290
Duncan v. Louisiana, 407
Duncan's Estate; In re, 154

Eccles v. Peoples Bank of Lakewood Village, California, 46, 51

Elmore v. American Motors Corporation, 240

Embola v. Tuppela, 148

Escola v. Coca Cola Bottling Co. of Fresno, 223

Fisher v. Taylor Motor Company, Inc. 138

Friend v. Childs Dining Hall Co., 201

G. Loewus and Co. v. Vischia, 150

Garner v. Teamsters, Chauffeurs and Helpers Local Union No. 776, 299

Gideon v. Wainwright, 127, 408

Gillette; United States v., 377, 383

Giordano v. United States, 282

Goodman v. Dicker, 191

Grand Lodge, International Assn. of Machinists v. King, 347

Greenman v. Yuba Power Products, Inc., 235

Hadley v. Baxendale, 162

Hall v. Butterfield, 138

Hamer v. Sidway, 146

Harrington v. Taylor, 148

Harris v. New York, 123

Henningsen v. Bloomfield Motors, Inc. and Chrysler Corporation, 227

Highway Truck Drivers and Helpers, Local 107 v. Cohen, 348

Hitchman Coal and Coke Company v. Mitchell, 276, *293*

Hochberg v. O'Donnell's Rest., Inc., 249

Hoffa; United States v.
    E.D. Tenn., S.D., 282
    6th Circuit Court of Appeals, 282, 413
    7th Circuit Court of Appeals, 282

Hotchkiss v. National City Bank of New York, 141

Hunt; Commonwealth v., 286

Hurley v. Woodsides, 156

Illinois v. Allen, 435

International Brotherhood of Teamsters, etc. Union Local 309 v. Hanke, 311

Johnson v. New Jersey, 127, 128

Kassab v. Central Soya, 243

Katz v. United States, 98, 389

Kirkpatrick v. Preisler, 69

Krauss v. Greenbarg, 164

Kridler v. Ford Motor Company, 247, 253

Kriegler v. Eichler Homes, 252

Krumsky v. Loesser, 261

Lefkowitz v. Great Minneapolis Surplus Store, 142

Linkletter v. Walker, 128

Local 357, International Brotherhood of Teamsters v. National Labor Relations Board, 280

Loewus and Co. v. Vischia, 150

Loomis v. Imperial Motors, Inc., 137

Loop v. Litchfield, 209

Losee v. Clute, 210

Lucy v. Zehmer, 138

MacDougall v. Ford Motor Co., 247, 253

MacPherson v. Buick Motor Co., 217

McAuliffe v. Mayor of New Bedford, 320

McBoyle v. United States, 86

Manton; United States v., 425

Marbury v. Madison, 79

218-220 Market Street Corp. v. Krich-Radisco, Inc., 176

Massachusetts v. Laird, 79

Mathis v. United States, 123

Miranda v. Arizona, 113, 389

Mora v. McNamara, 70, 78, 357

Morris v. Sparrow, 185

Morse v. Kenney, 194

Muse v. United States, 123

Muskrat v. United States, 41, 50-51

National Labor Relations Board v. Jones and Laughlin Steel Corp., 276, 296, 298

National Woodwork Manufacturers Association v. National Labor Relations Board, 314

Newsome v. Western Union Telegraph Co., 166

New York City Transit Authority v. Quill, 320

North Carolina State Board of Education v. Swann, 62

O'Brien; United States v., 361
Ohio v. Lafferty, 83
Oliver, In re, 400
Opinion of the Justices, 44, 50, 62
Orozco v. Texas, 123

Parrish v. Civil Service Commission of County of Alameda, 97
People ex rel. Karlin v. Culkin, 422
Philadelphia Ball Club v. Lajoie, 188
Pickelsimer v. Wainwright, 128
Pierce v. Society of Sisters, 55
Porter v. Wilson, 138
Powe; People v., 123
Powell v. McCormack, 72
Pullis; Commonwealth v., 283

Raffles v. Wichelhaus, 152
Reed v. Maley, 51, 52, 53
Reliance Cooperage Corp. v. Treat, 178, 181-82
Retail Clerks International Association, Local 1625 AFL-CIO v. Schermerhorn, 301
Richtmyer v. Mutual Live Stock Commission Company, 259
Rockingham County v. Luten Bridge Co., 177
Rosman v. Cuevas, 136

Salzhandler v. Caputo, 279
Schechter Poultry Corp. v. United States, 296
Schipper v. Levitt and Sons, Inc., 252
Schofield v. National Labor Relations Board, 279
Security Stove and Mfg. Co. v. American Ry. Express Co., 167

Sen v. Tile Layers Protective Association, 304
Sheppard v. Maxwell, 429
Sisson; United States v.
  District Court of Massachusetts, 371
  Supreme Court of the United States, 383, 384
Smith v. State, 85
Stephens v. Myers, 52, 53, 54
Stovall v. Denno, 127

Tehan v. United States ex rel. Shott, 128
Terry v. Ohio, 104, 125-126, 389
Thomas and Wife v. Winchester, 206, 252
Thornhill v. Alabama, 308
Tileston v. Ullman, 56
Tinker v. Des Moines Independent Community School District, 365
Torgesen v. Schultz, 215
Trial of William Penn and William Mead for Causing a Tumult, 399

United Mine Workers of America v. Red Jacket Consolidated Coal and Coke Company, 276

Vale v. Louisiana, 130
Vandermark v. Ford Motor Company, 237
Vegelahn v. Guntner, 290
Vuitch; United States v., 58

Watts v. United States, 377
Weinstein v. New York City Transit Authority, 322
Welsh v. United States, 377, 383
Wooden-Ware Company v. United States, 257
Worcester v. Georgia, 79
Wyman v. James, 97
Wyman v. Newhouse, 31, 38, 41

Table of Contents

Foreword v

Preface vii

Acknowledgments xi

Permissions to Reprint From Other Sources xiii

Statement of Format xv

Table of Cases xvi

1 In the Beginning Was the Word 1

Time, Place, and Law 2
Agriculture and Legal Growth 2
Language, Organization, and Technology 3
Planning and Law 4
Empire and Law 5
Three Types of Society 6
Law as a Molder of Society 7
Earthly Models for Divine Commands 8
Shipwreck, Money, and Law 9
Law as a Continuum 10
Law Is Not Self-Enforcing 11
The Role of Ritual in Procedure 12
The Role of the Fiction 13
Trade and Commerce Brought Equity 14
Legislation 16
Growth and Stagnation in Law 16
Law Outlasts Empire 17
A Fragmented Society and Law 18
Origins of English Law 19
Roman Law Did Not Die 20
Why English Law Is Special 21

Roman Components in English Law 22
The Long Thread 23
Uneven Development of Civilizations 24
What We Owe to Coke 25
References 27

2 *Law Limits Judging* 29

Introduction to Courts 29
Jurisdiction 31
    Wyman v. Newhouse 31
    Brewington v. Lowe 33
    Jurisdiction—Territorial, Personal, and Substantive 34
    Territorial Jurisdiction 34
    Personal Jurisdiction 37
    Substantive Jurisdiction 40
Justiciability 41
    Case or Controversy—The Kinds of Cases Courts Will Decide 41
    Criteria: Nature and Circumstances 41
    Muskrat v. United States 41
    Opinion of the Justices 44
    Eccles v. Peoples Bank of Lakewood Village, California 46
    The Autonomy of Courts 49
    Cases or Controversies of Trival Subject Matter 51
    Reed v. Maley 51
    Stephens v. Myers 52
    Causes of Action 53
    Standing—Parties Must Have a Real Interest 55
    Pierce v. Society of Sisters 55
    Tileston v. Ullman 56
    Growing Concepts of Justiciability 58
    Brown v. Board of Education 58
    Preface to Baker v. Carr 61
    Baker v. Carr 63
    Commentary on Baker v. Carr 68
    Mora v. McNamara 70
    Powell v. McCormack 72
Rulership 76
Questions 80

3 *Law Is Tender Toward Accused Persons* 81

Introduction 81
Needs of the State and Rights of the Citizen 83
    The Requirements of a Law Strictly Defining the Crime 83

   Ohio v. Lafferty 83

   McBoyle v. United States 86

  Significant Issues of Search and Seizure. 87

   Extent of Criminal Searches 87

    Chimel v. California. 87

   Administrative Searches 94

   Electronic Searches 98

    Katz v. United States 98

   Stop and Frisk. 104

   Terry v. Ohio 104

    Ballou v. Massachusetts 111

  Development of the Rights of Accused Persons. 111

  Expanding Applications of the Bill of Rights. 111

   Miranda v. Arizona 113

   People v. Powe 123

   Davis v. Mississippi 124

 Law and Liberty. 124

 Questions 131

4 *Law Makes the Promise Good* .132

 Introduction. 133

 Formation of Contracts—Essentials of the Agreement. 136

  Capacity to Contract 136

   Rosman v. Cuevas 136

  Intent to Contract 138

   Lucy v. Zenmer 138

   Balfour v. Balfour 141

  Examples of Offer and Acceptance 142

   Offer 142

   Lefkowitz v. Great Minneapolis Surplus Store 142

   Acceptance. 144

   Bullock v. Harwick 144

   Restatement of the Law of Contracts—Offer and Acceptance

   Defined. 146

  Examples of Consideration. 146

  Definition of Consideration 146

   Hamer v. Sidway 146

   Harrington v. Taylor. 148

   Embola v. Tuppela. 148

   Restatement of the Law of Contracts—Consideration Defined 149

  Mutuality of Obligation 150

   G. Loewus & Co. v. Vischia. 150

  Subject Matter 152

  Identity of Agreement 152

   Raffles v. Wichelhaus 152

Restatement of the Law of Contracts—Undisclosed
   Misunderstandings 153
Legality of Subject Matter 154
In re Duncan's Estate 154
Statute of Frauds 156
Hurley v. Woodsides 156
Charles R. Ablett Co. v. Sencer 157
Statute of Frauds—Original English Statute 159
Remedies for Breach of Contract—Society and the Broken Promise. 160
Remedies at Law. 162
Damages and the Expectation Interest 162
Hadley v. Baxendale 162
Krauss v. Greenbarg. 164
Newsome v. Western Union Telegraph Co. 166
Damages and the Reliance Interest. 167
Security Stove & Mfg. Co. v. American Ry. Express Co. 167
Damages and the Restitution Interest 170
Britton v. Turner 170
Other Considerations in Awarding Damages 172
Liquidated Damages and Penalties. 172
Clydebank Engineering and Shipbuilding Co., Ltd. v.
   Don Jose Yzquierdo y Castaneda 172
218-220 Market Street v. Krich-Radisco, Inc. 176
Mitigation of Damages. 177
Rockingham County v. Luten Bridge Co. 177
Reliance Cooperage Corp. v. Treat. 178
Commentary on Reliance Cooperage v. Treat 181
Remedies in Equity 183
Specific Performance 183
Bennett v. Moon. 183
Morris v. Sparrow. 185
Campbell Soup Co. v. Wentz 185
Injunctions 188
Philadelphia Ball Club v. Lajoie 188
Bradshaw v. Millikin 189
Remedies by Analogy to Contract 190
Recovery by Promissory Estoppel 191
Goodman v. Dicker 191
Recovery in Quasi Contract. 192
Cotnam v. Wisdom 192
Morse v. Kenney 194
Questions 197

5 *Law Clings to Consistency But Grows*. 198

Introduction 198

Torts and Contracts Distinguished.................................200
  Ash v. Childs Dining Hall Co........................200
  Friend v. Childs Dining Hall Co....................201
  A Lawyer Is Sometimes Needed...............................204
The Rise and Fall of a Legal Concept 206
  Thomas and Wife v. Winchester 206
  Loop v. Litchfield 209
  Losee v. Clute 210
  Devlin v. Smith 212
  Torgesen v. Schultz 215
  MacPherson v. Buick Motor Company 217
Consistency Is Not Always a Virtue...........................220
An Emerging Concept of Manufacturer's Liability 223
  Escola v. Coca Cola Bottling Company of Fresno.............223
  Henningsen v. Bloomfield Motors, Inc. 227
  Greenman v. Yuba Power Products, Inc...............235
  Vandermark v. Ford Motor Company 237
  Elmore v. American Motors Corporation.............240
  Kassab v. Central Soya 243
A New Day Needs a New Theory 247
Questions 253

6 Law Must Sometimes Embrace Expediency........255

Introduction 255
Cases Involving Innocent Victims 257
  Rights and Liabilities of Victims of Theft.................257
    Wooden-Ware Co. v. United States 257
    Richtmyer v. Mutual Live Stock Commission Company 259
  Rights and Liabilities of Victims of Swindle or Mistake.............261
    Krumsky v. Loeser...............................261
    Cowen v. Pressprich 262
Questions 269

7 Law of the Cases and Legislation Vie in Social Conflict 270

Introduction..271
Unionism and Case Law......................................283
  Labor Organization and Crime 283
    Commonwealth v. Pullis (Philadelphia Cordwainers' Case
      of 1806).....................................283
    Commonwealth v. Hunt 286
  Labor Organization and Tort 280
    Vegelahn v. Guntner 290

Labor Organization and Contract 293
   Hitchman Coal and Coke Company v. Mitchell................ 293
Summary of Major Labor Legislation 1914-1964.................... 295
Federal Versus State Jurisdiction Over Labor Disputes................ 298
  Federal Power—The Commerce Clause 298
  Examples of Federal Preemption.............................. 299
   Garner v. Teamsters, Local 776........................... 299
   Retail Clerks International Assn. v. Schermerhorn 301
Union Tactics and Federal-State Policies......................... 304
   Senn v. Tile Layers Protective Union....................... 304
   Thornhill v. Alabama 308
   International Brotherhood of Teamsters, Local 309 v. Hanke...... 311
Unionism and the Whole Society 314
  Unresolved Limits on Union Power........................... 314
   National Woodwork Manufacturers Association v.
    National Labor Relations Board 314
  Unresolved Limits on Public Power 317
   The Problem.. 317
   The Federal Situation 319
   Executive Order 10988—Employee-Management Cooperation
    in the Federal Service................................. 319
   The State Situation...................................... 319
   New York Anti-Strike Law (Condon-Wadlin Act)............. 320
   New York City Transit Authority v. Quill.................... 320
   Weinstein v. New York City Transit Authority................ 322
   Amnesty Act for Transit Workers........................... 323
   New York Public Employees Fair Employment Act (Taylor Law). 324
   Board of Education v. Shanker (injunction) 326
   Board of Education v. Shanker (contempt) 328
   City of New York v. De Lury 330
   Amendments to Taylor Law 332
Labor and Musical Chairs....................................... 332
Questions 336
Appendix—Statutory Material 337
   Clayton Act 337
   Norris-LaGuardia Act 337
   National Labor Relations Act (Wagner Act)................. 339
   Labor Management Relations Act (Taft-Hartley Act) 339
   Labor Management Reporting and Disclosure Act (Landrum-
    Griffin Act) 345
   Civil Rights Act of 1964................................. 351
   Employee-Management Cooperation in the Federal Service....... 352

8 Law is Ever and Anon Burdened with Dissent...... 355

Introduction... 355

Concerning Speech, Action, and War............................358
   Bond v. Floyd...358
   United States v. O'Brien 361
   Tinker v. Des Moines Independent Community School District......365
   United States v. Sisson 371
   Watts v. United States 377
Law and the World: What Price the Individual?....................380
Questions 385

9   Law is Meted Out Through Human Institutions.....386

Introduction...386
   Criminal Procedure 388
   Civil Procedure 391
The Trial 395
   The Judge 395
      A Note on The Trial of William Penn.......................399
         Bushell's Case 399
         In re Oliver 400
   The Jury 403
      Duncan v. Louisiana 407
   The Witness 408
   The Lawyer 413
      The Art of Cross Examination 413
      A Perjurer Unmasked by Lincoln 413
      A Sham Expert Pilloried by Wellman 415
      Lying—With or Without Motive.........................416
      Substitutes for Human Testimony.........................417
      Conviction of the Innocent...............................418
Justice and Professional Discipline..............................419
   Of the Lawyer...419
      People ex rel. Karlin v. Culkin 422
   Of the Judge 424
   Of the Media 426
      Sheppard v. Maxwell 429
      The Right of Fair Trial and Free Press......................434
   Questions 436

Epilogue—A Note on the Unique Tenth Commandment..438

Index 443

1   *In the Beginning Was the Word*

Time, Place, and Law 2
Agriculture and Legal Growth. 2
Language, Organization, and Technology. 3
Planning and Law. 4
Empire and Law 5
Three Types of Society 6
Law as a Molder of Society 7
Earthly Models for Divine Commands 8
Shipwreck, Money, and Law. 9
Law as a Continuum 10
Law Is Not Self-Enforcing 11
The Role of Ritual in Procedure 12
The Role of the Fiction 13
Trade and Commerce Brought Equity 14
Legislation. 16
Growth and Stagnation in Law 16
Law Outlasts Empire 17
A Fragmented Society and Law. 18
Origins of English Law. 19
Roman Law Did Not Die 20
Why English Law Is Special. 21
Roman Components in English Law 22
The Long Thread 23
The Uneven Development of Civilizations 24
What We Owe to Coke. 25
References 27

This is a book about law for human beings—after we had language. As the title of this chapter suggests, the law with which we shall deal involves words. Indeed, law is literally compounded of words.

There are some kinds of laws that are *not* made of words, such as Newton's law of gravitation or Einstein's special and general theories of relativity. One may talk *about* such laws, but they are best expressed mathematically. There are other laws without words, such as the law of the jungle, which may mean no law, or a rule of constant precaution (by man or beast), or a rule of territoriality under which a group of animals claim a jealously guarded territory for living among themselves. Unwritten rules and taboos (laws) existed among men before language evolved. For example, the complex rule against incest in primitive societies was one of the primordial and pervasive prohibitions by which, perhaps, society itself was formed.

TIME, PLACE, AND LAW

From the title of this section, *In the Beginning Was The Word*, which are the opening words of the Gospel according to St. John, the reader realizes that we are concerned with Western civilization. This concern with our Western Christian law is not because it is Western or Christian, or because we could not profitably study Egyptian or Chinese law (ancient or modern). Rather, our civilization, with its origins in Hebrew, Greek, and Roman cultures, was spread throughout Western Europe and the Americas by the driving power of Christianity. We confine ourselves, therefore, to Western law because law must exist with respect to a given civilization. For example, Russia was a society primarily in the Western tradition until the Bolshevik Revolution of 1917. Its laws of private property were not unlike ours, but those laws are no longer invariably appropriate to a communist society. Now, there are new Soviet laws just as applicable to communism as our Western laws are applicable to capitalism. Law, therefore, is a matter of time, place, and social purpose.

It is essential to remember that all civilizations are very recent—even in the life of man himself. The earth is at least 5–6 billion years old, and life on earth has existed continuously for 3–4 billion years. Of the various species that developed, only some remain, while many others have become extinct. Men, as distinguished from evolving apes, have been on the earth at least 600 thousand years; perhaps much longer. For most of that time, man was a predatory hunter, who foraged alone or in packs for the food (vegetable and animal) that he could find, collect, or subdue. Agriculture, and with it the birth of Western law, came only 10–11 thousand years ago.

AGRICULTURE AND LEGAL GROWTH

Except for the discovery of fire, agriculture was the most far-reaching technological change of the past, and the one upon which all civilizations are based.

Until agriculture, man lived by hand (and foot) to mouth and had no leisure or settled place for creative and innovative work and thought. Mrs. Peachum puts it well in "The Threepenny Opera,"[1]

> Whatever you may do, wherever you aspire,
> First feed the face, and then talk right and wrong
> For even the saintliest folks may act like sinners
> Unless they've had their customary dinners.

After the development of agriculture the complexities of man's life multiplied: settled communities; works of irrigation, such as the vast projects in the Valley of the Nile; organizations for building structures like the pyramids. In other words, after agriculture—actually quite late in the life of man—came civilization: cities, travel, trade, sailing, wars, engineering, astronomy, words, and law. Perhaps the best way to realize the recency of all civilizations is to note that the alphabet we use developed as late as about 1000 B.C.; hence the alphabet has existed for much less than one percent of man's life on earth. (Pictorial writing is somewhat older, as early as 3000 B.C. in Egypt, but not enough older to matter for our present purposes.)

LANGUAGE, ORGANIZATION, AND TECHNOLOGY

Language was, and is, a function of the organization of men for doing more than could be done by the two hands of a single man. Before history, that is, before written words, only artifacts tell what man did with the leisure that ensued from the development of agriculture. He rearranged nature and still does. The ancient and ubiquitous dolmens—in their simplest form, two or more unhewn but manually erected monoliths supporting a ten- or twelve-man capstone—tell the story. Their purpose is not certain, perhaps for marking some event, for worship, or for burial. But, they represent rearrangement of things found in nature. To put them up *did* require organization—several men working together at the command or direction of one man. Ten or twelve men lifting in sequence could not have raised the capstone. They must have lifted in unison, at a *word* of command. It is no fortuitous circumstance that the first dolmens occurred about 6,000 years ago, that is, about 5,000 years after the beginning of agriculture. It takes time for fundamental change to work out its consequential changes.

After the simple organization of men to gain the power of several pairs of hands, came technology. For example, the moving of heavy stones on rollers, found naturally in sections of tree trunks, or the floating of heavy stones on water in barges. Stonehenge in England was erected, with stones brought many miles by water and land, by tilting butt ends of upright stones into prepared

1. All superscript numbers correspond to REFERENCES at the end of this chapter.

pits and by shoring the massive lintels in small stages. This required planning, and if, in those islands, there was no writing (1900–1600 B.C.), orders and designs for cooperative works would have had to be remembered.[2] Technology has thus expanded (changed) from using the rolling log for moving stones, to the more recent wheel, to the telescope, steam engine, internal combustion motor, radio, television, jet engine, and spaceship.

Other change has occurred quite abstractly: the sudden insight, attributed to Moses, about the invisibility of a single god;[3] the Copernican discovery that the earth moved, made prior to the telescope and based on visual observation and mathematical analysis;[4] and the thought experiments of Einstein, particularly, the one of an imagined railroad train that proved simultaneity of two events is a matter of point of observation.[5]

In broad summary the physical causes of our civilization are (1) *agriculture,* which freed man from total preoccupation with food gathering and survival, (2) *organization*, which gave some men command of others to execute concepts beyond the powers of a single individual, and (3) *technology*, which subjects the power of physical phenomena to the imagination and will of men.

PLANNING AND LAW

Organization requires words, not necessarily written, but sufficient to at least communicate commands for instantaneous execution, such as the lifting of the capstone of a dolmen. Technology, however, requires planning, and as the technology grows more and more complex, the planning must be further and further in advance of the execution; such as the planning for the Great Pyramid built by the Egyptian pharaoh, Zoser (2700–2650 B.C.). Long-range planning requires a record of the plan because time elapses between the origination of the plan and its execution. Obviously, it is no accident that the earliest record of Egyptian writing (pictorial) bears a date only some 300 years earlier than that of Zoser's Great Pyramid.

Conceivably the record of the planning for the Great Pyramid could have been in the form of architects' drawings and therefore without words. Consider, however, the Egyptian irrigation systems. For centuries this land has survived by using and then controlling the soil-distributing floods of the Nile and by diverting its waters for the same purpose to an ever-widening expanse of reclaimed desert. Such systems of irrigation call for the administration of rules and regulations: when may a tiller of the soil open the sluice gate to his bit of land; how long may he keep it open; how much water may he take, and by what approved method?[6] Those rules and regulations were law then; they are law in Egypt today; and they will be law long after the Aswan Dam. Moreover, such law about water use, where water is scarce and makes the difference between life and death, will be constantly changing as the technology for water conservation and distribution changes. Laws of this type must be in words.

The laws for the distribution of water were the edicts of the Egyptian king. (The word "pharaoh" meant "great house" but gradually became a kind of shorthand for all the attributes and powers of the ruler.) John A. Wilson says that the three divine attributes of Egyptian kingship were (1) "authoritative utterance" or "creative command," (2) "perception" or "understanding," and (3) "justice."[7] Of course, these were the attributes of a rulership in any of the early civilizations. They are the requisites of rulership in any time, although in our present Western civilization they are not superstitiously thought to be embodied in one person—god incarnate, as in the case of the pharaohs.

The phrases and words used by the Egyptians to describe the powers and capacities of their god-related kings make a point about at least one source of law. In a land where only a few inches, plus or minus, in the height of the Nile meant famine, bountiful crops, or riotous destruction, the ability of the ruler to perceive (forecast) the coming behavior of the life-giving and life-taking river *would be* the basis of the "creative command." The pharaohs kept their observers far up river, at the second cataract, and thus had advance information on which to base their commands. In that respect, law was simply the informed command of the ruler. The law, however, was also the basis of a vast administrative system. What had been observed about the Nile at the second cataract and was speedily transmitted to the pharaoh, by only a few of his men, would determine rules of conduct with respect to water a thousand miles downstream. Hence, there would be many pharaoh's men announcing and enforcing laws concerning water. In one respect, therefore, law is the basis for administering the business of survival. Law is one of the instruments of social control—one of the techniques in Toynbee's interaction between challenge and response: man challenged by the Nile waters, by arctic snows, by jungle animals, or by arid desert. The response to the challenge calls for law emanating from the "perception" and "understanding" of rulers.

EMPIRE AND LAW

Law may be employed to create the conviction among conquered peoples that the conqueror is just. The Code of Hammurabi (about 2000 B.C.) seems to be an example. This King of Babylon had his laws inscribed on a pillar of stone some eight feet high, which was found in Iran in the winter of 1901–1902 and can now be seen in the Louvre. The inscription of this famous collection of laws, not really a code because it lacks comprehensiveness, is surmounted by a bas-relief of Shamash, the sun-god and god of justice. The Code deals with offenses against property, land and houses, trade and commerce, marriage, assaults, agriculture, wages, and slaves. There are many omissions, such as parricide, kidnapping, cattle stealing, pirating of water, and misconduct in cooperative irrigation. There are evidences that such offenses abounded, but the Code does not deal with them. Based on evidence found in the epilogue to the Code, Hammurabi's intent was to convince his extensive empire that he was a just and equitable ruler. This desire supports Reinhold Niebuhr's maxim that government, whether nation or empire, must rest not only on force, which indeed Hammurabi had used devastatingly in his campaigns, but also on some ideal of equity, justice, or peace.[8] In another respect, therefore, law is a cohesive factor in large communities of diverse and disparate elements; law supports the idea of justice.

THREE TYPES OF SOCIETY

In these Egyptian and Babylonian references we have been speaking of a type of social organization that Heilbroner calls the command society—in modern terminology, the dictatorship. Throughout most of history, rulership has been autocratic. The command of the ruler has been the predominant factor in social control. Today, certain Communist-controlled societies are command societies. Even those newer states that have erupted initially in a democratic form have frequently and promptly lapsed into forms of autocracy.

Heilbroner identifies the second type of society as the status society. This status society also makes a point about law. India is the clearest example. The castes of India may have been imposed by conquerors from the north about 2000 B.C. as a means of controlling (and working) the indigenous population. This caste system has historically determined, even to a considerable extent today, what work a man must and must not do. The four castes are: (1) priests, scholars, and teachers, the highest caste and known as Brahmans; (2) soldiers and rulers; (3) husbandmen, merchants, and artisans; and (4) servants. A fifth division of traditional Indian society is the outcasts, those without caste (the untouchables). The castes in the original teachings of that amorphous body of beliefs known as Hinduism were said to have sprung from the creator Brahma: the first from his mouth; the second from his arms; the third from his thighs; and the fourth from his feet.[9]

Since Indian independence, the caste system is slowly changing, but it is still a good example of social control by status. To be born into a given caste determines a man's work, his food, his marriage—his life. The castes are autonomous and to a large extent self-ruling, although they are *interdependent* with respect to the total economy of the society. Intracaste disputes were, and to some extent are still, handled by village councils. As a status society, law is rooted in custom and supported by divine sanction (the will of the gods). Administration of law is more decentralized than in the Egyptian example.

The market society, to employ Heilbroner's term for the third type, is quite recent. It can be equated with democracy. It is that society which, from an economic point of view, Adam Smith described definitively in *Wealth of Nations.* It is a society in which the individual is allowed extensive and multiple rights to pursue his own wishes, desires, and impulses, both rational and irrational. It is a society that Adam Smith reasoned would be good because, although he conceded the acquisitive, accumulative, even predatory nature of man, he argued that the excesses would be smoothed out by the mysterious "hidden hand" of the marketplace. In other words, the market society is the capitalistic, democratic society—affluent, troubled, and youthful —compared with the command and status societies.[10] Except for the present chapter, this book is about the rights, the duties, and the administration thereof in the market society.

LAW AS A MOLDER OF SOCIETY

In the creation of the Hebrew nation, law served a quite different purpose from that of cohesive factor in Hammurabi's empire, which was so vast in the ancient valleys of the Tigris and the Euphrates that he called himself "the king obeyed by the four quarters." Moses' task was not to rule with justice and equity over conquered peoples but rather to mold the Joseph clans, which Ramses II had enslaved between the Nile Delta and the upper Red Sea, into a people fit to be called a nation. He led these skeptical, complaining, unruly people in a successful revolt from Egypt and brought them to the Oasis of Kadesh, attributing the miraculous feat to Yahweh. There, or more probably along the way near Mt. Sinai (or Horeb, the exact location of the mountain in the Sinai peninsula still eludes scholars), Moses received the Ten Commandments, the Decalogue. This is one of the clearest cases of attributing law to divine command, and it is one of the foundations of Western philosophical dispute that has lasted for centuries. (Moses' date falls approximately after 1225 B.C.) The issue is whether law preexists its discovery and enunciation by man or arises only as man conceives law and enunciates it. Did God or Moses write the Ten Commandments?[11]

The usual reference for the text of the Ten Commandments is Exodus 20:2–17, but parts or differing versions of the Decalogue may be found in Deuteronomy. Shorn of elaboration, the Ten Commandments are:

I.   I am Yahweh, thy God, who brought thee out of the house of slaves: Thou shalt have no other gods before me.

II. Thou shalt not make unto thee a graven image.

III. Thou shalt not take the name of Yahweh, thy God, in vain.

IV. Remember the sabbath day to make it holy.

V.   Honor thy father and thy mother.

VI.   Thou shalt not kill.

VII.   Thou shalt not commit adultery.

VIII. Thou shalt not steal.

IX.   Thou shalt not bear false witness against thy neighbor.

X.   Thou shalt not covet.

EARTHLY MODELS FOR DIVINE COMMANDS

The form and content of this code appears, on analysis, to parallel closely the covenants of suzerainty, prevalent in Asia Minor in Moses' time, by which a superior bound an inferior to obligations defined by the superior. Such covenants were usual in the Hittite Bronze Age as the procedure by which a great lord or king imposed certain conditions of peace (or the obligation to make war on the king's behalf) upon a vassal. The significant innovation, or even revolution, that Moses accomplished was to transfer the indigenous practice of suzerainty covenanting from a flesh and blood overlord or emperor to a supreme and unique deity. In one respect, it was an expression of protest against imperialism with its hierarchies of mundane subserviences and dominances. Yet, the stipulations of the Decalogue define the interests of an earthly suzerain that the vassal is bound to respect as much as the interests of a one and only god. The First Commandment excludes relationships with other sovereign powers—"no other gods before me." Unwaivering trust of the suzerain was mandatory, and murmuring against him violated the covenant.

The reference in the First Commandment to "other gods" presupposes the existence of gods other than Yahweh. Nevertheless, the prohibition of any recognition of, or relations with, such other gods laid the foundations for monotheism. Any "other god" with whom one had no relationship became unreal and ultimately nonexistent.

The ethical dictates of the Decalogue (meaning "ten words," a compression probably coerced by the number of human fingers) are exactly what an earthly ruler would require for the internal peace of his realm. Murder, theft, adultery, false oaths, false accusations, insubordination of children, religious controversy—all are among the most common causes of internal strife. The content of the Decalogue was not markedly different from the customary laws of pagan antiquity.

There was, however, something unique in the Mosaic concept that distinguished the nascent Hebrew nation from other peoples of the time: obedience to the commands of Yahweh took precedence over other concerns. Consequently, temporal blessings and calamities became dependent upon ethical or moral norms. On the other hand, the "covenant" was not a case of *quid pro quo*: obedience in exchange for Yahweh's favor. This god would not stoop to bargaining in such fashion or in any fashion.[12]

The Hebrews of the Exodus were a benighted lot. (A full reading of Exodus or a complete reading of Thomas Mann's fascinating and scholarly account of the Exodus[13] will make that plain.) The case of the Ten Commandments presents an eloquent record of law as a moral or ethical pacesetter. The commands were enforced by Yahweh's threats and promises (the stick and the carrot) and were coerced by Joshua's police force, called "avenging angels," until the unwonted law got under the skin of the motley crew of ex-slaves and became a matter of conscience. Mann causes Moses to summarize the concept of conscience:[14]

> In the stone of the mountains I engraved the ABC of human conduct, but no less shall it be graven in your flesh and blood, O Israel, so that everyone who breaks one of the ten commandments shall shrink within himself and before God, and it shall be cold about his heart because he overstepped God's bound. Well I know, and God He too knows well, that His commands will not be obeyed, but will be rebelled against over and over again. But everyone who breaks the laws shall from now on grow icy cold about the heart, because they are written in the flesh and blood and he knows the Word will avail.

In still another respect, therefore, law, to use the psychologist's term, is a conditioner to upgrade human conduct.

SHIPWRECK, MONEY, AND LAW

Law evolves from what people do as well as from the aspirations of leaders such as Moses. Eight hundred years before the Ten Commandments a high civilization was developing in Crete, and the Minoans became the leading sea traders of the Mediterranean. When the Minoan civilization, centered at Knossos, fell to Mycenaean invaders from the Grecian mainland about 1400 B.C., the center of the Aegean sea trade passed to the mainland, only to die as the predatory kings of the Homeric era exhausted lands to plunder. It arose again in the Archaic period (800–500 B.C.) as the pressure of population on the Grecian mainland forced colonization of the islands. Sometime in this antiquity, the islanders of Rhodes formed a sea code in the heyday of their commerce when their ships sailed throughout the Mediterranean. Parts of this maritime law, such as the law of jettison and general average, have survived today, not only in record but also in practice.[15]

Under the law of jettison and general average, when cargo is thrown overboard to save a ship, compensation to the owner of the jettisoned cargo is made by contribution levied on the owners of the remaining cargo and the owners of the ship, because it was for their benefit that the goods were sacrificed. The Egyptians never needed such a relatively complicated but obviously fair rule because, as sophisticated as their civilization became, they remained predominantly a river people. In one respect, therefore, law arises from economic and technological modes of life, whatever they are and however they change.

A development, such as the invention of coined money, can result in a new law, not necessarily concerning coinage but, rather, concerning the social conflict that ultimately ensues from the innovation. Around 700 B.C. the Kingdom of Lidia, which was the trade intermediary between the Greek cities on the coast of Asia Minor and the Asiatic interior, began issuing pieces of metal stamped by the state to guarantee uniformity of weight and quality. These pieces were of high value and were useful principally in international trade. In the 6th century, B.C., an even more revolutionary coinage by Greek cities, such as Athens, of small change occurred. One consequence was the great expansion of internal trade. The agora of the Greek city, originally a place for political and religious meetings, became a marketplace. Another and related consequence was the shift from subsistence farming to specialized agriculture for the marketplace. Such a radical change caught many landowners in economic dislocation, and the only relief that the new money offered was lending at usurious rates. Small farmers were forced to borrow not only on the security of their lands but also of their persons. Among the principal reforms of Solon (594 B.C.) were laws cancelling all debts on land, freeing all debt slaves, and forbidding the securing of debts by the person.[16] The laws of Solon did not end the social strife of the period, but the point is that law can *cause* social changes, as in the case of the Hebrews, and can be *caused* by social change, as followed the introduction of coined money in Greece.

LAW AS A CONTINUUM

Although law changes and new law arises as social, economic, and technological changes occur, law nevertheless tends to be a continuum—each generation respectful of the past but never wholly bound by it, except when violent political revolution occurs. Rome, from the early kingships, through republicanism, to world imperialism, is the classic historical example (some 13 centuries) of continuity in legal development.

The traditional date for the founding of Rome is 753 B.C., over 100 years before Solon. About 450 B.C., according to a tradition that scholars respect in varying degrees, the XII Tables of Roman law were produced. Strangely, no complete copy has survived, but the fact of the XII Tables is deduced, not only from fragments but also from Roman writers such as Cicero, who says that in his youth, 400 years later, it was still customary for boys to memorize the code.

Almost everything about Roman life was practical, and it was a very practical reason that forced the incorporation of the unwritten, customary law of the Romans into written tables. There were no ceremonious offerings of the code to a sun-god, as the bas-relief of Hammurabi's pillar depicts, nor any commands from a god speaking to a prophet on a thunderous, smoking Sinai. Quite simply, the plebeians, Roman common people, demanded the writing so that the patrician magistrates could not play fast and loose with the rules. Thus, among the many fundamentals bequeathed by Roman law to Western civilization is the tradition of generality and certainty. Law must not be whimsical or irregular in its application. It must be uniform, applying alike to persons involved in all similar cases. From the Roman records we have the clear example of a body of magistrates regularly empowered, as a separate function, to hear and decide disputes, and whose announced principles for proceeding with cases and their decisions were made a record and became precedents for later magistrates.

From about 300 B.C. there arose a class of men who made the study of law their special interest. At first they were not professional lawyers but gave free legal advice to gain advancement in their own public careers. By the beginning of the Christian era, Augustus had authorized certain of these jurists to give opinions with the emperor's authority. By about 110–180 A.D., one of the greatest of the Roman jurists Gaius was interpreting, classifying, and organizing in his writings a half millenium of Roman law. Consequently, the legal scene in Rome became quite like our modern one: judges (magistrates), jurists (lawyers representing clients), and established procedures for litigation.

LAW IS NOT SELF-ENFORCING

Procedure is a word that we must briefly consider. It is one thing to have a rule of law like "Thou shalt not steal." But, no rule of law is self-enforcing. If a man *does* steal, what then? The case is never quite that simple. One accused of stealing may say that the "thing" had been *given* to him by the owner or that it was in his possession because he had *borrowed* it or because the owner had *left* it in the house of the accused. These defenses may be true. Who knows, if it is one man's word against another's?

In our American society the concept of law enforcement by the processes of apprehending the accused person and bringing him to trial before judge and jury is so commonplace that we understand with difficulty the long, slow process by which the procedures for the enforcement of law developed. Yet, it is important to know something about those laborious ages or to be aware of the scholarly speculation about them, in order to appreciate contemporary administration of justice (imperfect as it may sometimes seem). We must therefore consider additional information about the beginnings of law.

We have spoken of codes, such as the Code of Hammurabi, the Ten Commandments, and the Roman XII Tables. But such codes are not the beginnings of law. Successful ways of doing things that grow into habit and custom come first. Strangely enough, judging develops before law. Sir Henry Maine, in *Ancient Law*, looks to the Greek Homer for clues about the ancient role played by judging. Themis, who much later became the Greek goddess of justice, in her original role provided judgments. She is described in the *Iliad* as "the assessor of Zeus." She was thought to have an inventory of "judgments," which rulers and even gods obtained from her. Homer does not even employ the word, law. There were only judgments, "Themistes," named after the goddess.

Sir Henry says that in this period (Homeric legends occur about 1200 B.C.), "[t]he only authoritative statement of right and wrong is a judicial sentence after the facts, not one presupposing a law which has been violated, but one which is breathed for the first time by a higher power into the judges' mind at the moment of adjudication."[17] The reader should recall this mythology when, later in this book, the inevitable question will arise, whether judges (and juries, for that matter) *make* law or are *bound* by law.

Judging is both an ancient and a contemporary institution in the ordering of society. But before judging, habit, or custom, there was just primordial conduct; for example, self-help. An owner (possessor may be more precise because ownership is a philosophical concept, whereas possession is a visible reality), fancying his possession taken by another, might well go after it with whatever force and with whatever injury or death the recapture or attempt to recapture might involve. Thomas Mann, in *The Tables of the Law,* brilliantly describes the reluctance of the Hebrews to give up this self-help in favor of the judging process.

THE ROLE OF RITUAL IN PROCEDURE

The transition from self-help to submission to judging involved the psychological accommodation typical of many cultural developments. To illustrate by using our case of dispute of possession of the "thing," consider a form of submission to judging in early Roman law. Each party, when making his assertion of ownership, grasps the thing in dispute and lays a wand on it, after which the magistrate intervenes and says: "Let go both of you." Plainly, the procedure begins, as in the case of self-help, with each party asserting the intent of physical contest (the grasping); then, the physical contest having been symbolized, the parties sublimate their forceful impulses to an intellectual submission to the judging process. The case could be lost to the plaintiff by the least deviation from the ritual. Thus, a kind of magic overhung a rite so powerful that it could supersede self-help.*

---

* ". . . Certainly the most ancient judicial proceeding known to us is the Legis Actio Sacramenti of the Romans, out of which all the later Roman law of Actions may be proved to have

Before writing, the knowledge of the magic ritual and words by which parties could avoid self-help belonged, as one may readily imagine, to those who first had the aptitude for conceiving the rites and the words—kings and rulers with natural ability and assumed access to divine sources, then aristocracies of priests, nobles, and practitioners (medicine men in today's primitive societies). The *word* itself had magic, as our opening quotation from the first chapter of St. John indicates.

Omitting many interesting, not to say amusing, steps from self-help to rituals and words symbolizing self-help, men of all societies, believing in the divine inspiration of rulers and aristocracies, submitted to procedures for settling disputes. This is the process of the development of law: after self-help come judgments; from judgments come increasing submission to judgments; and from the multiplicity of judgments come customs and, if the society is progressive like Roman society was, the reduction of customary laws to writing. Thereafter, the problem is to reconcile the static writing to the dynamic progression of the society and to simplify the procedures for sublimating to the judging process the natural impulse toward self-help. In modern studies of law there are two usual categories: (1) substantive law, as in any of the codes we have mentioned, and (2) procedural law, as in the antique Roman ritual just described. We have just glimpsed the origins of those categories and the distinctions between them.

THE ROLE OF THE FICTION

It is not too early to speak of the processes by which law, after it has reached the written stage (and may thereby fall behind social progress), is changed, i.e. brought into closer alignment with the social condition. Sir Henry Maine

---

grown. Gaius carefully describes its ceremonial. Unmeaning and grotesque as it appears at first sight, a little attention enables us to decipher and interpret it.

"The subject of litigation is supposed to be in Court. If it is moveable, it is actually there. If it be immoveable, a fragment or sample of it is brought in its place; land, for instance, is represented by a clod, a house by a single brick. In the example selected by Gaius, the suit is for a slave. The proceeding begins by the plaintiff's advancing with a rod, which as Gaius expressly tells, symbolized a spear. He lays hold of the slave and asserts a right to him with the words, *"Hunc ego hominem ex Jure Quiritium meum esse dico secundum suam causam sicut dixi;"* and then saying, *"Ecce tibi Vindictam imposui,"* he touches him with the spear. The defendant goes through the same series of acts and gestures. On this the Praetor intervenes, and bids the litigants relax their hold, *"Mittite ambo hominem."* They obey, and the plaintiff demands from the defendant the reason of his interference, *"Postulo anne dicas quâ ex causâ vindicaveris,"* a question which is replied to by a fresh assertion of right, *"Jus peregi sicut vindictam imposui."* On this, the first claimant offers to stake a sum of money, called a Sacramentum, on the justice of his own case, *"Quando tu injuria provocasti, D oeris Sacramento te provoco,"* and the defendant in the phrase, *"Similiter ego te,"* accepts the wager. The subsequent proceedings were no longer of a formal kind, but it is to be observed that the Praetor took security for the Sacramentum, which always went into the coffers of the State." (Henry Summer Maine, *Ancient Law,* London, J. M. Dent & Sons, 1917, pp. 220–221.)

thinks that the earliest of these processes is the *legal fiction*, a concept that the reader of this book will continuously encounter, sometimes with considerable intellectual aversion. Take an illustration from early Roman law, if for no other reason than to see that the fiction in law is not just a devilish invention of modern judges. In early Roman times Roman law applied only to Roman citizens. A foreigner in Rome had no rights under any applicable law. Indeed, he himself could be seized like an ownerless piece of property by any Roman. Early Rome, like the Greek cities, however, enjoyed trade with the merchants of the Mediterranean. Because of this travel and intercourse, there *were* foreigners in Rome (some important), and they would get into misunderstandings and controversies. Why not? Yet, no law applied to the foreigner. Consequently, the practice arose under which a foreigner would assert before a magistrate that he *was* a Roman citizen when in fact he was not. The magistrate, however, would not permit the assertion (called averment in the law) to be denied. Why? So that the magistrate could take jurisdiction and decide the case. This did not mean that the magistrate would decide the case in favor of the foreigner. It simply meant that Roman society had become more metropolitan than Roman law. Because it was not immediately possible to change the law, the judges resorted to the fiction of Roman citizenship in certain cases; otherwise Rome would have become unattractive to traders (unhealthy for business) or, worse still, foreigners would not come peacefully but in force to take the city. (Some centuries later, Roman citizenship was widely extended to the peoples of the Roman provinces.) The fiction of citizenship was procedural—a device to get the case in court. We shall see that fictions have also played, and continue to play, an important role in substantive law.

TRADE AND COMMERCE BROUGHT EQUITY

For the second method by which law has kept pace with social development, we look again at early Rome. If the reader thinks we are spending considerable time in ancient Rome, he is right. Law, engineering, and imperial administration were Rome's three marks of genius. When we look to Rome for the origins of much modern legal thought and practice, we look to exactly the right, and only, place. Although Rome initially established her dominance over the Italian peninsula, under the kings and in the early days of the republic she remained, despite the superiority of her legal developments, a provincial town, but proud of herself, sure of her superior ways, and clannish about Rome for Romans. Hence, the establishment of the rule that the civil law of Rome was for Romans only, as we have seen in the discussion of the fiction.

No great city can be an island. Trade and commerce brought outsiders (foreigners), and even after the fiction gave Roman magistrates jurisdiction to try a case, what about the substantive law? Laws drawn from customs of

Roman farmers were not enough for the more complicated transactions of Mediterranean shipping practices and overseas commerce. Before that Rome had to take account of persons who came to Rome from within the peninsula. It was during this period that the concept of a class of judges who could take account of the customs and laws of other Italian communities, and later of all the communities of the Mediterranean world, evolved. These special judges looked for customs, rules, and laws common to all the communities whose citizens came to Rome for trade, commerce, and all forms of social intercourse. As the volume of cases increased through expanding, Mediterranean-wide exchanges of trade and culture, the special judges, called Praetors, built through their edicts a body of law that was a complex of Roman and non-Roman law and that came to be known as the law of nations.

The law of nations was not international law in the modern sense. Its fundamental was what the judges found to be common to many non-Roman communities, which themselves later came under Roman imperial power, whose citizens came to Rome. Sir Henry Maine says that the Latin word applied to this process of recognizing foreign laws was *equitas*, which meant levelling. Hence, Roman civil law, which assured to Romans all kinds of class distinctions and privileges, was diluted. From this Latin word *equitas* comes, Maine says, our modern law term *equity*.

Meanwhile, the Greek stoic philosophers had conceived laws of nature, good in and of themselves because they belonged to some earlier and idyllic state of man. As Greek culture grew influential in Rome, this concept of naturally good law seized upon the very practical Roman concept of laws common to all nations. Thus, the terms the law of nations, natural law, and equity, are commingled in legal writings, and some harm has been done by a widespread, albeit quite vague, notion that equity is law that is more just and reasonable than other law. Nevertheless, equity stands as the second device, after the fiction, for changing law.

In equity a body of rules arises to stand beside the original civil laws; equity, claiming inherent validity for its principles, deals with real cases that fall outside the original body of law. Equity, unlike the fiction, is not subversive of original civil law; it openly declares its special virtues and makes rules that are new to the old law. For example, the absolute conception of ownership in Roman law left no room for the possible rights of the one in *possession*. Such was the Roman civil law. Roman equity, however, would leave a *possessor* in possession until the alleged owner proved his title. Originally, equity represented a much more advanced stage of thought than the fiction.

Today, the whole body of American civil law, concerning rights of persons and property rights, is divided into "law" and "equity," and for the most part, the same courts administer both bodies of principles. Certain real distinctions between the law and equity still exist. For example, if one wishes money damages because his neighbor's intentionally loud radio has injured one's mental health, the suit is "at law" for money. If one wishes to put a stop to the overly loud radio playing, the suit is "in equity" for an injunction. Money damages at law; injunction in equity is an over-simplified but useful distinction.

LEGISLATION

Legislation is and was the third method by which law is ameliorated.[18] Contrary to our modern concept of division of powers among the executive, legislative, and judicial, legislation, as a modifying technique in the development of law, may emanate historically from a king or ruler as well as from the legislature in a republic. Legislation is like equity because it makes no pretense of reconciling itself to existing law, as the fiction does. Legislation is unlike equity because it depends on the naked power of the ruler or the legislature, whereas equity claims inherent rightness for its justification. Legislation may be whimsical, as demonstrated in the statement of the first great American Chief Justice John Marshall, "[t]he power to tax is the power to destroy." Legislation *may take account* of existing civil law, and legislation may be *influenced* by principles of equity, but legislation does not hesitate to make new law contravening old law. In modern American jurisprudence the distinction is drawn between (1) *case law*, meaning the decisions of judges either under principles of law or of equity, and (2) *statutory law*, meaning the acts of the legislatures. In the United States we have, within the memory of many men now living, a clear case of legislation's overturning case law in the field of labor-management relations. Such cases and legislation appear in Chapter 7.

GROWTH AND STAGNATION IN LAW

Law, like art or music, has periods of vitality and excellence and periods of stagnation and mediocrity. For example, the art of archaic Greece and that of the Periclean Age are superior to later Grecian art. To take another case, the music of Bach and Beethoven of the 18th century represents an especially creative period when compared with earlier and later periods. In the case of Roman law, which had so profound an effect on Western civilization, the period of dynamic development was lengthy. If we measure from the date of the XII Tables to the year 200 A.D. (when Roman law became static and retrospective), we have a period of some 600 years. During that time, Rome, beginning as a bucolic little town in an agricultural state, became through trade, conquest, and empire, mistress of the Mediterranean, Western Europe, the British Isles, the Near East, and North Africa. Roman law grew as Rome grew.

Among the many reasons assigned by historians for the fall of Rome is the decline of faith in the old pagan gods. In any case, the Christian communities in the first and second centuries had developed their own internal rules. Pollock and Maitland say that, "internally they were developing what was to become a system of constitutional and governmental law, which would endow the overseer *(episcopus)* of every congregation with manifold powers." The greatest of these overseers became the one at Rome because of the tradition that the apostle Peter founded that church. Thus, contemporaneously with the decline of dynamic development of Roman law, a new vitality was emerging in the Christian communities. Law in these communities, originally illegal in pagan Rome, was god-given in the Mosaic sense. Roman law had long since gotten away from the gods and had become a product of human thought, reason, and experience. But Christian law was divine, arbitrary, and authoritarian. Pollock and Maitland say:[19]

> . . . Long before the year 300 jurisprudence, the one science of the Romans, was stricken with sterility; it was sharing the fate of art. Its eyes were turned backward to the departed great. . . .
> It is on a changed world that we look in the year 400. After the one last flare of persecution (303), Christianity became a lawful religion (313). In a few years it, or rather one species of it, had become the only lawful religion. The "confessor" of yesterday was the persecutor of today. Heathenry, it is true, died hard in the West; but already about 350 a pagan sacrifice was by the letter of the law a capital crime. Before the end of the century, cruel statutes were being made against heretics of all sorts and kind.

As the Roman emperors lost their power and prestige the papacy became increasingly dominant, often in secular as well as religious affairs. Religion makes law—even civil law.

The reader will have occasion to remember, as he proceeds in this book, these origins of church or canon law. Such law has a long history, and its remnants are apparent today in the contest over prayers and religious teaching in public schools. To take another contemporary example, in an American state that permits dissemination of artificial contraception information, there is a conflict between civil law and Catholic Church law, which, for about a thousand years (from the 5th to the 15th centuries) reigned supreme in Europe.

LAW OUTLASTS EMPIRE

If we date the beginning of the decline of the Roman Empire with the decline of vitality in the development of Roman law, the full period extends from 200 A.D. to 476 A.D., longer than the United States is old. Even so, that decline was only the fall of the Western Empire. The Eastern Roman Empire, seated at Byzantium, which was renamed Constantinople (now Turkish Istanbul), continued for almost another 1,000 years. It is, therefore, something of an anomaly that the great collection, consolidation, organization, and codification of all Roman law occurred long after the zenith of the Western Empire, in which that law had its beginnings and most dynamic growth. This codification occurred under Justinian I (483–565 A.D.), a non-Roman probably of Slavic descent. Scholars, headed by Tribonian and working under the decree of Justinian, attempted to systematize Roman law by reducing it to order after a thousand years of development and after it had become static. They produced a comprehensive, systematic, and thorough compendium that came to be known much later as the *Corpus Juris.* Complete copies have survived.

Corpus Juris contains a general survey of the whole field of Roman law; there is also the *Digest,* the most important part intended for practitioners and judges and containing the law in concrete form, plus selections from 39 noted classical jurists, such as Gaius (mentioned earlier in this chapter). A collection of imperial legislation also exists. The original work was done with surprising speed, within the period 529–535 A.D. This work was of slight immediate consequence in Western Europe; certainly not after Islam became the rule of the Mediterranean and all of Western Europe was cut off from its long established cosmopolitan contacts with the East. (There is scarcely a great city in Western Europe today, except Berlin, that is not built upon the site of a city of the Roman Empire.) A date to remember in this connection is that Charles Martel turned back the Islamic invaders at Tours in 732. Islam controlled the Mediterranean for 500 years, and the old Roman cities, deprived of their trade with the outside world, died on the vine. Yet, the Christian bishops remained in the wasting cities and often became the chief source of government.[20]

A FRAGMENTED SOCIETY AND LAW

In the long period in which Roman law was of none or little consequence in Western Europe, jurisdictions were fragmented. It was a period of feudalism, of disorganization, and of lawlessness in the countryside.[21] However, Christian law, canon law, the law of the now all-powerful medieval Church, governed from Rome, prevailed. Just one example: The Church imposed an absolute prohibition against usury, which meant, unlike present prohibitions against an excessive interest rate, *no interest at all or any profit* on any transaction at all. It was a long period of a generally profitless society. Profit was a sin.[22] The economy was largely a manorial economy: production on the manor was for consumption. The so-called Dark Ages were five-hundred years of land holding, land grabbing, fighting, crusading, and worshipping, during which the divine laws of the Church were supreme and the idea of man-made, humanistic law was in almost complete eclipse.

The vigor of the medieval Church rule against usury was quite possible in the society of that time. Feudalism was a social order in which land tenure and personal allegiance and individual status (lords, vassals, sub-vassals, knights, squires, and serfs) were everything, and trade was almost nothing. It was easy for the Church to impose a rule, based upon texts in Deuteronomy (XXIII:19, 20), that forbade trade at a profit and helped to control the feudal administration of land (the Church itself ultimately became one of the largest holders). In one aspect, therefore, law often tends to "fit" the times.

Mosaic law tended to *make-over* the people of the Exodus, just as the 1954 United States Supreme Court's decision in Brown v. Board of Education tended to *make-over* our communities with respect to segregated education. During medieval feudalism, Church law on usury fitted the times. Later, that ingenious lawyer-theologian, Calvin, reworked the rationale, so that by the time of Puritanism in the 17th century, a profit, far from being a sin, became one of the marks of godliness in the "Protestant ethic."[23] Calvin, reasoning very much as lawyers have always reasoned, pointed out that usury, which Deuteronomy permitted as between Jew and Gentile, could not be wrong *per se*; otherwise it would have been prohibited absolutely. Then, embracing the New Testament concept of universal brotherhood, he argued that usury became a matter of conscience. Interest could be exacted but not against the poor in distress and, in any case, within reason. Thus, the foundation was laid for the borrowing of capital that modern industry would soon require. Law, even church law, *changes* with the times. Technology (the coming industrial revolution) was about to *change* law, just as technology *made* law when Grecian sea commerce was in its prime 25 centuries earlier.

ORIGINS OF ENGLISH LAW

Despite this fragmentation of rulership among lords, barons, earls, and kings, bodies of law *were* written. One of the most significant of these for later development was the statement of Germanic customs, known as *Lex Salica*. It was rude and primitive, dated sometime between the 5th and the 6th centuries. It is distinctive in not being particularly pagan; on the other hand, it is not particularly Christian. It was written in Latin but free from the Roman taint. It consisted of German folk laws, largely a tariff of offenses and atonements. By virtue of the Norman conquest (1066), the German *Lex Salica* became one of the ancestors of English law. Even the jury system, which Englishmen and Americans still regard as a virtuous part of their legal systems, has a Germanic origin. The original essence of the jury seems to lie in a body of neighbors summoned by some public officer to give, under oath, true answers to questions. These questions were usually of a royal nature; that is, from some Germanic rulership. Pollock and Maitland cite some examples.[24]

> Name all the landowners of your district and say how much land each of them has.
>
> Name all the persons in your district whom you suspect of murder, robbery, or rape.
>
> Is Roger guilty of having murdered Ralph?
>
> Or whether [sic] of the two has the greater right to Blackacre, William or Hugh?
>
> And so forth.

The learned authors conclude: "Such is now the prevailing opinion, and it has triumphed in this country [England] over the natural disinclination of Englishmen to admit that this 'palladium of our liberties' [the jury] is in its origin, not English but Frankish [Germanic], not popular but royal."[25]

Despite its immediate irrelevance during the feudal period, we must return briefly to *Corpus Juris* in order to complete the account of how that monumental work, still highly regarded in all Western juridical works, fared.

ROMAN LAW DID NOT DIE

In the 11th century there was a revival of interest in Roman law, especially in the Italian university at Bologna. How such revivals occur is sometimes obscure, but usually some scholar or body of scholars engenders them. We shall omit the names here, except for Lanfranc soon to be mentioned in our account of how Roman law came to England. We must skip many interesting developments and drive through to the ultimate triumph of *Corpus Juris* in the modern world. In the present nations of Western Europe, Roman law collated and preserved in both *Corpus Juris* and in the early 19th century *Napoleonic Code* is literally the foundation of modern jurisprudence. Furthermore, the influence of Roman law through those codes extends into any part of the world that has been colonized or otherwise affected by any of the continental nations of Western Europe. For example, because France colonized our American state of Louisiana, Roman law can be found in the Civil Code of that state. In one sense, we may say that any body of law that has a long period of development in a dynamic society, such as Rome, and has been the subject of significant scholarship during the height of its development and afterwards, as in the case of the *Corpus Juris,* never dies. Roman law had no such dominating influence in England, however, as it did on the Continent— a significant fact for Americans because England is the mother of American institutions.

With this brief history of English law, we shall complete this section. Some 8,000 years ago, the ocean broke through the isthmus joining an Atlantic peninsula to the Western World's mainland space. This created the flood of salt water that made the Straits of Dover. Thus, the destiny of England began.[26] This island has not been conquered in the last 900 years, although Phillip of Spain and the Spanish Armada, Louis XIV, Napoleon, Kaiser Wilhelm, and Hitler all made an attempt. The last conquest of England was that of William the Conqueror of Normandy who defeated the English Harold at the Battle of Hastings in 1066. Before then, there had been many conquests. The island was conquered by the Roman Caesar in 55 B.C. When Rome abandoned England in the early 5th century, the deep-shadowed period partly characterized by the legends of King Arthur ensued. These were not authenticated by writings of the times; otherwise they would not be legends. They are mentioned here because, like so many legends, they ultimately turned out to be valid and because they do show the deep Christian influence attributed by later writers to early England.

After the Romans, and in the dim period of the 5th to the 10th centuries, came, in order, Jutes, Angles and Saxons, Danes, Norwegians, and, finally, that great and critical invasion and conquest by the Normans. The point is that England, although a tiny island, is a microcosm of the melting pot that has boiled throughout all history and prehistory. When peoples move, whether in conquest or peacefully, they bring their customs and their laws.

WHY ENGLISH LAW IS SPECIAL

English law was at once separate from, and also a part and a consequence of, continental law. As we begin to consider briefly the development of law in England, we should note the effect of the English climate.

Arthur Bryant reasons that there arose a national distrust for long-term planning and that the capacity for adaptation may have arisen from constant experience with weather vagaries. He editorializes that in war—an activity in which the expected rarely happens—the English, although always unprepared for conflict planned by others, have usually been victorious. For our purposes, we see in this analysis of the British character one of the reasons why English law has developed on a case-by-case method and is to a considerable extent void of fixed dogma, the *a priori* of Roman and continental law.[27]

With climate it is necessary to emphasize also the mixture of races and peoples in such a small patch of geography. As Arthur Bryant states the case, there were long skulls and broad, short builds and tall, dark pigmentation and blond; such intermixture in so small an island has made its people many-sided and versatile. Left to themselves the Anglo-Saxons of a thousand years ago, who were florid large-limbed, blue-eyed, and phlegmatic, might have settled down into a sluggish complacency. But they were harried by the Danes and Norsemen and later conquered by the clear-minded, ruthless Normans. In the face of these powerful minorities they struggled for their customs, institutions, language—and original laws.

One must not overlook in the development of early English law the fact that because of the Channel, the early inhabitants of the islands were not threatened across a land frontier and so had no immediate and constant need to entrust their rulers with standing military forces or despotic rights over private liberties. The threats were from overseas and therefore not so imminent. (Throughout this book the fact will appear that when national security is threatened, internal freedom suffers.) Hence, from the earliest periods English authority was normally exercised only after those subject to it had had an opportunity to make their views known. From the early Saxon Witenagemot (a kind of town meeting) to 20th century Parliament, from the village hustings and manor court to the trade union lodge and parish council, there has nearly always been some working machinery in England by which those in authority could test the opinion of those over whom that authority was exercised. Arthur Bryant concludes: "Government was conducted subject to the right of the governed to criticize and, within lawful limits, to oppose." As this book progresses, the reader will have occasion to question to what extent the right to oppose includes the right to disobey. Is the burning of draft cards merely an expression of an ancient English civil liberty or is it treason?

The English development of law includes the attempt to make private liberty compatible with public order. "Freedom within a framework of discipline became their ideal," Bryant summarizes. They achieved it through the sovereignty of law. By law, the English meant an enforceable compact between themselves and their rulers, deriving not from unilaterally imposed force, as in the case of Yahweh and Moses, but from freely given assent. Law, rather than the executive, became the ultimate English sovereign. This comports with our oft-repeated claim that we have a government of laws not of men.

ROMAN COMPONENTS IN ENGLISH LAW

We must not hastily conclude that the development of English law, which must also mean the development of American law, was free of all out-island influence. First of all, the Romans, at the turn of the Christian era, brought Roman law, most of which probably died with the Roman abandonment of England. Yet, the Christian missionaries continued with Christian law. Augustine, a Benedictine monk, arrived from Italy at the head of 40 missionary monks in 597 and became the first Archbishop of Canterbury. The invading Jutes, Angles, Saxons, and Germanic peoples brought their customs and laws with their conquests. These legal influences may be somewhat speculative because they occurred in the darker period of English history, but beginning with William the Conqueror, we can be more certain.

In 1070, William made Lanfranc, the legal scholar and Italian churchman, Archbishop of Canterbury. Lanfranc founded an illustrious school at Bec in Normandy and was an associate of William's; he was educated in civil law; he was an able advocate, who had then turned to theology and became learned in the dogmas of the Church. He made many reforms in England, but for our purpose, the most important was the establishment of ecclesiastical courts. Thus, with William and Lanfranc that long partnership between secular and ecclesiastical law, between king and archbishop, began. An uneasy partnership it was—sometimes a struggle to the death, as between King Henry II and Thomas á Becket, whose murder in Canterbury Cathedral was the outcome of the continuing contest between secular law and ecclesiastical law. This "Murder in the Cathedral," dramatized by T. S. Eliot, came just 100 years after William the Conqueror had appointed Lanfranc his archbishop. The struggle was to continue for 500 years and end in a violent form with the killings of Archbishop Laud in 1645 and King Charles I four years later by the Puritans under Cromwell.

If, indeed, it is one of the glories of English law that it escaped the Roman taint (monarchical philosophy of government), nevertheless the influence was there. Maitland, who extols the escape, points out that Bracton, who produced the first important work on English law, was a pupil at Bologna and there learned "what a law book should be."

THE LONG THREAD

We now see a long continuum of transmitted law. Thomas Mann speculates that Hammurabi's Code was known to Moses. Greek philosophy influenced Roman law, and Roman lawyers (called jurisconsults) and their writings laid the foundation for Justinian's Code. Then came the emerging and finally dominant Christianity and its ecclesiastical law prevalent throughout the Middle Ages. This ecclesiastical law was at once a castback to Moses and an evangelical forward thrust into England, personified in the learned, first Norman Archbishop of Canterbury, Lanfranc. We may therefore deduce another maxim: not only does law not die but it moves. It knows no territorial boundaries; it moves with conquest, and it moves in the person of learned men entrusted by conquerors with the dual powers of judging and the administration of justice.

One reason we can note the movement of law, both in time and space, is the uneven development of civilizations. For example, the great step pyramid of Zoser in Egypt was built approximately a thousand years before Stonehenge in England. Given the facts that Stonehenge is a remarkable astronomical structure and that the movement and the erection of its great monoliths and lintels required considerable primitive engineering, the accomplishment of

Stonehenge cannot be compared with the Zoser pyramid of a thousand years earlier and certainly not with the great Egyptian temples and palaces at Karnak. Stonehenge and Karnak bear roughly the same dates, 1900–1600 B.C. All one needs to do, however, is to observe the remains of Stonehenge at Salisbury and Karnak on the Nile, near Luxor, to see how vastly more monumental was the construction at Karnak than at Stonehenge and what a wealth of artistry at Karnak compared with none at Stonehenge.

Striking comparisons could be made with respect to many civilizations. Take another example: almost two thousand years separate the great architecture of the Classical world, the Acropolis and its Parthenon at Athens, and the great architecture of the Christian world, the churches, particularly St. Peter's in Rome. When the Parthenon was built at Athens, the Romans were still farmers with a few household "sanitary gods," as they have been called. In Greece, highly sophisticated dramas, Sophocles' "Oedipux Rex" and "Antigone," for example, were in production in open-air theaters, so skillfully designed that acoustically they were superior to many contemporary theaters and symphony halls—this was seven centuries before Hadrian built the presently standing Roman Pantheon.

THE UNEVEN DEVELOPMENT OF CIVILIZATIONS

To depart from these physical evidences of the unequal and uneven pace at which civilizations have developed, let us take an example from uneven developments in law. Almost 25 centuries separate the time in which Moses was breaking the Hebrew ex-slaves of the practice of vengeance (self-help)—curbing "the eye for an eye and tooth for a tooth" concept of recriminatory justice and conditioning the ex-slaves to submit to judgments—from the time in which English law was struggling to work out of the blood feud (self-help) by substituting money payments for revenge. Pollock and Maitland say that on the eve of the Norman conquest, as regards the malefactor, the community might in that time assume one of four attitudes: (1) it might make war upon him; (2) it might leave him exposed to the vengeance of those whom he has wronged; (3) it might suffer him to make atonement; (4) it might inflict on him a determinative punishment, death, mutilation or the like. In the Anglo-Saxon law over two millenia after Moses, the offender might be left unprotected against those who had suffered by his misbehavior, or the offender might be left to the right of those he had injured to revenge themselves (the blood feud in which the injured kin could avenge the wrong not only on the person of the malefactor but also on his belongings).

The English law at this stage would have a life or lives for a life, persons not being of equal value; for example, six serfs must perish to balance the death of one lord. One more comparison is sufficient: in Julius Caesar's time there were traffic jams in the Roman Forum, and Caesar was decreeing parking restrictions for oxcarts. This was sixteen hundred years before the time of the English Sir Edward Coke, who prosecuted Sir Walter Raleigh on thinly supported charges of treason, and the highest court in the land could and did deliver the following sentence:[28]

> "That you shall be had from hence to the place whence you came [the Tower], there to remain until the day of execution. And from thence you shall be drawn upon a hurdle through the open streets to the place of execution, there to be hanged and cut down alive, and your body shall be opened, your heart and bowels plucked out, and your privy members cut off and thrown into the fire before your eyes. Then your head to be stricken off from your body, and your body shall be divided into four quarters, to be disposed of at the King's pleasure. And God have mercy upon your soul."

James I commuted the sentence to imprisonment, but the cruel sentence was not unusual and many similar ones were carried out.

WHAT WE OWE TO COKE

When we come forward from such great names as William the Conqueror and Lanfranc of the 11th century, passing by Henry II and Thomas á Becket in the 12th, and leap to Elizabeth I and Sir Edward Coke in the 17th, we move through six hundred years of English history with a speed that would be absurd if we were writing history but not unreasonable when we are considering the idea of law. The reader has gained some understanding of the sweeps of time in which the complex of ideas that we call law has slowly developed. Indeed, he might well imagine from the great names and great events, some shocking to our contemporary sensitivities and some revelatory, how early some concepts of freedom and law—now commonplace—emerged.

So, we come to that critical and great period in English history in which, literally, the foundations for American democracy were hammered out. This is the period of Elizabeth, daughter of Henry VIII and Queen of England until her death in 1603, and of her successor James I, whose ascension to the throne united England and Scotland and who ruled until his death in 1629. This is the period in which these two sovereigns enjoyed first the services and then the curbing influence of one of the greatest names in Anglo-American jurisprudence, Sir Edward Coke. He could prosecute Sir Walter Raleigh and could produce and subscribe to so horrendous a sentence as the one just quoted and later in his life could thwart his sovereign James I in his, to us now foolish, notion that royal will should be the law of the land. It was for this notion that Charles I, son of James I, lost his head (figuratively and literally) 24 years after the death of James I. And it was Edward Coke who, in a reversal of himself as dramatic as that of the reversal of Saul of Tarsus, would stand up to James

I and say, "The king is subject to God and the law," and who, in his 76th year having come close to losing his own head, could counsel the Commons on the famous Petition of Right. "Shall I," Coke demanded, "be made a tenant-at-will for my liberties, having property in my own house but not liberty in my person? There is no such tenure in all Littleton! I leave it as bare as Aesop's crow. It is a maxim, *The common law hath admeasured the King's prerogative,* that in no case it can prejudice the inheritance of the subjects. It is against law that men should be committed and no cause shown. I would not speak this, but that I hope my gracious King will hear of it. Yet it is not I, Edward Coke, that speaks it but the records that speak it."[29]

Notice that Edward Coke does not speak in his own right. Rather, he depends on an established body of law, English law, documented by Bracton (d. 1268), commented on by other English scholars, reduced to a record of cases by others in the Domesday books, and by Lord Coke himself in his famous record of law and law cases called *Institutes.*

In the 17th century English law reached that point at which Roman law had arrived in the 2nd century A.D. There were scholars of the law in both periods. In the English period there were law schools called "Inns of Court," so ancient that Pollock and Maitland did not undertake to ferret out their beginnings. By Coke's time, bodies of lawyers skilled in practice were under a professional obligation to teach, and they did. Coke himself was a pupil in one of the Inns called "Inner Temple." Later he taught, and the American democrat Roger Williams was a pupil of Coke before leaving England for the Colonies.

There are a number of landmark cases in Lord Coke's administration as Chief Justice in England. Perhaps the greatest of them, although several others might qualify, is Bonham's Case. Dr. Thomas Bonham had practiced medicine in London without a certificate from the Royal College of Physicians. The College censors arrested him and put him in the Fleet, whereupon Bonham brought action for false imprisonment. The censors' defense lay in their College statute of incorporation, empowering them to regulate all London physicians and punish infractions with fine and imprisonment. Coke noted that the statute gave the College one-half of each fine collected, thus making the censors at once judge and party to every case they brought to the court. There was, said Coke, a maxim of the common law: No man ought to be judge of his own cause. On this maxim alone, said Coke, the statute of incorporation should be disallowed, adding, "that in many cases *the common law will control acts of Parliament and some times adjudge them to be utterly void; For when an Act of Parliament is against common right and reason, or repugnant, or impossible to be performed, the common law will control it and adjudge such Act to be void.*"[30]

Catherine Drinker Bowen in *The Lion and the Throne* eloquently demonstrates how such a case traveled the Atlantic and echoed through the centuries. When the Stamp Act was passed in Parliament, New England protested that it was "an act against natural equity." From Boston to Virginia trumpets blew. The Massachusetts Assembly declared the Stamp Act invalid, "against Magna Charta and the natural rights of Englishmen, and therefore, according to the Lord Coke, null and void."[31]

Today, it is commonplace to read in American newspapers that the Supreme Court of the United States has nullified an act of Congress; yet that power, supported by no military force, rests on the rationale of a towering figure in Anglo-American history. His reason, his example, and his power of thought came across the Atlantic in the frail ships that moved the early colonists. Hundreds, some of them lawyers but not all of them, knew, and remembered, and asserted on American shores the principles of law established in England. Thus, as in all times, when men move they bring their laws.

REFERENCES

1. Weill, Kurt, "The Threepenny Opera," English adaptation of lyrics by Marc Blitzstein; music by Kurt Weill; original lyrics by Bert (Bertolt) Brecht (as recorded by MGM from production at Theater de Lys, New York, New York).

2. Hawkins, Gerald S., *Stonehenge Decoded,* Garden City, New York, Doubleday, 1965, p. 71.

3. Mann, Thomas, *The Tables of the Law,* New York, Knopf, 1945.

4. Kuhn, Thomas S., *The Copernican Revolution,* New York, Modern Library (Random House), 1959.

5. Gardner, Martin, *Relativity for the Million,* Macmillan, New York, 1963, pp. 40–43.

6. Wilson, John A., *The Burden of Egypt,* Chicago, University of Chicago Press, 1951, pp. 10, 11, 19.

7. Wilson, p. 102.

8. Niebuhr, Reinhold, *The Structure of Nations and Empire,* New York, Scribner's, 1959, p. 35.

9. Thomas, P., *Epics, Myths and Legends of India,* Bombay, D. B. Taraporevala Sons, 1961, Chap. II.

10. Heilbroner, Robert L., *The Making of Economic Society,* Englewood Cliffs, New Jersey, Prentice-Hall, 1962.

11. Mann, *supra.* ref. (3).

12. *The Interpreter's Dictionary of the Bible;* articles on "God, Names of; Law in the Old Testament; and Ten Commandments," New York, Abingdon Press, 1962.

13. Mann, *supra* (3).

14. Mann, *supra* (3), p. 62.

15. Ballentine, James A., *Law Dictionary,* Rochester, New York, The Lawyers Co-operative Publishing Co., 1948, *Lex Rhodia de Jactu.*

16. *An Encyclopedia of World History,* William L. Langer (ed.), Boston, Houghton-Mifflin, (rev. ed.) 1968, p. 65.

17. Maine, Henry Sumner, *Ancient Law,* London, J. M. Dent and Sons, 1917, p. 5.

18. For a complete discussion of the Fiction, Equity, and Legislation see Maine, *supra* (16), Chaps. II and III.

19. Pollock and Maitland, *History of English Law,* Cambridge, University Press, 1952, Vol. I, pp. 2, 3.

20. Pirenne, Henri, *Economic and Social History of Medieval Europe,* New York, Harcourt, Brace and World, 1937, pp. 3–14. Also, see Lopez, Robert, *The Birth of Europe,* New York, M. Evans and Co., 1967, pp. 77–81.

21. See generally Reade, Charles, *The Cloister and the Hearth,* New York, Modern Library (Random House), and in particular Chaps. XXIV–XXXVIII. Also, see generally Turner, Albert M., *The Making of the Cloister and the Hearth,* Chicago, University of Chicago Press, 1938.

22. On "usury," see generally Nelson, Benjamin N., *The Idea of Usury,* Princeton, Princeton University Press, 1949.

23. Tawney, R. H., *Religion and the Rise of Capitalism,* New York, Harcourt, Brace and World, 1926, Chap. IV.

24. Pollock and Maitland, *supra* (19), Vol. I, p. 139.

25. Pollock and Maitland, *supra* (19), Vol. I, pp. 141–142.

26. Bryant, Arthur, *The Story of England—Makers of the Realm,* London, Collins Clear-Type Press, (3rd. impression) 1954, p. 14.

27. Bryant, *supra* (26), p. 16 et. seq.

28. Bowen, Catherine Drinker, *The Lion and The Throne,* Boston, Little, Brown and Co., 1957, p. 217.

29. Bowen, *supra* (28), p. 484.

30. Bowen, *supra* (28), p. 315.

31. Bowen, *supra* (28), pp. 315–316.

2 Law Limits Judging

Introduction to Courts 29
Jurisdiction 31
    Wyman v. Newhouse 31
    Brewington v. Lowe. 33
  Jurisdiction—Territorial, Personal, and Substantive. 34
    Territorial Jurisdiction 34
    Personal Jurisdiction 37
    Substantive Jurisdiction 40
Justiciability 41
  Case or Controversy—The Kinds of Cases Courts Will Decide 41
  Criteria: Nature and Circumstances 41
    Muskrat v. United States. 41
    Opinion of the Justices 44
    Eccles v. Peoples Bank of Lakewood Village, California 46
  The Autonomy of Courts 49
  Cases or Controversies of Trivial Subject Matter 51
    Reed v. Maley. 51
    Stephens v. Myers. 52
  Causes of Action. 53
  Standing—Parties Must have a Real Interest 55
    Pierce v. Society of Sisters 55
    Tileston v. Ullman 56
Growing Concepts of Justiciability 58
  Brown v. Board of Education 58
  Preface to Baker v. Carr 61
  Baker v. Carr 63
  Commentary on Baker v. Carr. 68
  Mora v. McNamara. 70
  Powell v. McCormack 72
Rulership 76
Questions 80

INTRODUCTION TO COURTS

The function of the courts is to decide cases of dispute between or among parties. The parties must be real parties in interest; the dispute must be real; and the case must be the kind that courts will decide.

A real party in interest is one who is immediately, personally, peculiarly affected in a way in which no other person is affected. In other words, a person (two or more persons may have exactly the same right or complaint) who comes before a court must come because he is the injured one. No one else may assert his right for him; such an interloper, such an intermeddler is not a real party in interest. Don Quixote would never have had standing in a court of justice; he might well go around jousting with windmills and redressing the fancied wrongs of a fair maiden, but the maiden's wrongs were not wrongs to Don Quixote in a legal sense. He would have been promptly ejected from a court of justice because he would not have been a real party in interest.

Just as the parties must be real in the sense of being specially and peculiarly affected by the resolution of the issue, the issue itself must be real. The dispute is not real if the parties before the court are not truly adversary. Another test of the reality of the dispute is whether the issue ostensibly before the court is a feigned issue—the nonadversary party intending to resolve some undisclosed issue and possibly an issue affecting the rights of persons not before the court.

Not only must the dispute be real, it must also be currently real. An issue that may have been intensely meaningful at some time in the past but, by reason of passage of time or change in circumstances, is no longer of immediate consequence to a person who comes before a court will not be entertained. There are two aspects of immediacy: one is called unripe controversy, a case that is incipient or embryonic or emerging but not yet of immediate significance, and the other is the moot case, where the issue has passed its zenith and has declined into unreality.

Finally, the case must be the kind that courts will entertain. A dispute between parties concerning the existence of God is not a kind of dispute that courts will undertake to resolve. On the other hand, a dispute over a boundary between farms or city lots is precisely the kind of case that courts *will* entertain. "Good fences make good neighbors," but if Robert Frost's neighbors disagree as to the boundary, then the courts will function.

The Roman poet Catullus thought that justice itself was nothing more than those principles that emerge as courts resolve disputes between parties to litigation. The precise illustration Catullus used was questions of boundary as between property owners. Indeed, the word "boundary" might be extended from questions of land ownership to questions of any legal right or of conflicting legal rights. There is, for example, a right of free speech guaranteed by the First Amendment to the Constitution of the United States. Nevertheless, as Justice Oliver Wendell Holmes declared, the right of free speech does not include a right to falsely cry "fire" in a crowded theater. There is a boundary to every right beyond which that right does not extend, and it is that boundary upon which the courts will pass.

There are many important issues among people that have personal, even social consequences, but not every issue will gain a court's attention. For instance, a male guest invited to a seven o'clock dinner party who appeared without a tie or jacket would deeply offend his hostess and, perhaps, cause her severe social damage. But this is not the kind of offense of which the courts will take notice.

While the concept that there must be appropriate subject matter in a controversy before courts will be moved to action (in legal parlance, "to take jurisdiction") is firm, it does undergo, like most concepts, dynamic changes. Although it is unlikely that courts will ever interest themselves in points of social etiquette, they are now undertaking issues that involve questions of a nature that heretofore courts would not touch. For example, in Brown v. Board of Education (1954), *infra,* seven decades after the Fourteenth Amendment to the Constitution of the United States was ratified, the Supreme Court intervened in the administration of local schools to impose new definitions of equality of educational opportunity. Again, in Baker v. Carr (1961), *infra,* the Supreme Court of the United States after long years of declining jurisdiction over questions of state politics imposed upon the states the principle of "one man, one vote."

When these three indispensable elements exist—real parties in interest, real dispute, and appropriate subject matter—the case is called justiciable.

JURISDICTION

WYMAN v. NEWHOUSE
United States Court of Appeals, Second Circuit, 93 F.2d 313 (1937).

MANTON, Circuit Judge.   This appeal is from a judgment entered dismissing the complaint on motion before trial. The action is on a judgment entered by default in a Florida state court, a jury having assessed the damages. The recovery there was for money loaned, money advanced for appellee, and for seduction under promise of marriage.

Appellee's [Newhouse] answer pleads facts supporting his claim that he was fraudulently enticed into the Florida jurisdiction, appellant's [Wyman] state of residence, for the sole purpose of service of process. A motion by the plaintiff-appellant to strike out this defense and for summary judgment   .   .   .   was denied. For the purpose of such a motion, the facts alleged in the answer are deemed to be true.   .   .   .   Affidavits were submitted in support of and in opposition to these motions, and thereupon appellee moved to dismiss the complaint. The motion was granted.

Appellant and appellee were both married, but before this suit appellant's husband died. They had known each other for some years and had engaged in meretricious relations.

The affidavits submitted by the appellee [are] deemed to be true for the purpose of testing the alleged error of dismissing the complaint established that he was a resident of New York and never lived in Florida. On October 25, 1935, while appellee was in Salt Lake City, Utah, he received a telegram from the appellant, which read: "Account illness home planning leaving. Please come on way back. Must see you." Upon appellee's return to New York he received a letter from appellant stating that her mother was dying in Ireland; that she was leaving the United States for good to go to her mother; that she could not go without seeing the appellee once more; and that she wanted to discuss her affairs with him before she left. Shortly after the receipt of this letter, they spoke to each other on the telephone, whereupon the appellant repeated, in a hysterical and distressed voice, the substance of her letter. Appellee promised to go to Florida in a week or ten days and agreed to notify her when he would arrive. This he did, but before leaving New York by plane he received a letter couched in endearing terms and expressing love and affection for him, as well as her delight at his coming. Before leaving New York, appellee telegraphed appellant, suggesting arrangements for their accommodations together while in Miami, Fla. She telegraphed him at a hotel in Washington, D.C., where he was to stop en route, advising him that the arrangements requested had been made. Appellee arrived at 6 o'clock in the morning at the Miami Airport and saw the appellant standing with her sister some 75 feet distant. He was met by a deputy sheriff who, upon identifying appellee, served him with process in a suit for $500,000. A photographer was present who attempted to take his picture. Thereupon a stranger introduced himself and offered to take appellee to his home, stating that he knew a lawyer who was acquainted with the appellant's attorney. The attorney whom appellee was advised to consult came to the stranger's home and seemed to know about the case. The attorney invited appellee to his office, and upon his arrival he found one of the lawyers for the appellant there. Appellee did not retain the Florida attorney to represent him. He returned to New York by plane that evening and consulted his New York counsel, who advised him to ignore the summons served in Florida. He did so, and judgment was entered by default. Within a few days after the service of process, the appellant came to New York and sought an interview with the appellee. It resulted in their meeting at the home of the appellee's attorney. She was accompanied by her Florida counsel.

These facts and reasonable deductions therefrom convincingly establish that the appellee was induced to enter the jurisdiction of the state of Florida by a fraud perpetrated upon him by the appellant in falsely representing her mother's illness, her intention to leave the United States, and her love and affection for him, when her sole purpose and apparent thought was to induce him to come within the Florida jurisdiction so as to serve him in an action for damages. Appellant does not deny making these representations. All her statements of great and undying love were disproved entirely by her appearance at the airport and participation in the happenings there. She never went to Ireland to see her mother, if indeed the latter was sick at all.

In asking for judgment based on these Florida proceedings, appellant relies upon article 4, section 1, of the United States Constitution, providing that "Full Faith and Credit shall be given in each State to the public Acts, Records, and Judicial Proceedings of every other State." Congress has provided that judicial proceedings duly authenticated, "shall have such faith and credit given to them in every court within the United States as they have by law or usage in the courts of the State from which they are taken." 28 U.S.C.A. The first inquiry is what faith and credit would be given to this judgment within the state of Florida. On these facts, the service of process was fraudulent, and under the circumstances we think would have been vacated there.   .   .   .

This judgment is attacked for fraud perpetrated upon the appellee which goes to the jurisdiction of the Florida court over his person. A judgment procured fraudulently, as here, lacks jurisdiction and is null and void. . . . A fraud affecting the jurisdiction is equivalent to a lack of jurisdiction. . . . A judgment recovered in a sister state, through the fraud of the party procuring the appearance of another, is not binding on the latter when an attempt is made to enforce such judgment in another state. . . .

Judgment affirmed.

BREWINGTON v. LOWE
Supreme Court of Indiana, 1 Ind. 21 (1848).

[The plaintiff, Joshua Brewington, brought suit in the Dearborn Circuit Court against George P. Lowe, the defendant, for trespassing on certain parcels of Brewington's land. The defendant pleaded that the properties were not located in Dearborn County but were located in Ohio and Ripley Counties and that consequently the Dearborn Circuit Court did not have jurisdiction over the case.

This issue was submitted for trial where it was admitted that the various properties were located in territories that had been stricken or attempted to be stricken from Dearborn County to form Ohio County and to add to the territory of Ripley County. The plaintiff offered testimony to establish that the legislative acts which purported to detach portions of Dearborn County were unconstitutional and void. He asserted that the courts of Dearborn County still had jurisdiction over the suits for trespass to these properties because the properties had not been effectively removed from that county. This testimony was excluded by the Dearborn Circuit Court on the ground that it was not proper for the court to hear testimony purporting to show the several acts of legislature were unconstitutional. That court granted judgment for defendant.]

SMITH, J.

In the history given of this case by the counsel for the plaintiff, and his statement is confirmed by the counsel for the defendant, we are informed that this suit was not instituted to settle any matter really in controversy between the nominal parties, but as a device by certain persons, who believed "that the legislature had been imposed upon as to the quantity of land in Dearborn county," when the acts above referred to were passed, and were desirous to test the constitutionality of those acts by bringing them in question in some way before a judicial tribunal. These persons accordingly procured surveys to be made of the territory embraced within the counties of Dearborn and Ohio, and then instituted this action avowedly for the purpose of testing the constitutionality of the acts of the legislature forming the counties of Ripley and Ohio by describing closes in the different counts of the declaration situate in each of the several pieces of territory which had been taken by those acts from the county of Dearborn, and thus raising an issue as to the jurisdiction of the Dearborn Circuit Court within the territory thus detached.

We think these proceedings were instituted under a mistaken apprehension of the proper functions of the judiciary. Courts of justice are established to try questions pertaining to the rights of individuals. An action is the form of a suit given by law for the recovery of that which is one's due, or a legal demand of one's right. . . . In such actions, if there is found to be a conflict of laws as they relate to the particular case under consideration, whether such conflict arises from constitutional reasons or otherwise, there can be no doubt that, from the very nature of the case, a decision must be rendered according to the laws which are paramount. But Courts will not go out of their proper sphere to determine the constitutionality or unconstitutionality of a law. They will not declare a law unconstitutional or void in the abstract, for that would be interfering with the legislative power which is separate and distinct. It is only from the necessity of the case, when they are compelled to notice such law as bearing upon the rights of the parties to a question legally presented for adjudication, that they will go into an examination of its validity, and then the decision has reference only to that particular question, except so far as it may operate as a precedent, when it may afterwards become necessary to decide similar cases. But unless some individual right, directly affecting the parties litigant, is thus brought in question so that a judicial decision becomes necessary to settle the matters in controversy between them relative thereto, the Courts have no jurisdiction; and it would be a perversion of the purposes for which they were instituted, and an assumption of functions that do not belong to them, to undertake to settle abstract questions of law in whatever shape such questions may be presented. The impropriety of doing so in the present case is manifest from the facts, that the question professed to be litigated, considered with reference either to the point of law attempted to be raised, or the importance of the interests involved, is one of very grave character, and the parties who would be chiefly affected by its decision are not before the Court, and have no opportunity of being heard. Indeed, it is well settled that Courts will not take cognizance of fictitious suits, instituted merely to obtain judicial opinions upon points of law. . . .

As we are distinctly informed by both parties that this is a fictitious suit, without inquiring into the grounds upon which the judgment was rendered, as it was for the defendant and only for costs, the judgment below will be affirmed at the plaintiff's cost in this Court.

PER CURIAM.   The judgment is affirmed with costs.

JURISDICTION—TERRITORIAL, PERSONAL, AND SUBSTANTIVE

Territorial Jurisdiction

Why did it matter in Brewington v. Lowe whether the land in question was in Dearborn County or in one of the other counties, Ohio or Ripley? It did matter because one aspect of jurisdiction, that is, the authority of a court, is territorial. A court has authority, has the power to judge, only within a specified boundary.

Territoriality is probably fundamental to the conduct and to the social organization of all animals, including man. When a bird sings on a treetop, it is claiming a territory; it is warning others of the same species not to invade. When a scented animal ejects an odoriferous substance, this may be a territorial claim.

In any polytheistic society the gods have limited territorial jurisdiction. Even today, particularly in India or Egypt, the traveler will encounter local village ceremonies in honor of local gods not recognized as having any authority beyond the confines of the village or a limited area.

A classical case in Judeo-Christian lore is that of Ruth and Naomi. Ruth, a Moabitess, elected because of her personal affection and attachment to Naomi, a Hebrew, to remain in Bethlehem, saying:

> [T]hy people *shall be* my people,
> and thy God my God.

Thus, it is an ancient tradition of all animals, including man, that authority, divine or secular, be recognized in terms of territorial limits.

Throughout most of man's history, territorial limits have been established by fighting. This is true of the family, the tribe, the clan, and, later, the nation; it was true of the empires of Caesar Augustus and of Genghis Khan. It is true today in the bipolar world represented by the United States of America and the Union of Soviet Socialist Republics. One of the substitutes for fighting, sometimes employed among nations, is a treaty for determining national boundaries, such as the treaty between the United States and Canada for the establishment of one of the longest undefended boundaries in history.

Within a relatively stable community, such as the United States, territorial boundaries develop through original settlements; through later agreements among those settlements with respect to boundaries; and through acts of Congress in establishing, first, territories and, then, converting territories into states by other orderly processes. Territoriality in the United States means, therefore, division of the nation into states, each with fixed boundaries, and division of states into counties, cities, boroughs, townships, and other municipal subdivisions. In modern times these subdivisions of a state are established by acts of the legislature. The jurisdiction, the authority, of courts is coextensive with territorial boundaries.

In the United States there are 51 systems of courts: one for the United States as a whole, known as the federal court system, and one for each of the fifty states. Each of these 51 systems has its subdivisions. In the federal system the District Court is the court of first instance; that is, the court where litigation must usually begin. This court is sometimes called the trial court or the court of *nisi prius,* the court of first impression. Even in the federal system the districts do not overlap state boundaries. Many of the states have several federal districts. The next category in the hierarchy of federal courts is the United States Court of Appeals. There are ten of these courts each encompassing a judicial circuit comprising several federal district courts. In addition, there is an eleventh circuit of the United States Court of Appeals which has jurisdiction over the District of Columbia. The highest court in the nation is, of course, the Supreme Court of the United States.

In general, the organization of courts in the several states is substantially the same as the organization of the federal courts. There will always be a lowest court, a court where the case is first instituted and is tried before a judge and a jury (if the case is the kind that requires a jury). Then there will usually be a system of intermediate courts, roughly comparable to the federal circuit courts of appeals, and, finally, a highest court, the supreme court of the state. Among the states, however, there is no uniformity of terminology. There are states in which the supreme court is not the name of the highest court. In some states the court of appeals is the highest court, and in others the court of appeals is an intermediate court. In some states the court of first instance, that is, the lowest court, is called the court of common pleas. In other states it is called a circuit court or a district court. However, there is no magic in this terminology. There are in both the federal and the state judicial systems three levels: the lowest, where litigation starts, the intermediate, and the highest. The intermediate and the highest courts are called appellate courts.[1]

It is the litigant's right of appeal that necessitates the structure of judicial systems just defined. The litigant who loses his case in the lowest court may appeal to the intermediate court, or sometimes directly to the highest court. However, most often he must appeal from the lowest court to the intermediate court and from the intermediate court to the highest court. In the lowest court the case is "tried," meaning that evidence is introduced and a record is kept of the evidence and the procedures. In the appellate courts the case is not "tried," in the sense that new evidence is introduced. Rather, the case is argued on points of law that are involved with respect to the record.

In general, there is a single judge in the lowest court, and there are several judges in the appellate courts (sometimes three, five, seven, or in the Supreme Court of the United States, nine). In the lowest courts the single judge may make a record of the reasons for his decision and judgment, but he is usually not required to make such a record. In appellate courts a record is almost invariably made. With few exceptions a record is kept of the reasons for the appellate courts' decisions. It is this record that informs lawyers and judges

---

[1]The names of various special courts appear in both the state and the federal hierarchies. Without any attempt to be exhaustive, some of these special courts are called: justices of the peace, always in quite restricted local jurisdictions; municipal courts of limited jurisdiction over subject matter, such as police and traffic courts, or over small claims of limited money amounts—a few hundred or perhaps a few thousand dollars; domestic relations courts; juvenile courts; rent and housing courts.

There is a tendency to proliferate courts to deal with special problems of social organizations. This has long been true in the development of English law, and it is no less true in modern times. We have not yet created special courts for "social dropouts," but such a development is not beyond the realm of speculation.

In the federal judicial system the case is the same. There are special courts for patents, customs, claims against the Federal Government, federal taxes, and there is a special system of courts for the District of Columbia. There are military courts to deal with offenses against military laws, both in the field and in the noncombatant sections of the military establishment.

The important thing to remember is that however specialized the court or however either minor or sophisticated its jurisdiction may be, the case, subject to only a very few limitations having to do with trivia of money amounts or of subject matter, may be appealed and work its way into the system of appellate jurisdiction of these three major levels.

of the rules of law that guide lawyers in advising clients and that usually control judges in future decisions. Thus, Anglo-American law develops case-by-case because the record of a previous relevant case is usually a precedent for the next case.

Records in early times were recorded and reported by voluntary reporters. Now, for many years, we have had official court reporters who are authorized by the several courts to publish the record of the appellate proceedings and the court's reasons for the decision. Thus, in the case that furnished the occasion for this commentary on territorial jurisdiction and appellate procedures, the caption of the case is

BREWINGTON v. LOWE

Supreme Court of Indiana, 1 Ind. 21 (1848).

The "1 Ind." refers to the Indiana official, published, printed, bound volume in which the case is reported and recorded. The "21" is the page number of that volume on which the report of the case begins. For every case in the book, some such reference to a report, usually called the citation, will appear.

Let us return now to the problems of territoriality in jurisdiction. Brewington sued Lowe in the Dearborn County Circuit Court for alleged trespass on Brewington's land. Lowe replied that the land was not in Dearborn County but in Ohio and Ripley Counties. If, in fact, the land was not in Dearborn county, the Dearborn County Court, the court of first impression or of original jurisdiction, would have no authority over the case—because of the territorial nature of the jurisdiction of courts. The trouble in the case was that Brewington and Lowe were in collusion. The trespass was not real. Brewington did not care whether Lowe came on his land or not. They had feigned the trespass in order to intrigue or deceive the court into deciding whether the legislature had acted constitutionally in changing the boundaries of Dearborn County. The court would not hear or decide that issue because the ostensible issue, namely the alleged trespass, was a false or feigned issue.

Personal Jurisdiction

Territorial jurisdiction, in terms of the boundaries just discussed, may be thought of as one side of the coin. The other side of the judicial coin is the concept of persons or property within the territory over which the court has jurisdiction. A court in Dearborn County would have had jurisdiction over all persons residing in Dearborn County and over all property located within Dearborn County, but it would have had no jurisdiction over persons residing or property located in Ohio County or Ripley County.

In law, as in all other disciplines, generalities are subject to exceptions. A court in Dearborn County would have had jurisdiction over a nonresident of that county who chanced to enter Dearborn County, if, while such a person was present in Dearborn County, the necessary legal proceedings had been instituted against him. (See Introduction to Chapter 9, p. 391 et seq., *infra.*) The caution with which courts assert this right to take jurisdiction over a person not regularly a resident in the court's territory is strikingly exemplified in the case of Wyman v. Newhouse. In that case Mr. Newhouse, weakened by ambivalent and amorous impulses, was tricked into coming within the territorial jurisdiction of a Florida court. There a judgment was entered against him because he did not appear in response to the summons that was served upon him. Such judgment is called a judgment by default. The Federal District Court in the Southern District of New York State and the Circuit Court of Appeals for the Second Federal Circuit held that the judgment of the Florida court was invalid because of the trickery by which Mr. Newhouse was brought within the territorial limits of the Florida court.

Article IV, Section 1, of the Constitution of the United States provides that "Full faith and credit shall be given in each State to the public acts, records, and judicial proceedings of every other State." Under this provision the Federal District Court in New York State and the Federal Second Circuit Court of Appeals would have had jurisdiction to enforce the judgment of the Florida court, but those courts refused to enforce that judgment because of the fraud perpetrated on Mr. Newhouse by Mrs. Wyman in enticing him into the jurisdiction of the Florida court.

There are alternatives to jurisdiction obtained by reason of the presence of a person in the territorial jurisdiction of the court. If, for example, Mr. Newhouse had owned property in Florida, Mrs. Wyman might have brought an action against him under a procedure by which she would have seized upon his property. On proper publication of notice of the action, Mr. Newhouse would have been required to enter his defense or suffer judgment by default. This is called an action *in rem.* It is an action that ensues because courts have jurisdiction over property rights within a given territory. The judgment, however, would not have been valid against Mr. Newhouse generally—only to the extent of the value of the property or the amount of the judgment, whichever might be less.

There are other alternatives, such as in the modern statutes of some states, that provide that a motorist who travels within the boundaries of a state of which he is not a resident may nevertheless be sued. To visualize such a case, suppose a motorist, a resident of the State of California, is motoring within the State of New Jersey. He encounters an accident. An injured party considers it the fault of the Californian and may serve a notice of suit upon the Secretary of State of New Jersey. The Secretary of State will mail to the registered address of the Californian, obtained by the license plate number on his car, a notice of the suit. Under such a proceeding the Californian must appear to defend himself or suffer the risk of a judgment by default, which can then be enforced against him in California under the "full faith and credit" provision of the Constitution, *supra.*

There are apparent exceptions to the rule that a court has jurisdiction only with respect to property and persons within its territorial boundaries. The consequences of a decision, order, injunction, or mandate issued by a court within its jurisdiction may extend beyond the jurisdiction proper. Take the situation of a corporation resident within the territorial jurisdiction of a court or suable for one reason or another within that jurisdiction. For the purposes of this discussion, a corporation is a person in exactly the same sense that a natural flesh-and-blood being is a person. The rules of territoriality apply to corporations exactly as they apply to natural persons. A corporation, like a person, may have far-flung interests and enterprises. For example, assume a corporation that is suable in a federal district court in the State of New York. Assume that that corporation is a holding company, which means that the corporation actually conducts no business of its own except to own and vote the stock of other corporations. In this case, let us suppose that the holding company, subject to the jurisdiction of a federal district court in New York State, owns all of the stock of another corporation, called a subsidiary, whose business is entirely that of producing and exporting oil from Saudi Arabia. Suppose that the subsidiary agrees with other corporations producing and exporting oil from Saudi Arabia on the price at which the oil will be sold. Such an agreement in the United States would contravene the American antitrust laws. Assume, however, that such an agreement would not contravene the laws of Saudi Arabia.

The federal district court in New York State may see fit to order the holding company (commonly known as a parent company) to so vote the stock in the subsidiary corporation as to effect a termination of the price-fixing agreement in Saudi Arabia. Such an order carries with it a penalty. The court may punish the holding company for contempt by fining it or even imprisoning the officers of the holding company if they fail to so vote the stock in the subsidiary company as to effect a change of management or whatever is necessary to terminate the price-fixing agreement. Clearly, although the federal district court in New York has no jurisdiction in Saudi Arabia, an order issued in that district would have, under the circumstances described, exactly the same effect as if the federal court in New York did have jurisdiction in Saudi Arabia. Basic principles, perfectly valid and effective for the great majority of situations, do have in practical operation exceptions that, while not real in principle, are real in practical consequences.[2]

[2]Folsom, Victor C., "Toward a Rule of Reason in the Extraterritorial Application of the Antitrust Laws," *Problems and Solutions,* reprinted from the Proceedings of the Southwestern Legal Foundations' Symposium Private Investors Abroad, Matthew Bender and Co., Albany, New York, 1967.

Despite the alternatives and *de facto* exceptions to territorial and personal jurisdiction, the general rule holds, and the reader may cling tightly to the broad proposition that, by and large, courts have jurisdiction only within a confined territory over persons residing and property lying within that territory. This is a generality, subject only to the proposition that no generality is wholly true. As Austin Scott of the Harvard Law School faculty remarked, "Nobody knows any law until he knows it all," adding, "and nobody knows it all."

Substantive Jurisdiction

Jurisdiction over the subject matter of the litigation is a third aspect of the jurisdiciton of courts. The clearest case of limitations upon jurisdiction of courts over the subject matter is in the federal system. Section 2 of Article III in the United States Constitution limits the jurisdiction of federal courts to cases arising under the Constitution, to the laws and treaties of the United States, and to other special types of cases, including controversies between citizens of different states.

Usually these conditions of federal jurisdiction are referred to as either "a federal question," which means a question that arises under the Constitution or the laws of the United States, or "diversity of citizenship," which means a controversy that exists between citizens of different states.

Unless there is diversity of citizenship, there must be a constitutional question or a question of federal law; that is, there must be a federal law dealing with the matter at issue. A striking illustration of this proposition may be noted in connection with the assassination of President Kennedy in Dallas, Texas, in the year 1963. If his assassin had lived to be prosecuted for murder, that prosecution could not have occurred in the federal courts because of the absence of a law making murder generally a federal crime. The prosecution would have had to occur in the jurisdiction of the Texas court in which the assassination occurred.[3]

In both state and federal courts there are various types of limitations of jurisdiction over subject matter: a police court cannot grant a divorce; a traffic court cannot administer the estate of a deceased person; a juvenile court cannot entertain the prosecution of an adult for a bank robbery.

Frequently appellate jurisdiction is limited by money amounts. In many states there are provisions that a case cannot go to the highest court in the state unless more than a certain amount of money is at issue. On the other hand, if it is a case of punishment for an alleged crime in which life or liberty is involved, in general, the case will always go to the highest court of the state

---

[3]It is now a federal crime to kill, kidnap, or assault the President, Vice President, and President-elect of the United States or any person in immediate succession to the presidency. The penalty is a maximum of life imprisonment except in the case of killing, in which event the death penalty is permissive. 79 Stat. 580 (1965), 18 U.S.C.A. § 1751 (1967 Supp.)

in which the case arose. If there are questions of due process of law under the Fourteenth Amendment, the case may go to the Supreme Court of the United States; for example, the recent cases in which persons convicted in state courts have had their convictions overturned by the Supreme Court because the police interrogated the accused person without the presence of counsel for the accused person.

In summary, a federal court has jurisdiction only if a provision of the United States Constitution or a federal law is involved. In the case of Wyman v. Newhouse, the federal court in New York State had jurisdiction because the "full faith and credit" provision of the United States Constitution was involved. The second general basis for federal jurisdiction, that is, the diversity of citizenship, is illustrated by our hypothetical example of the nonresident motorist. A citizen of New Jersey having been injured in the accident mentioned in that illustration might travel to the State of California and bring an action against the Californian either in a court of the State of California or in a federal court within the State of California. In either such case the court would have jurisdiction over the Californian because of his residence in the territorial jurisdiction of the court, either state or federal. If the suit were brought in the federal court, it would then be on the ground of diversity of citizenship. One other limitation, however, might frustrate the New Jersey plaintiff. If the amount of his claim were less than $10,000, he could not bring the action in a federal court because, by federal statute, the amount in controversy in diversity cases must exceed that figure. Thus, we have in this commentary illustrations of territorial jurisdiction, personal jurisdiction, and substantive jurisdiction.

JUSTICIABILITY

CASE OR CONTROVERSY—THE KINDS OF CASES COURTS WILL DECIDE

Criteria: Nature and Circumstances

MUSKRAT v. UNITED STATES
Supreme Court of the United States, 219 U.S. 346 (1911).

[This case arises under an act of the United States Congress which purported to increase the number of Indians qualified to participate in the division of certain Cherokee Indian lands. Congress was naturally doubtful about the constitutionality of such legislation and so it included in the act provisions whereby four designated Cherokees, two of whom held interests under the then existing land grants and two of whom were to be enrolled under the new grants, were to institute a suit against the United States in the Court of Claims for the purpose of testing the validity of the act. The act further provided for the right of appeal to the Supreme Court by either party upon the final judgment of the Court of Claims and for the payment of all attorneys' fees out of the United States Treasury.

The question presented in the case is whether Congress can by statute confer jurisdiction on the United States Supreme Court to determine the constitutionality of acts of Congress.]

Mr. Justice DAY delivered the opinion of the Court.

.   .   .   .

The first question in these cases, as in others, involves the jurisdiction of this court to entertain the proceeding, and that depends upon whether the jurisdiction conferred is within the power of Congress, having in view the limitations of the judicial power as established by the Constitution of the United States.

Section 1 of Article III of the Constitution provides:

"The judicial power of the United States shall be vested in one Supreme Court and in such inferior courts as the Congress may from time to time ordain and establish."

Section 2 of the same Article provides:

"The judicial power shall extend to all cases, in law and equity, arising under this Constitution, the laws of the United States, and treaties made, or which shall be made, under their authority; to all cases affecting ambassadors, other public ministers, and consuls; to all cases of admiralty and maritime jurisdiction; to controversies to which the United States shall be a party; to controversies between two or more States; between a State and citizens of another State; between citizens of different States; between citizens of the same State claiming lands under grants of different States, and between a State, or the citizens thereof, and foreign states, citizens or subjects."

.   .   .   .

It therefore becomes necessary to inquire what is meant by the judicial power thus conferred by the Constitution upon this court, and with the aid of appropriate legislation upon the inferior courts of the United States. "Judicial power," says Mr. Justice Miller in his work on the constitution, "is the power of a court to decide and pronounce a judgment and carry it into effect between persons and parties who bring a case before it for decision." Miller on the Constitution, 314.

As we have already seen by the express terms of the Constitution, the exercise of the judicial power is limited to "cases" and "controversies." Beyond this it does not extend, and unless it is asserted in a case or controversy within the meaning of the Constitution, the power to exercise it is nowhere conferred.

What, then, does the Constitution mean in conferring this judicial power with the right to determine "cases" and "controversies"? A "case" was defined by Mr. Chief Justice Marshall as early as the leading case of Marbury v. Madison, 1 Cranch, 137, to be a suit instituted according to the regular course of judicial procedure. And what more, if anything, is meant in the use of the term "controversy"? That question was dealt with by Mr. Justice Field, at the circuit, in the case of In re Pacific Railway Commission, 32 Fed. Rep 241, 245. Of these terms that learned Justice said:

"The judicial article of the Constitution mentions cases and controversies. The term 'controversies,' if distinguishable at all from 'cases,' is so in that it is less comprehensive than the latter, and includes only suits of a civil nature.   .   .   .   By cases and controversies are intended the claims of litigants brought before the courts for determination by such regular proceedings as are established by law or custom for the protection or enforcement of rights, or the prevention, redress, or punishment of wrongs. Whenever the claim of a party under the Constitution, law, or treaties of the United States takes such a form that the judicial power is capable of acting upon it, then it has become a case. The term implies the existence of present or possible adverse parties whose contentions are submitted to the court for adjudication."

The power being thus limited to require an application of the judicial power to cases and controversies, is the act which undertook to authorize the present suits to determine the constitutional validity of certain legislation within the constitutional authority of the court? This inquiry in the case before us includes the broader question, when may this court, in the exercise of the judicial power, pass upon the constitutional validity of an act of Congress? That question has been settled from the early history of the court, the leading case on the subject being Marbury v. Madison, *supra.*

In that case Chief Justice Marshall, who spoke for the court, was careful to point out that the right to declare an act of Congress unconstitutional could only be exercised when a proper case between opposing parties was submitted for judicial determination; that there was no general veto power in the court upon the legislation of Congress; and that the authority to declare an act unconstitutional sprung from the requirement that the court, in administering the law and pronouncing judgment between the parties to a case, and choosing between the requirements of the fundamental law established by the people and embodied in the Constitution and an act of the agents of the people, acting under authority of the Constitution, should enforce the Constitution as the supreme law of the land. The Chief Justice demonstrated, in a manner which has been regarded as settling the question, that with the choice thus given between a constitutional requirement and a conflicting statutory enactment, the plain duty of the court was to follow and enforce the Constitution as the supreme law established by the people. And the court recognized, in Marbury v. Madison and subsequent cases, that the exercise of this great power could only be invoked in cases which came regularly before the courts for determination, for, said the Chief Justice, in Osborn v. Bank of United States, 9 Wheat. 819, speaking of the third Article of the Constitution conferring judicial power.

"This clause enables the judicial department to receive jurisdiction to the full extent of the Constitution, laws, and treaties of the United States, when any question respecting them shall assume such a form that the judicial power is capable of acting on it. That power is capable of acting only when the subject is submitted to it by a party who asserts his rights in the form prescribed by law. It then becomes a case, and the Constitution declares that the judicial power shall extend to all cases arising under the Constitution, laws, and treaties of the United States."

.   .   .   .

Applying the principles thus long settled by the decisions of this court to the act of Congress undertaking to confer jurisdiction in this case, we find that . . .   there is neither more nor less in this procedure than an attempt to provide for a judicial determination, final in this court, of the constitutional validity of an act of Congress. Is such a determination within the judicial power conferred by the Constitution, as the same had been interpreted and defined in the authoritative decisions to which we have referred? We think it is not. That judicial power, as we have seen, is the right to determine actual controversies arising between adverse litigants, duly instituted in courts of proper jurisdiction. The right to declare a law unconstitutional arises because an act of Congress relied upon by one or the other of such parties in determining their rights is in conflict with the fundamental law. The exercise of this, the most important and delicate duty of this court, is not given to it as a body with revisory power over the action of Congress, but because the rights of the litigants in justiciable controversies require the court to choose between the fundamental law and a law purporting to be enacted within constitutional authority, but in fact beyond the power delegated to the legislative branch of the Government. . . .

The questions involved in this proceeding as to the validity of the legislation may arise in suits between individuals, and when they do and are properly brought before this court for consideration they, of course, must be determined in the exercise of its judicial functions. For the reasons we have stated, we are constrained to hold that these actions present no justiciable controversy within the authority of the court, acting within the limitations of the Constitution under which it was created. As Congress, in passing this act as a part of the plan involved, evidently intended to provide a review of the judgment of the Court of Claims in this court, as the constitutionality of important legislation is concerned, we think the act cannot be held to intend to confer jurisdiction on that court separately considered. . . .

The judgments will be reversed and the cases remanded to the Court of Claims, with directions to dismiss the petitions for want of jurisdiction.

OPINION OF THE JUSTICES
Correspondence and Public Papers of John Jay, Vol. 3, p. 486 (1793).

[In an early application of the doctrine of separation of powers within the Federal Government of the United States, the Supreme Court refused to give an advisory opinion concerning the meaning of a treaty to Thomas Jefferson, then Secretary of State to President George Washington. In 1793 the Justices of the Supreme Court of the United States received the following letter, sent to them in the President's behalf by his Secretary of State.]

Philadelphia, July 18, 1793

Gentlemen:
    The war which has taken place among the powers of Europe produces frequent transactions within our ports and limits, on which questions arise of considerable difficulty, and of greater importance to the peace of the United States. These questions depend for their solution on the construction of our treaties, on the laws of nature and nations, and on the laws of the land, and are often presented under circumstances *which do not give a cognizance of them to the tribunals of the county.* Yet, their decision is so little analogous to the ordinary functions of the executive, as to occasion embarrassment and difficulty to them. The President therefore would be much relieved if he found himself free to refer questions of this description to the opinions of the judges of the Supreme Court of the United States, whose knowledge of the subject would secure us and their authority insure the respect of all parties. He has therefore asked the attendance of such of the judges

as could be collected in time for the occasion, to know, in the first place, their opinion, whether the public may, with propriety, be availed of their *advice on these questions?* And if they may, to present, for their advice the abstract questions which have already occurred, or may soon occur, from which they will themselves strike out such as any circumstances might, in their opinion, forbid them to pronounce on. I have the honour to be with sentiments of the most perfect respect, gentlemen,

Your most obedient and humble servant,
Thomas Jefferson

The following are some of the questions submitted by the President to the Justices:

1. Do the treaties between the United States and France give to France or her citizens, a *right,* when at war with a power with whom the United States are at peace, to fit out originally in and from the ports of the United States vessels armed for war, with or without commission?

2. If they give such a *right,* does it extend to all manner of armed vessels, or to particular kinds only? If the latter, to what kinds does it extend?

3. Do they give to France or her citizens, in the case supposed a right to refit or arm anew vessels, which, before their coming within any port of the United States, were armed for war, with or without commission?

4. If they give such a *right,* does it extend to all manner of armed vessels, or to particular kinds only? If the latter, to what kinds does it extend? Does it include an *augmentation* of force, or does it only extend to replacing the vessel in *status quo?*

.   .   .   .

19. If any armed vessel of a foreign power at war with another, with whom the United States are at peace, shall make prize of the subjects or property of its enemy within the territory or jurisdiction of the United States, have not the United States a right to cause restitution of such prizes? Are they bound, or not, by the principles of neutrality to do so, if such prize shall be within their power?

20. To what distance, by the laws and usages of nations, may the United States exercise the right of prohibiting the hostilities of foreign powers at war with each other within rivers, bays, and arms of the sea, and upon the sea along the coasts of the United States?

21. Have vessels, armed for war under commission from a foreign power, a right, without the consent of the United States, to engage within their jurisdiction seamen or soldiers for the service of such vessels, being citizens of that power, or of another foreign power, or citizens of the United States?

.   .   .   .

25. May we, within our own ports, sell ships to both parties, prepared merely for merchandise? May they be pierced for guns?

26. May we carry either or both kinds to the ports of the belligerent powers for sale?

27. Is the principle, that free bottoms make free goods, and enemy bottoms make enemy goods, to be considered as now an established part of the law of nations?

28. If it is not, are nations with whom we have no treaties, authorized by the law of nations to take out of our vessels enemy passengers, not being soldiers, and their baggage?

29.   May an armed vessel belonging to any of the belligerent powers follow *immediately* merchant vessels, enemies, departing from our ports, for the purpose of making prizes of them? If not, how long ought the former to remain, after the latter have sailed? And what shall be considered as the place of departure, from which the time is to be counted? And how are the facts to be ascertained?

Chief Justice JAY and the Associate Justices replied to the President directly, as follows:

August 8, 1793

Sir:

We have considered the previous question stated in a letter written by your direction to us by the Secretary of State on the 18th of last month, [regarding] the lines of separation drawn by the Constitution between the three departments of the government. These being in certain respects checks upon each other, and our being judges of a court in the last resort, are considerations which afford strong arguments against the propriety of our extra-judicially deciding the questions alluded to, especially as the power given by the Constitution to the President, of calling on the heads of departments for opinions, seems to have been *purposely* as well as expressly united to the *executive* departments.

We exceedingly regret every event that may cause embarrassment to your administration, but we derive consolation from the reflection that your judgment will discern what is right, and that your usual prudence, decision, and firmness will surmount every obstacle to the preservation of the rights, peace, and dignity of the United States.

ECCLES v. PEOPLES BANK OF LAKEWOOD VILLAGE, CALIFORNIA
Supreme Court of the United States, 333 U.S. 426 (1947).

[In admitting the respondent, a state bank, to membership in the Federal Reserve System, the Board of Governors prescribed a condition that if the Transamerica Corporation, a powerful bank holding company, acquired stock in the bank, the bank would withdraw from membership within 60 days after written notice from the Board. Subsequently, Transamerica acquired slightly less than 11% of the bank's stock.

The bank, fearing enforcement of the condition, sued the Board seeking a declaratory judgment[4] that the condition was invalid and an injunction against its enforcement. The

---

[4]Under statutes such as the Uniform Declaratory Judgment Act, which was first proposed in 1922 by the National Conference of Commissioners on Uniform State Laws and which has been adopted by a majority of the states, and the Federal Declaratory Judgment Act and other like statutes, a court may declare the rights, status, and other legal relations of parties seeking such declaration, whether further relief is or could be claimed. It is thought that such statutes represent a great advance in judicial methods and concepts. It should be emphasized that under the various statutes it is generally necessary that an actual controversy exists before the courts can take jurisdiction.

The United States Declaratory Judgment Act, 48 Stat. 955 (1934), as amended, 28 U.S.C. 2201-02 (1964), provides in part:

§ § 2201. Creation of remedy.

In a case of actual controversy within its jurisdiction, except with respect to Federal taxes, any court of the United States, upon the filing of an appropriate pleading, may declare the rights

Board of Governors, under the direction of chairman Marriner S. Eccles, disavowed any present intention of enforcing the condition, on the ground that it had satisfied itself that the bank's independence had not been affected and that the public interest required no action. The District Court for the District of Columbia denied the bank the relief sought. On appeal, the Court of Appeals for the District of Columbia reversed the decision and held that the condition was invalid. The case then went to the Supreme Court of the United States.]

Mr. Justice FRANKFURTER delivered the opinion of that court.

. . . . .

A declaratory judgment, like other forms of equitable relief, should be granted only as a matter of judicial discretion, exercised in the public interest. . . . Especially where governmental action is involved, courts should not intervene unless the need for equitable relief is clear, not remote or speculative.

The actuality of the plaintiff's need for a declaration of his rights is therefore of decisive importance. And so we turn to the facts of the case at bar. The Bank has always insisted that it is independent of Transamerica; the Board of Governors has sustained the claim. The Bank stands on its right to remain in the Federal Reserve System; the Board acknowledges that right. The Bank disclaims any intention to give up its independence; the Board of Governors, having imposed the condition to safeguard this independence, disavows any action to terminate the Bank's membership, so long as the Bank maintains the independence on which it insists. What the Bank really fears, and for which it now seeks relief, is that under changed conditions, at some future time, it may be required to withdraw from membership, and if this happens, so the argument runs, the Comptroller of the Currency, one of the Directors of the Federal Deposit Insurance Corporation, has agreed with the Federal Reserve Board to refuse application by the Bank for deposit insurance as a non-member.

Thus the Bank seeks a declaration of its rights *if* it should lose its independence, or *if* the Board of Governors should reverse its policy and seek to invoke the condition even though the Bank remains independent and *if* then the Directors of the Federal Deposit Insurance Corporation should not change their policy not to grant deposit insurance to the Bank as a non-member of the Federal Reserve System. The concurrence of these contingent events, necessary for injury to be realized, is too speculative to warrant anticipatory judicial determinations. Courts should avoid passing on questions of public law even short of constitutionality that are not immediately pressing. Many of the same reasons are present which impel them to abstain from adjudicating constitutional claims against a statute before it effectively and presently impinges on such claims.

It appears that the respondent could, if it wishes, protect itself from the loss of its independence through adoption of bylaws forbidding any further sale or pledge of its shares to Transamerica or its affiliates. . . . To this the Bank replies that even if

and other legal relations of any interested party seeking such declaration, whether or not further relief is or could be sought. Any such declaration shall have the force and effect of a final judgment or decree and shall be reviewable as such [Emphasis added.]

The National Conference of Commissioners on Uniform State Laws, mentioned above, is an organization of scholars appointed by the various states for the promotion of the uniformity of legislation where such uniformity is deemed desirable and practical.

its independence is maintained, the Board of Governors may change its policy, and seek enforcement of Condition No. 4, whether or not such enforcement is required by "the public interest" in having independent banks, which the condition now serves. Such an argument reveals the hypothetical character of the injury on the existence of which a jurisdiction, rooted in discretion is to be exercised. In the light of all this, the difficulties deduced from the present uncertainty regarding the future enforcement or the condition, possibly leading to uninsured deposits, are too tenuous to call for adjudication of important issues of public law.^A We are asked to contemplate as a serious danger that a body entrusted with some of the most delicate and grave responsibilities in our Government will change a deliberately formulated policy after urging it on this court against the Bank's standing to ask for relief.

.　.　.　.

A determination of administrative authority may of course be made at the behest of one so immediately and truly injured by regulation claimed to be invalid, that his need is sufficiently compelling to justify judicial intervention even before completion of the administrative process. But, as we have seen, the Bank's grievance here is too remote and insubstantial, too speculative in nature, to justify an injunction against the Board of Governors, and therefore equally inappropriate for a declaration of rights. . . .

Where administrative intention is expressed but has not come to fruition　.　.　.　, or where that intention is unknown　.　.　.　, we have held that the controversy is not yet ripe for equitable intervention. Surely, when a body such as the Federal Reserve Board has not only not asserted a challenged power but has expressly disclaimed its intention to go beyond the legitimate "public interest" confided to it, a court should stay its hand.

Judgment reversed.

The CHIEF JUSTICE and Mr. Justice DOUGLAS took no part in the consideration or decision of this case.[5]

Mr. Justice REED, with whom Mr. Justice BURTON joins, dissenting.

In order to get admission into the Federal Reserve System, the respondent was required to put into its charter a provision which was allegedly beyond the power of

---

^AThe Bank asserted, in its affidavits, not that lack of confidence had deterred depositors, but that deposits had been so heavy that capital expansion was in order, but might be disadvantaged by fear of prospective investors to risk personal assessment if deposits were uninsured.

[5]The reader will notice that in the Eccles case the CHIEF JUSTICE and Mr. Justice DOUGLAS took no part in the consideration or in the decision of the case. This is a privilege that judges may exercise. There are always good reasons why a particular judge may not participate in a particular case. He may have been involved in the matter, either as a lawyer or as an official of government, prior to having become a judge or justice. He may have some private financial interest that might render him apparently partial or in some way interested in the outcome. There are many such situations. The reader will frequently see in this book the notation in a report that a particular judge or justice did not participate. This is usually called "disqualification." The judge himself usually makes the decision as to whether or not he will disqualify himself. There are, however, cases in which a lawyer on one side or the other will suggest to the judge that he should disqualify himself. Even under such a circumstance the judge's determination as to his suitability for participating in the case, often called "sitting in the case," will usually be final.

President Richard M. Nixon nominated to the Supreme Court of the United States Clement Furman Haynsworth, Jr. One of the grounds for rejection of his nomination by the United States

the Board of Governors of the System to require. It seems obvious that the requirement was a restriction on the market for the respondent's stock and therefore detrimental to the conduct of its business, a continuing threat of the Board to exclude respondent from the benefits of the System.

Respondent desired to be free of what it regarded as an illegal requirement. The Board of Governors has not agreed that it will never enforce the prohibition but holds it as a threat to force the respondent to resign from the System upon acquisition of control by those deemed undesirable by the Board.

Certainly, as I see it, there is not only the possibility of future injury but a present injury by reason of the threat to the marketability of respondent's stock. It may have a substantial bearing upon the willingness of customers to establish banking relations with it, especially major relationships looking toward long and close associations of interests. It requires no elaboration to convince me that the threat is a real and substantial interference by allegedly illegal governmental action. As that threat has taken a definite form by the enforced agreement for withdrawal, we have not something that may happen but a concrete written notice requiring withdrawal by this respondent from the System on the happening of a fact which is contrary to the Board's idea of a legitimate public interest. Whether the Board's idea of a legitimate public interest is correct is the very point at issue.

In such circumstances there is a justiciable controversy, the claim of a right and a present threat to deprive a particular person of the right claimed. The damage from its actual or threatened enforcement is, of course, irremediable. Any bank would be seriously injured by even an effort to oust it from the System. This gives jurisdiction under the Declaratory Judgment Act.   . . .

I would decide the case on the merits.[6]

The Autonomy of Courts

Why would the Supreme Court of the United States refuse to entertain a case involving distribution of lands and funds among Cherokee Indians, when the Congress of the United States had so clearly conferred jurisdiction upon the Court of Claims and upon the Supreme Court to determine the validity of the legislation in question? Except for the restrained and temperate language of the Supreme Court, it appears to have been almost disrespectful to Congress. The reason for the Supreme Court's rejection of the case is deeply rooted in legal history.

Senate (November 21, 1969) was that he had failed to disqualify himself in certain cases involving corporations in which he held stock.

[6]In Brockington v. Rhodes, 396 U.S. 41 (1969), the plaintiff brought suit against Governor Rhodes of Ohio to force the Governor to place the plaintiff's name on the 1968 ballot for election to the United States House of Representatives. The plaintiff was denied relief in the first instance and took a series of appeals. The case reached the United States Supreme Court during the October Term of 1969, almost one year after the election had been held. The Supreme Court dismissed the case as being moot, since it was then impossible to grant the requested relief. For a discussion of mootness, see p. 30, *supra*.

The concept of division of governmental powers among the three branches, the executive, the legislative, and the judicial, is clearly articulated in the United States Constitution but did not originate with the Constitution. The division existed in English law; it existed in Roman law; it is a division typical of many, if not almost all, organized societies. Even in an embryonic society, such as that of the Hebrews depicted in the Book of Exodus, the judging function, although exercised by the executive (Moses), is identified as a separate function. In a much more sophisticated society, such as the democracy of the Greeks, the three divisions are delineated: the people as a whole act as the legislature, the executive (Pericles, for example) acts as statesman and military leader, and the old men of the community act as the court (the Areopagus).

Courts in all climates, in all lands, in all historical times (certainly in the last 2500 years) have acquired a separateness from the other roles of government. This has given them an autonomy, a standing, an acceptance by society, which enables them to determine for themselves, within rather broad limits, what the judicial function will and will not be. Of course, no court would undertake to put a law on the statute books, or declare war, or make a treaty. On the other hand, within the concept of litigation, that is, disputes between and among parties (personal, corporate, or official), the courts possess broad discretion in borderline questions about jurisdiction and justiciability. In this section we identify some of the principles that the courts employ in exercising that discretion.

The Act of Congress in question in the Muskrat case had the effect of increasing the number of persons entitled to participate in the division of Cherokee lands and funds. Naturally, Congress must have had some doubt about the validity of this legislation. It diminished the rights of the existing class of Cherokee Indians by creating a new and enlarged class of participants. Congress, and perhaps all the Cherokee Indians, would have liked to know whether Congress could diminish the rights, with respect to distribution of lands and funds, of some Cherokee Indians in order to create rights in others.

The Supreme Court said, however, that there was no controversy here as between an identified individual and another identified individual with adverse interests. Nothing had been done under the Act of Congress that changed the distribution of the lands and the funds. The Muskrat case stands for the proposition that not even Congress can require the Federal judiciary to take jurisdiction where the historical criteria for justiciability—case or controversy involving adversary parties—are absent.

Quite similar is the correspondence in the Opinion of the Justices. President George Washington wished an opinion about the meaning of certain treaties. The Supreme Court would not give him the desired opinion because it would have been extrajudicial. And, significantly, it was for the Court itself to decide the question of whether the matter presented by the request was at that stage justiciable.

The Federal Congress and the legislatures of many states have attempted to relax the criteria for rules about justiciability in the so-called declaratory judgment acts (see p. 46, *supra*). Such statutes generally provide that in cases of actual controversy the court shall have the power to declare the rights and other legal relations of any interested party, whether further relief is imminently requested. It should be noted that the Muskrat case arose in 1911. The Eccles case arose in 1947, after the enactment of the Federal Declaratory Judgment Act. Yet, even under that Act, the majority of the Supreme Court refused to take jurisdiction of the Eccles case on the ground that the controversy was not yet ripe. The minority of the Court thought otherwise and, to this writer, seems to have been more correct than the majority.

The reader may well review the case of Eccles v. Peoples Bank of Lakewood to determine how he thinks about the issue. Does he think, as the majority of the Supreme Court reasoned, that the case had "not yet come to fruition," or does he think, as the minority reasoned, that the Peoples Bank of Lakewood was suffering "a present injury by reason of the threat to the marketability of [the bank's] stock" and the possible disinclination of customers to deal with a bank whose status in the Federal Reserve System was uncertain?

For the first time in this book, one encounters in the Eccles case the significant role that dissenting opinions play in the decision-making process of the courts. As noted in the commentary on jurisdiction, appellate courts are manned by several judges. The judges, or justices as they are called in the Supreme Court of the United States, frequently disagree. The majority set forth their reasons in the report of the case and likewise, the minority set forth their reasons for their dissenting views. The majority views make the law. The dissents, however, are an important record for consideration by the public and by legal students and scholars, and they sometimes influence decisions in later cases.

Cases or Controversies of Trivial Subject Matter

REED v. MALEY
Court of Appeals of Kentucky, 115 Ky. 816 (1903).

PAYNTER, J.   The petition makes substantially the following averments: That the plaintiff was a married woman; that on October 19, 1898, whilst sitting near the window in her house, the defendant approached near it, and proposed to her to have sexual intercourse with him; that she indignantly refused the proposal; that the defendant thereby committed a trespass against her person; that she was frightened, and caused great mortification and shame; and in consequence of which she was greatly excited and damaged. It was not averred that the defendant entered her house or was in reach of her, so as to put her in fear. The court sustained a demurrer to and dismissed the petition on the ground that it did not state a cause of action. In an action for an assault the petition must allege the facts which constitute the assault, and in alleged trespass it is essential to state the facts which constitute it. . . .   No facts were averred which showed that the defendant made an assault upon the plaintiff, hence did not inflict any injury upon her person.

The sole question presented for consideration is, will a cause of action lie in favor of a woman against a man who solicits her to have sexual intercourse with him? If it will, the petition states a cause of action; otherwise it does not. This is a novel case, but the novelty of the case is no reason for denying a recovery if the cause of action can be made to rest upon some sound principle of law. The fact that learned counsel have been unable to cite any case involving the question here for our determination strongly conduces to show that the legal profession for centuries has labored under the impression that a civil action will not lie on a state of facts like those averred in the petition, for it is probable that, during past generations, applications have been made to them for the institution of actions like this one. If such applications have been made, it is probable that they have been made by good and virtuous women; and certainly there is no moral or social reason why the members of the legal profession should not have instituted such actions to recover damages for the wounded feelings and humiliation good women have suffered from such proposals, if such an action in their judgment could have been maintained. The solicitation for such intimacy is not equivalent to charging a woman with the want of chastity; therefore, if made under circumstances that would make a charge of unchastity a slander and actionable, no action for slander could be maintained on account of such solicitation   .   .   .   As there was no assault upon or trespass against the person of the plaintiff, and no physical injury produced, it seems to us that no recovery can be had. It is well settled that mental suffering may be taken into consideration in estimating damages in cases of physical injury. In such cases there may be a recovery for physical and mental suffering arising from physical injury. The objection to a recovery for injury occasioned without physical impact is the difficulty of testing the statements of the alleged sufferer, the remoteness of the damages, and the metaphysical character of the injury considered apart from physical pain.   .   .   .   Society and the moral sentiments of the people strongly condemn conduct like that with which the appellee is charged, but there is no principle of law known to us which will enable a party to maintain a civil action upon facts like those here under consideration.   .   .   .   .

The judgment is affirmed.[7]

STEPHENS v. MYERS
Nisi Prius, 4 C. & P. 349 (1830).

Assault: The declaration stated that the defendant threatened and attempted to assault the plaintiff. Plea: Not guilty.

---

[7]Note that Reed v. Maley is a civil case. Many states have statutes making conduct similar to that found in Reed v. Maley a crime. Witness, for example, a Pennsylvania statute concerning the malicious use of telephones which provides:

"Whoever telephones another person and addresses to or about such other person any lewd, lascivious or indecent words or language, or whoever anonymously telephones another person repeatedly for the purpose of annoying, molesting or harassing such other person or his or her

It appeared that the plaintiff was acting as chairman at a parish meeting, and sat at the head of a table, at which table the defendant also sat, there being about six or seven persons between him and the plaintiff. The defendant having, in the course of some angry discussion which took place, been very vociferous, and interrupted the proceedings of the meeting, a motion was made that he should be turned out, which was carried by a very large majority. Upon this the defendant said he would rather pull the chairman out of the chair than be turned out of the room, and immediately advanced with his fist clenched toward the chairman, but was stopped by the churchwarden, who sat next but one to the chairman, at a time when he was not near enough for any blow he might have meditated to have reached the chairman, but the witnesses said that it seemed to them that he was advancing with an intention to strike the chairman.

TINDAL, C. J., in his summing up, said: It is not every threat, when there is no actual personal violence, that constitutes an assault; there must, in all cases, be the means of carrying the threat into effect. The question I shall leave to you will be, whether the defendant was advancing at the time, in a threatening attitude, to strike the chairman, so that his blow would almost immediately have reached the chairman if he had not been stopped; then, though he was not near enough at the time to have struck him, yet, if he was advancing with that intent, I think it amounts to an assault in law. If he was so advancing that, within a second or two of time, he would have reached the plaintiff, it seems to me it is an assault in law. If you think he was not advancing to strike the plaintiff, then only can you find your verdict for the defendant; otherwise you must find it for the plaintiff, and give him such damages as you think the nature of the case requires.

Verdict for the plaintiff. Damages 1s.[one shilling].

Causes of Action

This commentary arises from a comparison of facts in the cases of Reed v. Maley and Stephens v. Myers. One may wonder why an obviously offensive action, such as Maley's indecent proposal to a married woman sitting in the window of her house, would not be entertained by the court, whereas the trivial action of parish member Myers in raising his fist and moving in the direction of chairman Stephens would be entertained by the court. The answer lies in what is called the cause of action.

It has long since become established in Anglo-American law that mere words do not constitute an assault. On the other hand, the demonstrated intent of one person to strike another is the simplest form of assault; the wrongful entry on the property of one person by another person is trespass; the failure to pay a debt has from ancient times constituted the cause of action known as "debt;" the wrongful retention by one person of the personal property of another gives rise to a cause of action for its recovery long known as "reple-

family, shall be deemed guilty of the misdemeanor of being a disorderly person, and, upon conviction, shall be fined in any sum not exceeding five hundred dollars ($500), to which may be added imprisonment in the county jail not exceeding six months. . . . " Act of June 24, 1939, P.L. 872, § 414.1, as amended, Purdon's Pa. Stat. Ann. tit. 18, § 4414.1 (1961).

vin." There were in English law numerous such specified causes of action, and the aggrieved party could institute his appropriate cause of action by obtaining from a magistrate a so-called writ for that particular cause of action. By the 12th century, many writs in English law were already quite precisely defined. The litigant had to decide the precise nature of the cause of action. A litigant could not obtain from a magistrate a writ for debt and under that writ make a claim for trespass. Indeed, the rigidity was more acute than even that illustration. A litigant who obtained a writ for debt in the amount of 20 pounds and proved up a debt of 19 pounds would lose his case entirely because he had asked that the writ issue for an amount that he did not succeed in proving. These rigidities have long since abated.

Today, it is not necessary that the litigant do more than make a short and plain statement of the grounds upon which he claims the court's attention. This is the rule in the federal courts, and it is the rule in most of the courts of the fifty states, although there are variations among the states as to the degree of technicality that the litigant's formal approach to the court must take.

Nevertheless, the law as a substantive body changes slowly, and by the same token, the rules of procedure change slowly. Hence, even in modern times the boundaries of an historical form of action still constitute a body of thought that lawyers and judges rely upon for determining what cases are and what cases are not justiciable. The definition in advance of what forms of conduct or misconduct are actionable informs the citizenry of rights and obligations normal to a given organized society.

A distinction may be made here between those causes of action that arise out of case law, known as common law, and those that arise out of legislative enactments, known as statutory law. Common law causes of action, while quite numerous, are not unlimited. These causes of action do change from time to time, and judges, by interpretation, bring sets of facts within the concept of the cause of action that at some other time, in some other court, might not have been so treated. For example, in the case of Stephens v. Myers the parish member's offensive words alone would not have constituted an assault. Perhaps, just the raising of his fist alone would not have constituted an assault, but the movement by Myers toward Stephens under all the circumstances brought the facts within the common law cause of action of assault.

The reader will recall from Chapter 1 that legislation is one method by which society creates rights or duties or prohibitions not within the body of common or case law. In the footnote to Reed v. Maley there is an illustration of this use of legislation to add a dimension, so to speak, to the common law. Although Maley's offensive proposal from the sidewalk was not actionable, if he had made the same proposal over the telephone, in many jurisdictions by statute his words would have been a crime.

In summary, we can say that while there are few forms of misconduct that cannot be brought before a court, either by a private litigant alleging injury or by the state charging a crime, there are boundaries, definitions, and limitations on what is actionable. The elements and components of the complaint must fall within some generally recognized right, wrong, permission or prohibition. This is simply the good sense of orderliness and predictability in the administration of justice.

STANDING—PARTIES MUST HAVE A REAL INTEREST

PIERCE v. SOCIETY OF SISTERS
Supreme Court of the United States, 268 U.S. 510 (1925).

Mr. Justice McREYNOLDS delivered the opinion of the Court.

These appeals are from decrees [of the district court] . . . which granted preliminary orders restraining appellants from threatening or attempting to enforce the Compulsory Education Act adopted November 7, 1922, under the initiative provision of her Constitution by the voters of Oregon. Jud. Code, § 266. They present the same points of law; there are no controverted questions of fact. Rights said to be guaranteed by the federal Constitution were specially set up, and appropriate prayers asked for their protection.

The challenged Act, effective September 1, 1926, requires every parent, guardian or other person having control or charge or custody of a child between eight and sixteen years to send him "to a public school for the period of time a public school shall be held during the current year" in the district where the child resides; and failure so to do is declared a misdemeanor. There are exemptions—not specially important here—for children who are not normal, or who have completed the eighth grade, or who reside at considerable distances from any public school, or whose parents or guardians hold special permits from the County Superintendent. The manifest purpose is to compel general attendance at public schools by normal children, between eight and sixteen, who have not completed the eighth grade. And without doubt enforcement of the statute would seriously impair, perhaps destroy, the profitable features of appellees' business and greatly diminish the value of their property.

Appellee, the Society of Sisters, is an Oregon corporation, organized in 1880, with power to care for orphans, educate and instruct the youth, establish and maintain academies or schools, and acquire necessary real and personal property. It has long devoted its property and effort to the secular and religious education and care of children, and has acquired the valuable good will of many parents and guardians. It conducts interdependent primary and high schools and junior colleges, and maintains orphanages for the custody and control of children between eight and sixteen. In its primary schools many children between those ages are taught the subjects usually pursued in Oregon public schools during the first eight years. Systematic religious instruction and moral training according to the tenets of the Roman Catholic Church are also regularly provided. All courses of study, both temporal and religious, contemplate continuity of training under appellee's charge; the primary schools are essential to the system and the most profitable. It owns valuable buildings, especially constructed and equipped for school purposes. The business is remunerative—the annual income from primary schools exceeds thirty thousand dollars—and the successful conduct of this requires long time contracts with teachers and parents. The Compulsory Education

Act of 1922 has already caused the withdrawal from its schools of children who would otherwise continue, and their income has steadily declined. The appellants, public officers, have proclaimed their purpose strictly to enforce the statute.

After setting out the above facts the Society's bill alleges that the enactment conflicts with the right of parents to choose schools where their children will receive appropriate mental and religious training, the right of the child to influence the parents' choice of a school, the right of schools and teachers therein to engage in a useful business or profession, and is accordingly repugnant to the Constitution and void. And, further, that unless enforcement of the measure is enjoined the corporation's business and property will suffer irreparable injury.

.   .   .   .   The [district] court ruled [upon the motions for preliminary injunctions] that the Fourteenth Amendment guaranteed appellees against the deprivation of their property without due process of law consequent upon the unlawful interference by appellants with the free choice of patrons, present and prospective. It declared the right to conduct schools was property and that parents and guardians, as a part of their liberty, might direct the education of children by selecting reputable teachers and places. Also, that these schools were not unfit or harmful to the public, and that enforcement of the challenged statute would unlawfully deprive them of patronage and thereby destroy their owners' business and property. Finally, that the threats to enforce the Act would continue to cause irreparable injury; and the suits were not premature.

No question is raised concerning the power of the State reasonably to regulate all schools, to inspect, supervise and examine them, their teachers and pupils; to require that all children of proper age attend some school, that teachers shall be of good moral character and patriotic disposition, that certain studies plainly essential to good citizenship must be taught, and that nothing be taught which is manifestly inimical to the public welfare.

The inevitable practical result of enforcing the Act under consideration would be destruction of appellees' primary schools, and perhaps all other private primary schools for normal children within the State of Oregon. These parties are engaged in a kind of undertaking not inherently harmful, but long regarded as useful and meritorious. Certainly there is nothing in the present records to indicate that they have failed to discharge their obligations to patrons, students or the State. And there are no peculiar circumstances or present emergencies which demand extraordinary measures relative to primary education.

.   .   .   .

The suits were not premature. The injury to appellees was present and very real, not a mere possibility in the remote future. If no relief had been possible prior to the effective date of the Act, the injury would have become irreparable. Prevention of impending injury by unlawful action is a well recognized function of courts of equity.

The decrees below are affirmed.

TILESTON v. ULLMAN
Supreme Court of the United States, 318 U.S. 44 (1943).

PER CURIAM.   This case comes here on appeal to review a declaratory judgment of the Supreme Court of Errors of Connecticut that §§ 6246 and 6562 of the General

Statutes of Connecticut of 1930—prohibiting the use of drugs or instruments to prevent conception, and the giving of assistance or counsel in their use—are applicable to appellant, a registered physician, and as applied to him are constitutional.   .   .   .

.   .   . Appellant alleged that the statute, if applicable to him, would prevent his giving professional advice concerning the use of contraceptives to three patients whose condition of health was such that their lives would be endangered by child-bearing, and that appellees, law enforcement officers of the state, intend to prosecute any offense against the statute and "claim or may claim" that the proposed professional advice would constitute such an offense. The complaint set out in detail the danger to the lives of appellant's patients in the event that they should bear children, but contained no allegation asserting any claim under the Fourteenth Amendment of infringement of appellant's liberty or his property rights. The relief prayed was a declaratory judgment as to whether the statutes are applicable to appellant and if so whether they constitute a valid exercise of constitutional power "within the meaning and intent of Amendment XIV of the Constitution of the United States prohibiting a state from depriving any person of life without due process of law." On stipulation of the parties the state superior court ordered these questions of law reserved for the consideration and advice of the Supreme Court of Errors. That court, which assumed without deciding that the case was an appropriate one for a declaratory judgment, ruled that the statutes "prohibit the action proposed to be done" by appellant and "are constitutional."

We are of the opinion that the proceedings in the state courts present no constitutional question which appellant has standing to assert. The sole constitutional attack upon the statutes under the Fourteenth Amendment is confined to their deprivation of life—obviously not appellant's but his patients'. There is no allegation or proof that appellant's life is in danger. His patients are not parties to this proceeding and there is no basis on which we can say that he has standing to secure an adjudication of his patients' constitutional right to life, which they do not assert in their own behalf. .   .   . No question is raised in the record with respect to the deprivation of appellant's liberty or property in contravention of the Fourteenth Amendment, nor is there anything in the opinion or judgment of the Supreme Court of Errors which indicates or would support a decision of any question other than those raised in the superior court and reserved by it for decision of the Supreme Court of Errors. That court's practice is to decline to answer questions not reserved. .   .   .   .

Since the appeal must be dismissed on the ground that appellant has no standing to litigate the constitutional question which the record presents, it is unnecessary to consider whether the record shows the existence of a genuine case or controversy essential to the exercise of the jurisdiction of this Court.

Dismissed.[8]

---

[8]In 1961 the Connecticut statutes involved in Tileston v. Ullman were once again before the courts in the case of Poe v. Ullman. The plaintiffs, Mr. and Mrs. Poe, sought a declaratory judgment on the question of the constitutionality of the statutes. Mrs. Poe had borne three infants, each with multiple congenital abnormalities. They all died. The plaintiffs alleged that the Connecticut statutes precluded Mrs. Poe from obtaining obviously needed contraceptive information. On appeal from the Supreme Court of Errors of Connecticut, the Supreme Court of the United States dismissed the suit, in a five to four decision, written by Justice Frankfurter, finding that because the statutes in question had not been applied in over eighty years, there was a tacit agreement by

GROWING CONCEPTS OF JUSTICIABILITY

BROWN v. BOARD OF EDUCATION (BROWN I)
Supreme Court of the United States, 347 U.S. 686 (1954).

[The decision of the Supreme Court in Plessy v. Ferguson, 163 U.S. 537 (1896), sustained a Louisiana statute requiring "equal but separate accommodations" for white and Negro railway passengers. In Plessy, Justice Brown, speaking for the majority, declared: "The object of the [Fourteenth] Amendment was undoubtedly to enforce the absolute equality of the two races before the law, but in the nature of things it could not have intended to abolish distinctions based upon color, or to enforce social, as distinguished from political equality, or a commingling of the two races upon terms unsatisfactory to either. Laws permitting, and even requiring, their separation in places where they are liable to be brought into contact do not necessarily imply the inferiority of either race to the other, and have been generally, if not universally, recognized as within the competency of the state legislatures in the exercise of their police power. The most common instance of this is connected with the establishment of separate schools for white and colored children, which has been held to be a valid exercise of the legislative power even by courts of States where the political rights of the colored race have been longest and most earnestly enforced."

Almost six decades after its decision in Plessy, the Supreme Court in Brown v. Board of Education faced squarely the applicability of the doctrine of "separate but equal" to public schools.]

Mr. Chief Justice WARREN delivered the opinion of the Court.

These cases come to us from the States of Kansas, South Carolina, Virginia, and Delaware. They are premised on different facts and different local conditions, but a common legal question justifies their consideration together in this consolidated opinion.

Connecticut authorities not to enforce the law. Hence, the majority held in effect that the case was not ripe. Justice Douglas, one of the four dissenting justices, castigated the "tacit agreement" reason, saying with great good sense that "no lawyer would advise his clients to rely on that 'tacit agreement.'" Poe v. Ullman, 367 U.S. 497, 512 (1961).

At long last the inescapable circumstances for adjudication of the constitutional question about contraceptive information arose in 1965 in the case of Griswold v. Connecticut. The State of Connecticut brought charges against Mrs. Griswold, who was the executive director, and Dr. Buxton, who was the medical director of the Planned Parenthood League of Connecticut, for openly giving a married woman contraceptive advice. They were convicted in the Connecticut courts. On appeal the United States Supreme Court held the statutes null and void because of "the zone of privacy (for the marital relation) created by several fundamental constitutional guarantees," particularly the First, Third, Fourth, and Fifth Amendments. Griswold v. Connecticut, 381 U.S. 479, 486 (1965).

The Griswold case is limited to the distribution of contraceptive information to married persons. Note the wave of abortion reform. The New York Legislature legalized abortions and Blue Cross of New York City said it will pay benefits to both married and single women (*New York Times,* June 27, 1970, p. 1). A federal court in Illinois declared the Illinois statute prohibiting abortions unconstitutional as a violation of a woman's right to privacy. Doe v. Scott, 8 Cr.L.Rptr. 2406 (D.C. N.111. 1971), while a federal court in North Carolina declared valid North Carolina's prohibition of abortions as coming within the state's power to protect children. Corkey v. Edwards, 8 Cr.L.Rptr. 2405 (D.C. W.N.C. 1971). The United States Supreme Court upheld a District of Columbia statute that prohibits abortion "unless necessary for preservation of the mother's life or health," including mental health. United States v. Vuitch, 9 Cr.L.Rptr. 3071 (1971).

In each of the cases, minors of the Negro race, through their legal representatives, seek the aid of the courts in obtaining admission to the public schools of their community on a nonsegregated basis. In each instance, they have been denied admission to schools attended by white children under laws requiring or permitting segregation according to race. This segregation was alleged to deprive the plaintiffs of the equal protection of the laws under the Fourteenth Amendment. In each of the cases other than the Delaware case, a three-judge federal district court denied relief to the plaintiffs on the so-called "separate but equal" doctrine announced by this Court in Plessy v. Ferguson, 163 U.S. 537. Under that doctrine, equality of treatment is accorded when the races are provided substantially equal facilities, even though these facilities be separate. In the Delaware case, the Supreme Court of Delaware adhered to that doctrine, but ordered that the plaintiffs be admitted to the white schools because of their superiority to the Negro schools.

The plaintiffs contend that segregated public schools are not "equal" and cannot be made "equal," and that hence they are deprived of the equal protection of the laws. Because of the obvious importance of the question presented, the Court took jurisdiction. Argument was heard in the 1952 Term, and reargument was heard this Term on certain questions propounded by the Court.

Reargument was largely devoted to the circumstances surrounding the adoption of the Fourteenth Amendment in 1868. It covered exhaustively consideration of the Amendment in Congress, ratification by the states, then existing practices in racial segregation, and the views of proponents and opponents of the Amendment. This discussion and our own investigation convince us that, although these sources cast some light, it is not enough to resolve the problem with which we are faced. At best, they are inconclusive. The most avid proponents of the post-War Amendments undoubtedly intended them to remove all legal distinctions among "all persons born or naturalized in the United States." Their opponents, just as certainly, were antagonistic to both the letter and the spirit of the Amendments and wished them to have the most limited effect. What others in Congress and the state legislatures had in mind cannot be determined with any degree of certainty.

An additional reason for the inconclusive nature of the Amendment's history, with respect to segregated schools, is the status of public education at that time. In the South, the movement toward free common schools, supported by general taxation, had not yet taken hold. Education of white children was largely in the hands of private groups. Education of Negroes was almost nonexistent, and practically all of the race were illiterate. In fact, any education of Negroes was forbidden by law in some states. Today, in contrast, many Negroes have achieved outstanding success in the arts and sciences as well as in the business and professional world. It is true that public school education at the time of the Amendment had advanced further in the North, but the effect of the Amendment on Northern States was generally ignored in the congressional debates. Even in the North, the conditions of public education did not approximate those existing today. The curriculum was usually rudimentary; ungraded schools were common in rural areas; the school term was but three months a year in many states; and compulsory school attendance was virtually unknown. As a consequence, it is not surprising that there should be so little in the history of the Fourteenth Amendment relating to its intended effect on public education.

In the first cases in this Court construing the Fourteenth Amendment, decided shortly after its adoption, the Court interpreted it as proscribing all state-imposed discriminations against the Negro race.[B] The doctrine of "separate but equal" did not make its appearance in this Court until 1896 in the case of Plessy v. Ferguson, supra, involving not education but transportation. American courts have since labored with the doctrine for over half a century. In this Court, there have been six cases involving the "separate but equal" doctrine in the field of public education. . . . In none of these cases was it necessary to re-examine the doctrine to grant relief to the Negro plaintiff. [In these six cases the Court found that the separate treatment accorded the Negro plaintiffs was not "equal."] . . .

In the instant cases, that question is directly presented. Here, unlike Sweatt v. Painter [339 U.S. 629, one of the six cases referred to above], there are findings below that the Negro and white schools involved have been equalized, or are being equalized, with respect to buildings, curricula, qualifications and salaries of teachers, and other "tangible" factors. Our decision, therefore, cannot turn on merely a comparison of these tangible factors in the Negro and white schools involved in each of the cases. We must look instead to the effect of segregation itself on public education.

In approaching this problem, we cannot turn the clock back to 1868 when the Amendment was adopted, or even to 1896 when Plessy v. Ferguson was written. We must consider public education in the light of its full development and its present place in American life throughout the Nation. Only in this way can it be determined if segregation in public schools deprives these plaintiffs of the equal protection of the laws.

Today, education is perhaps the most important function of state and local governments. Compulsory school attendance laws and the great expenditures for education both demonstrate our recognition of the importance of education to our democratic society. It is required in the performance of our most basic public responsibilities, even service in the armed forces. It is the very foundation of good citizenship. Today it is a principal instrument in awakening the child to cultural values, in preparing him for later professional training, and in helping him to adjust normally to his environment. In these days, it is doubtful that any child may reasonably be expected to succeed in life if he is denied the opportunity of an education. Such an opportunity, where the state has undertaken to provide it, is a right which must be made available to all on equal terms.

We come then to the question presented: Does segregation of children in public schools solely on the basis of race, even though the physical facilities and other "tangible" factors may be equal, deprive the children of the minority group of equal educational opportunities? We believe that it does.

· · ·

[B]In re Slaughter-House Cases, 1873, 16 Wall. 36, 67–72; Strauder v. West Virginia, 1880, 100 U.S. 303, 307–308:
"It ordains that no State shall deprive any person of life, liberty, or property, without due process of law, or deny to any person within its jurisdiction the equal protection of the laws. What is this but declaring that the law in the States shall be the same for the black as for the white; that all persons, whether colored or white, shall stand equal before the laws of the States, and, in regard to the colored race, for whose protection the amendment was primarily designed, that no discrimination shall be made against them by law because of their color? The words of the amendment, it is true, are prohibitory, but they contain a necessary implication of a positive immunity, or right, most valuable to the colored race,—the right to exemption from unfriendly legislation against them distinctively as colored,—exemption from legal discriminations, implying inferiority in civil society, lessening the security of their enjoyment of the rights which others enjoy, and discriminations which are steps towards reducing them to the condition of a subject race." . . .

. . . Whatever may have been the extent of psychological knowledge at the time of Plessy v. Ferguson, this finding is amply supported by modern authority.[c] Any language in Plessy v. Ferguson contrary to this finding is rejected.

We conclude that in the field of public education the doctrine of "separate but equal" has no place. Separate educational facilities are inherently unequal. Therefore, we hold that the plaintiffs and others similarly situated for whom the actions have been brought are, by reason of the segregation complained of, deprived of the equal protection of the laws guaranteed by the Fourteenth Amendment. . . .

. . . . .

It is so ordered.[9]

Preface to Baker v. Carr

The case of Baker v. Carr, one of the most significant and far-reaching decisions in the entire history of the Supreme Court of the United States, will try the reader's patience. It is standard practice of good law teachers to suggest to law students that usually more than one reading is essential to a full understanding of the case. Certainly, that is true of Baker v. Carr. The following commentary should be of assistance.

There is general understanding that the powers of the government of the United States are divided among the executive, the legislative, and the judicial. These powers are separate and distinct, and in their exercise, no clear impingement of one power upon any other power is constitutionally permissible. A perusal of Articles I, II, and III of the Constitution of the United States will be helpful.

The reader will recall that in Brewington v. Lowe the Supreme Court of Indiana would not intervene to determine whether the state legislature had validly established boundaries among Ohio, Ripley, and Dearborn Counties. At that time (1848), and indeed before and until Baker v. Carr, such a question or the question of the districting of a state for the election of officials was deemed political. Therefore, the courts were inclined to adopt an hands-off policy in deference to the doctrine of division of powers, by assuming that a political question belonged exclusively to the legislative branch. It was not that

[c]K. B. Clark, Effect of Prejudice and Discrimination on Personality Development (Midcentury White House Conference on Children and Youth, 1950); Witmer and Kotinsky, Personality in the Making (1952), c. VI; Deutscher and Chein, The Psychological Effects of Enforced Segregation: A Survey of Social Science Opinion, 26 J. Psychol. 259 (1948); Chein, What are the Psychological Effects of Segregation Under Conditions of Equal Facilities?, 3 Int. J. Opinion and Attitude Res. 229 (1949); Brameld, Educational Costs, in Discrimination and National Welfare (MacIver, ed., 1949). 44-48; Frazier, The Negro in the United States (1949), 674-681. And see generally Myrdal, An American Dilemma (1944).

[9]Several months after its decision in the principal case, the Supreme Court devoted four days to the argument about the manner in which the transition from segregated to unitary school systems would be achieved. After careful consideration of many viewpoints, the Court held that the primary responsibility for abolishing segregated schools rested with local school authorities

the word "political" necessarily barred judicial review of an issue. It was rather that the word was a euphemism for the reluctance of courts to invade an area that, until Baker v. Carr, the courts had deemed wise to leave to the legislative branch.

The Opinion of the Justices is another illustration firmly rooted in this respect for the division of powers. The Justices of the Supreme Court of the United States would not advise President Washington, upon the request of his Secretary of State, with respect to the meaning of a treaty of the United States because, as the Justices said in their letter, the President as Chief Executive could call upon the heads of departments for opinions. In other words, the making of a treaty and the conduct of foreign relations under the Constitution of the United States belonged to that branch of the government called the executive, and the judiciary would not interfere. The case was included in this book earlier for the proposition that there must be an actual controversy between or among litigants before a court will act, but a re-reading of the case also shows that division of powers was very much in the Justices' minds.

We come now to a decision of the Supreme Court of the United States that is a landmark case and will ever remain in that rare category. The reader will see by what deference to semantics a court changes the law. He will see how offensive this process is to a dissenting member of a court, not to mention that portion of the public that disagrees with the decision. He will see in action the organic process, sometimes called the glory of Anglo-American law: its capacity for growth. He will observe the coming of new law in a changing environment.

that the change from segregated to unitary school systems was to be made "at the earliest practicable date" and with "all deliberate speed." The problem of delays by local school authorities during the transition period was to be the responsibility of the local courts which were empowered to grant additional time to enable the ruling in the principal case to be carried out in an effective manner. Brown v. Board of Education, 349 U.S. 294 (1955), known as Brown II.

As late as the second half of the 1960's, the records in a number of Supreme Court cases showed that certain school districts had as yet taken no voluntary, effective steps to desegregate public schools. Seemingly, as the result of this situation, on October 29, 1969, the United States Supreme Court in a Per Curiam opinion announced that "the standard of allowing 'all deliberate speed' for desegregation is no longer constitutionally permissible." The Court continued that "under explicit holdings of this Court the obligation of every school district is to terminate dual school systems at once and to operate now and hereafter only unitary schools." Alexander v. Holmes County Board of Education, 396 U.S. 19, 20 (1969).

In North Carolina State Board of Education v. Swann 39 L.W. 4449 (1971), the Supreme Court set forth guidelines to implement its decisions in Brown v. Board of Education and Alexander v. Holmes. In an unanimous opinion by Chief Justice Burger the Court held that the lower federal courts can require state school authorities to adopt large scale busing programs to achieve unitary school systems. For guidance on the extent of racial mixing that is required under its decision, the Court stated that the lower federal courts can consider the white-to-black ratio of an entire school system and aim for that ratio in each school. Although the Court stated that such ratios were only starting points for desegregation plans, it emphasized that the existence of any all-white or all-black schools after such plans were drawn must be minor and unintentional or necessitated by risks to the health or welfare of the children caused by extensive busing.

BAKER v. CARR
Supreme Court of the United States, 369 U.S. 186 (1961).

Mr. Justice BRENNAN delivered the opinion of the Court.

This civil action was brought under 42 U.S.C. §§ 1983 and 1988 to redress the alleged deprivation of federal constitutional rights. The complaint, alleging that by means of a 1901 statute of Tennessee apportioning the members of the General Assembly among the State's 95 counties, "these plantiffs and others similarly situated, are denied the equal protection of the laws accorded them by the Fourteenth Amendment to the Constitution of the United States by virtue of the debasement of their votes," was dismissed by a three-judge court. . . . We hold that the dismissal was error, and remand the cause to the District Court for trial and further proceedings consistent with this opinion.

.   .   .   .

. . . Tennessee's standard for allocating legislative representation among her counties is the total number of qualified voters resident in the respective counties, subject only to minor qualifications. Decennial re-apportionment in compliance with the constitutional scheme was effected by the General Assembly each decade from 1871 to 1901. . . . In 1901 the General Assembly abandoned separate enumeration in favor of reliance upon the Federal Census and passed the Apportionment Act here in controversey. In more than 60 years since that action, all proposals in both Houses of the General Assembly for reapportionment have failed to pass.

Between 1901 and 1961, Tennessee has experienced substantial growth and redistribution of her population. . . . The relative standings of the counties in terms of qualified voters have changed significantly. It is primarily the continued application of the 1901 Apportionment Act to this shifted and enlarged voting population which gives rise to the present controversy.

.   .   .   .

In holding that the subject matter of this suit was not justiciable, the District Court relied on Colegrove v. Green, 328 U.S. 549, and later *per curiam* cases.[10] . . . We understand the District Court to have read the cited cases as compelling the conclusion that since the appellants sought to have a legislative apportionment held

---

[10]In Colegrove v. Green, a 1946 case, the Court focused on a federal district court action to enjoin Illinois officials from proceeding with an election of the United States Congressmen. The appellants contended that the Illinois law apportioning Congressional districts was unconstitutional because the districts were not of approximate equality in population. Only seven justices of the Supreme Court participated in the decision, owing to the death of Chief Justice Stone and the absence of Justice Jackson. Justice Frankfurter announced the judgment of the Court that dismissed the appellants' complaint on the ground that the issue was a "political question." He was joined in this opinion by two Justices—Burton and Reed. Justice Rutledge concurred on other grounds in the result reached by Justices Frankfurter, Reed, and Burton, and thus cast the deciding vote. Justice Frankfurter stated: "[T]his controversy concerns matters that bring courts into immediate and active relations with party contests. From the determination of such issues this Court has traditionally remained aloof. It is hostile to the democratic system to involve the judiciary in the politics of the people. . . . The short of it is that the Constitution has conferred upon Congress exclusive authority to secure fair representation by the States in the popular House and left to that House determination whether States have fulfilled their responsibili-

unconstitutional, their suit presented a "political question" and was therefore nonjusticiable. We hold that this challenge to an apportionment presents no nonjusticiable "political question." The cited cases do not hold the contrary.

Of course the mere fact that the suit seeks protection of a political right does not mean it presents a political question. Such an objection "is little more than a play upon words."   .   .   .   Rather, it is argued that apportionment cases, whatever the actual wording of the complaint, can involve no federal constitutional right except one resting on the guaranty of a republican form of government,[D] and that complaints based on that clause have been held to present political questions which are nonjusticiable.

We hold that the claim pleaded here neither rests upon nor implicates the Guaranty Clause and that its justiciability is therefore not foreclosed by our decisions of cases involving that clause. The District Court misinterpreted Colegrove v. Green and other decisions of this Court on which it relied. Appellants' claim that they are being denied equal protection is justiciable, and if "discrimination is sufficiently shown, the right to relief under the equal protection clause is not diminished by the fact that the discrimination relates to political rights."   .   .   .

[Mr. Justice Brennan set out four categories of cases which traditionally have been held to be political questions. They are (1) cases concerning foreign relations, (2) cases involving the enacting process of legislative acts, (3) cases involving the determination of the dates of duration of hostilities, and (4) cases concerning the status of Indian tribes. Justice Brennan demonstrated that cases in these categories which involve a political question contain one or more elements which identify it as essentially a function of separation of powers. Justice Brennan then enumerated the criteria which distinguish political questions from ordinary cases and controversies. He continued:]

.   .   .   .

Unless one of these formulations is inextricable from the case at bar, there should be no dismissal for nonjusticiability on the ground of a political question's presence. The doctrine of which we treat is one of "political questions," not one of "political cases." The courts cannot reject as "no law suit" a bona fide controversy as to whether some action denominated "political" exceeds constitutional authority. The cases we have reviewed show the necessity for discriminating inquiry into the precise facts and posture of the particular case, and the impossibility of resolution by any semantic cataloguing.

.   .   .   .

We come, finally to the ultimate inquiry whether our precedents as to what constitutes a nonjusticiable "political question" bring the case before us under the umbrella

---

ties.   .   .   .   Whether Congress faithfully discharges its duty or not, the subject has been committed to the exclusive control of Congress.   .   .   .   Courts ought not to enter this political thicket."

Justice Black was joined in dissent by Justices Douglas and Murphy, all of whom thought that the issue presented was a justiciable case or controversy.

[D]"The United States shall guarantee to every State in this Union a Republican Form of Government, and shall protect each of them against Invasion; and on Application of the Legislature, or of the Executive (when the Legislature cannot be convened) against domestic Violence." U.S. Const., Art. IV, §4.

of that doctrine. A natural beginning is to note whether any of the common characteristics which we have been able to identify and label descriptively are present. We find none: The question here is the consistency of state action with the Federal Constitution. We have no question decided, or to be decided, by a political branch of government coequal with this Court. Nor do we risk embarrassment of our government abroad, or grave disturbance at home if we take issue with Tennessee as to the constitutionality of her action here challenged. Nor need the appellants, in order to succeed in this action, ask the Court to enter upon policy determinations for which judicially manageable standards are lacking. Judicial standards under the Equal Protection Clause are well developed and familiar, and it has been open to courts since the enactment of the Fourteenth Amendment to determine, if on the particular facts they must, that a discrimination reflects *no* policy, but simply arbitrary and capricious action.

This case does, in one sense, involve the allocation of political power within a State, and the appellants might conceivably have added a claim under the Guaranty Clause. Of course, as we have seen, any reliance on that clause would be futile. But because any reliance on the Guaranty Clause could not have succeeded, it does not follow that appellants may not be heard on the equal protection claim which in fact they tender. True, it must be clear that the Fourteenth Amendment claim is not so enmeshed with those political question elements which render Guaranty Clause claims nonjusticiable as actually to present a political question itself. But we have found that not to be the case here.

.   .   .   .

We conclude then that the nonjusticiability of claims resting on the Guaranty Clause which arises from their embodiment of questions that were thought "political," can have no bearing upon the justiciability of the equal protection claim presented in this case. Finally, we emphasize that it is the involvement in Guaranty Clause claims of the elements thought to define "political questions," and no other feature, which could render them nonjusticiable. Specifically, we have said that such claims are not held nonjusticiable because they touch matters of state governmental organization. Brief examination of a few cases demonstrates this.

When challenges to state action respecting matters of "the administration of the affairs of the State and the officers through whom they are conducted" have rested on claims of constitutional deprivation which are amenable to judicial correction, this Court has acted upon its view of the merits of the claim. For example, in Boyd v. Nebraska ex rel. Thayer, 143 U.S. 135, we reversed the Nebraska Supreme Court's decision that Nebraska's Governor was not a citizen of the United States or of the State and therefore could not continue in office.   .   .   .   And only last Term, in Gomillion v. Lightfoot, 364 U.S. 339, we applied the Fifteenth Amendment to strike down a redrafting of municipal boundaries which effected a discriminatory impairment of voting rights, in the face of what a majority of the Court of Appeals thought to be a sweeping commitment to state legislatures of power to draw and redraw such [municipal] boundaries.

Gomillion was brought by a Negro who had been a resident of the City of Tuskegee, Alabama, until the municipal boundaries were so recast by the State Legislature as to exclude practically all Negroes. The plaintiff claimed deprivation of the right to vote in municipal elections.   .   .   .   This Court's answer to the argument that States enjoyed unrestricted control over municipal boundaries was:

"Legislative control of municipalities, no less than other state power, lies within the scope of relevant limitations imposed by the United States Constitution.   . . .
The opposite conclusion, urged upon us by respondents, would sanction the achievement by a State of any impairment of voting rights whatever so long as it was cloaked in the garb of realignment of political subdivisions. 'It is inconceivable that guarantees embedded in the Constitution of the United States may thus be manipulated out of existence.'" [Gomillion v. Lightfoot, 364 U.S. at 344-345.]

To [the] argument, that Colegrove v. Green, [see footnote 10, *supra*] was a barrier to hearing the merits of the [Gomillion] case, the Court responded that Gomillion was lifted "out of the so-called 'political' arena and into the conventional sphere of constitutional litigation" because here was discriminatory treatment of a racial minority violating the Fifteenth Amendment. [The Court in Gomillion said:]

"A statute which is alleged to have unconstitutional deprivations of petitioners' rights is not immune to attack simply because the mechanism employed by the legislature is a redefinition of municipal boundaries. . . .   While in form this is merely an act redefining metes and bounds, if the allegations are established, the inescapable human effect of this essay in geometry and geography is to despoil colored citizens, and only colored citizens, of their theretofore enjoyed voting rights. That was not Colegrove v. Green.

"When a State exercises power wholly within the domain of state interest, it is insulated from federal judicial review. But such insulation is not carried over when state power is used as an instrument for circumventing a federally protected right." 364 U.S. at 347.

We conclude that the complaint's allegations of a denial of equal protection present a justiciable constitutional cause of action upon which appellants are entitled to a trial and a decision. The right asserted is within the reach of judicial protection under the Fourteenth Amendment.

The judgment of the District Court is reversed and the cause is remanded for further proceedings consistent with this opinion.

Reversed and remanded.

Mr. Justice WHITTAKER did not participate in the decision of this case. [The separate concurring opinions of Mr. Justice Douglas, Mr. Justice Clark, and Mr. Justice Stewart are omitted. The dissenting opinion of Mr. Justice Harlan, in which Mr. Justice Frankfurter joined, is, likewise, omitted. In their opinions, Mr. Justice Clark and Mr. Justice Harlan were concerned with the question of what approach the courts will take when faced with the mathematically cumbersome problem of legislative redistricting.]

Mr. Justice FRANKFURTER, whom Mr. Justice HARLAN joins, dissenting.

The Court today reverses a uniform course of decision established by a dozen cases, including one by which the very claim now sustained was unanimously rejected only five years ago. The impressive body of rulings thus cast aside reflected the equally uniform course of our political history regarding the relationship between population and legislative representation—a wholly different matter from denial of the franchise to individuals because of race, color, religion or sex. Such a massive repudiation of the experience of our whole past in asserting destructively novel judicial power demands a detailed analysis of the role of this Court in our constitutional scheme. Disregard of inherent limits in the effective exercise of the Court's "judicial Power" not only presages the futility of judicial intervention in the essentially political conflict of forces by which the relation between population and representation has time out of mind been and now is determined. It may well impair the Court's position as the ultimate organ of "the supreme Law of the Land" in that vast range of legal problems, often strongly entangled in popular feeling, on which this Court must pronounce. The Court's authority—possessed of neither the purse nor the sword—ultimately rests on sustained public confidence in its moral sanction. Such feeling must be nourished by the Court's complete detachment, in fact and in appearance, from political entanglements and by abstention from injecting itself into the clash of political forces in political settlements.

. . . One of the Court's supporting [concurring] opinions, as elucidated by commentary, unwittingly affords a disheartening preview of the mathematical quagmire (apart from divers judicially inappropriate and elusive determinants) into which this Court today catapults the lower courts of the country without so much as adumbrating the basis for a legal calculus as a means of extrication. Even assuming the indispensable intellectual disinterestedness on the part of judges in such matters, they do not have accepted legal standards or criteria or even reliable analogies to draw upon for making judicial judgments. To charge courts with the task of accommodating the incommensurable factors of policy that underlie these mathematical puzzles is to attribute, however flatteringly, omnicompetence to judges. The Framers of the Constitution persistently rejected a proposal that embodied this assumption and Thomas Jefferson never entertained it.

.   .   .   .

At first blush, this charge of discrimination based on legislative underrepresentation is given the appearance of a more private, less impersonal claim, than the assertion that the frame of government is askew. Appellants appear as representatives of a class that is prejudiced as a class, in contradistinction to the polity in its entirety. However, the discrimination relied on is the deprivation of what appellants conceive to be their proportionate share of political influence. This, of course, is the practical effect of any allocation of power within the institutions of government. Hardly any distribution of political authority that could be assailed as rendering government non-republican would fail similarly to operate to the prejudice of some groups, and to the advantage of others, within the body politic. It would be ingenuous not to see, or consciously blind to deny, that the real battle over the initiative and referendum, or over a delegation of power to local rather than state-wide authority, is the battle between forces whose influence is disparate among the various organs of government to whom power may be given. No shift of power but works a corresponding shift in political influence among the groups composing a society.

The notion that representation proportioned to the geographic spread of population is so universally accepted as a necessary element of equality between man and man that it must be taken to be the standard of a political equality preserved by the Fourteenth Amendment—that it is, in appellants' words "the basic principle of representative government"—is, to put it bluntly, not true. However desirable and however desired by some among the great political thinkers and framers of our government, it has never been generally practiced, today or in the past. It was not the English system, it was not the colonial system, it was not the system chosen for the national government by the Constitution, it was not the system exclusively or even predominantly practiced by the States at the time of adoption of the Fourteenth Amendment, it is not predominantly practiced by the States today. Unless judges, the judges of this Court, are to make their private views of political wisdom the measure of the Constitution—views which in all honesty cannot but give the appearance, if not reflect the reality, of involvement with the business of partisan politics so inescapably a part of apportionment controversies—the Fourteenth Amendment, "itself a historical product," Jackman v. Rosenbaum Co., 260 U.S. 21, 31, provides no guide for judicial oversight of the representation problem.

·   ·   ·   ·

Although the District Court had jurisdiction in the very restricted sense of power to determine whether it could adjudicate the claim, the case is of that class of political controversy which, by the nature of its subject, is unfit for federal judicial action. The judgment of the District Court, in dismissing the complaint for failure to state a claim on which relief can be granted, should therefore be affirmed.

Commentary on Baker v. Carr

Despite the agonizing in Mr. Justice Frankfurter's dissent, the action of the majority of the United States Supreme Court became the law for the State of Tennessee. The Constitution is the supreme law of the land. The Supreme Court held that Tennessee's election districts were not in conformity with the Constitution—in legal effect they were gerrymandered. Therefore, officials of Tennessee elected in unconstitutional districts would be usurpers in office without valid warrant to exercise the powers of office. Innumerable questions would arise: the power to levy taxes, not to mention the power to borrow money; to carry on public improvements; to commit the state to the obligations that are necessary to conduct the business of a state. Everyone of such questions could, in the end, come to the Supreme Court of the United States, and it would be possible that the Supreme Court would hold all of the acts of Tennessee officials unwarranted, unlawful, unenforceable, and null and void. Predictably, the legislature of the State of Tennessee went into immediate, not to say hectic, action as did the legislatures of a considerable number of states.

The immediate consequences of the Supreme Court's decision in Baker v. Carr have been well summarized:

> Yet the fact that 20 of the 50 states had embarked on redrawing their legislative maps could not in itself be taken as the end of the tale. In state after state, the courts examined the newly submitted districting patterns and—in most cases—found them sorely inadequate. In Tennessee, the birthplace of Baker v. Carr, plans were sent back and forth from capitol to courthouse three or more times, and at each juncture the judges announced that the latest revision was still unsatisfactory. 'The rural bloc has demonstrated that it will seek every means of avoiding compliance—even cheating by a few seats—in an effort to preserve as much of its

authority as possible,' a correspondent in Nashville reported. [See *New York Times,* November 10, 1963.] As a final resort Tennessee issued a call for a constitutional convention to draw up an apportionment scheme. But even here the question would arise as to the manner in which the delegates to such a convention were chosen; clearly one ground for challenging an apportionment plan would be to say that legislative districts created by an unrepresentative convention were themselves invalid. All in all, the states that redistricted during 1963 and 1964 only went through the motions of reform, with the result that appeals against these new plans began to follow Baker v. Carr up the well-trod road to the United States Supreme Court. (Hacker, Andrew, *Congressional Districting—The Issue of Equal Representation,* The Brookings Institution, Washington, D. C., 1964, p. 37.)

Judge Miller of the Federal District Court for the Middle District of Tennessee attempted to put an end to the long drawn history of Baker v. Carr when he declared on November 15, 1965, that the Tennessee 1965 Apportionment Act was constitutional. (Baker v. Carr, 247 F. Supp. 629.) Judge Miller stated that "not every citizen has heard of Baker v. Carr, but it is perhaps not fanciful to suggest that the impact of the Supreme Court's decision . . .   has been felt by the courts. Since that decision, there have been literally hundreds of published opinions dealing with apportionment. And published opinions do not tell the whole story. In this case alone, the single-spaced docket entries require more than 13 pages, and the file is measured not in pages but in feet." Judge Miller placed Baker v. Carr on the retired docket.

In upholding the constitutionality of the 1965 Tennessee Apportionment Act, Judge Miller approved a plan that provided for forming Senate districts with an average of 63,420 qualified voters and House districts with an average of 21,140 qualified voters. Judge Miller held that the 1965 Act still met the Supreme Court "one man, one vote" requirement even though deviations from the average were as much as 15 percent, plus or minus. He noted that such deviations were necessary to preserve county lines and to avoid combining small rural and medium size counties with larger urban counties.

Compare Judge Miller's decision with the United States Supreme Court decision in the case of Kirkpatrick v. Preisler, 384 U.S. 526 (1969). The Kirkpatrick case involved the second attempt since 1965 by Missouri to comply with the Baker v. Carr standards. Based on the 1960 United States census figures, absolute equality among Missouri's ten Congressional districts would have required a population of 431,981 in each Congressional district. However, the districts created by the 1967 Missouri Apportionment Act varied from 12,260 below that number to 13,542 above. In percentage terms, the most populous district was 3.13% above that number, and the least populous was 2.83% below. On the average the deviation was 1.6%.

The Federal District Court in Kirkpatrick found that the 1967 Missouri Act did not meet the Baker v. Carr standard "as nearly as practicable" and that Missouri had failed to adduce any acceptable justification for the variance. On appeal the Supreme Court rejected Missouri's argument that there is a fixed numerical or percentage population variance small enough to be considered *de minimis*. The Supreme Court also agreed with the District Court that Missouri had not satisfactorily justified the population variances when it claimed the variances were necessary to avoid fragmenting political subdivisions by drawing Congressional district lines along existing county, municipal, or other political subdivision boundaries.

MORA v. McNAMARA
Supreme Court of the United States 389 U.S. 934 (1967).

[The petitioners in this case lost their suit for a declaratory judgment that the Vietnam War was "illegal." The District Court held that the petitioners sought judicial review of a political question beyond the jurisdiction of the court. The Court of Appeals affirmed the District Court's holding. The petitioners then sought a writ of certiorari from the Supreme Court. This request was denied. However, two justices dissented, and the case is included because the issue of justiciability is on the very razor's edge of division of federal powers.]

Mr. Justice STEWART, with whom Mr. Justice DOUGLAS joins, dissenting.

The petitioners were drafted into the United States Army in late 1965, and six months later were ordered to a West Coast replacement station for shipment to Vietnam. They brought this suit to prevent the Secretary of Defense and the Secretary of the Army from carrying out those orders, and requested a declaratory judgment that the present United States military activity in Vietnam is "illegal." The District Court dismissed the suit, and the Court of Appeals affirmed.

There exist in this case questions of great magnitude. . . .

I. Is the present United States military activity in Vietnam a "war" with the meaning of Article I, Section 8, Clause 11, of the Constitution?

II. If so, may the Executive constitutionally order the petitioners to participate in that military activity, when no war has been declared by the Congress?

III. Of what relevance to Question II are the present treaty obligations of the United States?

IV. Of what relevance to Question II is the Joint Congressional ("Tonkin Gulf") Resolution of August 10, 1964?

(a) Do present United States military operations fall within the terms of the Joint Resolution?

(b) If the Joint Resolution purports to give the Chief Executive authority to commit United States forces to armed conflict limited in scope only by his own absolute discretion, is the Resolution a constitutionally impermissible delegation of all or part of Congress' power to declare war?

These are large and deeply troubling questions. Whether the Court would ultimately reach them depends, of course, upon the resolution of serious preliminary issues of justiciability. We cannot make these problems go away simply by refusing to hear the case of three obscure Army privates. I intimate not even tentative views upon any of these matters, but I think the Court should squarely face them by granting certiorari and setting this case for oral argument.

Mr. Justice DOUGLAS, with whom Mr. Justice STEWART concurs, dissenting.

The questions posed by Mr. Justice Stewart cover the wide range of problems which the Senate Committee on Foreign Relations recently explored, in connection with the SEATO Treaty of February 19, 1955, and the Tonkin Gulf Resolution.

Mr. Katzenbach, representing the Administration, testified that he did not regard the Tonkin Gulf Resolution to be "a declaration of war" and that while the Resolution was not "constitutionally necessary" it was "politically, from an international viewpoint and from a domestic viewpoint, extremely important." He added:

"The use of the phrase 'to declare war' as it was used in the Constitution of the United States had a particular meaning in terms of the events and the practices which existed at the time it was adopted. . . .

"[I]t was recognized by the Founding Fathers that the President might have to take emergency action to protect the security of the United States, but that if there was going to be another use of the armed forces of the United States, that was a decision which Congress should check the Executive on, which Congress should support. It was for that reason that the phrase was inserted in the Constitution.

"Now, over a long period of time, . . . there have been many uses of the military forces of the United States for a variety of puposes without a congressional declaration of war. But it would be fair to say that most of these were relatively minor uses of force. . . .

.   .   .   .   .   .

"A declaration of war would not, I think, correctly reflect the very limited objectives of the United States with respect to Vietnam. It would not correctly reflect our efforts there, what we are trying to do, the reasons why we are there, to use an outmoded phraseology, to declare war."[11]

The view that Congress was intended to play a more active role in the initiation and conduct of war than the above statements might suggest has been espoused by Senator Fulbright (Cong. Rec., Oct. 11, 1967, pp. 14683-14690), quoting Thomas Jefferson who said:

"We have already given in example one effectual check to the Dog of war by transferring the power of letting him loose from the Executive to the Legislative body, from those who are to spend to those who are to pay."[E]

---

[11]The report of the proceedings before the Senate Committee on Foreign Relations referred to in this opinion is in Hearing on S. Res. No. 151, 90th Cong. 1st Sess., at 80–1, 87, 145 (1967).

[E]15 Papers of Jefferson 397 (Boyd ed., Princeton 1958). In the Federalist No. 69, at 465 (Cooke ed. 1961), Hamilton stated:

"[T]he President is to be Commander in Chief of the army and navy of the United States. In this respect his authority would be nominally the same with that of the King of Great-Britain, but in substance much inferior to it. It would amount to nothing more than the supreme command and direction of the military and naval forces, as first General and Admiral of the confederacy; while that of the British King extends to the *declaring* of war and to the *raising* and *regulating* of fleets and armies; all which by the Constitution under consideration would appertain to the Legislature."

. . . .

A host of problems is raised. Does the President's authority to repel invasions and quiet insurrections, do his powers in foreign relations and his duty to execute faithfully the laws of the United States, including its treaties, justify what has been threatened of petitioners? What is the relevancy of the Gulf of Tonkin Resolution and the yearly appropriations in support of the Vietnam effort?

. . . .

"Certainly it is not the function of the Judiciary to entertain private litigation—even by a citizen—which challenges the legality, the wisdom, or the propriety of the Commander-in-Chief in sending our armed forces abroad or to any particular region." Johnson v. Eisentrager, 339 U.S. 763, 789.

We do not, of course, sit as a committee of oversight or supervision. What resolutions the President asks and what the Congress provides are not our concern. With respect to the Federal Government, we sit only to decide actual cases or controversies within judicial cognizance that arise as a result of what the Congress or the President or a judge does or attempts to do to a person or his property.

In Ex parte Milligan, 4 Wall. 2, the Court relieved a person of the death penalty imposed by a military tribunal, holding that only a civilian court had power to try him for the offense charged. Speaking of the purpose of the Founders in providing constitutional guarantees, the Court said:

"They knew . . .   the nation they were founding, be its existence short or long, would be involved in war; how often or how long continued, human foresight could not tell; and that unlimited power, wherever lodged at such a time, was especially hazardous to freemen. For this, and other equally weighty reasons, they secured the inheritance they had fought to maintain, by incorporating in a written constitution the safeguards which *time* had proved were essential to its preservation. Not one of these safeguards can the President, or Congress, or the Judiciary disturb, except the one concerning the writ of habeas corpus." *Id.,* 125.

The fact that the political branches are responsible for the threat to petitioners' liberty is not decisive. As Mr. Justice Holmes said in Nixon v. Herndon, 273 U.S. 536, 540:

"The objection that the subject matter of the suit is political is little more than a play upon words. Of course the petition concerns political action but it alleges and seeks to recover for private damage. That private damage may be caused by such political action and may be recovered for in a suit at law hardly has been doubted for over two hundred years, since Ashby v. White, 2 Ld. Raym. 938, 3 *id.* 320, and has been recognized by this Court."

These petitioners should be told whether their case is beyond judicial cognizance. If it is not, we should then reach the merits of their claims, on which I intimate no views whatsoever.

POWELL v. McCORMACK
Supreme Court of the United States, 395 U.S. 486 (1969).

[Adam Clayton Powell, Jr., duly elected from the 18th Congressional District of New York to the United States House of Representatives for the 90th Congress, was, for alleged irregularities in his official conduct, excluded from his seat, stripped of his powerful position as chairman of the House Committee on Education and Labor, and denied his Congressional salary for the period in question. He was not expelled under the provisions of Article I, § 5 of the United States Constitution which might have been done by a two-thirds vote; rather he was excluded (prevented from taking the oath of office) by a majority vote under the claim of a constitutional delegation to Congress to determine the qualifications of its members.

Powell and some of the voters in his district filed suit in the Federal District Court of the District of Columbia claiming that the House had acted unconstitutionally in excluding him since, he argued, the only basis for exclusion would be failure to meet the standing requirements of age, citizenship and residence contained in Article I, § 2 —requirements the House found he had met. The District Court dismissed Powell's complaint "for want of jurisdiction of the subject matter," and the Court of Appeals affirmed the dismissal on other grounds. The Supreme Court granted certiorari and determined that the District Court erred in dismissing Powell's complaint, and further, that Powell was entitled to a declaratory judgment that he was unlawfully excluded from the 90th Congress.

Thereafter, Powell was elected to the 91st Congress by the same constituency. This time, however, he was permitted to take his seat subject to payment of a $25,000 fine assessed by the action of the House.

Provisions of the United States Constitution pertaining to this case are:

Article I, § 5, cl. 1, 2.

"Each House shall be the judge of the elections, returns and qualifications of its own members, and a majority of each shall constitute a quorum to do business; but a smaller number may adjourn from day to day, and may be authorized to compel the attendance of absent members, in such manner, and under such penalties as each House may provide.

"Each House may determine the rules of its proceedings, punish its members for disorderly behavior, and, with the concurrence of two thirds, expel a member."

Article I, § 2, cl. 2.

"No person shall be a representative who shall not have attained to the age of twenty-five years, and been seven years a citizen of the United States, and who shall not, when elected, be an inhabitant of that State in which he shall be chosen."

Mr. Chief Justice Warren delivered the opinion of the United States Supreme Court which is excerpted below.]

Mr. Chief Justice WARREN speaking for the Court.

. . . .

In deciding generally whether a claim is justiciable, a court must determine whether "the duty asserted can be judicially identified and its breach judicially determined, and whether protection for the right asserted can be judicially molded." Baker v. Carr, *supra*, [369 U.S. 186] at 198. Respondents do not seriously contend that the duty asserted and its alleged breach cannot be judicially determined. If petitioners are correct, the House had a duty to seat Powell once it determined he met the standing

requirements set forth in the Constitution. It is undisputed that he met those requirements and that he was nevertheless excluded.

Respondents do maintain, however, that this case is not justiciable because, they
assert, it is impossible for a federal court to "mold effective relief for resolving this
case." Respondents emphasize that petitioners asked for coercive relief against the
officers of the House, and, they contend, federal courts cannot issue mandamus or
injunctions compelling officers or employees of the House to perform specific official
acts. Respondents rely primarily on the Speech or Debate Clause to support this
contention.

We need express no opinion about the appropriateness of coercive relief in this case,
for petitioners sought a declaratory judgment, a form of relief the District Court could
have issued. The Declaratory Judgment Act, 28 U.S.C. § 2201 (1964 ed.), provides that
a district court may "declare the rights . . . of any interested party   . . .
whether or not further relief is or could be sought." The availability of declaratory relief
depends on whether there is a live dispute between the parties, . . .   and a request
for a declaratory relief may be considered independently of whether other forms of
relief are appropriate. See United Public Workers v. Mitchell, 330 U.S. 75, 93 (1947).
. . . We thus conclude that in terms of the general criteria of justiciability, this case
is justiciable.

.   .   .   .   .

Respondents' first contention is that this case presents a political question because
under Art. I, § 5, there has been a "textually demonstrable constitutional commitment"
to the House of the "adjudicatory power" to determine Powell's qualifications. Thus
it is argued that the House, and the House alone, has power to determine who is
qualified to be a member.

In order to determine whether there has been a textual commitment to a co-ordinate
department of the Government, we must interpret the Constitution. In other words,
we must first determine what power the Constitution confers upon the House through
Art. I, § 5, before we can determine to what extent, if any, the exercise of that power
is subject to judicial review. Respondents maintain that the House has broad power
under § 5, and, they argue, the House may determine which are the qualifications
necessary for membership. On the other hand, petitioners allege that the Constitution
provides that an elected representative may be denied his seat only if the House finds
he does not meet one of the standing qualifications expressly prescribed by the Constitution. [Article I, § 2, cl. 2.]

If examination of § 5 disclosed that the Constitution gives the House judicially
unreviewable power to set qualifications for membership and to judge whether prospective members meet those qualifications, further review of the House determination
might well be barred by the political question doctrine. On the other hand, if the
Constitution gives the House power to judge only whether elected members possess the
three standing qualifications set forth in the Constitution, further consideration would
be necessary to determine whether any of the other formulations of the political
question doctrine are "inextricable from the case at bar." Baker v. Carr, *supra,* at 217.

In other words, whether there is a "textually demonstrable constitutional commitment of the issue to a coordinate political department of government" and what is the
scope of such commitment are questions we must resolve for the first time in this case.

For, as we pointed out in Baker v. Carr, *supra,* "[d]eciding whether a matter has in any measure been committed by the Constitution to another branch of government, or whether the action of that branch exceeds whatever authority has been committed, is itself a delicate exercise in constitutional interpretation and is the responsibility of this Court as ultimate interpreter of the Constitution." *Id.,* at 211.

In order to determine the scope of any "textual commitment" under Art. I, § 5, we necessarily must determine the meaning of the phrase to "judge the qualifications of its members." Petitioners argue that the records of the debates during the Constitutional Convention, available commentary from the post-Convention, pre-ratification period, and early congressional applications of Art. I, § 5, support their construction of the section. Respondents insist, however, that a careful examination of the pre-Convention practices of the English Parliament and American colonial assemblies demonstrates that by 1787, a legislature's power to judge the qualifications of its members was generally understood to encompass exclusion or expulsion on the ground that an individual's character or past conduct rendered him unfit to serve. When the Constitution and the debates over its adoption are thus viewed in historical perspective, argue respondents, it becomes clear that the "qualifications" expressly set forth in the Constitution were not meant to limit the long recognized legislative power to exclude or expel at will, but merely to establish "standing incapacities," which could be altered only by a constitutional amendment. Our examination of the relevant historical materials leads us to the conclusion that petitioners are correct and that the Constitution leaves the House without authority to *exclude* any person, duly elected by his constituents, who meets all the requirements for membership expressly prescribed in the Constitution. [The standing qualifications of Article I, § 2.]

.   .   .   .   .

Had the intent of the Framers [of the Constitution] emerged from these materials [pre-Constitutional Convention practices in both the English Parliament and the colonial assemblies, records of the debates during the Constitutional Convention, commentary from the post-Conventional and pre-ratification period, and early applications of the power to expel under Article I, § 5] with less clarity, we would nevertheless have been compelled to resolve any ambiguity in favor of a narrow construction of the scope of Congress' power to exclude members-elect. A fundamental principle of our representative democracy is, in Hamilton's words, "that the people should choose whom they please to govern them." 2 Elliot's Debates 257. As Madison pointed out at the Convention, this principle is undermined as much by limiting whom the people can select as by limiting the franchise itself. In apparent agreement with this basic philosophy, the Convention adopted his suggestion limiting the power to expel. To allow essentially that same power to be exercised under the guise of judging qualifications, would be to ignore Madison's warning borne out in . . . some of Congress, own post-Civil War exclusion cases, against "vesting an improper & dangerous power in the Legislature." 2 Farrand 249. Moreover, it would effectively nullify the Convention's decision to require a two-third vote for expulsion. Unquestionably, Congress has an interest in preserving its institutional integrity, but in most cases that interest can be sufficiently safeguarded by the exercise of its power to punish its members for disorderly behavior and, in extreme cases, to expel a member with the concurrence of two-thirds. In short, both the intention of the Framers, to the extent it can be determined, and an examination of the basic principles of our democratic system persuade us that the Constitution does not vest in the Congress a discretionary power to deny membership by a majority vote.

For these reasons, we have concluded that Art. I, § 5, is at most a "texually demonstrable commitment" to Congress to judge only the qualifications expressly set forth in the Constitution. Therefore, the "textual commitment" formulation of the political question doctrine does not bar federal courts from adjudicating petitioners' claims.

.   .   .   .

To summarize, we have determined the following: .   .   . We have jurisdiction over the subject matter of this controversy.   .   .   . The case is justiciable.

Further, analysis of the "textual commitment" under Art. I, § 5 .   .   . has demonstrated that in judging the qualifications of its members Congress is limited to the standing qualifications prescribed in the Constitution. Respondents concede that Powell met these. Thus, there is no need to remand this case to determine whether he was entitled to be seated in the 90th Congress. Therefore, we hold that, that since Adam Clayton Powell, Jr., was duly elected by the voters of the 18th Congressional District of New York and was not ineligible to serve under any provision of the Constitution, the House was without power to exclude him from its membership.

Petitioners seek additional forms of equitable relief, including mandamus for the release of Petitioner Powell's back pay. The propriety of such remedies, however, is more appropriately considered in the first instance by the courts below. Therefore, .   .   . the judgment of the Court of Appeals for the District of Columbia Circuit is reversed and the case is remanded to that court with instructions to enter a declaratory judgment and for further proceedings consistent with this opinion.

It is so ordered.

[Mr. Justice Douglas in a concurring opinion noted that this case is but a logical extension of the "one man, one vote" principle, since it establishes that there is no constitutional basis for excluding a person who is lawfully elected just because he "is repulsive to the Establishment in Congress."

Mr. Justice Stewart dissented on the ground that the House action in seating Powell in the 91st Congress had rendered the lawsuit moot, since the action was brought to question the House's action in excluding Powell from the 90th Congress.][12]

RULERSHIP

Although the Constitution of the United States separates the powers of government into three branches, it is apparent that a high degree of restraint in the

[12]The August 19, 1969 PITTSBURGH PRESS, p. 12, reports that the attorneys for the House of Representatives wrote to the Federal District Court for the District of Columbia, after the United States Supreme Court's remand, that Rep. Adam Clayton Powell, Jr., was not entitled to pay for the period of his exclusion and that the action should be dismissed. The House attorneys wrote:

"We are instructed by our clients to advise your Honor that the House, with all due respect, does not agree with the decision of the Supreme Court in this matter.

"The House believes that the decision and mandate of the court constitute an unwarranted action inconsistent with the separation of powers provided by the Constitution."

exercise of these powers is required. The Constitution is, to use a common figure of speech, painted with a broad brush. There is wide latitude for interpretation, as among the delineations that *prima facie* define the separate powers of the legislature, the executive, and the judiciary. It is the legislature and the executive in which the power of *action* is reposed. It is the judiciary in which the power to *nullify* legislative or executive action on constitutional grounds is reposed.

In Baker v. Carr, however, the Supreme Court itself became an initiator of political action. The social implications involve far-reaching consequences, some of which may be predictable.

Because most of man's past has been nomadic and then agricultural (some 11,000 years), he has had little experience with urbanism. Now, in the short period of a few decades, urbanism is the rule, not the exception. Soon, in America—the same trend is appearing all over the world—eight out of ten persons will live in urban communities. Furthermore, American urban communities are increasingly composed of racial and cultural minorities, which are tending in certain cities to become political majorities. This trend is a consequence of (1) the preservation of antiquated city boundaries and (2) the flight from the cities to suburbia.

The doctrine of Baker v. Carr, popularly known as the concept of "one man, one vote," compels a vast rearrangement and realignment of political power from wide dispersion throughout agrarian areas into a few areas of high concentration of population. On the other hand, and just for that reason, there could be a reaction in favor of metropolitanism and the creation of larger urban political units to neutralize the influence of concentrations of voters within the confined boundaries of the old cities. The concept of integration in education, as directed by the United States Supreme Court in Brown v. Board of Education, could find its counterpart in integration of political power under the doctrine of Baker v. Carr.

We should also note the movement to annul, in part at least, the Baker v. Carr doctrine of "one man, one vote" because it is a modern application of Sir Henry Maine's proposition that the rigidity of case law (for example, the Supreme Court's rejection in Kirkpatrick of any variance from absolute equality in apportionment) may be ameliorated by legislation—in this case, constitutional amendment.

Under Article V of the United States Constitution, on the application of the legislatures of two-thirds of the several states, a convention for proposing amendments must be called. An amendment proposed by such a convention becomes a part of the Constitution when ratified by the legislatures of three-fourths of the several states or by conventions in three-fourths thereof (one or the other mode of ratification may be proposed by Congress). Thirty-two states have made, in one form or another, applications for a constitutional convention to propose an amendment concerning the doctrine established in Baker

v. Carr. Assuming the validity of those applications, about which some editorial doubts have been raised, applications from two more states would require such a convention, whose ultimate purpose would be to annul, amend, alter or in some manner impinge on the presently asserted powers of the judiciary to tell the states how they must apportion their population among the several districts of the states for the purpose of electing state legislators.

We cannot reject the temptation to raise a constitutional and quite logical question worthy of the talents of the best medievalist (how many angels can dance on the point of a pin?). Assume, as we may, that some of the legislatures that have petitioned for a constitutional convention are malapportioned under the standards of Baker v. Carr. Do such malapportioned legislatures have the power to petition for an amendment to the Constitution that, if enacted, might validate its existing apportionment despite the doctrine of "one man, one vote?" Assume a constitutional amendment producing that result, and further assume that the Supreme Court of the United States would hold the amendment unconstitutional because the doctrine of Baker v. Carr, which the amendment would undo, has been violated. One may speculate that if the Supreme Court, given its prestigious position in American society, should render the decision just postulated, public opinion would support it, and the amendment to the Constitution would be abortive for unconstitutionality. One may also speculate that the Supreme Court might well acquiesce in the constitutional amendment because throughout its history, particularly in the 20th century, the Court has shown considerable flexibility. (At one period in the 1930's, the erstwhile conservative Chief Justice Hughes was casting the deciding vote in support of New Deal legislation in 5–4 decisions and was known as the "man on the flying trapeze.")[13]

Baker v. Carr stands as a case of affirmative judicial action against the legislative. What about Mora v. McNamara? In that case, in a broad sense, the court refused to take an action against the executive that, if it had been taken, would have been comparable to the action that was taken against the State of Tennessee in Baker v. Carr. The court in Mora v. McNamara was asked to render a declaratory judgment that the "present United States military activity in Vietnam is illegal." By refusing to review the case, the Supreme Court of the United States accepted by implication the rationale of the courts below that the question was political and therefore not justiciable. But was the question in Baker v. Carr not political? On that score, one will need to ponder the difference, if any, between the two cases. Of course, it is less serious business for the Supreme Court to tell the State of Tennessee that it must give "one man, one vote" than to tell the President of the United States, in his

---

[13] An excellent account of this period is found in *The Struggle for Judicial Supremacy, A Study of a Crisis in American Power Politics*, by Robert H. Jackson, who later became a Justice of the United States Supreme Court.

capacity as Commander-in-Chief of the Armed Forces, that he cannot maintain troops abroad in armed conflict. This is not to say that the Supreme Court will never grasp such a nettle.[14]

In Powell, there may be the making of an impasse between the United States Supreme Court and the House of Representatives. If the House should refuse to restore Powell's lost pay as the letter of his counsel suggests (see footnote 12, *supra*), the Court will be powerless to enforce what would appear to be the logical consequence of its decision. Such an impasse would not be without precedent. In 1832, in the case of Worcester v. Georgia, 6 Peters 534, Chief Justice Marshall rendered an illustrious opinion in which he declared void as violating the Constitution, laws, and treaties of the United States certain acts of the Georgia Legislature under which the State had asserted jurisdiction over the Cherokee Nation in derogation of the relations which had already been established between the United States and the Cherokee Indians. It is said that Congress was excited by Marshall's opinion, Georgia enraged, and President Jackson agitated and belligerent. While Governor Lumpkin of Georgia was crying "Usurpation!" and declaring that he would meet the decision "with the spirit of determined resistance," President Jackson defied the Chief Justice asserting "John Marshall has made his decision—*now let him enforce it!*" Marshall's decree was never enforced.[15]   So it may be with Chief Justice Warren's decree in the Powell case.

The cases in the final portion of this section demonstrate that the Constitution of the United States is sufficiently self-explanatory on most, but not *all,* issues. They demonstrate the statement of Charles Evans Hughes that "The Constitution is what the judges say it is."[16] He made the remark when he was Governor of New York—a plain-spoken expression of the doctrine of judicial interpretation that John Marshall had enunciated more than 100 years earlier in Marbury v. Madison. It is only in the outer reaches of the national interest in domestic tranquility and in national security that the justices will always appear to some dissident portion of the people to have gone too far in constitutional interpretation—to have gone beyond their branch of rulership. On the distant horizons of the constitutionality of asserted powers, whether executive, legislative, or judicial, one may discern that judges are rulers, as well as executives and legislators.

---

[14]Even more dramatic than Mora v. McNamara was the United States Supreme Court's refusal to entertain a bill of complaint from the Commonwealth of Massachusetts, acting on behalf of all the citizens, to question the constitutionality of the war in Indochina. Massachusetts v. Laird, 39 L.W. 3196 (1970).

[15]Beveridge, Albert J., *The Life of John Marshall,* Vol. IV, Boston and New York, Houghton Mifflin, 1919, pp. 539–552.

[16]Pearson, D., *The Nine Old Men,* Garden City, New Jersey, Doubleday, 1936, p. 94.

QUESTIONS

1. The title of this chapter is "Law Limits Judging." Name the concepts involved in the limiting of judging and the components thereof.

2. In the Preface the statement is made that "Law may make the environment; and, of equal importance, the environment may make law." Name the two cases in this chapter which most clearly illustrate the environment's making law. Why?

3. If you are a resident of California and flee the scene of an automobile accident in which you were involved in New Jersey, when you get back to California are you necessarily home free? Give the legal basis for your answer.

4. Can you bring a suit against an atheist for a declaratory judgment that God exists? Explain your answer.

5. In Reed v. Maley you are more revolted than amused; and in Stephens v. Myers you are more amused than revolted. In one case there was a cause of action; in the other, not. Why?

6. The phrase, "real party in interest," is involved in two cases in this chapter. Name the cases and use them to illustrate the meaning of the word, "standing," or the phrase, "real party in interest."

7. Article III, Section 2, of the Constitution of the United States provides that, "The judicial power shall extend to all cases, in law and equity, arising under this Constitution. . . . " Why was it necessary to refer to equity as well as to law? What is the distinction? What is the origin of equity (see Chapter 1)?

8. Article I, Section 5, paragraph 2, of the Constitution provides that, "Each House may determine the rules of its proceedings, punish its members for disorderly behavior, and, with the concurrence of two thirds, expel a member." Suppose that two-thirds of the members of the House of Representatives should expel a member for no stated reason (the fact being that the expelled member was a professed and authenticated member of the Communist Party in the United States). On a legal action of the Adam Clayton Powell type brought by the communist for reinstatement in his seat, what decision do you think the Supreme Court of the United States would render, and why? If the Supreme Court should order the communist reinstated and the House should refuse, what could the Supreme Court do? What cases in this chapter would help you in considering this question?

3 Law is Tender Toward Accused Persons

Introduction 81
Needs of the State and Rights of the Citizen 83
 The Requirements of a Law Strictly Defining the Crime 83
  Ohio v. Lafferty 83
  McBoyle v. United States 86
 Significant Issues of Search and Seizure 87
  Extent of Criminal Searches 87
  Chimel v. California 87
  Administrative Searches 94
  Electronic Searches 98
  Katz v. United States 98
  Stop and Frisk 104
  Terry v. Ohio 104
  Ballou v. Massachusetts 111
Development of the Rights of Accused Persons 111
 Expanding Applications of the Bill of Rights 111
  Miranda v. Arizona 113
  People v. Powe 123
  Davis v. Mississippi 124
Law and Liberty 124
Questions 130

INTRODUCTION

Our society establishes rules for its protection against offensive actions of individuals. An offense against society in Western democracies is a political question resolved by the legislative branch of government. Once the legislature has defined the offense, the detection, apprehension, and prosecution of the offender, called an accused person, becomes a function of the executive branch. The determination of the innocence or guilt of the accused person is a judicial function, involving judge and jury. The assessment of punishment is usually a judicial function for the judge only. (Occasionally, a statute will prohibit or mandate certain penalties or leave to the jury the discretion between penalties.)

The field of law involving definition, detection, apprehension, prosecution, and punishment of offenses against society is called criminal law. It is to be distinguished from all other law known as civil law—civil law not in the continental sense discussed in Chapter 1 but rather all law that is not criminal law. The gamut of offenses against society established by the legislative branch is extensive. It includes not only the trilogy of murder, rape, and arson, but also the fixing of prices or the "fixing" of a traffic ticket, the selling of milk on Sunday or below a price fixed by the government, the tossing of a paper cup onto a highway, spitting on the floor of a public building, salacious talk over the telephone, the careless setting of a forest fire, the giving of a false fire alarm. The gamut runs from treason to trespass; from pornography to poaching; from shooting to shouting; from defecation in public to duels in private. The punishments range from death to reprimand.

The definition of offenses against society and the assessment of penalties—crime and punishment—create great controversy. Laws imposing Prohibition, recognition of God, the censorship of speech or writing, or conscription for military service are all highly controversial. The ethical question of whether a law deemed unjust may be disobeyed, initiated by Thoreau, followed by Mahatma Gandhi, and returned to America in the civil rights controversies of the 1960's, still persists. In general, in Western democracies, when the legislature enacts a law defining an offense against society and prescribing the punishment, the dissidents must conform or suffer the penalty. Henry David Thoreau did not believe in the Mexican War, so he refused to pay his taxes and went to jail.

Whether or not there is an ethical right to disobey an assertedly unjust law, a characteristic of law is that it *is* disobeyed. For example, those laws of physics or chemistry, mentioned in Chapter 1, *cannot* be disobeyed. One cannot violate the rule that two molecules of hydrogen and one of oxygen make water. On the other hand, one can violate the Fifth Commandment, *Thou Shalt Not Kill.*

Another aspect of law is that it is never self-enforcing. Law creates rights and obligations, but rights are effectuated and obligations are enforced by the institutions of law: policemen for apprehension and protection; grand jury and prosecutor for the charging of offenses and the prosecution of the charge (see Chapter 9, p. 388, *infra*); court and jury for the determination of innocence or guilt. The cases in this section primarily concern one aspect of criminal law —the issue of effective policemanship versus the right of the individual to be secure in his person and in his abode, unmolested by the state, unless for appropriate reasons the state determines that he must sacrifice his privacy so that society may remain unoffended.

The title of this section indicates the direction in which our American law is moving. The proposition that a crime must be clearly defined before the courts may adjudge that a crime has occurred and set a penalty is well established and uncontroverted. We learned that principle from the Romans who, more than two thousand years ago, forced the patricians, who were inclined to adjudge crime and assess penalties arbitrarily, to codify Roman law in writing in the XII Tables. The issue today does not concern the legislative definitions of crime but rather the methods to be employed in the enforcement of the statutory declaration. The purpose of this section is to introduce the reader to the complexities and difficulties of forming judgments between the needs of the state to be secure and the rights of the citizen to be free from oppression.

NEEDS OF THE STATE AND RIGHTS OF THE CITIZEN

THE REQUIREMENTS OF A LAW STRICTLY DEFINING THE CRIME

OHIO v. LAFFERTY
Court of Common Pleas of Ohio, Fifth Circuit, Tappan (Ohio) 113 (1817).

Lafferty was convicted, on three separate indictments, for selling unwholesome provisions.

Wright, for the defendant, moved, in arrest of judgement "for that there is no law of this state against selling unwholesome provisions." He observed, that the indictment was bottomed upon the common law of England, which was not in force in this state, it never having been adopted by our constitution or recognized by our laws or judicial decisions: that the 4th section of the 3d article of the constitution, limited and confined the jurisdiction of the court to offences declared such by the statute laws. He admitted that the offence charged, was an offence against the public, which at common law was indictable and punishable where the common law was in force; but that, in this state, as the common law was not in force; and no statute had declared it criminal, it was not an act which could be prosecuted criminally.

Beebe, contra. That the section of the constitution quoted and relied upon by Wright, as limiting the jurisdiction of the court to statutory offences, was not fairly construed; it should be considered as referring the courts to the statute law, for the extent of their several jurisdictions in criminal cases; and so considered the statute law which gave to the supreme court jurisdiction in all capital cases, and to the courts of common pleas jurisdiction in all cases not capital, without any specification of indictable offences; did point out the manner and the cases in which this section of the constitution intended the duties of the courts should be divided, and that it did not exclude a common law jurisdiction.

TAPPAN, President Judge.   The question raised on this motion, whether the common law is a rule of decision in this state? is one of very great interest and importance, and one upon which contradictory opinions have been holden both at the bar and upon the bench.

No just government ever did, nor probably ever can, exist, without an unwritten or common law. By the common law, is meant those maxims, principles, and forms of judicial proceeding, which have no written law to prescribe or warrant them, but which, founded on the laws of nature and the dictates of reason, have by usage and custom, become interwoven with the written laws; and, by such incorporation, form a part of the municipal code of each state or nation, which has emerged from the loose and erratic habits of savage life, to civilization, order, and a government of laws.

For the forms of process, indictment, and trial, we have no statute law directing us; and for almost the whole law of evidence, in criminal as well as in civil proceedings, we must look to the common law, for we have no other guide. Can it be said, then, that the common law is not in force, when, without its aid and sanction, justice cannot be administered; when even the written laws cannot be construed, explained, and enforced, without the common law, which furnishes the rules and principles of such construction?

We may go further and say, that not only is the common law necessarily in force here, but that its authority is superior to that of the written laws; for it not only furnishes the rules and principles by which the statute laws are construed, but it ascertains and determines the validity and authority of them. It is, therefore, that Lord Hobart said, that a statute law against reason, as to make a man a judge in his own cause, was void.

As the laws of nature and reason are necessarily in force in every community of civilized men, (because nature is the common parent, and reason the common guardian of man) so with communities as with individuals, the right of self-preservation is a right paramount to the institution of written law; and hence the maxim, *the safety of the people is the supreme law,* needs not the sanction of a constitution or statute to give it validity and force; but it cannot have validity and force, as law, unless the judicial tribunals have power to punish all such actions as directly tend to jeopardize that safety; unless, indeed, the judicial tribunals are the guardians of public morals and the conservators of the public peace and order. Whatever acts, then, are wicked and immoral in themselves, and directly tend to injure the community, are crimes against the community, which not only *may,* but *must,* be repressed and punished, or government and social order cannot be preserved. It is this salutary principle of the common law, which spreads its shield over society, to protect it from the incessant activity and novel inventions of the profligate and unprincipled, inventions which the most perfect legislation could not always foresee and guard against.

But although the common law, in all countries, has its foundation in reason and the laws of nature, and therefore is similar in its general principles, yet in its application it has been modified and adapted to various forms of government; as the different orders of architecture, having their foundation in utility and graceful proportion, rise in various forms of symmetry and beauty, in accordance with the taste and judgment of the builder. It is also a law of liberty; and hence we find, that when North America was colonized by emigrants who fled from the pressure of monarchy and priestcraft in the old world, to enjoy freedom in the new, they brought with them the common law of England, (their mother country) claiming it as their birth-right and inheritance. In their charters from the crown, they were careful to have it recognized as the foundation on which they were to erect their laws and governments: not more anxious was Aeneas to secure from the burning ruins of Troy his household Gods, than were these first settlers of America to secure to themselves and their children the benefits of the common law of England. From thence, through every stage of the colonial governments, the common law was in force, so far as it was found necessary or useful. When the revolution commenced, and independent state governments were formed; in the midst of hostile collisions with the mother country, when the passions of men were inflamed, and a deep and general abhorrence of the tyranny of the British government was felt; the sages and patriots who commenced that revolution, and founded those state governments, recognized in the common law a guardian of liberty and social order. The common law of England has thus always been the common law of the colonies and states of North America; not indeed in its full extent, supporting a monarchy, aristocracy, and hierarchy, but so far as it was applicable to our more free and happy habits of government.

. . . . .

But suppose that the position is a correct one, that the principles of the common law have no force or authority in this state, and what are the consequences? They are these: that there are no legal forms of process, of indictments, or trial; there is no law of evidence; and the statute laws cannot be enforced, but must remain inoperative from the uncertain signification of the terms used in defining criminal offences. Beside, the constitution gives jurisdiction to this court in criminal matters, "in such cases *and in such manner as may be pointed out by law;"* and as we have no statute pointing out the manner in which such jurisdictions shall be exercised, the consequence follows that it cannot be lawfully exercised in any manner whatever.

On the whole, therefore, it may be concluded, that were the written laws wholly silent on the subject, the principles and maxims of the common law must, of necessity, be the rule and guide of judicial decision, in criminal as well as civil cases: to supply the defects of a necessarily imperfect legislation, and to prevent "the will of the judge, that law of tyrants," being substituted in the room of known and settled rules of law in the administration of justice.

And that by the ordinance of congress, the constitution and laws of the state, a common law jurisdiction in criminal cases is established and vested in this court. The motion in arrest is, therefore, overruled.

The defendant was fined 50 dollars in each case, with costs.[1]

---

[1]The rule enunciated in Ohio v. Lafferty did not last long—even in Ohio. It was subsequently overruled in 1861 in Smith v. State, 12 Ohio St. 466. Justice Peck speaking for the court said: "It must be borne in mind that we have no common law offenses in this state. No act or omission, however hurtful or immoral in its tendencies, is punishable as a *crime* in Ohio, unless such act or omission is specially enjoined or prohibited by the statute laws of the state." 12 Ohio St. at 469.

The rule of the Smith case brought Ohio into line with the general proposition that without a law, there can be no crime and no punishment. Hence, for an act to be a crime, it must be prohibited and made punishable by a statute existing at the time the act is committed.

McBOYLE v. UNITED STATES

Supreme Court of the United States, 283 U.S. 25 (1931).

Mr. Justice HOLMES delivered the opinion of the Court.

The petitioner was convicted of transporting from Ottawa, Illinois, to Guymon, Oklahoma, an airplane that he knew to have been stolen, and was sentenced to serve three years' imprisonment and to pay a fine of $2,000. The judgment was affirmed by the Circuit Court of Appeals for the Tenth Circuit. 43 F.2d 273. A writ of certiorari was granted by this Court on the question whether the National Motor Vehicle Theft Act applies to aircraft. Act of October 20, 1919, c. 89, 41 Stat. 324; U.S. Code, Title 18, sec. 408. That Act provides: "Sec. 2. That when used in this Act: (a) The term 'motor vehicle' shall include an automobile, automobile truck, automobile wagon, motor cycle, or any other self-propelled vehicle not designed for running on rails; . . . Sec. 3. That whoever shall transport or cause to be transported in interstate or foreign commerce a motor vehicle, knowing the same to have been stolen, shall be punished by a fine of not more than $5,000, or by imprisonment of not more than five years, or both."

Section 2 defines the motor vehicles of which the transportation in interstate commerce is punished in sec. 3. The question is the meaning of the word 'vehicle' in the phrase "any other self-propelled vehicle not designed for running on rails." No doubt etymologically it is possible to use the word to signify a conveyance working on land, water or air, and sometimes legislation extends the use in that direction, e.g., land and air, water being separately provided for, in the Tariff Act, September 22, 1922, c. 356, sec. 401(b), 42 Stat. 858, 948. But in everyday speech 'vehicle' calls up the picture of a thing moving on land. Thus in Rev. Stats. sec. 4, intended, the Government suggests, rather than restrict the definition, vehicle include every contrivance capable of being used "as a means of transportation on land." And this is repeated, expressly excluding aircraft, in the Tariff Act, June 17, 1930, c. 997, sec 401(b); 46 Stat. 590, 708. So here, the phrase under discussion calls up the popular picture. For after including automobile truck, automobile wagon and motor cycle, the words "any other self-propelled vehicle not designed for running on rails" still indicate that a vehicle in the popular sense, that is a vehicle running on land, is the theme. It is a vehicle that runs, not something, not commonly called a vehicle, that flies. Airplanes were well known in 1919, when this statute was passed; but it is admitted that they were not mentioned in the reports or in the debates in Congress. It is impossible to read words that so carefully enumerate the different forms of motor vehicles and have no reference of any kind to aircraft, as including airplanes under a term that usage more and more precisely confines to a different class. The counsel for the petitioner have shown that the phraseology of the statute as to motor vehicles follows that of earlier statutes of Connecticut, Delaware, Ohio, Michigan and Missouri, not to mention the late Regulation of Traffic for the District of Columbia, Title 6, c. 9, sec. 242, none of which can be supposed to leave the earth.

Although it is not likely that a criminal will carefully consider the text of the law before he murders or steals, it is reasonable that a fair warning should be given to the world in language that the common world will understand, of what the law intends to do if a certain line is passed. To make the warning fair, so far as possible the line should be clear. When a rule of conduct is laid down in words that evoke in the common mind only the picture of vehicles moving on land, the statute should not be extended to aircraft, simply because it may seem to us that a similar policy applies, or upon the speculation that, if the legislature had thought of it, very likely broader words would have been used.   .   .   .

Judgment reversed.

SIGNIFICANT ISSUES OF SEARCH AND SEIZURE

Extent of Criminal Searches

CHIMEL v. CALIFORNIA
Supreme Court of the United States, 395 U.S. 752 (1969).

[The Fourth Amendment to the United States Constitution provides:

The right of the people to be secure in their persons, houses, papers, and effects, against unreasonable searches and seizures, shall not be violated, and no warrants shall issue, but upon probable cause, supported by oath or affirmation, and particularly describing the place to be searched, and the persons or things to be seized.

In 1914, in the case of Weeks v. United States, 232 U.S. 383, the Supreme Court ruled that "the Fourth Amendment barred the use of evidence secured through an illegal search and seizure." Just what was an illegal or unreasonable search and seizure that demanded the exclusion of the seized property as evidence was to be determined on a case-by-case approach.

A crucial point in the definitional process of unreasonable searches and seizures occurred in 1947 when the Court decided the case of Harris v. United States, 331 U.S. 145. In Harris, the petitioner was taken in custody by officers of the Federal Bureau of Investigation (F.B.I.) under a valid warrant for his arrest in connection with an interstate scheme involving both forgery and fraud. Pursuant to the petitioner's arrest, which took place in the living room of his apartment, the F.B.I., hoping to find the cancelled forged checks, made an intensive five-hour search of the other three rooms of the petitioner's apartment. As the search neared its end, one of the F.B.I. agents discovered a sealed envelope marked "George Harris, personal papers" in a bedroom bureau drawer. The agent tore open the envelope and found 19 "draft cards" bearing the stamp of Local Board No. 7 of Oklahoma County. The agent then confiscated the "draft cards," which subsequently were used as evidence against the petitioner in a prosecution that resulted in his being convicted on 16 counts of an indictment charging him with the unlawful possession, concealment, and alteration of "draft cards" in violation of Section 11 of the Selective Training and Service Act of 1940. On appeal the United States Supreme Court upheld the petitioner's conviction, reasoning that (a) since the arrest was lawful, the search incident to the arrest was also lawful, and (b) since the search was lawful, the contraband "draft cards" seized during the lawful search could be used as evidence to sustain a conviction against the petitioner without violating his Fourth Amendment rights.

The Harris case stood as the law of the land from 1947 until it was expressly overruled by the Supreme Court in 1969 in the Chimel case. The report of the Chimel case is reproduced here.]

Mr. Justice STEWART delivered the opinion of the Court.

This case raises basic questions concerning the permissible scope under the Fourth Amendment of a search incident to a lawful arrest.

The relevant facts are essentially undisputed. Late in the afternoon of September 13, 1965, three police officers arrived at the Santa Ana, California, home of the petitioner with a warrant authorizing his arrest for the burglary of a coin shop. The officers knocked on the door, identified themselves to the petitioner's wife, and asked if they might come inside. She ushered them into the house, where they waited 10 or 15 minutes until the petitioner returned home from work. When the petitioner entered the house, one of the officers   .   .   . asked for permission to "look around." The petitioner objected, but was advised that "on the basis of the lawful arrest," the officers would nonetheless conduct a search. No search warrant had been issued.

Accompanied by the petitioner's wife, the officers then looked through the entire three-bedroom house, including the attic, the garage, and a small workshop. In some rooms the search was relatively cursory. In the master bedroom and sewing room, however, the officers directed the petitioner's wife to open drawers and "to physically move contents of the drawers from side to side so that [they] might view any items that would have come from [the] burglary." After completing the search, they seized numerous items—primarily coins, but also several medals, tokens, and a few other objects. The entire search took between 45 minutes and an hour.

At the petitioner's subsequent state trial on two charges of burglary, the items taken from his house were admitted into evidence against him, over his objection that they had been unconstitutionally seized. He was convicted, and the judgments of conviction were affirmed by both the California District Court of Appeal, 61 Cal. Rptr. 714, and the California Supreme Court, 67 Cal. Rptr. 421.   .   .   .   We granted certiorari in order to consider the petitioner's substantial constitutional claims. 393 U.S. 958.

.   .   .   This brings us directly to the question whether the warrantless search of the petitioner's entire house can be constitutionally justified as incident to that arrest. The decisions of this Court bearing upon that question have been far from consistent, as even the most cursory review makes evident.

Approval of a warrantless search incident to a lawful arrest seems first to have been articulated by the Court in 1914 as dictum in Weeks v. United States, 232 U.S. 383, in which the Court stated: "What then is the present case? Before answering that inquiry specifically, it may be well by a process of exclusion to state what it is not. It is not an assertion of the right on the part of the Government, always recognized under English and American law, to search the person of the accused when legally arrested to discover and seize the fruits or evidences of crime." Id., at 392.

That statement made no reference to any right to search the *place* where an arrest occurs, but was limited to a right to search the "person." Eleven years later the case of Carroll v. United States, 267 U.S. 132, brought the following embellishment of the Weeks statement: "When a man is legally arrested for an offense, whatever is found upon his person *or in his control* which it is unlawful for him to have and which may be used to prove the offense may be seized and held as evidence in the prosecution." Id., at 158. (Emphasis added.)

Still, that assertion too was far from a claim that the "place" where one is arrested may be searched so long as the arrest is valid. Without explanation, however, the principle emerged in expanded form a few months later in Agnello v. United States,

269 U.S. 20—although still by way of dictum: "The right without a search warrant contemporaneously to search persons lawfully arrested while committing crime and to search the place where the arrest is made in order to find and seize things connected with the crime as its fruits or as the means by which it was committed, as well as weapons and other things to effect an escape from custody, is not to be doubted. See Carroll v. United States, 267 U.S. 132, 158; Weeks v. United States, 232 U.S. 383, 392." 269 U.S., at 30.

And in Marron v. United States, 275 U.S. 192, two years later, the dictum of Agnello appeared to be the foundation of the Court's decision. In that case federal agents had secured a search warrant authorizing the seizure of liquor and certain articles used in its manufacture. When they arrived at the premises to be searched, they saw "that the place was used for retailing and drinking intoxicating liquors." *Id.*, at 194. They proceeded to arrest the person in charge and to execute the warrant. In searching a closet for the items listed in the warrant they came across an incriminating ledger, concededly not covered by the warrant, which they also seized. The Court upheld the seizure of the ledger by holding that since the agents had made a lawful arrest, "[t]hey had a right without a warrant contemporaneously to search the place in order to find and seize the things used to carry on the criminal enterprise." *Id.*, at 199.

That the Marron opinion did not mean all that it seemed to say became evident, however, a few years later in Go-Bart Importing Co. v. United States, 282 U.S. 344, and United States v. Lefkowitz, 285 U.S. 452. In each of those cases the opinion of the Court was written by Mr. Justice Butler, who had authored the opinion in Marron. In Go-Bart, agents had searched the office of persons whom they had lawfully arrested, and had taken several papers from a desk, a safe, and other parts of the office. The Court noted that no crime had been committed in the agents' presence, and that although the agent in charge "had an abundance of information and time to swear out a valid [search] warrant, he failed to do so." 282 U.S., at 358. In holding the search and seizure unlawful, the Court stated: "Plainly the case before us is essentially different from Marron v. United States, 275 U.S. 192. There, officers executing a valid search warrant for intoxicating liquors found and arrested one Birdsall who in pursuance of a conspiracy was actually engaged in running a saloon. As an incident to the arrest they seized a ledger in a closet where the liquor or some of it was kept and some bills beside the cash register. These things were visible and accessible and in the offender's immediate custody. There was no threat of force or general search or rummaging of the place." 282 U.S., at 358. This limited characterization of Marron was reiterated in Lefkowitz, a case in which the Court held unlawful a search of desk drawers and a cabinet despite the fact that the search had accompanied a lawful arrest. 285 U.S., at 465.

The limiting views expressed in Go-Bart and Lefkowitz were thrown to the winds, however, in Harris v. United States, 331 U.S. 145, decided in 1947. In that case, officers had obtained a warrant for Harris' arrest on the basis of his alleged involvement with the cashing and interstate transportation of a forged check. He was arrested in the living room of his four-room apartment, and in an attempt to recover two canceled checks thought to have been used in effecting the forgery, the officers undertook a thorough search of the entire apartment. Inside a desk drawer they found a sealed envelope marked "George Harris, personal papers." The envelope, which was then torn open, was found to contain altered selective service documents, and those documents were used to secure Harris' conviction for violating the Selective Training and Service Act of 1940. The Court rejected Harris' Fourth Amendment claim, sustaining the search as "incident to arrest." *Id.,* at 151.

Only a year after Harris, however, the pendulum swung again. In Trupiano v. United States, 334 U.S. 699, agents raided the site of an illicit distillery, saw one of several conspirators operating the still, and arrested him, contemporaneously "seiz[ing] the illicit distillery." *Id.,* at 702. The Court held that the arrest and others made subsequently had been valid, but that the unexplained failure of the agents to procure a search warrant—in spite of the fact that they had had more than enough time before the raid to do so—rendered the search unlawful. The opinion stated:

"It is a cardinal rule that, in seizing goods and articles, law enforcement agents must secure and use search warrants wherever reasonably practicable. . . . This rule rests upon the desirability of having magistrates rather than police officers determine when searches and seizures are permissible and what limitations should be placed upon such activities. . . . To provide the necessary security against unreasonable intrusions upon the private lives of individuals, the framers of the Fourth Amendment required adherence to judicial processes wherever possible. And subsequent history has confirmed the wisdom of that requirement.

.   .   .   .

"A search or seizure without a warrant as an incident to a lawful arrest has always been considered to be a strictly limited right. It grows out of the inherent necessities of the situation at the time of the arrest. But there must be something more in the way of necessity than merely a lawful arrest." *Id.,* at 705, 708.

In 1950, two years after Trupiano, came United States v. Rabinowitz, 339 U.S. 56, the decision upon which California primarily relies in the case now before us. In Rabinowitz, federal authorities had been informed that the defendant was dealing in stamps bearing forged overprints. On the basis of that information they secured a warrant for his arrest, which they executed at his one-room business office. At the time of the arrest, the officers "searched the desk, safe, and file cabinets in the office for about an hour and a half," *id.,* at 59, and seized 573 stamps with forged overprints. The stamps were admitted into evidence at the defendant's trial, and this Court affirmed his conviction, rejecting the contention that the warrantless search had been unlawful. The Court held that the search in its entirety fell within the principle giving law enforcement authorities "[t]he right 'to search the place where the arrest is made in order to find and seize things connected with the crime. . . . '" *Id.,* at 61. Harris was regarded as "ample authority" for that conclusion. *Id.,* at 63. The opinion rejected the rule of Trupiano that "in seizing goods and articles, law enforcement agents must secure and use search warrants wherever reasonably practicable." The test, said the Court, "is not whether it is reasonable to procure a search warrant, but whether the search was reasonable." *Id.,* at 66.

Rabinowitz has come to stand for the proposition, *inter alia,* that a warrantless search "incident to a lawful arrest" may generally extend to the area that is considered to be in the "possession" or under the "control" of the person arrested. And it was on the basis of that proposition that the California courts upheld the search of the petitioner's entire house in this case. That doctrine, however, at least in the broad sense in which it was applied by the California courts in this case, can withstand neither historical nor rational analysis.

Even limited to its own facts, the *Rabinowitz* decision was, as we have seen, hardly founded on an unimpeachable line of authority. As Mr. Justice Frankfurter commented in dissent in that case, the "hint" contained in *Weeks* was, without persuasive justification, "loosely turned into dictum and finally elevated to a decision." 339 U.S., at 75. And the approach taken in cases such as Go-Bart, Lefkowitz, and Trupiano was essentially disregarded by the Rabinowitz Court.

Nor is the rationale by which the State seeks here to sustain the search of the petitioner's house supported by a reasoned view of the background and purpose of the Fourth Amendment. Mr. Justice Frankfurter wisely pointed out in his *Rabinowitz* dissent that the Amendment's proscription of "unreasonable searches and seizures" must be read in light of "the history that gave rise to the words"—a history of "abuses so deeply felt by the Colonies as to be one of the potent causes of the Revolution. . . . " 339 U.S., at 69. The Amendment was in large part a reaction to the general warrants and warrantless searches that had so alienated the colonists and had helped speed the movement for independence. In the scheme of the Amendment, therefore, the requirement that "no Warrants shall issue, but upon probable cause," plays a crucial part. As the Court put it in McDonald v. United States, 335 U.S. 451:

"We are not dealing with formalities. The presence of a search warrant serves a high function. Absent some grave emergency, the Fourth Amendment has interposed a magistrate between the citizen and the police. This was done not to shield criminals nor to make the home a safe haven for illegal activities. It was done so that an objective mind might weigh the need to invade that privacy in order to enforce the law. The right of privacy was deemed too precious to entrust to the discretion of those whose job is the detection of crime and the arrest of criminals. . . . And so the Constitution requires a magistrate to pass on the desires of the police before they violate the privacy of the home. We cannot be true to that constitutional requirement and excuse the absence of a search warrant without a showing by those who seek exemption from the constitutional mandate that the exigencies of the situation made that course imperative." *Id.,* at 455–456. . . .

. . . . .

. . . When an arrest is made, it is reasonable for the arresting officer to search the person arrested in order to remove any weapons that the latter might seek to use in order to resist arrest or effect his escape. Otherwise, the officer's safety might well be endangered, and the arrest itself frustrated. In addition, it is entirely reasonable for the arresting officer to search for and seize any evidence on the arrestee's person in order to prevent its concealment or destruction. And the area into which an arrestee might reach in order to grab a weapon or evidentiary items must, of course, be governed by a like rule. A gun on a table or in a drawer in front of one who is arrested can be as dangerous to the arresting officer as one concealed in the clothing of the person arrested. There is ample justification, therefore, for a search of the arrestee's person and the area "within his immediate control"—construing that phrase to mean the area from within which he might gain possession of a weapon or destructible evidence.

There is no comparable justification, however, for routinely searching rooms other than that in which an arrest occurs—or, for that matter, for searching through all the desk drawers or other closed or concealed areas in that room itself. Such searches, in the absence of well-recognized exceptions, may be made only under the authority of a search warrant. The "adherence to judicial processes" mandated by the Fourth Amendment requires no less.

This is the principle that underlay our decision in Preston v. United States, 376 U.S. 364. In that case three men had been arrested in a parked car, which had later been towed to a garage and searched by police. We held the search to have been unlawful under the Fourth Amendment, despite the contention that it had been incidental to a valid arrest. Our reasoning was straightforward: "The rule allowing contemporaneous searches is justified, for example, by the need to seize weapons and other things which might be used to assault an officer or effect an escape, as well as by the need to prevent the destruction of evidence of the crime—things which might easily happen where the weapon or evidence is on the accused's person or under his immediate control. But these justifications are absent where a search is remote in time or place from the arrest." *Id.,* at 367.[A] . . .

It is argued in the present case that it is "reasonable" to search a man's house when he is arrested in it. But that argument is founded on little more than a subjective view regarding the acceptability of certain sorts of police conduct, and not on considerations relevant to Fourth Amendment interests. Under such an unconfined analysis, Fourth Amendment protection in this area would approach the evaporation point. It is not easy to explain why, for instance, it is less subjectively "reasonable" to search a man's house when he is arrested on his front lawn—or just down the street—than it is when he happens to be in the house at the time of arrest.[B] As Mr. Justice Frankfurter put it: "To say that the search must be reasonable is to require some criterion of reason. It is no guide at all either for a jury or for district judges or the police to say that an 'unreasonable search' is forbidden—that the search must be reasonable. What is the test of reason which makes a search reasonable? The test is the reason underlying and expressed by the Fourth Amendment: the history and the experience which it embodies and the safeguards afforded by it against the evils to which it was a response." United States v. Rabinowitz, 339 U.S., at 83 (dissenting opinion). Thus, although "[t]he recurring questions of the reasonableness of searches" depend upon "the facts and circumstances—the total atmosphere of the case," *id.,* at 63, 66 (opinion of the Court), those facts and circumstances must be viewed in the light of established Fourth Amendment principles.

It would be possible, of course, to draw a line between Rabinowitz and Harris on the one hand, and this case on the other. For Rabinowitz involved a single room, and Harris a four-room apartment, while in the case before us an entire house was searched. But such a distinction would be highly artificial. The rationale that allowed the searches and seizures in Rabinowitz and Harris would allow the searches and seizures in this

---

[A]Our holding today is of course entirely consistent with the recognized principle that, assuming the existence of probable cause, automobiles and other vehicles may be searched without warrants "where it is not practicable to secure a warrant because the vehicle can be quickly moved out of the locality or jurisdiction in which the warrant must be sought." Carroll v. United States, 267 U.S. 132, 153; see Brinegar v. United States, 338 U.S. 160.

[B]Some courts have carried the Rabinowitz approach to just such lengths. See, e.g., Clifton v. United States, 224 F. 2d 329 (C. A. 4th Cir.), cert. denied, 350 U.S. 894 (purchaser of illicit whiskey arrested in back yard of seller; search of one room of house sustained); *United States* v. *Jackson,* 149 F. Supp. 937 (D. C. D. C.), rev'd on other grounds, 102 U.S. App. D. C. 109, 250 F. 2d 772) (suspect arrested half a block from his rented room; search of room upheld). But see *James* v. *Louisiana,* 382 U.S. 36 *(per curiam).*

case. No consideration relevant to the Fourth Amendment suggests any point of rational limitation, once the search is allowed to go beyond the area from which the person arrested might obtain weapons or evidentiary items. The only reasoned distinction is one between a search of the person arrested and the area within his reach on the one hand, and more extensive searches on the other.[c]

The petitioner correctly points out that one result of decisions such as Rabinowitz and Harris is to give law enforcement officials the opportunity to engage in searches not justified by probable cause, by the simple expedient of arranging to arrest suspects at home rather than elsewhere. We do not suggest that the petitioner is necessarily correct in his assertion that such a strategy was utilized here, but the fact remains that had he been arrested earlier in the day, at his place of employment rather than at home, no search of his house could have been made without a search warrant. In any event, even apart from the possibility of such police tactics, the general point so forcefully made by Judge Learned Hand in United States v. Kirschenblatt, 16 F. 2d 202, remains: "After arresting a man in his house, to rummage at will among his papers in search of whatever will convict him, appears to us to be indistinguishable from what might be done under a general warrant; indeed, the warrant would give more protection, for presumably it must be issued by a magistrate. True, by hypothesis the power would not exist, if the supposed offender were not found on the premises; but it is small consolation to know that one's papers are safe only so long as one is not at home." *Id.,* at 203.

Rabinowitz and Harris have been the subject of critical commentary for many years, and have been relied upon less and less in our own decisions. It is time, for the reasons we have stated, to hold that on their own facts, and insofar as the principles they stand for are inconsistent with those that we have endorsed today, they are no longer to be followed.

Application of sound Fourth Amendment principles to the facts of this case produces a clear result. The search here went far beyond the petitioner's person and the area from within which he might have obtained either a weapon or something that could have been used as evidence against him. There was no constitutional justification, in the absence of a search warrant, for extending the search beyond that area. The scope of the search was, therefore, "unreasonable" under the Fourth and Fourteenth Amendments, and the petitioner's conviction cannot stand.

Reversed.

---

[c]It is argued in dissent that so long as there is probable cause to search the place where an arrest occurs, a search of that place should be permitted even though no search warrant has been obtained. This position seems to be based principally on two premises: first, that once an arrest has been made, the additional invasion of privacy stemming from the accompanying search is "relatively minor"; and second, that the victim of the search may "shortly thereafter" obtain a judicial determination of whether the search was justified by probable cause. With respect to the second premise, one may initially question whether all of the States in fact provide the speedy suppression procedures the dissent assumes. More fundamentally, however, we cannot accept the view that Fourth Amendment interests are vindicated so long as "the rights of the criminal" are "protect[ed] . . . against introduction of evidence seized without probable cause." The Amendment is designed to prevent, not simply to redress, unlawful police action. In any event, we cannot join in characterizing the invasion of privacy that results from a top-to-bottom search of a man's house as "minor." And we can see no reason why, simply because some interference with an individual's privacy and freedom of movement has lawfully taken place, further intrusions should automatically be allowed despite the absence of a warrant that the Fourth Amendment would otherwise require.

[The concurring opinion of Mr. Justice Harlan is omitted.]

Mr. Justice WHITE, with whom Mr. Justice BLACK joins, dissenting.

Few areas of the law have been as subject to shifting constitutional standards over the last 50 years as that of the search "incident to an arrest." There have been a remarkable instability in this whole area, which has seen at least four major shifts in emphasis. Today's opinion makes an untimely fifth. In my view, the Court should not now abandon the old rule.

. . . .

Such rapid reversals had occurred before, but they are rare. Here there had been two about-faces, one following hard upon the other. Justice Frankfurter objected in this language: "Especially ought the Court not reenforce needlessly the instabilities of our day by giving fair ground for the belief that Law is the expression of chance—for instance, of unexpected changes in the Court's composition and the contingencies in the choice of successors." [United States v. Rabinowitz, 339 U.S. 56, 86 (1950) (dissenting opinion).] . . .

The rule which has prevailed, but for very brief or doubtful periods of aberration, is that a search incident to an arrest may extend to those areas under the control of the defendant and where items subject to constitutional seizure may be found. The justification for this rule must, under the language of the Fourth Amendment, lie in the reasonableness of the rule. . . . In terms, then, the Court must decide whether a given search is reasonable. The Amendment does not proscribe "warrantless searches" but instead it proscribes "unreasonable searches" and this Court has never held nor does the majority today assert that warrantless searches are necessarily unreasonable.

. . . .

An arrested man, by definition conscious of the police interest in him, and provided almost immediately with a lawyer and a judge, is in an excellent position to dispute the reasonableness of his arrest and contemporaneous search in a full adversary proceeding. I would uphold the constitutionality of this search contemporaneous with an arrest since there was probable cause both for the search and for the arrest, exigent circumstances involving the removal or destruction of evidence, and a satisfactory opportunity to dispute the issues of probable cause shortly thereafter. In this case, the search was reasonable.[2]

Administrative Searches

In Abel v. United States, 362 U.S. 217 (1959), Abel was arrested in his hotel room in New York City by agents of the Immigration and Naturalization

---

[2]In Chambers v. Maroney, 399 U.S. 42 (1970), the police upon probable cause, but without a warrant, stopped an automobile and arrested its occupants. The automobile was then driven to the police station, where the police, still operating without a warrant (the car being in their custody) made a thorough search of the car and found two .38 caliber pistols and other incriminating evidence. The United States Supreme Court upheld the search of the car, the seizure of the articles, and the admission of these seized articles into evidence against the petitioner at his trial for robbery. Compare Carroll v. United States and Brinegar v. United States, in footnote A, p. 92, *supra*.

Service (I.N.S.). The attention of the I.N.S. was drawn to Abel by officers of the F.B.I. who learned through an informer named Hayhanen, a recently defected Russian spy, that Abel was engaged in espionage. Hayhanen was not at that time willing to testify against Abel; instead of arresting and prosecuting him, the F.B.I. decided to bring Abel to the attention of the I.N.S. with a view toward deportation.

The I.N.S. concluded that if Abel were, as suspected, an alien he would be subject to deportation because he had failed to comply with the legal duty of aliens to notify the Attorney General every January of their address in the United States. With an administrative arrest warrant issued by the district director of the I.N.S., two I.N.S. agents went to Abel's apartment. They were accompanied by several F.B.I. men who had no warrant. It was agreed that before Abel was arrested the F.B.I. would "interview" Abel in an attempt to persuade him to "cooperate."

When Abel released the catch on his door three F.B.I. agents entered the room. Abel, who was nude, was told to put on a pair of undershorts and to sit on the bed, which he did. When he did not "cooperate" the F.B.I. agents signalled to the I.N.S. agents who then entered the room, placed Abel under arrest and searched his person and his room for the purpose of discovering weapons and documentary evidence of his "alienage." They found a birth certificate for "Martin Collins" (forged) and a piece of paper containing a coded message. A later search of Abel's belongings, undertaken at the head-quarters of the I.N.S., uncovered a birth certificate for "Emil Goldfus" (Emil Goldfus had died in 1903 at the age of one year), an international certificate of vaccination issued to "Martin Collins," and a bank book containing the account of "Emil Goldfus."

As soon as Abel had been taken away, the F.B.I. agents obtained permission from the hotel management to search the room. They found a hollow pencil containing microfilm and a block of wood containing a "cipher pad."

Mr. Justice Frankfurter, who delivered the opinion of the Court, said that "the question in this case is whether seven items were properly admitted into evidence at the petitioner's trial for conspiracy to commit espionage. All seven items were seized by officers of the Government without a search warrant. The seizures did not occur in connection with the exertion of the criminal process against petitioner. They arose out of his administrative arrest by the United States Immigration and Naturalization Service as a preliminary to his deportation. A motion to suppress these items as evidence, duly made in the District Court, was denied after a full hearing. . . . Petitioner was tried, convicted and sentenced to thirty years' imprisonment and to the payment of a fine of $3,000. The Court of Appeals affirmed. . . .

"The main claims which petitioner pressed upon the Court may be thus summarized: (1) the administrative arrest was used by the Government in bad faith; (2) administrative arrests as preliminaries to deportation are unconstitutional; and (3) regardless of the validity of the administrative arrest here, the searches and seizures through which the challenged items came into the Government's possession were not lawful ancillaries to such an arrest. . . . "

The majority of the Court in Abel held that (1) since two lower courts had heard the facts on bad faith and found none, the Supreme Court would not look into that matter; (2) the search was less exhaustive than in Harris and valid—although incident to an administrative arrest rather than a criminal procedure; and (3) the hollow pencil and the block of wood containing microfilm found by the F.B.I. in the wastebasket, after Abel was taken away, were admissible in evidence because Abel had abandoned these items in the wastebasket after he had checked out.

Abel's sentence of thirty years and a fine of $3,000 were affirmed, Justices Douglas and Black dissenting. (Abel was later returned to Russia in an exchange for Francis Gary Powers, the American U-2 pilot shot down over Russian territory.)[3]

The legality of administrative inspections to detect violations of municipal health, fire, housing, or welfare regulations, or violations of federal immigration and revenue laws was again considered in the case of Camara v. Municipal Court, 387 U.S. 523 (1967). Camara had violated a criminal provision of the San Francisco Housing Code by refusing to permit a warrantless inspection of his residence.

The United States Supreme Court reversed Camara's conviction. Applying the Fourth Amendment through the "due process" clause of the Fourteenth Amendment to the state administrative searches, the Court declared that "[we] cannot agree that the Fourth Amendment interests at stake in these inspection cases are merely 'peripheral.' It is surely anomalous to say that the individual and his private property are fully protected by the Fourth Amendment only when an individual is suspected of criminal behavior." 387 U.S. at 530.

The Camara case creates some difficult problems for local government, which has the responsibility of preventing the development of conditions that are dangerous to public health and safety, such as rat infestation or fire hazards. Every man's home is his castle, immune from unlawful entry, but does that mean that he may harbor, beyond detection, conditions that jeopardize his neighbor? The Supreme Court has said that "since the holding [in Camara] emphasizes the controlling standard of reasonableness, nothing we say today is intended to foreclose prompt inspections, even without a warrant, that the law has traditionally upheld in emergency situations." 387 U.S. at 539. Nevertheless, the question remains: what is an emergency?

[3]See the NEW YORK TIMES, February 10, 1962.

A recent development in the area of administrative searches, in several states, is the unannounced searches of homes of indigents who are receiving public assistance in order to determine welfare eligibility. In one such case, Parrish v. Civil Service Commission of County of Alameda, 66 Cal.2d 260 (1967), the plaintiff asked to be reinstated as a county social worker after he had been discharged for insubordination because he refused to participate in an unannounced early morning search for the purpose of detecting the presence of "unauthorized males." (In California, the amount of a grant to a needy child is computed after considering the income of any adult male "assuming the role of spouse" to the child's mother, whether he is married to her or not. The male "assuming the role of spouse" is often characterized as an "unauthorized male.")

The Supreme Court of California held that the county had failed to obtain a warrant or to secure consent to search homes of welfare recipients to determine welfare eligibility; therefore administrative searches without warrant were unconstitutional—except in emergencies. The Court also held that even if consent had been obtained, the county could not constitutionally condition the continued receipt of public assistance upon the giving of such consent. The Court found that these searches transgress constitutional limitations; therefore Parrish must be reinstated to his former position as a county social worker. To be compared with Parrish is Wyman v. James, United States Supreme Court, No. 69, 1970 Term, in which a New York State statute mandating daylight visits in the premises of relief recipients was upheld.

The obvious question remains whether in Chimel the Supreme Court implicitly overruled Abel. As Mr. Justice Frankfurter has poignantly stated, in this area of a search incident to an arrest or incident to a warrant other than a warrant issued by a magistrate in a criminal procedure—the pendulum has been swinging furiously. Indeed, we might reasonably predict that the pendulum has not yet ceased to swing. The reader will become aware of the practice, frequently indulged by the Supreme Court of the United States, of throwing a doubt upon a case like Abel without expressly overruling it. Harris was expressly overruled. Nothing was said about Abel. It is therefore left to lawyers, criminals, and the interested public to use their several best judgments as to whether Abel is still the law.

A perennial conflict besets our land. Crime is big business; billions of dollars are taken from our economy by lawbreakers. The detection of these criminals is a sophisticated business that is largely carried on by ordinary human beings, who are not highly paid (as much perhaps as society can afford). Obviously, these law enforcement agencies composed of fallible human beings need some flexibility. On the other hand, the freedom of a single individual is precious in our society. It is often said that it is better that a hundred criminals go free than that one innocent citizen be mistreated by the law or deprived of his liberty. This is the dichotomy. There is no instantaneous solution.

Electronic Searches

KATZ v. UNITED STATES
Supreme Court of the United States, 389 U.S. 347 (1967).

Mr. Justice STEWART delivered the opinion of the Court.

The petitioner was convicted in the District Court for the Southern District of California under an eight-count indictment charging him with transmitting wagering information by telephone from Los Angeles to Miami and Boston, in violation of a federal statute. At trial the Government was permitted, over the petitioner's objection, to introduce evidence of the petitioner's end of the telephone conversations, overheard by FBI agents who had attached an electronic listening and recording device to the outside of the public telephone booth from which he had placed his calls. In affirming his conviction, the Court of Appeals rejected the contention that the recordings had been obtained in violation of the Fourth Amendment, because "[t]here was no physical entrance into the area occupied by [the petitioner]." We granted certiorari in order to consider the constitutional questions thus presented.

The petitioner has phrased those questions as follows:

"A. Whether a public telephone booth is a constitutionally protected area so that evidence obtained by attaching an electronic listening recording device to the top of such a booth is obtained in violation of the right to privacy of the user of the booth.

"B. Whether physical penetration of a constitutionally protected area is necessary before a search and seizure can be said to be violative of the Fourth Amendment to the United States Constitution."

We decline to adopt this formulation of the issues. In the first place, the correct solution of Fourth Amendment problems is not necessarily promoted by incantation of the phrase "constitutionally protected area." Secondly, the Fourth Amendment cannot be translated into a general constitutional "right to privacy." That Amendment protects individual privacy against certain kinds of governmental intrusion, but its protections go further, and often have nothing to do with privacy at all. Other provisions of the Constitution protect personal privacy from other forms of governmental invasion. But the protection of a person's *general* right to privacy—his right to be let alone by other people—is, like the protection of his property and of his very life, left largely to the law of the individual States.

Because of the misleading way the issues have been formulated, the parties have attached great significance to the characterization of the telephone booth from which the petitioner placed his calls. The petitioner has strenuously argued that the booth was a "constitutionally protected area." The Government has maintained with equal vigor that it was not. But this effort to decide whether or not a given "area," viewed in the abstract, is "constitutionally protected" deflects attention from the problem presented by this case. For the Fourth Amendment protects people, not places. What a person knowingly exposes to the public, even in his own home or office, is not a subject of Fourth Amendment protection. . . . But what he seeks to preserve as private, even in an area accessible to the public, may be constitutionally protected. . . .

The Government stresses the fact that the telephone booth from which the petitioner made his calls was constructed partly of glass, so that he was as visible after he entered it as he would have been if he had remained outside. But what he sought to exclude when he entered the booth was not the intruding eye—it was the uninvited ear. He did not shed his right to do so simply because he made his calls from a place where he might be seen. No less than an individual in a business office, in a friend's apartment, or in a taxicab, a person in a telephone booth may rely upon the protection of the Fourth Amendment.One who occupies it, shuts the door behind him, and pays the toll that permits him to place a call, is surely entitled to assume that the words he utters into the mouthpiece will not be broadcast to the world. To read the Constitution more narrowly is to ignore the vital role that the public telephone has come to play in private communication.

The Government contends, however, that the activities of its agents in this case should not be tested by Fourth Amendment requirements, for the surveillance technique they employed involved no physical penetration of the telephone booth from which the petitioner placed his calls. It is true that the absence of such penetration was at one time thought to foreclose further Fourth Amendment inquiry, Olmstead v. United States, 277 U.S. 438, 457, 464, 466; Goldman v. United States, 316 U.S. 129, 134, 136, for that Amendment was thought to limit only searches and seizures of tangible property. But "[t]he premise that property interests control the right of the Government to search and seize has been discredited." Warden v. Hayden, 387 U.S. 294, 304. Thus, although a closely divided Court supposed in Olmstead that surveillance without any trespass and without the seizure of any material object fell outside the ambit of the Constitution, we have since departed from the narrow view on which that decision rested. Indeed, we have expressly held that the Fourth Amendment governs not only the seizure of tangible items, but extends as well to the recording of oral statements, overheard without any "technical trespass under local property law." Silverman v. United States, 365 U.S. 505, 511. Once this much is acknowledged, and once it is recognized that the Fourth Amendment protects people—and not simply "areas"—against unreasonable searches and seizures, it becomes clear that the reach of that Amendment cannot turn upon the presence or absence of a physical intrusion into any given enclosure.

We conclude that the underpinnings of Olmstead and Goldman have been so eroded by our subsequent decisions that the "trespass" doctrine there enunciated can no longer be regarded as controlling. The Government's activities in electronically listening to and recording the petitioner's words violated the privacy upon which he justifiably relied while using the telephone booth and thus constituted a "search and seizure" within the meaning of the Fouth Amendment. The fact that the electronic device employed to achieve that end did not happen to penetrate the wall of the booth can have no constitutional significance.

The question remaining for decision, then, is whether the search and seizure conducted in this case complied with constitutional standards. In that regard, the Government's position is that its agents acted in an entirely defensible manner: They did not begin their electronic surveillance until investigation of the petitioner's activities had established a strong probability that he was using the telephone in question to transmit gambling information to persons in other States, in violation of federal law. Moreover, the surveillance was limited, both in scope and in duration, to the specific purpose of establishing the contents of the petitioner's unlawful telephonic communications. The agents confined their surveillance to the brief periods during which he used the telephone booth, and they took great care to overhear only the conversations of the petitioner himself.

Accepting this account of the Government's actions as accurate, it is clear that this surveillance was so narrowly circumscribed that a duly authorized magistrate, properly notified of the need for such investigation, specifically informed of the basis on which it was to proceed, and clearly apprised of the precise intrusion it would entail, could constitutionally have authorized, with appropriate safeguards, the very limited search and seizure that the Government asserts in fact took place. Only last Term we sustained the validity of such an authorization, holding that, under sufficiently "precise and discriminate circumstances," a federal court may empower government agents to employ a concealed electronic device "for the narrow and particularized purpose of asscertaining the truth of the . . . allegations" of a "detailed factual affidavit alleging the commission of a specific criminal offense." Osborn v. United States, 385 U.S. 323, 329-330. Discussing that holding, the Court in Berger v. New York, 388 U.S. 41, said that "the order authorizing the use of the electronic device" in Osborn "afforded similar protections to those . . . of conventional warrants authorizing the seizure of tangible evidence." Through those protections, "no greater invasion of privacy was permitted than was necessary under the circumstances." *Id.,* at 57.ᴰ Here, too, a similar judicial order could have accommodated "the legitimate needs of law enforcement" by authorizing the carefully limited use of electronic surveillance.

The Government urges that, because its agents relied upon the decisions in Olmstead and Goldman, and because they did no more here than they might properly have done with prior judicial sanction, we should retroactively validate their conduct. That we cannot do. It is apparent that the agents in this case acted with restraint. Yet the inescapable fact is that this restraint was imposed by the agents themselves, not by a judicial officer. They were not required, before commencing the search, to present their estimate of probable cause for detached scrutiny by a neutral magistrate. They were not compelled, during the conduct of the search itself, to observe precise limits established in advance by a specific court order. Nor were they directed, after the search had been completed, to notify the authorizing magistrate in detail of all that had been seized. In the absence of such safeguards, this Court has never sustained a search upon the sole ground that officers reasonably expected to find evidence of a particular crime and voluntarily confined their activities to the least intrusive means consistent with that end. Searches conducted without warrants have been held unlawful "notwithstanding facts unquestionably showing probable cause," Agnello v. United States, 269 U.S. 20, 33, for the Constitution requires "that the deliberate, impartial judgment of a judicial officer . . . be interposed between the citizen and the police. . . . " Wong Sun v.

ᴰAlthough the protections afforded the petitioner in Osborn were "similar . . . to those . . . of conventional warrants," they were not identical. A conventional warrant ordinarily serves to notify the suspect of an intended search. But if Osborn had been told in advance that federal officers intended to record his conversations, the point of making such recordings would obviously have been lost: the evidence in question could not have been obtained. In omitting any requirement of advance notice, the federal court that authorized electronic surveillance in Osborn simply recognized, as has this Court, that officers need not announce their purpose before conducting an otherwise authorized search if such an announcement would provoke the escape of the suspect or the destruction of critical evidence. . . .

United States, 371 U.S. 471, 481-482. "Over and again this Court has emphasized that the mandate of the [Fourth] Amendment requires adherence to judicial processes," United States v. Jeffers, 342 U.S. 48, 51, and that searches conducted outside the judicial process, without prior approval by judge or magistrate, are *per se* unreasonable under the Fourth Amendment—subject only to a few specifically established and well-delineated exceptions. . . .

It is difficult to imagine how any of those exceptions could ever apply to the sort of search and seizure involved in this case. Even electronic surveillance substantially contemporaneous with an individual's arrest could hardly be deemed an "incident" of that arrest. . . . And, of course, the very nature of electronic surveillance precludes its use pursuant to the suspect's consent.

The Government does not question these basic principles. Rather, it urges the creation of a new exception to cover this case. It argues that surveillance of a telephone booth should be exempted from the usual requirement of advance authorization by a magistrate upon a showing of probable cause. We cannot agree. Omission of such authorization "bypasses the safeguards provided by an objective predetermination of probable cause, and substitutes instead the far less reliable procedure of an after-the-event justification for the . . . search, too likely to be subtly influenced by the familiar shortcomings of hindsight judgment." Beck v. Ohio, 379 U.S. 89, 96. And bypassing a neutral predetermination of the *scope* of a search leaves individuals secure from Fourth Amendment violations "only in the discretion of the police." *Id.,* at 97.

These considerations do not vanish when the search in question is transferred from the setting of a home, an office, or a hotel room, to that of a telephone booth. Wherever a man may be, he is entitled to know that he will remain free from unreasonable searches and seizures. The government agents here ignored "the procedure of antecedent justification . . . that is central to the Fourth Amendment," a procedure that we hold to be a constitutional precondition of the kind of electronic surveillance involved in this case. Because the surveillance here failed to meet the condition, and because it led to the petitioner's conviction, the judgment must be reversed.

It is so ordered.

[Mr. Justice Marshall took no part in the consideration or decision of this case.

The opinions of Mr. Justice Douglas, with whom Mr. Justice Brennan joins, concurring, and of Mr. Justice Harlan, concurring, and of Mr. Justice White, concurring, are omitted.]

Mr. Justice BLACK dissenting.

If I could agree with the Court that eavesdropping carried on by electronic means (equivalent to wiretapping) constitutes a "search" or "seizure," I would be happy to join the Court's opinion. For on that premise my Brother Stewart set out methods in accord with the Fourth Amendment to guide States in the enactment and enforcement of laws passed to regulate wiretapping by government. . . . Notwithstanding these good efforts of the Court, I am still unable to agree with its interpretation of the Fourth Amendment.

My basic objection is twofold: (1) I do not believe that the words of the Amendment will bear the meaning given them by today's decision, and (2) I do not believe that it is the proper role of the Court to rewrite the Amendment in order "to bring it into harmony with the times" and thus reach a result that many people believe to be desirable.

While I realize that an argument based on the meaning of words lacks the scope, and no doubt the appeal, of broad policy discussions and philosophical discourses on such nebulous subjects as privacy, for me the language of the Amendment is the crucial place to look in constructing a written document such as our Constitution. The Fourth Amendment says that

"The right of the people to be secure in their persons, houses, papers, and effects, against unreasonable searches and seizures, shall not be violated, and no Warrants shall issue, but upon probable cause, supported by Oath or affirmation, and particularly describing the place to be searched, and the persons or things to be seized."

The first clause protects "persons, houses, papers, and effects, against unreasonable searches and seizures. . . . " These words connote the idea of tangible things with size, form, and weight, things capable of being searched, seized, or both. The second clause of the Amendment still further establishes its Framers' purpose to limit its protection to tangible things by providing that no warrants shall issue but those "particularly describing the place to be searched and the person or things to be seized." A conversation overheard by eavesdropping whether by plain snooping or wiretapping, is not tangible and, under the normally accepted meanings of the words, can neither be searched nor seized. In addition the language of the second clause indicates that the Amendment refers to something not only tangible so it can be seized but to something already in existence so it can be described. Yet the Court's interpretation would have the Amendment apply to overhearing future conversations which by their very nature are nonexistent until they take place. How can one "describe" a future conversation, and if not, how can a magistrate issue a warrant to eavesdrop one in the future? It is argued that information showing what is expected to be said is sufficient to limit the boundaries of what later can be admitted into evidence; but does such general information really meet the specific language of the Amendment which says "particularly describing"? Rather than using language in a completely artificial way, I must conclude that the Fourth Amendment simply does not apply to eavesdropping.

·   ·   ·   ·

I do not deny that common sense requires and that this Court often has said that the Bill of Rights' safeguards should be given a liberal construction. This principle, however, does not justify construing the search and seizure amendment as applying to eavesdropping or the "seizure" of conversations. The Fourth Amendment was aimed directly at the abhorred practice of breaking in, ransacking and searching homes and other buildings and seizing peoples' personal belongings without warrants issued by magistrates. The Amendment deserves, and this Court has given it, a liberal construction in order to protect against warrantless searches of buildings and seizures of tangible personal effects. But until today this Court has refused to say that eavesdropping comes within the ambit of Fourth Amendment restrictions. See, e.g., Olmstead v. United States, 277 U.S. 438 (1928), and Goldman v. United States, 316 U.S. 129 (1942).

·   ·   ·   ·

The Fourth Amendment protects privacy only to the extent that it prohibits unreasonable searches and seizures of "persons, houses, papers and effects." No general right is created by the Amendment so as to give this Court the unlimited power to hold unconstitutional everything which affects privacy. Certainly the Framers, well acquainted as they were with the excesses of governmental power, did not intend to grant this Court such omnipotent lawmaking authority as that. The history of governments proves that it is dangerous to freedom to repose such powers in courts.

For these reasons I respectfully dissent.[4]

[4]Congress enacted and President Johnson signed into law on June 19, 1968, the "Omnibus Crime Control and Safe Streets Act of 1968," whose basic purpose is to assist State and local governments in reducing the incidence of crime and to increase the effectiveness and the coordination of law enforcement systems at all levels of government. Here are portions of Title III of the Act, which is designated "Wiretapping and Electronic Surveillance," and was drafted to meet the standards delineated in Katz.

Wiretapping and Electronic Surveillance
82 Sta. 212-223 (1968), 18 U.S.C.A. §§ 2510-2520 (Supp. 1969).

§ 2516. Authorization for interception of wire or oral communications

(1) The Attorney General, or any Assistant Attorney General specially designated by the Attorney General, may authorize an application to a Federal judge of competent jurisdiction for, and such judge may grant . . . an order authorizing or approving the interception of wire or oral communications by the Federal Bureau of Investigation, or a Federal agency having responsibility for the investigation of the offense as to which the application is made. . . .

(2) The principal prosecuting attorney of any State, or the principal prosecuting attorney of any political subdivision thereof, if such attorney is authorized by a statute of that State to make application to a State court judge of competent jurisdiction for an order authorizing or approving the interception of wire or oral communications, may apply to such judge for, and such judge may grant . . . an order authorizing or approving the interception of wire or oral communications by investigative or law enforcement officers having responsibility for the investigation of the offense as to which the application is made. . . .

§ 2518. Procedure for interception of wire or oral communications

(1) Each application for an order authorizing or approving the interception of a wire or oral communication shall be made in writing upon oath or affirmation to a judge of competent jurisdiction and shall state the applicant's authority to make such application. Each application shall include the following information:

(a) the identity of the investigative or law enforcement officer making the application, and the officer authorizing the application;

(b) a full and complete statement of the facts and circumstances relied upon by the applicant, to justify his belief that an order should be issued, including (i) details as to the particular offense that has been, is being, or is about to be committed, (ii) particular description of the nature and location of the facilities from which or the place where the communication is to be intercepted, (iii) a particular description of the type of communications sought to be intercepted, (iv) the identity of the person, if known, committing the offense and whose communications are to be intercepted;

(c) a full and complete statement as to whether or not other investigative procedures have been tried and failed or why they reasonably appear to be unlikely to succeed if tried or to be too dangerous;

(d) a statement of the period of time for which the interception is required to be maintained. . . .

. . . .

(5) No order entered under this section may authorize or approve the interception of any wire or oral communication for any period longer than is necessary to achieve the objective of the authorization, nor in any event longer than thirty days. Extensions of an order may be granted.
. . . . The period of extension shall be no longer than the authorizing judge deems necessary to achieve the purposes for which it was granted and in no event for longer than thirty days. . . .

Stop and Frisk

TERRY v. OHIO

Supreme Court of the United States, 392 U.S. 1 (1968).

Mr. Chief Justice WARREN delivered the opinion of the Court.

This case presents serious questions concerning the role of the Fourth Amendment in the confrontation on the street between the citizen and the policeman investigating suspicious circumstances.

Petitioner Terry was convicted of carrying a concealed weapon and sentenced to the statutorily prescribed term of one to three years in the penitentiary. Following the denial of a pretrial motion to suppress, the prosecution introduced in evidence two revolvers and a number of bullets seized from Terry and a codefendant, Richard Chilton, by Cleveland Police Detective Martin McFadden. At the hearing on the motion to suppress this evidence, Officer McFadden testified that while he was patrolling in plain clothes in downtown Cleveland at approximately 2:30 in the afternoon of October 31, 1963, his attention was attracted by two men, Chilton and Terry, standing on the corner of Huron Road and Euclid Avenue. He had never seen the two men before, and he was unable to say precisely what first drew his eye to them. However, he testified that he had been a policeman for 39 years and a detective for 35 and that he had been assigned to patrol this vicinity of downtown Cleveland for shoplifters and pickpockets for 30 years. He explained that he had developed routine habits of observation over the years and that he would "stand and watch people or walk and watch people at many intervals of the day." He added, "Now, in this case when I looked over they didn't look right to me at the time."

His interest aroused, Officer McFadden took up a post of observation in the entrance to a store 300 to 400 feet away from the two men. "I get more purpose to watch them when I seen their movements," he testified. He saw one of the men leave the other one and walk southwest on Huron Road, past some stores. The man paused for a moment and looked in a store window, then walked on a short distance, turned around and walked back toward the corner, pausing once again to look in the same store window. He rejoined his companion at the corner, and the two conferred briefly. Then the second man went through the same series of motions, strolling down Huron Road, looking in the same window, walking on a short distance, turning back, peering in the store window again, and returning to confer with the first man at the corner. The two men

---

§ 2511. Interception and disclosure of wire or oral communications prohibited

(1)Except as otherwise specifically provided in this chapter any person who—

(a) willfully intercepts, endeavors to intercept, or procures any other person to intercept or endeavor to intercept, any wire or oral communication;

(b) willfully uses, endeavors to use, or procures any other person to use or endeavor to use any electronic, mechanical, or other device to intercept any oral communication . . . shall be fined not more than $10,000 or imprisoned not more than five years, or both.

.   .   .

(2)(c) It shall not be unlawful under this chapter for a person acting under color of law to intercept a wire or oral communication, where such person is a party to the communication or one of the parties to the communication has given prior consent to such interception.

repeated this ritual alternately between five and six times apiece—in all, roughly a dozen trips. At one point, while the two were standing together on the corner, a third man approached them and engaged them briefly in conversation. This man then left the two others and walked west on Euclid Avenue. Chilton and Terry resumed their measured pacing, peering, and conferring. After this had gone on for 10 to 12 minutes, the two men walked off together, heading west on Euclid Avenue, following the path taken earlier by the third man.

By this time Officer McFadden had become thoroughly suspicious. He testified that after observing their elaborately casual and oft-repeated reconnaissance of the store window on Huron Road, he suspected the two men of "casing a job, a stick-up," and that he considered it his duty as a police officer to investigate further. He added that he feared "they may have a gun." Thus, Officer McFadden followed Chilton and Terry and saw them stop in front of Zucker's store to talk to the same man who had conferred with them earlier on the street corner. Deciding that the situation was ripe for direct action, Officer McFadden approached the three men, identified himself as a police officer and asked for their names. At this point his knowledge was confined to what he had observed. He was not acquainted with any of the three men by name or by sight, and he had received no information concerning them from any other source. When the men "mumbled something" in response to his inquiries, Officer McFadden grabbed petitioner Terry, spun him around so that they were facing the other two, with Terry between McFadden and the others, and patted down the outside of his clothing. In the left breast pocket of Terry's overcoat Officer McFadden felt a pistol. He reached inside the overcoat pocket, but was unable to remove the gun. At this point, keeping Terry between himself and the others, the officer ordered all three men to enter Zucker's store. As they went in, he removed Terry's overcoat completely, retrieved a .38 caliber revolver from the pocket and ordered all three men to face the wall with their hands raised. Officer McFadden proceeded to pat down the outer clothing of Chilton and the third man, Katz. He discovered another revolver in the outer pocket of Chilton's overcoat, but no weapons were found on Katz. The officer testified that he only patted the men down to see whether they had weapons, and that he did not put his hands beneath the outer garments of either Terry or Chilton until he felt their guns. So far as appears from the record, he never placed his hands beneath Katz's outer garments. Officer McFadden seized Chilton's gun, asked the proprietor of the store to call a police wagon, and took all three men to the station, where Chilton and Terry were formally charged with carrying concealed weapons.

On the motion to suppress the guns the prosecution took the position that they had been seized following a search incident to a lawful arrest. The trial court rejected this theory, stating that it "would be stretching the facts beyond reasonable comprehension" to find that Officer McFadden had had probable cause to arrest the men before he patted them down for weapons. However, the court denied the defendant's motion on the ground that Officer McFadden, on the basis of his experience, "had reasonable cause to believe . . . that the defendants were conducting themselves suspiciously, and some interrogation should be made of their action." Purely for his own protection, the court held, the officer had the right to pat down the outer clothing of these men, whom he had reasonable cause to believe might be armed. The court distinguished between an investigatory "stop" and an arrest, and between a *"frisk"* of the outer clothing for weapons and a full-blown search for evidence of crime. The frisk, it held, was essential to the proper performance of the officer's investigatory duties, for without it "the answer to the police officer may be a bullet, and a loaded pistol discovered during the frisk is admissible."

.　　　.　　　.

I.

.　.　. Unquestionably petitioner was entitled to the protection of the Fourth Amendment as he walked down the street in Cleveland. . . . The question is whether in all the circumstances of this on-the-street encounter, his right to personal security was violated by an unreasonable search and seizure.

We would be less than candid if we did not acknowledge that this question thrusts to the fore difficult and troublesome issues regarding a sensitive area of police activity —issues which have never been before squarely presented to this Court. Reflective of the tensions involved are the practical and constitutional arguments pressed with great vigor on both sides of the public debate over the power of the police to "stop and frisk" —as it is sometimes euphemistically termed—suspicious persons.

On the one hand, it is frequently argued that in dealing with the rapidly unfolding and often dangerous situations on city streets the police are in need of an escalating set of flexible responses, graduated in relation to the amount of information they possess. For this purpose it is urged that distinctions should be made between a "stop" and an "arrest" (or a "seizure" of a person), and between a "frisk" and a "search." Thus, it is argued, the police should be allowed to "stop" a person and detain him briefly for questioning upon suspicion that he may be connected with criminal activity. Upon suspicion that the person may be armed, the police should have the power to "frisk" him for weapons. If the "stop" and the "frisk" give rise to probable cause to believe that the suspect has committed a crime, then the police should be empowered to make a formal "arrest," and a full incident "search" of the person. This scheme is justified in part upon the notion that a "stop" and a "frisk" amount to a mere "minor inconvenience and petty indignity," which can properly be imposed upon the citizen in the interest of effective law enforcement on the basis of a police officer's suspicion.

On the other side the argument is made that the authority of the police must be strictly circumscribed by the law of arrest and search as it has developed to date in the traditional jurisprudence of the Fourth Amendment. It is contended with some force that there is not—and cannot be—a variety of police activity which does not depend solely upon the voluntary cooperation of the citizen and yet which stops short of an arrest based upon probable cause to make such an arrest. The heart of the Fourth Amendment, the argument runs, is a severe requirement of specific justification for any intrusion upon protected personal security, coupled with a highly developed system of judicial controls to enforce upon the agents of the State the commands of the Constitution. Acquiescence by the courts in the compulsion inherent in the field interrogation practices at issue here, it is urged, would constitute an abdication of judicial control over, and indeed an encouragement of, substantial interference with liberty and personal security by police officers whose judgment is necessarily colored by their primary involvement in "the often competitive enterprise of ferreting out crime." Johnson v. United States, 333 U.S. 10, 14 (1948). This, it is argued, can only serve to exacerbate police-community tensions in the crowded centers of our Nation's cities.

.　　　.　　　.

Having thus roughly sketched the perimeters of the constitutional debate over the limits on police investigative conduct in general and the background against which this case presents itself, we turn our attention to the quite narrow question posed by the facts before us: whether it is always unreasonable for a policeman to seize a person and subject him to a limited search for weapons unless there is probable cause for an arrest. . . .

II.

Our first task is to establish at what point in this encounter the Fourth Amendment becomes relevant. That is, we must decide whether and when Officer McFadden "seized" Terry and whether and when he conducted a "search." There is some suggestion in the use of such terms as "stop" and "frisk" that such police conduct is outside the purview of the Fourth Amendment because neither action rises to the level of a "search" or "seizure" within the meaning of the Constitution. We emphatically reject this notion. It is quite plain that the Fourth Amendment governs "seizures" of the person which do not eventuate in a trip to the station house and prosecution for crime —"arrests" in traditional terminology. It must be recognized that whenever a police officer accosts an individual and restrains his freedom to walk away, he has "seized" that person. And it is nothing less than sheer torture of the English language to suggest that a careful exploration of the outer surfaces of a person's clothing all over his or her body in an attempt to find weapons is not a "search." Moreover, it is simply fantastic to urge that such a procedure performed in public by a policeman while the citizen stands helpless, perhaps facing a wall with his hands raised, is a "petty indignity." It is a serious intrusion upon the sanctity of the person, which may inflict great indignity and arouse strong resentment, and it is not to be undertaken lightly.

. . .

In this case there can be no question, then, that Officer McFadden "seized" petitioner and subjected him to a "search" when he took hold of him and patted down the outer surfaces of his clothing. We must decide whether at this point it was reasonable for Officer McFadden to have interfered with petitioner's personal security as he did. And in determining whether the seizure and search were "unreasonable" our inquiry is a dual one—whether the officer's action was justified at its inception, and whether it was reasonably related in scope to the circumstances which justified the interference in the first place.

III.

If this case involved police conduct subject to the Warrant Clause of the Fourth Amendment, we would have to ascertain whether "probable cause" existed to justify the search and seizure which took place. However, that is not the case. We do not retreat from our holdings that the police must, whenever practicable, obtain advance judicial approval of searches and seizures through the warrant procedure see, *e.g.,* Katz v. United States, 389 U.S. 347 (1967), . . . or that in most instances failure to comply with the warrant requirement can only be excused by exigent circumstances, see, *e.g.,* Warden v. Hayden, 387 294 (1967) (hot pursuit); . . . But we deal here with an entire rubric of police conduct—necessarily swift action predicated upon the on-the-spot observations of the officer on the beat—which historically has not been, and as a practical matter could not be, subjected to the warrant procedure. Instead, the conduct involved in this case must be tested by the Fourth Amendment's general proscription against unreasonable searches and seizures.

Nonetheless the notions which underlie the warrant procedure and the requirement of probable cause remain fully relevant in this context. In order to assess the reasonableness of Officer McFadden's conduct as a general proposition, it is necessary "first to focus upon the governmental interest which allegedly justifies official intrusion upon the constitutionally protected interests of the private citizen," for there is "no ready test for determining reasonableness other than by balancing the need to search [or seize] against the invasion which the search [or seizure] entails." Camara v. Municipal Court, 387 U.S. 523, 534, 536–537 (1967). And in justifying the particular intrusion the police officer must be able to point to specific and articulable facts which, taken together with rational inferences from those facts, reasonably warrant that intrusion. The scheme of the Fourth Amendment becomes meaningful only when it is assured that at some point the conduct of those charged with enforcing the laws can be subjected to the more detached, neutral scrutiny of a judge who must evaluate the reasonableness of a particular search or seizure in light of the particular circumstances. And in making that assessment it is imperative that the facts be judged against an objective standard: would the facts available to the officer at the moment of the seizure or the search "warrant a man of reasonable caution in the belief" that the action that was taken was appropriate? . . .   Anything less would invite intrusions upon constitutionally guaranteed rights based on nothing more substantial than inarticulate hunches, a result this Court has consistently refused to sanction. . . .   And simple "'good faith on the part of the arresting officer is not enough.' . . .   If subjective good faith alone were the test, the protections of the Fourth Amendment would evaporate, and the people would be 'secure in their persons, houses, papers, and effects' only in the discretion of the police." Beck v. Ohio, [379 U.S. 89, 96, 97 (1964)].

Applying these principles to this case, we consider first the nature and extent of the governmental interests involved. One general interest is of course that of effective crime prevention and detention; it is this interest which underlies the recognition that a police officer may in appropriate circumstances and in an appropriate manner approach a person for the purposes of investigating possibly criminal behavior even though there is no probable cause to make an arrest. It was this legitimate investigative function Officer McFadden was discharging when he decided to approach petitioner and his companions. He had observed Terry, Chilton, and Katz go through a series of acts, each of them perhaps innocent in itself, but which taken together warranted further investigation. There is nothing unusual in two men standing together on a street corner, perhaps waiting for someone. Nor is there anything suspicious about people in such circumstances strolling up and down the street, singly or in pairs. Store windows, moreover, are made to be looked in. But the story is quite different where, as here, two men hover about a street corner for an extended period of time, at the end of which it becomes apparent that they are not waiting for anyone or anything; where these men pace alternately along an identical route, pausing to stare in the same store window roughly 24 times; where each completion of this route is followed immediately by a conference between the two men on the corner; where they are joined in one of these conferences by a third man who leaves swiftly; and where the two men finally follow the third and rejoin him a couple of blocks away. It would have been poor police work indeed for an officer of 30 years' experience in the detection of thievery from stores in this same neighborhood to have failed to investigate this behavior further.

The crux of this case, however, is not the propriety of Officer McFadden's taking steps to investigate petitioner's suspicious behavior, but rather, whether there was justification for McFadden's invasion of Terry's personal security by searching him for weapons in the course of that investigation. We are now concerned with more than the governmental interest in investigating crime; in addition, there is the more immediate interest of the police officer in taking steps to assure himself that the person with whom he is dealing is not armed with a weapon that could unexpectedly and fatally be used against him. Certainly it would be unreasonable to require that police officers take unnecessary risks in the performance of their duties. American criminals have a long tradition of armed violence, and every year in this country many law enforcement officers are killed in the line of duty, and thousands more are wounded. Virtually all of these deaths and a substantial portion of the injuries are inflicted with guns and knives.

In view of these facts, we cannot blind ourselves to the need for law enforcement officers to protect themselves and other prospective victims of violence in situations where they may lack probable cause for an arrest. When an officer is justified in believing that the individual whose suspicious behavior he is investigating at close range is armed and presently dangerous to the officer or to others, it would appear to be clearly unreasonable to deny the officer the power to take necessary measures to determine whether the person is in fact carrying a weapon and to neutralize the threat of physical harm.

We must still consider, however, the nature and quality of the intrusion on individual rights which must be accepted if police officers are to be conceded the right to search for weapons in situations where probable cause to arrest for crime is lacking. Even a limited search of the outer clothing for weapons constitutes a severe, though brief, intrusion upon cherished personal security, and it must surely be an annoying, frightening, and perhaps humiliating experience. . . .

.   .   .   .   .   .

.   .   .   An arrest is a wholly different kind of intrusion upon individual freedom from a limited search for weapons, and the interests each is designed to serve are likewise quite different. An arrest is the initial stage of a criminal prosecution. It is intended to vindicate society's interest in having its laws obeyed, and it is inevitably accompanied by future interference with the individual's freedom of movement, whether or not trial or conviction ultimately follows. The protective search for weapons, on the other hand, constitutes a brief, though far from inconsiderable, intrusion upon the sanctity of the person. It does not follow that because an officer may lawfully arrest a person only when he is apprised of facts sufficient to warrant a belief that the person has committed or is committing a crime, the officer is equally unjustified, absent that kind of evidence, in making any intrusions short of an arrest. Moreover, a perfectly reasonable apprehension of danger may arise long before the officer is possessed of adequate information to justify taking a person into custody for the purpose of prosecuting him for a crime. . . .

Our evaluation of the proper balance that has to be struck in this type of case leads us to conclude that there must be a narrowly drawn authority to permit a reasonable search for weapons for the protection of the police officer, where he has reason to believe that he is dealing with an armed and dangerous individual, regardless of whether he has probable cause to arrest the individual for a crime. The officer need not be absolutely certain that the individual is armed; the issue is whether a reasonably prudent man in the circumstances would be warranted in the belief that his safety or that of others was in danger. . . . And in determining whether the officer acted reasonably in such circumstances, due weight must be given, not to his inchoate and unparticularized suspicion or "hunch," but to the specific reasonable inferences which he is entitled to draw from the facts in light of his experience. . . .

IV.

We must now examine the conduct of Officer McFadden in this case to determine whether his search and seizure of petitioner were reasonable, both at their inception and as conducted. . . .

The scope of the search in this case presents no serious problem in light of these standards. Officer McFadden patted down the outer clothing of petitioner and his two companions. He did not place his hands in their pockets or under the outer surface of their garments until he had felt weapons, and then he merely reached for and removed the guns. He never did invade Katz's person beyond the outer surfaces of his clothes, since he discovered nothing in his pat down which might have been a weapon. Officer McFadden confined his search strictly to what was minimally necessary to learn whether the men were armed and to disarm them once he discovered the weapons. He did not conduct a general exploratory search for whatever evidence of criminal activity he might find.

V.

We conclude that the revolver seized from Terry was properly admitted in evidence against him. At the time he seized petitioner and searched him for weapons, Officer McFadden had reasonable grounds to believe that petitioner was armed and dangerous, and it was necessary for the protection of himself and others to take swift measures to discover the true facts and neutralize the threat of harm if it materialized. The policeman carefully restricted his search to what was appropriate to the discover of the particular items which he sought. Each case of this sort will, of course, have to be decided on its own facts. We merely hold today that where a police officer observes unusual conduct which leads him reasonably to conclude in light of his experience that criminal activity may be afoot and that the persons with whom he is dealing may be armed and presently dangerous; where in the course of investigating this behavior he identifies himself as a policeman and makes reasonable inquiries; and where nothing in the initial stages of the encounter serves to dispel his reasonable fear for his own or others' safety, he is entitled for the protection of himself and others in the area to conduct a carefully limited search of the outer clothing of such persons in an attempt to discover weapons which might be used to assault him. Such a search is a reasonable search under the Fourth Amendment, and any weapons seized may properly be introduced in evidence against the person from whom they were taken.

Affirmed.

. . .

[The concurring opinions of Mr. Justice Black, Mr. Justice Harlan, and Mr. Justice White are omitted. Mr. Justice Douglas dissented.]

BALLOU v. MASSACHUSETTS, 403 F.2d 982 (1st Cir. 1968), cert. denied, 394 U.S. 909 (1969). In Ballou, the Boston police, acting on an unidentified informant's tip, went to a cafe where, the informant had said, there were three men (whom he named) with firearms. Two of the Boston officers involved recognized that one of the three men named by the informant was known to have served time on a gun-carrying charge, to carry a gun, and to be a friend of a leader involved in a current gang war. Pursuant to this information the police proceeded to the cafe, and upon their arrival patted down the first of the three men with his permission and found nothing. Next, without asking permission, they patted down the defendant and found a revolver. The defendant was convicted in a state court of carrying a concealed weapon, and on appeal the conviction was affirmed.

The defendant sought review of his case in the Massachusetts Federal District Court by petitioning for a writ of habeas corpus. The District Court denied the writ, and the First Circuit Court of Appeals affirmed the denial. The Court of Appeals, relying on Terry, held that the factual situation in the instant case supported a "reasonable suspicion" on the part of the officers and thus justified their search of defendant. The Court of Appeals felt that "the course of action decided upon here—to follow the tip and investigate—was properly responsive to all the information the officers possessed and the governmental interests of crime prevention and detection." The Court did, however, note that it was aware that the stop-and-frisk practice on an anonymous tip opened the possibility of capricious police harassment, but it emphasized its decision in this case was grounded upon the fact that these safeguards were met: that the tip must be accurate, specific, and capable of being substantially corroborated by observation; that the tip must be linked to other known facts by the police; and that the police must respond to the tip in good faith.

DEVELOPMENT OF THE RIGHTS OF ACCUSED PERSONS

EXPANDING APPLICATIONS OF THE BILL OF RIGHTS

The first ten amendments to the Constitution of the United States, known as the Bill of Rights, are generally prohibitions against the *federal* government. For example, *inter alia,* the First Amendment guarantees freedom of religion and freedom of speech; the Second provides for a militia; the Third provides against quartering soldiers in people's homes; and the Fourth guarantees the security of persons, houses, papers and effects against unreasonable searches and seizures. The Fifth Amendment provides for a grand jury or other procedures before a person may be held for a crime; it guarantees that an accused person need not be a witness against himself and that no person may be deprived of life, liberty or property without due process of law. The Sixth

Amendment guarantees a speedy, public trial and the right to have the assistance of counsel in defense; the Seventh provides for trial by jury; the Eighth provides that excessive bail shall not be required nor cruel and unusual punishments inflicted; the Ninth provides, in general, that the powers enumerated for the federal government shall not be construed to deny others retained by the people; and the Tenth expressly provides that powers not delegated to the United States are reserved to the states.

Much of the texts of the first ten amendments evolved from that era in which Lord Coke counseled the Commons regarding the Petition of Rights, granted by the Crown in 1628. In general, the guarantees in the first eight amendments to the Constitution are guarantees exacted from the federal government as protections for the people against the federal government.

Most of the relationships between a person and government, however, are relationships between that person and the state and local community in which he resides and which has jurisdiction over him. Policemanship is the most obvious example of those relationships. It is the laws of the city, of the county, and of the state that are the source of most of the impact of government on the person and that are the source of most of the rights of the person against government.

Many of the states have in their constitutions counterparts of the federal Bill of Rights, but there are many and important differences in the texts of state constitutions. Furthermore, state courts differ among themselves and with the United States Supreme Court in the interpretation of apparently identical constitutional provisions. For a considerable portion of American judicial history, the states have largely been free to determine through their own state judicial processes the quality, the character, and the extent of the citizen's rights against government. Municipal ordinances, county ordinances, and criminal laws of the state have historically been matters determined by the state.

The passage of the Fourteenth Amendment to the Constitution in 1868 added a new factor to this question of the rights of persons against government. The apparently predominant purpose of this Amendment was to establish, beyond question, that former Negro slaves were citizens of the United States. However, the Amendment contains language on which a very large amount of contemporary federal adjudication now rests. The Amendment provides that no state shall "deprive any person of life, liberty, or property, without due process of law; nor deny to any person within its jurisdiction the equal protection of the laws." Just as the first eight of the first ten amendments were prohibitions against the federal government in favor of *persons,* the Fourteenth Amendment constitutes a prohibition against the *states* in favor of *persons.*

The full meaning of the general provisions of the Fourteenth Amendment emerged slowly. Indeed, only within recent decades have the more significant civil liberties interpretations of the Fourteenth Amendment occurred. The *states* under that Amendment are prohibited from abridging the privileges or immunities of citizens, from depriving persons of life, liberty, or property without due process of law, and from denying persons equal protection of the laws. These are broad phrases. The term "due process of law" is one of the most ancient of phrases in English jurisprudence. Determining what is due process of law often involves an historical investigation. The Supreme Court is now looking to the first eight amendments to find those privileges, immunities, rights to life, liberty or property, and rights to equal protection of the law upon which the states may not impinge.

Let us take some illustrations. A chief of police issues a shoot-to-kill order in a riot-situation. A city council approves a zoning plan with certain areas restricted to white, Anglo-Saxon Protestants. A county government refuses Jehovah's Witnesses the right to erect a tabernacle for temporary use in a public park. A state governor quarters a large body of militia within the confines of city boundaries at a time when there are no riots, no burnings, and no emergencies of any sort. These illustrations are drawn from current events in America, but there could be many more. Any one of them may or may not involve one of the liberties that federal courts will consider under the Fourteenth Amendment.

Note that these illustrations involve actions, in some cases by legislative bodies and in other cases by the executive. Any official of state government, from the local dog catcher to the governor, may take an action that may involve the Fourteenth Amendment. The litigation involving the legality of such legislative or executive action may be instituted in the courts of the state in question or in the federal courts. The considerations that determine where the litigation arises does not concern us here.

Now, suppose that in any one of these cases or in any other case a state supreme court held that the governmental official's action was legal. In accordance with the modern interpretation of the Fourteenth Amendment, covering the privileges or immunities of citizens, the life, liberty and property of citizens, and their equal protection under the law, the litigation may not end with the supreme court of the state. The Supreme Court of the United States may elect to review the case, render an opinion, and deliver a judgment that would require whatever agency of the state is involved—the governor, the state legislature, the county government, the city council, the chief of police, or the state supreme court itself—to revise or to abrogate the action of the state. Thus, although they originated in state courts, cases such as some of those in this section reach the United States Supreme Court.

MIRANDA v. ARIZONA
Supreme Court of the United States, 384 U.S. 436 (1966).

[The Supreme Court granted *certiorari* in four cases involving the issue of the apprisement of constitutional rights to defendants held in police custody. In the title case,

Miranda v. Arizona, the facts are expressed by Chief Justice Warren as follows: "On March 13, 1963, petitioner, Ernesto Miranda, was arrested at his home and taken in custody to a Phoenix police station. He was there identified by the complaining witness. The police then took him to 'Interrogation Room No. 2' of the detective bureau. There he was questioned by two police officers. The officers admitted at trial that Miranda was not advised that he had a right to have an attorney present. Two hours later, the officers emerged from the interrogation room with a written confession signed by Miranda. At the top of the statement was a typed paragraph stating that the confession was made voluntarily, without threats or promises of immunity and 'with full know-ledge of my legal rights, understanding any statement I make may be used against me.'

"At his trial before a jury, the written confession was admitted into evidence over the objection of defense counsel, and the officers testified to the prior oral confession made by Miranda during the interrogation. Miranda was found guilty of kidnapping and rape. He was sentenced to 20 to 30 years' imprisonment on each count, the sentences to run concurrently. On appeal, the Supreme Court of Arizona held that Miranda's constitutional rights were not violated in obtaining the confession and affirmed the conviction. 98 Ariz. 18, 401 P.2d 721. In reaching its decision, the [Arizona] court emphasized heavily the fact that Miranda did not specifically request counsel."]

Mr. Chief Justice WARREN delivered the opinion of the Court.

The cases before us raise questions which go to the roots of our concepts of American criminal jurisprudence: the restraints society must observe consistent with the Federal Constitution in prosecuting individuals for crime. More specifically, we deal with the admissibility of statements obtained from an individual who is subjected to custodial police interrogation and the necessity for procedures which assure that the individual is accorded his privilege under the Fifth Amendment to the Constitution not to be compelled to incriminate himself.

We dealt with certain phases of this problem recently in Escobedo v. Illinois, 378 U.S. 478 (1964). There, as in the four cases before us, law enforcement officials took the defendant into custody and interrogated him in a police station for the purpose of obtaining a confession. The police did not effectively advise him of his right to remain silent or of his right to consult with his attorney. Rather, they confronted him with an alleged accomplice who accused him of having perpetrated a murder. When the defen-dant denied the accusation and said "I didn't shoot Manuel, you did it," they hand-cuffed him and took him to an interrogation room. There, while handcuffed and standing, he was questioned for four hours until he confessed. During this interroga-tion, the police denied his request to speak to his attorney, and they prevented his retained attorney, who had come to the police station, from consulting with him. At his trial, the State, over his objection, introduced the confession against him. We held that the statements thus made were constitutionally inadmissible.

This case has been the subject of judicial interpretation and spirited legal debate since it was decided two years ago. . . .

. . . We have undertaken a thorough re-examination of the Escobedo decision and the principles it announced, and we reaffirm it. That case was but an explication of basic rights that are enshrined in our Constitution—that "No person . . . shall be compelled in any criminal case to be a witness against himself," and that "the accused shall . . . have the Assistance of Counsel"—rights which were put in jeopardy in that case through official overbearing. . . .

.   .   .   .

Our holding will be spelled out with some specificity in the pages which follow but briefly stated it is this: the prosecution may not use statements, whether exculpatory or inculpatory, stemming from custodial interrogation of the defendant unless it demonstrates the use of procedural safeguards effective to secure the privilege against self-incrimination. By custodial interrogation, we mean questioning initiated by law enforcement officers after a person has been taken into custody or otherwise deprived of his freedom of action in any significant way. As for the procedural safeguards to be employed, unless other fully effective means are devised to inform accused persons of their right of silence and to assure a continuous opportunity to exercise it, the following measures are required. Prior to any questioning, the person must be warned that he has a right to remain silent, that any statement he does make may be used as evidence against him, and that he has a right to the presence of an attorney, either retained or appointed. The defendant may waive effectuation of these rights, provided the waiver is made voluntarily, knowingly and intelligently. If, however, he indicates in any manner and at any stage of the process that he wishes to consult with an attorney before speaking there can be no questioning. Likewise, if the individual is alone and indicates in any manner that he does not wish to be interrogated, the police may not question him. The mere fact that he may have answered some questions or volunteered some statements on his own does not deprive him of the right to refrain from answering any further inquiries until he has consulted with an attorney and thereafter consents to be questioned.

The Constitutional issue we decide in each of these cases is the admissibility of statements obtained from a defendant questioned while in custody and deprived of his freedom of action. In each, the defendant was questioned by police officers, detectives, or a prosecuting attorney in a room in which he was cut off from the outside world. In none of these cases was the defendant given a full and effective warning of his rights at the outset of the interrogation process. In all the cases, the questioning elicited oral admissions, and in three of them, signed statements as well which were admitted at their trials. They all thus share salient features—incommunicado interrogation of individuals in a police-dominated atmosphere, resulting in self-incriminating statements without full warnings of constitutional rights.

An understanding of the nature and setting of this in-custody interrogation is essential to our decisions today. The difficulty in depicting what transpires at such interrogations stems from the fact that in this country they have largely taken place incommunicado. From extensive factual studies undertaken in the early 1930's, including the famous Wickersham Report to Congress by a Presidential Commission, it is clear that police violence and the "third degree" flourished at that time. In a series of cases decided by this Court long after these studies, the police resorted to physical brutality—beating, hanging, whipping—and to sustained and protracted questioning incommunicado in order to extort confessions. The Commission on Civil Rights in 1961 found much evidence to indicate that "some policemen still resort to physical force to obtain confessions," 1961 Comm'n on Civil Rights Rep., Justice, pt. 5, 17. The use of physical brutality and violence is not unfortunately relegated to the past or to any part of the country. Only recently [1965] in Kings County, New York, the police brutally beat, kicked and placed lighted cigarette butts on the back of a potential witness under interrogation for the purpose of securing a statement incriminating a third party.

The examples given above are undoubtedly the exception now, but they are sufficiently widespread to be the object of concern.   .   .   .

Again we stress that the modern practice of in-custody interrogation is psychologically rather than physically oriented. As we have stated before, "Since Chambers v. Florida, 309 U.S. 227, this Court has recognized that coercion can be mental as well as physical, and that the blood of the accused is not the only hallmark of an unconstitutional inquisition." Blackburn v. Alabama, 361 U.S. 199, 206 (1960). Interrogation still takes place in privacy. Privacy results in secrecy and this in turn results in a gap in our knowledge as to what in fact goes on in the interrogation rooms. A valuable source of information about present police practices, however, may be found in various police manuals and texts which document procedures employed with success in the past, and which recommend various other effective tactics. These texts are used by law enforcement agencies themselves as guides.

The officers are told by the manuals that the "principal psychological factor contributing to a successful interrogation is *privacy*—being alone with the person under interrogation." Inbau & Reid, Criminal Interrogation and Confessions (1962), at 1.   .   .   .

To highlight the isolation and unfamiliar surroundings, the manuals instruct the police to display an air of confidence in the suspect's guilt and from outward appearance to maintain only an interest in confirming certain details. The guilt of the subject is to be posited as a fact. The interrogator should direct his comments toward the reasons why the subject committed the act, rather than to court failure by asking the subject whether he did it. Like other men, perhaps the subject has had a bad family life, had an unhappy childhood, had too much to drink, had an unrequited desire for women. The officers are instructed to minimize the more seriousness of the offense, to cast blame on the victim or society. These tactics are designed to put the subject in a psychological state where his story is but an elaboration of what the police purport to know already —that he is guilty. Explorations to the contrary are dismissed and discouraged.

.   .   .   .

The manuals suggest that the suspect be offered legal excuses for his actions in order to obtain an initial admission of guilt. Where there is a suspected revenge-killing, for example, the interrogator may say:

"Joe, you probably didn't go out looking for this fellow with the purpose of shooting him. My guess is, however, that you expected something from him and that's why you carried a gun—for your own protection. You knew him for what he was, no good. Then when you met him he probably started using foul, abusive language and he gave some indication that he was about to pull a gun on you, and that's when you had to act to save your own life. That's about it, isn't it, Joe?"

Having then obtained the admission of shooting, the interrogator is advised to refer to circumstantial evidence which negates the self-defense explanation. This should enable him to secure the entire story. Our text notes that "Even if he fails to do so, the inconsistency between the subject's original denial of the shooting and his present admission of at least doing the shooting will serve to deprive him of a self-defense 'out' at the time of trial." Inbau & Reid, *supra* at 40.

When the techniques described above prove unavailing, the texts recommend they be alternated with a show of some hostility. One ploy often used has been termed the "friendly-unfriendly" or the "Mutt and Jeff" act:

"   .   .   .   In this technique, two agents are employed, Mutt, the relentless investigator, who knows the subject is guilty and is not going to waste any time. He's sent a dozen men away for this crime and he's going to send the subject away for the full term. Jeff, on the other hand, is obviously a kindhearted man. He has a family himself. He has a brother who was involved in a little scrape like this. He disapproves of Mutt and his tactics and will arrange to get him off the case if the subject will cooperate. He can't hold Mutt off for very long. The subject would be wise to make a quick decision. The technique is applied by having both investigators present while Mutt acts out his role. Jeff may stand by quietly and demur at some of Mutt's tactics. When Jeff makes his plea for cooperation, Mutt is not present in the room." Inbau & Reid, *supra,* at 58–59.

.   .   .   .

From these representative samples of interrogation techniques, the setting prescribed by the manuals and observed in practice becomes clear. In essence, it is this: To be alone with the subject is essential to prevent distraction and to deprive him of any outside support. The aura of confidence in his guilt undermines his will to resist. He merely confirms the preconceived story the police seek to have him describe. Patience and persistence, at times relentless questioning, are employed.   .   .   .

Even without employing brutality, the "third degree" or the specific strategies described above, the very fact of custodial interrogation exacts a heavy toll on individual liberty and trades on the weakness of individuals.   .   .   .

In these cases, we might not find the defendants' statements to have been involuntary in traditional terms. Our concern for adequate safeguards to protect precious Fifth Amendment rights is, of course, not lessened in the slightest. In each of the cases, the defendant was thrust into an unfamiliar atmosphere and run through menacing police interrogation procedures. The potentiality for compulsion is forcefully apparent, for example, in Miranda where the indigent Mexican defendant was a seriously disturbed individual with pronounced sexual fantasies, and in Stewart, in which the defendant was an indigent Los Angeles Negro who had dropped out of school in the sixth grade. To be sure, the records do not evince overt physical coercion or patented psychological ploys. The fact remains that in none of these cases did the officers undertake to afford appropriate safeguards at the outset of the interrogation to insure that the statements were truly the product of free choice.

.   .   .   .

The warnings required and the waiver necessary in accordance with our opinion today are, in the absence of a fully effective equivalent, prerequisites to the admissibility of any statement made by a defendant. No distinction can be drawn between statements which are direct confessions and statements which amount to "admissions" of part or all of an offense.   .   .   .

The principles announced today deal with the protection which must be given to the privilege against self-incrimination when the individual is first subjected to police interrogation while in custody at the station or otherwise deprived of his freedom of action in any significant way.   .   .   .   Under the system of warnings we delineate today or under any other system which may be devised and found effective, the safeguards to be erected about the privilege must come into play at this point.

Our decision is not intended to hamper the traditional function of police officers in investigating crime. . . .   When an individual is in custody on probable cause, the police may, of course, seek out evidence in the field to be used at trial against him. Such investigation may include inquiry of persons not under restraint. . . .

.   .   .   .

To summarize, we hold that when an individual is taken into custody or otherwise deprived of his freedom by the authorities and is subjected to questioning, the privilege against self-incrimination is jeopardized. Procedural safeguards must be employed to protect the privilege, and unless other fully effective means are adopted to notify the person of his right of silence and to assure that the exercise of the right will be scrupulously honored, the following measures are required. He must be warned prior to any questioning that he has the right to remain silent, that anything he says can be used against him in a court of law, that he has the right to the presence of an attorney, and that if he cannot afford an attorney one will be appointed for him prior to any questioning if he so desires. Opportunity to exercise these rights must be afforded to him throughout the interrogation. After such warnings have been given, and such opportunity afforded him, the individual may knowingly and intelligently waive these rights and agree to answer questions or make such a statement. But unless and until such warnings and waiver are demonstrated by the prosecution at trial, no evidence obtained as a result of interrogation can be used against him.

IV.

A recurrent argument made in these cases is that society's need for interrogation outweighs the privilege. . . .

.   .   .   .

In announcing these principles, we are not unmindful of the burdens which law enforcement officials must bear, often under trying circumstances. We also fully recognize the obligation of all citizens to aid in enforcing the criminal laws. This Court, while protecting individual rights, has always given ample latitude to law enforcement agencies in the legitimate exercise of their duties. The limits we have placed on the interrogation process should not constitute an undue interference with a proper system of law enforcement. . . .   Although confessions may play an important role in some convictions, the cases before us present graphic examples of the overstatement of the "need" for confessions. In each case authorities conducted interrogations ranging up to five days in duration despite the presence, through standard investigating practices, of considerable evidence against each defendant. . . .

.   .   .   .

Over the years the Federal Bureau of Investigation has compiled an exemplary record of effective law enforcement while advising any suspect or arrested person, at the outset of an interview, that he is not required to make a statement, that any statement may be used against him in court, that the individual may obtain the services of an attorney of his own choice and, more recently, that he has a right to free counsel if he is unable to pay. A letter received from the Solicitor General in response to a question from the Bench makes it clear that the present pattern of warnings and respect for the rights of the individual followed as a practice by the FBI is consistent with the procedure which we delineate today. . . .

V.

.   .   . From the testimony of the officers and by the admission of respondent, it is clear that Miranda was not in any way apprised of his right to consult with an attorney and to have one present during the interrogation, nor was his right not to be compelled to incriminate himself effectively protected in any other manner. Without these warnings, the statements were inadmissible.   .   .   .

[The judgment of the Supreme Court of Arizona in Miranda v. Arizona is reversed.]

Mr. Justice CLARK, dissenting in No. 759 [Miranda v. Arizona].   .   .   .

The rule prior to today—as Mr. Justice Goldberg, the author of the Court's opinion in Escobedo, stated it in Haynes v. Washington—depended upon "totality of circumstances evidencing an involuntary   .   .   .   admission of guilt." 373 U.S., at 514.   .   .   .

I would continue to follow that rule. Under the "totality of circumstances" rule   .   .   . , I would consider in each case whether the police officer prior to custodial interrogation added the warning that the suspect might have counsel present at the interrogation and, further, that a court would appoint one at his request if he was too poor to employ counsel. In the absence of warnings, the burden would be on the State to prove that counsel was knowingly and intelligently waived or that in the totality of the circumstances, including the failure to give the necessary warnings, the confession was clearly voluntary.

Mr. Justice HARLAN, whom Mr. Justice STEWART and Mr. Justice WHITE join, dissenting.

I. INTRODUCTION

.   .   . I believe that reasoned examination will show that the Due Process Clauses provide an adequate tool for coping with confessions and that, even if the Fifth Amendment privilege against self-incrimination be invoked, its precedents taken as a whole do not sustain the present rules. Viewed as a choice based on pure policy, these new rules prove to be a highly debatable if not one-sided appraisal of competing interests, imposed over widespread objection, at the very time when judicial restraint is called for by the circumstances.

II. CONSTITUTIONAL PREMISES

It is most fitting to begin an inquiry into the constitutional precedents by surveying the limits on confessions the Court has evolved under the Due Process Clause of the Fourteenth Amendment   .   .   .

This   .   .   . line of decisions, testing admissibility by the Due Process Clause, began in 1936, with Brown v. Mississippi, 297 U.S. 278, and must now embrace somewhat more than 30 full opinions of the Court. While the voluntariness rubric was repeated in many instances, *e.g.,* Lyons v. Oklahoma, 322 U.S. 596, the Court never pinned it down to a single meaning but on the contrary infused it with a number of different values. To travel quickly over the main themes, there was an initial emphasis on reliability, *e.g.,* Ward v. Texas, 316 U.S. 547, supplemented by concern over the legality and fairness of the police practices, *e.g.,* Ashcraft v. Tennessee, 322 U.S. 143, in an "accusatorial" system of law enforcement, Watts v. Indiana, 338 U.S. 49, 54, and eventually by close attention to the individual's state of mind and capacity for effective choice, *e.g.,* Gallegos v. Colorado, 370 U.S. 49. The outcome was a continuing re-evaluation on the facts of each case of *how much* pressure on the suspect was permissible.

. . . [W]ith over 25 years of precedent the Court has developed an elaborate, sophisticated, and sensitive approach to admissibility of confessions. It is "judicial" in its treatment of one case at a time, see Colomba v. Connecticut, 367 U.S. 568, 635 (concurring opinion of THE CHIEF JUSTICE), flexible in its ability to respond to the endless mutations of fact presented, and ever more familiar to the lower courts. Of course, strict certainty is not obtained in this developing process, but this is often so with constitutional principles, and disagreement is usually confined to that borderland of close cases where it matters least.

. . . The Court's opinion in my view reveals no adequate basis for extending the Fifth Amendment's privilege against self-incrimination to the police station. Far more important, it fails to show that the Court's new rules are well supported, let alone compelled, by Fifth Amendment precedents. Instead, the new rules actually derive from quotation and analogy drawn from precedents under the Sixth Amendment, which should properly have no bearing on police interrogation.
. . . Historically, the privilege against self-incrimination did not bear at all on the use of extra-legal confessions, for which distinct standards evolved.
. . . Even those who would readily enlarge the privilege must concede some linguistic difficulties since the Fifth Amendment in terms proscribes only compelling any person "in any criminal case to be a witness against himself." . . .

The . . . premise is that pressure on the suspect must be eliminated though it be only the subtle influence of the atmosphere and surroundings. The Fifth Amendment, however, has never been thought to forbid all pressure to incriminate one's self in the situations covered by it. On the contrary, it has been held that failure to incriminate one's self can result in denial of removal of one's case from state to federal court, Maryland v. Soper, 270 U.S. 9; in refusal of a military commission, Orloff v. Willoughby, 345 U.S. 83; in denial of a discharge in bankruptcy, Kaufman v. Hurwitz, 176 F. 2d 210; and in numerous other adverse consequences. . . . This is not to say that short of jail or torture any sanction is permissible in any case; policy and history alike may impose sharp limits. . . . However, the Court's unspoken assumption that *any* pressure violates the privilege is not supported by the precedents and it has failed to show why the Fifth Amendment prohibits that relatively mild pressure the Due Process Clause permits.

A closing word must be said about the Assistance of Counsel Clause of the Sixth Amendment, which is never expressly relied on by the Court but whose judicial precedents turn out to be linchpins of the confession rules announced today. To support its requirement of a knowing and intelligent waiver, the Court cites Johnson v. Zerbst, 304 U.S. 458; appointment of counsel for the indigent suspect is tied to Gideon v. Wainwright, 372 U.S. 335, and Douglas v. California, 372 U.S. 353; the silent-record doctrine is borrowed from Carnley v. Cochran, 369 U.S. 506, as is the right to an express offer of counsel. All these cases imparting glosses to the Sixth Amendment concerned counsel at trial or on appeal. While the Court finds no pertinent differences between judicial proceedings and police interrogation, I believe the differences are so vast as to disqualify wholly the Sixth Amendment precedents as suitable analogies in the present cases.

.   .   .   .   .

III. POLICY CONSIDERATIONS

Examined as an expression of public policy, the Court's new regime proves so dubious that there can be no due compensation for its weakness in constitutional law. . . .

.   .   .   .   .

What the Court largely ignores is that its rules impair, if they will not eventually serve wholly to frustrate, an instrument of law enforcement that has long and quite reasonably been thought worth the price paid for it. There can be little doubt that the Court's new code would markedly decrease the number of confessions. . . .

How much harm this decision will inflict on the law enforcement cannot fairly be predicted with accuracy. Evidence on the rule of confessions is notoriously incomplete. . . . We do know that some crimes cannot be solved without confessions, that ample expert testimony attests to their importance in crime control, and that the Court is taking a real risk with society's welfare in imposing its new regime on the country. The social costs of crime are too great to call the new rules anything but a hazardous experimentation.

While passing over the costs and risks of its experiment, the Court portrays the evils of normal police questioning in terms which I think are exaggerated. Albeit stringently confined by the due process standards interrogation is no doubt often inconvenient and unpleasant for the suspect. However, it is no less so for a man to be arrested and jailed, to have his house searched, or to stand trial in court, yet all this may properly happen to the most innocent given probable cause, a warrant, or an indictment. Society has always paid a stiff price for law and order, and peaceful interrogation is not one of the dark moments of the law.

This brief statement of the competing considerations seems to me ample proof that the Court's preference is highly debatable at best and therefore not to be read into the Constitution. However, it may make the analysis more graphic to consider the actual facts of one of the four cases reversed by the Court. Miranda v. Arizona serves best, being neither the hardest nor easiest of the four under the Court's standards.

On March 3, 1963, an 18-year old girl was kidnapped and forcibly raped near Phoenix, Arizona. Ten days later, or the morning of March 13, petitioner Miranda was arrested and taken to the police station. At this time Miranda was 23 years old, indigent, and educated to the extent of completing half the ninth grade. He had "an emotional illness" of the schizophrenic type, according to the doctor who eventually examined him; the doctor's report also stated that Miranda was "alert and oriented as to time, place, and person," intelligent within normal limits, competent to stand trial, and sane within the legal definition. At the police station, the victim picked Miranda out of a lineup, and two officers then took him into a separate room to interrogate him, starting about 11:30 a.m. Though at first denying his guilt, within a short time Miranda gave a detailed oral confession and then wrote out in his own hand and signed a brief statement admitting and describing the crime. All this was accomplished in two hours or less without any force, threats or promises and—I will assume this though the record is uncertain,   .   .   .   —without any effective warnings at all.

Miranda's oral and written confessions are now held inadmissible under the Court's new rules. One is entitled to feel astonished that the Constitution can be read to produce this result. These confessions were obtained during brief, daytime questioning conducted by two officers and unmarked by any of the traditional indicia of coercion. They assured a conviction for a brutal and unsettling crime, for which the police had and quite possibly could obtain little evidence other than the victim's identifications, evidence which is frequently unreliable. There was, in sum, a legitimate purpose, no perceptible unfairness, and certainly little risk of injustice in the interrogation. Yet the resulting confessions, and the responsible course of police practice they represent, are to be sacrificed to the Court's own finespun conception of fairness which I seriously doubt is shared by many thinking citizens in this country.

.   .   .   .

The Court in closing its general discussion invokes the [F.B.I.] practice   .   .   . as lending weight to its new curbs on confession for all the States.   .   .   .   Differing circumstances may make this comparison quite untrustworthy, but in any event the FBI falls sensibly short of the Court's formalistic rules. For example, there is no indication that FBI agents must obtain an affirmative "waiver" before they pursue their questioning. Nor is it clear that one invoking his right to silence may not be prevailed upon to change his mind. And the warning as to appointed counsel apparently indicated only that one will be assigned by the judge when the suspect appears before him; the thrust of the Court's rules is to induce the suspect to obtain appointed counsel before continuing the interview.   .   .   .

.   .   .   .

IV. CONCLUSIONS

All four of the cases involved here present express claims that confessions were inadmissible, not because of coercion in the traditional due process sense, but solely because of lack of counsel or lack of warnings concerning counsel and silence. For the reasons stated in this opinion, I would adhere to the due process test and reject the new requirements inaugurated by the Court.   .   .   .

.   .   .   .

[Mr. Justice White, with whom Mr. Justice Harlan and Mr. Justice Stewart joined, also dissented.][5]

[5]The procedures to be followed by police during "in custody" interrogations announced in Miranda apply not only to investigations of violent crimes, such as arson, rape and murder, but also to "in custody" interrogations of such nonviolent breaches of law as income tax evasion. In

PEOPLE v. POWE (Ind. # 3425/65, Supreme Court of Kings County, Brooklyn, New York, 1966). The following transcript of the proceedings heard before the Honorable Michael Kern, Justice, is *one* example of the communities' reaction to the effect of Miranda on criminal jurisprudence.

MISS HELLER [The prosecuting attorney.]:   If your Honor please, on indictment number 3425 of 1965, Joan Powe, charged with the crime of manslaughter in the first degree, and assault in the second degree, with great reluctance, because of the United States Supreme Court decision in People vs. Miranda, that I must stand here and dismiss this case, because the only evidence in the case is the admission by the defendant to the beating of her four year old child with a rubber hose and a broomstick, all because the child soiled a bed.

Were it not for this decision, we would have been ready to prosecute this case and let this defendant be punished. And therefore, as I said, your Honor, it is with great reluctance that I have to stand here and dismiss this case.

THE COURT: Miss Heller, I have assumed you have inquired very thoroughly into the whole matter to determine whether or not there is some testimony or some evidence other than the alleged statement made by the defendant?

MISS HELLER: Yes, your Honor. I spoke to the first officer on the scene, Patrolman Owen Brodeur and the Detective, Detective Baumann of the 73rd Squad, and both advised me, the only evidence in the case is the admission of the defendant as to what took place on the day of the occurrence, November 2, 1965.

THE COURT: And that admission was not made by the defendant in conformity with Miranda against Arizona, is that correct?

MISS HELLER: That is correct.

Mathis v. United States, 391 U.S. 1 (1968), the petitioner was serving a sentence in a Florida prison when he was questioned about certain tax returns by an Internal Revenue Service Investigator during "a routine tax investigation." The crucial issue in Mathis as in all other Miranda-type cases is whether the person being interrogated was "in custody at the station or otherwise deprived of his freedom of action in any way." The Supreme Court held that Mathis was "in custody" and that the Government's failure to give the requisite warnings before questioning Mathis necessitated exclusion at his trial of any statements made by him. To the same effect is Orozco v. Texas, 394 U.S. 324 (1969), where the Supreme Court held inadmissible evidence seized from petitioner by several police officers who were investigating a homicide and who questioned petitioner at 4 a.m. in his bedroom without first giving him the Miranda warnings. On the other hand, when two income tax defendants were questioned in their own offices by Internal Revenue Service agents without being given the Miranda warnings and later questioned at the Internal Revenue Service office after being given the warnings, all statements made by them were held admissible in evidence at their income tax evasion trials. Cohen v. United States, 405 F.2d 34 (8th Cir. 1968), *cert. denied,* 394 U.S. 943 (1969); Muse v. United States, 405 F.2d 41 (8th Cir. 1968), *cert. denied,* 393 U.S. 1117 (1969).

A right to have counsel present at a preliminary hearing was accorded a suspect in Coleman v. Alabama, 90 S.Ct. 1999 (1970). The Court split on whether the Sixth Amendment's guarantee of counsel "In all criminal prosecutions . . ." includes preliminary hearings. Chief Justice Burger dissented on the ground that the Sixth Amendment could not require counsel for a suspect at a stage earlier than the grand jury since admittedly the suspect is not entitled to counsel before that body. (See Criminal Procedure, p. 388, 408.)

In Harris v. New York, 8 Cr.L.Rptr. 3139 (1971), the Supreme Court contracted rather than expanded the rule announced in Miranda. The Court in Harris, to prevent a defendant from committing perjury on the witness stand, held that a confession obtained in violation of Miranda could be used for cross-examination although that same confession could not have been used as affirmative prosecution evidence to prove the defendant's guilt.

THE COURT: Equally with great reluctance, Miss Heller, I will grant the motion. The indictment is dismissed.

MISS HELLER: And I will have a formal plea statement, your honor drawn up—a formal statement of dismissal in the file on this case.

THE COURT: Yes. All right.

THE DEFENDANT: Thank you, your Honor, from all my heart.

THE COURT: Don't thank me. Thank the United States Supreme Court.

THE DEFENDANT: I thank the United States Supreme Court.

THE COURT: Don't thank me at all. You killed this child and you ought to go to jail. The trouble is that there is insufficient evidence because of the decision of the United States Supreme Court in the Miranda case. Don't thank me and don't thank the District Attorney.

The indictment is dismissed.

DAVIS v. MISSISSIPPI, 394 U.S. 721 (1969). In Davis, the petitioner was one of 40–50 Negro youths interrogated at police headquarters, at school or on the street by the Meridian police who were investigating a rape, and in addition petitioner was one of 24 Negro youths taken, without a warrant, to police headquarters and questioned briefly, fingerprinted, and released. One week later petitioner was driven by Meridian police to Jackson, Mississippi, where he was confined overnight before he was returned to confinement in the Meridian jail and fingerprinted a second time. The petitioner's fingerprints, along with the fingerprints of fourteen others, were sent for analysis to F.B.I. headquarters in Washington, D.C. The F.B.I. reported that the petitioner's fingerprints matched those taken from the window of the rape victim. The petitioner was then tried and convicted of rape at a trial in which the fingerprint data were introduced into evidence. The United States Supreme Court reversed petitioner's conviction on the ground that he was arrested, detained, and questioned without probable cause and thus the fingerprints were not admissible in evidence. Justice Stewart dissented claiming that, "we do not deal here with a confession wrongfully obtained or with property wrongfully seized—so tainted as to be forever inadmissible as evidence against a defendant." He argued that "fingerprints are not 'evidence' in the conventional sense that weapons or stolen goods might be. Like the color of a man's eyes, his height, or his very physiognomy, the tips of his fingers are an inherent and unchanging characteristic of the man. And physical impressions of his fingertips can be exactly and endlessly reproduced . . . [and thus are] 'evidence' that can be identically reproduced and lawfully used at any subsequent trial."

LAW AND LIBERTY

Give me your tired, your poor,
Your huddled masses yearning to breathe free,
The wretched refuse of your teeming shore.
Send these, the homeless, tempest-tossed to me,
I lift my lamp beside the golden door.[6]

[6]Inscription, taken from the sonnet "The New Colossus," was written by Emma Lazarus and originally published in 1889.

This invitation engraved on the base of the Statue of Liberty in New York harbor is no more self-implementing than a criminal statute is self-enforcing. What one observes in such cases as Miranda is the long painstaking, deliberate process by which the tired, the poor, and the wretched gain freedom. In this commentary we shall examine the social price for Miranda-type freedom.

Concern for the individual did not arise with the United States Constitution. In the most ancient societies records disclose forms of civil liberties. In the Mosaic laws there are very detailed provisions for the protection of maid servants. In both Greek and Roman society there were carefully articulated civil liberties, even for slaves. Concern for "the aimless, helpless, and hopeless" was *not* introduced for the first time in the third quarter of the twentieth century. The decisions of the so-called "Warren Court," charged on the one hand as licenses for crime and hailed on the other hand as charters of liberty, are simply the twentieth century increment to a long record of adjustment of relationships between the state and the subject or the citizen. The process is deeply rooted in Hebrew, Greek, and Roman law.

Nor is the antipathy of order for liberty new. The price of order may be loss of liberty, and the price of liberty may be disorder. The law stands between the two and strikes a balance between how much order a state is to be permitted, at what price to the individual, and how much liberty the individual is to be permitted, at what price to the state. This resolution is a never-ending process. The quality and nature of the process is disclosed by the Miranda case, which left aghast many who believe in "common sense" in the affairs of men. One never knows the extent to which such anguished cries as ensued after Miranda influence the Court in the next comparable case. (As Finley Peter Dunn (Mr. Dooley) was given to saying, "The Supreme Court follows the newspapers.") This influence may have been felt in Harris v. New York, p. 123.

In the Terry case, following Miranda, the Court seems to favor the security of the state against the liberty of the individual. In Miranda a confessed criminal was temporarily exonerated (he was tried again without the confession and convicted); in the Terry case some furtive characters were put up against a wall in public and forced to submit to the indignity of a policeman's hand entering some portions of their personal garments.

Miranda reads like a rule book for a police headquarters, whereas Terry adopts the standard of the reasonableness of an experienced police officer. Suppose the police officer were inexperienced. What would the rule be under that circumstance? Miranda imports inflexible dictate. Terry is flexible—what is called the case-by-case approach—which means that the frisk was all right in Terry but that it might not be valid in other cases with different facts and circumstances. Miranda says to the police, "You have no discretion." Terry says, "Use your head; be reasonable."

Miranda says that the police, in the case of a suspect in custody, may not use a confession in court to prove guilt unless the suspect has first been informed, in addition to his other constitutional rights, of his right to have a lawyer present at the police interrogation. The rule in Miranda eliminates all possibility of a police interrogation's being so impeccable psychologically and so devoid of all mental or physical brutality that an ensuing confession could be admitted without further safeguards. No rule of reason such as that permitted to police officers on the public street in Terry is applicable within the police station. It is assumed that no police officer would ever accord an accused his constitutional rights unless a lawyer is present. The assumption of Miranda is that society will be best served if the accused person remains forever silent. That is what the lawyer will advise the accused person to do.

What lies behind a rule that seems to cast the weight of the law in favor of liberty and against order—order in the sense of the social norm? Why should it be made so difficult for the police to follow expeditious resolutions of the vast number of offenses that harass the morality and the security of society? Every police officer knows the prostitutes in his district. Nevertheless, in a given case, he must proceed with such finesse and maneuver that it becomes extremely difficult for him to establish what he already knows. Every police officer in every district knows the numbers writers, the bookmakers, the pickpockets, the shoplifters, and the potential rapists, arsonists, and murderers. Yet, after one of those offenses, a suspect in custody may not be interrogated for the purpose of eliciting a confession without an invitation to a lawyer. Many offenses are minor, even innocuous, but the policeman's oath requires him to detect all criminal offenses and assemble evidence against the offender. Miranda makes no distinction between major and minor offenses and thus often requires the police to use an anvil to kill a mouse. What amounts to the practical necessity of a lawyer's presence before any offender, minor or major, may be interrogated by the police obviously puts a serious burden on policemanship. At the least, the requirement would impede that process by which what the police already know and what offenders already know cannot simply be conceded by the accused person in the daily routine of criminality and law enforcement.

Society asserts certain norms. By and large, these norms are affected by the conscience of the citizenry because a majority of the citizenry believe in the norms. The "golden rule," the conscience, the law-abiding impulse are all better enforcement agencies than the policemanship in our society. Nevertheless, the number of deviants is large in the gross and significant in the percentage. Policemanship is a tried and true technique. If the work of policemanship is unduly encumbered with procedures, the economics of performance may become so costly that society cannot or will not pay. In addition, if the policeman is confronted with evidence that society distrusts him as much as it does the criminal, his morale and efficiency are drastically reduced. The difficulty with Miranda, therefore, is its inflexible dogma, which is distinguished from the philosophy of reasonableness in Terry.

As we mentioned in Chapter 1, there are several techniques by which inflexible law, that is, law that has gone beyond reasonable discretion in its application, gets changed. Legislation is one of these methods. The legislature intervenes to ameliorate the rigors of the court-made law. We have currently a dramatic illustration of that process in the Omnibus Crime Control and Safe Streets Act of 1968. Under Title II of that Act a confession obtained in a federal case in violation of the dictates of Miranda would not be automatically excluded; rather the trial judge in a federal case would determine whether the confession was "voluntary." In determining that question, the court under the new Act may consider a number of factors, including whether the defendant was advised prior to questioning of his rights to the assistance of counsel and whether there was in fact assistance of counsel; however no one of the factors will be conclusive. In other words, Congress has now undertaken in a federal criminal case to leave to a trial judge discretion of the same type in a Miranda situation that the Supreme Court of the United States left to the policeman himself in a Terry situation.

The Act did not, however, settle the issue of admissible confessions raised by Miranda. The intervention of Congress attempts to correct what is widely regarded as an excess of judicial power, namely, the dogma of Miranda with respect to confessions. But the attempt by Congress to dictate to the federal judiciary the procedures for admitting or excluding a confession may contravene the concept of division of powers. Certainly, it may be expected that this Act of Congress will be challenged, and it will be the Supreme Court of the United States that will, in the end, determine whether Congress has the power to curtail its jurisdiction on the subject of confessions.

Meanwhile, there is the obvious question about the fate of those who were convicted prior to Miranda under identical or similar denials of constitutional protection. One week after its decision in Miranda, the Supreme Court held that Miranda would apply to those cases only in which the trial began *after* Miranda.[7] In fact, at the time the Supreme Court elected to hear the Miranda case there were 80 similar cases pending on applications to be heard. The Court selected four, including Miranda, and all the others were rejected. The Supreme Court explained this administration of justice *by chance* by saying that the fact that the parties involved in the decision were the only litigants so situated who received the benefit of the new rule is "an unavoidable consequence of the necessity that constitutional adjudications not stand as mere dictum."[8] Thus, Miranda was clearly given only a prospective effect.

On the other hand, in Gideon v. Wainwright, 372 U.S. 335 (1963), the accused was denied an appointed counsel at his trial for breaking and entering a poolroom with intent to commit a misdemeanor. Gideon's conviction was

[7]Johnson v. New Jersey, 384 U.S. 719 (1966).
[8]Stovall v. Denno, 388 U.S. 293 at 301 (1967).

reversed by the Supreme Court of the United States on the ground that his constitutional right to counsel at his trial—by appointment at taxpayers' expense if necessary—had been violated. Later, the Supreme Court accepted the petitions of ten persons similarly convicted, and in Florida prisons, and sent the cases to the Florida Supreme Court for consideration in the light of Gideon.[9] Hence, Miranda was applied only prospectively, but Gideon was applied both prospectively and retrospectively. Why?

The Supreme Court's rationale for the apparent inconsistencies between the treatment of Miranda type convicts and Gideon type convicts is: for the police to interrogate and obtain a confession from the accused person in a police station, while denying the constitutional right to counsel, is not so serious a denial as for a judge at the trial to deny, by refusing to appoint, counsel in the courtroom. An examination of the cases would not add much, if anything, to the distinction here simply stated. Obviously there are priorities in and among constitutional rights.[10]

If there is a dichotomy between order and liberty in which law plays its meditating role, it is also true that force is the handmaiden of order, liberty, and law. If there is only order—without liberty and law—the force is whimsical, arbitrary, and brutal, as in Nazi Germany in which order was everything and liberty and law were nothing. If there is only liberty, the force is unofficial, largely unorganized, and sporadic in its employment, as in the "hot summers" of the mid-1960's in which concepts of segmental power, as distinguished from the power of a totally established society, produced the burning and looting of cities. If there is rapport between order and liberty, as in stable societies, force is nevertheless a factor. But it is the force of ideally neutral policemanship in which its functions are to apprehend offenders against clearly defined prohibitions, to assemble the preliminary evidences of violation of those prohibitions, and to hold the offender pending the action of the law—all within those ancient rights, privileges, and immunities of the citizen against the state, known in the Anglo-Saxon world as "due process of law."

The force necessary for the operation of the ideally neutral policemanship is nevertheless an embarrassment in modern societies. The nature of the embarrassment is stated by Reinhold Niebuhr:[11]

> . . . Dominion is a necessity of community from the lowest to the highest, from the most primordial to the latest forms of communal life. This dominion validates itself to the community as a prerequisite of its order; but every form of dominion, except possibly the first dominion of fatherhood, contains an embarrassment to the moral consciousness of man. That embarrassment consists in the fact that the dominion and authority are established from motives of self-interest. The

---

[9]Pickelsimer v. Wainwright, 375 U.S. 2 (1963).

[10]See, generally, Linkletter v. Walker, 381 U.S. 618 (1965); Tehan v. United States ex rel. Shott, 382 U.S. 406 (1966); Johnson v. New Jersey, 384 U.S. 719 (1966).

[11]Niebuhr, Reinhold, *The Structure of Nations and Empire,* pp. 33–34, Scribner's, New York, 1959.

integral and parochial communities are organized and ordered by the classes in the community which hold the most significant social power.

The embarrassment of which Niebuhr speaks was eloquently demonstrated in the disorder, burning, looting, violence, and death in the American ghettos and on the American university and college campuses during the late 1960's. The establishments needed to preserve order. Yet, in the very process of the requisite policemanship, the ranks of the violators of order swelled—apparently not from conviction about the causes of the original disruption but, rather, from antipathy simply to the use of force, any force.

The fundamental issues were frequently obscured by charges of excessive use of force by the police and by countercharges from the police of extreme provocation. Looking through such rationalizations, we find that there was a prevalent embarrassment about the use of established force on the city streets and on the campuses because "the internal force of cohesion" was weak in the "hot summers" and during the campus crises; hence force lacked its usual moral sanctions.

If the internal cohesion—predominant belief in the rightness of the economic and social mores—strengthens, order can be restored and maintained by force; otherwise creeping revolution can run its full course and a new scheme, in which much of old law will be irrelevant, will emerge. In the latter case the process could be long and painful because nihilism seems to be the only clearly identifiable theme in the disorders of the sixth decade of the twentieth century.

For the large segment of American society that believes a case like Miranda makes neutral policemanship inordinately difficult and expensive, it is important to recall the remarkably recent periods in our own Anglo-Saxon culture in which incredibly brutal punishments—cruel and unusual in the terms of the Eighth Amendment to the Constitution—were the order of the day. Witness the sentence on Sir Walter Raleigh for treason cited in Chapter 1 (see p. 25):[12]

> "That you shall be had from hence to the place whence you came [the Tower], there to remain until the day of execution. And from thence you shall be drawn upon a hurdle through the open streets to the place of execution, there to be hanged and cut down alive, and your body shall be opened, your heart and bowels plucked out, and your privy members cut off and thrown into the fire before your eyes. Then your head to be stricken off from your body, and your body shall be divided into four quarters, to be disposed of at the King's pleasure. And God have mercy upon your soul."

Critics of Miranda must remember that within only two centuries before Sir Walter Raleigh, the Inquisition tortured men on the rack for the crime of

---

[12]Bowen, Catherine Drinker, *The Lion and The Throne,* p. 217, Little, Brown, New York, 1957. (James I commuted the sentence to imprisonment. *Id.,* at p. 222.)

heresy. Just the sight of the instruments of torture caused Galileo to deny his own discovery that the earth rotates about the sun and not the reverse. If one is offended that because of Miranda a rapist would have gone free except for a subsequent trial and conviction, he should note that under Miranda, Galileo would never have made his absurd retraction. In the future the doctrine of Miranda may shield not only "the aimless, helpless, and hopeless," but also you and me.

What one sees today is the eternal swing of the pendulum between order on the right and liberty on the left. Law is both the suspension point of the pendulum and the mechanism of the pendulum's perpetual motion—the spring forever wound taut. In the long arc, from the Inquisition through the Pax Britannica and the Victorian Era to Hitler, the social cosmos moved from torture through security to torture. In the short arc, the social microcosm moved in a smaller but nonetheless significant path from Miranda through Terry to the Omnibus Crime Control and Safe Streets Act of 1968. Whatever the circumstances, the pendulum will forever swing either on so short a radius that one may see the movement in any newspaper or on so long a radius that only the historian may retrospectively observe the movement.

The Harris To Chimel oscillation is a pertinent illustration of the small-arc swing. The vigorous dissents in both cases—a bare 20 years apart—attest to the inconclusive state of the law on the extent of searches properly incident to a legal arrest on an accused person's premises. One might predict that in the end more latitude will be allowed arresting officers to determine on the premises the extent of the search, as the law in Terry allows the arresting officer (for his protection) some discretion as to the search of the person arrested away from his premises. Why should the premises be immune when the protection of the public is involved? That will be the continuing issue.

For example, Congress passed the District of Columbia Court Reform and Criminal Procedure Act of 1970 (P.L. 91–358), approved by the President July 29, 1970. This act, although confined to the District of Columbia, has been officially suggested as a model for all urban communities. Among other provisions, the act grants police officers in the District of Columbia the right to break and enter without notice and (popularly called "no knock") to arrest or to search incident to the arrest or with a warrant if, for one reason, notice (knocking) would be likely to result in destruction of evidence, such as narcotics or other contraband.

A month earlier the Supreme Court ruled in a narcotics case that an entry incident to an arrest made on the front steps of the house of a suspect was unjustified. Vale v. Louisiana, 399 U.S. 30 (1970).

One may safely predict that the no knock provision will be challenged in the Supreme Court of the United States. Whatever the outcome, it is certain that the pendulum has not yet come to rest.

QUESTIONS

1. Was Judge Tappan entirely wrong in holding that the Common Law was in force in the American colonies and in the states? If he was only partly wrong, in what respect was he right and in what respect was he wrong?

2. Do you think that Mr. Justice Holmes would have decided the case differently in McBoyle if the airplane had been taxied across the state line, never having left the ground?

3. What is interstate commerce?

4. In Chimel the phrase "by way of dictum" is used. What does the phrase mean?

5. What does Chimel show about:
    (a) Immutability of law
    (b) Utility of minority dissent

6. In Katz do you agree with the majority opinion by Mr. Justice Stewart or with the dissent by Mr. Justice Black? Why?

7. How does the Omnibus Crime Control and Safe Streets Act of 1968 illustrate Sir Henry Maine's proposition about Legislation? (See Chapter 1, "Legislation.")

8. In Terry do you think Mr. Chief Justice Warren spent an inordinate amount of time in justifying what seems like a rountine police action to frustrate three petty criminals? Why?

9. Do you think that Miss Heller and the Court were justifiably sardonic in People v. Powe? Why?

4   Law Makes The Promise Good

Introduction 133
Formation of Contracts—Essentials of the Agreement 136
   Capacity to Contract 136
      Rosman v. Cuevas 136
   Intent to Contract 138
      Lucy v. Zehmer 138
      Balfour v. Balfour 141
   Examples of Offer and Acceptance 142
      Offer 142
      Lefkowitz v. Great Minneapolis Surplus Store 142
      Acceptance 144
      Bullock v. Harwick 144
      Restatement of the Law of Contracts—Offer and Acceptance Defined . . . 146
   Examples of Consideration 146
      Definition of Consideration 146
      Hamer v. Sidway 146
      Harrington v. Taylor 148
      Embola v. Tuppela 148
      Restatement of the Law of Contracts—Consideration Defined 149
   Mutuality of Obligation 150
      G. Loewus & Co. v. Vischia 150
   Subject Matter 152
      Identity of Agreement 152
      Raffles v. Wichelhaus 152
      Restatement of the Law of Contracts—Undisclosed Misunderstandings . . 153
      Legality of Subject Matter 154
      In re Duncan's Estate 154
   Statute of Frauds 156
      Hurley v. Woodsides 156
      Charles R. Ablett Co. v. Sencer 157
      Statute of Frauds—Original English Statute 159
   Remedies for Breach of Contract—Society and the Broken Promise 160

Remedies at Law. 162
  Damages and Expectation Interest. 162
    Hadley v. Baxendale 162
    Krauss v. Greenbarg 164
    Newsome v. Western Union Telegraph Co.. 166
  Reliance Interest. 167
    Security Stove & Mfg. Co. v. American Ry. Express Co. 167
  Restitution Interest 170
    Britton v. Turner 170
  Other Considerations in Awarding Damages. 172
  Liquidated Damages and Penalties. 172
    Clydebank Engineering and Shipbuilding Co., Ltd.
      v. Don Jose Yzquierdo y Castaneda 172
    218-220 Market Street v. Krich-Radisco, Inc.. 176
  Mitigation of Damages 177
    Rockingham County v. Luten Bridge Co. 177
    Reliance Cooperage Corp. v. Treat 178
    Commentary on Reliance Cooperage Corp. v. Treat 181
Remedies in Equity. 183
  Specific Performance. 183
    Bennett v. Moon 183
    Morris v. Sparrow. 185
    Campbell Soup Co. v. Wentz 185
  Injunctions 188
    Philadelphia Ball Club v. Lajoie. 188
    Bradshaw v. Millikin 189
Remedies by Analogy to Contract. .190
  Recovery by Promissory Estoppel 191
    Goodman v. Dicker. 191
  Recovery in Quasi Contract. 192
    Cotnam v. Wisdom 192
    Morse v. Kenney 194
Questions 197

INTRODUCTION

We deal in this chapter with a class of cases, called contracts, in which society enforces obligations voluntarily assumed between and among individuals.

Society has a vested interest in the enforcement of obligations voluntarily assumed. One could conceive of a society in which no one was expected to keep his word. In such a case, the ordinary transactions of an industrial society or, for that matter, the ordinary transactions of a nonindustrial, primitive society would be difficult, if not impossible, to make. The business of life, of even the slightest economic complexity, depends on the right of individuals to enforce obligations voluntarily assumed by other individuals. This is particularly true when heavy technology requires great accumulation of capital and long-range planning requires dependable future commitments. We are speaking of a Western, capitalistic society in which the state plays the role of the enforcing agency between and among contracting parties—individuals, corporations, and other entities. We are concerned with a capitalistic society in which property rights and expectations based on contract are as much a concern of the state as of the parties themselves. As we saw in Chapter 1, law is a function of a particular time and a particular society. A society in which self-help is forbidden will open its courts for recompense to a party who is injured by the default, called breach of contract, of the other contracting party. Only in the courts may the injured party hope for relief and then under rather well-defined rules.

The concept of a promise that the law will enforce had a long, historical struggle. In *Ancient Law,** Sir Henry Maine says that the Romans commingled the ideas of contract and conveyance (transfer of property) in the single word *nexum,* meaning the parties were bound by some mystical bond. If the transaction, for example, was the sale of a slave, the seller and the buyer were in nexum (bound to each other until the exchange of the slave for the money was completed, whereupon they were both released from nexum.) If the slave were delivered but the money not paid, the buyer was still in nexum. It was a step, but a long step, in Roman law for nexum to mean that both parties remained in nexum even though nothing was delivered and nothing was paid. Today we substitute the term *executory contract* for the Roman nexum.

Later, in English law the promissory oath was a precursor of contract. O. W. Holmes and Pollock and Maitland* point to the long struggle to obtain recognition of such promises in the civil courts. Ecclesiastical courts, presided over by Christian prelates, would hear a case of breach of the *promissory oath* because the sinner in default must in some way be exonerated from the wrath of God, in whose name the breached oath had been taken. This, of course, was small comfort to the victim of the default.

The development of the concept of contract to its modern high estate parallels the development of modern civilization. Heilbroner* says that in all history there have been three forms of society: the Command, the Status, and the Market society. The first two have predominated in the past, with status as the most predominant feature of both. The absolute ruler functioned in the interstices between status institutions (family, clan, tribe, and later, the feudal manor), and his rule reached the individual only through these status institutions. The concept of contract slowly replaced status as the determiner of the rights and obligations of the individual. He was free to arrange his activities and his future by agreements. The proof of this rule is found in the modern proposition that minors and insane persons cannot contract because they lack the competence to arrange their personal affairs.

*See REFERENCES, Chapter 1.

This basic concept of contract makes possible the modern market society, in which every individual may higgle and haggle and bargain and fend for himself and in which each possesses rights against government itself. Rousseau distorted the concept of contract into the notion of the *social contract,* to be made by each with all other men, as the only valid sanction of government. This drastic alteration of the concept of contract does not detract from Sir Henry Maine's proposition that it is contract that has destroyed status in the development of Western civilization. It is possible to say, therefore, that it is contract—the freedom of contract—on which the modern market society and its attendant democracy rest.

The abolition of status by contract, however, is not total. In contemporary society, particularly in a highly industrialized society, status is not wholly absent. Although the employer-employee contract has replaced the master-slave status, the modern worker contracts, for the greater part, not on his own behalf but through his union. His status is that of a union member, and his rights against his employers ensue from that fact rather than from an individual contract.

Nexum, the mystical bond in a superstitious Roman society, was the best the Romans, whose politics and wars were determined by the auguries to be read in the flight of birds, could conceive. The concept of contract was improved but still remained inchoate in a religious English society, which was content to leave the promisor under false oath to the wrath of God and the mercies of the Church. In our modern era of rationalism in which scientism replaces superstition and religion, the contract emerges from components far more precisely determined than in those societies to which we must, nevertheless, look for its origins. No age is an island.

Let us present a few elementary propositions involved in constructing a modern contract that the courts will enforce. Begin with the basic proposition that a simple promise made by one person to another person standing alone is unenforceable. If *A* says to *B,* "I will give you $100," and there is nothing more than that naked promise, a promise to make a gift, then the promise is unenforceable because society is not interested. If, on the other hand, *A* says to *B,* "I will give you $100 to drive me to California," and *B* does, then a binding contract has been made. If *A* refuses to pay the $100, *B* may recover and, in the case stated, may recover the full $100. This is called an "executed contract"—the only type of contract that, at one state in the development of Western law, could be enforced.

Suppose, however, that after *A* said to *B,* "I will give you $100 to drive me to California," *B* asked, "When?" Then, *A* replied, "Tomorrow at 10 A.M.," and *B* said, "I accept your offer"—this would be called an "executory contract." Suppose, further, that at 10 A.M. *B* was present, able, and willing to drive to California, and *A* said, "I have changed my mind because *C* will drive me to California for nothing." *A* has now broken a promise that the law will enforce, not necessarily by awarding $100, as in the case of the executed contract, but by awarding what the law calls "damages." Cases in this section delineate some of the criteria for determining "damages."

In modern times an exchange of promises is sufficient to make a contract. For example, a contract to build a skyscraper must rest on mutual promises for the obvious reason that several years are required for performance. Long-range planning is one of the necessary functions in a society of heavy technology and great enterprises. There are many relationships in heavy technology that extend into the future for 10–15 years or as much as a half century. For example, it is not at all unusual for an owner of coal mines to make contracts of such duration to supply a particular industrial consumer of coal. It is not at all unusual for a producer of electricity to make contracts for such an extended period to supply industrial operations in cities and communities. The sanctity of contract makes modern society viable.

Despite the central role that contract plays in the affairs of mankind, it lies within the power of a contracting party to fail or refuse to perform his contract —for a good reason or for no reason. A party who exercises the power to breach his contract will not be immediately punished by society. Nevertheless, society will go after his pocketbook in favor of the party damaged by the default, and in some cases will require him to do what he promised to do.

A contract may be as simple as an exchange of promises on a street corner or in a bar, as one of the cases in this chapter demonstrates. On the other hand, a contract may be expressed in thousands of words—the product of days, weeks, or months of negotiations and pages of lawyers' refined verbiage. In either case the problem of the courts is to discover first the obligations that the parties mutually assumed, and then, if there is a breach, what is the appropriate remedy.

FORMATION OF CONTRACTS—ESSENTIALS OF THE AGREEMENT

CAPACITY TO CONTRACT

ROSMAN v. CUEVAS
Superior Court of Los Angeles County, California, 1 Cal. Rptr. 485 (1959).

HULS, Judge.   Respondent sued appellant and her husband and had judgment against her for a balance due on a conditional sales contract for the purchase of an automobile. At the trial, counsel stipulated that the contract had been executed between her husband and appellant as buyers and the automobile seller, who was plaintiff's assignor. Appellant answered by a general denial and an affirmative defense that at the time of entering into the contract, appellant lacked capacity to contract, having lost her civil rights upon her conviction of a felony. The sole issue is whether appellant had *capacity to make the contract* and that the seller, assignor, knew of her incapacity at the time it entered into the contract. The husband was not served and is not a party to the action or the judgment. . . . Aside from the facts stipulated, the only oral testimony was by appellant, who testified she had told the seller that she had no capacity to sign the contract because her parole stipulated that she could not sign anything, but was told by the seller she was to sign to prove she had taken the car off the lot. . . .

Civil Code, § 1556 reads: "All persons are capable of contracting, except minors, persons of unsound mind, and persons deprived of civil rights." Appellant, having been deprived of her civil rights by her conviction, is incapable of contracting by the fiat of the statute.

In the case before us, the appellant parolee purchaser of the auto should not be prevented from asserting the defense of her incapacity to contract, especially where the uncontradicted evidence shows that, after objecting to signing because of her legal incapacity, she was lured into signing by the seller, after her husband had signed, in order that she might get the car off the lot. . . .

"It is essential that in any contract * * *, there must exist parties competent to enter into the contract and there must be a mutual understanding of what is being done." In re Estate of Ginsberg, 1936, 11 Cal.App.2d 210, 216, 53 P.2d 397, 399.

We think the better view is that such a contract as is here in question . . . and under the circumstances here in evidence, is void and not merely voidable. Violation of parole by a parolee is cause for revocation of his parole, and is tantamount to the imposition of a penalty by statute. "The imposition by statute of a penalty implies a prohibition of the act to which the penalty is attached, and a contract founded upon such act is void." Tevis v. Blanchard, 1954, 122 Cal.App.2d 731, 738, 266 P.2d 85, 90. . . .

The judgment is reversed with directions to enter judgment for defendant that plaintiff take nothing.[1]

---

[1] In contrast to Rosman v. Cuevas where the court declared the alleged agreement void, many cases involving persons lacking capacity to contract, i.e., minors, insane persons, intoxicated persons, persons under guardianship, and married women at common law, hold that the alleged contract is voidable, and not void. A voidable contract remains in full force and effect until disaffirmed by the incompetent party; whereas a void agreement is never given legal effect. A voidable contract may be disaffirmed by an incompetent either within the period of his incompetency (curiously despite his lack of capacity) or within a reasonable time after competency is acquired.

In addition to electing to disaffirm, a party to a voidable contract may avoid it by claiming in his defense to a suit on the contract that he was incompetent at the time of the making of the agreement. If the contract is executory, the defendant's incompetency is an absolute defense. On the other hand, if the contract has been executed, many cases hold that the disaffirming party need not return the other party to the *status quo ante* but must, where possible, return what he has received from the other party and still retains in his possession.

In Loomis v. Imperial Motors, Inc., 88 Idaho 74, 396 P.2d (1964), the minor plaintiff, one day before reaching majority, disaffirmed the contract, returned the car, and received from the defendant dealer the full purchase price of the car, even though the defendant argued that a reasonable rental value for the use of the car should be assessed against the plaintiff. Also, following the rule that the incompetent seeking to disaffirm a contract need make complete restoration only where

INTENT TO CONTRACT

LUCY v. ZEHMER
Supreme Court of Appeals of Virginia, 196 Va. 493 (1954).

BUCHANAN, Justice.   This suit was instituted by W. O. Lucy and J. C. Lucy, complainants, against A. H. Zehmer and Ida S. Zehmer, his wife, defendants, to have specific performance of a contract by which it was alleged the Zehmers had sold to W. O. Lucy a tract of land owned by A. H. Zehmer in Dinwiddie county containing 471.6 acres, more or less, known as the Ferguson farm, for $50,000.   .   .   .

The instrument sought to be enforced was written by A. H. Zehmer on December 20, 1952, in these words: "We hereby agree to sell to W. O. Lucy the Ferguson Farm complete for $50,000.00, title satisfactory to buyer," and signed by the defendants, A. H. Zehmer and Ida S. Zehmer.

The answer of A. H. Zehmer admitted that at the time mentioned W. O. Lucy offered him $50,000 cash for the farm, but that he, Zehmer, considered that the offer was made in jest; that so thinking, and both he and Lucy having had several drinks, he wrote out "the memorandum" quoted above and induced his wife to sign it; that he did not deliver the memorandum to Lucy, but that Lucy picked it up, read it, put it in his pocket, attempted to offer Zehmer $5 to bind the bargain, which Zehmer refused to accept, and realizing for the first time that Lucy was serious, Zehmer assured him that he had no intention of selling the farm and that the whole matter was a joke. Lucy left the premises insisting that he had purchased the farm.

Depositions were taken and the decree appealed from was entered holding that the complainants had failed to establish their right to specific performance, and dismissing their bill. The assignment of error is to this action of the court.

.   .   .   .

The defendants insist that the evidence was ample to support their contention that

possible is Fisher v. Taylor Motor Company, Inc., 249 N.C. 617, 107 S.E.2d 94 (1959), where it was held that a minor could recover $550 of the $600 he paid for a car and keep the wrecked vehicle stipulated to be worth $50, although the car had depreciated in value and had been worth only $400 immediately preceding the accident. To a similar effect is Adamowski v. Curtiss-Wright Flying Service, Inc., 300 Mass. 281, 15 N.E.2d 467 (1938), where the minor plaintiff, nearly one year after reaching majority, disaffirmed a contract for flying instructions and recovered the money he had paid for the lessons, although obviously he could make no restoration.

Because the rule which requires complete restoration only where possible often works a hardship on innocent parties, some courts have held that an incompetent who seeks to disaffirm, and who does not have in his possession the property received from the other party, must return the equivalent of the value actually received before the contract will be avoided. Some courts apply this rule only where the failure to return the property is due to the fault of the one seeking to disaffirm; whereas other courts apply it in all cases. An example of the latter is Hall v. Butterfield, 59 N.H. 354 (1879), where it was held that the minor plaintiff in order to disaffirm the contract had to pay the other party the reasonable value of the goods received and used. Likewise, in Porter v. Wilson, 106 N.H. 270, 209 A.2d 730 (1965), it was held that the minor plaintiff in order to disaffirm his contract for an attorney's services in connection with his guardianship proceedings had to pay the reasonable value of the attorney's services as determined by the court.

The theory of these last-mentioned decisions is one of "benefit received" and is closely akin to the standard rule that a minor is always liable on a contract for "necessaries" upon receiving them. The definition of what is a "necessary" is quite flexible and varies with the facts in the individual case, often ranging from food, clothing, and shelter to a college education.

the writing sought to be enforced was prepared as a bluff or dare to force Lucy to admit that he did not have $50,000; that the whole matter was a joke; that the writing was not delivered to Lucy and no binding contract was ever made between the parties.

It is an unusual, if not bizarre, defense. When made to the writing admittedly prepared by one of the defendants and signed by both, clear evidence is required to sustain it.

In this testimony Zehmer claimed that he "was high as a Georgia pine," and that the transaction "was just a bunch of two doggoned drunks bluffing to see who could talk the biggest and say the most." That claim is inconsistent with his attempt to testify in great detail as to what was said and what was done. It is contradicted by other evidence as to the condition of both parties, and rendered of no weight by the testimony of his wife that when Lucy left the restaurant she suggested that Zehmer drive him home. The record is convincing that Zehmer was not intoxicated to the extent of being unable to comprehend the nature and consequences of the instrument he executed, and hence that instrument is not to be invalidated on that ground. . . . It was in fact conceded by defendants' counsel in oral argument that under the evidence Zehmer was not too drunk to make a valid contract.

The evidence is convincing also that Zehmer wrote two agreements, the first one beginning "I hereby agree to sell." Zehmer first said he could not remember about that, then that "I don't think I wrote but one out." Mrs. Zehmer said that what he wrote was "I hereby agree," but that the "I" was changed to "We" after that night. The agreement that was written and signed is in the record and indicates no such change. Neither are the mistakes in spelling that Zehmer sought to point out readily apparent.

The appearance of the contract, the fact that it was under discussion for forty minutes or more before it was signed; Lucy's objection to the first draft because it was written in the singular, and he wanted Mrs. Zehmer to sign it also; the rewriting to meet that objection and the signing by Mrs. Zehmer; the discussion of what was to be included in the sale, the provision for the examination of the title, the completeness of the instrument that was executed, the taking possession of it by Lucy with no request or suggestion by either of the defendants that he give it back, are facts which furnish persuasive evidence that the execution of the contract was a serious business transaction rather than a casual, jesting matter as defendants now contend.

. . . .

If it be assumed, contrary to what we think the evidence shows, that Zehmer was jesting about selling his farm to Lucy and that the transaction was intended by him to be a joke, nevertheless the evidence shows that Lucy did not so understand it but considered it to be a serious business transaction and the contract to be binding on the Zehmers as well as on himself. The very next day he arranged with his brother to put up half the money and take a half interest in the land. The day after that he employed an attorney to examine the title. The next night, Tuesday, he was back at Zehmer's place and there Zehmer told him for the first time, Lucy said, that he wasn't going to sell and he told Zehmer, "You know you sold that place fair and square." After receiving the report from his attorney that the title was good he wrote to Zehmer that he was ready to close the deal.

Not only did Lucy actually believe, but the evidence shows he was warranted in believing, that the contract represented a serious business transaction and a good faith sale and purchase of the farm.

In the field of contracts, as generally elsewhere, "We must look to the outward expression of a person as manifesting his intention rather than to his secret and unexpressed intention. The law imputes to a person an intention corresponding to the reasonable meaning of his words and acts." First Nat. Exchange Bank of Roanoke v. Roanoke Oil Co., 169 Va. 99.

At no time prior to the execution of the contract had Zehmer indicated to Lucy by word or act that he was not in earnest about selling the farm. They had argued about it and discussed its terms, as Zehmer admitted, for a long time. Lucy testified that if there was any jesting it was about paying $50,000 that night. The contract and the evidence show that he was not expected to pay the money that night. Zehmer said that after the writing was signed he laid it down on the counter in front of Lucy. Lucy said Zehmer handed it to him. In any event there had been what appeared to be a good faith offer and a good faith acceptance, followed by the execution and apparent delivery of a written contract. Both said that Lucy put the writing in his pocket and then offered Zehmer $5 to seal the bargain. Not until then, even under the defendants' evidence, was anything said or done to indicate that the matter was a joke. Both of the Zehmers testified that when Zehmer asked his wife to sign he whispered that it was a joke so Lucy wouldn't hear and that it was not intended that he should hear.

The mental assent of the parties is not requisite for the formation of a contract. If the words or other acts of one of the parties have but one reasonable meaning, his undisclosed intention is immaterial except when an unreasonable meaning which he attaches to his manifestations is known to the other party. Restatement of the Law of Contracts, Vo. 1, § 71, p. 74.

" * * * The law, therefore, judges of an agreement between two persons exclusively from those expressions of their intentions which are communicated between. * * * " Clark on Contracts 4 ed., § 3, p. 4.

An agreement or mutual assent is of course essential to valid contract but the law imputes to a person an intention corresponding to the reasonable meaning of his words and acts. If his words and acts, judged by a reasonable standard, manifest an intention to agree, it is immaterial what may be the real but unexpressed state of his mind.

So a person cannot set up that he was merely jesting when his conduct and words would warrant a reasonable person in believing that he intended a real agreement.

Whether the writing signed by the defendants and now sought to be enforced by the complainants was the result of a serious offer by Lucy and a serious acceptance by the defendants, or was a serious offer by Lucy and an acceptance in secret jest by the defendants, in either event it constituted a binding contract of sale between the parties.

.   .   .   .   .

The complainants are entitled to have specific performance of the contract sued on. The decree appealed from is therefore reversed and the cause is remanded for the entry of a proper decree requiring the defendants to perform the contract in accordance with the prayer of the bill.

Reversed and remanded.[2]

---

[2]The case of Lucy v. Zehmer is said to be an example of the objective theory of contracts. Judge Learned Hand has described the objective theory as that in which:

"A contract has, strictly speaking, nothing to do with the personal, or individual, intent of the

BALFOUR v. BALFOUR
In the Court of Appeal [England], L.R. 2 K.B. 571 (1919).

The plaintiff sued the defendant (her husband) for money which she claimed to be due in respect of an agreed allowance of £30 a month. The alleged agreement was entered into under the following circumstances. The parties were married in August, 1900. The husband, a civil engineer, had a post under the Government of Ceylon as Director of Irrigation, and after the marriage he and his wife went to Ceylon, and lived there together until the year 1915, except that in 1906 they paid a short visit to this country, and in 1908 the wife came to England in order to undergo an operation, after which she returned to Ceylon. In November, 1915, she came to this country with her husband, who was on leave. They remained in England until August, 1916, when the husband's leave was up and he had to return. The wife however on the doctor's advice remained in England. On August 8, 1916, the husband being about to sail, the alleged parol agreement sued upon was made. The plaintiff, as appeared from the judge's note, gave the following evidence of what took place: "In August, 1916, defendant's leave was up. I was suffering from rheumatic arthritis. The doctor advised my staying in England for some months, not to go out till November 4. On August 8 my husband sailed. He gave me a cheque from 8th to 31st for £24, and promised to give me £30 per month until I returned." Later on she said: "My husband and I wrote the figures together on August 8; £34 shown. Afterwards he said £30." In cross-examination she said that they had not agreed to live apart until subsequent differences arose between them, and that the agreement of August, 1916, was one which might be made by a couple in amity. Her husband in consultation with her assessed her needs, and said he would send £30 per month for her maintenance. She further said that she then understood that the defendant would be returning to England in a few months, but that he afterwards wrote to her suggesting that they had better remain apart. In March, 1918, she commenced proceedings for restitution of conjugal rights, and on July 30 she obtained a decree nisi. On December 16, 1918, she obtained an order for alimony.

Sargant J. held that the husband was under an obligation to support his wife, and the parties had contracted that the extent of that obligation should be defined in terms of so much a month. The consent of the wife to that arrangement was a sufficient consideration to constitute a contract which could be sued upon.

He accordingly gave judgment for the plaintiff.

The husband appealed.

.   .   .   .   .

ATKIN, L. J.   The defence to this action on the alleged contract is that the defendant, the husband, entered into no contract with his wife, and for the determination of that it is necessary to remember that there are agreements between parties which do not result in contracts within the meaning of that term in our law. The ordinary example is where two parties agree to take a walk together, or where there is an offer

parties. A contract is an obligation attached by the mere force of law to certain acts of parties, usually words, which ordinarily accompany and represent a known intent. If, however, it were proved by twenty bishops that either party when he used the words intended something else than the usual meaning which the law imposes them, he would still be held, unless there were some mutual mistake or something else of the sort." Hotchkiss v. National City Bank of New York, 200 F. 287, 283 (S.D.N.Y. 1911).

and an acceptance of hospitality. Nobody would suggest in ordinary circumstances that those agreements result in what we know as a contract, and one of the most usual forms of agreement which does not constitute a contract appears to me to be the arrangements which are made between husband and wife.

It is quite common, and it is the natural and inevitable result of the relationship of husband and wife, that the two spouses should make arrangements between themselves —agreements such as are in dispute in this action—agreements for allowances, by which the husband agrees that he will pay to his wife a certain sum of money, per week, or per month, or per year, to cover either her own expenses or the necessary expenses of the household and of the children of the marriage, and in which the wife promises either expressly or impliedly to apply the allowance for the purpose for which it is given. To my mind those agreements, or many of them, do not result in contracts at all, and they do not result in contracts even though there may be what as between other parties would constitute consideration for the agreement. The consideration, as we know, may consist either in some right, interest, profit or benefit accruing to one party, or some forbearance, detriment, loss or responsibility given, suffered or undertaken by the other. That is a well-known definition, and it constantly happens, I think, that such arrangements made between husband and wife are arrangements in which there are mutual promises, or in which there is consideration in form within the definition that I have mentioned. Nevertheless they are not contracts, and they are not contracts because the parties did not intend that they should be attended by legal consequences.

.   .   .   .

The only question in this case is whether or not this promise was of such a class or not. For the reasons given by my brethren it appears to me to be plainly established that the promise here was not intended by either party to be attended by legal consequences. I think the onus was upon the plaintiff, and the plaintiff has not established any contract. The parties were living together, the wife intending to return. The suggestion is that the husband bound himself to pay £30 a month under all circumstances, and she bound herself to be satisfied with that sum under all circumstances, and although she was in ill-health and alone in this country, that out of that sum she undertook to defray the whole of the medical expenses that might fall upon her, whatever might be the development of her illness, and in whatever expenses it might involve her. To my mind neither party contemplated such a result. I think that the parol evidence upon which the case turns does not establish a contract. I think that the letters do not evidence such a contract, or amplify the oral evidence which was given by the wife, which is not in dispute. For these reasons I think the judgment of the Court below was wrong and that this appeal should be allowed.

EXAMPLES OF OFFER AND ACCEPTANCE

Offer

LEFKOWITZ v. GREAT MINNEAPOLIS SURPLUS STORE
Supreme Court of Minnesota, 251 Minn. 188 (1957).

MURPHY, Justice.   This is an appeal from an order of the Municipal Court of Minneapolis denying the motion of the defendant for amended findings of fact, or, in the alternative, for a new trial. The order for judgment awarded the plaintiff the sum of $138.50 as damages for breach of contract.

This case grows out of the alleged refusal of the defendant to sell to the plaintiff a certain fur piece which it had offered for sale in a newspaper advertisement. . . .

On April 13, the defendant . . . published [two] advertisements in . . . [a] newspaper as follows:

Saturday 9 A.M.
2 Brand New Pastel
Mink 3-Skin Scarfs
Selling for $89.50
Out they go
Saturday. Each $1.00
1 Black Lapin Stole
Beautiful,
worth $139.50 .... $1.00
First Come
First Served

The record supports the findings of the court that . . . following the publication of the above-described ads the plaintiff was the first to present himself at the appropriate counter in the defendant's store and on each occasion demanded the coat and the stole so advertised and indicated his readiness to pay the sale price of $1. On both occasions, the defendant refused to sell the merchandise to the plaintiff, stating on the first occasion that by a "house rule" the offer was intended for women only and sales would not be made to men, and on the second visit that plaintiff knew defendant's house rules.

.   .   .

The defendant contends that a newspaper advertisement offering items of merchandise for sale at a named price is a "unilateral offer" which may be withdrawn without notice. He relies upon authorities which hold that, where an advertiser publishes in a newspaper that he has a certain quantity or quality of goods which he wants to dispose of at certain prices and on certain terms, such advertisements are not offers which become contracts as soon as any person to whose notice they may come signifies his acceptance by notifying the other that he will take a certain quantity of them. Such advertisements have been construed as an invitation for an offer of sale on the terms stated, which offer, when received may be accepted or rejected and which therefore does not become a contract of sale until accepted by the seller; and until a contract has been so made, the seller may modify or revoke such prices or terms.   . . .

.   .   .   We are of the view on the facts before us that the offer by the defendant of the sale of the Lapin fur was clear, definite, and explicit, and left nothing open for negotiation. The plaintiff having successfully managed to be the first one to appear at the seller's place of business to be served, as requested by the advertisement, and having offered the stated purchase price of the article, he was entitled to performance on the part of the defendant. We think the trial court was correct in holding that there was in the conduct of the parties a sufficient mutuality of obligation to constitute a contract of sale.

The defendant contends that the offer was modified by a "house rule" to the effect that only women were qualified to receive the bargains advertised. The advertisement contained no such restriction. This objection may be disposed of briefly by stating that, while an advertiser has the right at any time before acceptance to modify his offer, he does not have the right, after acceptance, to impose new or arbitrary conditions not contained in the published offer.   .   .   .

Affirmed.

Acceptance

BULLOCK v. HARWICK

Supreme Court of Florida, 30 S.2d 539 (1947).

CHILLINGWORTH, Associate Justice.   This is an appeal from a final decree dismissing a bill for specific performance.   .   .   .

.   .   .   .   .

After a series of preliminary letters and telegrams the vendor, the principal defendant in the suit below, and appellee here, sent a telegram as follows:

"Re Purchase Stock Colombian Export Line by Bullock Stop Harwick to Deliver all Colombian Stock Resignation Officers Records to Bullock in Exchange for Bank Draft Payable to Harwick of Miami Beach First National Bank in Amount of Seventy-Five Thousand Dollars Stop Colombian Export Indebtedness Consists Mortgage Due Miami Beach Heights of Seventy-Five Thousand Dollars of Record Nothing Otherwise Stop Harwick Agrees Pay Interest on this Mortgage to Closing Date Stop No Commissions Acknowledged by Buyer or Seller Harwick Pays Judge Southerland Fee Two Thousand Dollars on Closing Stock Deal Stop No Escrows Necessary Stop Any Prior Understandings or Implications Void Stop Closing Judge Southerland Office Stop Harwick Expects Arrive Miami About September 21st."

On September 24th, the vendor and the vendee, plaintiff-appellant, met in the office of an attorney in Miami Beach. The vendor expected to close the sale at that time. He asserted that he had in his pocket all of the original stock certificates, the resignations of the three officers of the corporation, and that he had with him the corporate minute book. But he did not expose the certificates of the resignations. Doubt is cast upon his actual possession of these certificates. He testified that he had obtained them from a safety deposit box on the morning of September 24th, only readily to admit his obvious mis-statement, when confronted by evidence of the bank vault officials showing that he had made no entry to the box on that day, or prior thereto, or that he was even then authorized to have access to the box. He did not have the stock record book with him, or any evidence of the fact that the only indebtedness of the corporation was the purchase money mortgage due on the property or that the corporation was in good standing at the time.

The vendee did not have with him a bank draft of any nature, nor did he have the requisite amount in cash or a certified check or cashier's check. The vendee asserted that he had funds available which could be readily obtained as soon as the vendor was in a position to do the things he was required to do by his offer. None of the purchase price was ever paid. No writing was ever signed by the vendee. While the evidence is conflicting, it is reasonably manifest that the vendor did not definitely withdraw the offer, nor did the vendee definitely accept the offer. Neither, by words or conduct, clearly evidenced the obligations he desired to assume, or his real intentions. At the conclusion of the conference the vendor, in relating his parting words to the vendee, said: "I told him I would be back in a few days; if I was interested further I would get in touch with him." The vendee was no more precise in his attitude than the vendor.

The parties separated. No further action was taken by the vendor except to phone the attorney who arranged the conference and with whom they had met the day before. The vendor inquired of the attorney whether the attorney thought that the vendee really had the cash for the transaction and would go through with the deal. In response to an affirmative answer, he made no further statement.

On December 26, 1945, about three months later, the vendee made a tender of $75,000 cash to the attorney for the vendor. Upon its rejection the vendee immediately filed suit for specific performance.

The record tells a tale of two skillful and wary traders in action. The vendor was willing to close the deal September 24th and apparently willing vaguely and indifferently to keep the offer open. But he specifically declined to sign a contract, or execute any further writing, or to produce any evidence of a present ability to fully perform, until the cash, or its equivalent, was actually in sight. The vendee, anxious to keep the offer open, was careful not to accept in writing. He, being either unwilling or unable to produce the cash and also unwilling to be bound in law for the purchase price, was also vague and indifferent about any definite verbal acceptance of the offer. After September 24th, the vendor and vendee saw each other a number of times, usually in a restaurant where they would have lunch, but neither ever approached the other about the sale or the prospects of closing any sale. One may fairly infer that had the market value of this property gone down, rather than up, between September 24th and December 26th, no suit would have been filed by the purchaser. Without the institution of this suit, the purchaser would not have been bound at any time to pay the purchase price of this property, unless he had done something more than he had done prior to then.

Pomeroy's Specific Performance of Contracts, 3rd Edition, Paragraphs 63, 64 and 66, clearly expresses the law, in the following excerpts: "As the acceptance is the means by which the minds of two parties are brought to an agreement, it must be so expressed as to show that there is an actual assent, a meeting of the two minds, and that there is an assent upon exactly the same matters. To produce a concluded contract the acceptance must, therefore, possess certain fundamental requisites. First. It must be absolute, unambiguous, unequivocal, without condition or reservation. * * * Second. As the assent of the parties should be given to exactly the same matters, the acceptance must not vary from the terms of the offer, either by way of omission, addition, or alteration; if it does vary in either of these modes, no contract is concluded thereby, the transaction remains in the state of negotiation, and neither party is bound. * * * The acceptance may be in writing, by parol, or by act. * * * In whatever mode the assent is signified, whether by writing, by words, or by conduct, it must be actually expressed in some overt manner, by some overt acts; a mere mental intention to accept an offer, however carefully formed, will not create a contract."

This Court held in Prescott v. Mutual Benefit Health & Accident Association, 133 Fla. 510, in an opinion by Justice Buford, that a mere offer not assented to constitutes no contract, for there must be not only a proposal but an acceptance, and, so long as the proposal was not acceded to, it is binding on neither party and may be retracted.

Therefore we hold that it was not clearly established that there was a definite acceptance by the vendee on September 24th and that the offer was effectually withdrawn by the action and words of the vendor on September 24th and confirmed by his conduct thereafter. The acceptance of December 26th was too late.

Affirmed.

RESTATEMENT OF THE LAW OF CONTRACTS—
Offer and Acceptance Defined[3]

§ 24. OFFER DEFINED

An offer is a promise which is in its terms conditional upon an act, forbearance or return promise being given in exchange for the promise or its performance. . . .

Comment:

a. In an offer for an informal unilateral contract the promise is conditional upon an act other than a promise being given. . . . In an offer for a bilateral contract the offeror's promise is always conditional upon a return promise being given. The return promise may be in the form of assent to the proposal in the offer. . . . The promise must not be merely performable on a certain contingency.

. . . . .

§ 52. ACCEPTANCE DEFINED

Acceptance of an offer is an expression of assent to the terms thereof made by the offeree in a manner requested or authorized by the offeror. If anything except a promise is requested as consideration no contract exists until part of what is requested is performed or tendered. If a promise is requested, no contract exists . . . until the promise is expressly or impliedly given.

EXAMPLES OF CONSIDERATION

Definition of Consideration

HAMER v. SIDWAY
Court of Appeals of New York, 124 N.Y. 538 (1891).

PARKER, J.   The question which provoked the most discussion by counsel on this appeal, and which lies at the foundation of plaintiff's asserted right of recovery, is whether by virtue of a contract defendant's testator William E. Story became indebted to his nephew William E. Story, 2d, on his twenty-first birthday in the sum of five thousand dollars. The trial court found as a fact that "on the 20th day of March, 1869,

---

[3]The Restatement of the Law of Contracts is a product of The American Law Institute (A.L.I.). The A.L.I. was formed because of concern for the vast and expanding volumes of court decisions th at established new and often irreconcilable decisions, resulting in an increasing uncertainty in the law. The organization meeting of the A.L.I. was held in 1923 and was attended by members of the United States Supreme Court, representatives from the United States Circuit Courts of

* * * William E. Story agreed to and with William E. Story, 2d, that if he would refrain from drinking liquor, using tobacco, swearing, and playing cards or billiards for money until he should become 21 years of age, then he, the said William E. Story, would at that time pay him, the said William E. Story, 2d, the sum of $5000 for such refraining, to which the said William E. Story, 2d, agreed," and that he "in all things fully performed his part of said agreement."

The defendant contends that the contract was without consideration to support it, and, therefore, invalid. He asserts that the promisee by refraining from the use of liquor and tobacco was not harmed but benefited; that that which he did was best for him to do independently of his uncle's promise, and insists that it follows that unless the promisor was benefited, the contract was without consideration, a contention which, if well founded, would seem to leave open for controversy in many cases whether that which the promisee did or omitted to do was, in fact, of such benefit to him as to leave no consideration to support the enforcement of the promisor's agreement. Such a rule could not be tolerated, and is without foundation in the law. The Exchequer Chamber, in 1875, defined consideration as follows: "A valuable consideration in the sense of the law may consist either in some right, interest, profit, or benefit accruing to the one party, or some forbearance, detriment, loss, or responsibility given, suffered, or undertaken by the other." Courts "will not ask whether the thing which forms the consideration does in fact benefit the promisee or a third party, or is of any substantial value to any one. It is enough that something is promised, done, forborne, or suffered by the party to whom the promise is made as consideration for the promise made to him." Anson's Prin. of Con. 63.

.   .   .   .

In Talbott v. Stemmons, 89 Ky. 222, the step-grandmother of the plaintiff made with him the following agreement: "I do promise and bind myself to give my grandson, Albert R. Talbott, $500 at my death, if he will never take another chew of tobacco or smoke another cigar during my life from this date up to my death, and if he breaks this pledge he is to refund double the amount to his mother." The executor of Mrs. Stemmons demurred to the complaint on the ground that the agreement was not based on a sufficient consideration. The demurrer was sustained and an appeal taken therefrom to the Court of Appeals, where the decision of the court below was reversed. In the opinion of the court it is said that "the right to use and enjoy the use of tobacco was a right that belonged to the plaintiff and not forbidden by law. The abandonment of its use may have saved him money or contributed to his health; nevertheless, the surrender of that right caused the promise, and having the right to contract with reference to the subject-matter, the abandonment of the use was a sufficient considera-

Appeals, the highest courts of a majority of States, the Association of American Law Schools, the American and State Bar Associations, and the National Conference of Commissioners on Uniform State Laws. The A.L.I. was formed in the belief that to clarify, simplify, and render the law more certain, the first step must be the preparation of an orderly restatement of the case law as developed by common law decisions and statutory interpretations. The Restatement of the Law of Contracts is one such compilation.

The Restatements often guide the courts in interpreting and reconciling existing case law and in developing new concepts. In the interest of showing the reader not only the excellent work done by the A.L.I. but also the use of the Restatements in ordering the legal process, certain selected portions of the Restatements will be reproduced here and in Chapter 5.

tion to uphold the promise." Abstinence from the use of intoxicating liquors was held to furnish a good consideration for a promissory note in Lindell v. Rokes, 60 Mo. 249. The cases cited by the defendant on this question are not in point. . . .

. . .

Order reversed and judgment of special term affirmed.

HARRINGTON v. TAYLOR
Supreme Court of North Carolina, 225 N.C. 690 (1945).

PER CURIAM. The plaintiff in this case sought to recover of the defendant upon a promise made by him under the following peculiar circumstances:

The defendant had assaulted his wife, who took refuge in plaintiff's house. The next day the defendant gained access to the house and began another assault upon his wife. The defendant's wife knocked him down with an axe, and was on the point of cutting his head open or decapitating him while he was laying on the floor, and the plaintiff intervened, caught the axe as it was descending, and the blow intended for defendant fell upon her hand, mutilating it badly, but saving defendant's life.

Subsequently, defendant orally promised to pay the plaintiff her damages; but, after paying a small sum, failed to pay anything more. . . .

. . .

The question presented is whether there was a consideration recognized by our law as sufficient to support the promise. The Court is of the opinion that, however much the defendant should be impelled by common gratitude to alleviate the plaintiff's misfortune, a humanitarian act of this kind, voluntarily performed, is not such consideration as would entitle her to recover at law.

The judgment [of the trial court] . . . is affirmed.

EMBOLA v. TUPPELA
Supreme Court of Washington, 127 Wash. 285 (1923).

Action by Henry Embola against John Tuppela, by C. H. Farrell, his guardian ad litem. Judgment for plaintiff, and defendant appeals.

Affirmed.

PEMBERTON, J. John Tuppela joined the gold seekers' rush to Alaska, and after remaining there a number of years prospecting was adjudged insane, and committed to an asylum in Portland, Ore. Upon his release, after a confinement of about four years, he found that his mining properties in Alaska had been sold by his guardian. In May of 1918 Tuppela, destitute and without work, met respondent at Astoria, Ore. They had been close friends for a period of about 30 years. Respondent advanced money for his support, and in September brought him to Seattle to the home of Herman Lindstrom, a brother-in-law of respondent. Tuppela had requested a number of people to advance money for an undertaking to recover his mining property in Alaska, but found no one who was willing to do so. The estimated value of this mining property was about $500,000. In the month of September [1918] Tuppela made the following statement to respondent:

"You have already let me have $270. If you will give me $50 more so I can go to Alaska and get my property back, I will pay you ten thousand dollars when I win my property."

Respondent accepted this offer, and immediately advanced the sum of $50. In January, 1921, after extended litigation, Tuppela recovered his property. Tuppela, remembering his agreement with respondent, requested Mr. Cobb, his trustee, to pay the full amount, and upon his refusal so to do this action was instituted to collect the same.

The answer of the appellant denies the contract, and alleges that, if it were made, it is unconscionable, not supported by adequate consideration, procured through fraud, and is usurious. The appellant also alleges that the amount advanced did not exceed $100, and he has paid $150 into the registry of the court for the benefit of respondent.

The court found in favor of the respondent, and from the judgment entered this appeal is taken.

It is contended by appellant that the amount advanced is a loan, and therefore usurious, and that the sum of $300 is not an adequate consideration to support a promise to repay $10,000. It is the contention of respondent that the money advanced was not a loan, but an investment; that the transaction was in the nature of a grubstake contract, which has been upheld by this court. . . .

This is not a case wherein respondent advanced money to carry on prospecting. The money was advanced to enable appellant to recover his mining property. Appellant had already been advised by an attorney that he could not recover this property. The risk of losing the money advanced was as great in this case as if the same had been advanced under a grubstake contract. Where the principal sum advanced is to be repaid only on some contingency that may never take place, the sum so advanced is considered an investment, and not a loan, and the transaction is not usurious.

"To constitute usury it is essential that the principal sum loaned shall be repayable at all events and not put in hazard absolutely. If it is payable only on some contingency then the transaction is not usurious. . . . " 27 R.C.L. sec. 21, p. 220.

The fact that the money advanced was not to be returned until appellant won his property, a contingency at that time unlikely to occur, supports the finding that the consideration was not inadequate. To the contention that the contract was procured through fraud the testimony shows that appellant voluntarily offered to pay the $10,000, and at the time was of sound and disposing mind, and considered that the contract was fair and to his advantage.

The trial court having found that there was no fraud, and that the contract was not unconscionable, we should uphold these findings unless the evidence preponderates against them. . . . We are satisfied that the evidence supports the findings.

The judgment is affirmed.

RESTATEMENT OF THE LAW OF CONTRACTS—
Consideration Defined

§ 75. DEFINITION OF CONSIDERATION

(1) Consideration for a promise is

(a) an act other than a promise, or
(b) a forbearance, or
(c) the creation, modification or destruction of a legal relation, or
(d) a return promise,
bargained for and given in exchange for the promise.
(2) Consideration may be given to the promisor or to some other person. It may be given by the promisee or by some other person.

Mutuality of Obligation

G. LOEWUS & CO. v. VISCHIA
Supreme Court of New Jersey, 2 N.J. 54 (1949).

OLIPHANT, Justice.   Plaintiff-appellant appeals from a judgment of non-suit entered against it in the former Supreme Court, Essex County Circuit.

Plaintiff was a wholesale liquor distributor owning and operating a wine bottling plant in the City of Newark. Defendant owned and operated a winery in the City of Paterson. On March 31, 1942 the parties entered into two contracts. One provided for the sale of plaintiff's wine bottling equipment to defendant, the other, upon which this cause is predicated, was a "requirements" contract which by its terms was to continue in force for sixteen months and to be renewed automatically unless terminated under its provisions.

The complaint was in four counts. By stipulation the causes of action set forth in the third and fourth counts were settled and judgment entered in favor of the plaintiff thereon. This appeal is from a judgment entered for the defendant on the first and second counts, which claimed damages for failure of the defendant to fill orders given him by plaintiff pursuant to the contract sued on. The first count was for damages for loss of profits on orders given between May 14, 1942 and May 14, 1943 and not filled, the second count was to recover anticipated profits on orders plaintiff claims to have given defendant between July 30, 1943 and July 31, 1944. The cause was tried by the court, sitting without a jury.

The pertinent portions of the contract are as follows:

"1. Vischia agrees to sell to Loewus all types of domestic wines; said wines shall be bottled by Vischia under labels designated by Loewus; said wines shall be bottled and furnished to Loewus pursuant to such orders therefor as are received from time to time by Vischia from Loewus. Loewus agrees to place orders with Vischia from time to time for such wine as it may require under labels bearing brand or trade names which are its exclusive property.

"3. It is agreed that the provisions of the preceding paragraphs shall apply to the brand names 'Sunlight' and 'Ramona' now being used by Loewus and to such other brand names as are used on individual orders of 500 cases or more received by Vischia from Loewus. It is further agreed that in so far as other brand names applied to wine which is not ordered in such quantities are concerned, and in so far as wine bearing the private label of any particular retailer is concerned, Vischia shall bottle and furnish the same to Loewus pursuant to this agreement, provided that in such event Vischia may impose the following additional charge above the cost fixed in paragraph 2, etc.

"5. Vischia agrees to maintain at all times adequate equipment, staff and force of employees to meet the requirements of Loewus and guarantees (except for matters beyond his control) that he will fill in proper and sufficient manner all orders received from Loewus within one week after the receipt of the order.

"7. Nothing hereinbefore or hereafter contained shall in any wise restrict the freedom of Loewus to purchase all imported wines, or domestic wines bottled by others under labels which are not the exclusive property of Loewus by ownership or lease.

"8. It is agreed that in the event Vischia fails for any reason whatever to fill an order submitted by Loewus within seven days after the receipt thereof, Loewus may proceed without restriction to place such order and obtain the ordered product elsewhere."

Judge William A. Smith, in finding for the defendant, held the contract did not require or bind plaintiff to purchase from defendant any more wine than it wanted or desired, but even if it did the amount which defendant might be required to furnish was too uncertain to render the contract definite enough to be enforceable and that it was not enforceable as to the orders given but not filled.

The court below found as a fact that defendant was unable to reasonably estimate what supply plaintiff would require of him and that if plaintiff was obligated to give defendant all his orders the contemplated business was of such a character that, under the contract for the requirements of the business, neither party was in a position to make a reasonable estimate of what those orders might be.

The basic question before us is whether the contract is mutual and enforceable or whether it is unilateral, lacks mutuality and hence is unenforceable.

While under the contract plaintiff was assured of an ample supply of wine, it was, nevertheless, only required to purchase such wines from defendant as it might "require under labels bearing its brand or trade names which are its exclusive property."

By the terms of paragraph 7 it is apparent, however, there was nothing in the contract to prevent plaintiff from purchasing all the necessary wine to meet the requirements from others than defendant so long as it did not use labels bearing brand or trade names which were its exclusive property. As a matter of fact it appears no orders were placed with defendant under this contract for wines under brands which were the exclusive property of plaintiff. On the contrary a brand belonging to defendant was used.

Before the contract in suit was entered into the business of plaintiff was the buying and selling at wholesale bottled wines and in part the bottling of wines under its own brands and selling these at wholesale. When the contract was entered into plaintiff changed its business to that of buying bottled goods solely and re-selling them at wholesale. A new business was created the requirements of which were unknown.

Both parties in this cause rely largely on Ferenczi v. The National Sulphur Co., Cir.Ct. 1933, 11 N.J.Misc. 262, 166 A. 477, 478, an opinion by Judge, now Justice Ackerson, sitting at the Hudson Circuit. As there said "In passing upon the validity of contracts of this character the general rule is that it will be presumed that the parties thereto intended to make a binding and enforceable obligation. Baker v. Murray, 137 Okl. 288, 279 P. 340. As between two equally reasonable constructions, we should adopt the one which makes the contract valid, as against that reaching a contrary result. Pittsburgh Plate Glass Co. v. Vhneuer Glass Co., 6 Cir., 253 F. 161." . . .

With regard to "requirement" contracts providing for the furnishing of such material as one may need or require they are, by the weight of authority, held mutual and binding on the parties where, from the nature of the purchaser's business the quantity of the goods needed is subject to a reasonably accurate estimate. The basis of the rule is that the purchaser's obligation to buy to the extent of his requirements or needs supplies mutuality. Ferenczi v. The National Sulphur Co., supra, and the cases therein cited.

In considering the validity of purely executory contracts the rule is that "where the promise has for its subject-matter something, which by the terms of the contract is left to depend for its very existence upon the future election of the promisor, it will not form a valid consideration for an executory contract, but where such subject-matter, in the normal and bona fide course of events as contemplated by both parties, is not thus left dependent, it will form such valid consideration, although there may be elements of quantity, requirement, selection, etc., agreed to be left to the future discretion of the promisor." Atlantic Pebble Co. v. Lehigh Valley R. R. Co., Err. & App.1916, 89 N.J.L. 336, 341, 98 A. 410, 412; Ferenczi v. The National Sulphur Co., supra.

In Williston on Sales, § 464a, Rev.Ed., it is stated: "It is true, as a general rule, that if it is wholly optional with one party to a bilateral agreement whether he shall perform or not, there is no legal contract. The promise of that party in such a bargain is illusory; that is, though in form a promise, it is so qualified that the promisor really engages himself for nothing and his illusory promise is insufficient consideration to support a counterpromise. A promise to buy such a quantity of goods as the buyer may thereafter order or to take goods in such quantities 'as may be desired' or as the buyer 'may want' is not sufficient consideration since the buyer may refrain from buying at his option and without incurring legal detriment himself or benefiting the other party."

In the case sub judice the undertaking of the plaintiff is left to depend for its very existence upon its future election as to whether it will purchase from defendant any bottled wine under its own exclusive brands, or whether it will purchase all or a considerable part thereof from others under other brands.

The contract is unilateral, lacks mutuality and hence is unenforceable.

The judgment below is affirmed.

SUBJECT MATTER

Identity of Agreement

RAFFLES v. WICHELHAUS
In the Court of Exchequer, 159 Eng. Rep. 375 (1864).

Declaration.   For that it was agreed between the plaintiff and the defendants, to wit, at Liverpool, that the plaintiff should sell to the defendants, and the defendants buy of the plaintiff, certain goods, to wit, 125 bales of Surat cotton, guaranteed middling fair merchant's Dhollorah, to arrive ex Peerless from Bombay; and that the cotton should be taken from the quay, and that the defendants would pay the plaintiff for the same at a certain rate, to wit, at the rate of 17-1/4 d. per pound, within a certain time then agreed upon after the arrival of the said goods in England. Averments: that the said goods did arrive by the said ship from Bombay in England, to wit, at Liverpool, and the plaintiff was then and there ready and willing and offered to deliver the said goods to the defendants, etc. Breach: that the defendants refused to accept the said goods or pay the plaintiff for them.

Plea.   That the said ship mentioned in the said agreement was meant and intended by the defendants to be the ship called the Peerless, which sailed from Bombay, to wit, in October; and that the plaintiff was not ready and willing and did not offer to deliver to the defendants any bales of cotton which arrived by the last mentioned ship, but instead thereof was only ready and willing, and offered to deliver to the defendants 125 bales of Surat cotton which arrived by another and different ship, which was also called the Peerless, and which sailed from Bombay, to wit, in December.

Demurrer, and joinder therein.

Milward, in support of the demurrer. The contract was for the sale of a number of bales of cotton of a particular description, which the plaintiff was ready to deliver. It is immaterial by what ship the cotton was to arrive, so that it was a ship called the "Peerless." The words "to arrive ex 'Peerless'," only mean that if the vessel is lost on the voyage, the contract is to be at an end. [Pollock, C.B. It would be a question for the jury whether both parties meant the same ship called the "Peerless."] That would be so if the contract was for the sale of a ship called the "Peerless"; but it is for the sale of cotton on board a ship of that name. [Pollock, C.B. The defendant only bought that cotton which was to arrive by a particular ship. It may as well be said that if there is a contract for the purchase of certain goods in warehouse A, that is satisfied by the delivery of goods of the same description in warehouse B.] In that case there would be goods in both warehouses; here it does not appear that the plaintiff had any goods on board the other "Peerless." [Martin, B. It is imposing on the defendant a contract different from that which he entered into. Pollock, C.B. It is like a contract for the purchase of wine coming from a particular estate in France or Spain, where there are two estates of that name.] The defendant has no right to contradict by parol evidence, a written contract good upon the face of it. He does not impute misrepresentation or fraud, but only says that he fancied the ship was a different one. Intention is of no avail, unless stated at the time of the contract. [Pollock, C.B. One vessel sailed in October and the other in December.] The time of sailing is no part of the contract.

Mellish (Cohen with him), in support of the plea. There is nothing on the face of the contract to show that any particular ship called the "Peerless" was meant; but the moment it appears that two ships called the "Peerless" were about to sail from Bombay there is a latent ambiguity, and parol evidence may be given for the purpose of showing that the defendant meant one Peerless and the plaintiff another. That being so, there was no consensus ad idem, and therefore no binding contract. He was then stopped by the court.

PER CURIAM. There must be judgment for the defendants.

RESTATEMENT OF THE LAW OF CONTRACTS—
Undisclosed Misunderstandings

§ 71. UNDISCLOSED UNDERSTANDING OF OFFEROR OR OFFEREE, WHEN MATERIAL

. . . [T]he undisclosed understanding of either party of the meaning of his own words and other acts, or of the other party's words and other acts, is material in the formation of contracts in the following cases and in no others:

(a) If the manifestations of intention of either party are uncertain or ambiguous, and he has no reason to know that they may bear a different meaning to the other party from that which he himself attaches to them, his manifestations are operative in the formation of a contract only in the event that the other party attaches to them the same meaning.

(b) If both parties know or have reason to know that the manifestations of one of them are uncertain or ambiguous and the parties attach different meanings to the manifestations, this difference prevents the uncertain or ambiguous manifestations from being operative as an offer or an acceptance.

(c) If either party knows that the other does not intend what his words or other acts express, this knowledge prevents such words or other acts from being operative as an offer or an acceptance.

Comment:

a. The mental assent of the parties is not requisite for the formation of a contract. If the words or other acts of one of the parties have but one reasonable meaning, his intention is material only in the exceptional case, stated in Clause (c), that an unreasonable meaning which he attaches to his manifestations is known to the other party. If the manifestations of the parties have more than one reasonable meaning, it must be determined which of the possible meanings is to be taken. If either party has reason to know that the other will give the manifestations only one of these meanings and in fact the manifestations are so understood, the party conscious of the ambiguity is bound in accordance with that understanding. On the other hand, if a party has no reason to suppose that there is ambiguity, he may assert that his words or other acts bear the meaning that he intended, that being one of their legitimate meanings, and he will not be bound by a different meaning attached to them by the other party.

Illustrations:

1. A offers B to sell goods shipped from Bombay ex steamer "Peerless." B expresses assent to the proposition. There are, however, two steamers of the name "Peerless." It may be supposed, firstly, that A knows, or has reason to know this fact, and that B neither knows nor has reason to know it; secondly, conversely, that B knows or has reason to know it and that A does not; thirdly, that both know or have reason to know of the ambiguity; or, fourthly, that neither of them knows or has reason to know it at the time when the communications between them take place. In the case first supposed there is a contract for the goods from the steamer which B has in mind. In the second case there is a contract for the goods from the steamer which A has in mind. In the third and fourth cases there is no contract unless A and B in fact intend the same steamer. In that event there is a contract for goods from that steamer.

2. A says to B, "I offer to sell you my horse for $100." B, knowing that A intends to offer to sell his cow, not his horse for that price, and that the use of the word "horse" is a slip of the tongue, replies, "I accept." There is no contract for the sale of either the horse or the cow.

Legality of Subject Matter

IN RE DUNCAN'S ESTATE
Supreme Court of Colorado, 87 Colo. 149 (1930).

WHITFORD, C. J.   Charles M. Duncan died intestate. The defendant in error, his third wife, survived him. The plaintiff in error was appointed administrator of his estate.

The widow petitioned the court for an order requiring the administrator to pay her the widow's allowance under the statute. The administrator resisted her petition, and set up an antenuptial contract, as a bar to the claim for an allowance. The alleged antenuptial contract is as follows:

"This agreement made and entered into this sixteenth day of December, 1924, between Charles M. Duncan, physician, party of the first part, and Mrs. Hattie E. Gibson, party of the second part, Witnesseth, that the said parties hereby mutually agree, that in the event of legally entering into a state of matrimony and living together as man and wife, it is the intention that such relationship shall be continued in to the satisfaction of both parties, and to their mutual happiness. This agreement further witnesseth, that should at any time a condition exist that would disturb the harmony of the married life and domestic relations of said parties, they agree to a legal separation, with the following stipulations: The party of the first part agrees to make a settlement with the party of the second part at the rate of $100.00 for each year they shall have lived together as man and wife, the said settlement to be paid in the lawful money of the United States of America, or its equivalent. The said party of the second part agrees to accept said settlement within 24 hours of the time the said parties shall have ceased to live together as man and wife. The said party of the second part further agrees to vacate the house, rooms or premises the said parties shall have occupied, and to take from said house, rooms or premises all articles of household goods, furnishings, and wearing apparel which are her personal property, within 24 hours of receiving the foregoing settlement, and with no expense to the said party of the first part. In consideration of the foregoing, the party of the second part does hereby further agree to forever release the said party of the first part, his heirs and assigns, from any and all claims for alimony, support, maintenance, dower, or wife's or widow's rights; and not to contest any action for divorce that may be brought by the party of the first part."

In less than one year thereafter the parties separated, following which the wife signed a receipt, which is as follows, to wit:

"I hereby acknowledge the receipt of the sum of $110.00, in full settlement of all claims I have against C. M. Duncan, by or on account of our marriage relations, which have been mutually discontinued, or any claim for alimony or support from and after this date."

The county court denied the widow's claim for an allowance. On trial de novo in the district court, on appeal, that court held the antenuptial agreement void, and entered judgment in favor of the widow. To reverse that judgment the administrator comes here on error.

The judgment of the district court must be affirmed. The contract provides for a future separation and divorce. The receipt was given in pursuance of that contract. They will be taken and considered together.

The antenuptial contract was a wicked device to evade the laws applicable to marriage relations, property rights, and divorces, and is clearly against public policy and decency. It was nothing more, in effect, than an attempt, on the part of the deceased, in whose favor the contract was drawn, to legalize prostitution, under the name of marriage, at the price of $100 per year. It was the establishing of a companionate marriage, to exist only so long as neither party objected to a continuance. The wife, under its terms, was made a base hireling. The man could enjoy her companionship, under its covenant, for a single night, and then discard her, or he might continue his companionship with her for a week, or a fortnight, or longer if it pleased his fancy, and then he could, under its terms, capriciously and arbitrarily reject her, and put her adrift by paying the price, at the rate of $100 per year; and thereupon, at his bidding, she must gather up her personal belongings and leave the house within 24 hours, without any rights, either as wife or widow, and then, as a finale, she would be obliged silently to submit to his action of divorce, without a right to contest the same in court, no matter how vile, false, or unjust the charges made against her reputation or character.

The contract is utterly void. It is against public policy. The marriage relation lies at the foundation of our civilization. Marriage promotes public and private morals, and advances the well-being of society and social order. The marriage relation is so sacred in character that it is indissoluble except in conformity with legislative requirements and the solemn decree of a court. It cannot be annulled by contract, or at the pleasure of the parties.

The judgment is affirmed.

STATUTE OF FRAUDS

HURLEY v. WOODSIDES
Court of Appeals of Kentucky, 21 Ky. Law Rep. 1073 (1899).

Appeal from circuit court, Crittenden county. Action by G. F. Hurley against J. L. Woodsides to recover damages for breach of contract. Judgment for defendant, and plantiff appeals. Affirmed.

BURNAM, J.   Appellant alleged that on the 30th of October, 1897, he verbally contracted to lease from appellee a tract of 25 acres of timbered land, for the period of five years; that, under the contract, he was to clear up 5 acres of the land in the winter of 1897–98, 10 acres in the winter of 1898–99, and 10 acres in the winter of 1899–1900, and was to have the free use of the land so cleared up for three years thereafter; that appellee agreed to erect a dwelling house, smoke house, kitchen, and stable on the leased premises for his occupancy, and was to furnish a team of oxen with which to break up the land as soon as it was cleared, and that he was also to remove all logs lying upon the land at the time of the lease, and was to erect a tobacco barn for his use; that it was a part of the agreement that the contract was to be put in writing, and, relying upon appellee's promise to do so, he moved his personal effects into an old house located upon the land until the new one was finished, and gave up the premises previously occupied by him; that after such removal appellee denied that he had agreed to furnish the cattle to break up the land, or to remove the logs, or to erect a tobacco barn, and refused to sign a contract embracing these stipulations; and that such refusal necessitated an abandonment on his part of the leased premises. He says that, as a result of this failure on the part of appellee to comply with his contract, he has been damaged in $100, cost of removing his effects, $50 for time lost in hunting up another place, $200 in prospective profits which he would have realized by reason of his bargain, and $300 by reason of having been induced to surrender the premises formerly occupied by him, making in the aggregate the sum of $650. The court sustained a general demurrer to the petition, and from that judgment this appeal is prosecuted.

Section 470 of the Kentucky Statutes provides: "No action shall be brought to charge any person upon any contract for the sale of real estate, or any lease thereof, for a longer term than one year, nor upon any agreement which is not to be performed within one year from the making thereof, unless the promise, contract, agreement, or some memorandum or note thereof be in writing and signed by the party to be charged therewith." Under this provision of the statute, the alleged verbal contract was not binding or enforceable upon the parties thereto, for the reason that it was a contract for the lease of real estate for a longer term than one year, and was an agreement which was not to be performed within one year from the making thereof; and, as the contract itself was not enforceable between the parties, no action for damages for refusing to execute it or to reduce it to writing can be maintained, as "it would leave but little, if anything, of the statute of frauds, to hold that a party might be mulcted in damages for refusing to execute in writing a verbal agreement which, unless in writing, is invalid under the statute of frauds." . . .

For reasons indicated, the judgment is affirmed.

CHARLES R. ABLETT CO. v. SENCER
City Court of New York, 130 Misc. Rep. 416 (1927).

Action by the Charles R. Ablett Company against Philip Sencer. Verdict for plaintiff. On defendant's motion to set aside verdict, and for new trial. Motion denied.

SHIENTAG, J.   Plaintiff and defendant entered into an agreement on April 12, 1927, for the sale of a certain quantity of electric bulbs for the sum of $550. The defendant gave the plaintiff his check on the same day for the full amount of the purchase price, and obtained from the plaintiff a receipted bill for the merchandise in question. Subsequently the defendant, the drawer, stopped payment on the check. The plaintiff brings suit on the check, and the only defense with which we are here concerned is that of the statute of frauds. There was no acceptance and actual receipt of any part of the goods by the defendant. The plaintiff having made no point of it, I shall assume for the purpose of this motion that there was no memorandum in writing by the party sought to be held on the contract.

The plaintiff contends that the defendant's check, although subsequently dishonored, constituted a payment of the purchase price within the meaning of the statute, thus dispensing with the necessity of a writing. This year marks the 250th anniversary of the enactment of the statute of frauds in England, section 17 of which, in substantially its original form, is in force in this state today. Section 85, subd. 1, of the Personal Property Law. Considering the nature and age of the statute, it is not surprising that there has been such a wide difference of opinion among jurists and legal scholars concerning its usefulness and efficacy. . . .

With the wisdom of legislation, as such, courts can have no concern. It is important, however, in construing the statute in the light of modern conditions, to consider some of the reasons which led to its enactment. The original statute of frauds was stated to have been passed "for the prevention of many fraudulent practices which are commonly endeavored to be upheld by perjury and subornation of perjury." Holdsworth points out that in 1677, when the statute went into effect, trial by jury was still in the stage where a jury might decide a case upon its own knowledge of the facts. Furthermore, under the then existing rules of evidence, "neither of the parties to an action, nor their husbands or wives, nor any person who had any interest in the result of the litigation, were competent witnesses." 6 Holdsworth, 388. A man sued on an oral contract, not being permitted to testify himself, was practically helpless in the face of any attempted perjury. The intention of the statute obviously was, as summed up by the Earl of Halsbury, L. C., in Norton v. Davison (L. R. 1899) Q. B. 401: "That mere words of mouth should not be sufficient to establish a contract for the sale of goods exceeding the prescribed value, but that something besides should be necessary for that purpose." Page 404.

So the statute in the original form provided in substance that no contract for the sale of goods of the value of £10 sterling or upwards should be allowed to be good unless some note or memorandum in writing of the bargain be made and signed by the parties to be charged therewith (in New York the party to be charged) or their duly authorized agents.

The requirement of a writing was dispensed with if certain acts were performed, viz: (1) If the buyer shall accept and actually receive a part of the goods sold; or (2) if the buyer shall give something in earnest to bind the bargain or in part payment. On this motion I am concerned solely with the second exception. "The giving of earnest and the part payment of the price are two facts independent of the bargain, capable of proof by parol, and the framers of the statute of frauds said in effect that either of them, if proven in addition to parol proof of the contract itself, is a sufficient safeguard against fraud and perjury to render the contract good without a writing." Benjamin on Sales (6th Ed.) p. 255. Today the giving of earnest and part payment are practically synonymous. Some overt act is what the framers wanted in addition to words of mouth. The statute places no limitation on the manner in which payment shall be made.

The payment may be in the form of any personal property. "The statute requires that he should pay some part of the purchase money. No doubt it must be taken, in its spirit, to mean anything or part of anything given, by way of consideration, which is money or money's worth. But the object was to have something pass between the parties besides mere words; some symbol like earnest money (2 Black. Com. 448).   . . . One object of the statute was to prevent perjury. The method taken was to have something done; not to rest everything upon mere oral agreement." Cowen, J., in Artcher v. Zeh, 5 Hill, 200, 205.   . . .

Is the delivery by the vendee to the vendor of the former's check for the purchase price in and of itself a payment within the statute, regardless of what may thereafter become of the check? What is meant by the term "payment" as used in the statute? "Payment is not a technical term," says Mr. Justice Maule in Maillard v. Duke of Argyle, 6 Man. & G. 40; "it has been imported into law proceedings from the exchange, and not from law treatises."   . . .   "* * * Checks are in common use, and pass from hand to hand. It is the usual and ordinary way of transacting business of any magnitude, and courts take judicial notice of such custom." Rohrbach v. Hammill, 162 Iowa, 131, 143 N. W. 872, 875. In Gould v. Town of Oneonta, 71 N. Y. 298, 307, the court said: "Cash payment of such large sums is usually made by check. In such a case the check may be regarded as the representative of the money."

Since that case was decided it has become the practice in the commercial world to make substantially all payments, large or small, by check.

A check bearing the date on which it is issued   . . .   is the commonly accepted method of payment in the business world today, and has largely supplanted the use of currency as a medium for barter and exchange. The giving of such a check is an overt act more easily proved, and less susceptible to misconstruction or perjury than the payment of a sum in currency. . . . It is objected that a draft or check of a debtor is only conditional payment, and not satisfaction of the debt for which it is given, in the absence of some agreement to the contrary. That, it is submitted, has nothing to do with the application of the statute of frauds. The statute is not concerned with the legal effect of the payment; it says nothing about the payment being in satisfaction, wholly or in part, of the vendor's claim. The purpose of the statute is fully satisfied by the physical delivery of the instrument, the overt act indicating that there was a bargain between the parties. How is this outward manifestation affected by what may subsequently happen to the instrument or other article that the buyer delivers to the seller at the time of the bargain?

. . . . .

The purpose of the statute as so declared is accomplished regardless of what may thereafter happen to the check. It is the delivery and acceptance of the check which constitute the overt act required by the statute. . . .

. . . . .

In the instant case the check is for the full amount of the purchase price, and when the check was delivered to the seller he gave the buyer a receipted bill for the merchandise sold. Obviously the check in this case was received as a payment. The written exhibits so indicate, and I so find. . . . [T]he vendee's check, although it was subsequently dishonored, was given in payment within the meaning of section 85 of the Personal Property Law. The defense of the statute of frauds must therefore fail.

Statute of Frauds—Original English Statutes

Most states have statutes that provide certain promises will not be enforced unless they are evidenced by a writing. This requirement is derived from the English Statute of Frauds, originally enacted in 1677. Below are portions of the original English statute.

THE STATUTE OF FRAUDS,
An Act for Prevention of Frauds and Perjuries, Stat. 29, Car. II, c. 3 (1677).

Section 4. And be it further enacted by the authority aforesaid, That from and after the said four and twentieth day of June [1677] no action shall be brought

(1) whereby to charge any executor or administrator upon any special promise, to answer damages out of his own estate;

(2) or whereby to charge the defendant upon any special promise to answer for the debt, default or miscarriages of another person;

(3) or to charge any person upon any agreement made upon consideration of marriage; or

(4) upon any contract or sale of lands, tenements or hereditaments, or any interest in or concerning them;

(5)   or upon any agreement that is not to be performed within the space of one year from the making thereof;

(6)   unless the agreement upon which such action shall be brought, or some memorandum or note thereof, shall be in writing, and signed by the party to be charged therewith or some other person thereunto by him lawfully authorized.

.   .   .   .

Section 17. And be it further enacted by the authority aforesaid, That from and after the said four and twentieth of June no contract for the sale of any goods, wares and merchandizes, for the price of ten pounds sterling or upwards, shall be allowed to be good except the buyer shall accept part of the goods so sold, and actually receive the same, or give something in earnest to bind the bargain, or in part of payment, or that some note or memorandum in writing of the said bargain be made and signed by the parties to be charged by such contract, or their agents thereunto lawfully authorized.

REMEDIES FOR BREACH OF CONTRACT—SOCIETY AND THE BROKEN PROMISE

The most impeccably formed contract can be broken by either of the parties. At the moment of the breach, the contract becomes a scrap of paper. It is worthless to the injured party, that is, the party injured by the breach, unless and until he proceeds in a court of law to enforce his rights and to assert against the defaulting party that party's obligations. The procedures by which an injured party under a breach of contract must proceed are set forth in sufficient detail in Chapter 9, on "The Trial."

Society does not punish a person who defaults in the performance of his contractual obligation, as it punishes a criminal for his crime. Neither does it readily entertain a case against contract breakers, as it does against a tortfeasor for his tort (described in Chapter 5). Throughout history, society has been slow to proceed against a member whose sole offense has been failure to keep his contractual obligation to another member of society. Even during the formation of the Christian ethic and at the very zenith of Puritanism, in which a shrewd bargain was an aspect of godliness, defaulters in contract performance were not put in the stocks. That punishment might be exacted for nodding in church or for various forms of erotic behavior, but not for breach of a contract.

The principles of recompense for the injured party under a breach of contract have developed as slowly and as precisely as have the principles for determination of the formation, or creation, of the contract. Society through the courts seeks to develop criteria for determining what amounts of money, called damages, or what actions in kind called specific performance, must be required of the defaulter in order to place the injured party in the position in which he would have been if the contract had been performed.

Let us return to the case stated in the introduction to this chapter. One situation hypothesized was that *A*, having promised *B* a hundred dollars to drive him to California, and *B* having accepted, *A* then defaults. *B* cannot collect the full hundred dollars because he would have had to spend money for gasoline and would have suffered wear and tear and depreciation on his car. Suppose he had been necessarily going to California in any case, then would there have been any damages at all? It is unnecessary to elaborate or define the problems of determining just what it takes to put *B* in just the position he would have been in if *A* had kept the agreement. It is obvious that, even in such a simple case, there are problems of determining the principles of recompense correctly.

It is sometimes possible (1) to allow the injured party money damages in the amount that would give him the "expected fruits" of the bargain. On the other hand, it is sometimes possible (2) only to restore to the disappointed party what he is out of pocket by reason of expenditures made "in reliance" upon the promise of the other party. It is not always the case (3) that even a defaulting party is without rights against the non-defaulting party. A defaulting party who has partly performed and has conferred benefits upon the nondefaulting party in excess of the damage his default has caused may recover the value he has conferred upon the other party, who must restore to the defaulting party either in kind or in money that value. This latter is an example of "restitution."

The terms "expectation," "reliance," and "restitution" are not precise terms importing neat compartments into which every problem of damages must fit. They are useful words, however, for thinking about a philosophy of damages for breach of contract.

Under some circumstances the parties to a contract may agree on an amount that will be paid in case of default, but there are severe limitations on their right to take that course. The amount may not be arbitrary or utterly unrelated to the amount of injury suffered by the non-defaulting party; nor can a nondefaulting party demand his pound of flesh. He may not callously allow the amount of damages to increase when, under some circumstances, he himself could take action to avoid or minimize his injury.

There are some subjects of contract with respect to which the non-defaulting party cannot be compensated by money. Land is one. Courts will require a seller of land to convey that precise land. Money is no adequate remedy. Likewise, if a certain unique chattel, for example, the Hope diamond or the horse Keno is the subject of the contract, then money compensation is inadequate—the chattel itself must be delivered.

This is an appropriate place to refer again to an oversimplification of the distinction between law and equity. For the great mass of breached contracts, money, the amount of which is to be determined under the principles enunciated in the cases in this section, is an adequate remedy. Money is the usual remedy—the remedy that is allowed in courts of law. When money is not an adequate remedy, when there must be delivery in kind, called specific performance, the action for that form of remedy must occur in equity.

There is a popular misconception that principles of equity are more flexible and are less rigid or less constraining on the injured party than are the principles of law. The layman likes the term equity and fears the term law. He fancies that equity will always conform to his idea of what justice for him would be. Such is not the case. The criteria for granting relief in equity are as well fixed as the criteria for determining the amount of money that is to be awarded at law.

There are breaches of contract for which neither money nor specific performance is an effective remedy. We may use the following illustration: Suppose that an opera singer contracts with an opera company to sing and defaults. She may be unique; therefore money damages are inadequate. Equity will not order her to sing because that would make her slave labor—even if equity got over that hurdle, she might sing flat; hence equity would have done more harm than good. However, equity can and will order her not to sing for any other opera company. She has the power to break her contract, but equity has the power to prevent her from selling her voice elsewhere. This is called injunction.

We have spoken of the principles of remedies, but principles do not preexist cases. They are deduced from the decisions of the cases. It is the intellectual struggle of the individual judge writing the rationale for the decision in the individual case that gives the law its awesome charm. It is this process,—sometimes fumbling and halting and sometimes as direct as the shaft from an archer's bow—by which the law has come to increasingly shrewd sanctions for making the promise good. And it is this process which interests us in all its living drama.

REMEDIES AT LAW

Damages and Expectation Interest

HADLEY v. BAXENDALE
In the Court of Exchequer, 9 Exch. 341, 156 Eng. Rep. 145 (1854).

[This is an action for damages for breach of contract. Plaintiff is a flour miller, and defendant is a reputable carrier. A crankshaft on a steam engine used by plaintiff in the milling process became broken, thereby preventing the operation of the mill until the shaft was repaired. Shortly after discovery of the break, plaintiff sent a servant to the office of defendant for the purpose of having the broken shaft transferred to Greenwich for repair. Plaintiff's servant told the defendant's clerk that operations in the flour mill were halted and that the broken shaft must be sent for repair immediately. The clerk replied that if the shaft was delivered to the carrier before noon on any day, it would be delivered to Greenwich on the following day. The plaintiff presented the broken shaft to the defendant for carriage, paid the tariff, and told the defendant's clerk that a special entry, if required, should be made to hasten the delivery of the shaft. The delivery of the shaft was delayed because of some neglect on the part of the defendant. The late delivery of the shaft caused a delay in the working of the mill, resulting in a loss of profits that would otherwise have been received. The defendant argued that these damages were too remote and thus that defendant should not be liable for them. The judge allowed the case to go to the jury, which returned a verdict for the plaintiff with damages £25 beyond the amount paid into court.]

ALDERSON, B.   We think that there ought to be a new trial in this case; but, in so doing, we deem it to be expedient and necessary to state explicitly the rule which the Judge, at the next trial, ought, in our opinion, to direct the jury to be governed by when they estimate the damages.

.   .   .   .

Now we think the proper rule in such a case as the present is this: [Where two parties have made a contract which one of them has broken, the damages which the other party ought to receive in respect of such breach of contract should be such as may fairly and reasonably be considered either arising naturally, i. e., according to the usual course of things, from such breach of contract itself, or such as may reasonably be supposed to have been in the contemplation of both parties, at the time they made the contract, as the probable result of the breach of it.] Now, if the special circumstances under which the contract was actually made were communicated by the plaintiffs to the defendants, and thus known to both parties, the damages resulting from the breach of such a contract, which they would reasonably contemplate, would be the amount of injury which would ordinarily follow from a breach of contract under these special circumstances so known and communicated. But, on the other hand, if these special circumstances were wholly unknown to the party breaking the contract, he, at the most, could only be supposed to have had in his contemplation the amount of injury which would arise generally, and in the great multitude of cases not affected by any special circumstances, from such a breach of contract. For, had the special circumstances been known, the parties might have specially provided for the breach of contract by special terms as to the damages in that case; and of this advantage it would be very unjust to deprive them.

Now the above principles are those by which we think the jury ought to be guided in estimating the damages arising out of any breach of contract. It is said, that other cases such as breaches of contract in the non-payment of money, or in the not making a good title to land, are to be treated as exceptions from this, and as governed by a conventional rule. But as, in such cases, both parties must be supposed to be cognizant of that well-known rule, these cases may, we think, be more properly classed under the rule above enunciated as to cases under known special circumstances, because there both parties may reasonably be presumed to contemplate the estimation of the amount of damages according to the conventional rule.

Now, in the present case, if we are to apply the principles above laid down, we find that the only circumstances here communicated by the plaintiffs to the defendants at the time the contract was made, were, that the article to be carried was the broken shaft of a mill, and that the plaintiffs were the millers of that mill. But how do these circumstances shew reasonably that the profits of the mill must be stopped by an unreasonable delay in the delivery of the broken shaft by the carrier to the third person? Suppose the plaintiffs had another shaft in their possession put up or putting up at the time, and that they only wished to send back the broken shaft to the engineer who made it; it is clear that this would be quite consistent with the above circumstances, and yet the unreasonable delay in the delivery would have no effect upon the intermediate profits of the mill. Or, again, suppose that, at the time of the delivery to the carrier, the machinery of the mill had been in other respects defective, then, also, the same results would follow. Here it is true that the shaft was actually sent back to serve as a model for a new one, and that the want of a new one was the only cause of the stoppage of the mill, and that the loss of profits really arose from not sending down the new shaft in proper time, and that this arose from the delay in delivering the broken one to serve as a model. But it is obvious that, in the great multitude of cases of millers sending off broken shafts to third persons by a carrier under ordinary circumstances, such consequences would not, in all probability, have occurred; and these special circumstances were here never communicated by the plaintiffs to the defendants. It follows, therefore, that the loss of profits here cannot reasonably be considered such a consequence of the breach of contract as could have been fairly and reasonably contemplated by both the parties when they made this contract. For such loss would neither have flowed naturally from the breach of this contract in the great multitude of such cases occurring under ordinary circumstances, nor were the special circumstances, which, perhaps, would have made it a reasonable and natural consequence of such breach of contract, communicated to or known by the defendants. The Judge ought, therefore, to have told the jury, that, upon the facts then before them, they ought not to take the loss of profits into consideration at all in estimating the damages. There must therefore be a new trial in this case.

Rule absolute.

KRAUSS v. GREENBARG
Third Circuit, United States Court of Appeals, 137 F.2d 56 (1943)

GOODRICH, Circuit Judge.   On July 30, 1940, the defendants who used the business name of King Kard Overall Company, received an award and contract from the War Department of the United States to supply 698,084 pairs of leggings. The contract called for deliveries of certain quantities of leggings at stated intervals and provided for a sum as liquidated damages for each day of delay. By a memorandum of the same date the defendants placed an order with the plaintiff, whose business was carried on under the name of American Cord and Webbing Company, for the webbing to be used in making the leggings. The order provided for certain quantities of webbing to be delivered at given dates.

On March 11, 1941, the webbing company started suit in the Eastern District of Pennsylvania to recover $15,326.13 for the webbing sold and delivered to the overall company pursuant to the latter's order. The buyers admitted nonpayment but filed a counterclaim for $22,740.99. The jury returned a verdict in favor of the overall company for the counterclaim. . . .   The webbing company filed this appeal.

The issues raised on this appeal concern the counterclaim. The theory of the counterclaim is that the webbing company did not maintain the scheduled deliveries of the webbing and as a result thereof the overall company could not meet its schedule with the Government. Because of this it incurred the per diem penalty provided for in the government contract for each day's delay in deliveries which amounted to $22,740.99. These special damages it seeks to charge to the webbing company. The latter admits that it failed to deliver the webbing as per schedule. It denies, however, liability on its part for the special damages sought.

The first question for us is to determine the law applicable to the controversy. The webbing company formally acknowledged the order by a letter sent from its New York office, all the prior negotiations having taken place in Philadelphia, where the overall company had its factory. We do not need to determine where the contract was consummated, however, for applying the Pennsylvania conflict of laws rule, as we must, Klaxon Company v. Stentor Electric Manufacturing Co., Inc., 1941, 313 U.S. 487, we find that the right to and measure of damages is governed by the law of the place of performance. . . . Here, the place of performance was at Philadelphia and the Pennsylvania rule of damages controls.

The rule governing special damages in contract cases applied in the Pennsylvania decisions has been that laid down in the leading English case of Hadley v. Baxendale, 9 Ex. 341 (1854). It is that special damages for breach of a contract are not recoverable unless they can fairly and reasonably be considered as arising naturally from the breach or as being within the contemplation of the parties, at the time the contract was made, as the probable result of the breach. [Citations of Pennsylvania cases relying upon Hadley v. Baxendale omitted.] Where the consequential damages claimed were within the contemplation of the parties at the time of the contracting as the probable result of the breach, their recovery has been allowed. [Further Pennsylvania citations omitted.] The question stressed as ultimately determinative   . . .   is whether at the time of making the contract the party who broke his promise knew that his breach would probably result in the kind of special damages claimed and thus could be said to have foreseen them. If he did, then he was liable for the consequential damages.

On this question in the case at bar we have a special finding by the jury. At the trial of the case the court submitted three questions to the jury. One asked whether Krauss [the webbing company] knew, at the time he made his contract with Greenbarg [the overall company], that the latter's contract with the Government provided that delay in delivery would subject it to a penalty. The jury answered yes. This finding, which is unassailed, establishes definitely that the webbing company knew and could have foreseen that if the webbing, which it undertook to furnish, was not delivered as scheduled in the contract and as a result the leggings could not be delivered on time, the overall company would incur the special damages it now claims.

The appellant makes the argument that mere contemplation of future harm is not sufficient to impose liability for that harm as special damages. There must have been virtually a tacit agreement to assume the risk of whatever harm was foreseeable. There is some judicial authority for this view in the highest court of this land. Globe Refining Company v. Landa Cotton Oil Company, 190 U.S. 540 (1903). There is likewise some support for the view in the native home of Hadley v. Baxendale. B. C. Saw-Mill Co. v. Nettleship, L.R. 3 C.P. 499 (1868); Horne v. The Midland Railway Company, L.R. 7 C.P. 583 (1872); L.R. 8 C.P. 131 (1873). The merits of this subsequent restriction on Hadley v. Baxendale have been argued at length. [Citations of treatises and periodicals omitted.] However, as this Court has said many times since Erie Railroad Co. v. Tompkins, 1938, 304 U.S. 64, our duty is to apply state law as we find it in the state decisions irrespective of what we may regard as its merits. Pennsylvania decisions have clearly held, we think, that knowledge of facts which makes special damages foreseeable imposes liability therefor.

.   .   .   .

Causation

The webbing company asserted at the trial, and introduced evidence tending to prove that its delay in furnishing webbing was not the sole cause for the overall company's delay in performance. It claimed as other contributing causes a landlord's distress and eviction at the buyer's factory, a removal by the overall company of its plant, a shortage of eyelets necessary to the manufacture of the leggings, and excessive delay by the manufacturer even after all the webbing had been delivered. Assigned as error, in view of this evidence, is the judge's charge to the jury that although there may have been other contributing causes, if the "primary" "real" "main" "chief" cause of the overall company's delay was the webbing company's failure to deliver on time, then the loss was chargeable to it. That delay, he charged had "to be sufficient in itself to have delayed his [overall company's] contract with the Government."[A] It is contended that in order to charge the penalty to ِhe webbing company, its failure to deliver on time had to be the sole cause of the damage claimed.

We think the trial judge's charge was not open to attack by the appellant. One of the legal tests which must be met in order for something which is a cause in fact to be a "legal cause" is that it shall have been a substantial factor in bringing about the harm. As thus used substantial denotes "the fact that the defendant's conduct has such an effect in producing the harm as to lead reasonable men to regard it as a cause, * * * ." Restatement, Torts (1931) § 431, comment a. . . . If a number of factors are operating one may so predominate in bringing about the harm as to make the effect produced by others so negligible that they cannot be considered substantial factors and hence legal causes of the harm produced. In that event liability attaches, the requisites of legal cause being shown, only to the one responsible for the predominating, or substantial, factor producing the harm. The trial judge in charging the jury, required no less than this.

As he himself says in the opinion on the motion for new trial, the charge in this respect may have been more favorable than the seller of the webbing was entitled to have. In any event, it is not open to attack by the latter.

.   .   .   .

The judgment of the District Court is affirmed.

NEWSOME v. WESTERN UNION TELEGRAPH CO.
Supreme Court of North Carolina, 153 N. C. 153 (1910).

BROWN, J.   .   .   .   The alleged negligence consists in transmitting a telegram to one Royal, Benson, N. C., ordering four gallons corn whisky to be sent by express to Mints

---

[A]The jury specifically found that the penalty incurred by the manufacturer was a loss directly and naturally resulting, as above defined by the trial judge, from the webbing company's failure to deliver on time. The finding itself is not assailed.

Siding, in Sampson county, N. C. The signature was transcribed on the delivered telegram as T. J. Sessons, instead of T. J. Newsome. The plaintiff alleges that he ordered the whisky by agreement with his raft hands, who were preparing to construct rafts and take his timber and rosin to Wilmington during a freshet in February, 1902, and that they refused to go into the water without it, in consequence of which he lost the benefit of the freshet, and was greatly endamaged.

The defendant requested an instruction that in no view of the evidence can plaintiff recover more than nominal damage, which was refused. The courts will be careful not to apply to a contract of this character a rule of damage which will impose upon the defendant an unreasonable and speculative liability, which an individual may avoid by declining to enter into the contract. The fact that the plaintiff informed the defendant's operator that he needed the whisky in order to get his rafting done will not allow us to hold the defendant to damages which from the very nature of the case must be purely speculative and remote. It should be borne in mind that the defendant, being a public agency, was compelled to accept the telegram, and to agree with the plaintiff, at the price fixed by the North Carolina Corporation Commission, to transmit it. Under such circumstances it cannot be said that the defendant contracted with reference to the damages claimed by the plaintiff simply because its agent was informed of the purpose for which the plaintiff wanted the whisky. While we apply the rule of Hadley v. Baxendale to this kind of a contract, yet that rule will not justify the imposition of remote and speculative damages upon a public service corporation.

.   .   .   .

The fact that the whisky was not sent may have caused the hands not to go into the water, but it is a far cry between constructing the raft at Thomas and marketing the product at Wilmington. The whisky may have arrived and still the raft remain unconstructed. The raft may have been constructed and loaded, and still never have reached Wilmington. It requires quite a stretch of the imagination to conceive that, had the four gallons of corn whisky arrived at Thomas, the raft would have been properly constructed, loaded, and safely conducted over a heavy freshet to Wilmington, and the merchandize duly and profitably marketed. Whisky is very potential at times, but it cannot be relied upon to produce such beneficent results as is claimed for it in this case. It is a singular fact in the county where the four gallons of corn whisky were expected to produce such unusual results its use was decried and its sale prohibited by law. It was contraband, outlawed, and dealing in it made a crime.

We are of opinion that the plaintiff is entitled to recover nominal damages only.

Reliance Interest

SECURITY STOVE & MFG. CO. v. AMERICAN RY. EXPRESS CO.
Kansas City Court of Appeals, Missouri, 227 Mo. App. 175 (1932).

BLAND, J.   This is an action for damages for the failure of defendant to transport, from Kansas City to Atlantic City, New Jersey, within a reasonable time, a furnace equipped with a combination oil and gas burner. The cause was tried before the court without the aid of a jury, resulting in a judgment in favor of plaintiff in the sum of $801.50 and interest, or in a total sum of $1,000.00. Defendant has appealed.

The facts show that plaintiff manufactured a furnace equipped with a special combination oil and gas burner it desired to exhibit at the American Gas Association Convention held in Atlantic City in October, 1926. The president of plaintiff testified that plaintiff engaged space for the exhibit for the reasons "that the Henry L. Dougherty Company was very much interested in putting out a combination oil and gas burner; we had just developed one, after we got through, better than anything on the market and we thought this show would be the psychological time to get in contact with the Dougherty Company"; that "the thing wasn't sent there for sale but primarily to show"; that at the time the space was engaged it was too late to ship the furnace by freight so plaintiff decided to ship it by express, and, on September 18th, 1926, wrote the office of the defendant in Kansas City, stating that it had engaged a booth for exhibition purposes at Atlantic City, New Jersey, from the American Gas Association, for the week beginning October 11th; that its exhibit consisted of an oil burning furnace, together with two oil burners which weighed at least 1,500 pounds; that, "In order to get this exhibit in place on time it should be in Atlantic City not later than October the 8th. What we want you to do is to tell us how much time you will require to assure the delivery of the exhibit on time."

Mr. Bangs, chief clerk in charge of the local office of the defendant, upon receipt of the letter, sent Mr. Johnson, a commercial representative of the defendant, to see plaintiff. Johnson called upon plaintiff taking its letter with him. Johnson made a notation on the bottom of the letter giving October 4th as the day that defendant was required to have the exhibit in order for it to reach Atlantic City on October 8th.

On October 1st, plaintiff wrote the defendant at Kansas City, referring to its letter of September 18th, concerning the fact that the furnace must be in Atlantic City not later than October 8th, and stating what Johnson had told it, saying: "Now Mr. Bangs, we want to make doubly sure that this shipment is in Atlantic City not later than October 8th and the purpose of this letter is to tell you that you can *have your truck call for the shipment between 12 and 1 o'clock on Saturday, October 2nd for this.*" (Italics plaintiff's) On October 2nd, plaintiff called the office of the express company in Kansas City and told it that the shipment was ready. Defendant came for the shipment on the last mentioned day, received it and delivered the express receipt to plaintiff. The shipment contained 21 packages. Each package was marked with stickers backed with glue and covered with silica of soda, to prevent the stickers being torn off in shipping. Each package was given a number. They ran from 1 to 21.

Plaintiff's president made arrangements to go to Atlantic City to attend the convention and install the exhibit, arriving there about October 11th. When he reached Atlantic City he found the shipment had been placed in the booth that had been assigned to plaintiff. The exhibit was set up, but it was found that one of the packages shipped was not there. This missing package contained the gas manifold, or that part of the oil and gas burner that controlled the flow of gas in the burner. This was the most important part of the exhibit and a like burner could not be obtained in Atlantic City.

Wires were sent and it was found that the stray package was at the "over and short bureau" of defendant in St. Louis. Defendant reported that the package would be forwarded to Atlantic City and would be there by Wednesday, the 13th. Plaintiff's president waited until Thursday, the day the convention closed, but the package had not arrived at the time, so he closed up the exhibit and left. About a week after he arrived in Kansas City, the package was returned by the defendant.

. . . . .

Plaintiff asked damages, which the court in its judgment allowed as follows: $147.00 express charges (on the exhibit); $45.12 freight on the exhibit from Atlantic City to Kansas City; $101.39 railroad and pullman fares to and from Atlantic City, expended by plaintiff's president and a workman taken by him to Atlantic City; $48.00 hotel room for the two; $150.00 for the time of the president; $40.00 for wages for plaintiff's other employee and $270.00 for rental of the booth, making a total of $801.51.

. . . . .

We think, under the circumstances in this case, that it was proper to allow plaintiff's expenses as its damages. Ordinarily the measure of damages where the carrier fails to deliver a shipment at destination within a reasonable time is the difference between the market value of the goods at the time of delivery and the time when they should have been delivered. But where the carrier has notice of peculiar circumstances under which the shipment is made, which will result in an unusual loss by the shipper in case of delay in delivery, the carrier is responsible for the real damage sustained from such delay if the notice given is of such character, and goes to such extent, in informing the carrier of the shipper's situation, that the carrier will be presumed to have contracted with reference thereto.   . . .

In the case at bar defendant was advised of the necessity of prompt delivery of the shipment. Plaintiff explained to Johnson the "importance of getting the exhibit there on time." Defendant knew the purpose of the exhibit and ought to respond for its negligence in failing to get it there. As we view the record this negligence is practically conceded. The undisputed testimony shows that the shipment was sent to the over and short department of the defendant in St. Louis. As the packages were plainly numbered this, prima facie, shows mistake or negligence on the part of the defendant. No effort was made by it to show that it was not negligent in sending it there, or not negligent in not forwarding it within a reasonable time after it was found.

. . . . .

Defendant contends that plaintiff "is endeavoring to achieve a return of the status quo in a suit based on a breach of contract. Instead of seeking to recover what he would have had, had the contract not been broken, plaintiff is trying to recover what he would have had, had there never been any contract of shipment"; "that the expenses sued for would have been incurred in any event. It is no doubt the general rule that where there is a breach of contract the party suffering the loss can recover only that which he would have had, had the contract not been broken, and this is all the cases decided upon which defendant relies,   . . .   But this is merely a general statement of the rule and is not inconsistent with the holdings that, in some instances, the injured party may recover expenses incurred in relying upon the contract, although such expenses would have been incurred had the contract not been breached.   . . .

In Sperry et al. v. O'Neill-Adams Co. (C.C.A.) 185 F. 231, the court held that the advantages resulting from the use of trading stamps as a means of increasing trade are so contingent that they cannot form a basis on which to rest a recovery for a breach of contract to supply them. In lieu of compensation based thereon the court directed a recovery in the sum expended in preparation for carrying on business in connection with the use of the stamps. The court said, loc. cit. 239:

"Plaintiff in its complaint had made a claim for lost profits, but, finding it impossible to marshal any evidence which would support a finding of exact figures, abandoned that claim. Any attempt to reach a precise sum would be mere blind guesswork. Nevertheless a contract, which both sides conceded would prove a valuable one, had been broken and the party who broke it was responsible for resultant damage. In order to carry out this contract, the plaintiff made expenditures which otherwise it would not have made. . . . The trial judge held, as we think rightly, that plaintiff was entitled at least to recover these expenses to which it had been put in order to secure the benefits of a contract of which defendant's conduct deprived it."

.   .   .

The case at bar was [not] to recover damages for loss of profits by reason of the failure of the defendant to transport the shipment within a reasonable time, so that it would arrive in Atlantic City for the exhibit. There were no profits contemplated. The furnace was to be shown and shipped back to Kansas City. There was no money loss, except the expenses, that was of such a nature as any court would allow as being sufficiently definite or lacking in pure speculation. Therefore, unless plaintiff is permitted to recover the expenses that it went to, which were a total loss to it by reason of its inability to exhibit the furnace and equipment, it will be deprived of any substantial compensation for its loss. The law does not contemplate any such injustice. It ought to allow plaintiff, as damages, the loss in the way of expenses that it sustained, and which it would not have been put to if it had not been for its reliance upon the defendant to perform its contract. . . .

.   .   .

The judgment is affirmed.
All concur.

Restitution Interest

BRITTON v. TURNER
Superior Court of Judicature of New Hampshire, 6 N.H. 481 (1834).

Assumpsit for work and labor, performed by the plaintiff, in the service of the defendant, from March 9th, 1831, to December 27, 1831.

The declaration contained the common counts, and among them a count in *quantum meruit,* for the labor, averring it to be worth one hundred dollars.

At the trial in the C. C. Pleas, the plaintiff proved the performance of the labor as set forth in the declaration.

The defence was that it was performed under a special contract—that the plaintiff agreed to work one year, from some time in March, 1831, to March, 1832, and that the defendant was to pay him for said year's labor the sum of one hundred and twenty dollars; and the defendant offered evidence tending to show that such was the contract under which the work was done.

Evidence was also offered to show that the plaintiff left the defendant's service without his consent, and it was contended by the defendant that the plaintiff had no good cause for not continuing in his employment.

There was no evidence offered of any damage arising from the plaintiff's departure, farther than was to be inferred from his nonfulfillment of the entire contract.

The court instructed the jury that if they were satisfied from the evidence that the labor was performed, under a contract to labor a year, for the sum of one hundred and twenty dollars, and if they were satisfied that the plaintiff labored only the time specified in the declaration, and then left the defendant's service, against his consent, and without any good cause, yet the plaintiff was entitled to recover, under his quantum meruit count, as much as the labor he performed was reasonably worth, and under this direction the jury gave a verdict for the plaintiff for the sum of $95.

The defendant excepted to the instructions thus given to the jury.

.   .   .   .

PARKER, J.   It may be assumed that the labor performed by the plaintiff, and for which he seeks to recover a compensation in this action, was commenced under a special contract to labor for the defendant the term of one year, for the sum of one hundred and twenty dollars, and that the plaintiff has labored but a portion of that time, and has voluntarily failed to complete the entire contract. It is clear, then, that he is not entitled to recover upon the contract itself, because the service, which was to entitle him to the sum agreed upon, has never been performed.

But the question arises, can the plaintiff, under these circumstances, recover a reasonable sum for the service he has actually performed, under the count in *quantum meruit?* Upon this, and questions of a similar nature, the decisions to be found in the books are not easily reconciled. It has been held, upon contracts of this kind for labor to be performed at a specified price, that the party who voluntarily fails to fulfil the contract by performing the whole labor contracted for, is not entitled to recover anything for the labor actually performed, however much he may have done toward the performance; and this has been considered the settled rule of law upon this subject.   .   .   .

That such a rule in its operation may be very unequal, not to say unjust, is apparent. A party who contracts to perform certain specified labor, and who breaks his contract in the first instance, without any attempt to perform it, can only be made liable to pay the damages which the other party has sustained by reason of such nonperformance, which in many instances may be trifling; whereas a party who in good faith has entered upon the performance of his contract, and nearly completed it, and then abandoned the further performance,—although the other party has had the full benefit of all that has been done, and has perhaps sustained no actual damage,—its fact subjected to a loss of all which has been performed, in the nature of damages for the nonfulfillment of the remainder, upon the technical rule, that the contract must be fully performed in order to [allow] a recovery of any part of the compensation.

By the operation of this rule, the party who attempts performance may be placed in a much worse situation than he who wholly disregards his contract, and the other party may receive much more, by the breach of the contract, than the injury which he has sustained by such breach, and more than he could be entitled to were he seeking to recover damages by an action.

The case before us presents an illustration. Had the plaintiff in this case never entered upon the performance of his contract, the damage could not probably have been greater than some small expense and trouble incurred in procuring another to do the labor which he had contracted to perform. But having entered upon the performance, and labored nine and a half months, the value of which labor to the defendant as found by the jury is $95, if the defendant can succeed in this defence, he in fact receives nearly five sixths of the value of a whole year's labor, by reason of the breach of contract by the plaintiff, a sum not only utterly disproportionate to any probable, not to say possible damage which could have resulted from the neglect of the plaintiff to continue the remaining two and a half months, but altogether beyond any damage which could have been recovered by the defendant, had the plaintiff done nothing towards the fulfillment of his contract.

.   .   .   .

The benefit and advantage which the party takes by the labor, therefore, is the amount of value which he receives, if any, after deducting the amount of damage; and if he elects to put this in defence he is entitled so to do, and the implied promise which the law will raise, in such a case, is to pay such amount of the stipulated price for the whole labor, as remains after deducting what it would cost to procure a completion of the residue of the service, and also any damage which has been sustained by reason of the nonfulfilment of the contract.

If in such case it be found that the damages are equal to or greater than the amount of the labor performed, so that the employer, having a right to the full performance of the contract has not upon the whole case received a beneficial service, the plaintiff cannot recover.

This rule, by binding the employer to pay the value of the service he actually receives, and the laborer to answer in damages where he does not complete the entire contract, will leave no temptation to the former to drive the laborer from his service, near the close of his term, by ill treatment, in order to escape from payment; nor to the latter to desert his service before the stipulated time, without a sufficient reason; and it will in most instances settle the whole controversy in one action, and prevent a multiplicity of suits and cross actions.

There may be instances, however, where the damage occasioned is much greater than the value of the labor performed, and if the party elects to permit himself to be charged for the value of the labor, without interposing the damages in defence, he is entitled to do so, and may have an action to recover his damages for the nonperformance, whatever, they may be.   .   .   .

And he may commence such action at any time after the contract is broken, notwithstanding no suit has been instituted against him; but if he elects to have the damages considered in the action against him, he must be understood as conceding that they are not to be extended beyond the amount of what he has received, and he cannot afterwards sustain an action for farther damages.

Applying the principles thus laid down, to this case, the plaintiff is entitled to judgment on the verdict.

OTHER CONSIDERATIONS IN AWARDING DAMAGES

Liquidated Damages and Penalties

CLYDEBANK ENGINEERING AND SHIPBUILDING COMPANY, LTD. AND OTHERS
v. DON JOSE RAMOS YZQUIERDO Y CASTANEDA
House of Lords, [1905] App. Cas. 6.

Appeal against a judgment of the Second Division of the Court of Session, Scotland.

The Spanish Government, represented by the respondents, sought to recover from the appellants the penalties alleged to have been incurred by the appellants under a contract dated June 4, 1896, for the construction of two torpedo-boat destroyers, afterwards named *Audaz* and *Osado*, and the penalties alleged to have been incurred by the appellants under another contract dated November 24, 1896, for the construction of two torpedo-boat destroyers, afterwards named *Pluton* and *Proserpina.*

These contracts were entered into between the then chief of the Spanish Royal Naval Commission in London, the commissary of that commission, in the name and representation of His Excellency the Spanish Minister of Marine in Madrid, for the Spanish Government, on the one part, and the appellants (inter alios) James and George Thomson, Limited, engineers and shipbuilders, Clydebank, Scotland, of the other part.

The contracts were for building four torpedo-boat destroyers for the Spanish Government. They contained the following clauses:

In the first, the contractors "undertake that the said vessels shall be finished, complete and ready for sea, the first vessel in six and three-quarter months, and the second in seven and three-quarter months, from the signing of this contract and accompanying specifications and plans."

The second contract dealt with the third and fourth vessels, and promised that these vessels should be delivered in six and a half and seven and a half months respectively. The contracts contained also this clause: "The penalty for later delivery shall be at the rate of £500 per week for each vessel not delivered by the contractors in the contract time."

The two vessels built under the first contract, namely, the *Audaz* and *Osado,* should under the terms of the contract have been delivered on April 23, 1897, respectively. They were in point of fact, not delivered until March 7, 1898.

The two vessels built under the other contract, namely, the *Pluton* and *Proserpina,* should under the terms of the contract have been delivered on June 14, and July 13, 1897, respectively; but the *Pluton* was not delivered until November 30, 1897, and the *Proserpina* until February 8, 1898.

The respondents, after receiving delivery, and paying the price of the vessels, claimed under the penalty clause in respect of each vessel; and on June 17, 1903 (1), the Second Division of the Court of Session, affirming the interlocutor of the Lord Ordinary (Lord Kyllachy), allowed a total of 135 weeks' delay, or damages of about £67,500 in all, with interest.

The appellants maintained that the penalty named in the contracts was not truly liquidated damages pre-estimated by the parties as the loss which might be sustained through a breach of the contract, but a penalty in the strict sense of the word, and therefore recoverable only to the extend to which actual loss or damage was proved by the respondents. In this view, the appellants maintained that on the most liberal estimate the only damages proved by the respondents amounted to £312 .

.   .   .   .

EARL OF HALSBURY L.C.   My Lords, this is a case in which a party to an agreement has admittedly broken it, and an action was brought for the purpose of enforcing the payment of a sum of money which, by the agreement between the parties, was fixed as that which the defenders were to pay in the event that has happened.

Two objects have been made to the enforcement of that payment. The first objection is one which appears upon the face of the instrument itself, namely, that it is a penalty, and not, therefore, recoverable as a pactional arrangement of the amount of damages resulting from the breach of contract. It cannot, I think, be denied—indeed, I think it has been frankly admitted by the learned counsel—that not much reliance can be placed upon the mere use of certain words. Both in England and in Scotland it has been pointed out that the Court must proceed according to what is the real nature of the transaction   . . . .

We come then to the question, What is the agreement here? and whether this sum of money is one which can be recovered as an agreed sum as damages, or whether, as has been contended, it is simply a penalty to be held over the other party in terrorem —whether it is, what I think gave the jurisdiction to the Courts in both countries to interfere at all in an agreement between the parties, unconscionable and extravagant, and one which no Court ought to allow to be enforced.

My Lords, it is impossible to lay down any abstract rule as to what it may or it may not be extravagant or unconscionable to insist upon without reference to the particular facts and circumstances which are established in the individual case. I suppose it would be possible in the most ordinary case, where people know what is the thing to be done and what is agreed to be paid, to say whether the amount was unconscionable or not. For instance, if you agreed to build a house in a year, and agreed that if you did not build the house for £ 50, you were to pay a million of money as a penalty, the extravagance of that would be at once apparent. Between such an extreme case as I have supposed and other cases, a great deal must depend upon the nature of the transaction —the thing to be done, the loss likely to accrue to the person who is endeavouring to enforce the performance of the contract, and so forth. It is not necessary to enter into a minute disquisition upon that subject, because the thing speaks for itself. But, on the other hand, it is quite certain, and an established principle in both countries, that the parties may agree beforehand to say, "Such and such a sum shall be damages if I break my agreement." The very reason why the parties do in fact agree to such a stipulation is that sometimes, although undoubtedly there is damages and undoubtedly damages ought to be recovered, the nature of the damage is such that proof of it is extremely complex, difficult, and expensive. If I wanted an example of what might or might not be said and done in controversies upon damages, unless the parties had agreed beforehand, I could not have a better example than that which the learned counsel has been entertaining us with for the last half-hour in respect of the damage resulting to the Spanish Government by the withholding of these vessels beyond the stipulated period. Supposing there was no such bargain, and supposing the Spanish Government had to prove damages in the ordinary way without insisting upon the stipulated amount of them, just imagine what would have to be the cross-examination of every person connected with the Spanish Administration such as is suggested by the commentaries of the learned counsel: "You have so many thousand miles of coast-line to defend by your torpedo-boat destroyers; what would four torpedo-boat destroyers do for that purpose? How could you say you are damaged by their non-delivery? How many filibustering expeditions could you have stopped by the use of four torpedo-boat destroyers?"

My Lords, I need not pursue that topic. It is obvious on the face of it that the very thing intended to be provided against by this pactional amount of damages is to avoid that kind of minute and somewhat difficult and complex system of examination which would be necessary if you were to attempt to prove the damage. As I pointed out to the learned counsel during the course of his argument, in order to do that properly and to have any real effect upon any tribunal determining that question, one ought to have before one's mind the whole administration of the Spanish Navy—how they were going to use their torpedo-boat destroyers in one place rather than another, and what would be the relative speed of all the boats they possessed in relation to those which they were getting by this agreement. It would be absolutely idle and impossible to enter into a question of that sort unless you had some kind of agreement between the parties as to what was the real measure of damages which ought to be applied.

Then the other learned counsel suggests that you cannot have damages of this character, because really in the case of a warship it has no value at all. That is a strange and somewhat bold assertion. If it was an ordinary commercial vessel capable of being used for obtaining profits, I suppose there would not be very much difficulty in finding out what the ordinary use of a vessel of this size and capacity and so forth would be, what would be the hire of such a vessel, and what would therefore be the equivalent in money of not obtaining the use of that vessel according to the agreement during the period which had elapsed between the time of proper delivery and the time at which it was delivered in fact. But, says the learned counsel, you cannot apply that principle to the case of a warship because a warship does not earn money. It is certainly a somewhat bold contention. I should have thought that the fact that a warship is a warship, her very existence as a warship capable of use for such and such a time, would prove the fact of damage if the party was deprived of it, although the actual amount to be earned by it, and in that sense to be obtained by the payment of the price for it, might not be very easily ascertained—not so easily ascertained as if the vessel were used for commercial purposes and where its hire as a commercial vessel is ascertainable in money. But, my Lords, is that a reason for saying that you are not to have damages at all? It seems to me it is hopeless to make such a contention, and although that would not in itself be a very cogent argument because the law might be so absurd, yet it would be a very startling proposition to say that you never could have agreed damages for the nondelivery of a ship of war although, under the very same words with exactly the same phraseology in the particular contract, you might have damages if it was a vessel used for commercial purposes; so that you would have to give a different construction to the very same words according to whether the thing agreed to be built was a warship or a ship intended for commercial purposes. My Lords, I think it is only necessary to state the contention to show that it is utterly unsound.

Then there comes another argument which, to my mind, is more startling still: the vessel was to be delivered at such and such a time; it was not delivered, but the fleet the Spanish Government had was sent out at such a time and the greater part of it was sunk, and, says the learned counsel, "If we had kept our contract and delivered these vessels they would have shared the fate of the other vessels belonging to the Spanish Government, and therefore in fact you have got your ships now, whereas if we had kept our contract they would have been at the bottom of the Atlantic." My Lords, I confess after some experience, I do not think I ever heard an argument of that sort before, and I do not think I shall often hear it again. Nothing could be more absurd than such a contention, which, if it were reduced to a compendious form such as one has in a marginal note, would certainly be a striking example of jurisprudence. I think I need say no more to show how utterly absurd such a contention is. I pass on to the other question.

It seems to me, when one looks to see what was the nature of the transaction in this case, it is hopeless to contend that the parties only intended this as something in terrorem. Both parties recognised the fact of the importance of time; it is a case in which time is of the essence of the contract and so regarded by both parties, and the particular sum fixed upon as being the agreed amount of damages was suggested by the defendants themselves, and to say that that can be unconscionable or something which the parties ought not to insist upon, that it was a mere holding out something in terrorem, after looking at the correspondence between the parties is, to my mind, not a very plausible suggestion. I have, therefore, come to the conclusion that the judgments of the Courts in Scotland are perfectly right in this respect, and I think there is no ground for the contention that this is not pactional damage agreed to between the parties—and for very excellent reason agreed to between the parties—at the time the contract was entered into.

.   .   .   .

Ordered that the appeal be dismissed with costs.

218–220 MARKET STREET CORP. v. KRICH-RADISCO, INC.
Court of Errors and Appeals of New Jersey, 124 N.J.L. 302 (1940).

PORTER, Justice.   This appeal is from a judgment recovered in the Essex County Circuit Court by the respondent on its counter-claim.

The action was for a breach of contract for the installation of an air conditioning system in the appellant's bar and restaurant. The claim was that the equipment installed was not as specified; that it was not satisfactory in doing the work intended and that it had not been installed within the time limited in the contract. The respondent denied any breach and counter claimed for the sum of $11,400, which was the unpaid balance of the contract price.

.   .   .   .

The first, and perhaps the main point, urged by appellant as reversible error is that the trial court was in error in directing a verdict against it on the fourth count of the complaint. This count sets up the provision of the contract, and charges its breach, it provided that the cooling system be installed and in operation by May 30, 1938, and failing in those respects the respondent shall pay $100 for every day thereafter until the installation and operation be completed as liquidated damages. We think that a legal question for the court rather than a factual one for the jury was presented on this motion as to the legality of this provision of the contract. We conclude that the court was right in granting the motion for two reasons: First—because the testimony, in our view, abundantly establishes the fact that the equipment was installed and in operation on the date mentioned. Secondly—whether that was the fact or not, we conclude that the sum of $100 per day is so out of proportion to any loss which the proofs indicate might result from such breach that is is in fact a penalty and not liquidated damages. We reach that conclusion from a consideration of the amount of the contract price; the nature of the work and its intended purpose; that the period during which this amount is payable is a continuing one and is not limited to the summer season and all the other circumstances of the case. It seems clear that this amount was not based upon damages which would likely flow from a breach but is rather an arbitrary figure unrelated to such damages or losses and was therefore a penalty. Moreover, no testimony was offered to show any loss of business or other specific damage suffered by appellant in the circumstances. This matter of proof of damages will be adverted to again later. The policy of the law is to allow real damages only. If the contract provides damages which will exceed real damages as same may be ascertainable by proof, or damages which are unconscionable or excessive under the circumstances the same are considered as penalties and are unlawful.

The judgment is affirmed.

Mitigation of Damages

ROCKINGHAM COUNTY v. LUTEN BRIDGE CO.
United States Circuit Court of Appeals, Fourth Circuit, 35 F.2d 301 (1929).

PARKER, Circuit Judge.   This was an action at law instituted in the court below by the Luten Bridge Company, as plaintiff, to recover of Rockingham County, North Carolina, an amount alleged to be due under a contract for the construction of a bridge. The county admits the execution and breach of the contract, but contends that notice of cancellation was given the bridge company before the erection of the bridge was commenced, and that it is liable only for the damages which the company would have sustained, if it had abandoned construction at that time.   . . .

The facts out of which the case arises, as shown by the affidavits and offers of proof appearing in the record, are as follows: On January 7, 1924, the board of commissioners of Rockingham county voted to award to plaintiff a contract for the construction of the bridge in controversy. Three of the five commissioners favored the awarding of the contract and two opposed it. Much feeling was engendered over the matter.   . . .

At . . . a regularly advertised called meeting held on February 21st, a resolution was unanimously adopted declaring that the contract for the building of the bridge was not legal and valid, and directing the clerk of the board to notify plaintiff that it refused to recognize same as a valid contract, and that plaintiff should proceed no further thereunder. This resolution also rescinded action of the board theretofore taken looking to the construction of a hard-surfaced road, in which the bridge was to be a mere connecting link. The clerk duly sent a certified copy of this resolution to plaintiff. . . . At the time of the passage of the . . . resolution, very little work toward the construction of the bridge had been done, it being estimated that the total cost of labor done and material on the ground was around $1,900; but, notwithstanding the repudiation of the contract by the county, the bridge company continued with the work of construction.

On November 24, 1924, plaintiff instituted this action against Rockingham county, and against Pruitt, Pratt, McCollum, Martin, and Barber, as constituting its board of commissioners. Complaint was filed, setting forth the execution of the contract and the doing of work by plaintiff thereunder, and alleging that for work done up until November 3, 1924, the county was indebted in the sum of $18,301.07. . . .

[The trial court directed a verdict for plaintiff in the amount of $18,301.07. Defendant appealed.]

Coming, then to the . . . question—i.e., as to the measure of plaintiff's recovery—we do not think that, after the county had given notice, while the contract was still executory, that it did not desire the bridge built and would not pay for it, plaintiff could proceed to build it and recover the contract price. It is true that the county had no right to rescind the contract, and the notice given plaintiff amounted to a breach on its part; but, after plaintiff had received notice of the breach, it was its duty to do nothing to increase the damages flowing therefrom. If A enters into a binding contract to build a house for B, B, of course, has no right to rescind the contract withouth A's consent. But if, before the house is built, he decides that he does not want it, and notifies A to that effect, A has no right to proceed with the building and thus pile up damages. His remedy is to treat the contract as broken when he receives the notice, and sue for the recovery of such damages as he may have sustained from the breach, including any profit which he would have realized upon performance, as well as any other losses which may have resulted to him. In the case at bar, the county decided not to build the road of which the bridge was to be a part, and did not build it. The bridge, built in the midst of the forest, is of no value to the county because of this change of circumstances. When, therefore, the county gave notice to the plaintiff that it would not proceed with the project, plaintiff should have desisted from further work. It had no right thus to pile up damages by proceeding with the erection of a useless bridge.

. . . . .

. . . It follows that there was error in directing a verdict for plaintiff for the full amount of its claim. The measure of plaintiff's damage, upon its appearing that notice was duly given not to build the bridge, is an amount sufficient to compensate plaintiff for labor and materials expended and expense incurred in the part performance of the contract, prior to its repudiation, plus the profit which would have been realized if it had been carried out in accordance with its terms. . . .

. . . The judgment below will accordingly be reversed, and the case remanded for a new trial.

Reversed.

RELIANCE COOPERAGE CORP. v. TREAT
United States Court of Appeals, Eighth Circuit, 195 F.2d 977 (1952).

[The plaintiff, Reliance Cooperage Corp., entered into a written contract with the defendant, Treat, on July 12, 1950. Reliance agreed to buy and Treat agreed to sell a quantity of staves totaling 300,000 white oak bourbon staves of four and one-half inches average width. The production of the staves was to begin as soon as possible and to be completed no later than December 31, 1950. The price agreed upon was 450 per thousand bourbon grade staves.

On August 12, 1950, Treat wrote Reliance a letter in which Treat stated that both his costs and the market price of bourbon staves were rising. According to Treat, at the time of his letter, the market price of such staves was $475–$500 per thousand. Treat's letter continued: "You see I can't compete . . . so if you want those staves I will have to get around whatever is the market from time to time."

During the trial, Treat testified that he telephoned Reliance, shortly after he wrote the letter above, to inform Reliance that he would not make any staves under the contract.

On October 6, 1950, Reliance formally notified Treat by letter that, "We want to make it very clear that we are looking forward to your strict compliance with all the obligations which you have undertaken in your agreement with us." Reliance's letter requested an immediate reply. None was forthcoming.

No staves were delivered, and Reliance brought this action for damages for breach of contract against Treat. The United States Disctrict Court for the Western District of Arkansas entered judgment for plaintiff for the sum of $500. Plaintiff appealed to the Eighth Circuit Court of Appeals. The Eighth Circuit reversed the case and remanded it with directions to grant a new trial limited to issues of damages.]

SANBORN, Circuit Judge.   The question for decision is whether the measure of the general damages recoverable by a purchaser for the nonperformance by a seller of an executory contract for the sale of goods is changed or affected by an unaccepted anticipatory repudiation of the contract by the seller.

.   .   .   .   .

The evidence [presented at the trial] as to the market price of staves on December 31, 1950, would have sustained a finding that it was more than the contract price but not in excess of $750.00 a thousand.

At the close of the evidence, the court was requested by the plaintiff to instruct the jury that the plaintiff was entitled to recover the difference between the contract price of the staves the defendant had promised to deliver on or before December 31, 1950, and the market price of similar staves on that date. The court denied the request.

.   .   .   .   .

We gather from the court's instructions that its opinion was that if the defendant had definitely notified the plaintiff prior to December 31, 1950, that he would not produce and deliver staves under the contract, and that if the plaintiff, notwithstanding its insistence that the contract be fulfilled, by a reasonable effort and without undue risk or expense could then have bought similar staves on the market, the measure of its damages would be the difference between what the plaintiff would have had to pay for staves at the time the defendant announced his refusal of performance and the contract price of such staves.

.   .   .   .   .

A concise statement of the general rule as applied to a sales contract is found in Claes and Lehenbeuter Mfg. Co. v. McCord, 65 Mo.App. 507, 509, in which the court said: "* * * The law is that, where the promisor before the time of performance expressly renounces his contract, the promisee is thereby entitled either to treat the contract as broken and sue at once for its breach without averring an offer or readiness to perform, or he may wait until the time of performance has expired, and then sue for the consequences of nonperformance." That this is still the law . . . is sufficiently evidenced by the following cases: Minneapolis-Moline Power Implement Co. v. Wright, 233 Mo.App. 409, 420–421; The Hiatt Investment Co. v. Buehler, 225 Mo.App. 151, 163–164; Wahl v. Cunningham, 320 Mo. 57 (decided by the Supreme Court of Missouri in banc). The case last cited points out that while as a general rule an action upon an executory contract cannot be maintained until the time for performance has expired, the repudiation of the contract by one of the parties before that time gives to the other party the option to treat the contract as ended and to sue for the damages resulting from the anticipatory breach. In other words, unless the injured party chooses to treat the contract as breached by the anticipatory repudiation, his claim for damages does not accrue until the expiration of the time for performance.

There is no doubt that a party to an executory contract such as that in suit may refuse to accede to an anticipatory repudiation of it and insist upon performance, and, if he does so, the contract remains in existence and is binding on both parties, and no actionable claim for damages arises until the time for performance expires.

It is our opinion that, under the undisputed facts in this case, the unaccepted anticipatory renunciation by the defendant of his obligation to produce and deliver staves under the contract did not impair that obligation or affect his liability for damages for the nonperformance of the contract, and that the measure of those damages was no different than it would have been had no notice of renunciation been given by the defendant to the plaintiff. If there had been no anticipatory repudiation of the contract, the measure of damages for nonperformance by the seller would have been the difference between the contract price and the market price of the staves on the date when delivery was due, and that is the measure which should have been applied in assessing damages in this case.

Moreover, the measure of damages would have been the same had the plaintiff accepted the anticipatory repudiation as an actionable breach of the contract. The plaintiff would still have been entitled to recover what it had lost by reason of the defendant's failure to produce and deliver by December 31, 1950, the staves contracted for, namely, the difference between the market price and the contract price of the staves on that date. The Comment in Restatement of the Law of Contracts, § 338, Measure of Damages for Anticipatory Breach, contains the following statement (page 549): "The fact that an anticipatory repudiation is a breach of contract (see § 318) does not cause the repudiated promise to be treated as if it were a promise to render performance at the date of the repudiation. Repudiation does not accelerate the time fixed for performance; nor does it change the damages to be awarded as the equivalent of the promised performance." . . .

It seems safe to say that ordinarily no obligation to mitigate damages arises until there are damages to mitigate. No damages for the nonperformance of the contract in suit accrued before December 31, 1950. Until that time the defendant, notwithstanding his anticipatory repudiation of the contract, was obligated and was at liberty to produce and deliver the staves, and had he done so the plaintiff would have been required to take and to pay for them. There is no justification for ruling that, after the plaintiff was advised that the defendant did not intend to perform, it must hold itself in readiness to accept performance from him and at the same time, at its own risk and expense, buy the staves contracted for upon the open market in the hope of reducing the defendant's liability for damages in case he persisted in his refusal to fulfill his obligations. The plaintiff did nothing to enhance its damages and seeks no special damages.

This same question as to mitigation of damages by a purchaser who insisted upon performance of a contract after a seller's anticipatory repudiation, arose in Continental Grain Co. v. Simpson Feed Co., D.C.E.D. Ark., 102 F.Supp. 354. In that case Judge Lemley, we think, correctly decided that the purchaser was not required to attempt to mitigate his damages by buying the commodity contracted for upon the open market. Judge Lemley said, page 363 of 102 F.Supp.:

"While we have found no Arkansas cases which are directly in point in connection with mitigation of damages, the general rule in the United States is that a buyer who refuses to accept a seller's anticipatory refusal to deliver the commodities contracted for, and who insists upon performance by the latter, is not required to go upon the open market and purchase upon receipt of notice that the seller does not intend to perform. He has a right to treat the notice as inoperative, to wait until the time for performance has passed, and then buy on the open market, charging the seller with the difference between the contract price of the goods and the market price which prevailed at the time that performance should have been forthcoming. . . .

"There are two reasons for this rule. First, to require the innocent party to make an immediate purchase or sale upon receipt of notice of the other's repudiation would encourage such repudiation on the part of the seller or of the buyer as the market rose or fell. See Fahey v. Updike Elevator Co., [102 Neb. 249, 166 N.W. 622]. Second, the immediate action of the innocent party might not have the effect of mitigating his damages, but might, on the other hand, enhance them. Williston on Contracts, Section 1397, Callan v. Andrews, 48 F.2d 118, 120, and Missouri Furnace Co. v. Cochran, 8 F. 463. . . . "

The doctrine of anticipatory breach by repudiation is intended to aid a party injured as a result of the other party's refusal to perform his contractual obligations, by giving to the injured party an election to accept or to reject the refusal of performance without impairing his rights or increasing his burdens. Any effort to convert the doctrine into one for the benefit of the party who, without legal excuse, has renounced his agreement should be resisted.

The plaintiff is entitled to recover as damages the amount by which on December 31, 1950, the market price of the staves contracted for exceeded their contract price. What the market price of such staves was on that date is a question of fact which has not as yet been determined.

The judgment is reversed and the case is remanded with directions to grant a new trial limited to the issue of the amount of damages.

COMMENTARY ON RELIANCE COOPERAGE CORP. v. TREAT

The Reliance Cooperage case was included as an illustration of a situation in which the doctrine of mitigation of damages does not apply. The court neatly excluded the application of that doctrine by pointing out that a seller who has agreed to deliver on a given date and who, before that date, repudiates his contract and notifies the buyer of his repudiation does not thereby impose on the buyer any obligation to minimize the damages that will fall on the seller for his default. The court reaches this conclusion because of the proposition that damages do not arise until the date for performance, despite the seller's earlier repudiation, and therefore there could be no obligation to mitigate. Well enough—the logic is impeccable.

Now we shall consider whether the basic philosophy of the case was correct. May it not be said that a seller, who knows that he is going to default and who knows that fact at some point of time in advance of the date for performance, is in fact doing a favor to the buyer to notify him of the intended nonperformance then and there? Indeed, the buyer's inconvenience, not to say injury, might be seriously enhanced if the seller simply kept to himself the secret of his intent not to perform.

In the case at hand, Reliance, a barrelmaker, undoubtedly had forward commitments to distillers of whiskey or makers of any other fluid normally kept in barrels. Staves are necessary in the making of barrels, and, to repeat, it might very well be argued that it was the duty of the seller to inform the buyer of his intent not to perform at the earliest possible moment, so that the barrelmaker, who could not make barrels without staves, could make alternative arrangements.

If one accepts this analysis, it is apparent that the reasoning in Reliance must fail. If there is a duty on the seller to notify the buyer as soon as the intent not to perform is established in his mind, then what about the duty of the buyer once the notification has been given? Does the buyer then have an obligation to forthwith establish the measure of the seller's damages? This could have readily been done in the Reliance case by the buyer's going onto the market and procuring the same quantity of staves. In that case the measure of the seller's damages would be the difference between the contract price for the staves and whatever higher price, if any, it cost the buyer to secure the contract-quantity of staves.

In fact, our reasoning is exactly that of the district court in Reliance. This reasoning was rejected on appeal by the Eighth Circuit Court of Appeals but has now been incorporated by legislation into the laws of 49 states. The Uniform Commercial Code (U.C.C.) provides that "the measure of damages for non-delivery or repudiation by the seller is the difference between the market price at the time when the buyer learned of the breach and the contract price." [U.C.C. § 2-713(1)]. This is a clear case of the intervention of legislation to alter a rule of case law. Reliance is overruled by a statute.

The legislation promulgated ensues from the work of the National Conference of Commissioners on Uniform State Laws. The Conference was formed in 1892 because of a concern to produce uniformity in the statutory enactments of the states in areas of the law of nation-wide importance.

Curiously the U.C.C. does not apply the same rule for measuring damages with respect to a buyer who repudiates the contract as it applies to a seller who repudiates. With respect to a repudiating buyer, the U.C.C. fixes the time for determination of damages at the contractual date for performance rather than at the time when the buyer notifies the seller of buyer's intent not to perform. The buyer's repudiation puts no obligation on the seller to mitigate the seller's damages. The seller may await the date scheduled by the contract for delivery and claim his damages as of that date. [U.C.C. § 2-708(1)]. There appears to be no explanation of these differing treatments in the U.C.C. of a repudiating seller and a repudiating buyer. Quite simply, the differentiation may be a mistake. Code draftsmen are not infallible.

REMEDIES IN EQUITY

Specific Performance

BENNETT v. MOON
Supreme Court of Nebraska, 110 Neb. 692 (1923).

[This action for specific performance was instituted by the plaintiff, Bennett, to compel the defendant, Moon, to execute a lease which the defendant had contracted in writing to execute. The plaintiff's action was prompted by the fact that the defendant was in possession of the property from February, 1920 until January, 1921, when he removed his effects and ceased to pay the stipulated rental.

The trial court refused to grant specific performance on the ground that the contract was not complete since the only provisions it contained were those concerning the proposed rental fee and the term for which the lease was to run.

The plaintiff appealed from the denial of specific performance. The Supreme Court of Nebraska reversed the decision of the trial court upon finding that the agreement to execute the lease, in its legal effect, was an agreement for a lease with the usual and ordinary covenants and provisions, and thus was a complete contract. The court remanded the case with instructions to the trial court to award specific performance of the contract to the plaintiff. Portions of the opinion of the Supreme Court of Nebraska concerning specific performance are printed below.]

COLBY, District Judge.

. . . . .

The first question presented for our determination is whether the district court had equitable jurisdiction to decree the specific performance of an executory contract to lease.

The rule of law seems to be well settled that courts of equity will take cognizance of actions requiring the specific performance of agreements concerning real property, and that the rule applies as well to leases as to deeds. This power of courts of equity is regarded as discretionary, yet it is limited to fixed and established equitable principles, and, unless exercised within these limitations, it has been adjudged to be arbitrary and capricious. It is generally held by the best judicial authorities that, under a proper state of facts, the right to the remedy of specific performance is perfect, and the court cannot, in any sense, exercise its discretion to deny relief. It has been announced that when a contract, of which equity has jurisdiction, conforms with certain equitable principles, which are quite limited in number, it is as much a matter of course for a court of equity to decree specific performance as for a court of law to give damages for a breach of the contract. The formula as to judicial discretion, therefore, is habitually used by the courts simply to indicate that the cases before the court are governed, not by legal rules, but by some well-established equitable principles.

Further, where the contracts involved concern land, or, in general, where land or any estate or interest in land is the subject-matter of the agreement, the jurisdiction to enforce specific performance is undisputed, and does not depend upon the inadequacy of the legal remedy in the particular case. To emphasize and restate the above principle, it is as much a matter of course for courts of equity to decree the specific performance of a contract for the conveyance or lease of real estate, which is in its nature unobjectionable, as it is for courts of law to give damages for its breach. Equity seems to have adopted this principle as a general governing rule. This is not because the land is fertile or rich in minerals, but because it is land, "a favorite and favored subject in England and every country of Anglo-Saxon origin." Land is assumed to have a peculiar value so as to give an equity for specific performance without reference to its quality or quantity.

The following extract from 5 Pomeroy, Equitable Remedies (2d Ed.) § 2184, plainly recognizes and enunciates the limitations upon the discretionary latitude applicable to suits for the specific performance of real estate contracts given to courts of equity:

"The granting the equitable remedy is, in the language ordinarily used, a matter of discretion, not arbitrary, capricious discretion, but of a sound judicial discretion, controlled by established principles of equity, and exercised upon a consideration of all the circumstances of each particular case. Where, however, the contract is in writing, is certain in its terms, is for a valuable consideration, is fair and just in all its provisions, and is capable of being enforced without hardship to either party, it is as much a matter of course for a court of equity to decree a specific performance as for a court of law to award a judgment of damages for its breach. This is the ordinary language of judges and text-writers. The term 'discretionary,' as thus used is in my opinion misleading and inaccurate. The remedy of specific performance is governed by the same general rules which control the administration of all other equitable remedies. The right to it depends upon elements, conditions and incidents, which equity regards as essential to the administration of all its peculiar modes of relief. When all these elements, conditions, and incidents exist, the remedial right is perfect in equity."

These limitations upon the discretionary powers of courts of equity have been approved by this court in the following language:

"Whether a decree for the specific performance of an agreement for the sale of real estate will be granted rests in the discretionary powers of the trial court sitting as a court of chancery. Such discretion, however, is not unlimited, and a decree is not to be given nor withheld arbitrarily and capriciously, but it is a judicial discretion, to be controlled and governed by equitable rules and principles." Hoctor-Johnston Co. v. Billings, 65 Neb. 214, 91 N.W. 183. See also Stanton v. Dreftkorn, 83 Neb. 36, 118 N.W. 1092; Waldon v. Lockhard, 96 Neb. 490, 148 N.W. 510.

The foregoing citations are sufficient to authorize us to answer in the affirmative the first question, and to show the recognized principle that equity takes cognizance of all actions requiring the specific performance of an agreement concerning real property or any estate or interest in land, including the execution of leases.

.   .   .   .

Under the established principles of equity and the facts, the plaintiff was entitled to the specific performance of the contract, and to have the defendant execute the lease tendered by the plaintiff and set forth in plaintiff's petition. The decree of the district court is reversed and the cause remanded, with instructions to require of the defendant his specific performance of the agreement as to leasing the premises in question.

Reversed.

MORRIS v. SPARROW
Supreme Court of Arkansas, 225 Ark. 1019 (1956).

ROBINSON, Justice. Appellee Archie Sparrow filed this suit for specific performance, seeking to compel appellant Morris to deliver possession of a certain horse, which Sparrow claims Morris agreed to give him as part consideration for work done by Sparrow. The appeal is from a decree requiring the delivery of the horse.

Morris owns a cattle ranch near Mountain View, Arkansas, and he also participates in rodeos. Sparrow is a cowboy, and is experienced in training horses; occasionally he takes part in rodeos. He lives in Florida; while at a rodeo in that state, he and Morris made an agreement that they would go to Morris' ranch in Arkansas and, later, the two would go to Canada. After arriving at the Morris ranch, they changed their plans and decided that, while Morris went to Canada, Sparrow would stay at the ranch and do the necessary work. The parties are in accord that Sparrow was to work 16 weeks for a money consideration of $400. But, Sparrow says that as an additional consideration he was to receive a brown horse called Keno, owned by Morris. However, Morris states that Sparrow was to get the horse only on condition that his work at the ranch was satisfactory, and that Sparrow failed to do a good job. Morris paid Sparrow the amount of money they agreed was due, but did not deliver the horse.

At the time Sparrow went to Morris' ranch, the horse in question was practically unbroken; but during his spare time, Sparrow trained the horse and, with a little additional training, he will be a first class roping horse.

First there is the issue of whether Sparrow can maintain, in equity, a suit to enforce, by specific performance, a contract for the delivery of personal property. Although it has been held that equity will not ordinarily enforce, by specific performance, a contract for the sale of chattels, it will do so where special and peculiar reasons exist which render it impossible for the injured party to obtain relief by way of damages in an action at law. . . . Moreover, specific performance is authorized by Ark.Stats. § 68–1468, which provides: "Where the seller has broken a contract to deliver specific or ascertained goods, a court having the powers of a court of equity may, if it thinks fit, on the application of the buyer, by its judgment or decreee direct that the contract shall be performed specifically, without giving the seller the option of retaining the goods on payment of damages. * * *" Certainly when one has made a roping horse out of a green, unbroken pony, such a horse would have a peculiar and unique value; if Sparrow is entitled to prevail, he has a right to the horse instead of its market value in dollars and cents.

Affirmed.

. . . .

CAMPBELL SOUP CO. v. WENTZ
United States Court of Appeals, Third Circuit, 172 F.2d 80 (1948).

GOODRICH, Circuit Judge. These are appeals from judgments of the District Court denying equitable relief to the buyer under a contract for the sale of carrots. . . .

The transactions which raise the issues may be briefly summarized. On June 21, 1947, Campbell Soup Company (Campbell) a New Jersy corporation, entered into a written contract with George B. Wentz and Harry T. Wentz, who are Pennsylvania farmers, for delivery by the Wentzes to Campbell of all the Chantenay red cored carrots to be grown on fifteen acres of the Wentz farm during the 1947 season. Where the contract was entered into does not appear. The contract provides, however, for delivery of the carrots at the Campbell plant in Camden, New Jersey. The prices specified in the contract ranged from $23 per ton according to the time of delivery. The contract price for January, 1948 was $30 a ton.

The Wentzes harvested approximately 100 tons of carrots from the fifteen acres covered by the contract. Early in January, 1948, they told a Campbell representative that they would not deliver their carrots at the contract price. The market price at that time was at least Chantenay $90 per ton, and red cored carrots were virtually unobtainable. The Wentzes then sold approximately 62 tons of their carrots to the defendant Lojeski, a neighboring farmer. Lojeski resold about 58 tons on the open market, approximately half to Campbell and the balance to other purchasers.

On January 9, 1948, Campbell, suspecting that Lojeski was selling it "contract carrots," refused to purchase any more, and instituted these suits against the Wentz brothers and Lojeski to enjoin further sale of the contract carrots to others, and to compel specific performance of the contract. The trial court denied equitable relief. We agree with the result reached, but on a different ground from that relied upon by the District Court.

.   .   . A party may have specific performance of a contract for the sale of chattels if the legal remedy is inadequate. Inadequacy of the legal remedy is necessarily a matter to be determined by an examination of the facts in each particular instance.

We think that on the question of adequacy of the legal remedy the case is one appropriate for specific performance. It was expressly found that at the time of the trial it was "virtually impossible to obtain Chantenay carrots in the open market." This Chantenay carrot is one which the plaintiff uses in large quantities, furnishing the seed to the growers with whom it makes contracts. It was not claimed that in nutritive value it is any better than other types of carrots. Its blunt shape makes it easier to handle in processing. And its color and texture differ from other varieties. The color is brighter than other carrots. The trial court found that the plaintiff failed to establish what proportion of its carrots is used for the production of soup stock and what proportion is used as identifiable physical ingredients in its soups. We do not think lack of proof on that point is material. It did appear that the plaintiff uses carrots in fifteen of its twenty-one soups. It also appeared that it uses these Chantenay carrots diced in some of them and that the appearance is uniform. The preservation of uniformity in appearance in a food article marketed throughout the country and sold under the manufacturer's name is a matter of considerable commercial significance and one which is properly considered in determining whether a substitute ingredient is just as good as the original.

The trial court concluded that the plaintiff had failed to establish that the carrots, "judged by objective standards," are unique goods. This we think is not a pure fact conclusion like a finding that Chantenay carrots are of uniform color. It is either a conclusion of law or of mixed fact and law and we are bound to exercise our independent judgment upon it. That the test for specific performance is not necessarily "objective" is shown by the many cases in which equity has given it to enforce contracts for articles—family heirlooms and the like—the value of which was personal to the plaintiff.

Judged by the general standards applicable to determining the adequacy of the legal remedy we think that on this point the case is a proper one for equitable relief. There is considerable authority, old and new, showing liberality in the granting of an equitable remedy. We see no reason why a court should be reluctant to grant specific relief when it can be given without supervision of the court or other time-consuming processes against one who has deliberately broken his agreement. Here the goods of the special type contracted for were unavailable on the open market, the plaintiff had contracted for them long ahead in anticipation of its needs, and had built up a general reputation for its products as part of which reputation uniform appearance was important. We think if this were all that was involved in the case specific performance should have been granted.

[The reason that we shall affirm instead of reversing with an order for specific performance is found in the contract itself. We think it is too hard a bargain and too one-sided an agreement to entitle the plaintiff to relief in a court of conscience. For each individual grower the agreement is made by filling in names and quantity and price on a printed form furnished by the buyer. This form has quite obviously been drawn by skilful draftsmen with the buyer's interests in mind.]

Paragraph 2 provides for the manner of delivery. Carrots are to have their stalks cut off and be in clean sanitary bags or other containers approved by Campbell. This paragraph concludes with a statement that Campbell's determination of conformance with specifications shall be conclusive.

The defendants attack this provision as unconscionable. We do not think that it is, standing by itself. We think that the provision is comparable to the promise to perform to the satisfaction of another and that Campbell would be held liable if it refused carrots which did in fact conform to the specifications.

The next paragraph allows Campbell to refuse carrots in excess of twelve tons to the acre. The next contains a covenant by the grower that he will not sell carrots to anyone else except the carrots rejected by Campbell nor will he permit anyone else to grow carrots on his land. Paragraph 10 provides liquidated damages to the extent of $50 per acre for any breach by the grower. There is no provision for liquidated or any other damages for breach of contract by Campbell.

The provision of the contract which we think is the hardest is paragraph 9, set out in the margin.[B] It will be noted that Campbell is excused from accepting carrots under certain circumstances. But even under such circumstances the grower, while he cannot say Campbell is liable for failure to take the carrots, is not permitted to sell them elsewhere unless Campbell agrees. This is the kind of provision which the late Francis H. Bohlen would call "carrying a good joke too far." What the grower may do with his product under the circumstances set out is not clear. He has covenanted not to store it anywhere except on his own farm and also not to sell to anybody else.

We are not suggesting that the contract is illegal. Nor are we suggesting any excuse

[B]"Grower shall not be obligated to deliver any Carrots which he is unable to harvest or deliver, nor shall Campbell be obligated to receive or pay for any Carrots which it is unable to inspect, grade, receive, handle, use or pack at or ship in processed form from its plants in Camden (1) because of any circumstance beyond the control of Grower or Campbell, as the case may be, or (2) because of any labor distrubance, work stoppage, slow-down, or strike involving any of Campbell's employees. Campbell shall not be liable for any delay in receiving Carrots due to any of the above contingencies. During periods when Campbell is unable to receive Grower's Carrots, Grower may with Campbell's written consent, dispose of his Carrots elsewhere. Grower may not, however, sell or otherwise dispose of any Carrots which he is unable to deliver to Campbell."

for the grower in this case who has deliberately broken an agreement entered into with Campbell. We do think, however, that a party who has offered and succeeded in getting an agreement as tough as this one is, should not come to a chancellor and ask court help in the enforcement of its terms. That equity does not enforce unconscionable bargains is too well established to require elaborate citation.

The plaintiff argues that the provisions of the contract are separable. We agree that they are, but do not think that decisions separating out certain provisions from illegal contracts are in point here. As already said, we do not suggest that this contract is illegal. All we say is that the sum total of its provisions drives too hard a bargain for a court of conscience to assist.

This disposition of the problem makes unnecessary further discussion of the separate liability of Lojeski, who was not a party to the contract, but who purchased some of the carrots from the Wentzes.

The judgments will be affirmed.

Injunctions

PHILADELPHIA BALL CLUB v. LAJOIE
Supreme Court of Pennsylvania, 202 Pa. 210 (1902).

POTTER, J.   The defendant in this case contracted to serve the plaintiff as a baseball player for a stipulated time. During that period he was not to play for any other club. He violated his agreement, however, during the term of his engagement, and, in disregard of his contract, arranged to play for another and a rival organization. The plaintiff, by means of this bill, sought to restrain him during the period covered by the contract. The court below refused an injunction, holding that to warrant the interference prayed for "the defendant's services must be unique, extraordinary, and of such a character as to render it impossible to replace him; so that his breach of contract would result in irreparable loss to the plaintiff." In the view of the court, the defendant's qualifications did not measure up to this high standard.   .   .   .

The learned judge who filed the opinion in the court below, with great industry and painstaking care, collected and reviewed the English and American decisions bearing up on the question involved, and makes apparent the wide divergence of opinion which has prevailed. We think, however, that in refusing relief unless the defendant's services were shown to be of such a character as to render it impossible to replace him he has taken extreme ground. It seems to us that a more just and equitable rule is laid down in Pom. Spec. Perf. p. 31, where the principle is thus declared: "Where one person agrees to render personal services to another, which require and presuppose a special knowledge, skill, and ability in the employe, so that in case of a default the same service could not easily be obtained from others, although the affirmative specific performance of the contract is beyond the power of the court, its performance will be negatively enforced by enjoining its breach. * * * The damages for breach of such contract cannot be estimated with any certainty, and the employer cannot, by means of any damages, purchase the same service in the labor market." We have not found any case going to the length of requiring, as a condition of relief, proof of the impossibility of obtaining equivalent service. It is true that the injury must be irreparable; but, as observed by Mr. Justice Lowrie in Com. v. Pittsburgh & C.R. Co., 24 Pa. 160: "The argument that there is no 'irreparable damage' would not be so often used by wrongdoers if they would take the trouble to discover that the word 'irreparable' is a very unhappily chosen one, used in expressing the rule that an injunction may issue to prevent wrongs of a repeated and continuing character, or which occasion damages which are estimated only by conjecture, and not by any accurate standard." We are therefore within the term whenever it is shown that no certain pecuniary standard exists for the measurement of the damages.   . . .

. . . [A]nother observation may be made, which is that the plaintiff, by the act of bringing this suit, has disavowed any intention of exercising the right to terminate the contract on its own part. This is a necessary inference from its action in asking the court to exercise its equity power to enforce the agreement made by the defendant not to give his services to any other club. Besides, the remedy by injunction is elastic and adaptable, and is wholly within the control of the court. If granted now, it can be easily dissolved whenever a change in the circumstances or in the attitude of the plaintiff should seem to require it. The granting or refusal of an injunction or its continuance is never a matter of strict right, but is always a question of discretion, to be determined by the court in view of the particular circumstances.

Upon a careful consideration of the whole case, we are of opinion that the provisions of the contract are reasonable.   . . .   The evidence shows no indications of any attempt at overreaching or unfairness. Substantial justice between the parties requires that the court should restrain the defendant from playing for any other club during the term of his contract with the plaintiff.

The specifications of error are sustained, and the decree of the court below is reversed, and the bill is reinstated; and it is ordered that the record be remitted to the court below for further proceedings in accordance with this opinion.

BRADSHAW v. MILLIKIN
Supreme Court of North Carolina, 173 N.C. 432 (1917).

Appeal from Superior Court, Richmond County; Webb, Judge.

Civil action by B. K. Bradshaw against J. E. Millikin. Motion to continue injunction to final hearing denied, and plaintiff appeals. Error.

These are the facts: Defendant sold and transferred to the plaintiff his barber business in the town of Hamlet, N.C., together with all of the furniture, fixtures, and other property used therein, and the good will of the business for a certain consideration, and also agreed that he would not in any manner, either directly or indirectly, engage in the same or any similar business in said town, for the period of two years from the execution of the contract, June 9, 1916, with this further condition:

"It is expressly understood that the stipulations aforesaid are to apply to and to bind the heirs, executors and administrators of the respective parties, and in case of failure, the parties bind themselves, each unto the other, in the sum of four hundred dollars, as liquidated damages, and not as a penalty, to be paid by the failing party."

The defendant did engage in the business of a barber in the town of Hamlet, N.C., within the two years, and plaintiff brought this action to enjoin him from continuing therein. The court held, and so adjudged, that the defendant should not be enjoined if he gave a good and sufficient bond in the sum of $500, upon condition that he pay the plaintiff such damages as he may suffer for the breach of this contract. The record is silent as to the important fact whether the bond was given by the defendant as required to be done by the order, but it was admitted here that it had been given, and that the restraining order was dissolved, and the parties desire the case to be decided on its merits.

WALKER, J. (after stating the facts as above). The plaintiff appealed, and his counsel contended here that he had a legal right to a continuance of the injunction to the final hearing, whether the bond was given or not, and in this we agree with him.

．　．　．　．

It is clear, upon examining the language of the agreement between the parties to this action, as applied to the subject of the sale and the situation at the time, that its object is to secure absolutely to the plaintiff the exclusive right, as against the defendant, to pursue the business of a barber in the town of Hamlet, and the latter, having sold his interest and good will, expressly stipulates not to engage in the business, and to pay certain fixed damages if there is a breach. There is nothing here to show any right or option in the defendant to continue the business upon payment of the money, or that the covenant would be satisfied by the payment of the sum stated, except by consent of the plaintiff, but it is an absolute agreement not to do certain acts and thereby interfere with the plaintiff's business. This is a distinct agreement, independent of the stipulation as to the money to be paid if he violates the contract, or in case of a breach of the condition. The substance of the whole paper is that the defendant covenants not to do a particular thing, and, if he does, that he will pay $400 as satisfaction, if plaintiff elects to sue for damages, but this does not prevent the court from enjoining him from doing that which he has agreed not to do. He did not purchase the right to disregard the contract by agreeing to pay damages for a breach of it, and in satisfaction thereof, for he had no such alternative right.

．　．　．　．

The court erred in refusing the injunction to the final hearing, and allowing defendant to give bond to stay its restraining power or in lieu of its exercise. Plaintiff is entitled to the specific relief by injunction and to any damages he may be able to prove up to the operation of the injunction order, when the defendant must cease his violation of the covenant by discontinuing the business.

．　．　．　．

Error.

REMEDIES BY ANALOGY TO CONTRACT

We have already noted that society came slowly to the decision to lend its courts to cases of breach of promise. So many other problems seemed more important: killings; mayhems; batteries; theft (of water in dry lands; of camels in desert lands; of wives in any land); trespasses on property; maidens' doweries; legitimacy of children; wills—a whole host of human actions and affairs for which the law devised forms of action long before the broken promise seemed to justify judicial attention.

Now, we see that once the promise is matched with another promise, or an action is taken in reliance on the promise, or a nonaction (some restraint or detriment) is suffered because of the promise, the rules are quite precise about making the promise good. We have sampled a sufficient number of cases of criteria for contract and criteria for and manner of relief when one or both parties break the contract to see how the law goes, and why.

Suppose, however, the facts do not make out a contract. Some essential of agreement is missing: no intent; no offer or no acceptance; no consideration. Yet the case is appealing. An obviously honest plaintiff has been frustrated in a reasonable expectation, or has rendered services under circumstances that did not permit the formalities of contract, or has acted from uncertain but ethical motives, without a lawyer at his elbow. What then? No contract, no relief—is that the attitude of the law?

The answer is found in the cases closing this chapter. The key to the rationale of these cases is in the concept of *analogy*. These cases are decided as if there were a contract when in fact there was no contract. Phrases such as promissory estoppel or implied contract or quasi contract emerge. True, there are principles. The law is not so loose as to recompense every person who encounters thwarted hopes or expectations, or who suffers a loss. But, just as in early Roman or English times the law yielded to the insistent appeals from suitors who suffered from defaulters under good and valid contracts, so in later times the law yields to the insistence of hardship cases and relaxes the necessity for contract formalities. Judges, like other men, are given to saying, "There ought to be a law," but unlike other men, judges have the power to rationalize that impulse.

RECOVERY BY PROMISSORY ESTOPPEL

GOODMAN v. DICKER
United States Court of Appeals, District of Columbia,
83 U.S. App. D.C. 353 (1948).

PROCTOR, Associate Justice.   This appeal is from a judgment of the District Court in a suit by appellees for breach of contract.

Appellants are local distributors for Emerson Radio and Phonograph Corporation in the District of Columbia. Appellees, with the knowledge and encouragement of appellants, applied for a "dealer franchise" to sell Emerson's products. The trial court found that appellants by their representations and conduct induced appellees to incur expenses in preparing to do business under the franchise, including employment of salesmen and solicitation of orders for radios. Among other things, appellants represented that the application had been accepted; that the franchise would be granted, and that appellees would receive an initial delivery of thirty to forty radios. Yet, no radios were delivered, and notice was finally given that the franchise would not be granted.

The case was tried without a jury. The court held that a contract had not been proven but that appellants were estopped from denying the same by reasons of their statements and conduct upon which appellees relied to their detriment. Judgment was entered for $1500, covering cash outlays of $1150 and loss of $350, anticipated profits on sale of thirty radios.

The main contention of appellants is that no liability would have arisen under the dealer franchise had it been granted because, as understood by appellees, it would have been terminable at will and would have imposed no duty upon the manufacturer to sell or appellees to buy any fixed number of radios. From this it is argued that the franchise agreement would not have been enforceable (except as to acts performed thereunder) and cancellation by the manufacturer would have created no liability for expenses incurred by the dealer in preparing to do business. Further, it is argued that as the dealer franchise would have been unenforceable for failure of the manufacturer to supply radios appellants would not be liable to fulfill their assurance that radios would be supplied.

We think these contentions miss the real point of this case. We are not concerned directly with the terms of the franchise. We are dealing with a promise by appellants that a franchise would be granted and radios supplied, on the faith of which appellees with the knowledge and encouragement of appellants incurred expenses in making preparations to do business. Under these circumstances we think that appellants cannot now advance any defense inconsistent with their assurance that the franchise would be granted. Justice and fair dealing require that one who acts to his detriment on the faith of conduct of the kind revealed here should be protected by estopping the party who has brought about the situation from alleging anything in opposition to the natural consequences of his own course of conduct. . . . In Dickerson v. Colgrove, 100 U.S. 578, 580, the Supreme Court, in speaking of equitable estoppel, said: "The law upon the subject is well settled. The vital principle is that he who by his language or conduct leads another to do what he would not otherwise have done, shall not subject such person to loss or injury by disappointing the expectations upon which he acted. Such a change of position is sternly forbidden. * * * This remedy is always so applied as to promote the ends of justice." . . .

In our opinion the trial court was correct in holding defendants liable for moneys which appellees expended in preparing to do business under the promised dealer franchise. These items aggregated $1150. We think, though, the court erred in adding the item of $350 for loss of profits on radios promised under an initial order. The true measure of damage is the loss sustained by expenditures made in reliance upon the assurance of a dealer franchise. As thus modified, the judgment is

Affirmed.

RECOVERY IN QUASI CONTRACT

COTNAM v. WISDOM
Supreme Court of Arkansas, 83 Ark. 601 (1907).

Appeal from Circuit Court, Pulaski County; R. J. Lea, Judge.

Action by F. L. Wisdom and another against T. T. Cotnam, administrator of A. M. Harrison, deceased, for services rendered by plaintiffs as surgeons to defendant's intestate. Judgment for plaintiffs. Defendant appeals. Reversed and remanded.

Instructions 1 and 2, given at the instance of plaintiffs, are as follows: "(1) If you find from the evidence that plaintiffs rendered professional services as physicians and surgeons to the deceased, A. M. Harrison, in a sudden emergency following the deceased's injury in a street car wreck, in an endeavor to save his life, then you are instructed that plaintiffs are entitled to recover from the estate of the said A. M. Harrison such sum as you may find from the evidence is a reasonable compensation for the services rendered. (2) The character and importance of the operation, the responsibility resting upon the surgeon performing the operation, his experience and professional training, and the ability to pay of the person operated upon, are elements to be considered by you in determining what is reasonable charge for the services performed by plaintiffs in the particular case."

HILL, C. J. (after stating the facts).

.   .   .   .

The first question is as to the correctness of this [the first] instruction. As indicated therein the facts are that Mr. Harrison, appellant's intestate, was thrown from a street car, receiving serious injuries which rendered him unconscious, and while in that condition the appellees were notified of the accident and summoned to his assistance by some spectator, and performed a difficult operation in an effort to save his life, but they were unsuccessful, and he died without regaining consciousness. The appellant says: "Harrison was never conscious after his head struck the pavement. He did not and could not, expressly or impliedly, assent to the action of the appellees. He was without knowledge or will power. However merciful or benevolent may have been the intention of the appellee, a new rule of law, of contract by implication of law, will have to be established by this court in order to sustain the recovery." Appellant is right in saying that the recovery must be sustained by a contract by implication of law, but is not right in saying that it is a new rule of law, for such contracts are almost as old as the English system of jurisprudence. They are usually called "implied contracts." More properly they should be called "quasi contracts" or "constructive contracts." . . .

The following excerpts from Sceva v. True, 53 N.H. 627, are peculiarly applicable here: "We regard it as well settled by the cases referred to in the briefs of counsel, many of which have been commented on at length by Mr. Shirley for the defendant, that an insane person, an idiot, or a person utterly bereft of all sense and reason by the sudden stroke of an accident or disease may be held liable, in assumpsit, for necessaries furnished to him in good faith while in that unfortunate and helpless condition. And the reasons upon which this rest are too broad, as well as too sensible and humane, to be overborne by any deductions which a refined logic may make from the circumstances that in such cases there can be no contract or promise, in fact, no meeting of the minds of the parties. The cases put it on the ground of an implied contract; and by this is not meant, as the defendant's counsel seems to suppose, an actual contract—that is, an actual meeting of the minds of the parties, an actual, mutual understanding, to be inferred from language, acts, and circumstances by the jury—but a contract and promise, said to be implied by the law, where, in point of fact, there was no contract, no mutual understanding, and so no promise. The defendant's counsel says it is usurpation for the court to hold, as a matter of law, that there is a contract and a promise, when all the evidence in the case shows that there was not a contract, nor the semblance of one. It is doubtless a legal fiction, invented and used for the sake of the remedy. If it was originally usurpation, certainly it has now become very inveterate, and firmly fixed in the body of the law. Illustrations might be multiplied, but enough has been said to show that when a contract or promise implied by law is spoken of, a very different thing is meant from a contract in fact, whether express or tacit. The evidence of an actual contract is generally to be found either in some writing made by the parties, or in verbal communications which passed between them, or in their acts and conduct considered in the light of the circumstances of each particular case. A contract implied by law, on the contrary, rests upon no evidence. It has no actual existence. It is simply a mythical creation of the law. The law says it shall be taken that there was a promise, when in point of fact, there was none. . . .

The court permitted to go to the jury the fact that Mr. Harrison was a bachelor, and that his estate would go to his collateral relatives, and also permitted proof to be made of the value of the estate, which amounted to about $18,500, including $10,000 from accident and life insurance policies. . . .

There was evidence in this case proving that it was customary for physicians to graduate their charges by the ability of the patient to pay. . . . This could not apply to a physician called in an emergency by some bystander to attend a stricken man whom he never saw or heard of before; and certainly the unconscious patient could not, in fact or in law, be held to have contemplated what charges the physician might properly bring against him. In order to admit such testimony, it must be assumed that the surgeon and patient each had in contemplation that the means of the patient would be one factor in determining the amount of the charge for the services rendered. While the law may admit such evidence as throwing light upon the contract and indicating what was really in contemplation when it was made, yet a different question is presented when there is no contract to be ascertained or construed, but a mere fiction of law creating a contract where none existed in order that there might be a remedy for a right. This fiction merely requires a reasonable compensation for the services rendered. The services are the same be the patient prince or pauper, and for them the surgeon is entitled to fair compensation for his time, service, and skill. It was therefore error to admit this evidence, and to instruct the jury in the second instruction that in determining what was a reasonable charge they could consider the "ability to pay of the person operated upon."

It was improper to let it go to the jury that Mr. Harrison was a bachelor and that his estate was left to nieces and nephews. This was relevant to no issue in the case, and its effect might well have been prejudicial. While this verdict is no higher than some of the evidence would justify, yet it is much higher than some of the other evidence would justify, and hence it is impossible to say that this was a harmless error.

Judgment is reversed, and cause remanded.

MORSE v. KENNEY
Supreme Court of Vermont, 87 Vt. 445 (1914).

Action by Cleo D. Morse against Patrick Kenney. Judgment for defendant, and plaintiff excepts. Judgment affirmed.

TAYLOR, J. This is an action of general assumpsit. Plea the general issue and trial by court. The plaintiff is a livery stable keeper and seeks to recover for the board and care of a certain horse. One Badlam was the owner of the horse in question which was being kept for him by the plaintiff. On May 25, 1911, the defendant, a farmer, went to the plaintiff's stable to purchase a horse for use on his farm. The plaintiff being absent, his servant, one Spaulding, who was in charge of the stable, told the defendant that the Badlam horse was for sale; that it was a good work horse, suitable for defendant's use on his farm; that it was able to draw reasonable loads; and that it was worth $50. Spaulding called Badlam by telephone and had some talk with him (the nature of which and whether in the hearing of the defendant does not appear from the findings), upon which he sold the horse to the defendant for $50. The defendant paid the purchase price to Spaulding for Badlam and took the horse home.

The defendant had not had much experience in dealing in horses and was not much acquainted with their value. He relied wholly upon Spaulding's representations, believing them to be true. The next day he attempted to use the horse and found it "weak in its hind quarters," unable to draw a small load, and unfit to perform ordinary farm work. The defendant at once returned the horse to the plaintiff's stable, found Spaulding there, claimed the horse was not as represented, and asked to leave the horse where he got it; but Spaulding refused to accept the horse back and would not allow the defendant to put it in the stable. The defendant hitched the horse to a ring just outside the stable and went immediately to Badlam's place of business, where he demanded the return of his money, which Badlam refused. On plaintiff's return later the same day he found the horse hitched outside; knowing that the defendant had left it there for Badlam he put it in the stable, fed and cared for it, and on the same day wrote the defendant: "Your mare is here and it is 25c a feed." Upon receiving this letter the defendant replied: "The mare you refer to is not mine. Therefore don't look to me for any pay for her feed." Plaintiff kept the horse until July 12th, when this suit was brought for its board and care.

Can the plaintiff recover in general assumpsit on the foregoing facts? If so, it must be upon the theory of an implied promise to pay for the board and care of the horse.

There are two kinds of implied contracts, as the term is ordinarily used in the books: (1) Where the minds of the parties meet and their meeting results in an unexpressed agreement; (2) where there is no meeting of minds. . . . The former class embraces true contracts which are implied in the sense that the fact of the meeting of minds is inferred. Such contracts are more accurately defined as resting upon an implied promise in fact. The latter class embraces contractual obligations implied by the law where none in fact exist.

In many cases where there is no contract, the law upon equitable grounds imposes an obligation often called quasi contractual. . . . Such obligations are not contracts in the proper sense, since they are created by law and not by the parties. . . . In such so-called contracts the law creates a fictitious promise for the purpose of allowing the remedy by action of assumpsit. Though created by law and clothed with the semblance of a contract, the obligation is not a contract at all. The proper term for such obligations is "quasi contracts," a term borrowed from the Roman law. . . . They are called "quasi contracts" because, as the term implies, they are not contracts at all, but have a semblance of contract in that they may be enforced by an action of assumpsit. . . . Much of the apparent confusion in the cases arises from a failure to distinguish clearly between implied contracts in fact and contracts implied in law or constructive contracts.

The plaintiff cannot maintain this action as upon an implied promise in fact, for such a promise is implied from the understanding of the parties, inferred as a question of fact from their conduct and the surrounding circumstances; such facts and circumstances as show, according to the ordinary course of dealing and the common understanding of men, a mutual intent to contract. . . . It is never inferred against the express understanding of the parties. . . . The defendant's assent is necessary to such a promise. . . .

The source of the obligation, as in express contracts, is the intention of the parties. . . . It is implied only when the facts warrant the inference of mutual expectation; the defendant expecting to pay for the service and the plaintiff performing it relying upon that understanding. . . . It is implied only in this: It is inferred from the conduct of the parties instead of from their spoken words; or, in other words, the contract is evidenced by conduct instead of by words.

Unless the party benefited has conducted himself in such a manner that his assent may fairly be inferred therefrom, he is not bound to pay. . . .

. . . . .

Applying these principles to the facts in this case it is evident that plaintiff cannot recover. The same result is reached whether the attempt by the defendant to rescind the sale is regarded as effectual or ineffectual. If effectual, then the horse was no longer his, and confessedly no principle of equity and good conscience would demand that the law imply a contract for its keeping against his express dissent. If ineffectual, and for that reason the horse remained his, when the plaintiff, knowing the circumstances under which the horse was left by the defendant outside his stable, saw fit to take charge of and care for it, he acted as a volunteer. It cannot be said that the horse was left in the plaintiff's possession so that a duty to care for it was cast upon him. . . . To be sure the defendant had asked Spaulding to receive the horse back, but this request was coupled with a demand for the return of the purchase money, and his request was denied.

The fact that the property is a live animal, in the absence of special circumstances raising a duty to care for it, does not change the situation. The [defendant] cannot be held liable on an implied contract to pay for that which he expressly declines to have done on his account, unless the law imposes upon him an obligation to do something which he declines to do, and which must be done to meet the legal requirement. There is no such obligation upon one to retain and preserve his property, whether it be live animals or anything else. He may abandon or destroy it, if he pleases (Keith v. De Bussigney et al., 179 Mass. 255), subject of course to prohibitions of the statute against cruelty to animals. The facts of this case do not disclose such necessity for the plaintiff's interference, on grounds of humanity or otherwise, as would authorize him to care for the horse at the defendant's expense against his protest. The general rule is as was said in State v. St. Johnsbury, 59 Vt. 332, 342,: "One cannot thrust himself upon me and make me his debtor whether I will or not." The plaintiff fails to bring himself within the exceptions to this rule. This being so, he must be taken at the best to be a mere volunteer and so precluded from recovering. . . .

Judgment affirmed.

QUESTIONS

1. What element essential for contract formation was lacking in the case of Rosman v. Cuevas? Could the result in Cuevas be different in a state other than California?

2. What is the distinction between a void contract and a voidable contract? Illustrate with cases.

3. What is the objective test for determination of whether a contract exists? What case in Chapter 4 illustrates the objective test?

4. Why is it good and legal consideration for the promise of the promisor that the promisee refrain from doing what in any case it is beneficial to the promisee not to do? On what case is this question founded?

5. Why will the courts in some cases refuse to enforce a contract which contains all of the elements essential to the formation of a contract? Cite the fact and rationale of a case in which this question is necessarily raised.

6. What is the Statute of Frauds? Where and when did the prototype Statute of Frauds arise? What were the original reasons for the Statute? Are such statutes usual today?

7. Name three concepts of criteria for determining damages for breach of contract and illustrate each one.

8. Describe a situation, explicated in one of the cases in this chapter, in which a rule of case law on measure of damages is upset by a rule of statutory law on measure of damages. Name the case. Explain why you agree or disagree with the rule of statutory law.

9. What is specific performance? To what types of contract does specific performance apply? Describe a principle of equity which defeated specific performance in a case in Chapter 4 where otherwise the conditions for specific performance applied. Name the case. Do you agree with the result?

10. What is the fiction? Refer to Chapter 1. Relate the concept of the fiction to other aspects of legal development which Sir Henry Maine treats in his comments on Roman law.

5 Law Clings to Consistency But Grows

Introduction. 198
Torts and Contracts Distinguished 200
    Ash v. Childs Dining Hall Co.. 201
    Friend v. Childs Dining Hall Co. 204
    A Lawyer Is Sometimes Needed 204
The Rise and Fall of a Legal Concept 206
    Thomas and Wife v. Winchester 206
    Loop v. Litchfield 209
    Losee v. Clute 210
    Devlin v. Smith 212
    Torgesen v. Schultz 215
    MacPherson v. Buick Motor Company 217
    Consistency Is Not Always a Virtue 220
An Emerging Concept of Manufacturer's Liability. 223
    Escola v. Coca Cola Bottling Company of Fresno 223
    Henningsen v. Bloomfield Motors, Inc. 227
    Greenman v. Yuba Power Products, Inc.. 235
    Vandermark v. Ford Motor Company. 237
    Elmore v. American Motors Corporation 240
    Kassab v. Central Soya 243
A New Day Needs a New Theory 247
Questions 253

INTRODUCTION

The cases in this chapter demonstrate how valiantly English law and American law seek to build on precedent. Our judges always attempt to justify today's decision in terms of yesterday's rationalization. Yet, the modes of man's life change, and as we saw in Chapter 1, technology, urbanism, trade, travel, and traffic make for changing ways of life and, hence, for changes in the cause and nature of conflict. These cases reflect this struggle for consistency in decision rationale in the face of mounting technological and economic complexities.

Many of the cases in this chapter are drawn from a branch of the law, called torts, in which society imposes upon its members certain standards of care, caution, prudence, and concern each for the other. Failure by any member of society to observe any of these standards is called a tort, which is actionable if another member of the society is thereby injured. The failure may be intentional, as when *A* deliberately strikes *B,* or it may be unintentional, as when a manufacturer carelessly produces a defective product. Carelessness is called negligence in the law. Historically, the principles have been the same, whether the parties in conflict are, on the one hand, a giant manufacturer or, on the other, the humblest of citizens. Departure from these principles subjects the offender to the involuntary imposition of money payments to the injured person. The existence of the word *tort,* from the medieval Latin, in modern English and American law is but one of many evidences of that long continuum mentioned in Chapter 1. The word came into English law with the Norman conquest.

Law may be divided into two broad categories: criminal law, where the state proceeds against the individual to correct him and punish him for offenses against society; and civil law, where an individual proceeds against another individual to seek recompense for an injury. (The individual may be a natural flesh and blood person or an artificial person, such as a corporation.) The civil law may be divided between: contract law, where individuals have voluntarily assumed mutual obligations, and society through its courts will assess damages against a defaulting party, as we saw in Chapter 4, and tort law, where an individual seeks recompense from another individual for the violation of a right or the doing of a wrong—a right that society has granted or a wrong that society has prohibited generally, and without the voluntary acquiescence of any particular individual. For example, a person who drives his automobile on the wrong side of the road and collides with another person's automobile is liable for the damage that ensues to the property and person of the driver who was on the right side of the road. Why? Because society has established rules for driving, without asking any particular individual, "By your leave, sir." Such a case in which one individual pays another money damages for an injury that results from the breach of a rule established by society belongs in the broad category of legal cases called torts.

The purpose of this chapter, however, is not to teach the whole of the law of torts any more than it is the purpose of this book to teach the whole of law. This chapter has a precise and particular purpose—to show how law develops from case to case; how judges struggle for precedents to follow; and finally how, when the rationale of the precedents no longer fits the changing technological and social modes, a new rationale—although rarely and reluctantly—emerges. It is the judicial process of making a rule for a particular set of facts, then applying that rule to every analogous set of facts, called *stare decisis,* that gives the law consistency, dependability, and predictability. Law is seldom revolutionary—almost always evolutionary. This stability is the pride and joy of the law.

Stability, however, can become sterility. We saw in Chapter 1 how Roman law, made originally for farmers and a bucolic village, changed to yield to the needs of trade and Mediterranean cosmopolitanism. Likewise, we shall see in this section how rules of liability change as the economy changes; for example, as the technology of mobility moves from custom-built, horse-drawn wagons to mass-produced, motor vehicles. This point is eloquently emphasized in the words of Mr. Justice O. W. Holmes:[1]

> . . . The life of the law has not been logic: it has been experience. The felt necessities of the time, the prevalent moral and political theories, intuitions of public policy, avowed or unconscious, even the prejudices which judges share with their fellow-men, have had a good deal more to do than the syllogism in determining the rules by which men should be governed. The law embodies the story of a nation's development through many centuries, and it cannot be dealt with as if it contained only the axioms and corollaries of a book of mathematics. In order to know what it is, we must know what it has been, and what it tends to become. We must alternately consult history and existing theories of legislation. But the most difficult labor will be to understand the combination of the two into new products at every stage. The substance of the law at any given time pretty nearly corresponds, so far as it goes, with what is then understood to be convenient; but its form and machinery, and degree to which it is able to work out desired results, depend very much upon its past.

We come now to a few cases that demonstrate the mental stress and strain by which the courts have developed, and are still developing, a doctrine to establish a seller's or manufacturer's liability to a remote buyer, a user of the manufactured product, or an innocent bystander if injury or loss ensues to one or more of them by reason of a defective product.

TORTS AND CONTRACTS DISTINGUISHED

ASH v. CHILDS DINING HALL CO.
Supreme Judicial Court of Massachusetts, 231 Mass. 86 (1918).

RUGG, C. J.   This is an action of tort. It rests solely upon allegations of negligence. The burden of proving that the proximate cause of the plaintiff's injury was the negligence of the defendant or its servants or agents rested on the plaintiff. It is well settled that the duty rests upon the keeper of an inn, restaurant, or other eating place

---

[1]Holmes, Oliver Wendell, Jr., *The Common Law,* pp. 1–2, Little Brown, Boston, (48th print.) 1923.

to use due care to furnish wholesome food, fit to eat. Failure in this respect resulting in injury is foundation for an action of negligence. . . .

The testimony of the plaintiff tended to show that she received injuries from the presence of a tack in a piece of blueberry pie which she was eating while a guest of the defendant in its restaurant. Her description was that "there lodged in her throat, in her right tonsil, a very thin small-headed tack, the head a little mite larger than a pin head. * * * It was a little longer than a carpet tack." It was not the same shape as a carpet tack. "It was thin, long and a very small head." The head was flat. "It was a black tack."

The pie was made by the defendant on its premises and served as food by its waitress to the plaintiff. The manager of the defendant testified that at that time its blueberries came in ordinary quart berry baskets, made of wood in which were tacks "hardly an eighth of an inch long, with a flat head, and that this was the first time in the eighteen years that he had been in the business that he had seen a tack in blueberries." There was other testimony to the effect that a high degree of care was exercised in the preparation of the blueberries for the pies. That is laid on one side, as it may not have been credited by the jury. But disbelief of the defendant's testimony as to the precautions used by it cannot take the place of evidence of negligence.

There is nothing in the record from which it can be inferred that the harm to the plaintiff resulted directly from any failure of duty on the part of the defendant. The precise cause of her injury is left to conjecture. It may as reasonably be attributed to a condition for which no liability attached to the defendant as to one for which it is responsible. Under such circumstances the plaintiff does not sustain the burden of fastening tortious conduct on the defendant by a fair preponderance of all the evidence, and a verdict ought to be directed [in favor of the defendant] accordingly. . . .

The tack was very small. It was so tiny that it readily might have become imbedded in a blueberry. If so, its color and shape were such that it would naturally escape the most careful scrutiny. It might as readily have stuck into a blueberry before it came to the possession of the defendant as afterward. The carelessness of some person for whom the defendant in no way was responsible might have caused its presence in the pie. The maker of the basket, some previous owner of the berry, or some other third person, is as likely to have been the direct cause of the tack being in the pie as the defendant or those for whose conduct it is liable. . . .

. . . The mere fact of injury does not show negligence. The burden of proof resting upon the plaintiff to establish that fact must be sustained by evidence either direct or inferential. . . . No question arises as to the contractual relations between the parties. . . .

Exceptions sustained.

FRIEND v. CHILDS DINING HALL CO.
Supreme Judicial Court of Massachusetts, 231 Mass. 65 (1918).

RUGG, C. J. The plaintiff introduced evidence tending to show that the defendant kept a restaurant in Boston, which she entered and ordered of a waitress of the defendant from its menu, "New York baked beans and corned beef." This food was served to her and she sat at a table to eat it. She further testified: "I started to eat the food and there were two or three dark pieces which I thought were hard beans, that is baked more than the others, and I put two in my mouth and bit down hard on them and * * * I was hurt. * * * I took those things out of my mouth and found they were stones."

There was no further evidence that the plaintiff had anything to do with the selection of the beans. She gave no instructions respecting the food other than to order it. There was no evidence of express warranty or that the defendant knew of the presence of the stones in the food. There was evidence of injury to the plaintiff. At the close of the evidence the plaintiff elected to rely upon a count for breach of an implied warranty of fitness to eat in a contract for food to be eaten on the premises of the defendant. The defendant introduced no evidence. The question is whether the plaintiff was entitled to go to the jury.

There is strong ground for holding that the contract made between one who keeps a restaurant and one who resorts there for food to be served and eaten on the premises is a sale of food.   .   .   .

.   .   . If it is a sale, then plainly it is governed by the Sales Act, St. 1908, c. 237, § 15(1), which is in these words: "Where the buyer, expressly or by implication makes known to the seller the particular purpose for which the goods are required, and it appears that the buyer relies on the seller's skill or judgment, whether he be the grower or manufacturer or not, there is an implied warranty that the goods shall be reasonably fit for such purpose."

It is manifest that at least it might be inferred, from the relations of the parties, that the guest who asks to be served food upon the premises of one who is the keeper of a restaurant makes known as the particular purpose for which the food is required that it is then and there to be eaten, and that he relies upon the latter's skill or judgment in the selection and preparation of the food. Hence there would be an implied warranty that it was reasonably fit for such purpose.

But there is authority to the effect that, when food is furnished to a guest by the keeper of a restaurant or inn, the transaction does not constitute a sale, that the title to the food does not pass, that the customer may consume so much as he pleases, but that he cannot carry away of the portion ordered that which he does not eat, or give or sell it to another; and that the charge made is not for the food alone, but includes the service rendered and the providing of a place in which to eat. It is stated in Beal on Innkeepers, § 169: "The title to food never passes as a result of the ordinary transaction of supplying food to a guest; or, as it was quaintly put in an old case 'He does not sell but utters his provision.'" Parker v. Flint, 12 Mod. 254.

Therefore it seems desirable to consider somewhat the relation of the guest to a keeper of a place where good is served [sic] for immediate consumption. It is ancient law that when one resorts to a tavern, inn or eating place, there for a consideration to be served with food for immediate consumption, and is received as a guest by the keeper, a duty is implied that the food shall be fit to eat. It has been said that:

"If a man goes into a tavern for refreshment, and corrupt drink or meat is there sold to him, which occasions his sickness, an action clearly lies against the tavern keeper; * * * an action lies against him without express warranty for it is a warranty in law." Keilway's Rep. 91; Burnby v. Bollett, 16 M. & W. 644, 646, 647, 654, where are the references to numerous older cases. "A taverner or vinter was bound as such to sell wholesome food and drink." Ames, Lectures on Legal History, p. 137, citing also cases from the Year Books. "If a man sells victuals which is corrupt without warranty an action lies, because it is against the commonwealth." Rosevel v. Vaughan, Cro. Jac. 196, 197. . . .

The relation between guest and host in a public house is one of contract. It seemingly is the result of those early authorities that it was an implied term or condition of that contract that the food and drink furnished should not be harmful, but appropriate for eating. There are numerous other illustrations in the law of contracts of an implied condition that the thing sold is merchantable. . . . Food for immediate use which is not fit to eat is not merchantable as food. This rule was held in Farrell v. Manhattan Market Co., 198 Mass. 271, to be applicable to cases where a purchaser buys from a dealer food at retail for immediate use. That rule now prevails generally in this country. . . .

. . . The exhaustive review of cases in the Farrell opinion demonstrated that it was the law both of England and of this commonwealth that in the absence of statute it was an implied term of every sale of provisions by a dealer for immediate use, where the selection was not made by the buyer, that the food was fit for consumption. The principles there discussed and the result there reached appeared to be equally applicable to the case at bar. It would be an incongruity in the law amounting at least to an inconsistency to hold with reference to many keepers of restaurants who conduct the business both of supplying food to guests and of putting up lunches to be carried elsewhere and not eaten on the premises, that, in case of want of wholesomeness, there is liability to the purchaser of a lunch to be carried away founded on an implied condition of the contract, but that liability to the guest who eats a lunch at a table on the premises rests solely on negligence. The guest of a keeper of an eating house or innkeeper is quite as helpless to protect himself against deleterious food or drink as is the purchaser of a fowl of a provision dealer. The opportunity for the innkeeper or restaurant keeper, who prepares and serves food to his guest, to discover and provide against deleterious food is at least as ample as is that of the retail dealer in foodstuffs. The evil consequences in the one case are of the same general character as in the other. Both concern the health and physical comfort and safety of human beings. On principle and on authority it seems to us that the liability of the proprietor of an eating house to his guest for serving bad food rests on an implied term of the contract and does not sound exclusively in tort, although of course he may be held for negligence if that is proved. Without repeating the reasoning of Farrell v. Manhattan Market Co., 198 Mass. 271, we are of the opinion that, on sound legal principles, it bears with equal force upon the facts here presented. Even if there were no common-law authority (which there is, as already pointed out), it would not be practicable to establish a distinction upon this point which could be supported in reason, between the liability of a retail dealer in meat for immediate consumption and of a victualer who serves food to guests to be eaten forthwith at his own table. Every argument which supports liability of the former tends to sustain liability of the latter with at least equal cogency. They appear to us to rest upon the same footing in principle.

It has been urged that public policy demands that the standard imposed upon a restaurant keeper ought to be that of reasonable care, and nothing more. Earnest argument is made to the effect that otherwise the opportunity for groundless litigation will be fostered. These considerations, when given their full weight, do not appear to us to overbalance the reasons which have been stated.

The baked beans served to the plaintiff with the stones of the size of and resembling beans might have been found to be not reasonably fit to be eaten. A foreign substance of that sort, with its possibilities for harm to teeth, may have been determined by the jury not proper to be served in food.

.   .   .   .

Our conclusion is that, whether the transaction established on the evidence between the plaintiff and defendant be treated as a sale of food, or as a contract for entertainment where the defendant simply "utters his provisions" (to use the neat phrase of Parker v. Flint, 12 Mod. 252, employed more than two centuries ago) for the benefit of the plaintiff, there was a case to be submitted to the jury.

In accordance with the terms of the report and with leave reserved with the consent of the jury .   .   .   verdict is to be entered for the plaintiff for $150.

So ordered.

[The dissenting opinion of Justice Crosby is omitted.]

A LAWYER IS SOMETIMES NEEDED

In the two cases just presented we encounter an apparent anomaly. The factual situations were almost identical. The likelihood of Childs locating a small-headed tack among the blueberries in a pie would be no greater than that of locating a small pebble among the beans in a plate of "New York beans and corned beef." Nevertheless in these two cases, both against the same restaurant and both decided by the same judge on the same day of the same year, one was decided for the defendant and one was decided for the plaintiff. Why?

The Ash case was brought in tort. This means that the lawyer who brought the case believed that he should charge Childs with negligence in failure to discover that there was a small tack among the blueberries in the pie. The appellate court in effect held that, in the absence of any other proof, that fact alone did not prove negligence (the court opined that a small tack could easily be sticking in a blueberry and thus might have been undiscoverable, despite the exercise of reasonable care). Therefore, the plaintiff, who certainly had an injury, failed to recover. She failed to recover because her lawyer brought the action in tort, in which it is necessary to prove negligence and such proof was not adduced.

Why then in the Friend case, in which the facts are about as analogous as one could imagine, did the plaintiff recover? Because she based her claim, that is, her lawyer based her claim, not on negligence but on implied warranty that the food in Childs was fit to eat. However, blueberry pie with a tack in it is not anymore fit to eat than a plate of beans with a stone in it is fit to eat. The unfitness of the food was a fact in both cases. What then was the magic of

Friend's bringing the case, not on the basis of negligence, which belongs to the law of torts, but on the basis of implied warranty, which belongs to the law of contracts?

Although the facts in Friend were almost identical with those in Ash, Friend used those facts to evoke a principle in the law of contracts rather than the principle of negligence in the law of torts. Friend went into the establishment; she encountered the representatives of Childs, the waitresses or other functionaries; she entered into a transaction in which Childs was the seller or purveyor of cooked food and she was the buyer. A relationship of this sort is called in the law, *privity*. If Friend had bought a can of beans off the shelf in a grocery store—a can of beans put up, or tinned, or canned, by some manufacturer whom Friend had never seen and on whose premises she had never entered—she would not have been in privity with the manufacturer.

Childs was just as careful in one case as in the other. It would have been as difficult to detect the defect in the plate of beans as in the blueberry pie. Why then, to ask again, should Friend have recovered? Because she cast her case in contract and not in tort!

Ordinarily, a contract is a voluntary engagement, as we noted in Chapter 4. Obviously, there was no verbally expressed contract in Friend v. Childs. Friend did not come in and say, "I will buy a plate of beans if you will guarantee that there are no stones in the beans." If she had said that and if Childs had served her a plate of beans on that condition, that would have been an express contract. But Friend did not make any such offer. She simply went in, as hundreds of other customers, looked at the menu, asked for a plate of beans, and they were served to her; therefore there was no express contractual warranty. What the court did in the Friend situation was to invoke one of the most ancient of legal devices—the fiction. This device was described in Chapter 1 as one of three ways in which the rigidity of law is ameliorated. Friend could not prove negligence against Childs, but she could, and did, invoke the principle of implied warranty that the plate of beans was fit to eat—a concept related to the law of contracts, not to the law of torts. The word "implied" itself imports some deviation from the strict concept of formal warranty or contract. To imply in law is to create a fiction.

We come now to the ultimate resolution of this apparent anomaly as between Ash and Friend. If the law had said in Ash that although there was no negligence (no breach by Childs of its duty to exercise due care towards its customers), nevertheless Ash has been hurt and therefore we are going to render a verdict against Childs, this would have been arbitrary and unreasoned. In other words, the law would not imply negligence where none was proved, but the law would and did imply a contractual warranty where none was expressed. Why? Because to have implied negligence where there was none would have been to ignore the very foundations of the law of torts. That would have been justice by one man, not by the law that generations of men had developed. On the other hand, contractual warranty could be implied without violence to the whole body of contract law. An implied contract is closer to actual contract than implied negligence is to no negligence.

THE RISE AND FALL OF A LEGAL CONCEPT

THOMAS AND WIFE v. WINCHESTER
Court of Appeals of New York, 6 N.Y. (2 Selden) 397 (1852).

Action in the supreme court, commenced in August, 1849, against Winchester and Gilbert, for injuries sustained by Mrs. Thomas, from the effects of a quantity of extract of belladonna, administered to her by mistake as extract of dandelion.

. . . The defendant Gilbert was acquitted by the jury under the direction of the court, and a verdict was rendered against Winchester, for eight hundred dollars. A motion for a new trial, made upon a bill of exceptions taken at the trial, having been denied at a general term in the sixth district, the defendant Winchester, brought this appeal. . . .

RUGGLES, CH. J. delivered the opinion of the court.   This is an action brought to recover damages from the defendant for negligently putting up, labeling and selling as and for the extract of *dandelion,* which is a simple and harmless medicine, a jar of the extract of *belladonna,* which is a deadly poison; by means of which the plaintiff Mary Ann Thomas, to whom, being sick, a dose of dandelion was prescribed by a physician, and a portion of the contents of the jar, was administered as and for the extract of dandelion, was greatly injured, etc.

The facts proved were briefly these: Mrs. Thomas being in ill health, her physician prescribed for her a dose of dandelion. Her husband purchased what was believed to be the medicine prescribed, at the store of Dr. Foord, a physician and druggist in Cazenovia, Madison county, where the plaintiffs reside.

A small quantity of the medicine thus purchased was administered to Mrs. Thomas on whom it produced very alarming effects; such as coldness of the surface and extremities, feebleness of circulation, spasms of the muscles, giddiness of the head, dilation of the pupils of the eyes, and derangement of the mind. She recovered, however, after some time, from its effects, although for a short time her life was thought to be in great danger. The medicine administered was *belladonna, and not dandelion.* The jar from which it was taken was labeled *"1/2 lb. dandelion, prepared by A. Gilbert, No. 108 John-street, N. Y. Jar 8 oz."* It was sold for and believed by Dr. Foord to be the extract of dandelion as labeled. Dr. Foord purchased the article as the extract of dandelion from Jas. S. Aspinwall, a druggist at New York. Aspinwall bought it of the defendant as extract of dandelion, believing it to be such. The defendant was engaged at No. 108 John-street, New York, in the manufacture and sale of certain vegetable extracts for medicinal purposes, and in the purchase and sale of others. The extracts manufactured by him were put up in jars for sale, and those which he purchased were put up by him in like manner. The jars containing extracts manufactured by himself and those containing extracts purchased by him from others, were labeled alike. Both were labeled like the jar in question, as "prepared by A. Gilbert." Gilbert was a person employed by the defendant at a salary, as an assistant in his business. The jars were labeled in Gilbert's name because he had been previously engaged in the same business on his own account at No. 108 John-street, and probably because Gilbert's labels rendered the articles more salable. The extract contained in the jar sold to Aspinwall, and by him to Foord, was not manufactured by the defendant, but was purchased by him from another manufacturer or dealer. The extract of dandelion and the extract of belladonna resembled each other in color, consistence, smell and taste; but may on careful examination be distinguished the one from the other by those who are well acquainted with these articles. Gilbert's labels were paid for by Winchester and used in his business with his knowledge and assent.

The defendant's counsel moved for a nonsuit on the following grounds:

1. That the action could not be sustained, as the defendant was the remote vendor of the article in question; and there was no connection, transaction or privity between him and the plaintiffs, or either of them.

.   .   .   .   .

The judge overruled the motion for a nonsuit, and the defendant's counsel excepted.

The judge among other things charged the jury, that if they should find from the evidence that either Aspinwall or Foord was guilty of negligence in vending as and for dandelion the extract taken by Mrs. Thomas, or that the plaintiff Thomas, or those who administered it to Mrs. Thomas were chargeable with negligence in administering it, the plaintiffs were not entitled to recover; but if they were free from negligence, and if the defendant Winchester was guilty of negligence in putting up and vending the extracts in question, the plaintiffs were entitled to recover, provided the extract administered to Mrs. Thomas was the same which was put up by the defendant and sold by him to Aspinwall and by Aspinwall to Foord.   .   .   .

.   .   .   .   .

The case depends on the first point taken by the defendant on his motion for a nonsuit; and the question is, whether the defendant, being a remote vendor of the medicine, and there being no privity or connection between him and the plaintiffs, the action can be maintained.

If, in labeling a poisonous drug with the name of a harmless medicine, for public market, no duty was violated by the defendant, excepting that which he owed to Aspinwall, his immediate vendee, in virtue of his contract of sale, this action cannot be maintained. If A. builds a wagon and sells it to B., who sells it to C., and C. hires it to D., who in consequence of the gross negligence of A. in building the wagon is overturned and injured, D. cannot recover damages against A., the builder. A.'s obligation to build the wagon faithfully, arises solely out of his contract with B. The public have nothing to do with it. Misfortune to third persons, not parties to the contract, would not be a natural and necessary consequence of the builder's negligence; and such negligence is not an act imminently dangerous to human life.

So, for the same reason, if a horse be defectively shod by a smith, and a person hiring the horse from the owner is thrown and injured in consequence of the smith's negligence in shoeing; the smith is not liable for the injury. The smith's duty in such case grows exclusively out of his contract with the owner of the horse; it was a duty which the smith owed to him alone, and to no one else. And although the injury to the rider may have happened in consequence of the negligence of the smith, the latter was not bound, either by his contract or by any considerations of public policy of safety, to respond for his breach of duty to any one except the person he contracted with.

This was the ground on which the case of Winterbottom v. Wright, 10 Mees. & Welsh. 109, was decided. A. contracted with the postmaster general to provide a coach to convey the mail bags along a certain line of road, and B. and others also contracted to horse the coach along the same line. B. and his co-contractors hired C., who was the plaintiff, to drive the coach. The coach, in consequence of some latent defect, broke down; the plaintiff was thrown from his seat and lamed. It was held that C. could not maintain an action against A. for the injury thus sustained. The reason of the decision is best stated by Baron Rolfe. A.'s duty to keep the coach in good condition, was a duty to the postmaster general, with whom he made his contract and not a duty to the driver employed by the owners of the horses.

But the case in hand stands on a different ground. The defendant was a dealer in poisonous drugs. Gilbert was his agent in preparing them for market. The death or great bodily harm of some person was the natural and almost inevitable consequence of the sale of belladonna by means of the false label.

Gilbert, the defendant's agent, would have been punishable for manslaughter if Mrs. Thomas had died in consequence of taking the falsely labeled medicine. Every man who, by his culpable negligence, causes the death of another, although without intent to kill, is guilty of manslaughter. . . . A chemist who negligently sells laudanum in a phial labeled as paregoric, and thereby causes the death of a person to whom it is administered, is guilty of manslaughter. Tesymond's case, 1 Lowin's Crown Cases, 169. "So highly does the law value human life that it admits no justification wherever life has been lost and the carelessness or negligence of one person has contributed to the death of another." Regina v. Swindall, 2 Car. & Kir. 238-3. And this rule applied not only where the death of one is occasioned by the negligent act of another, but where it is caused by the negligent omission of a duty of that other. 2 Car. & Kir. 368, 371. Although the defendant Winchester may not be answerable criminally for the negligence of his agent, there can be no doubt of his liability in a civil action, in which the act of agent is to be regarded as the act of the principal.

In respect to the wrongful and criminal character of the negligence complained of, this case differs widely from those put by the defendant's counsel. No such imminent danger existed in those cases. In the present case the sale of the poisonous article was made to a dealer in drugs, and not to a consumer. The injury therefore was not likely to fall on him, or on his vendee who was also a dealer; but much more likely to be visited on a remote purchaser as actually happened. The defendant's negligence put human life in imminent danger. Can it be said that there was no duty on the part of the defendant, to avoid the creation of that danger by the exercise of greater caution? or that the exercise of that caution was a duty only to his immediate vendee, whose life was not endangered? The defendant's duty arose out of the nature of his business and the danger to others incident to its mismanagement. Nothing but mischief like that which actually happened could have been expected from sending the poison falsely labeled into the market; and the defendant is justly responsible for the probable consequence of the act. The duty of exercising caution in this respect did not arise out of the defendant's contract of sale to Aspinwall. The wrong done by the defendant was in putting the poison, mislabeled, into the hands of Aspinwall as an article of merchandise to be sold and afterwards used as the extract of dandelion, by some person then unknown. The owner of a horse and cart who leaves them unattended in the street is liable for any damage which may result from his negligence. Lynch v. Nurdin, 1 Ad. & Ellis, N.S. 29. . . . The owner of a loaded gun who puts it into the hands of a child by whose indiscretion it is discharged, is liable for the damage occasioned by the discharge. 5 Maude & Sell. 194. The defendant's contract of sale to Aspinwall does not excuse the wrong done to the plaintiffs. It was a part of the means by which the wrong was effected. The plaintiffs' injury and their remedy would have stood on the same principle, if the defendant had given the belladonna to Dr. Foord without price, or if he had put in his shop without his knowledge, which would probably have led to its sale on the faith of the label.

In Longmeid v. Holliday, 6 Law and Eq.Rep. 562, the distinction is recognized between an act of negligence imminently dangerous to the lives of others, and one that is not so. In former case, the party guilty of the negligence is liable to the party injured, whether there be a contract between them or not; in the latter, the negligent party is liable only to the party with whom he contracted, and on the ground that negligence is a breach of the contract.

The defendant, on the trial, insisted that Aspinwall and Foord were guilty of negligence in selling the article in question for what it was represented to be in the label; and that the suit, if it could be sustained at all, should have been brought against Foord. The judge charged the jury that if they, or either of them were guilty of negligence in selling the belladonna for dandelion, the verdict must be for the defendant; and left the question of their negligence to the jury, who found on that point for the plaintiff. If the case really depended on the point thus raised, the question was properly left to the jury. But I think it did not. The defendant, by affixing the label to the jar, represented its contents to be dandelion; and to have been "prepared" by his agent Gilbert. The word "prepared" on the label, must be understood to mean that the article was manufactured by him, or that it had passed through some process under his hands, which would give him personal knowledge of its true name and quality. Whether Foord was justified in selling the article upon the faith of the defendant's label, would have been an open question in an action by the plaintiffs against him, and I wish to be understood as giving no opinion on that point. But it seems to me to be clear that the defendant cannot, in this case, set up as a defense, that Foord sold the contents of the jar as and for what the defendant represented it to be. The label conveyed the idea distinctly to Foord that the contents of the jar was the extract of dandelion; and that the defendant knew it to be such. So far as the defendant is concerned, Foord was under no obligation to test the truth of the representation. The charge of the judge in submitting to the jury the question in relation to the negligence of Foord and Aspinwall, cannot be complained of by the defendant.

. . .

Judgment affirmed.

LOOP v. LITCHFIELD
Court of Appeals of New York, 42 N.Y. 351 (1870).

HUNT, J.   A piece of machinery already made and on hand, having defects which weaken it, is sold by the manufacturer to one who buys it for its own use. . . . This piece of machinery is used by the buyer [Collister] for five years, and is then taken into possession of a neighbor, who uses it for his own purposes. While so in use, it flies apart by reason of its original defects, and the person using it is killed. Is the seller, upon this state of facts, liable to the representatives of the deceased party?   . . .

To maintain this liability, the appellants rely upon the case of Thomas v. Winchester, 6 N.Y., 2 Seld., 397.   . . .

.   .   .   .

The appellants recognize the principle of this decision, and seek to bring their case within it, by asserting that the fly wheel in question was a dangerous instrument. Poison is a dangerous subject. Gunpowder is the same. A torpedo is a dangerous instrument, as is a spring gun, a loaded rifle or the like. They are instruments and articles in their nature calculated to do injury to mankind, and generally intended to accomplish that purpose. They are essentially, and in their elements, instruments of danger. Not so, however, an iron wheel, a few feet in diameter and a few inches in thickness although one part may be weaker than another. If the article is abused by too long use, or by applying too much weight or speed, an injury may occur, as it may from an ordinary carriage wheel, a wagon axle, or the common chair in which we sit. There is scarcely an object in art or nature, from which an injury may not occur under such circumstances. Yet they are not in their nature sources of danger, nor can they, with any regard to the accurate use of language, be called dangerous instruments. That an injury actually occurred by the breaking of a carriage axle, the failure of the carriage body, the falling to pieces of a chair or sofa, or the bursting of a fly wheel, does not in the least alter its character.

It is suggested that it is no more dangerous or illegal to label a deadly poison as a harmless medicine than to conceal a defect in a machine and paint it over so that it will appear sound.   . . .   I answer, that the decision in Thomas v. Winchester was based upon the idea that the negligent sale of poisons is both at common law and by statute an indictable offence.   . . .   The injury in that case was a natural result of the act. It was just what was to have been expected from putting falsely labeled poisons in the market, to be used by whoever should need the true articles. It was in its nature an act imminently dangerous to the lives of others. Not so here. The bursting of the wheel and the injury to human life was not the natural result or the expected consequence of the manufacture and sale of the wheel. Every use of the counterfeit medicines would be necessarily injurious, while this wheel was in fact used with safety for five years.

.   .   .   .

Upon the facts as stated, assuming that the deceased had no knowledge of the defects complained of, and assuming that he was in the rightful and lawful use of the machine, I am of the opinion that the verdict cannot be sustained. The facts constitute no cause of action.

.   .   .   .

All concur. Judgment affirmed, and judgment absolute.ordered for the defendants.

LOSEE v. CLUTE
Commission of Appeals of New York, 51 N.Y. 494 (1873).

Appeal from judgment of the General Term of the Supreme Court in the fourth judicial district, affirming a judgment entered upon an order dismissing plaintiff's complaint on the trial.

The action was brought to recover damages caused to the property of the plaintiff by the explosion of a steam boiler while the same was owned and being used by the Saratoga Paper Company at their mill situated in the village of Schuylerville, Saratoga County and State of New York, on the thirteenth day of February, 1864, by means whereof the boiler was thrown on to the plaintiff's premises and through several of his buildings, thereby injuring and damaging the same.

The defendants, Clute, were made parties defendants to the action with the Saratoga Paper Company and Coe S. Buchanan and Daniel A. Bullard, trustees and agents of said company, on the ground that they were the manufacturers of the boiler, and made the same out of poor and brittle iron and in a negligent and defective manner, in consequence of which negligence said explosion occurred.

At the close of the evidence the complaint was dismissed as to the defendants Clute.

. . . . .

LOTT, CH. J.   It appears by the case that the defendants Clute manufactured the boiler in question for the Saratoga Paper Company, in which they were stockholders, for the purposes and uses to which it was subsequently applied by it; and the testimony tended to show that it was constructed improperly and of poor iron, that the said defendants knew at the time that it was to be used in the immediate vicinity of and adjacent to dwelling-houses and stores in a village, so that, in case of an explosion while in use, it would be likely to be destructive to human life and adjacent property, and that, in consequence of the negligence of the said defendants in the improper construction of the boiler, the explosion that took place occurred and damaged the plaintiff's property. The evidence also tended to show that the boiler was tested by the company to its satisfaction, and then accepted, and was thereafter used by it for about three months prior to the explosion, and that after such test and acceptance the said defendants had nothing whatever to do with the boiler, and had no care or management of it at the time of the explosion, but that the company had the sole and exclusive ownership, management and conduct of it.

In determining whether the complaint was properly dismissed, we must assume all the facts which the evidence tended to show as established, and the question is thereby presented whether the defendants have incurred any liability to the plaintiff. They contracted with the company, and did what was done by them for it and to its satisfaction, and when the boiler was accepted they ceased to have any further control over it or its management, and all responsibility for what was subsequently done with it devolved upon the company and those having charge of it, and the case falls within the principle decided by the Court of Appeals in The Mayor, etc., of Albany v. Cunliff, 2 Comst., 165, which is that [at] the most an architect or builder of a work is answerable only to his employees for any want of care or skill in the execution thereof, and he is not liable for accidents or injuries which may occur after the execution of the work; and the opinions published in that case clearly show that there is no ground of liability by the defendants to the plaintiff in this action. They owed *him* no *duty* whatever at the time of the explosion either growing out of contract or imposed by law.

It may be proper to refer to the case of Thomas v. Winchester, 2 Selden, 397, cited by the appellant's counsel, and I deem it sufficient to say that the opinion of Hunt, J., in Loop v. Litchfield, 42 N.Y. 351, clearly shows that the principle decided in that case has no application to this.

It appears from these considerations that the complaint was properly dismissed, and it follows that there was no case made for the consideration of the jury, and, consequently, there was no error in the refusal to submit it to them.

There was an exception taken to the exclusion of evidence to show that two persons were killed by this boiler in passing through a dwelling-house in its course, but as it is not urged on this appeal, it is, I presume, abandoned; but if not, it was matter, as the judge held at the trial, wholly immaterial to the issue between the parties in this action.

There is, for the reasons stated, no ground for the reversal of the judgment. It must, therefore, be affirmed, with costs.

All concur.

Judgment affirmed.

DEVLIN v. SMITH
Court of Appeals New York, 89 N.Y. 470 (1882).

This is an appeal from a judgment of the General Term, second department, affirming a judgment entered upon an order dismissing plaintiff's complaint, at the trial.   . . .

This action was commenced to recover damages for the benefit of the next of kin of Hugh Devlin, deceased, who was killed through the alleged negligence of the defendants.

The deceased, at the time he was killed, was upon a scaffold erected in the rotunda of the court-house, in Brooklyn, washing off the panels of the dome preparatory to its being painted; while thus engaged the portion of the scaffold upon which the deceased was at work broke and fell, precipitating him to the ground, a distance of ninety feet, thereby causing his death.

The defendant Smith entered into a contract with the board of supervisors, of the county of Kings, whereby he agreed to paint and fresco the inside of the county court-house, and furnish all the material and labor necessary therefor. In the performance of his contract it became necessary to have a scaffold erected in the rotunda of the court-house, and he made a contract with the defendant Stevenson to erect the scaffold in question, and to furnish the material therefor.

The scaffold erected consisted of six sections, one built on top of the other, and known as a rope and pole scaffold. Plank being laid across the ledgers, or horizontal poles and forming a flooring to enable the men to work upon the dome.

The portion of the scaffold that broke at the time of accident was not constructed like the other portions; the end of one of the top ledgers was not supported by an upright, but instead thereof, a piece of plank was used as a brace by resting the lower end upon the ledger below, the upper end being nailed to the end of the ledger in question.

The deceased, together with a fellow workman, was upon a plank resting on this ledger at the time it broke. The defendant Stevenson knew that the brace in question was nailed to the ledger as above described, he having examined it before the accident. The defendant Smith in whose employ the deceased was, had many contracts going on at the same time, and would go about each day from one job to another, remaining at each place about half an hour. The scaffold was not examined by the defendant Smith nor his superintendent until after the accident. .

RAPALLO, J.   Upon a careful review of all the testimony in this case, we are of opinion that there was sufficient evidence to require the submission to the jury of the question, whether the breaking down of the scaffold was attributable to negligence in its construction. It appears that the ledger which supported the plank upon which the deceased was sitting broke down without any excessive weight being put upon it, and without any apparent cause sufficient to break a well-constructed scaffold. One witness on the part of the plaintiff, accustomed to work on scaffolds and to see them built, testified that the upright which supported the end of the ledger should have been fastened to it by lashing with ropes, instead of by nailing, and that lashing would have made it stronger, giving as reasons for this opinion, that the springing of the planks when walked upon was liable to break nails or push them out, whereas lashings would only become tighter, and the witness testified that the kind of scaffold in question was generally fastened by lashing, and that it was not the proper way to support the end of the ledger which broke, with an upright nailed to the ledger, and that the ledger in question was fastened by nailing.

Another, a carpenter and builder, testified, that when, on account of the curving of a dome, it became necessary to put in a cripple, the cripple as well as the main uprights should be tied to the ledgers with rope; that the springing of the scaffold will break nails.

The appearances after the breakage were described to the jury, and a model of the scaffold was exhibited to them. Testimony touching the same points was submitted on the part of the defendants, and we think that on the whole evidence it was a question of fact for the jury, and not of law for the court, whether or not the injury was the result of the negligent construction of the scaffold.

The question of contributory negligence on the part of the deceased was also one for the jury. They had before them the circumstances of the accident. It appeared that the deceased was sitting on a plank, performing the work for which the scaffold had been erected. He was washing the interior wall of the dome, preparatory to its being painted. There was nothing to indicate that he was in an improper place, or that he unnecessarily exposed himself to danger, or did any act to contribute to the accident. It is suggested that he, or some of his fellow-servants, may have kicked against the upright or brace which supported the end of the ledger, and thus thrown it out of place, but there was no evidence which would entitle the court to assume that the accident occurred from any such cause. The case was, therefore, one in which the jury might have found from the evidence that the death was caused by the improper or negligent construction of the scaffold, and without any fault on the part of the deceased, and the remaining question is, whether, if those facts should be found, the defendants, or either of them, should be held liable in this action.

The defendant Smith claims that no negligence on his part was shown. He was a painter who had made a contract with the supervisors of Kings county to paint the interior of the dome of the county courthouse, and the deceased was a workman employed by him upon that work. As between Smith and the county, he was bound to furnish the necessary scaffolding; but he was not a scaffold-builder, nor had he any knowledge of the business of building scaffolds, or any experience therein. He did not undertake to build the scaffold in question himself, or by means of servants or workmen under his direction, but made a contract with the defendant Stevenson to erect the structure for a gross sum, and the work was done under that contract, by Stevenson, who employed his own workmen and superintended the job himself. Mr. Stevenson had been known to Smith as a scaffold-builder since 1844. His experience had been very large, and Smith had employed him before, and on this occasion the contract with him was for a first-class scaffold. There is no evidence upon which to base any allegation of incompetency on the part of Stevenson, nor any charge of negligence on the part of Smith in selecting him as a contractor, nor is there any evidence that Smith knew, or had reason to know, of any defect in the scaffold.

.   .   .   .

If any person was at fault in the matter it was the defendant Stevenson. It is contended, however, that even if through his negligence the scaffold was defective, he is not liable in this action because there was no privity between him and the deceased, and he owed no duty to the deceased, his obligation and duty being only to Smith.

As a general rule the builder of a structure for another party, under a contract with him, or one who sells an article of his own manufacture, is not liable to an action by a third party who uses the same with the consent of the owner or purchaser, for injuries resulting from a defect therein, caused by negligence. The liability of the builder or manufacturer for such defects is, in general, only to the person with whom he contracted. But, notwithstanding this rule, liability to third parties has been held to exist when the defect is such as to render the article in itself imminently dangerous, and serious injury to any person using it is a natural and probable consequence of its use. As where a dealer in drugs carelessly labeled a deadly poison as a harmless medicine, it was held that he was liable not merely to the person to whom he sold it, but to the person who ultimately used it, though it had passed through many hands. This liability was held to rest, not upon any contract or direct privity between him and the party injured, but upon the duty which the law imposes on every one to avoid acts in their nature dangerous to the lives of others. Thomas v. Winchester, 6 N.Y. 397. In that case Mayor, etc., v. Cunliff, 2 N.Y. 165, was cited as an authority for the position that a builder is liable only to the party for whom he builds. Some of the examples there put by way of illustration were commented upon, and among others the case of one who builds a carriage carelessly and of defective materials, and sells it, and the purchaser lends it to a friend, and the carriage, by reason of its original defect, breaks down and the friend is injured, and the question is put, can he recover against the maker? The comments of Ruggles, Ch. J., upon this supposititious case, in Thomas v. Winchester, and the ground upon which he answers the question in the negative, show clearly the distinction between the two classes of cases. He says that in the case supposed, the obligation of the maker to build faithfully arises only out of his contract with the purchaser. The public have nothing to do with it. Misfortune to third persons, not parties to the contract, would not be a natural and necessary consequence of the builder's negligence, and such negligence is not an act imminently dangerous to human life.

Applying these tests to the question now before us, the solution is not difficult. Stevenson undertook to build a scaffold ninety feet in height, for the express purpose of enabling the workmen of Smith to stand upon it to paint the interior of the dome. Any defect or negligence in its construction, which should cause it to give way, would naturally result in these men being precipitated from that great height. A stronger case where misfortune to third persons not parties to the contract would be a natural and necessary consequence of the builder's negligence, can hardly be supposed, nor is it easy to imagine a more apt illustration of a case where such negligence would be an act imminently dangerous to human life. These circumstances seem to us to bring the case fairly within the principle of Thomas v. Winchester.

Loop v. Litchfield, 42 N.Y. 351, was decided upon the ground that the wheel which caused the injury was not in itself a dangerous instrument, and that the injury was not a natural consequence of the defect, or one reasonably to be anticipated. Losee v. Clute, 51 N.Y. 494, was distinguished from Thomas v. Winchester, upon the authority of Loop v. Litchfield.

We think there should be a new trial as to the defendant Stevenson, and that it will be for the jury to determine whether the death of the plaintiff's intestate was caused by negligence on the part of Stevenson in the construction of the scaffold.

The judgment should be affirmed, with costs, as to the defendant Smith, and reversed as to the defendant Stevenson, and a new trial ordered as to him, costs to abide the event.

ANDREWS, CH. J., DANFORTH and FINCH, JJ., concur; EARL, J., concurs as to defendant Smith, and dissents as to defendant Stevenson. MILLER, J., absent; TRACY, J., not sitting.

Judgment accordingly.

TORGESEN v. SCHULTZ
Court of Appeals of New York, 192 N.Y. 156 (1908).

Appeal from a judgment of the Appellate Division of the Supreme Court in the first judicial department, entered April 12, 1906, affirming a judgment in favor of defendant entered upon a dismissal of the complaint by the court at a Trial Term.

WILLARD BARTLETT, J.   The plaintiff has suffered the loss of an eye by reason of the explosion of a siphon bottle of aerated water filled and put upon the market by the defendant corporation. The siphon had been charged at a pressure of 125 pounds to the square inch. The plaintiff was a domestic servant and on July 1, 1901, between one and two o'clock in the afternoon she received at the door of her employer's house in the city of New York two siphons which had been filled with water by the defendant and which had been purchased from a druggist who had obtained them from the defendant. The day was very hot, the registered temperature at the weather bureau being as follows: 1 P.M., 95 degrees; 2 P.M., 96 degrees; 3 P.M., 96 degrees; 4 P.M., 96 degrees; 5 P.M., 96 degrees; 6 P.M., 97 degrees; 7 P.M., 96 degrees, and 8 P.M., 93 degrees. Upon receiving the siphons the plaintiff took them to a room in the third story, where they remained until between 7 and 8 o'clock in the evening, when she carried them down stairs and placed them in a standing position in a pan containing ice, so that one side of each bottle was against the ice. As she turned away one of the siphons exploded with the result stated.

To show the necessity of taking precautions to prevent such explosions, and also to show the extent of the precautions actually taken by the defendant to that end, plaintiff's counsel read in evidence certain extracts from a printed circular of the defendant, and counsel for the defendant also read certain other extracts, all of which taken together are as follows:

"We take all possible precautions to guard against accidents by not allowing any siphons or bottles to leave our premises without first being thoroughly tested. On account of the sudden change of temperature any defect in the glass will at once cause the siphon bottle to break. The accompanying cut shows our siphon testing department. All siphon bottles are imported direct from Austria and are received in large casks. They are unpacked and filled with water at a temperature of from 98 to 100 F. They are then put in cages and subjected to a hydrostatic pressure of 350 lbs. to the square inch. This pressure is allowed to remain for about 30 seconds. Then it is reduced to a pressure of 100 lbs. to the square inch, and the entire cage containing five siphons is then submerged in a tank containing cracked ice and water. On account of the sudden change of temperature any defect in the glass will at once cause the siphon bottle to break. The second step in our test is the only definite method to discover flaws in the anneal of the glass, and is by far severer than any condition a siphon is ever subjected to in the ordinary run of our business."

The plaintiff also called as an expert witness an instructor in physics at Columbia University, who described a series of experimental tests which he had made upon a number of siphon bottles of aerated water sold by the defendant. These experiments were conducted by subjecting the siphons to conditions designed to reproduce approximately those which existed at the time when the explosion occurred by which the plaintiff was injured. Out of seventy-one bottles which were thus tested five exploded, and all of these explosions occurred within half a minute after the bottles were placed in contact with ice. It furthermore appeared that when the siphons came back to the defendant, after having once been distributed to its customers, they were not tested again, and that the defendant had no means of determining how many times the bottles were sent out after they had been filled and after they were returned for filling, although they were probably sent out a large number of times.

It is manifest that there was no contract relation between the plaintiff and the defendant, but the defendant is sought to be held liable under the doctrine of Thomas v. Winchester, 6 N.Y. 397, and similar cases based upon the duty of the vendor of an article dangerous in its nature, or likely to become so in the course of the ordinary usage to be contemplated by the vendor, either to exercise due care to warn users of the danger or to take reasonable care to prevent the article sold from proving dangerous when subjected only to customary usage. The principle of law invoked is that which was well stated by Lord Justice Cotton in Heaven v. Pender, L.R. [11 Q.B.D.] 503, as follows: "Any one who leaves a dangerous instrument, as a gun, in such a way as to cause danger, or who without due warning supplies to others for use an instrument or thing which to his knowledge, from its construction or otherwise is in such a condition as to cause danger, not necessarily incident to the use of such an instrument or thing, is liable for injury caused to others by reason of his negligent act."

.   .   .   .   .

.   .   .   The language of the defendant's circular tends to show that it was well aware that siphons charged under a pressure of 125 pounds to the square inch were liable to explode unless the bottles had been first subjected to an adequate test. This is plainly inferable from the statement: "We take all possible precautions to guard against accidents." There could be no possible occasion for this assertion unless accidents were likely to happen in the absence of proper precaution to avert them. The testimony of the expert witness to which we have referred tended to show, although, of course, it did not necessarily establish the fact, that the test described in the defendant's circular (which, it may fairly be assumed, was the severest test applied to the siphons) was insufficient to establish that the bottles would not explode when used as customers might be expected to use them. The defendant might reasonably be held chargeable with knowledge that it was customary, especially in hot weather, to place siphons charged with aerated water in contact with ice, and in view of this fact a jury might well find that the tests applied to such bottles should be such as to render it tolerably certain that they would not explode when thus used. As has already been suggested, the expert testimony indicated that the test actually employed by the defendant was not adequate to justify such a conclusion.

It may very well be that the defendant, if put to its proof on the subject, may establish the adequacy of its test and that nothing further can reasonably be required to be done to assure the safety of those making use of their charged siphons as against explosions of the character which injured the plaintiff, but upon the evidence as it stood at the close of her case I think there was enough to entitle the plaintiff to have the question of the defendant's negligence submitted to the jury.

The judgment should be reversed and a new trial granted, costs to abide the event.

CULLEN, CH. J., GRAY, HAIGHT, VANN, HISCOCK and CHASE, JJ., concur.

Judgment reversed, etc.

MACPHERSON v. BUICK MOTOR CO.
Court of Appeals of New York, 217 N.Y. 382 (1916).

Appeal, by permission, from a judgment of the Appellate Division of the Supreme Court in the third judicial department, entered January 8, 1914, affirming a judgment in favor of plaintiff entered upon a verdict.

. . . . .

CARDOZO, J.   The defendant is a manufacturer of automobiles. It sold an automobile to a retail dealer. The retail dealer resold it to the plaintiff. While the plaintiff was in the car, it suddenly collapsed. He was thrown out and injured. One of the wheels was made of defective wood, and its spokes crumbled into fragments. The wheel was not made by the defendant; it was bought from another manufacturer. There is evidence, however, that its defects could have been discovered by reasonable inspection, and that inspection was omitted. There is no claim that the defendant knew of the defect and willfully concealed it. . . .   The charge is one, not of fraud, but of negligence. The question to be determined is whether the defendant owed a duty of care and vigilance to any one but the immediate purchaser.

The foundations of this branch of the law, at least in this state, were laid in Thomas v. Winchester, 6 N.Y. 397. A poison was falsely labeled. The sale was made to a druggist, who in turn sold to a customer. The customer recovered damages from the seller who affixed the label. "The defendant's negligence," it was said, "put human life in imminent danger." A poison falsely labeled is likely to injure anyone who gets it. Because the danger is to be foreseen, there is a duty to avoid the injury. Cases were cited by way of illustration in which manufacturers were not subject to any duty irrespective of contract. The distinction was said to be that their conduct, though negligent, was not likely to result in injury to any one except the purchaser. We are not required to say whether the chance of injury was always as remote as the distinction assumes. Some of the illustrations might be rejected to-day. The *principle* of the distinction is for present purposes the important thing.

Thomas v. Winchester became quickly a landmark of the law. In the application of its principle there may at times have been uncertainty or even error. There has never in this state been doubt or disavowal of the principle itself. The chief cases are well known, yet to recall some of them will be helpful. Loop v. Litchfield, 42 N.Y. 351, is the earliest. It was the case of a defect in a small balance wheel used on a circular saw. The manufacturer pointed out the defect to the buyer, who wished a cheap article and was ready to assume the risk. The risk can hardly have been an imminent one, for the wheel lasted five years before it broke. In the meanwhile the buyer had made a lease of the machinery. It was held that the manufacturer was not answerable to the lessee. Loop v. Litchfield was followed in Losee v. Clute, 51 N.Y. 494, the case of the explosion of a steam boiler. That decision has been criticized   .   .   .   but it must be confined to its special facts. It was put upon the ground that the risk of injury was too remote. The buyer in that case had not only accepted the boiler, but had tested it. The manufacturer knew that his own test was not the final one. The finality of the test has a bearing on the measure of diligence owing to persons other than the purchaser.   .   .   .

These early cases suggest a narrow construction of the rule. Later cases, however, evince a more liberal spirit. First in importance is Devlin v. Smith, 89 N.Y. 470. The defendant, a contractor, built a scaffold for a painter. The painter's servants were injured. The contractor was held liable. He knew that the scaffold, if improperly constructed, was a most dangerous trap. He knew that it was to be used by the workmen. He was building it for that very purpose. Building it for their use, he owed them a duty, irrespective of his contract with their master, to build it with care.

From Devlin v. Smith we pass over intermediate cases and turn to the latest case in this court in which Thomas v. Winchester was followed. That case is Statler v. Ray Mfg. Co., 195 N.Y. 478, 480. The defendant manufactured a large coffee urn. It was installed in a restaurant. When heated, the urn exploded and injured the plaintiff. We held that the manufacturer was liable. We said that the urn "was of such a character inherently that, when applied to the purposes for which it was designed, it was liable to become a source of great danger to many people if not carefully and properly constructed."

It may be that Devlin v. Smith and Statler v. Ray Mfg. Co. have extended the rule of Thomas v. Winchester. If so, this court is committed to the extension. The defendant argues that things imminently dangerous to life are poisons, explosives, deadly weapons —things whose normal function is to injure or destroy. But whatever the rule in Thomas v. Winchester may once have been, it has no longer that restricted meaning. A scaffold (Devlin v. Smith, *supra*) is not inherently a destructive instrument. It becomes destructive only if imperfectly constructed. A large coffee urn (Statler v. Ray Mfg. Co., *supra*) may have within itself, if negligently made, the potency of danger, yet no one thinks of it as an implement whose normal function is destruction. What is true of the coffee urn is equally true of bottles of aerated water (Torgeson v. Schultz, 192 N.Y. 156). We have mentioned only cases in this court.   .   .   .

We hold, then, that the principle of Thomas v. Winchester is not limited to poisons, explosives, and things of like nature, to things which in their normal operation are implements of destruction. If the nature of a thing is such that it is reasonably certain to place life and limb in peril when negligently made, it is then a thing of danger. Its nature gives warning of the consequences to be expected. If to the element of danger there is added knowledge that the thing will be used by persons other than the purchaser, and used without new tests, then, irrespective of contract, the manufacturer of this thing of danger is under a duty to make it carefully. That is as far as we are required to go for the decision of this case. There must be knowledge of a danger, not merely possible, but probable. It is *possible* to use almost anything in a way that will make it dangerous if defective. That is not enough to charge the manufacturer with a duty independent of his contract. Whether a given thing is dangerous may be sometimes a question for the court and sometimes a question for the jury. There must also be knowledge that in the usual course of events the danger will be shared by others than the buyer. Such knowledge may often be inferred from the nature of the transaction. But it is possible that even knowledge of the danger and of the use will not always be enough. The proximity or remoteness of the relation is a factor to be considered. We are dealing now with the liability of the manufacturer of the finished product, who puts it on the market to be used without inspection by his customers. If he is negligent, where danger is to be foreseen, a liability will follow. We are not required at this time to say that it is legitimate to go back of the manufacturer of the finished product and hold the manufacturers of the component parts. To make their negligence a cause of imminent danger, an independent cause must often intervene; the manufacturer of the finished product must also fail in *his* duty of inspection. It may be that in those circumstances the negligence of the earlier members of the series is too remote to constitute, as to the ultimate user, an actionable wrong.   .   .   .   We leave that question open. We shall have to deal with it when it arises. The difficulty which it suggests is not present in this case. There is here no break in the chain of cause and effect. In such circumstances, the presence of a known danger, attendant upon a known use, makes vigilance a duty. We have put aside the notion that the duty to safeguard life and limb, when the consequences of negligence may be foreseen, grows out of contract and nothing else. We have put the source of the obligation where it ought to be. We have put its source in the law.

From this survey of the decisions, there thus emerges a definition of the duty of a manufacturer which enables us to measure this defendant's liability. Beyond all question, the nature of an automobile gives warning of probable danger if its construction is defective. This automobile was designed to go fifty miles an hour. Unless its wheels were sound and strong, injury was almost certain. It was as much a thing of danger as a defective engine for a railroad. The defendant knew the danger. It knew also that the car would be used by persons other than the buyer. This was apparent from its size; there were seats for three persons. It was apparent also from the fact that the buyer was a dealer in cars, who bought to resell. The maker of this car supplied it for the use of purchasers from the dealer just as plainly as the contractor in Devlin v. Smith supplied the scaffold for use by the servants of the owner. The dealer was indeed the one person of whom it might be said with some approach to certainty that by him the car would not be used. Yet the defendant would have us say that he was the one person whom it was under a legal duty to protect. The law does not lead us to so inconsequent a conclusion. Precedents drawn from the days of travel by stage coach do not fit the conditions of travel to-day. The principle that the danger must be imminent does not change, but the things subject to the principle do change. They are whatever the needs of life in a developing civilization require them to be.

.   .   .   .

In this view of the defendant's liability there is nothing inconsistent with the theory of liability on which the case was tried. It is true that the court told the jury that "an automobile is not an inherently dangerous vehicle." The meaning, however, is made plain by the context. The meaning is that danger is not to be expected when the vehicle is well constructed. The court left it to the jury to say whether the defendant ought to have foreseen that the car, if negligently constructed, would become "imminently dangerous." Subtle distinctions are drawn by the defendant between things inherently dangerous and things imminently dangerous, but the case does not turn upon these verbal niceties. If danger was to be expected as reasonably certain, there was a duty of vigilance, and this whether you call the danger inherent or imminent. In varying forms that thought was put before the jury. We do not say that the court would not have been justified in ruling as a matter of law that the car was a dangerous thing. If there was any error, it was none of which the defendant can complain.

We think the defendant was not absolved from a duty of inspection because it bought the wheels from a reputable manufacturer. It was not merely a dealer in automobiles. It was a manufacturer of automobiles. It was responsible for the finished product. It was not at liberty to put the finished product on the market without subjecting the component parts to ordinary and simple tests.   .   .   .   Under the charge of the trial judge nothing more was required of it. The obligation to inspect must vary with the nature of the thing to be inspected. The more probable the danger, the greater the need of caution. There is little analogy between this case and Carlson v. Phoenix Bridge Co., 132 N.Y. 273, where the defendant bought a tool for a servant's use. The making of tools was not the business in which the master was engaged. Reliance on the skill of the manufacturer was proper and almost inevitable. But that is not the defendant's situation. Both by its relation to the work and by the nature of its business, it is charged with a stricter duty.

.   .   .   .

The judgment should be affirmed with costs.

[The dissenting opinion by Willard Bartlett, Ch. J., is omitted.]

HISCOCK, CHASE, and CUDDEBACK, JJ., concur with CARDOZO, J., and HOGAN, J., concurs in result; WILLARD BARTLETT, CH. J., reads dissenting opinion; POUND, J., not voting.

Judgment affirmed.

CONSISTENCY IS NOT ALWAYS A VIRTUE

No chapter in this book so exemplifies the concept of law and the changing environment as this chapter, in which the impact of mass production on the manufacturer's liability is dramatically demonstrated.

Mass production is a recent phenomenon in even the most advanced societies. For a thousand years in Western Europe, from the fall of Rome until the time of Joan of Arc, production was for consumption. The feudal manor was self-sustaining in all of the essentials of life, except the knight's armor and arms. Trade and markets, in the modern sense of the terms, were absent. There were occasional fairs in which the traveling merchant displayed wares (exotic products from the East—jewels, gems, ivories, laces, embroideries and the like). But trade in the sense of routine access to established markets for the necessities of life did not exist.

As feudalism disintegrated under the impact of nascent nationalism, as population began to increase, as the rule of primogeniture left second, third, and fourth sons no place on the manor, and as towns began to evolve beyond the walls of the fortified castles, specialization developed. The butcher, the baker, the candlestick maker—these were real figures, with real specialties, who enjoyed real trade; and there was a personal relationship between the maker of the product and the buyer. This personal relationship the law calls *privity.* The rule was that for lack of privity there was no liability to a secondary or remote buyer or user for injury caused by a maker's defective product, however negligent the maker may have been.

Aspects of this personal relationship persisted into the 19th century. Not until the late 19th and 20th centuries and the full fruition of the Industrial Revolution, which is characterized by inventions ranging from the flying shuttle to the steam engine, does large scale production significantly alter the legal relationship between the maker and secondary or remote buyers or users of a product.

With the growth of mass production and the proliferation of products far beyond the absolute necessities of life, it became increasingly unlikely that the manufacturer of a product would personally encounter the buyer or the user of that product in the purchase transaction. How many Model T owners ever bought a car from Henry Ford or any officer of Ford Motor Company in person? Few, if any. Yet, the original rule was that Ford Motor Company would not be liable to an injured owner or user of a defective Model T, absent privity of contract. Nevertheless, precisely because the manufacturer—a complete stranger to the buyer or user—produces large numbers of identical products, the risk of a defective product increases and the care induced by an "eyeball to eyeball" relationship diminishes.

It was not until 1965 that Ralph Nader, a lawyer, in *Unsafe at Any Speed* was the first to effectively point out that automobile manufacturers *do* make some defective automobiles. This revelation came after four decades of multimillion car-years and carnage on the highways that was, in some substantial measure, caused by faulty automobiles.

What we observe in such cases as Thomas and Wife and MacPherson is the legal process by which the courts broke away from the rule of a manufacturer's nonliability for injury to a remote buyer or user of a defective product.

It was a harsh, albeit logical, rule that a manufacturer had no liability to a remote buyer, however severely injured by the manufacturer's product or however defectively and negligently the product was made. The law long needed an escape from so severe a rule and found it in such cases as Thomas and Wife in the *inherently dangerous instrumentality exception.* The exception avoided repudiation of privity generally; it dispensed with privity only if the product was *an instrumentality inherently capable of injury to the user and if, in addition to that inherent characteristic, the product had a defect that was a consequence of the negligence of the maker.*

The exception did no more than shift the problem of a manufacturer's liability for a defective, negligently made product from the necessity for privity to the question, "What is a dangerous instrumentality?" The court had no trouble in holding belladonna inherently dangerous, but a defective flywheel that came apart and a pressure boiler made of brittle and therefore defective iron were held not to be dangerous instrumentalities. On the other hand, a ninety-foot scaffold and an aerated water bottle were declared inherently dangerous.

A rationale or criterion for determining what products are inherently dangerous would be impossible to develop from these cases. There seems to be no problem about belladonna, but why is a flywheel with a defect not inherently dangerous? The centrifugal forces involved are tremendous. What would be more likely to cause injury than a flywheel that could come apart? If an iron boiler is not inherently dangerous, then why is a siphon bottle? Both are pressure vessels. If a ninety-foot scaffold is inherently dangerous, then how about an eighty-foot scaffold, or an eight-foot scaffold? At what number of feet does the scaffold become inherently dangerous?

The whole dilemma of the inherently dangerous instrumentality exception was finally resolved by Judge Cardozo (in the MacPherson case) who, following the penchant of great judges for preserving a rule, defined the exception in such broad terms as to make the exception more important than the rule. Yet, he did not abolish the requirement for privity. Judges are respectful of a rule even though they may avoid it by exception. The judge never knows when he may need to recall an all but forgotten rule for a set of circumstances that he cannot presently imagine.

Judge Cardozo, a lucid and brilliant writer within the conventions of the law, stated: "If the nature of the thing is such that it is reasonably certain to place life and limb in peril when negligently made it is then a thing of danger. Its nature gives warning of the consequences to be expected. If to the element of danger there is added knowledge that the thing will be used by persons other than the purchaser, and used without new tests, then, irrespective of contract, the manufacturer of this thing of danger is under a duty to make it carefully." Hence, with respect to almost any product the manufacturer could be liable to a remote buyer. The product might be anything from a hairnet to a space vehicle. The door was now wide open for converting the exception by redefinition of an inherently dangerous instrumentality into a new rule that, in effect, abolishes privity in cases of manufacturer's liability to remote buyers and users. Quite likely, Judge Cardozo was aware of the implications of the Mac-

Pherson ruling. Otherwise, why would he have said: "The principle that the danger [inherent in the defective thing] must be imminent does not change, but the things subject to the principle do change. They are whatever the needs of life in a developing civilization require them to be."

Nevertheless, it remained necessary in a case in which a remote buyer or user asserted liability against the manufacturer of a product from which an injury had been suffered to show negligence on the part of the manufacturer in the manufacturing process; later, regardless of negligence, evidence of a defect in the product was required. In the remaining cases in this section we shall see what has become of these requirements.

Meanwhile, a great change in rationale has occurred, but the change relates to technology. Ash and Friend were decided in Massachusetts in 1918, two years after MacPherson was decided in New York. Ash and Friend involved blueberry pie and baked beans with corn beef, respectively. MacPherson involved a Buick automobile. In Ash and Friend it made a critical difference whether the suit was brought in tort or in contract. In MacPherson, Judge Cardozo, impatient with historical complexities, says: "We have put aside the notion that the duty to safeguard life and limb, when the consequences of negligence may be foreseen, grows out of contract and nothing else. We have put the source of the obligation where it ought to be. We have put its source in the law." Loose talk from a great judge? Seemingly so. What moves him to depart from consistency? The difference between blueberry pie and baked beans with corn beef on the one hand and an automobile on the other. Technology and commerce change law in America today no less than, as we saw in Chapter 1, they changed law in ancient Rome.

AN EMERGING CONCEPT OF MANUFACTURER'S LIABILITY

ESCOLA v. COCA COLA BOTTLING CO. OF FRESNO
Supreme Court of California, 24 Cal.2d 453 (1944).

[This case is included for the new philosophy of manufacturer's liability enunciated in the concurring opinion of Justice Traynor. The reader will note the doctrine of *res ipsa loquitur* on which the majority rest the decision; but it is the Traynor opinion which demonstrates how the law tries to grow.]

GIBSON, Chief Justice.   Plaintiff, a waitress in a restaurant, was injured when a bottle of Coca Cola broke in her hand. She alleged that defendant company, which had bottled and delivered the alleged defective bottle to her employer, was negligent in selling "bottles containing said beverage which on account of excessive pressure of gas or by reason of some defect in the bottle was dangerous * * * and likely to explode." This appeal is from a judgment upon a jury verdict in favor of plaintiff.

Defendant's driver delivered several cases of Coca Cola to the restaurant, placing them on the floor, one on top of the other, under and behind the counter, where they remained at least thirty-six hours. Immediately before the accident, plaintiff picked up the top case and set it upon a near-by ice cream cabinet in front of and about three feet from the refrigerator. She then proceeded to take the bottles from the case with her right hand, one at a time, and put them into the refrigerator. Plaintiff testified that after she had placed three bottles in the refrigerator and had moved the fourth bottle about 18 inches from the case "it exploded in my hand." The bottle broke into two jagged pieces and inflicted a deep five-inch cut, severing blood vessels, nerves and muscles of the thumb and palm of the hand. Plaintiff further testified that when the bottle exploded, "It made a sound similar to an electric light bulb that would have dropped. It made a loud pop." Plaintiff's employer testified, "I was about twenty feet from where it actually happened and I heard the explosion." A fellow employee, on the opposite side of the counter, testified that plaintiff "had the bottle, I should judge, waist high, and I know that it didn't bang either the case or the door or another bottle * * * when it popped. It sounded just like a fruit jar would blow up * * *."

The witness further testified that the contents of the bottle "flew all over herself and myself and the walls and one thing and another."

The top portion of the bottle, with the cap, remained in plaintiff's hand, and the lower portion fell to the floor but did not break. The broken bottle was not produced at the trial, the pieces having been thrown away by an employee of the restaurant shortly after the accident. Plaintiff, however, described the broken pieces, and a diagram of the bottle was made showing the location of the "fracture line" where the bottle broke in two.

One of defendant's drivers, called as a witness by plaintiff, testified that he had seen other bottles of Coca Cola in the past explode and had found broken bottles in the warehouse when he took the cases out, but that he did not know what made them blow up.

Plaintiff then rested her case, having announced to the court that being unable to show any specific acts of negligence she relied completely on the doctrine of res ipsa loquitur.

Defendant contends that the doctrine of res ipsa loquitur does not apply in this case, and that the evidence is insufficient to support the judgment.

.   .   .   .

A chemical engineer for the Owens-Illinois Glass Company and its Pacific Coast subsidiary, maker of Coca Cola bottles, explained how glass is manufactured and the methods used in testing and inspecting bottles. He testified that his company is the largest manufacturer of glass containers in the United States, and that it uses the standard methods for testing bottles recommended by the glass containers association. A pressure test is made by taking a sample from each mold every three hours—approximately one out of every 600 bottles—and subjecting the sample to an internal pressure of 450 pounds per square inch, which is sustained for one minute. (The normal pressure in Coca Cola bottles is less than 50 pounds per square inch.) The sample bottles are also subjected to the standard thermal shock test. The witness stated that these tests are "pretty near" infallible.

It thus appears that there is available to the industry a commonly-used method of testing bottles for defects not apparent to the eye, which is almost infallible. Since Coca Cola bottles are subjected to these tests by the manufacturer, it is not likely that they contain defects when delivered to the bottler which are not discoverable by visual inspection. Both new and used bottles are filled and distributed by defendant. The used bottles are not again subjected to the tests referred to above, and it may be inferred that defects not discoverable by visual inspection do not develop in bottles after they are manufactured. Obviously, if such defects do occur in used bottles there is a duty upon the bottler to make appropriate tests before they are refilled, and if such tests are not commercially practicable the bottles should not be re-used. This would seem to be particularly true where a charged liquid is placed in the bottle. It follows that a defect which would make the bottle unsound could be discovered by reasonable and practicable tests.

Although it is not clear in this case whether the explosion was caused by an excessive charge or a defect in the glass there is a sufficient showing that neither cause would ordinarily have been present if due care had been used. Further, defendant had exclusive control over both the charging and inspection of the bottles. Accordingly, all the requirements necessary to entitle plaintiff to rely on the doctrine of res ipsa loquitur to supply an inference of negligence are present.

It is true that defendant presented evidence tending to show that it exercised considerable precaution by carefully regulating and checking the pressure in the bottles and by making visual inspections for defects in the glass at several stages during the bottling process. It is well settled, however, that when a defendant produces evidence to rebut the inference of negligence which arises upon application of the doctrine of res ipsa loquitur, it is ordinarily a question of fact for the jury to determine whether the inference has been dispelled.   .   .   .

The judgment is affirmed.

SHENK, CURTIS, CARTER, and SCHAUER, JJ., concurred.

TRAYNOR, J.   I concur in the judgment, but I believe the manufacturer's negligence should no longer be singled out as the basis of a plaintiff's right to recover in cases like the present one. In my opinion it should now be recognized that a manufacturer incurs an absolute liability when an article that he has placed on the market, knowing that it is to be used without inspection, proves to have a defect that causes injury to human beings. MacPherson v. Buick Motor Co., 217 N.Y. 382, established the principle, recognized by this court, that irrespective of privity of contract, the manufacturer is responsible for an injury caused by such an article to any person who comes in lawful contact with it.   .   .   .   In these cases the source of the manufacturer's liability was his negligence in the manufacturing process or in the inspection of component parts supplied by others. Even if there is no negligence, however, public policy demands that responsibility be fixed wherever it will most effectively reduce the hazards of life and health inherent in defective products that reach the market. It is evident that the manufacturer can anticipate some hazards and guard against the recurrence of others, as the public cannot. Those who suffer injury from defective products are unprepared to meet its consequences. The cost of an injury and the loss of time or health may be an overwhelming misfortune to the person injured, and a needless one, for the risk of injury can be insured by the manufacturer and distributed among the public as the cost of doing business. It is to the public interest to discourage the marketing of products having defects that are a menace to the public. If such products nevertheless find their way into the market it is to the public interest to place the responsibility for whatever injury they may cause upon the manufacturer, who, even if he is not negligent in the manufacture of the product, is responsible for its reaching the market. However intermittently such injuries may occur and however haphazardly they may strike, the risk of their occurrence is a constant risk and a general one. Against such a risk there should, be general and constant protection and the manufacturer is best situated to afford such protection.

The injury from a defective product does not become a matter of indifference because the defect arises from causes other than the negligence of the manufacturer, such as negligence of a submanufacturer of a component part whose defects could not be revealed by inspection   .   .   .   or unknown causes that even by the device of res ipsa loquitur cannot be classified as negligence of the manufacturer. The inference of negligence may be dispelled by an affirmative showing of proper care. If, the evidence against the fact inferred is "clear, positive, uncontradicted, and of such a nature that it cannot rationally be disbelieved, the court must instruct the jury that the nonexistence of the fact has been established as a matter of law." Blank v. Coffin, 20 Cal.2d 457, 461. An injured person, however, is not ordinarily in a position to refute such evidence or identify the cause of the defect, for he can hardly be familiar with the manufacturing process as the manufacturer himself is. In leaving it to the jury to decide whether the inference has been dispelled, regardless of the evidence against it, the negligence rule approaches the rule of strict liability. It is needlessly circuitous to make negligence the basis of recovery and impose what is in reality liability without negligence. If public policy demands that a manufacturer of goods be responsible for their quality regardless of negligence there is no reason not to fix that responsibility openly.

.   .   .

The liability of the manufacturer to an immediate buyer injured by a defective product follows without proof of negligence from the implied warranty of safety attending the sale. Ordinarily, however, the immediate buyer is a dealer who does not intend to use the product himself, and if the warranty of safety is to serve the purpose of protecting health and safety it must give rights to others than the dealer. In the words of Judge Cardozo in the MacPherson case: "The dealer was indeed the one person of whom it might be said with some approach to certainty that by him the car would not be used. Yet the defendant would have us say that he was the one person whom it was under a legal duty to protect. The law does not lead us to so inconsequent a conclusion." While the defendant's negligence in the MacPherson case made it unnecessary for the court to base liability on warranty, Judge Cardozo's reasoning recognized the injured person as the real party in interest and effectively disposed of the theory that the liability of the manufacturer incurred by his warranty should apply only to the immediate purchaser. It thus paves the way for a standard of liability that would make the manufacturer guarantee the safety of this product even when there is no negligence.

.   .   .

As handicrafts have been replaced by mass production with its great markets and transportation facilities, the close relationship between the producer and consumer of a product has been altered. Manufacturing processes, frequently valuable secrets, are ordinarily either inaccessible to or beyond the ken of the general public. The consumer no longer has means or skill enough to investigate for himself the soundness of a product, even when it is not contained in a sealed package, and his erstwhile vigilance has been lulled by the steady efforts of manufacturers to build up confidence by advertising and marketing devices such as trademarks.   .   .   .   Consumers no longer approach products warily but accept them on faith, relying on the reputation of the manufacturer or the trade mark. . . . Manufacturers have sought to justify that faith by increasingly high standards of inspection and a readiness to make good on defective products by way of replacements and refunds. . . . The manufacturer's obligation to the consumer must keep pace with the changing relationship between them; it cannot be escaped because the marketing of a product has become so complicated as to require one or more intermediaries. Certainly there is greater reason to impose liability on the manufacturer than on the retailer who is but a conduit of a product that he is not himself able to test. . . .

The manufacturer's liability should, of course, be defined in terms of the safety of the product in normal and proper use, and should not extend to injuries that cannot be traced to the product as it reached the market.

HENNINGSEN v. BLOOMFIELD MOTORS, INC. and CHRYSLER CORPORATION
Supreme Court of New Jersey, 32 N.J. 358 (1960).

FRANCIS, J. Plaintiff Clause H. Henningsen purchased a Plymouth automobile, manufactured by defendant Chrysler Corporation, from defendant Bloomfield Motors, Inc. His wife, plaintiff Helen Henningsen, was injured while driving it and instituted suit against both defendants to recover damages on account of her injuries. Her husband joined in the action seeking compensation for his consequential losses. The complaint was predicated upon breach of express and implied warranties and upon negligence. At the trial the negligence counts were dismissed by the court and the cause was submitted to the jury for determination solely on the issues of implied warranty of merchantability. Verdicts were returned against both defendants and in favor of the plaintiffs. Defendants appealed and plaintiffs cross-appealed from the dismissal of their negligence claim. . . .

The facts are not complicated, but a general outline of them is necessary to an understanding of the case.

On May 7, 1955 Mr. and Mrs. Henningsen visited the place of business of Bloomfield Motors, Inc., an authorized De Soto and Plymouth dealer, to look at a Plymouth. They wanted to buy a car and were considering a Ford or a Chevrolet as well as a Plymouth. They were shown a Plymouth which appealed to them and the purchase followed. The record indicates that Mr. Henningsen intended the car as a Mother's Day gift to his wife. He said the intention was communicated to the dealer. When the purchase order or contract was prepared and presented, the husband executed it alone. His wife did not join as a party.

The purchase order was a printed form of one page. On the front it contained blanks to be filled in with a description of the automobile to be sold, the various accessories to be included, and the details of the financing. . . .

. . . . . .

The reverse side of the contract contains 8 - 1/2 inches of fine print. . . . The page is headed "Conditions" and contains ten separate paragraphs consisting of 65 lines in all. The paragraphs do not have headnotes ot margin notes denoting their particular subject, as in the case of the "Owner Service Certificate" to be referred to later. In the seventh paragraph, about two-thirds of the way down the page, the warranty, which is the focal point of the case, is set forth. It is as follows:

"7. It is expressly agreed that there are no warranties, express or implied, *made* by either the dealer or the manufacturer on the motor vehicle, chassis, of parts furnished hereunder except as follows.

" 'The manufacturer warrants each new motor vehicle (including original equipment placed thereon by the manufactuer except tires), chassis or parts manufactured by it to be free from defects in material or workmanship under normal use and service. Its obligation under this warranty being limited to making good at its factory any part or parts thereof which shall, within ninety (90) days after delivery of such vehicle *to the original purchaser* or before such vehicle has been driven 4,000 miles, whichever event shall first occur, be returned to it with transportation charges prepaid and which its examination shall disclose to its satisfaction to have been thus defective; *this warranty being expressly in lieu of all other warranties expressed or implied, and all other obligations or liabilities on its part,* and it neither assumes no authorizes any other person to assume for it any other liability in connection with the sale of its vehicles * * *.' " (Emphasis ours.)

. . . . .

The new Plymouth was turned over to the Henningsens on May 9, 1955. No proof was adduced by the dealer to show precisely what was done in the way of mechanical or road testing beyond testimony that the manufacturer's instructions were properly followed. Mr. Henningsen drove it from the dealer's place of business in Bloomfield to their home in Keansburg. On the trip nothing unusual appeared in the way in which it operated. Thereafter, it was used for short trips on paved streets about the town. It had no servicing and no mishaps of any kind before the event of May 19. That day, Mrs. Henningsen drove to Asbury Park. On the way down and in returning the car performed in normal fashion until the accident occurred.

She was proceeding north on Route 36 in Highlands, New Jersy, at 20–22 miles per hour. The highway was paved and smooth, and contained two lanes for northbound travel. She was riding in the right-hand lane. Suddenly she heard a loud noise "from the bottom, by the hood." It "felt as if something cracked." The steering wheel spun in her hands; the car veered sharply to the right and crashed into a highway sign and a brick wall. No other vehicle was in any way involved. A bus operator driving in the left-hand lane testified that he observed plaintiffs' car approaching in normal fashion in the opposite direction; "all of a sudden [it] veered at 90 degrees * * * and right into this wall." As a result of the impact, the front of the car was so badly damaged that it was impossible to determine if any of the parts of the steering wheel mechanism or workmanship or assembly were defective or improper prior to the accident. The condition was such that the collision insurance carrier, after inspection, declared the vehicle a total loss. It had 468 miles on the speedometer at the time.

The insurance carrier's inspector and appraiser of damaged cars, with 11 years of experience, advanced the opinion, based on the history and his examination, that something definitely went "wrong from the steering wheel down to the front wheels" and that the untoward happening must have been due to mechanical defect or failure; "something down there had to drop off or break loose to cause the car" to act in the manner described.

As has been indicated, the trial court felt that the proof was not sufficient to make out a *prime facie* case as to the negligence of either the manufacturer or the dealer.

The case was given to the jury, therefore, solely on the warranty theory, with results favorable to the plaintiffs against both defendants.

I.

The Claim of Implied Warranty Against the Manufacturer

In the ordinary case of sale of goods by description an implied warranty of merchantability is an integral part of the transaction. R.S. 46:30–20, N.J.S.A. If the buyer, expressly or by implication, makes known to the seller the particular purpose for which the article is required and it appears that he has relied on the seller's skill or judgment, an implied warranty arises of reasonable fitness for that purpose. R.S. 46:30–21(1), N.J.S.A. The former type of warranty simply means that the thing sold is reasonably fit for the general purpose for which it is manufactured and sold. . . .

Of course such sales, whether oral or written, may be accompanied by an express warranty. Under the broad terms of the Uniform Sale of Goods Law any affirmation of fact relating to the goods is an express warranty if the natural tendency of the statement is to induce the buyer to make the purchase. R.S. 46:30–18, N.J.S.A. And over the years since the almost universal adoption of the act, a growing awareness of the tremendous development of modern business methods has prompted the courts to administer that provision with a liberal hand. . . .   Solicitude toward the buyer plainly harmonizes with the intention of the Legislature. That fact is manifested further by the later section of the act which preserves and continues any permissible implied warranty, despite an express warranty, unless the two are inconsistent. R.S. 45:30–21(6), N.J.S.A.

The uniform act codified, extended and liberalized the common law of sales. The motivation in part was to ameliorate the harsh doctrine of *caveat emptor*, and in some measure to impose a reciprocal obligation on the seller to beware. The transcendent value of the legislation, particularly with respect to implied warranties, rests in the fact that obligations on the part of the seller were imposed by operation of law, and did not depend for their existence upon express agreement of the parties. And of tremendous significance in a rapidly expanding commercial society was the recognition of the right to recover damages on account of personal injuries arising from a breach of warranty. R.S. 46:30–75, 76 N.J.S.A. . . .   The particular importance of this advance resides in the fact that under such circumstances strict liability is imposed upon the maker or seller of the product. Recovery of damages does not depend upon proof of negligence or knowledge of the defect.

As the Sales Act and its liberal interpretation by the courts threw this protective cloak about the buyer, the decisions in various jurisdictions revealed beyond doubt that many manufacturers took steps to avoid these ever increasing warranty obligations. Realizing that the act governed the relationship of buyer and seller, they undertook to withdraw from actual and direct contractual contact with the buyer. They ceased selling products to the consuming public through their own employees and making contracts of sale in their own names. Instead, a system of independent dealers was established; their products were sold to dealers who in turn dealt with the buying public, ostensibly solely in their own personal capacity as sellers. In the past in many instances, manufacturers were able to transfer to the dealers burdens imposed by the act and thus achieved a large measure of immunity for themselves. But, as will be noted in more detail hereafter, such marketing practices, coupled with the advent of large scale advertising by manufacturers to promote the purchase of these goods from dealers by members of the public, provided a basis upon which the existence of express or implied warranties was predicated, even though the manufacturer was not a party to the contract of sale.

.   .   .   .

With these considerations in mind, we come to a study of the express warranty on the reverse side of the purchase order signed by Claus Henningsen.   .   .   .

.   .   .   .

The terms of the warranty are a sad commentary upon the automobile manufacturers' marketing practices.   .   .   .

The manufacturer agrees to replace defective parts for 90 days after the sale or until the car has been driven 4,000 miles, whichever is first to occur, *if the part is sent to the factory, transportation charges prepaid, and if examination discloses to its satisfaction that the part is defective.* It is difficult to imagine a greater burden on the consumer, or less satisfactory remedy. Aside from imposing on the buyer the trouble of removing and shipping the part, the maker has sought to retain the uncontrolled discretion to decide the issue of defectiveness. Some courts have removed much of the force of that reservation by declaring that the purchaser is not bound by the manufacturer's decision.   .   .   .   Also, suppose, as in this case, a defective part or parts caused an accident and that the car was so damaged as to render it impossible to discover the precise part or parts responsible, although the circumstances clearly pointed to such fact as the cause of the mishap. Can it be said that the impossibility of performance deprived the buyer of the benefit of the warranty?

Moreover, the guaranty is against defective workmanship. That condition may arise from good parts improperly assembled. There being no defective parts to return to the maker, is all remedy to be denied?   .   .   .

The matters referred to represent only a small part of the illusory character of the security presented by the warranty. Thus far the analysis has dealt only with the remedy provided in the case of a defective part. What relief is provided when the breach of the warranty results in personal injury to the buyer? (Injury to third persons using the car in the purchaser's right will be treated hereafter.) As we have said above, the law is clear that such damages are recoverable under an ordinary warranty. The right exists whether the warranty sued on is express or implied.   .   .   .   And, of course, it has long since been settled that where the buyer or a member of his family driving with his permission suffers injuries because of negligent manufacture or construction of the vehicle, the manufacturer's liability exists.   .   .   .   But in this instance, after reciting that defective parts will be replaced at the factory, the alleged agreement relied upon by Chrysler provides that the manufacturer's "obligation under this warranty" is limited to that undertaking; further, that such remedy is "in lieu of all other warranties, express or implied, and all other obligations or liabilities on its part." The contention has been raised that such language bars any claim for personal injuries which may emanate from a breach of the warranty.   .   .   .

Putting aside for the time being the problem of the efficacy of the disclaimer provisions contained in the express warranty, a question of first importance to be decided is whether an implied warranty of merchantability by Chrysler Corportion accompanied the sale of the automobile to Claus Henningsen.

.   .   .   .

Chrysler points out that an implied warranty of merchantability is an incident of a contract of sale. It concedes, of course, the making of the original sale to Bloomfield Motors, Inc., but maintains that this transaction marked the terminal point of its contractual connection with the car. Then Chrysler urges that since it was not a party to the sale by the dealer to Henningsen, there is no privity of contract between it and the plaintiffs, and the absence of this privity eliminates any such implied warranty.

There is no doubt that under early common-law concepts of contractual liability only those persons who were parties to the bargain could sue for a breach of it. In more recent times a noticeable disposition has appeared in a number of jurisdictions to break through the narrow barrier of privity when dealing with sales of goods in order to give realistic recognition to a universally accepted fact. The fact is that the dealer and the ordinary buyer do not, and are not expected to, buy goods, whether they be foodstuffs or automobiles, exclusively for their own consumption or use. Makers and manufacturers know this and advertise and market their products on that assumption; witness, the "family" car, the baby foods, etc. The limitations of privity in contracts for the sale of goods developed their place in the law when marketing conditions were simple, when maker and buyer frequently met face to face on an equal bargaining plane and when many of the products were relatively uncomplicated and conducive to inspection by a buyer competent to evaluate their quality. . . .   With the advent of mass marketing, the manufacturer became remote from the purchaser, sales were accomplished through intermediaries, and the demand for the product was created by advertising media. In such an economy it became obvious that the consumer was the person being cultivated. Manifestly, the connotation of "consumer" was broader than that of "buyer." He signified such a person who, in the reasonable contemplation of the parties to the sale, might be expected to use the product. Thus, where the commodities sold are such that if defectively manufactured they will be dangerous to life or limb, then society's interests can only be protected by eliminating the requirement of privity between the maker and his dealers and the reasonably expected ultimate consumer. In that way the burden of losses consequent upon use of defective articles is borne by those who are in a position to either control the danger or make an equitable distribution of the losses when they do occur. As Harper & James put it, "The interest in consumer protection calls for warranties by the maker that *do* run with the goods, to reach all who are likely to be hurt by the use of the unfit commodity for a purpose ordinarily to be expected." 2 Harper & James, Law of Torts, 1571, 1572. . . .   As far back as 1932, in the well known case of Baxter v. Ford Motor Co., 12 P.2d 409 (Sup. Ct. 1932), affirmed 15 P.2d 1118, (Sup. Ct. 1932), the Supreme Court of Washington gave recognition to the impact of then existing commercial practices on the strait jacket of privity, saying:

"It would be unjust to recognize a rule that would permit manufacturers of goods to create a demand for their products by representing that they possess qualities which they, in fact, do not possess, and then, because there is no privity of contract existing between the consumer and the manufacturer, deny the consumer the right to recover if damages result from the absence of those qualities, when such absence is not readily noticeable." 12 P.2d at page 412.

.   .   .   .

Accordingly, we hold that under modern marketing conditions, when a manufacturer puts a new automobile in the stream of trade and promotes its purchase by the public, an implied warranty that it is reasonably suitable for use as such accompanies it into the hands of the ultimate purchaser. Absence of agency between the manufacturer and the dealer who makes the ultimate sale is immaterial.

II.

The Effect of the Disclaimer and Limitation of Liability Clauses on the Implied Warranty of Merchantability

.   .   .   .

The task of the judiciary is to administer the spirit as well as the letter of the law. On issues such as the present one, part of that burden is to protect the ordinary man against the loss of important rights through what, in effect, is the unilateral act of the manufacturer. The status of the automobile industry is unique. Manufacturers are few in number and strong in bargaining position. In the matter of warranties on the sales of their products, the Automotive Manufacturers Association has enabled them to present a united front. From the standpoint of the purchaser, there can be no arms length negotiating on the subject. Because his capacity for bargaining is so grossly unequal, the inexorable conclusion which follows is that he is not permitted to bargain at all. He must take or leave the automobile on the warranty terms dictated by the maker. He cannot turn to a competitor for better security.

Public policy is a term not easily defined. Its significance varies as the habits and needs of a people may vary. It is not static and the field of application is an ever increasing one. A contract, or a particular provision therein, valid in one era may be wholly opposed to the public policy of another.   . . .   Courts keep in mind the principle that the best interests of society demand that persons should not be unecessarily restricted in their freedom to contract. But they do not hesitate to declare void as against public policy contractual provisions which clearly tend to the injury of the public in some way.   . . .

Public policy at a given time finds expression in the Constitution, the statutory law and in judicial decisions. In the area of sale of goods, the legislative will has imposed an implied warranty of merchantability as a general incident of sale of an automobile by description. The warranty does not depend upon the affirmative intention of the parties. It is a child of the law; it annexes itself to the contract because of the very nature of the transaction.   . . .   The judicial process has recognized a right to recover damages for personal injuries arising from a breach of that warranty. The disclaimer of the implied warranty and exclusion of all obligations except those specifically assumed by the express warranty signify a studied effort to frustrate that protection. True, the Sales Act authorizes agreements between buyer and seller qualifying the warranty obligations. But quite obviously the Legislature contemplated lawful stipulations (which are determined by the circumstances of a particular case) arrived at freely by parties of relatively equal bargaining strength. The lawmakers did not authorize the automobile manufacturer to use its grossly disproportionate bargaining power to relieve itself from liability and to impose on the ordinary buyer, who in effect has no real freedom of choice, the grave danger of injury to himself and others that attends the sale of such a dangerous instrumentality as a defectively made automobile. In the framework of this case, illuminated as it is by the facts and the many decisions noted, we are of the opinion that Chrysler's attempted disclaimer of an implied warranty of merchantability and of the obligations arising therefrom is so inimical to the public good as to compel an adjudication of its invalidity. . . .

.   .   .   .   .

IV.

Proof of Breach of the Implied Warranty of Merchantability

Both defendants argue that the proof adduced by plaintiffs as to the happening of the accident was not sufficient to demonstrate a breach of warranty. Consequently, they claim that their motion for judgment should have been granted by the trial court. We cannot agree. In our view, the total effect of the circumstances shown from purchase to accident is adequate to raise an inference that the car was defective and that such condition was causally related to the mishap. . . . Thus, determination by the jury was required.

The facts . . . show that on the day of the accident, ten days after delivery, Mrs. Henningsen was driving in a normal fashion, on a smooth highway, when unexpectedly the steering wheel and the front wheels of the car went into the bizarre action described. Can it reasonably be said that the circumstances do not warrant an inference of unsuitability for ordinary use against the manufacturer and the dealer? Obviously there is nothing in the proof to indicate in the slightest that the most unusual action of the steering wheel was caused by Mrs. Henningsen's operation of the automobile on this day, or by the use of the car between delivery and the happening of the incident. Nor is there anything to suggest that any external force or condition unrelated to the manufacturing or servicing of the car operated as an inducing or even concurring factor.

It is a commonplace of our law that on a motion for dismissal all of the evidence and the inferences therefrom must be taken most favorably to the plaintiff. And if reasonable men studying the proof in that light could conclude that the car was not merchantable, the issue had to be submitted to the jury for determination. Applying that test here, we have no hesitation in holding that the settlement of the question of breach of warranty as to both defendants was properly placed in the hands of the jury. In our judgment, the evidence shown, as a matter of preponderance of probabilities, would justify the conclusion by the ultimate triers of the facts that the accident was caused by a failure of the steering mechanism of the car and that such failure constituted a breach of the warranty of both defendants.

.   .   .   .   .

It may be conceded that the opinion of the automobile expert produced by the plaintiffs in the present case was not entitled to very much probative force. However, his assertion in answer to the hypothethical question that the unusual action of the steering wheel and front wheels must have been due to a mechanical defect or failure of something from the steering wheel down to the front wheels, that "something down there had to drop off or break loose" to cause the car to act in the manner it did, cannot be rejected as a matter of law. Its evaluation under all of the circumstances was a matter for jury consideration. Defendants argue that the proof of his qualifications was not adequate to warrant the admission of his testimony. But the matter of an expert's competency to testify is primarily for the discretion of the trial court. An appellate tribunal will not interfere unless a clear abuse of discretion appears. . . .   In our view, the experience of the witness, as an automobile repairman and as an appraiser of damaged cars, was such as to preclude a holding by us that the trial court accepted his qualifications without any reasonable basis.

.   .   .

V.

The Defense of Lack of Privity Against Mrs. Henningsen

Both defendants contend that since there was no privity of contract between them and Mrs. Henningsen, she cannot recover for breach of any warranty made by either of them. On the facts, as they were developed, we agree that she was not a party to the purchase agreement. . . .   Her right to maintain the action, therefore, depends upon whether she occupies such legal status thereunder as to permit her to take advantage of a breach of defendants' implied warranties.

For the most part the cases that have been considered dealt with the right of the buyer or consumer to maintain an action against the manufacturer where the contract of sale was with a dealer and the buyer had no contractual relationship with the manufacturer. In the present matter, the basic contractual relationship is between Claus Henningsen, Chrysler, and Bloomfield Motors, Inc. The precise issue presented is whether Mrs. Henningsen, who is not a party to their respective warranties, may claim under them. In our judgment, the principles of those cases and the supporting texts are just as proximately applicable to her situation. We are convinced that the cause of justice in this area of the law can be served only by recognizing that she is such a person who, in the reasonable contemplation of the parties to the warranty, might be expected to become a user of the automobile. Accordingly, her lack of privity does not stand in the way of prosecution of the injury suit against the defendant Chrysler.

.   .   .

It is important to express the right of Mrs. Henningsen to maintain her action in terms of a general principle. To what extent may lack of privity be disregarded in suits on such warranties? . . .   [I]t is our opinion that an implied warranty of merchantability chargeable to either an automobile manufacturer or a dealer extends to the purchaser of the car, members of his family, and to other persons occupying or using it with his consent. It would be wholly opposed to reality to say that use by such persons is not within the anticipation of parties to such a warranty of reasonable suitability of an automobile for ordinary highway operation. Those persons must be considered within the distributive chain.

.   .   .

Under all of the circumstances outlined above the judgments in favor of the plaintiffs and against the defendants are affirmed.

For affirmance: Chief Justice WEINTRAUB and Justices BURLING, JACOBS, FRANCIS, PROCTOR and SCHETTINO—6.

For reversal: None

GREENMAN v. YUBA POWER PRODUCTS, INC.
Supreme Court of California, 59 Cal. 2d 57 (1963).

[The reader will notice that the writer of the opinion in this case is the same Justice Traynor who, 19 years earlier, wrote the concurring opinion in Escola v. Coca Cola, *supra* p. 223, urging a new doctrine of manufacturer's absolute liability to a remote user of a defective product.]

TRAYNOR, Justice.   Plaintiff brought this action for damages against the retailer and the manufacturer of a Shopsmith, a combination power tool that could be used as a saw, drill, and wood lathe. He saw a Shopsmith demonstrated by the retailer and studied a brochure prepared by the manufacturer. He decided he wanted a Shopsmith for his home workshop, and his wife bought and gave him one for Christmas in 1955. In 1957 he bought the necessary attachments to use the Shopsmith as a lathe for turning a large piece of wood he wished to make into a chalice. After he had worked on the piece of wood several times without difficulty, it suddenly flew out of the machine and struck him on the forehead, inflicting serious injuries. About ten and a half months later, he gave the retailer and the manufacturer written notice of claimed breaches of warranties and filed a complaint against them alleging such breaches and negligence.

After a trial before a jury, the court ruled that there was no evidence that the retailer was negligent or had breached any express warranty and that the manufacturer was not liable for the breach of any implied warranty. Accordingly, it submitted to the jury only the cause of action alleging breach of implied warranties against the retailer and the causes of action alleging negligence and breach of express warranties against the manufacturer. The jury returned a verdict for the retailer against plaintiff and for plaintiff against the manufacturer in the amount of $65,000. The trial court denied the manufacturer's motion for a new trial and entered judgment on the verdict. The manufacturer and plaintiff appeal. Plaintiff seeks a reversal of the part of the judgment in favor of the retailer, however, only in the event that the part of the judgment against the manufacturer is reversed.

Plaintiff introduced substantial evidence that his injuries were caused by defective design and construction of the Shopsmith. His expert witnesses testified that inadequate set screws were used to hold parts of the machine together so that normal vibration caused the tailstock of the lathe to move away from the piece of wood being turned permitting it to fly out of the lathe. They also testified that there were other more positive ways of fastening the parts of the machine together, the use of which would have prevented the accident. The jury could therefore reasonably have concluded that the manufacturer negligently constructed the Shopsmith. The jury could also reasonably have concluded that statements in the manufacturer's brochure were untrue, that they constituted express warranties[A] and that plaintiff's injuries were caused by their breach.

[A]In this respect the trial court limited the jury to a consideration of two statements in the manufacturer's brochure: (1) "WHEN SHOPSMITH IS IN HORIZONTAL POSITION— Rugged construction of frame provides rigid support from end to end. Heavy centerless-ground steel tubing insurers perfect alignment [sic] of components." (2) "SHOPSMITH maintains its accuracy because every component has positive locks that hold adjustments through rough or precision work."

The manufacturer contends, however, that plaintiff did not give it notice of breach of warranty within a reasonable time and that therefore his cause of action for breach of warranty is barred by section 1769 of the Civil Code. Since it cannot be determined whether the verdict against it was based on the negligence or warranty cause of action or both, the manufacturer concludes that the error in presenting the warranty cause of action to the jury was prejudicial.

Section 1769 of the Civil Code provides: "In the absence of express or implied agreement of the parties, acceptance of the goods by the buyer shall not discharge the seller from liability in damages or other legal remedy for breach of any promise or warranty in the contract to sell or the sale. But, if, after acceptance of the goods, the buyer fails to give notice to the seller of the breach of any promise or warranty within a reasonable time after the buyer knows, or ought to know of such breach, the seller shall not be liable therefor."

Like other provisions of the uniform sales act (Civ. Code, §§ 1721–1800), section 1769 deals with the rights of the parties to a contract of sale or a sale. It does not provide that notice must be given of the breach of a warranty that arises independently of a contract of sale between the parties. Such warranties are not imposed by the sales act, but are the product of common-law decisions that have recognized them in a variety of situations.   .   .   .

.   .   .   We conclude, therefore, that even if plaintiff did not give timely notice of breach of warranty to the manufactuer, his cause of action based on the representations contained in the brochure was not barred.

Moreover, to impose strict liability on the manufacturer under the circumstances of this case, it was not necessary for plaintiff to establish an express warranty as defined in section 1732 of the Civil Code.[B] A manufacturer is strictly liable in tort when an article he places on the market, knowing that it is to be used without inspection for defects, proves to have a defect that causes injury to a human being. Recognized first in the case of unwholesome food product, such liability has now been extended to a variety of other products that create as great or greater hazards if defective. Peterson v. Lamb Rubber Co., 54 Cal.2d 339, 347 [grinding wheel]; Vallis v. Canada Dry Ginger Ale, Inc., 190 Cal. App. 2d 35, 42–44 [bottle]; Jones Burgermeister Brewing Corp., 198 Cal. App. 2d 198, 204 [bottle]; Gottsdanker v. Cutter Laboratories, 182 Cal. App. 2d 602, 607 [vaccine]; McQuaide v. Bridgport Brass Co., D.C., 190 F. Supp. 252, 254 [insect spray]; Bowles v. Zimmer Manufacturing Co., 7 Cir., 277 F.2d 868, 875 [surgical pin]; Thompson v. Reedman, D.C., 199 F. Supp. 120, 121 [automobile]; Chapman v. Brown, D.C., 198 F. Supp. 78, 118, 119, affd. Brown v. Chapman, 9 Cir., 304 F.2d 149 [skirt]; B. F. Goodrich Co. v. Hammond, 10 Cir., 269 F.2d 501, 504 [automobile tire]; Markovich v. McKesson and Robbins, Inc., 106 Ohio App. 265 [home permanent]; Graham v. Bottenfield's Inc., 176 Kan. 68 [hair dye]; General Motors Corp. v. Dodson, 47 Tenn. App. 438 [automobile]; Henningsen v. Bloomfield Motors, Inc., 32 N.J. 358 [automobile]; Hinton v. Republic Aviation Corporation, D.C., 180 F. Supp. 31, 33 [airplane].

[B]"Any affirmation of fact or any promise by the seller relating to the goods is an express warranty if the natural tendency of such affirmation or promise is to induce the buyer to purchase the goods, and if the buyer purchases the goods relying thereon. No affirmation of the value of the goods, nor any statement purporting to be a statement of the seller's opinion only shall be construed as a warranty."

Although in these cases strict liability has usually been based on the theory of an express or implied warranty running from the manufacturer to the plaintiff, the abandonment of the requirement of a contract between them, the recognition that the liability is not assumed by agreement but imposed by law . . .   and the refusal to permit the manufacturer to define the scope of its own responsibility for defective products . . . make clear that the liability is not one governed by the law of contract warranties but by the law of strict liability in tort. Accordingly, rules defining and governing warranties that were developed to meet the needs of commercial transactions cannot properly be invoked to govern the manufacturer's liability to those injured by their defective products unless those rules also serve the purposes for which such liability is imposed.

. . . The purpose of such [strict] liability is to insure that the costs of injuries resulting from defective products are borne by the manufacturers that put such products on the market rather than by the injured persons who are powerless to protect themselves. Sales warranties serve this purpose fitfully at best. . . .   In the present case, for example, plaintiff was able to plead and prove an express warranty only because he read and relied on the representations of the Shopsmith's ruggedness contained in the manufacturer's brochure. Implicit in the machine's presence on the market, however, was a representation that it would safely do the jobs for which it was built. Under these circumstances, it should not be controlling whether plaintiff selected the machine because of the statements in the brochure, or because of the machine's own appearance of excellence that belied the defect lurking beneath the surface, or because he merely assumed that it would safely do the jobs it was built to do. It should not be controlling whether the details of the sales from manufacturer to retailer and from retailer to plaintiff's wife were such that one or more of the implied warranties of the sales act arose. . . .   "The remedies of injured consumers ought not to be made to depend upon the intricacies of the law of sales." Ketterer v. Armour & Co., D.C., 200 F. 323, 323; Klein v. Duchess Sandwich Co., 14 Cal.2d 272. To establish the manufacturer's liability it was sufficient that plaintiff proved that he was injured while using the Shopsmith in a way it was intended to be used as a result of a defect in design and manufacture of which plaintiff was not aware that made the Shopsmith unsafe for its intended use.

.   .   .   .   .

The judgment is affirmed.

GIBSON, C.J., and SCHAUER, McCOMB, PETERS, TOBRINGER, and PEEK, JJ., concur.

VANDERMARK v. FORD MOTOR COMPANY
Supreme Court of California, 61 Cal.2d 256 (1964).

TRAYNOR, Justice.   In October 1958 plaintiff Chester Vandermark bought a new Ford automobile from defendant Lorimer Diesel Engine Company, an authorized Ford dealer doing business as Maywood Bell Ford. About six weeks later, while driving on the San Bernardino Freeway, he lost control of the car. It went off the highway to the right and collided with a light post. He and his sister, plaintiff Mary Tresham, suffered serious injuries. They brought this action for damages against Maywood Bell Ford and the Ford Motor Company, which manufactured and assembled the car. They pleaded causes of action for breach of warranty and negligence. The trial court granted Ford's motion for a nonsuit on all causes of action and directed a verdict in favor of Maywood Bell on the warranty causes of action. The jury returned a verdict for Maywood Bell on the negligence causes of action, and the trial court entered judgment on the verdict. Plaintiffs appeal.

Vandermark had driven the car approximately 1500 miles before the accident. He used it primarily in town, but drove it on two occasions from his home in Huntington Park to Joshua Tree in San Bernardino County. He testified that the car operated normally before the accident except once when he was driving home from Joshua Tree. He was in the left-hand west-bound lane of the San Bernardino Freeway when traffic ahead slowed. He applied the brakes and the car "started to make a little dive to the right and continued on across the two lanes of traffic till she hit the shoulder. Whatever it was then let go and I was able to then pull her back into the road." He drove home without further difficulty, but before using the car again, he took it to Maywood Bell for the regular 1000-mile new car servicing. He testified that he described the freeway incident to Maywood Bell's service attendant, but Maywood Bell's records do not indicate that any complaint was made.

After the car was serviced, Vandermark drove it in town on short trips totaling approximately 300 miles. He and his sister then set out on another trip to Joshua Tree. He testified that while driving in the right-hand lane of the freeway at about 45 to 50 miles per hour, "the car started to make a little shimmy or weave and started pulling to the right. * * * I tried to pull back, but it didn't seem to come, so I applied my brakes gently to see if I could straighten her up, but I couldn't seem to pull her back to the left. So, I let off on the brakes and she continued to the right, and I tried again to put on the brakes and she wouldn't come back, and all of a sudden this pole was in front of me and we smashed into it." Plaintiff Tresham testified to a substantially similar version of the accident. A witness for plaintiffs, who was driving about 200 feet behind them, testified that plaintiffs' car was in the right-hand lane when he saw its taillights come on. The car started to swerve and finally skidded into the light post. An investigating officer testified that there were skid marks leading from the highway to the car.

Plaintiffs called an expert on the operation of hydraulic automobile brakes. In answer to hypothetical questions based on evidence in the record and his own knowledge of the braking system of the car, the expert testified as to the cause of the accident. It was his opinion that the brakes applied themselves owing to a failure of the piston in the master cylinder to retract far enough when the brake pedal was released to uncover a bypass port through which hydraulic fluid should have been able to escape into a reservoir above the master cylinder. Failure of the piston to uncover the bypass port led to a closed system and a partial application of the brakes, which in turn led to heating that expanded the brake fluid until the brakes applied themselves with such force that Vandermark lost control of the car. The expert also testified that the failure of the piston to retract sufficiently to uncover the bypass port could have been caused by dirt in the master cylinder, a defective or wrong-sized part, distortion of the fire wall, or improper assembly or adjustment. The trial court struck the testimony of the possible causes of the failure of the piston to retract, on the ground that there was no direct evidence that any one or more of the causes existed, and it rejected plaintiffs' offer to prove that all of the possible causes were attributable to defendants. These rulings were erroneous, for plaintiffs were entitled to establish the existence of a defect and defendants' responsiblity therefor by circumstantial evidence, particularly when, as in this case, the damage to the car in the collision precluded determining whether or not the master cylinder assembly had been properly installed and adjusted before the accident.

Accordingly, for the purposes of reviewing the nonsuit in favor of Ford and the directed verdict in favor of Maywood Bell on the warranty causes of action, it must be taken as established that when the car was delivered to Vandermark, the master cylinder assembly had a defect that caused the accident. Moreover, since it could reasonably be inferred from the description of the braking system in evidence and the offer of proof of all possible causes of defects that the defect was owing to negligence in design, manufacture, assembly, or adjustment, it must be taken as established that the defect was caused by some such negligence.

Ford contends, however, that it may not be held liable for negligence in manufacturing the car or strictly liable in tort for placing it on the market without proof that the car was defective when Ford relinquished control over it. Ford points out that in this case the car passed through two other authorized Ford dealers before it was sold to Maywood Bell and that Maywood Bell removed the power steering unit before selling the car to Vandermark.

In Greenman v. Yuba Power Products, Inc., 59 Cal.2d 57, 62, 27 Cal. Rptr. 697, 700, we held that "A manufacturer is strictly liable in tort when an article he places on the market, knowing that it is to be used without inspection for defects, proves to have a defect that causes injury to a human being." Since the liability is strict it encompasses defects regardless of their source, and therefore a manufacturer of a completed product cannot escape liability by tracing the defect to a component part supplied by another. Goldberg v. Kolsman Instrument Corp., 12 N.Y.2d 432, 437, 240 N.Y.S.2d 592. Moreover, even before such strict liability was recognized, the manufacturer of a completed product was subject to vicarious liability for the negligence of his suppliers or subcontractors that resulted in defects in the completed product. Dow v. Holly Manufacturing Co. 49 Cal.2d 720, 726, 727, 321 P.2d 736. These rules focus responsibility for defects, whether negligently or nonnegligently caused, on the manufacturer of the completed product, and they apply regardless of what part of the manufacturing process the manufacturer chooses to delegate to third parties. It appears in the present case that Ford delegates the final steps in that process to its authorized dealers. It does not deliver cars to its dealers that are ready to be driven away by the ultimate purchasers but relies on its dealers to make the final inspections, corrections, and adjustments necessary to make the cars ready for use. Since Ford, as the manufacturer of the completed product, cannot delegate its duty to have its cars delivered to the ultimate purchaser free from dangerous defects, it cannot escape liability on the ground that the defect in Vandermark's car may have been caused by something one of its authorized dealers did or failed to do.

Since plaintiffs introduced or offered substantial evidence that they were injured as a result of a defect that was present in the car when Ford's authorized dealer delivered it to Vandermark, the trial court erred in granting a nonsuit on the causes of action by which plaintiff sought to establish that Ford was strictly liable to them. Since plaintiffs also introduced or offered substantial evidence that the defect was caused by some negligent conduct for which Ford was responsible, the trial court also erred in granting a nonsuit on the causes of action by which plaintiffs sought to establish that Ford was liable for negligence.

Plaintiffs contend that Maywood Bell is also strictly liable in tort for the injuries caused by the defect in the car and that therefore the trial court erred in directing a verdict for Maywood Bell on the warranty causes of action. Maywood Bell contends that the rule of strict liability in the Greenman case applies only to actions against manufacturers brought by injured parties with whom the manufacturers did not deal. It contends that it validly disclaimed warranty liability for personal injuries in its contract with Vandermark. . . .

Retailers like manufacturers are engaged in the business of distributing goods to the public. They are an integral part of the overall producing and marketing enterprise that should bear the cost of injuries resulting from defective products. . . . In some cases the retailer may be the only member of that enterprise reasonably available to the injured plaintiff. In other cases the retailer himself may play a substantial part in insuring that the product is safe or may be in a position to exert pressure on the manufacturer to that end; the retailer's strict liability thus serves as an added incentive to safety. Strict liability on the manufacturer and retailer alike affords maximum protection to the injured plaintiff and works no injustice to the defendants, for they can adjust the costs of such protection between them in the course of their continuing business relationship. Accordingly, as a retailer engaged in the business of distributing goods to the public, Maywood Bell is strictly liable in tort for personal injuries caused by defects in cars sold by it. . . .

Since Maywood Bell is strictly liable in tort, the fact that it restricted its contractual liability to Vandermark is immaterial. Regardless of the obligations it assumed by contract, it is subject to strict liability in tort because it is in the business of selling automobiles, one of which proved to be defective and caused injury to human beings. . . .

Although plaintiffs sought to impose strict liability on Maywood Bell on the theory of sales-act warranties, they pleaded and introduced substantial evidence of all the facts necessary to establish strict liability in tort. Accordingly, the trial court erred in directing a verdict for Maywood Bell on the so-called warranty causes of action.

. . . . .

The judgment on nonsuit in favor of Ford Motor Company is reversed. The judgment in favor of Maywood Bell Ford on the negligence causes of action is affirmed and in all other respects the judgment in favor of Maywood Bell Ford is reversed.

GIBSON, C. J., and SCHAUER, McCOMB, PETERS, TOBRINER and PEEK, JJ., concur.

ELMORE v. AMERICAN MOTORS CORPORATION
Supreme Court of California, 75 Cal. Rptr. 652 (1969).

[An automobile driven by Elmore went out of control and collided with one driven by Waters. Elmore suffered injuries that deprived her of any memory of the accident, and Waters was killed. There was evidence that the drive shaft of Elmore's car disengaged and caused the accident. Suits were brought on behalf of both Elmore and Waters and were consolidated. The only question discussed in the following portion of the opinion is whether American Motors, the defendant manufacturer, and Mission Rambler, the defendant retailer, of the defective automobile, should be liable for the death of Waters, the deceased driver of the other car.]

PETERS, Justice.

"A manufacturer is strictly liable in tort when an article he places on the market, knowing that it is to be used without inspection for defects, proves to have a defect that causes injury to a human being." Greenman v. Yuba Power Products, Inc., 59 Cal.2d 57, 62; Vandermark v. Ford Motor Co., 61 Cal.2d 256, 260–261. Similarly, a retailer engaged in the business of distributing automobiles to the public is strictly liable in tort for personal injuries caused by defects in cars sold by it. Vandermark v. Ford Motor Co., *supra*, 61 Cal.2d 256, 263.

The authors of the restatement have refrained from expressing a view as to whether the doctrine of strict liability of the manufacturer and retailer for defects is applicable to third parties who are bystanders and who are not purchasers or users of the defective chattel. (Rest.2d Torts, § 402A, com. o.)[2]   The authors pointed out that as yet (1965) no case had applied strict liability to a person who was not a user or consumer. Two recent cases, however, have held manufacturers of defective goods strictly liable in tort for injuries caused to persons who were mere bystanders and were not users or consumers. Piercefield v. Remington Arms Company, 375 Mich. 85, 133 N.W.2d 129, 134–136 (1965); Mitchell v. Miller, 26 Conn. Sup. 142, 214 A.2d 694, 697–699 (1965).[3] . . .   Several cases, most of them earlier, have refused to extend the doctrine in favor of the bystander. See Prosser, The Fall of the Citadel, 50 Minn.L.Rev. 791, 820, fn. 154. In Vandermark v. Ford Motor Co., *supra,* one of the plaintiffs was a passenger in the car, but we did not discuss the issue of liability to her separately from the issue of liability to the owner-driver.

In Greenman v. Yuba Power Products, Inc., *supra,* 59 Cal.2d 37, 63, we pointed out that the purpose of strict liability upon the manufacturer in tort is to insure that "the

[2]Restatement of the Law of Torts, 2d. § 402 A (1965):

(1) One who sells any product in a defective condition unreasonably dangerous to the user or consumer or to his property is subject to liability for physical harm thereby caused to the ultimate user or consumer, or to his property, if

(a) the seller is engaged in the business of selling such a product, and

(b) it is expected to and does reach the consumer without substantial change in the condition in which it is sold.

(2) The Rule stated in Subsection (1) applies, although

(a) the seller has exercised all possible care in the preparation and sale of his product, and

(b) the user or consumer has not bought the product from or entered into any contractual relation with the seller.

Comment *o.*   Injuries to non-users and non-consumers.

Thus far the courts, in applying the rule stated in this section, have not gone beyond allowing recovery to users and consumers. . . .

[3]In Piercefield, the Michigan Supreme Court held that an action for breach of implied warranty could be maintained by the plaintiff, an innocent bystander, against the manufacturer, wholesaler and retailer of a defective shot gun shell which exploded causing metal fragments to become lodged in the plaintiff's brain. In Mitchell, the Superior Court of Connecticut held that a tort action for damages would lie against an automobile manufacturer in favor of the estate of the deceased who was killed when the automobile's defective transmission disengaged, thus allowing the car to roll down an incline and to strike the deceased while he was playing golf on the seventeenth fairway.

costs of injuries resulting from defective products are borne by the manufacturers that put such products on the market rather than by the injured persons who are powerless to protect themselves." We further pointed out that the rejection of the view that such liability was governed by contract warranties rather than tort rules was shown by cases which had recognized that the liability is not assumed by agreement but imposed by law and which had refused to permit the manufacturer to define its own responsibility for defective products (59 Cal.2d at p. 63.) Similarly, in Vandermark v. Ford Motor Co., *supra*, 61 Cal.2d 256, 263, we held that, since the retailer is strictly liable in tort, the fact that it restricted its contractual liability was immaterial.

These cases make it clear that the doctrine of strict liability may not be restricted on a theory of privity of contract. Since the doctrine applies even where the manufacturer has attempted to limit liability, they further make it clear that the doctrine may not be limited on the theory that no representation of safety is made to the bystander.

The liability has been based upon the existence of a defective product which caused injury to a human being, and in both Greenman and Vandermark we did not limit the rules stated to consumers and users but instead used language applicable to human beings generally.

It has been pointed out that an injury to a bystander "is often a perfectly foreseeable risk of the maker's enterprise, and the considerations for imposing such risks on the maker without regard to his fault do not stop with those who undertake to use the chattel. [A restriction on the recovery by bystanders] is only the distorted shadow of a vanishing privity which is itself a reflection of the habit of viewing the problem as a commercial one between traders, rather than as part of the accident problem." 2 Harper and James, The Law of Torts (1956) p. 1572, fn. 6.

If anything, bystanders should be entitled to greater protection than the consumer or user where injury to bystanders from the defect is reasonably foreseeable. Consumers and users, at least, have the opportunity to inspect for defects and to limit their purchases to articles manufactured by reputable manufacturers and sold by reputable retailers, where as the bystander ordinarily has no such opportunities. In short, the bystander is in greater need of protection from defective products which are dangerous, and if any distinction should be made between bystanders and users, it should be made, contrary to the position of defendants, to extend greater liability in favor of the bystanders [than users].

An automobile with a defectively connected drive shaft constitutes a substantial hazard on the highway not only to the driver and passenger of the car but also to pedestrians and other drivers. The public policy which protects the driver and passenger of the car should also protect the bystander, and where a driver or passenger of another car is injured due to defects in the manufacture of an automobile and without any fault of their own, they may recover from the manufacturer of the defective automobile.

[The court next discussed the strict liability in tort of a retailer as that concept was developed in Vandermark. The court saw no reason why that doctrine of Vandermark should not be applied in this case in favor of Waters, the innocent bystander. The court then in summary concluded:]

All of the foregoing considerations are as applicable to the bystander's action as that of the purchaser or user, and we are satisfied that the doctrine of strict liability in tort is available in an action for personal injuries by a bystander against the manufacturer and the retailer.

The judgments are reversed.

TRAYNOR, C. J., and McCOMB, TOBRINER, MOSK, BURKE and SULLIVAN, JJ., concur.

KASSAB v. CENTRAL SOYA
Supreme Court of Pennsylvania, 432 Pa. 217 (1968).

ROBERTS, Justice.   Appellants, man and wife, are engaged in the business of breeding Charolais cattle. On December 14, 1961 they placed an order for cattle feed with defendant-appellee, Pritts. This feed was to be blended by Pritts according to a formula previously used by appellants for their cattle and previously blended by Pritts. One of the ingredients in appellants' formula was commercially packaged feed supplement known as "Cattle Blend," manufactured by defendant-appellee Central Soya. Pritts blended the feed supposedly according to appellants' formula whereupon it was fed to Mr. and Mrs. Kassab's herd. Shortly thereafter the cows in the herd began to abort and the breed bull began behaving in a manner which tended to cast doubt upon his masculinity. He was eventually pronounced sterile.

Fearing that the feed supplement used in appellants' formula had somehow caused the malfunctioning of the Kassab's cattle, a chemical analysis was made which revealed the presence of a drug known as "stilbestrol" in the feed, and more particularly in the feed supplement, Cattle Blend. Although appellees contest this fact the trial judge, sitting without a jury, found on the basis of competent evidence that stilbestrol was in the feed, a finding which this Court will not disturb on appeal. It is conceded by all concerned that stilbestrol is customarily added to feed for *beef* cattle since it has a tendency to make the cattle gain weight. However, it is also conceded that stilbestrol is a synthetic hormone which tends to accentuate the female characteristics in animals, inducing heat and abortions in cows and sterility in bulls. Accordingly, feed containing this drug is not recommended for breed cattle. In fact, a federal regulation requires that feed containing stilbestrol be so labeled and that this label state, inter alia, that the feed is not to be fed to breeding or dairy animals. 21 Code of Federal Regulations § 121.241 (1963). It is finally conceded that no such label appeared on the bag of Cattle Blend used by Pritts in compounding appellants' feed formula. Obviously, Central Soya mistakenly packed its stilbestrol-added feed supplement into a bag supposed to contain a supplement without stilbestrol. Therefore, although appellants ordered feed without stilbestrol, and although Pritts thought that this is what he had mixed, in fact the feed sold to appellants did not conform to the mixture ordered.

Alleging (1) that the stilbestrol in the feed caused their cows to abort and their bull to become sterile; and (2) that community knowledge of what the herd had eaten resulted in appellants' inability to sell their stock except at beef prices thus greatly diminishing the value of appellants' property, Mr. and Mrs. Kassab commenced this action in assumpsit against Pritts and Central Soya. The case was heard before a judge sitting without a jury.   .   .   .   [T]he court announced a verdict for defendants, and orally (later in a written opinion) stated that, although it found that stilbestrol was present in the feed contrary to the formula ordered, nevertheless there should be a verdict for defendants because the court believed defendants' expert who testified that the amount of drug in the feed could not have caused the abortions and sterility complained of. This appeal followed.

.   .   .   [A]ppellants maintain that the court below, having found as a fact that stilbestrol was in the feed contrary to the formula ordered, had no choice but to find for them on the issue of liability, since the tainted feed constituted a clear breach of the implied warranty of merchantability and of the warranty of fitness for a particular purpose. With this contention we agree. The court declared that it was basing its decision of no breach of warranty on its finding that plaintiffs failed to establish that the tainted feed caused any injury to their cattle. But the question of injury, we believe, goes only to the amount of damages and will not affect a finding that the contract itself was breached. Accordingly, on the facts as found appellants were at least entitled to a verdict in their favor for nominal damages.

We reach this conclusion as to liability for breach of warranty only after rejecting the arguments of the two defendant-appellees that they are individually not liable under the implied warranty provisions of the Uniform Commercial Code.[4] Appellee Central Soya, the feed supplement manufacturer, argues that it cannot be liable for breach of any implied warranty because it was not in privity with appellants.

---

[4]The Uniform Commercial Code is presently the law in 49 states. The Code was first published in 1952 by the American Law Institute and the National Conference of Commissioners on Uniform State Laws. Codes prepared by the National Conference of Commissioners differ from the Restatements (see footnote 3, chapter 4, p. 146, *supra*) in that they are intended to be adopted by state legislatures. The Restatements, on the other hand, have as their purpose the reconciliation and interpretation of case law and the development of new concepts—all in the hope that the Restatements will be influential, albeit not controlling, with judges.

Below are the Implied Warranty Sections of the Uniform Commercial Code:

§ 2-314.   Implied Warranty: Merchantability; Usage of Trade (1968)

(1) Unless excluded or modified   .   .   .   a warranty that the goods shall be merchantable is implied in a contract for their sale if the seller is a merchant with respect to goods of that kind. Under this section the serving for value of drink to be consumed either on the premises or elsewhere is a sale.

(2) Goods to be merchantable must be at least such as

(a) pass without objection in the trade under the contract description; and

(b) in the case of fungible goods, are of fair average quality within the description; and

(c) are fit for the ordinary purposes for which such goods are used; and

(d) run within the variations permitted by the agreement, of even kind, quality and quantity within each unit and among all units involved; and

(e) are adequately contained, packaged, and labeled as the agreement may require; and

(f) conform to the promises or affirmation of fact made on the container or label if any.

(3) Unless excluded or modified   .   .   .   other implied warranties may arise from course of dealing or usage of trade.

§ 2-315.   Implied Warranty: Fitness for Particular Purpose

Where the seller at the time of contracting has reason to know any particular purpose for which the goods are required and that the buyer is relying on the seller's skill or judgment to select or furnish suitable goods, there is unless excluded or modified   .   .   .   an implied warranty that the goods shall be fit for such purpose.

There is, of course, no doubt that the feed supplied by Central Soya failed to meet the requirements of [the implied warranty of] merchantability. Section 2-314 of the code lists, inter alia, the following requirements that goods must meet to be merchantable: they must be "fit for the ordinary purposes for which such goods are used" and must be "adequately contained, packaged, and labeled as the agreement may require." It was properly found below that the Cattle Blend supplied by Central Soya was *not* fit for the ordinary purpose of feeding to breed cattle and was *not* properly labeled. But Soya disclaims liability because appellants purchased the feed from Pritts and cannot therefore maintain an action in assumpsit against Soya, a remote manufacturer.

Indeed, were we to continue to adhere to the requirement that privity of contract must exist between plaintiff and defendant in order to maintain an action in assumpsit for injuries caused by a breach of implied warranty, there would be no doubt that Soya could escape liability under the authority of Miller v. Preitz, 422 Pa. 383, 221 A.2d 320 (1966). However, we take this opportunity today to reconsider one of our holdings in that case, and accordingly this Court is now of the opinion that Pennsylvania should join the fast growing list of jurisdictions that have eliminated the privity requirement in assumpsit suits by purchasers against remote manufacturers for breach of implied warranty. That aspect of Miller must therefore be overruled.

As far back as 1931 the seeds of discontent were sown in the field of privity when Justice Cardozo said in Ultramares Corp. v. Touche, 255 N.Y. 170, 174 N.E. 441, 445 (1931): "The assault upon the citadel of privity is proceeding in these days apace." Since that historic decision the citadel has all but crumbled to dust in this area of product liability. Courts and scholars alike have recognized that the typical consumer does not deal at arms length with the party whose product he buys. Rather, he buys from a retail merchant who is usually little more than an economic conduit. It is not the merchant who has defectively manufactured the product. Nor is it usually the merchant who advertises the product on such a large scale as to attract consumers. We have in our society literally scores of large, financially responsible manufacturers who place their wares in the stream of commerce not only with the realization, but with the avowed purpose, that these goods will find their way into the hands of the consumer. Only the consumer will use these products; and only the consumer will be injured by them should they prove defective. Yet the law in Pennsylvania continued to permit these manufacturers to escape contractual liability for harm caused consumers by defective merchandise simply because the manufacturer technically did not *sell* directly to the consumer. There was no privity of contract between them. No one denied the *existence* of absolute liability under the code for breach of implied warranty. But this warranty ran not to the injured party, but rather to the middleman who merely sold to the injured party, thus ignoring commercial reality and encouraging multiplicity of litigation.

We realize that prior to the adoption of section 402a of the Restatement of Torts by this Court, see Webb v. Zern, 422 Pa. 424, 220 A.2d 853 (1966), a rather compelling argument against discarding privity in assumpsit actions for breach of warranty existed. Under the Uniform Commercial Code, once a breach of warranty has been shown, the defendant's liability, assuming of course the presence of proximate cause and damages, is absolute. Lack of negligence on the seller's part is no defense. Therefore, prior to the adoption of section 402a, it could be said that to dispense with privity would be to allow recovery in contract without proof of negligence, while requiring a showing of negligence in order to recover for the same wrong against the same defendant if suit were brought in tort. To permit the result of a lawsuit to depend solely on the caption atop plaintiff's complaint is not now, and has never been, a sound resolution of identical controversies.

However, with Pennsylvania's adoption of Restatement 402a, the same demands of legal symmetry which once supported privity now destroy it. Under the Restatement, if an action be commenced in tort by a purchaser of a defective product against a remote manufacturer, recovery may be had without a showing of negligence, and without a showing of privity, for any damage inflicted upon the person or property of the plaintiff as a result of this defective product. The language of the Restatement is both clear and emphatic:

"(1) One who sells any product in a defective condition unreasonably dangerous to the user or consumer or to his property is subject to liability for physical harm thereby caused to the ultimate user or consumer, or to his property, if
(a) the seller   .   .   .   [is engaged in the business] of selling such a product, and
(b) it is expected to and does reach the user or consumer without substantial change in the condition in which it is sold.
(2) The rule stated in Subsection (1) applies although
(a) the seller has exercised all possible care in the preparation and sale of his product, and
(b) the user or consumer has not bought the product from or entered into any contractual relation with the seller."

Thus, in the present case, for example, appellants' complaint alleging that their property (cattle) was damaged (rendered valueless as breeding stock) by virtue of the physical harm caused when these animals ate appellee-Soya's defective feed would have been sufficient to state a valid cause of action had it been captioned "Complaint in Trespass." However, because appellants elected to style their complaint as one in assumpsit for breach of warranty under the code, the requirement of privity would prevent these identical allegations from making out a good cause of action. This dichotomy of result is precisely the same evil which, prior to the Restatement, prevented the abolition of privity. It now compels this abolition.

.   .   .   .

To retain this tort-contract dichotomy with its haphazard, crazy quilt of exceptions and appendages can only cause Justice Voelker's language (speaking for the Supreme Court of Michigan when that tribunal abolished the privity requirement) to ring painfully true for the law of *this* Commonwealth. In commenting on the state of Michigan law under privity it was said: "A court lacking a clear and understandable rule of its own can scarcely be expected to impart it to others. Legal confusion has inevitably resulted. Aggrieved plaintiffs have scarcely known whether to sue in deceit or fraud or for negligence or breach of warranty—or indeed whether it was worthwhile to sue at all." Spence v. Three Rivers Builders & Masonry Supply, Inc., 353 Mich. 120, 90 N.W.2d 873, 878 (1958). We therefore hold that the lack of privity between appellants and Soya cannot insulate the latter from liability for breach of warranty.

.   .   .   .

Finally, we must address ourselves to the issue of recoverable damages for this breach of warranty. As we noted earlier in this opinion, the court below erred when it concluded that no *breach of warranty* existed because appellants did not prove that the stilbestrol present in the feed actually caused the cows to abort and the bull to become sterile. The breach of warranty was made out, and appellees shown liable at least for nominal damages, simply by proof that stilbestrol was in fact present in the feed contrary to the formula ordered. However, since there was sufficient evidence to sustain the lower court's finding that the abortions and sterility were not proximately caused by this stilbestrol, we have no choice but to hold that appellants have not demonstrated that particular element of damages.

Nevertheless, because the court below erroneously held that no breach of warranty occurred, it refused to hear any testimony on the second element of damages set forth in appellants' amended complaint wherein it is alleged that the value of the herd has been seriously affected by the cattle buying community's knowledge that these animals ate tainted feed. We believe that . . . appellants should be allowed to recover for the diminution in value of their cattle provided they can establish that this diminution proximately resulted from appellees' breach of warranty. It does not matter whether the cattle lost value because they in fact could not reproduce, or because no one in the community would buy them out of a reasonable fear that the stilbestrol they ate might cause reproductive disorders. For, if either be true, it can fairly be said that appellants' property has been damaged due to the feed sold by appellees. We thus must vacate the judgment below and remand this cause to afford appellants an opportunity to demonstrate, if they can, that their cattle have become unmarketable as breeding animals and that this fact is a proximate result of the ingestation of appellees' feed.

The judgment of the Court of Common Pleas of Washington County is vacated, and the record remanded for further proceedings consistent with this opinion.[5]

A NEW DAY NEEDS A NEW THEORY

A Coca Cola bottle exploded in the hand of a waitress, and the injury was severe. The majority of a California court thought that case should be resolved under an ordinary principle of tort law known as *res ipsa loquitur*—the thing speaks for itself. This relatively ancient principle holds that negligence is to be imputed to the maker of the thing if the thing, for unexplained and unexplainable reasons, does cause injury. If the maker cannot refute the implication of negligence, the case is then treated as if negligence had been pleaded and proved. The question of whether the maker of the thing has refuted the implication of negligence is for the jury. In the Escola case there was proof of statistical testing of one bottle out of every 600—a technique, according to an expert witness, that was "pretty near infallible" and therefore assurance

---

[5]The Pennsylvania Superior Court in MacDougall v. Ford Motor Co., 214 Pa. Superior Ct. 384 (1969), a Restatement § 402A case, held that the plaintiffs need not prove a specific defect in design or construction in order to prevail. The court allowed a defective condition in the automobile to be inferred from proof of a malfunction. See also Kridler v. Ford Motor Co., 422 F.2d 1182 (3d Cir. 1970), holding that in an action for breach of warranty under Pennsylvania law the plaintiff need prove only that a malfunction of the machine was the proximate cause of the accident. Other recent automobile cases in this line are: Cintrone v. Hertz Truck Leasing, 45 N.J. 434 (1965) and Cordle v. Renault, Inc., 361 F.2d 332 (6th Cir. 1966).

against delivery to the public of a Coca Cola bottle that would explode. The jury disregarded that proof and accepted the implication of negligence under the doctrine of *res ipsa loquitur.*

Justice Traynor in his Escola concurring opinion was satisfied with the result but not with the reason. He urged that if public policy demands that a manufacturer of goods be responsible for their quality regardless of negligence, there is good reason to openly fix that responsibility. One of the glories of the process of judge-made law is such a concurring opinion in which a great judge, entirely satisfied that justice was served in the case at hand, nevertheless enunciates a new concept, broader than the old, for justice in future cases.

Nineteen years later in the Greenman case Justice Traynor found the occasion to press the concept of manufacturer's absolute liability as an insurer of the remote user or consumer against injury from a defective product. He had spoken in Escola as if a mass producer, however that term might ultimately be defined, should be absolutely liable for an injury on the appealing sociological ground that the mass producer could better bear the cost of the injury than the individual consumer or user. This was a clear forecast of some higher measure of manufacturer's liability. In the Greenman case *defect* was stressed and relied upon. There was testimony that improper screws had been used. Something had been done wrongly or inadequately in the construction of the device that the plaintiff's wife trustingly purchased as a Christmas present for her woodworking husband. Justice Traynor, having staked out an advanced minority position in Escola, found the occasion here to implement it in the Greenman case.

Similarly, in Vandermark there was evidence of something amiss in the automobile in question. Justice Traynor did not in this case insist that a mass producer of automobiles is absolutely liable regardless of defect. It is true that the evidence of defect was most tenuous. It was "iffy" kind of evidence. An expert testified concerning what could have been wrong with the master cylinder of the braking system, but he had no way of knowing whether anything was actually wrong with the braking system of the car. Nevertheless, when Justice Traynor noted such evidence, however trivial, he made a genuflection to the rule requiring proof of defect. His reasoning is probably circular: if there is an unexplained, perhaps unexplainable, injury from a product, then there must have been a defect. This illogicality lies in the judicial subconscious. For the record the jurist stresses the evidence of defect however trivial.

In Henningsen again there was some evidence of something amiss. The court noted: "Suddenly she [the driver] heard a loud noise 'from the bottom, by the hood.' It 'felt as if something cracked.'" Yet, in Henningsen the liability was cast in implied warranty, not in tort—as the majority held in Escola and the entire court held in Greenman. Now, in Pennsylvania's Kassab the ultimate leap is taken: the action in Pennsylvania may be in either tort or implied warranty with nothing hanging on which.

The court in Henningsen said: "In our view, the total effect of the circumstances shown from the purchase to the accident is adequate to raise an inference that the car was defective and that such condition was causally related to the mishap." It must now be apparent that, although the courts have not adopted the 1944 philosophy of Justice Traynor that the manufacturer is an insurer against injury from a defective product, they have come to receive as evidence of (a) negligence or (b) defect such trivia as to amount to little, if any, proof. This condition enables the lawyer to perform one of his principal functions, that is, to predict what the result will be if, as, and when a certain hypothetical case becomes a case in fact. For example, suppose that in Henningsen the lady had not heard any noise, or suppose that, unhappily, she had died in the accident and could not testify. Suppose, further, that the car had been so utterly demolished as to preclude any form of automotive autopsy; and just to make the case airtight, suppose that there were no witnesses. Then what?

Let us predict that in this hypothetical case the manufacturer would be held liable, not to Mrs. Henningsen, but rather to her next of kin to whom her cause of action legally survives. Upon what theory? We have seen that the exception of the "inherently dangerous instrumentality" no longer serves a sensible purpose. It would offend common sense that American industry in producing 8–9 million automobiles per annum is producing that number of inherently dangerous instrumentalities. We must conclude that the old rule of privity is gone, whether the action is in tort for negligence, as in Thomas and Wife, or in implied warranty of fitness for the intended purpose of the thing, as in Henningsen. We must conclude that the rule of privity is waived in favor not only of a wife or a child, but also in favor of a servant in the household, some distant relative or guest, and ultimately, in favor of a person such as Waters in the opposite lane of a highway or Mitchell, a bystander injured while playing golf. Both vertical and horizontal privity are passing. When the rule goes, the dangerous instrumentality exception goes. Hence, the product may be something as innocuous as a rug, shoe, dry cell battery, paper cup, light bulb, or hula skirt.[6]

We must conclude that it is no longer necessary for an injured plaintiff to prove manufacturer's negligence. That would be too great a burden. How could an impecunious plaintiff discover the technical deviations from standards of due care that faultlessly occur in cavernous plant expanses where the inexorable movements of gears grind out in faceless unconcern the mass of products that the masses trustingly and eagerly await? That burden of proof would certainly be too great in an age when the factory totally dwarfs the individual.

[6]Wright, Kenneth B., *The Defective Product and Strict Liability,* American Bar Association, Law Notes, April 1969. For a case involving a martini olive, see Hochberg v. O'Donnell's Rest., Inc., 39 L.W. 2449 (D.C. Ct.APP. 1971).

A plaintiff, using a manufactured thing for the purposes for which the manufacturer intended it or might reasonably have expected it to be used, will recover for injury caused by the thing, if the thing is defective. The modern plaintiff is left with the necessity of proving defect, and only defect. The facts in Escola, Henningsen, Greenman, and Vandermark show what minimal evidence will prove defect.

We now ask what would be the answer to our hypothetical Henningsen case: no evidence of defect; both car and lone driver demolished; no witnesses; only unspeaking and unspeakable devastation. We must accept these bare facts— at least for the moment. Obviously, the defendant manufacturer would have moved to dismiss the complaint on the ground that there was no proof of defect. The next of kin of the deceased would have first contended that no proof of defect was necessary, citing how trivial the proof of defect was in Henningsen and later cases. Now, more than likely, the defendant manufacturer in the hypothetical case would have employed the statistical inspection methods used in Escola. But the plaintiff's argument would be as follows: Defective automobiles *are* made. Manufacturers *do* call in large numbers of automobiles for the cure of admitted defects. The question whether the demolished car *was* such a one is, therefore, for the jury. It seems probable that the court would send the case to the jury, which in the real world means that the plaintiff, in the context of the background of the cases in this section (the teaching of which would have been imparted by the court's instructions to the jury), would recover without tangible proof of defect. The rule that is emerging is one of absolute liability (without proof of defect) to be fixed upon the mass producer in favor of an injured remote user or consumer of the mass-produced product or anyone else, including a bystander, unfortunate enough to be present and injured by the misbehavior of the product.

The logical reason for the rule of absolute liability is more difficult to ascertain. The cases in this section disclose, as the cases in any area of the law would disclose, a persistent intent and attempt by the courts to be logical and consistent. These cases begin with the proposition that a manufacturer is liable in tort for a negligently or defectively made product only if, in the first instance, he stood face to face with the purchaser of his product. This was called privity.

The rule seemed harsh. The dangerous instrumentality became an ameliorating exception. Yet the exception became as difficult as the rule. We begin, therefore, in this closing analysis to look for something other than logic to explain the rise and fall of the exception. Apparently, it was applied to favor the new technology. A flywheel, an indispensable element of the steam engine, and the boiler, a fundamental of the engine, were instrumentalities held to be not inherently dangerous. One can but specualte that the law was being tender to the new technology.

In all but the tick of a second hand on the clock of man's existence, work has been done by the muscles of man and animals or by the natural forces of nature, wind, and water. Then came Watt and a man-made source of energy. The law would naturally be tender to the alleviation of man's toil. It felt no such tenderness to a lethal drug, which is ancient in the cultures of man, whether it is belladonna, some medicine man's concoction, or some witch's brew. It felt no such tenderness toward a high scaffolding, which is as ancient as the Sumerian Hanging Gardens, the columns at Karnac, or the monoliths and lintels at Stonehenge.

The law was indeed tender to the new technology—while it was new. When the new technology matured into the internal combustion engine and emerged in the form of traffic jams and lethal smog, the law became less tender. When new technology passes from innovation to banality, it is easier for the law to make the manufacturer absolutely liable. The exception of the dangerous instrumentality was intended to be logical, but it was forced by technology and banality to illogicality. Hence, the exception and the rule both failed.

Our prediction in this closing commentary holds that a mass producer of a product widely sold and widely bought in society is absolutely liable to an injured user of one of those products, whether or not the user can prove either negligence or defect. If this judgment is correct, then is this prediction merely out of the legal fingertips, or is it a logical progression of heretofore established concepts? In legal candor it must be considered the former.

Therefore we look for what, in strict legal analysis, must be considered a nonlegal reason for the new rule. One cannot do better than Justice Traynor. In 1944 he said: "In my opinion it should now be recognized that a manufacturer incurs an absolute liability when an article that he has placed on the market, knowing that it is to be used without inspection, proves to have a defect that causes injury to human beings." Justice Traynor moved directly to a socioeconomic concept: the mass producer can afford to insure the risk because he can pass on the cost, actuarially determined, to the consumer.

Mass production is a complex of fragmented responsibilities, all neatly gathered into the ultimate determination of profit and loss. Business, whether that of a hawker at a county fair or that of a giant producer of automobiles, exists to produce a product or service, to sell it at a price higher than the aggregate of all costs, and thus to produce a profit. Every section, every element, every authority, every responsibility in the total process looks to its profit. If it were otherwise, business would not exist. Business does not do well on losses. That method has been tried and tried well. It does not work as the records of the bankruptcy courts attest.

It is therefore inherent in the mass production process that risks will be taken, corners will be cut in order to reduce costs, and inspection will be statistical, not piece by piece. It is also inherent in the mass production process that risks of the product will be passed to the consuming public. Hence, if there is an ensuing legal rationale other than O. W. Holmes' "convenience," it lies in this aspect, and this inevitable aspect, of mass production, namely, the inexorable pressures to reduce costs so that there will be profits and the inexorable consequence of occasional product risks passed on by the manufacturer to the consumer. By the same token the manufacturer, once absolutely liable, will actuarially determine his higher costs and pass them on in the form of higher prices to the consumer. Justice Traynor would find these higher costs the consequences of justice by his formula.

It is the genius of the law in Anglo-American culture that it proceeds case by case; that it does not play the role of deity; that it does not propose to lay out a blueprint for the best of all possible worlds; that it does not pretend to prior apperception. And, yet, it is an admirable aspect of legal development that occasionally logic comes to an end and consistency fails. When that happens, then the candor of Mr. Justice Holmes shines forth in such a statement as:[7]

> The truth is, that the law is always approaching, and never reaching, consistency. It is forever adopting new principles from life at one end, and it always retains old ones from history at the other, which have not yet been absorbed or sloughed off. It will become entirely consistent only when it ceases to grow.

Clearly, the postulated rule of absolute liability for injury suffered from a mass-produced product will not be free of difficulty in application. It will be no less difficult in borderline cases to determine who is a mass producer than it was to determine what was a dangerous instrumentality. Obviously, there will be no problem about any of the big three automobile manufacturers or any of the big soft drink bottlers, just for examples. But how about a small shop that converts stock cars for racing or for the police? How about Mrs. X, a widow, who makes a few fruit cakes each year for sale through some women's exchange?

A policeman injured in a converted stock car will present exactly the same case as the coachman in the wagon wheel case mentioned in Thomas and Wife. A Christmas dinner guest at the house of a hostess who never saw Mrs. X, encountering a piece of black stone the size of a raisin in the fruit cake, will present the same problem as in Ash and Friend. The automobile converter and Mrs. X obviously are not mass producers. It seems likely, therefore, that a new rule of absolute liability will not apply to such small producers as they are and will always be.[8] Contrary to conventions—one law for the big; another law

---

[7]Holmes, Oliver Wendell, Jr., *The Common Law,* p. 36, Little Brown, Boston (48th print.), 1909; 1923.

[8]In Schipper v. Levitt & Sons, Inc., 44 N.J. 70, 207 A.2d 314 (1965), the New Jersey Supreme Court held a builder of mass produced homes strictly liable for injuries sustained by the child of a purchaser's lessee who was scalded by excessively hot water drawn from the bathroom faucet which the builder had defectively installed. To similar effect is Kriegler v. Eichler Homes, 269 Cal. Appellate Ct. 2d. 224, 74 Cal. Rptr. 749 (1969), in which the California Court of Appeals for the First Appellate District held that a builder of mass produced homes was strictly liable in tort for damages to the owner's property caused by the corrosion of the radiant heating system that had been installed eight years before the injury was sustained.

for the small? So it seems. Why not? Yet courts must say who are big and who are little. There is no end to the judging process.

There are, and will be, types of manufacturers whose categories will challenge our future courts. For example, the space vehicle manufacturer or a manufacturer of one of its almost innumerable components. Certainly such manufacturers are not mass producers—not now when one launching pad, rocket system, capsule, terrestrial control complex are the work of years. There is no production line spitting off automobiles or a bottling machine ejecting soft drinks. Rather, the "manufacturer," if he can be called such, is a systems manager, who coordinates, integrates, and makes a multiple-element complex greater than the sum of its parts.

There were originally 113 significant engineering orders that had not been completed, and on final delivery, 22 engineering orders that were not recorded as having been accomplished in the space vehicle complex in which three American astronauts were incinerated or asphyxiated at Cape Kennedy in January, 1967.[9] Who, if anyone, is liable to their widows?

Very well! The ultimate will not be a landing on the moon, Mars, or some other astro-body, but also the space platform, on which men and women will live, no longer earthbound, as our men and women have never lived since man emerged 500,000, perhaps 2,000,000 or more years ago. (The anthropologists are constantly pushing true man's date deeper into the primordial past.) Someday, eager men and women will have passage on a space platform for astro-cruising through the music of the spheres. Some of them will be doomed never to return. There will be no more evidence of what happened than in our hypothetical Henningsen case. Who will be liable and upon what theory? Could we have a clearer view of the environment's changing law than in the kaleidoscope of cases from Thomas v. Winchester to MacDougall v. Ford Motor and Kridler v. Ford Motor?

QUESTIONS

1. Belladonna is a poison; it is also a medicine in certain cases. Suppose that the physician had prescribed belladonna but dandelion had been supplied by reason of mislabeling. In other words, in Thomas v. Winchester, suppose we have just the converse as between belladonna and dandelion. Suppose the patient had suffered grievously unto death for lack of the prescribed medicine. What result would the court have reached in 1852? Would that result be different today?

2. In the dangerous instrumentality exception to the rule requiring privity, what fundamental, logical distinction would you make between belladonna and a scaffold? A clue to the distinction will be found in Judge Cardozo's opinion in MacPherson.

[9]Lewis, Richard S., *Appointment on the Moon,* p. 391, Viking Press, New York, 1968.

3. Something is said about the doctrine of *res ipsa loquitur* in Escola and also something is said by the author about that doctrine in the commentary entitled, "A New Day Needs a New Theory." Do you see any identity between the doctrine of *res ipsa loquitur* and Judge Traynor's concept of absolute liability of the manufacturer for injury to a remote buyer, user, or bystander from a defective product?

4. The reader will recall what a critical difference in result ensued from a suit in tort in Ash and a suit in implied warranty in Friend. Would such a difference obtain today? If not, what cases in this chapter so hold?

5. If manufacturers of defective products are to be liable to everyone and anyone who suffers injury from the product, then manufacturers have one of two choices: either to take greater precautions to avoid defects or to treat the damages they must pay for injuries as the cost of manufacture. In either case the manufacturers' cost will increase, and the prices to consumers will increase. In other words, if the manufacturer becomes in effect an insurer of his product against injury to everyone and anyone, then it is the consumer who must pay the bill. Is this social justice?

6. The reader will have noted that all of the rationale about absolute liability of the manufacturer for a defective product is founded upon the fact of mass production. What about a defective product which is not mass produced? In that case would you adhere to the rule of privity?

6 Law Must Sometimes Embrace Expediency

Introduction. 255
Cases Involving Innocent Victims. 257
  Rights and Liabilities of Victims of Theft 257
    Wooden-Ware Co. v. United States 257
    Richtmyer v. Mutual Live Stock Commission Company. 259
  Rights and Liabilities of Victims of Swindle or Mistake 261
    Krumsky v. Loeser 261
    Cowen v. Pressprich. 262
Questions 269

INTRODUCTION

In this chapter a few cases are presented to illustrate the inadequacy of a natural sense of justice. Judges, no less than other men, often believe themselves possessed of a dependable and innate sense of what is right and what is wrong. This is sometimes called the conscience. Some cases in other chapters of this book demonstrate that judges, like ordinary men, appeal to conscience as the final arbitrator. When a judge appeals to conscience he makes law no less than when he appeals to logic or to precedent. When an ordinary man appeals to conscience, he merely approves or disapproves law. From the point of view of social control in the individual case, as well as the setting of precedent, the conscience of a judge is effectual, while that of the layman is ineffectual, unless the point of conscience is held by enough men to assemble the political power to employ the legislative process to make new law.

Some cases in other chapters of this book demonstrate the role of emotion in the judging process. The outraged conscience of the judge, verging on contempt for one party or the other, or righteous indignation are emotions that aid the decision-making process. They shine through the judicial writing, sometimes blatantly, when some "wise and just" judge decides to unsettle an old rule in order that "justice" may be done in some new set of circumstances in the changing environment.

However, the cases in this section demonstrate the difficulty that a natural sense of right and wrong encounters when one of two blameless parties must suffer by reason of the misconduct of a third party who has fled the jurisdiction. No thought is generated by leveling judicial rage at the escaped culprit. It would be comforting if every frustrating controversy could be neatly handled by Solomon's formula for the discovery of the true mother, by Cardozo's sense of the absurd in MacPherson, or by Francis' outrage over the fine print in Henningsen. Emotion as well as reason is father to thought, but not in every situation and particularly not when one of two equally innocent parties must lose.

In this chapter one may feel a strong inclination to emulate the wisdom of Solomon by dividing the losses between the two innocents, because neither conscience nor outrage will avail for the answer. The law, however, does not avoid in so facile a manner its obligation to decide the hard case. In looking for the rationale of decision in the "hard cases," where no obvious just result appears, more often than not, logic turns to convenience. Consider the case in which a thief takes the property of A and sells it to B, who buys it in good faith with utterly no knowledge of the theft. Who must suffer the loss, A or B? Suppose the property stolen from A is worth much more in the market where B bought and paid for it than it was worth where the thief stole it from A; suppose the converse. Why does the law distress itself with such questions? Why not leave A and B where the thief left them—the thief himself having been hanged, as he would have been a few decades ago in the American West for the theft of a horse or of cattle; or resting secure and impecunious in jail; or having fled to some Shangri-La. Must A lose because B bought innocently; must B return the stolen property to A and lose what he paid for it? Suppose B no longer possesses the property. Must B pay A its value; if so, as of what time and market?

The inadequacy of the formulations of some of our greatest Western-World thinkers about justice and law will be illuminated by the cases in this section. Consider Aristotle and Aquinas, as rendered and quoted by Mortimer Adler:[1]

Whether it is stated in terms of the good of other individuals or in terms of the common good of a community (domestic or political), * * * justice seems to consider the actions of a man as they affect the well-being, not of himself, but of others. "Justice, alone of the virtues," says Aristotle, "is thought to be 'another's good,' because it is related to our neighbor." Concerned with what is due another, justice involves the element of duty or obligation. "To each one," Aquinas writes, "is due what is his own," and "it evidently pertains to justice," he adds, "that a

[1]Adler, Mortimer J., *A Syntopicon of Great Books of the Western World*, p. 853, Encyclopaedia Britannica, Chicago, 1952.

man give another his due." That is why "justice alone, of all the virtues, implies the notion of duty." Doing good to others or not injuring them, when undertaken as a matter of strict justice, goes no further than to discharge the debt which each man owes every other.

But what is *A*'s debt to *B* or *B*'s to *A,* within the meaning of the Aristotelian concept of neighborliness, when the whole problem of who stands the loss is occasioned by *C,* an unneighborly thief?

CASES INVOLVING INNOCENT VICTIMS

RIGHTS AND LIABILITIES OF VICTIMS OF THEFT

WOODEN-WARE COMPANY v. UNITED STATES
Supreme Court of the United States, 106 U.S. 432 (1882).

Mr. Justice MILLER delivered the opinion of the court.

This is a writ of error, founded on a certificate of division of opinion between the judges of the Circuit Court.

The facts, as certified, out of which this difference of opinion arose appear in an action in the nature of trover, brought by the United States for the value of two hundred and forty-two cords of ash timber, or wood suitable for manufacturing purposes, cut and removed from that part of the public lands known as the reservation of the Oneida tribe of Indians, in the State of Wisconsin. This timber was knowingly and wrongfully taken from the land by Indians, and carried by them some distance to the town of Depere, and there sold to the E. E. Bolles Wooden-ware Company, the defendant, which was not chargeable with any intentional wrong or misconduct or bad faith in the purchase.

The timber on the ground, after it was felled, was worth twenty-five cents per cord, or $60.71 for the whole, and at the town of Depere, where defendant bought and received it, three dollars and fifty cents per cord, or $850 for the whole quantity. The question on which the judges divided was whether the liability of the defendant should be measured by the first or the last of these valuations.

It was the opinion of the circuit judge that the latter was the proper rule of damages, and judgment was rendered against the defendant for that sum.

We cannot follow counsel for the plaintiff in error through the examination of all the cases, both in England and this country, which his commendable research has enabled him to place upon the brief. In the English courts the decisions have in the main grown out of coal taken from the mine, and in such cases the principle seems to be established in those courts, that when suit is brought for the value of the coal so taken, and it has been the result of an honest mistake as to the true ownership of the mine, and the taking was not a wilful trespass, the rule of damages is the value of the coal as it was in the mine before it was disturbed, and not its value when dug out and delivered at the mouth of the mine. . . .

The doctrine of the English courts on this subject is probably as well stated by Lord Hatherley in the House of Lords, in the case of Livingstone *v.* Rawyards Coal Co., 5 App. Cas. 25, as anywhere else. He said: "There is no doubt that if a man furtively, and in bad faith, robs his neighbor of his property, and because it is underground is probably for some little time not detected, the court of equity in this country will struggle, or I would rather say, will assert its authority to punish the fraud by fixing the person with the value of the whole of the property which he has so furtively taken, and making him no allowance in respect of what he has so done, as would have been justly made to him if the parties had been working by agreement." But "when once we arrive at the fact that an inadvertence has been the cause of the misfortune, then the simple course is to make every just allowance for outlay on the part of the person who has so acquired the property, and to give back to the owner, so far as is possible under the circumstances of the case, the full value of that which cannot be restored to him *in specie."*

There seems to us to be no doubt that in the case of a wilful trespass the rule as stated above is the law of damages both in England and in this country, though in some of the State courts the milder rule has been applied even in this class of cases. Such are some that are cited from Wisconsin. Weymouth *v.* Chicago & Northwestern Railway Co., 17 Wis. 550; Single *v.* Schneider, 24 Wis. 299.

On the other hand, the weight of authority in this country as well as in England favors the doctrine that where the trespass is the result of inadvertence or mistake, and the wrong was not intentional, the value of the property when first taken must govern; or if the conversion sued for was after value had been added to it by the work of the defendant, he should be credited with this addition.   .   .   .

While these principles are sufficient to enable us to fix a measure of damages in both classes of torts where the original trespasser is defendant, there remains a third class, where a purchaser from him is sued, as in this case, for the conversion of the property to his own use. In such case, if the first taker of the property were guilty of no wilful wrong, the rule can in no case be more stringent against the defendant who purchased of him than against his vendor.

But the case before us is one where, by reason of the wilful wrong of the party who committed the trespass, he was liable, under the rule we have supposed to be established, for the value of the timber at Depere the moment before he sold it, and the question to be decided is whether the defendant who purchased it then with no notice that the property belonged to the United States, and with no intention to do wrong, must respond by the same rule of damages as his vendor should if he had been sued.

It seems to us that he must. The timber at all stages of the conversion was the property of plaintiff. Its purchase by defendant did not divest the title nor the right of possession. The recovery of any sum whatever is based upon that proposition. This right, at the moment preceding the purchase by defendant at Depere, was perfect, with no right in any one to set up a claim for work and labor bestowed on it by the wrong-doer. It is also plain that by purchase from the wrong-doer defendant did not acquire any better title to the property than his vendor had. It is not a case where an innocent purchaser can defend himself under that plea. If it were, he would be liable to no damages at all, and no recovery could be had. On the contrary, it is a case to which the doctrine of *caveat emplor* applies, and hence the right of recovery in plaintiff.

On what ground, then, can it be maintained that the right to recover against him should not be just what it was against his vendor the moment before he interfered and acquired possession? If the case were one which concerned additional value placed upon the property by the work or labor of the defendant after he had purchased, the same rule might be applied as in case of the inadvertent trespasser.

But here he has added nothing to its value. He acquired possession of property of the United States at Depere, which, at that place, and in its then condition, is worth $850, and he wants to satisfy the claim of the government by the payment of $60. He founds his right to do this, not on the ground that anything *he* has added to the property has increased its value by the amount of the difference between these two sums, but on the proposition that in purchasing the property he purchased of the wrong-doer a right to deduct what the labor of the latter had added to its value.

If, as in the case of an unintentional trespasser, such right existed, of course defendant would have bought it and stood in his shoes; but as in the present case, of an intentional trespasser, who had no such right to sell, the defendant could purchase none.

. . . .

To hold that when the government finds its own property in hands but one removed from these wilful trespassers, and asserts its right to such property by the slow processes of the law, the holder can set up a claim for the value which has been added to the property by the guilty party in the act of cutting down the trees and removing the timber, is to give encouragement and reward to the wrong-doer, by providing a safe market for what he has stolen and compensation for the labor he has been compelled to do to make his theft effectual and profitable.

We concur with the circuit judge in this case, and the judgment of the Circuit Court is affirmed.

RICHTMYER v. MUTUAL LIVE STOCK COMMISSION COMPANY
Supreme Court of Nebraska, 122 Neb. 317 (1932).

BLACKLEDGE, District Judge.   This action is by the plaintiff, appellee, for the conversion of certain cattle which were stolen from his ranch in Cherry county; and its object, to recover the value of the cattle from the defendant, which as a livestock commission merchant, some seven days after the theft, received the cattle of Omaha on shipment from the thief, and sold them in the usual course on the market.

In the briefing and submission of the case in this court, all assignments of error are eliminated except the one which involve the proper measure of damage to be applied in the case.

The defendant contends that, the jury having found for plaintiff upon the identity of the cattle, it is liable to plaintiff in some amount, as having handled and disposed of the stolen property, but insists that the value for which it may be held to account is that in Omaha where it received and dealt with the property. It claims to have acted innocently and in good faith, without knowledge of the prior theft and conversion; and this fact is conceded by plaintiff, who states in his brief: "We wish to make it clear that we do not charge the defendant with any culpability."

The plaintiff contends, and the trial court adopted the theory, that the proper measure of damage was the value of the cattle in Cherry county at the time of the original taking by the thief, with interest from that date. Evidence was either received or excluded in the trial in accordance with that theory, and the jury were so instructed.

The cattle were pure bred registered Herefords, valuable for breeding purposes. They were sold on the market as ordinary beef cattle, netting the shipper some $1,000. Their value as pure breds in Cherry county is amply sustained by the evidence at $3,500, which the jury found. The defendant was not permitted to show the value of such cattle at Omaha.

Both parties concede that the general rule for the measure of damages for conversion is the value of the property at the time and place of conversion, with interest from that date. Here they part company, however, and each seeks to apply that statement, as an unbending and all-inclusive rule, to the facts of his own case. Plaintiff urges that his loss occurred at the original taking, and that this unalterably fixes the time and place governing the value to be allowed, regardless of the remoteness of time or place when and where they came into posession of defendant, or of the innocence or culpability of the defendant, who had no part in the original taking and became liable solely by having, in the usual course of business, handled and disposed of the stolen property, and regardless also of the condition or value of the property at the time defendant came into possession.

.   .   .   .

That the general rule hereinbefore stated of the measure of damages for conversion is the law of this state, there can be no doubt.   .   .   .

It does not follow, however, that it is so unyielding and all inclusive that no account should be taken of the facts attendant upon the conversion, the entrance of defendant into the zone of liability, or the location or condition of the property at that time. Courts have often considered the condition of the converted property as it came into the hands of the defendant, and, upon comparison with its condition when originally taken, modified the measure of damage as it is hereinbefore stated. This has generally occurred in cases wherein the property had been increased in value by some process of trade or manufacture. In some instances the plaintiff was awarded the value as increased, upon the ground that it was made by the wrong-doer himself who should not be permitted to thus profit by his own act and in effect compel an involuntary sale by plaintiff. Wooden-ware Co. v. United States, 106 U.S. 432. In Pine River Logging & Improvement Co. v. United States, 186 U.S. 279, it is said: "The cases involving this distinction and in line with the Wooden-Ware case are abundant, both in the federal and state courts, and are too numerous even for citation."

In many cases the courts rest a distinction upon the ground that the defendant, not being an intentional wrong-doer, came innocently into possession of the property, and allow the defendant credit for any increase in value contributed by him, although holding him to account for the condition of the property as it came into his hands.   .   .   .

.   .   .   .

This all leads to the conclusion that in such cases "the time and place of conversion" to be considered, and which controls on the question of value, is that fixed by the acts of the defendant in its dealing with the property, rather than the original taking in which defendant had no part. The trial court was in error in excluding evidence as to the value of the property at Omaha, and in instructing the jury that the value in Cherry county on the date of the theft was the only value to be considered. This gives to the plaintiff full compensation for his loss in so far as the defendant had any connection with it, holds defendant responsible for the full value of that in which it dealt, without attaching additional penalty for the acts of another, and seems to us a just and salutary rule.

It is not to be understood, however, that the value of the property in Cherry county, so recently before the conversion by defendant, becomes immaterial in the case. The limits of the inquiry should not in this case be so confined. The value there at that time might well tend to show the value on shipment to Omaha. Also whether the cattle in question were pure breds or only beef cattle was one of the issues in the case. We judicially know the relative location of the counties and cities in the state and approximate distances and the general routes of travel; and that Omaha is the principal live stock market in the state and probably the one most accessible from Cherry county. It seems reasonable that in this investigation the values at either place would be relevant in fixing the actual value of the property at the time and place of the acts of the defendant in relation thereto.

For the reasons stated, the judgment of the district court is reversed and a new trial awarded.

Reversed.

RIGHTS AND LIABILITIES OF VICTIMS OF SWINDLE OR MISTAKE

A bailment in law exists when goods are received by one to be held in trust for a specific purpose and are to be returned when that purpose is ended. This simplistic definition will suffice for the following two cases.

KRUMSKY v. LOESER
Supreme Court of New York, Appellate Term, 75 N.Y. Supp. 1012 (1902).

GREENBAUM, J.   Defendants appeal from a judgment rendered against them in the municipal court, Fifth district. The facts upon which the controversy between the parties hinges are practically undisputed. The plaintiff is a manufacturer of ladies' wrappers. The defendants are the proprietors of a large department store in Brooklyn. The parties had never had business relations with each other. On April 19, 1901, two swindlers purporting to represent the defendants ordered a bill of goods of the plaintiff, with directions to deliver them to the defendants' place of business. The plaintiff, after satisfying himself of the financial ability of defendants, as he asserts, sent the goods to the defendants by an expressman. It appears that the defendants' establishment is in the habit of receiving about 350 packages from various houses daily, and that the goods were received under the assumption that they had been ordered by the defendants. Later in the day the man in charge of the receiving department of the defendants was called up on the telephone by a person who represented himself to be the plaintiff, and who stated that the case of wrappers had been delivered to the defendants by mistake, and that the goods would be called for. Shortly after this conversation a person called with an order, purporting to be signed by plaintiff, addressed to the defendants, requesting the redelivery of the case to bearer. The order explained that the mistake was occasioned by wrongly addressing the goods to the defendants, instead of "E. Losier, Savannah, Ga.," and expressed the hope that the defendants had not been inconvenienced. The goods were thereupon handed over to the bearer of the order. It subsequently transpired that the plaintiff and the defendants were the victims of a swindle, and the question is presented as to which of the parties must bear the loss of the goods.

The plaintiff attempts to fasten a liability upon the defendants as gratuitous bailees, upon the theory of the defendants' negligence in accepting the goods and delivering them up to a stranger. Were defendants bailees? A bailment must be predicated upon some contractual relation, express or implied, upon the delivery of the goods, between the bailor and bailee. In this case the goods were by trick, the result of a fraud practiced upon plaintiff, thrust upon the defendants, who thus for a short time were unconsciously and unknowingly the custodians of the plaintiff's goods. Where one becomes possessed of another's goods by chance or accident, no bailment obligation will arise unless the possessor is aware and has knowledge of the fact that goods have come into his possession which belong to another. In the case at bar the knowledge that the defendants became possessed of the goods not belonging to them was communicated to them by the swindler to enable him to carry out his scheme of obtaining the property of the plaintiff. If I am apprised by another that a certain article belonging to him was sent to me by mistake, am I not justified in assuming, from the very fact of such party first making me aware of its possession, that he is the true owner, and entitled to its return? Am I obligated or beholden to the real owner, if I have been deceived, to account for the value of the article thus secured from me through trick? I think not. If, however, by any process of reasoning, the duty of a gratuitous bailee could be fastened upon the defendants, then I am of opinion that, inasmuch as they would only be chargeable in that case with gross negligence, First Nat. Bank v. Ocean Nat. Bank, 60 N.Y. 278, they should not be here held liable. They were certainly no more negligent than was the plaintiff in parting with his goods. The defendants, indeed, acted in the matter as any ordinarily prudent man could have been expected to act under the circumstances. . . . .

Judgment reversed, and new trial ordered, with costs to appellants to abide event. All concur.

COWEN v. PRESSPRICH
Supreme Court of New York, Appellate Term, 192 N.Y. Supp. 242 (1922).

MULLAN, J.   Conversion, for the defendants' alleged wrongful delivery of a bond. The parties on both sides are stock exchange brokers. Plaintiffs had agreed to sell and deliver to defendants a bond of the Oregon Short Line Railroad of the par value of $1,000. To fill that order, plaintiffs ordered the bond from a third bond house, and the latter, by mistake, sent plaintiffs an Oregon & California Railroad bond, and plaintiffs, also by mistake, sent this Oregon & California bond to defendants. There is no controversy as to the manner of the sending. Plaintiffs handed the Oregon & California bond to Goldberg, a youth of 17 years, who was one of plaintiffs' two messengers or "runners," as they seem to be called. With the bond was a memorandum (also called "slip" or "statement") briefly describing an Oregon Short Line bond. The bond and slip were inclosed together in an envelope. Goldberg took the envelope to defendants' place of business in a Wall Street office building. Defendants' suite of offices had two entrance doors from the office building hall, one for general use, and the other for persons, such as Goldberg, making deliveries. Goldberg entered at the latter door, and was then in a tiny outside room, described as about two feet by six feet. There was no door for passage between this small outside room and an inside, and presumably larger, room.

Deliveries were made by dropping papers in a slot in one of the partitions partly forming this small outer room. Above the slot was a window of opaque glass that swung inwards. That window was kept closed unless or until the person acting for defendants at the delivery window should desire to talk to one making a delivery, when he would open the window. Next to the partition containing that slot and window, and in the inner room, was a desk at which was kept seated either a member of defendants' firm or a clerk. At the time here in question there were two persons at that desk, Mr. Quackenbush, of the defendants' firm, and an employee, one Campbell. Goldberg dropped the envelope through the slot. His testimony was:

"I waited until he [the person at the desk] took it in, and then I left. * * * I told him I will call back for a check. Q. Why didn't you ask for the receipt? A. Well, I was in a hurry; I had many deliveries that day, and I had to make them * * * Q. How long would you say you were in that delivery room in front of that delivery window —from the time you put the bond in until you left? A. It was from a minute to a minute and a half."

Goldberg could not recall whether the person at the other side of the window said anything. He thought, but was not sure, that there was "somebody" else in the little outside room when he was there. It does not appear from Goldberg's testimony whether or not the delivery window was open during any part of his stay while making the delivery. Mr. Quackenbush testified as follows:

"Q. Will you tell us what took place at the time of that delivery. A. It was about 10:30 in the morning. Mr. Campbell and myself stood there making up our loans, when a bond shoots through the window like a streak of lightning; it goes right down my desk—that was my desk about the width of this table (indicating stenographer's table) —right down in front of us. As it rolls over, I opened it up; just pulled the bond open that way instantly (indicating). The statement called for an Oregon Short Line five bond; I could see immediately that the bond was an Oregon & California, and we handle thousands of them. Q. What did you do then? A. I immediately opened the window. Q. Where was that; right in front of you? A. Right like that (indicating), and I yelled 'Cowen.' A young man steps right up, and I says, 'Make your statement agree with the bond.' The Court: Sir? The Witness: 'Make your statement agree with the bond.' He mumbled, 'Alright,' and takes the bond and goes out immediately like that. Q. And he took it? A. He took it. Q. When you say man— A. A young boy 19 or 20 years old. Q. What did you do then; close the window? A. Closed the window; went about my work. Q. You were expecting from Cowen & Co. at that time a Short Line bond, were you not? A. Yes; we had purchased one, looking for it. Q. You were looking for it? A. Yes; some day. Q. And you say you instantly found it was not— A. It was not more than 15 seconds. Q. And you were under no contract to purchase from Cowen & Co. a California bond? A. No, sir. Q. How long would you say it took between the time that bond came into your slot on to your desk and the time you opened the window and yelled 'Cowen'? A. Not a second more that 15. Q. Fifteen seconds? A. Not a second more than that. Q. When you opened the window where did the boy come? A. To my left from the main door. Q. You heard the Goldberg boy testify, did you not, that when he put that bond into your window, he waited about a minute and a half; is that correct? A. I will say no. Q. Did you hear him say anything? A. Nothing. Q. The only thing you know is seeing the bond shoot into the window. A. Exactly. Q. Was there a receipt on that bond to be signed by you? A. No, sir; it was not. Q. It was merely a sale memorandum? A. Exactly. Q. Neither one of them is the young man to whom you delivered the bond? A. No, sir. Q. You delivered the bond to some one else? A. Neither one of those [plaintiffs] boys."

Mr. Campbell substantially corroborated Mr. Quackenbush's version.

Concededly the boy to whom Quackenbush returned the bond delivered by Goldberg was not Goldberg, but some unidentified boy who made away with the bond. The bond was of the bearer type, fully negotiable.

The defendants have refused to make good the plaintiffs' loss, contending that they were chargeable only with due diligence, and that, accepting the version of the plaintiffs as given by Goldberg, it appears that they exercised all the care required of them. The plaintiffs contend that there was an absolute obligation on the part of the defendants to redeliver the bond to the plaintiffs, and that no question of negligence enters into the case. They also argue that, if the negligence question does enter, there was sufficient evidence to warrant a finding that the defendants did not, in fact, exercise due care. The learned trial judge did not state the ground of his decision in plaintiffs' favor.

A person who has been put, through no act or fault of his own, in such a situation as that in which the defendants were put upon the delivery to them of the wrong bond, has come to be known as "involuntary bailee," . . . or bailee by casualty, . . . or constructive or quasi bailee. . . .

In the field of voluntary bailments, whether they be for hire or be otherwise coupled with an interest on the part of the bailee, or whether they be merely gratuitous, no rule is better settled than that it is the duty of the bailee to deliver the bailed article to the right person, and that delivery to the wrong person is not capable of being excused by any possible showing of care or good faith or innocence. . . .

Such distinctions as have been drawn between the duties of voluntary bailees for compensation and voluntary gratuitous bailees relate solely to the degree of care the bailee should exercise in respect of the custody of the thing bailed. In respect of delivery to the proper person, no such distinction is drawn; the duty in both cases is absolute.

What, then, is the difference, if any, between the duty of a voluntary gratuitous bailee and that of a wholly involuntary bailee? There is an astonishing paucity of decision and text opinion upon the subject. I think, however, that all that can be found upon it points to the conclusion that the involuntary bailee, as long as his lack of volition continues, is not under the slightest duty to care for or guard the subject of the bailment, and cannot be held, in respect of custody, for what would even be the grossest negligence in the case of a voluntary bailment . . . but that, in case the involuntary bailee shall exercise any dominion over the thing so bailed, he becomes as responsible as if he were a voluntary bailee. 1 Halsbury, p. 528, par. 1078; Story, Bailments [7th Ed.] §§ 85 to 88; Smith V. N. & L. R. R., [27 N.H. 86]; T. J. Moss Tie Co. v. Kreilich, 80 Mo. App. 304; Hiort v. Bott, L. R., 9 Ex. 86 [1873-74].

In Hiort v. Bott, *supra,* the plaintiff shipped barley to defendant, at the same time sending to defendant an invoice stating that the barley was ordered by defendant through G., described in the invoice as a broker acting for both parties, and with the invoice was a "delivery order" that made the barley deliverable to the order of "consignor or consignee." The defendant had not ordered the barley, and had never had any dealings with either the plaintiff or G. A few days later G. called upon defendant, informed defendant that the shipment to him was made by mistake, and asked defendant to indorse the delivery order to him, G. The defendant complied, and G., concededly an imposter, obtained the barley and absconded. It was held that, as the defendant by reason of his affirmative act exercised dominion over the barley, thus causing a misdelivery, he was liable in conversion as matter of law. . . .

    . . . . .

I am of the opinion that the Krumsky Case [Krumsky v. Loeser, 75 N.Y. Supp. 1012 (App. Term)] is clearly distinguishable from that at bar. As I read the opinion there, the holding of the court was predicated upon two considerations, neither of which touches the instant case, namely, that the possession of the defendants there was due to a trick and a fraud and defendants' total lack of knowledge of the true owner. . . .

    . . . . .

I have reached the conclusion that while, at first blush, it may seem to be imposing upon the defendants an unduly severe rule of conduct to hold them to an absolute liability, the rule is no more severe than the occasion calls for. The Exchequer judges in the Hiort Case were reluctant to hold the defendant there to the rule of absolute liability, but they were, nevertheless, unanimous in doing so; and I think the rule worked more harshly there than it would here. There, the parties never had any relations with each other. Here the plaintiffs were at least attempting to fill an order given by the defendants. The defendants could easily have protected themselves by telephoning the plaintiffs that the wrong bond had been delivered, or they could have sent the bond back to the plaintiffs by one of their own messengers. Instead, they chose to take the chance of delivering it to the wrong messenger. As the delivery window was closed when the bond was dropped through the slot, and remained closed for an appreciable time, they could not have known what messenger had made the delivery.

    . . . . .

For the reasons stated, I vote to affirm.

Judgment affirmed, with $25 costs, with leave to defendants to appeal to the Appellate Division.

LEHMAN, J. (dissenting).   I agree in all material particulars with the statement of facts contained in the opinion of Mr. Justice Mullan. . . .

    . . . . .

. . . It is to be noted . . . that the complaint does not allege any negligence on the part of the defendants, and I agree with Mr. Justice Mullan that no such issue was litigated, and that the judgment can be sustained only if, as a matter of law, the defendants' mistake in returning the bond to the wrong messenger constituted a conversion of the bond or at least a breach of an implied agreement on their part to return the bond only to the plaintiffs.

While the slot in the window constituted an invitation to deliver at that place securities intended for the defendants, it is evident that it constituted an invitation only to deliver securities which the defendants were under some obligation to receive. Obviously no person could by slipping in other securities impose upon the defendants without their consent any affirmative obligation to care for these securities, to pay for them, or even to receive them. The plaintiffs never intended to deliver to the defendants an Oregon & California Railroad bond. By their mistake the plaintiffs divested themselves of possession of the bond, but they did not transfer to the defendants either title or right to possession if they demanded the return of the bond. The defendants had not consented to accept the bond as a deposit, they claimed no title to it, and they were not subject to any trust or obligation as bailees, for a bailment arises only through an express or implied contract. They were put in posession of the bond without any agreement on their part, express or implied, to accept the deposit of the bond; and, though persons who come into possession of the property of others without their consent are sometimes for convenience called "involuntary" or "quasi bailees," they incur no responsibility to the true owner in respect thereof. It is only where they commit some "over act" of interference with the property that an implied contract of bailment is created. Halsbury's Laws of England, vol. 1, § 1078.

It can hardly be contended, however, that every "overt act" of interference with the property creates an implied obligation of bailment. Undoubtedly an "involuntary bailee" need not abandon the property, but he may, without incurring further liability, at least take steps to preserve and care for the property. As stated by Mr. Justice Mullan, it is only in case the involuntary bailee shall exercise any dominion over the thing so bailed that he becomes as responsible as if he were a voluntary bailee. The exercise of dominion, as I understand it, necessarily involves some act inconsistent with the complete right of dominion of the real owner, at least to the extent that it would be wrongful unless performed by some person to whom the owner had transferred the right to possession. In other words, an implied contract of bailment with its consequent obligations arises only where a person in possession of the property of another does some act which is inconsistent with the view that he does not accept the possession which has been thrust upon him.

The "overt act" which it is claimed constituted an improper interference with or act of dominion over the plaintiffs' property consists of a delivery of the bond to a stranger who had no title to it. If the defendants had attempted to transfer to this stranger any title or right of possession of their own, then, of course, they could not claim that they had never accepted possession of the bond as bailees. They would then be on the horns of a dilemma, for they would have either denied the right of the true owner and thereby converted the property to their own use or would have exercised a right which was theirs only if they accepted the deposit of the bond left with them. In the case of Hiort v. Bott, L. R. 9 Exch. 86, relied on for authority by Mr. Justice Mullan, the defendant had in fact attempted to transfer to a stranger his own ostensible title to the goods, and he had no actual title unless he first accepted an attempted delivery of the goods by the true owner to himself. The defendant in that case had not received the barley into his possession, but had received merely a delivery order which made the barley deliverable "to the order of consignor or consignee," and, as pointed out by Bramwell, B., "if the defendant had done nothing at all, it would have been delivered to the plaintiffs." In the language of Cleasby, B., "he had no duty to perform in relation to the goods and was a mere stranger, except that by mistake he had been made consignee, and so had an ostensible title and could dispose of the goods." Knowing that the ostensible title was vested in him only by mistake, the defendant was induced by fraud to indorse the delivery order and thereby transfer to a third party the ostensible title to the barley.

The defendant could not indorse the delivery order unless he had title to the barley either in his own right or as agent for the true owner. He did not claim title in his own right, and, if he had done so knowing that the ostensible title had been transferred to him only by mistake, such act would in itself have constituted a conversion. His act was lawful, therefore, only if he had accepted title as an agent. The fraud of the alleged broker induced him to believe that he had authority as agent of the true owner to transfer title, but he voluntarily assumed to act as agent of the owner and to accept title as such agent. By voluntarily doing an act which would be lawful only if he accepted title either in his own right or as agent of the owner, he was not in a position to say that possession of the property was thrust on him without his consent. He did in fact accept the title as agent of the owner, and he then was bound to transfer the title only in accordance with authority actually given by the owner, and no mistake, however innocent, can avail an agent as an excuse for any other delivery.

It seems to me quite clear that this was the real ground of the decision in the case of Hiort v. Bott, supra, and the facts in the case before us are so clearly distinguishable that it can in no wise be regarded as any authority for the contention of these plaintiffs, and in fact the reasoning of the opinions rendered in that case supports the contention of the defendants herein. In the present case the defendants were put in possession of the bond by mistake; they discovered the mistake promptly, and thereafter they committed no "overt act" of interference with the bond except that they attempted to divest themselves of this possession by delivering the bond to a person whom they believed to be the messenger of the plaintiffs. That act was not only consistent with the continued title and right of dominion in the plaintiffs, but was an honest attempt to restore possession to the true owners. It certainly cannot be contended that the defendants were bound at their peril to wait until the plaintiffs came to their office and physically took away their property; they could take proper steps to divest themselves of the possession thrust upon them by mistake without thereby impliedly agreeing, contrary to their clear intention, to accept possession as bailees with the consequent obligations flowing from such relation. It is quite immaterial whether we call these defendants bailees or not if we keep in mind the fact that the possession of these goods was thrust upon them by mistake of the plaintiffs and without their invitation or consent, and that therefore any liability for failure to return the goods to the true owner upon demand must be the result of some act voluntarily done by the defendant thereafter. An attempt to return the bond to the true owner or to the person who delivered it cannot be considered as inconsistent with a recognition of the complete ownership and right of dominion by the true owner, and certainly shows no intent to accept the possession thrust upon the defendants by plaintiffs' mistake, and I fail to see how, in the absence of such elements, any implied contract of bailment can arise. If in making an attempt to return the goods, which was lawful and proper in itself, the defendants used means which were not reasonable and proper, and as a result thereof the goods were lost or misdelivered, then the defendants would be liable for negligence or possibly for conversion, for every man is responsible for his own acts; but, if the defendants had a right to divest themselves of possession and attempt to return the goods, then, in the absence of some obligation resting upon contract to deliver the goods only to the true owner or upon his order, I do not see how the mere fact that through innocent mistake the defendants handed the bond to the wrong messenger could constitute a conversion. The defendants could not properly disregard entirely the mistake in the delivery of the bonds. Common courtesy and prudence, if not the law, certainly placed upon them the duty to take some steps by which the plaintiffs would be apprised of their mistake and enabled to regain their property. The defendants might have placed the bond in a safe and telephoned to the plaintiffs to call for the bond, but they were under the impression that the messenger who delivered the bond was still present, and they gave the bond to him as a means of carrying out their evident duty to apprise the plaintiffs of their error and revest possession in them.   .   .   .

While no case has been cited which is exactly parallel to the present case, it seems to me that in several cases in the courts of this state these considerations have been assumed, even if not expressly stated.   .   .   .   The case of Krumsky v. Loeser, 37 Misc. Rep. 504, 75 N.Y. Supp. 1012, seems to me more directly in point, and I think the decision is necessarily based upon the same view of the law of bailments as I have taken. I cannot see that there is any possible distinction in principle in regard to the obligations arising from possession which has been thrust upon the defendant either by fraud practiced on the true owner or by mistake of the true owner. While that case may perhaps logically be distinguished from the present case in that there the defendant did not know the true owner and was induced to give up possession of the goods to a thief through fraud, yet in my opinion these circumstances do not logically affect the rule that a person in possession of goods without his consent is not liable for conversion merely because he delivers them to a stranger in an attempt to revest possession in the true owner, though they may affect the question of the defendant's negligence and whether he has acted reasonably and properly, but only these questions.   .   .   ..   I cannot see that, except in regard to the question of negligence, there is any logical distinction in regard to the effect of delivery to a stranger where the owner is known and where he is not known. In each case the holder has assumed to revest possession in the true owner and by mistake has delivered it to a stranger, and in neither case has he assumed any right of his own to dispose of the goods, and thereby exercised dominion over them; but in both cases the question still always remains whether the holder in so acting was free from negligence.

Even if under these pleadings we could consider the question of negligence, I find no evidence upon this question to sustain a judgment in favor of the plaintiffs. There is no doubt that the defendants acted in good faith and in the honest belief that they were handing back the bond to the messenger who delivered it. They had assumed no obligation of any kind to the plaintiffs; any act they performed was for the plaintiffs' benefit, and it was through plaintiffs' mistake that they were called upon to act at all in the premises. Doubtless, if they had foreseen the possibility of mistake, they would not have delivered the bond to the wrong messenger; but it was not unreasonable to suppose that the messenger might be waiting or that, if he had left, no thief would be in the office who would claim to represent the plaintiffs. They probably committed an error of judgment, but for such error they cannot be held liable. Since they owed no obligation to the plaintiffs and acted in good faith under the reasonable belief that they were returning the bond to the messenger who delivered it, I see no ground for imposing upon them liability for the loss of a bond which would never have been lost but for the plaintiffs' mistake, due apparently to the plaintiffs' negligence.

.   .   .   .

For these reasons, it seems to me that the judgment should be reversed, with costs, and the complaint dismissed, with costs.

The decision in this case was appealed to the Supreme Court, Appellate Division. Six months after the opinion printed above was rendered, the Appellate

Division dismissed the judgment of the Appellate Term in favor of the plaintiff and ordered judgment for the defendant based on the dissenting opinion of Lehman, J. 194 N.Y. Supp. 926 (1922).

QUESTIONS

1. Would it have made a difference in the amount of damages Wooden-Ware would have been required to pay if the Indians had cut the timber by inadvertence, that is, by an honest mistake? If so, why?

2. A test of whether you have reached an understanding of Question 1 and the answer will come if you can give an opinion as to whether, in the light of the rationale in Wooden-Ware, the court went wrong in Richtmyer. You may therefore address yourself to what, if any, strict logic the court followed in Richtmyer. If the court did not follow strict logic in Richtmyer, then what pragmatic considerations moved the court?

3. What underlying simplistic principle would seem to have determined the decision in Krumsky and the ultimate decision in Cowen? If you discover such a principle, you will find that it was not cleanly enunciated in either case. Why, in your opinion?

4. Do the differing interpretations of Hiort v. Bott by Judge Mullan and Judge Lehman leave you with a comparison of the relative intellectual capacities of the two judges? If so, in whose favor?

7 Law of the Cases and Legislation Vie in Social Conflict

Introduction	271
Unionism and Case Law	283
Labor Organization and Crime	283
Commonwealth v. Pullis (The Philadelphia Cordwainers' Case of 1806)	283
Commonwealth v. Hunt	286
Labor Organization and Tort	290
Vegelahn v. Guntner	290
Labor Organization and Contract	293
Hitchman Coal & Coke Company v. Mitchell	293
Summary of Major Labor Legislation 1914–1964	294
Federal versus State Jurisdiction Over Labor Disputes	298
Federal Power—The Commerce Clause	298
Examples of Federal Preemption	299
Garner v. Teamsters, Local 776	299
Retail Clerks International Assn. v. Schermerhorn	301
Union Tactics and Federal-State Policies	304
Senn v. Tile Layers Protective Union	304
Thornhill v. Alabama	308
International Brotherhood of Teamsters, Local 309 v. Hanke	311
Unionism and the Whole Society	314
Unresolved Limits on Union Power	314
National Woodwork Manufacturers Association v. National Labor Relations Board	314
Unresolved Limits on Public Power	317
The Problem	317
The Federal Situation	319
Executive Order 10988—Employee-Management Cooperation in the Federal Service	319
The State Situation	319

New York Anti-Strike Law (Condon-Wadlin Act). 320
New York City Transit Authority v. Quill 320
Weinstein v. New York City Transit Authority 322
Amnesty Act for Transit Workers. 323
New York Public Employees Fair Employment Act (Taylor Law). 324
Board of Education v. Shanker (injunction) 326
Board of Education v. Shanker (contempt). 328
City of New York v. De Lury. 330
Amendments to Taylor Law. 332
Labor and Musical Chairs 332
Questions 336
Appendix—Statutory Material. 337
Clayton Act. 337
Norris-LaGuardia Act 337
National Labor Relation Act (Wagner Act) 339
Labor Management Relations Act (Taft-Hartley Act). 339
Labor Management Reporting and Disclosure Act (Landrum-Griffin
Act). 345
Civil Rights Act of 1964 351
Employee Management Cooperation in the Federal Service. 352

INTRODUCTION

In this chapter the reader will observe in stark relief the processes by which the changing social and economic environment in the second and third quarters of the twentieth century made new labor law. In that period 200 years of the industrial revolution and 100 years of groping unionism came to an apogee and labor law changed—dramatically. This chapter is a treasure of proof of the interaction between law and environment—in this case, proof that a changing environment does compel a change in law. The reader will also observe the heavy impact of legislation upon case law and the ensuing struggle between legislation and case law in the resolution of social and economic conflict.

In Chapter 1 the roles of the fiction, of equity, and of legislation were described as separate factors in the amelioration of rigidities of case law. However, while legislation at times ameliorates and even reverses case law, case law also interprets legislation and *ameliorates it.* The role of case law in interpreting legislation is most clearly demonstrated when the legislation provides an administrative body, such as the National Labor Relations Board, with the power to decide cases that arise under the legislation.

Administrative bodies are ancient in governmental organization. Even in late feudal England, the Privy Council tended to be dominated by experts and specialists. Its functions were a commingled complex of executive, legislative, and judicial functions. Under the Tudors the Council was an arm of royal authority. With the coming of the Stuarts in the early 17th century and thereafter, an increasing differentiation of function among the three branches of government was compelled by the rising power of Parliament and the increasing independence of the courts. In contemporary times administrative bodies have proliferated on the theory that as governmental interventions in the economic and social life of the community increase, there must be expert administrative bodies with quasi-judicial powers to administer the legislative interventions.

In 1887, because of the alleged machinations of the Standard Oil Company in securing trade advantages by special freight rate rebates, the United States Congress decided to regulate the railroads by establishing the Interstate Commerce Commission as an administrative body with presumptive expertise about transportation. Since that major development, the creation of expert regulatory bodies with powers to decide cases under statutes designed to ameliorate or supplement case law, or to make law where there was none before, has grown apace. Trade practices under antitrust laws, commodity exchanges, radio, television, oil and gas, telephones and other utilities, exports, imports, maritime activities, airways, stock exchanges—to mention only some of the subjects of governmental regulation—have all come under the jurisdiction of administrative bodies. A branch of law, known as administrative law, has arisen, and while it is not as fundamental as the law of crimes, contracts, torts, or property, administrative law over the past half century has received increasingly respectful attention in American law schools.

The fundamental legal principle about administrative bodies is that their decisions cannot be exempted from review and reversal by the courts. Since the days of the Tudors and the Stuarts, the lines of demarcation of separation of powers among the legislative, executive, and judicial branches have become constitutionally clear—relatively. In addition, administrative bodies are the creatures of the legislature. They cannot be invested with uncontrolled discretion because that would constitute an unconstitutional delegation of legislative power; nor can the legislature render its creatures immune from review by the courts because that would be in derogation of the separate judicial power.

With this background of firmly established constitutional certainties, we examine here the struggle between case law and legislation including its administrative body for labor-management relations. The National Labor Relations Board, created by Congress in 1935, is a late addition to that long line of presumptively expert bodies standing between the legislature and the courts—this time in an era of confrontation between workers, empowered in unionism, and management, invested with control of the machine processes. Initially, this chapter deals with the historical struggle between organized labor and the individual or corporate management for control of the productive and distributive functions of industry. Finally, this section presents the current struggle between organized labor and the government and the public for control of the economy and the quantity and quality of public services—everything from garbage collection to education. The American people are confronted with the fundamental issue: how much labor power? This issue is not yet settled. More history is to come. To predict it one must cast a backward look.

In 1806 in the Philadelphia Cordwainers case (*infra,* p. 283), the court held the attempt to form a union a criminal conspiracy, saying:

> A combination to raise their wages may be considered in a twofold point of view: one is to benefit themselves * * * the other is to injure those who do not join their society. The rule of law condemns both.

Nevertheless, unionism pressed its claim of workers' rights to organize:

1827 – The Mechanics Union of Trades Association was founded in Philadelphia.

1834 – The National Trades' Union was founded "to promote the moral, physical, and intellectual condition of the working classes, and to advance their pecuniary interest."

1866 – The National Labor Union with a full-time president at $1,000 a year was established.

1878 – The Knights of Labor became a national organization, with the slogan, "An injury to one is the concern of all," and with its membership open to all "except lawyers, bankers, stock brokers, professional gamblers, and anybody who had anything to do with the sale of intoxicating beverages."

1881 – The Federation of Organized Trades and Labor Unions, patterned on the British Trades Union Congress, got its start and lived to sponsor the famous movement for the eight-hour day.

1886 – The American Federation of Labor was born at Columbus, Ohio. It elected Samuel Gompers its first president and attained by 1920 a membership of over 4 million, which was to decline by 1933 to little more than 2 million and rise again to over 10 million in 1955. Then, in that year, it merged with the Congress of Industrial Organizations in an "honorable organic unity," whose membership became more than 16 million organized working men in 1966.

One of the chief determinants of the direction labor was to take Samuel Gompers' firm insistence that "our problems are primarily industrial," and his stout rejection of all temptations to form a "labor party." The long shadow of Gompers points the continuing philosophical course of American labor—"bread and butter" unionism—and at the same time, of course, cake.

At the turn of the century and in the early decades of the 20th century, the legal and extra-legal struggle was bitter, just as it had been long before Gompers. On July 6, 1892, two barges moved up the Monongahela river loaded with

Pinkerton agents. At the end of that bloody day ten were dead, three agents and seven strikers, and 60 were wounded. Later, 8,000 Pennsylvania Guardsmen came to keep the peace. On November 21, Frick cabled Carnegie the news:[1]

> Strike officially called off yesterday. Our victory is now complete and most gratifying. Do not think we will ever have any serious labor trouble again.

"Ever" was too long, and Carnegie himself knew it. Nevertheless, he replied to Frick from Rome:

> Think I'm about ten years older. Europe has rung with Homestead, Homestead, until we are all sick of the name; but it is all over now. Ever your pard, A.C.

And yet Carnegie knew that it was not over. In later life his writings show his ambivalence. One pamphlet brought a letter from Grover Cleveland who defeated Harrison, as some say, because of the Homestead strike. Cleveland said to Carnegie:[2]

> You must capture and keep the heart of any *working man* before his hands will do their best.

In the last decade of the nineteenth century, however, American management did not understand Grover Cleveland's prescient comment—William James was sowing the seeds for a deeper psychological knowledge at Harvard University, but the social sciences were not yet in flower. It was to be another two decades before the phrase "human relations" was generally employed. Indeed, as late as 1933 the picture of the coal mines and steel mills of western Pennsylvania and West Virginia was a mélange of NRA, Roosevelt, Phil Murray, John L. Lewis, insurgent workers, tear gas, deputies, and some deaths. But the workingman's heart was not captured, nor his union recognized.

The rapid expansion of unionism in the 1930's rested not so much on right actions by unions as on wrong actions by employers. The findings of the LaFollette Committee Reports (1937, 1939) make a record that employers would like to forget and that workers do not forget. The Committee disclosed that 1,475 companies were clients of detective agencies during the years 1933–1936; these agencies provided "espionage, strike breaking" services; expenditures by 300 companies "on espionage, munitions, and strike breaking" amounted to nearly $9,500,000; spies were operating in practically every union in the country, 100 of them held union office (one became a union treasurer to keep the company informed on union membership). Facts such as these, unspoken but unforgotten, condition labor-management relations to this day.

Unionism in the United States encountered the law of the cases on three

---

[1]O'Connor, Harvey, *Steel-Dictator,* pp. 90 ff., John Day, New York, 1935.

[2]Long, Haniel, *Pittsburgh Memoranda,* p. 19, Writers' Edition, Santa Fe, New Mexico, 1935.

fronts: (a) unionism as a crime, (b) unionism as tortious interference with enterprise, and (c) unionism as tortious interference with contracts. The cases in this chapter demonstrate the frustration of unionism by the application of principles drawn through those three fields of law and the eventual intervention of legislation, induced by union power, to redress industrial and business power.

The industrial, business, and financial men in the post-civil war American boom and, for that matter, in the early decades of the 20th century were inclined to identify their decisions and their attitudes with the will of God. They were post-Puritans and were deeply convinced that the affairs of enterprise, which they often found in their hands as the result of their own unrestrained enterprise, were a disposition of providence itself. In the anthracite coal strike of 1902 a leading representative of the operators wrote to assure a citizen of Wilkes Barre, Pennsylvania, "The rights and interests of the laboring man will be protected and cared for—not by the labor agitators, but by the Christian men to whom God in his infinite wisdom has given control of the property interests of the country."[3]

If law at a given time is the will of the prevailing economic class, the actions of the courts in labor matters in the late 19th and early 20th centuries amply justified that definition. As early as 1842 the concept of unionism as a crime was abandoned in the Massachusetts case of Commonwealth v. Hunt, 4 Met. 111 (*infra,* p. 286); however, the concepts of unionism as tortious interference with enterprise itself or as tortious interference with the right of the employer to make individual contacts with workers against unionism, called "yellow-dog" contracts, continued well into the 20th century.

The employment of the injunction in federal courts became an almost invariable tool. The procedure was quite simple. Counsel for the employer would draw a bill in equity, alleging that if a strike occurred the business enterprise and property of the employer would be irreparably damaged. Such allegations, supported by sworn affidavits, laid the foundation for equitable jurisdiction in any court; and in the federal courts, jurisdiction was specifically rested upon the commerce clause of the United States Constitution (Art. I, sec. 8, cl. 3), which gave the federal government in all of its branches including the judicial, power over any interference with interstate commerce. The injunction, punishable by fines and jail sentences if violated, would then issue *ex parte,*—the workers not being heard in the first instance. The case would be set for hearing on the merits later, but the strike fever had been cooled. The tactical court victory usually went to the employer.

Despite the marshalling of substantially all of the forces of the national establishment against unionism, the movement grew. By 1930 union power was sufficient at the national level to force the Senate refusal of the confirma-

---

[3]Allen, Frederick Lewis, *The Big Change,* p. 83, Harpers, New York, 1952.

tion of President Hoover's appointment of the eminently qualified Circuit Court of Appeals Judge John J. Parker to the United States Supreme Court. Three years earlier Judge Parker had applied the Supreme Court's rule sustaining "yellow-dog" contracts so that organization of the coal fields of United Mine Workers of America was impeded.[4] As a lower court judge, Parker had simply done his judicial duty by following the Supreme Court decision in the Hitchman Coal case (infra, p. 293). Nevertheless, the political power of organized labor was sufficient to punish him for applying the case law, as it then stood, which protected the right of an employer to make a contract with an employee stating that the employee would not join a union.

Hard on the heels of the significant rejection of Parker's nomination came the Norris-LaGuardia Act in 1932 (Appendix, infra, p. 337). This was the second major intervention of legislation at the national level in the application of the law to favor the cause of unionism. [The Clayton Act of 1914 had exempted unions from the anti-trust laws of the United States (Appendix, infra, p. 337).] Labor was now (1932) strong enough to move the United States Congress to use its legislative power to impose on the federal courts a prohibition against the utilization of the inherent power of equity courts to employ the injunction. The legislation quite simply decreed that the injunction should not be used in labor disputes. There were exceptions with respect to violence and other unlawful acts, but the naked power of the federal courts to enjoin a strike in its very incipiency was abolished. The Norris-LaGuardia Act was followed by comparable legislation in many of the industrial states of the Union.

Then came the National Labor Relations Act (July 5, 1935) (Appendix, infra, p. 339), known by the name of its author Senator Robert Wagner of New York. This New Deal law marked the third major intervention by government in the long struggle between management and labor over union claims of right to bargain for employees. The Act was unequivocally in support of labor. It proclaimed the right of workers to organize; established procedures for selection of bargaining units and for union elections within these units; gave to a union that had a majority of the workers in any unit the right to represent all of the workers in that unit; and required management to bargain collectively with such a union. On April 12, 1937, the United States Supreme Court, still composed of the "nine old men," sustained the Act.[5] On that day an old order ended.

The Act led to such results as management's decision, in March 1937, that United States Steel Corporation would recognize the steelworkers' union-organizing committee (SWOC). Meanwhile, sitdown strikes, although ulti-

[4]United Mine Workers of America v. Red Jacket Consolidated Coal & Coke Co., 18 F.2d 839 (4th Cir. 1927).

[5]National Labor Relations Board v. Jones & Laughlin Steel Corp., 301 U.S. 1 (1937).

mately held illegal by the United States Supreme Court, had softened General Motors Corporation. After these milestones, union membership mounted, particularly in the Congress of Industrial Organizations (CIO), and surprised industrialists everywhere found themselves looking for industrial relations directors.

The Wagner Act made collective bargaining an instrument of American national policy. Other nations, while practicing collective bargaining, do not rely as heavily on its processes; for example, in Australia and in the Scandinavian countries industrial courts are involved in wage determination. But, since 1935 we have been committed almost exclusively to collective bargaining in private industry. The issue is not yet settled with respect to the employees of government. Furthermore, the Wagner Act does not permit a union to bargain only for its members. It requires that the union bargain for *all* of the employees, including nonunion workers, in the bargaining unit that under the terms of the Act has been found appropriate. This fact was a shock to employers, and its full significance has been slowly perceived by both employers and unions.

Management is not given, anymore than mankind generally, to full analysis or completely logical scrutiny of the phrases that express its feelings. It was not so much that management felt that employees who belonged to a union were disloyal, but rather that employees who had not joined a union had demonstrated a *special* brand of loyalty to management. The Wagner Act, therefore, produced an acute emotional reaction in management, as well as in union leadership. The employer found himself powerless to reward a loyal nonmember with a larger pay envelope, and the union found itself powerless to discriminate against the nonmember.

The term "free rider" was quick to emerge. Unions, pointing to their legal responsibility to represent all employees in the lawful unit, asked why nonmembers should receive all of the benefits of union representation and bear none of the cost, that is, be exempt from payment of union initiation fees and dues. The union's charge against a free rider was and still is countered with the charge of compulsory unionism—a tax on the right to work. Following the Wagner Act, management often resisted union demands that all employees be required to join the union and pay dues, giving as a reason "loyalty to our loyal employees." In many cases this was a good reason but not the *real* reason. The real motive was to fight a holding action. Many people in the late 1930's believed that the "excesses" of the New Deal, including unionism, would someday abate.

But now, almost four decades later, a philosophical argument over compulsory unionism continues with such vigor that one must not question the sincerity of the participants on either side. There are 19 states with laws or constitutional provisions, often called "right-to-work laws," that protect in various ways the privilege of an employee to work whether or not he is paying dues to a union. These laws attest to the vigor of the conviction that union membership should not be a condition of employment. The arguments in support of the alleged free rider and of the liberty for the individual to take employment free of a tax in the form of union dues are impressive. The unions are challenged on their own ground. It is said that the term "free rider" would be applicable only if the union is in fact getting something for the nonmember that he would not have otherwise obtained. This argument is buttressed by economists who find that unions have had no effect on the general wage level; instead blind forces such as market, monetary, and fiscal factors determine the general wage level.[6] For this reason it is argued that there is actually no bonus for the alleged free rider. In any case, so the argument runs, it should be the individual, free, American citizen who decides whether the union has benefited him and, therefore, whether he chooses to pay dues. Any factor other than his subjective determination is branded as an invasion of his liberty.

There is no doubt that the proponents of liberty have a good philosophical argument, but here theory gets hit by hard fact. One cannot remain unconcerned if unionism actually does involve a tax on the right to work. On the other hand, one cannot ignore the important reality that the dues-paying 51 percent of the employees of a unit can stop working in protest if the other 49 percent are not paying dues.

By 1940 picket lines were usual around the plants of many American corporations. "Dues picketing," it was called. Employees who had paid their dues were admitted; all others were excluded. In many cases this was the equivalent of closing the plant. Heavy industries such as steel or glass, where high melting temperatures compel continuous operations, depend on many specialized functions. A few dozen men, kept out of the plant for nonpayment of dues, would leave certain crucial functions unmanned; hence the whole process would stop, although thousands of dues-paying employees had entered the gates.

Feelings between dues-paying and nondues-paying employees ran high. There was dissension not only at the plant gates but also within the plants. Dues-paying members were berating nondues-paying employees. Inexorable machines can stand almost anything but the failure of human hands to attend them regularly, on strict schedule. American pragmatism began to operate on the philosophical issue of the individual's right to work versus the union's need to collect dues.

One plan required neither the "closed shop," under which management may hire only such employees as the union designates, nor the "union shop," under

[6]Hazard, Leland, "Wage Theory—A Management View," in *New Concepts in Wage Determination* (George Taylor and Frank Pierson, eds.), pp. 32–50, McGraw Hill, New York, 1957.

which management, while free to hire anyone, must fire him if he fails to join the union or, having joined, loses his "good standing."

Many managers and some politicians were against either the closed shop or the union shop because of the requirement that the employee be in "good standing" with his union. Good standing can mean anything—not being black or white, not being a Methodist or a Catholic, or, of equally great economic consequence, being too energetic at work in the shop[7] or too vocal on the union floor.[8] There was great hesitation to *contract* such power into union hands or such restrictions on management's ability to select and keep necessary manpower. But, it would be quite another matter, so the argument ran, to require an employee to pay *reasonable and limited* sums to be bargained out between management and union as initiation fees and monthly dues. Thus, whether an employee was a member or not, he would be required to pay such amounts as a fee because the union was his legal representative in collective bargaining.

Employers have many necessary rules that govern the employee's access to a job. Some of the rules, such as those requiring special clothing, cost the employee money. There was no difference, it was argued in 1940, between such rules and one requiring an employee to keep peace in the shop by paying to an organization, *empowered by law* to represent him, certain sums of money bearing a reasonable relationship to his pay. A typical amount was $2 for the initial payment and monthly payments of 1 percent of gross earnings. In the first decade after the Wagner Act, management worked out compromises of a pragmatic nature. The process was aided by management's discovery that their "loyal employees" would join the union and pay dues when a big issue was up. Then, the issue resolved, would stop paying. In one sense, requiring a worker to pay dues to a union to which he does not choose to belong is unfair. In another and practical sense, *it is* fair—simply one of those workaday compromises that society asks the individual to make to further group action. Senator Robert A. Taft took the latter view during the Congressional procedures leading up to the Labor Management Relations Act of 1947, known as the Taft-Hartley Act (Appendix, *infra*, p. 339). This law establishes the important distinction between the union shop and what came to be known as the "agency shop"—now the only legal shop.

Under the agency shop an employer can decide who will work for him and

---

[7] In Scofield v. National Labor Relations Board, 394 U.S. 423 (1969), the United States Supreme Court sustained a union rule that precluded employees from accepting earnings under a company incentive plan above a ceiling set by the union and contained in the collective bargaining contract, despite the wish of the dissident members to work for the extra earnings and the wish of the company to pay them.

[8] In Salzhandler v. Caputo, 316 F.2d 445 (2d Cir.), *cert. denied,* 375 U.S. 946 (1963), the court held that the union could not lawfully punish a member who criticized the handling of union funds by taking away his right to participate in union affairs for a period of five years.

for how long. A union cannot decide who may work, or for whom, or for how long. A worker can decide for whom he will work and if, after employment, pays amounts (bargained between employer and union) equal to initiation fee and regular dues to the union, he will not be fired on the demand of the union even though the union decides he is in bad standing. All this is because in an agency shop the worker does not have to be admitted to the union before he can get a job or at any time thereafter, and he will not be fired on the demand of the union except for failure to make the specified payments. He can decide for whom he will work and for how long, but he cannot decide to take a free ride on the union that bargains with his employer for his wages, hours, and working conditions.

The closed shop and the union shop are now illegal, with the exception of hiring halls,[9] since 1947, when the Taft-Hartley Act was passed by Congress.

Labor's score in Federal legislation during the second quarter century included one great gain, the Wagner Act (1935) guaranteeing labor the right to organize unions and requiring management to bargain with them. At 12-year intervals after the Wagner Act there were two moderate losses for labor. In the Taft-Hartley Act (1947) Congress curbed union violence, secondary boycotts, closed and union shops, and provided for a limited injunction against strikes involving a national emergency. In the 1959 legislation Congress placed even tighter restrictions on secondary boycotts, hot cargo agreements, and organizational picketing. More importantly, the new law provided a workers' bill of rights against their own unions, required reporting from unions, and gave policing powers over some internal union affairs to the Federal Government agencies.

The pendulum had swung far to the right since the late 1930's when an employer appeared at his peril before the Wagner Act's National Labor Relations Board. Since that time the Federal courts and the Congress had sharply dampened the revolutionary zeal with which the New Deal set out to equalize the power of labor with that of management.

American national policy was, however, still strongly in support of unionism. The fundamentals of the Wagner Act were intact—the right of workers to unions of their own choosing and the obligation of employers to bargain

---

[9]Hiring halls are essentially employment agencies operated by unions. Under the hiring hall provisions of a collective bargaining agreement between a union and an employer, the employer must check at the hiring hall for available workmen before employing any new men. This arrangement serves to eliminate scouting for jobs by the individual workman and searches for workers by employers.

Section 8(a)(3) of the Labor Management Relations Act, 1947 (Taft-Hartley Act), 61 Stat. 140-141, 29 U.S.C. § 15 (Appendix, *infra*, p. 351), along with Section 8(f) of the Labor Management Reporting and Disclosure Act of 1959 (Landrum-Griffin Act), 73 Stat. 545, 29 U.S.C. § 158 (Appendix, *infra*, p. 000), make allowances for hiring halls. The United States Supreme Court upheld the hiring hall device in Local 357 International Brotherhood of Teamsters v. National Labor Relations Board, 365 U.S. 667 (1961), so long as it was not used by the union to create a closed shop.

with them. Still far from their goals were the rightists who wanted Congress to bar industry-wide bargaining, restore to employers the right of injunction, and subject unions to the antitrust laws.[10]

Labor's reception of the 1959 Landrum-Griffin Act was substantially more temperate than its reaction to the Taft-Hartley Act twelve years earlier. The phrase "slave-labor law" swept the ranks of unionism in 1947. President Truman vetoed the Act and both houses of Congress promptly passed the law over his veto. Repeal of the Taft-Hartley Act was an issue as late as the presidential election of 1952. But the Act resisted all repeal efforts and stands without major modification. One may predict that the Landrum-Griffin Act will also remain intact, but it will not diminish honest union power.

Meanwhile, management in the years preceding the Landrum-Griffin legislation indulged some delusions of its own. In early 1958 a New York congressman delivered on the floor of the House a speech that had wide circulation and great influence throughout the ranks of management. He proved to his satisfaction and to the alarm of industrialists that as the Congress was then constituted, no legislation could pass that labor opposed. Within 18 months of his speech and without significant changes in the composition of the Congress, the labor reform legislation of 1959 was passed, despite the vocal opposition of the principal, national labor leaders.

There had been more than a little union mania after the Wagner Act aligned government with labor. Union membership soared in the late 1930's. Union leadership was not adequate in numbers or experience for its new administrative problems. Capping the confusion of the new era were the internecine conflicts between the older craft-minded American Federation of Labor and the new industry-minded Congress of Industrial Organizations. Hard on the heels of these new-found powers and unwanted problems came World War II.

Despite remarkable administrative success in wage controls under the World War II War Labor Board, the public, deeply aware that national survival was at stake, did not regard frequent labor stoppages in basic industries with equanimity. War mothers with sons on the shelled beaches of Normandy and in the hot seas of the Asian front had little patience with jurisdictional strikes at home. Refinements of collective bargaining and labor-management relations that seemed of the greatest significance to the new generation of labor statesmen left much of the general public unimpressed.

Six hundred million dollars of union dues each year presented too much

[10]Meanwhile management and labor made substantial progress in developing better grievance procedures and more effective no-strike clauses operative during the term of the contract.

This book does not include a description of grievance procedures and arbitration under labor-management contracts. Such materials properly belong in manuals concerning the techniques of personnel management. It cannot be overemphasized, however, that if labor gives up its right to strike during the term of the contract, management must also give up the right to say a final "No" at the end of a worker's grievance. Binding arbitration of grievances arising during the period of the contract, usually three years, is the price management must pay for a no-strike clause.

temptation for some labor leaders. Two and a half years (1957-1959) of investigation and public hearings by the Committee on Improper Activities in the Labor or Management Field shocked and sobered the American people, including some top labor leaders themselves. Senator John L. McClellan's work as Chairman of that Committee certainly ranks with the work of Senator LaFollette twenty years earlier.

The shortest way to characterize the findings of the McClellan Committee is to summarize some of the Committee's charges against James R. Hoffa, president, subject to protracted court proceedings, of the Teamsters. He was charged with granting union charters to men with long criminal records, keeping jailed Teamster officials on the union payroll, manipulating hundreds of thousands of union dollars for his personal benefit, making millions more available to his friends without membership approval, profiting from conflict-of-interest business arrangements set up for him and his wife by employers dependent on the union's good will, using strong-arm tactics to maintain and extend one-man rule, and conspiring with racketeers to defeat his own union's organizing efforts in the New York taxicab field. Much of the Senate testimony dealt with financial abuses in Local 299, of which Hoffa was president. The Committee also charged that Hoffa's announced intention to weld all transportation unions—land, sea, and air—into a single front would make him more powerful than the government itself.

The American public observed with keen interest that despite the dreary recital of Committee charges of misappropriation of union funds and association with gangsters and despite expulsion from the AFL-CIO, Hoffa's 1,600,000-member union continued to adhere unquestioningly to his leadership. The Congress, having started with a project in 1935 to balance the power of labor with the power of management, found itself 25 years later with the problem of balancing corruption and gangsterism with righteousness and law.[11]

[11]In March, 1964, in the Federal District Court for the Eastern District of Tennessee, James Hoffa was convicted of bribing a jury and sentenced to eight years in federal prison. See United States v. Hoffa, 349 F.2d 20 (6th Cir., 1965). After a multitude of unsuccessful attempts to prevent his incarceration, Hoffa began serving his sentence at the Lewisburg, Pennsylvania federal penitentiary on March 7, 1967. Under federal law, Hoffa becomes eligible for parole after serving one-third of his sentence or, in this case, two years and eight months. In addition to being convicted in March, 1964, of jury tampering, in August, 1964, in the Federal District Court for the Northern District of Illinois, Hoffa was convicted and sentenced to five years in prison for mail fraud, wire fraud, and conspiracy to procure loans from the Teamsters Union Pension Fund. See United States v. Hoffa, 367 F.2d 698 (7th Cir., 1966).

Early in 1969, the United States Supreme Court ordered the Federal District Court in both Hoffa cases to review the wiretap, mail tap, and informer evidence presented by the Government to determine whether it was seized in violation of Hoffa's Fourth Amendment rights and if so to award him a new trial. Giordano v. United States, 394 U.S. 310 (1969). In the summer of 1969, the Illinois court denied Hoffa a new trial. On January 2, 1970, the Tennessee court, in response to the United States Supreme Court's mandate for a review, again found against Hoffa on his constitutional claims. United States v. Hoffa, 307 F.Supp. 1129 (E.D. Tenn. S.D. 1970). NEW YORK TIMES, July 15, 1969, p. 25, col. 5.

We shall now examine the key cases and, in a closing commentary, the unresolved issue of the strike as an instrument of economic policy in either private enterprise or public employment.

UNIONISM AND CASE LAW

LABOR ORGANIZATION AND CRIME

COMMONWEALTH v. PULLIS
(PHILADELPHIA CORDWAINER'S CASE OF 1806)
Philadelphia Mayor's Court, 3 Commons and Gilmore,
A Documentary History of American Industrial Society 59–248 (1958).

[This case is the first recorded "labor relations" case in the United States. It involves a group of journeymen cordwainers (boot and shoemakers) who were indicted for combining, conspiring and confederating to refuse to work for any employer who paid less than a fixed rate. The selections that follow are taken from the summation of both the facts and the law applicable to this case as rendered by Moses Levy, the trial court judge (recorder), in his charge to the jury.]

Recorder LEVY delivered the following charge.

. . . This jury will act without fear or favour; without partiality or hatred; regardless whether they make friends or enemies by their verdict—they will do their duty—they will, after the rule of law has been investigated and laid down by the court, find a verdict in conformity to the justice of the case.

If this, gentlemen, is your disposition, there are only two objects for your consideration. First. What the rule of law is on this subject? Second. Whether the defendants acted in such a manner as to bring them within that rule?

[Here the recorder referred to books of authority.]

What are the offences alleged against them? They are contained in the charges of the indictment.

[Here he recited from the indictment the first and second counts.]

These are the questions for our consideration, and it lies with you to determine how far the evidence supports the charges, and how the principles of the law bear upon them.

It is proper to consider, is such a combination consistent with the principles of our law, and injurious to the public welfare? The usual means by which the prices of work are regulated, are the demand for the article and the excellence of its fabric. Where the work is well done, and the demand is considerable, the prices will necessarily be high. Where the work is ill done, and the demand is inconsiderable, they will unquestionably be low. If there are many to consume, and few to work, the price of the article will be high: but if there are few to consume, and many to work, the article must be low. Much will depend too, upon these circumstances, whether the materials are plenty or scarce; the price of the commodity, will in consequence be higher or lower. These are the means by which prices are regulated in the natural course of things. To make an artificial regulation, is not to regard the excellence of the work or quality of the material, but to fix a positive and arbitrary price, governed by no standard, controlled by no impartial person, but dependant on the will of the few who are interested; this is the unnatural way of raising the price of goods or work. This is independent of the number of customers, or of the quality of the material, or of the number who are to do the work. It is an unnatural, artificial means of raising the price of work beyond its standard, and taking an undue advantage of the public. Is the rule of law bottomed upon such principles, as to permit or protect such conduct? Consider it on the footing of the general commerce of the city. Is there any man who can calculate (if this is tolerated) at what price he may safely contract to deliver articles, for which he may receive orders, if he is to be regulated by the journeymen in an arbitrary jump from one price to another? It renders it impossible for a man, making a contract for a large quantity of such goods, to know whether he shall lose or gain by it. If he makes a large contract for goods to-day, for delivery at three, six, or nine months hence, can he calculate what the prices will be then, if the journeymen in the intermediate time, are permitted to meet and raise their prices, according to their caprice or pleasure? Can he fix the price of his commodity for a future day? It is impossible that any man can carry on commerce in this way. There cannot be a large contract entered into, but what the contractor will make at his peril. He may be ruined by the difference of prices made by the journeymen in the intermediate time. What then is the operation of this kind of conduct upon the commerce of the city? It exposes it to inconveniences, if not to ruin; therefore, it is against the public welfare. How does it operate upon the defendants? We see that those who are in indigent circumstances, and who have families to maintain, and who get their bread by their daily labour, have declared here upon oath, that it was impossible for them to hold out; the masters might do it, but they could not: and it has been admitted by the witnesses for the defendants, that such persons, however sharp and pressing their necessities, were obliged to stand to the turn-out, or never afterwards to be employed. They were interdicted from all business in future, if they did not continue to persevere in the measures, taken by the journeymen shoemakers. Can such a regulation be just and proper? Does it not tend to involve necessitous men in the commission of crimes? If they are prevented from working for six weeks, it might induce those who are thus idle, and have not the means of maintenance, to take other courses for the support of their wives and children. It might lead them to procure it by crimes—by burglary, larceny, or highway robbery! A father cannot stand by and see, without agony, his children suffer; if he does, he is an inhuman monster; he will be driven to seek bread for them, either by crime, by beggary, or a removal from the city. Consider these circumstances as they affect trade generally. Does this measure tend to make good workmen? No: it puts the botch incapable of doing justice to his work, on a level with the best tradesman. The master must give the same wages to each. Such a practice would take away all the excitement to excel in workmanship or industry. Consider the effect it would have upon the whole community. If the masters say they will not sell under certain prices, as the journeymen declare they will not work at certain wages, they, if persisted in, would put the whole body of the people into their power. Shoes and boots are articles of the first necessity. If they could stand out three or four weeks in winter, they might raise the price of boots to thirty, forty, or fifty dollars a pair, at least for some time, and until a competent supply could be got from other places. In every point of view, this measure is pregnant with public mischief and private injury,

. . . tends to demoralize the workmen, . . . destroy the trade of the city, and leaves the pockets of the whole community to the discretion of the concerned. . . .

What is the case now before us? . . . A combination of workmen to raise their wages may be considered in a two fold point of view: one is to benefit themselves [and] the other is to injure those who do not join their society. The rule of law condemns both. If the rule be clear, we are bound to conform to it even though we do not comprehend the principle upon which it is founded. We are not to reject it because we do not see the reason of it. It is enough, that it is the will of the majority. It is law because it is their will—if it is law, there may be good reasons for it though we cannot find them out. But the rule in this case is pregnant with sound sense and all the authorities are clear upon the subject. Hawkins, the greatest authority on the criminal law, has laid it down, that a combination to maintaining one another, carrying a particular object, whether true or false, is criminal. . . .

In the profound system of law, (if we may compare small things with great) as in the profound systems of Providence . . . there is often great reason for an institution, though a superficial observer may not be able to discover it. Obedience alone is required in the present case, the reason may be this. One man determines not to work under a certain price and it may be individually the opinion of all: in such a case it would be lawful in each to refuse to do so, for if each stands, alone, either may extract from his determination when he pleases. In the turn-out of last fall, if each member of the body had stood alone, fettered by no promises to the rest, many of them might have changed their opinion as to the price of wages and gone to work; but it has been given to you in evidence, that they were bound down by their agreement, and pledged by mutual engagements, to persist in it, however contrary to their own judgment. The continuance in improper conduct may therefore well be attributed to the combination. The good sense of those individuals was prevented by this agreement, from having its free exercise. . . . Is it not restraining, instead of promoting, the spirit of '76 when men expected to have no law but the constitution, and laws adopted by it or enacted by the legislature in conformity to it? Was it the spirit of '79, that either masters or journeymen, in regulating the prices of their commodities should set up a rule contrary to the law of their country? General and individual liberty was the spirit of '76. It is our first blessing. It has been obtained and will be maintained. . . . Though we acknowledge it is the hard hand of labour that promise the wealth of a nation, though we acknowledge the usefulness of such a large body of tradesmen and agree they should have every thing to which they are legally entitled; yet we conceive they ought to ask nothing more. They should neither be the slaves nor the governors of the community.

The sentiments of the court, not an individual of which is connected either with the masters or journeymen; all stand independent of both parties . . . are unanimous. They have given you the rule as they have found it in the book, and it is now for you to say, whether the defendants are guilty or not. The rule they consider as fixed, they cannot change it. It is now, therefore, left to you upon the law, and the evidence, to find the verdict. If you can reconcile it to your consciences, to find the defendants not guilty, you will do so; if not, the alternative that remains, is a verdict of guilty.

The jury retired, about 9 o'clock, and were directed by the court to seal up their verdict. . . . Next morning the following circumstances took place.

Mr. Franklin requested the jury to be polled.

It was granted by the court.

On calling over the jury list, Mr. Wm. Henderson, the fifth on the Roster, said, The clerk will find a paper inclosed in the bill of indictment containing the verdict of the jury, subscribed with their names. The clerk then read the paper referred to.

The reporter took it down in these words: We find the defendants guilty of a combination to raise their wages, Subscribed by the 12 jurors.

.   .   .   .

And the court fined the defendants eight dollars each, with costs of suit, and to stand committed till paid.

COMMONWEALTH v. HUNT
Supreme Judicial Court of Massachusetts, 4 Metcalf 111 (1842).

[John Hunt and six others were indicted for combining and agreeing not to work for any master bootmaker who employed any workmen or journeymen who were not members of the Boston Journeymen Bootmakers' Society. A second count of the same indictment charged that John Hunt and the others did compel one Isaac B. Wait, a master cordwainer in Boston, to dismiss Jeremiah Horne, a journeyman bootmaker, because Jeremiah Horne refused to pay the Society a penalty levied upon him for breaching Society rules. The third count of the indictment alleged that the defendants in pursuit of their conspiracy had deprived Jeremiah Horne of the right to make a following in his occupation and thus "did greatly impoverish him."

At the trial the defendants were found guilty of criminal conspiracy as charged in the indictment. The defendants claimed that the trial judge erred in refusing to charge the jury as requested by defendants' counsel that "the indictment did not set forth any agreement to do a criminal act, or to do any act by criminal means; and that the agreements, therein set forth, did not constitute a conspiracy indictable by any law of this Commonwealth. . . . " On appeal, in a landmark decision, Chief Justice Lemuel Shaw overruled the decision of the trial court.]

SHAW, C. J.

.   .   .   .

Let us, then, first consider how the subject of criminal conspiracy is treated by elementary writers. The position cited by Chitty from Hawkins, by way of summing up the result of the cases, is this: "In a word, all confederacies wrongfully to prejudice another are misdemeanors at common law, whether the intention is to injure his property, his person, or his character." And Chitty adds, that "the object of conspiracy is not confined to an immediate wrong to individuals; it may be to injure public trade, to affect public health, to violate public police, to insult public justice, or to do any act in itself illegal." 3 Chit. Crim. Law, 1139.

Several rules upon the subject seem to be well established, to wit, that the unlawful agreement constitutes the gist of the offence, and therefore that it is not necessary to charge the execution of the unlawful agreement. . . . And when such execution is charged, it is to be regarded as proof of the intent, or as an aggravation of the criminality of the unlawful combination.

.   .   .   .   .

From this view of the law respecting conspiracy, we think it an offence which especially demands the application of that wise and humane rule of the common law, that an indictment shall state, with as much certainty as the nature of the case will admit, the facts which constitute the crime intended to be charged. This is required, to enable the defendant to meet the charge and prepare for his defence, and, in case of acquittal or conviction, to show by the record the identity of the charge so that he may not be indicted a second time for the same offence. It is also necessary, in order that a person, charged by the grand jury for one offence, may not substantially be convicted, on his trial, of another. This fundamental rule is confirmed by the Declaration of Rights, which declares that no subject shall be held to answer for any crime or offence, until the same is fully and plainly, substantially and formally described to him.

From these views of the rules of criminal pleading, it appears to us to follow, as a necessary legal conclusion, that when the criminality of a conspiracy consists in an unlawful agreement of two or more persons to compass or promote some criminal or illegal purpose, that purpose must be fully and clearly stated in the indictment; and if the criminality of the offence, which is intended to be charged, consists in the agreement to compass or promote some purpose, not of itself criminal or unlawful, by the use of fraud, force, falsehood, or other criminal or unlawful means, such intended use of fraud, force, falsehood, or other criminal or unlawful means, must be set out in the indictment.   .   .   .

.   .   .   .   .

With these general views of the law, it becomes necessary to consider the circumstances of the present case, as they appear from the indictment itself, and from the bill of exceptions filed and allowed.

.   .   .   .   .

Stripped   .   .   .   of   .   .   .   introductory recitals and alleged injurious consequences, and of the qualifying epithets attached to the facts, the averment is this; that the defendants and others formed themselves into a society, and agreed not to work for any person, who should employ any journeyman or other person, not a member of such society, after notice given him to discharge such workman.

The manifest intent of the association is, to induce all those engaged in the same occupation to become members of it. Such a purpose is not unlawful. It would give them a power which might be exerted for useful and honorable purposes, or for dangerous and pernicious ones. If the latter were the real and actual object, and susceptible of proof, it should have been specially charged. Such an association might be used to afford each other assistance in times of poverty, sickness and distress; or to raise their intellectual, moral and social condition; or to make improvement in their art; or for other proper purposes. Or the association might be designed for purposes of oppression and injustice. But in order to charge all those, who become members of an association, with the guilt of a criminal conspiracy, it must be averred and proved that the actual, if not the avowed object of the association, was criminal. An association may be formed, the declared objects of which are innocent and laudable, and yet they may have secret articles, or an agreement communicated only to the members, by which they are banded together for purposes injurious to the peace of society or the rights of its members. Such would undoubtedly be a criminal conspiracy, on proof of the fact, however meritorious and praiseworthy the declared objects might be. The law is not to be hoodwinked by colorable pretences. It looks at truth and reality, through whatever disguise it may assume. But to make such an association, ostensibly innocent, the subject of prosecution as a criminal conspiracy, the secret agreement, which makes it so, is to be averred and proved as the gist of the offence. But when an association is formed for purposes actually innocent, and afterwards its powers are abused, by those who have the control and management of it, to purposes of oppression and injustice, it will be criminal in those who thus misuse it, or give consent thereto, but not in the other members of the association. In this case, no such secret agreement, varying the objects of the association from those avowed, is set forth in this count of the indictment.

Nor can we perceive that the objects of this association, whatever they may have been, were to be attained by criminal means. The means which they proposed to employ, as averred in this count, and which, as we are now to presume, were established by the proof, were, that they would not work for a person, who, after due notice, should employ a journeyman not a member of their society. Supposing the object of the association to be laudable and lawful, or at least not unlawful, are these means criminal? The case supposes that these persons are not bound by contract, but free to work for whom they please, or not to work, if they so prefer. In this state of things, we cannot perceive, that it is criminal for men to agree together to exercise their own acknowledged rights, in such a manner as best to subserve their own interests. One way to test this is, to consider the effect of such an agreement, where the object of the association is acknowledged on all hands to be a laudable one. Suppose a class of workmen, impressed with the manifold evils of intemperance, should agree with each other not to work in a shop in which ardent spirit was furnished, or not to work in a shop with any one who used it, or not to work for an employer, who should, after notice, employ a journeyman who habitually used it. The consequences might be the same. A workman, who should still persist in the use of ardent spirit, would find it more difficult to get employment; a master employing such an one might, at times, experience inconvenience in his work, in losing the services of a skillful but intemperate workman. Still it seems to us, that as the object would be lawful, and the means not unlawful, such an agreement could not be pronounced a criminal conspiracy.

From this count in the indictment, we do not understand that the agreement was, that the defendants would refuse to work for an employer, to whom they were bound by contract for a certain time, in violation of that contract; nor that they would insist that an employer should discharge a workman engaged by contract for a certain time, in violation of such contract. It is perfectly consistent with every thing stated in this count, that the effect of the agreement was, that when they were free to act, they would not engage with an employer, or continue in his employment, if such employer, when free to act, should engage with a workman, or continue a workman in his employment, not a member of the association. If a large number of men, engaged for a certain time, should combine together to violate their contract, and quit their employment together, it would present a very different question. Suppose a farmer, employing a large number of men, engaged for the year, at fair monthly wages, and suppose that just at the moment that his crops were ready to harvest, they should all combine to quit his service, unless he would advance their wages, at a time when other laborers could not be obtained. It would surely be a conspiracy to do an unlawful act, though of such a character, that if done by an individual, it would lay the foundation of a civil action only, and not of a criminal prosecution. It would be a case very different from that stated in this count.

The second count, omitting the recital of unlawful intent and evil disposition, and omitting the direct averment of an unlawful club or society, alleges that the defendants, with others unknown, did assemble, conspire, confederate and agree together, not to work for any master or person who should employ any workman not being a member of a certain club, society or combination, called the Boston Journeymen Bootmaker's Society, or who should break any of their by-laws, unless such workmen should pay to said club, such sum as should be agreed upon as a penalty for the breach of such unlawful rules, &c; and that by means of said conspiracy they did compel one Isaac B. Wait, a master cordwainer, to turn out of his employ one Jeremiah Horne, a journeyman boot-maker, &c. in evil example, &c. So far as the averment of a conspiracy is concerned, all the remarks made in reference to the first count are equally applicable to this. It is simply an averment of an agreement amongst themselves not to work for a person, who should employ any person not a member of a certain association. It sets forth no illegal or criminal purpose to be accomplished, nor any illegal or criminal means to be adopted for the accomplishment of any purpose. It was an agreement, as to the manner in which they would exercise an acknowledged right to contract with others for their labor. It does not aver a conspiracy or even an intention to raise their wages; and it appears by the bill of exceptions, that the case was not put upon the footing of a conspiracy to raise their wages. Such an agreement, as set forth in this count, would be perfectly justifiable under the recent English statute, by which this subject is regulated. *St.* 6 Geo. IV. *C.* 129. See Roscoe Crim. Ev. (2d Amer. ed.) 368, 369.

As to the latter part of this count, which avers that by means of said conspiracy, the defendants did compel one Wait to turn out of his employ one Jeremiah Horne, we remark, in the first place, that as the acts done in pursuance of a conspiracy, as we have before seen, are stated by way of aggravation, and not as a substantive charge; if no criminal or unlawful conspiracy is stated, it cannot be aided and made good by mere matter of aggravation. If the principal charge falls, the aggravation falls with it. . . .

. . . . . .

The third count, reciting a wicked and unlawful intent to impoverish one Jeremiah Horne, and hinder him from following his trade as a boot-maker, charges the defendants, with others unknown, with an unlawful conspiracy, by wrongful and indirect means, to impoverish said Horne and to deprive and hinder him, from his said art and trade and getting his support thereby, and that, in pursuance of said unlawful combination, they did unlawfully and indirectly hinder and prevent, &c. and greatly impoverish him.

If the fact of depriving Jeremiah Horne of the profits of his business, by whatever means it might be done, would be unlawful and criminal, a combination to compass that object would be an unlawful conspiracy, and it would be unnecessary to state the means. . . .

Suppose a baker in a small village had the exclusive custom of his neighborhood, and was making large profits by the sale of his bread. Supposing a number of those neighbors, believing the price of his bread too high, should propose to him to reduce his prices, or if he did not, that they would introduce another baker; and on his refusal, such other baker should, under their encouragement, set up a rival establishment, and sell his bread at lower prices; the effect would be to diminish the profit of the former baker, and to the same extent to impoverish him. And it might be said and proved, that the purpose of the associates was to diminish his profits, and thus impoverish him, though the ultimate and laudable object of the combination was to reduce the cost of bread to themselves and their neighbors. The same thing may be said of all competition in every branch of trade and industry; and yet it is through that competition, that the best interests of trade and industry are promoted. It is scarcely necessary to allude to the familiar instances of opposition lines of conveyance, rival hotels, and the thousand other instances, where each strives to gain custom to himself, by ingenious improvements, by increased industry, and by all the means by which he may lessen the price of commodities, and thereby diminish the profits of others.

We think, therefore, that associations may be entered into, the object of which is to adopt measures that may have a tendency to impoverish another, that is, to diminish his gains and profits, and yet so far from being criminal or unlawful, the object may be highly meritorious and public spirited. The legality of such an association will therefore depend upon the means to be used for its accomplishment. If it is to be carried into effect by fair or honorable and lawful means, it is, to say the least, innocent; if by falsehood or force, it may be stamped with the character of conspiracy. It follows as a necessary consequence, that if criminal and indictable, it is so by reason of the criminal means intended to be employed for its accomplishment; and as a further legal consequence, that as the criminality will depend on the means, those means must be stated in the indictment. If the same rule were to prevail in criminal, which holds in civil proceedings—that a case defectively stated may be aided by a verdict—then a court might presume, after verdict, that the indictment was supported by proof of criminal or unlawful means to effect the object. But it is an established rule in criminal cases, that the indictment must state a complete indictable offence, and cannot be aided by the proof offered at the trial.

. . . [L]ooking solely at the indictment, disregarding the qualifying epithets, recitals and immaterial allegations, and confining ourselves to facts so averred as to be capable of being traversed and put in issue, we cannot perceive that it charges a criminal conspiracy punishable by law. The exceptions must therefore be sustained, and the judgment arrested.[12]

LABOR ORGANIZATION AND TORT

VEGELAHN v. GUNTNER
Supreme Judicial Court of Massachusetts, 167 Mass. 92 (1896).

Bill in Equity, filed December 7, 1891, against fourteen individual defendants and two trades unions, alleging that the plaintiff was engaged in business as a manufacturer of

---

[12]Commonwealth v. Hunt foreshadowed the gradual decline of the application of the criminal law to union organizing activities in the United States. One of the last reported labor cases involving the doctrine of criminal conspiracy is State v. Donaldson, 32 N.J.L. 151 (Sup. Ct. 1867). This case was repealed by the New Jersey Legislature in 1883. England, on the other hand, abolished the criminal conspiracy doctrine by Parliamentary decree in 1875. See Gregory, Charles

furniture, in the premises numbered 141, 143, 145, and 147 North Street in Boston, and employed a large number of men in carrying on his business there, that there were in Boston certain associations named as defendants, which were composed of persons engaged in similar occupations to that of the individual defendants, of whom the defendant Guntner was agent; that on or about October 11, 1894, the plaintiff received a communication from the defendant unions as follows: "Your upholsterers do hereby kindly submit enclosed Price-list for your earnest consideration, the object is to institute a more equal competition this we would asked to go into effect on and after Oct. 29, 1894, and we kindly request that after said date Nine hours constitute a day's work", that on or about November 21, 1894, without notice and without warning, all of the individual defendants, except Guntner, struck, and left the plaintiff's employment and premises in a body; that since that date the plaintiff had endeavored to carry on his business, and to employ other men to fill the places of the defendants, but the defendants, their agents and servants, had wilfully and maliciously patrolled the streets in front of his premises in groups and squads continuously, and had used indecent language and epithets to those working in his employ in the places made vacant by the defendants, that they had wilfully and maliciously blocked up the doorway and entrance of his premises, and there intercepted, interfered with, and intimidated persons who desired to visit the premises for the purpose of engaging in the employment of the plaintiff, and for the purpose of trading with the plaintiff; that they had wilfully and maliciously intimidated and threatened the persons whom he had employed to take their places with bodily harm if they continued in the plaintiff's employment, and had caused certain new men so employed to leave his employment, . . . that the defendants, their agents and servants, had been and were a nuisance and obstruction to persons travelling on the street, and to persons in the employ of the plaintiff, and to persons intending to trade with the plaintiff at his premises; that all acts of the defendants were a part of a scheme to prevent persons from entering the employment of the plaintiff and from continuing in his employment, that the business carried on by the plaintiff was a large one, and the good will was of considerable value, in both of which the plaintiff had already been injured; and that, if the defendants were permitted to continue their acts, both the business and the good will would be further seriously injured and destroyed.

. . . . .

ALLEN, J.   The principal question in this case is whether the defendants should be enjoined against maintaining the patrol. . . .

The patrol was maintained as one of the means of carrying out the defendants' plan, and it was used in combination with social pressure, threats of personal injury or unlawful harm, and persuasion to break existing contracts. It was thus one means of intimidation indirectly to the plaintiff, and directly to persons actually employed, or seeking to be employed, by the plaintiff, and of rendering such employment unpleasant or intolerable to such persons. Such an act is an unlawful interference with the rights both of employer and of employed. An employer has a right to engage all persons who are willing to work for him, at such prices as may be mutually agreed upon; and persons employed or seeking employment have a corresponding right to enter into or remain

O., *Labor and the Law* (2d ed.), pp. 30–31, Norton, New York, 1958; Nelles, Walter, "Commonwealth v. Hunt," 32 *Colum. L. Rev.* 1128 (1932).

in the employment of any person or corporation willing to employ them. These rights are secured by the Constitution itself. . . .   No one can lawfully interfere by force or intimidation to prevent employers or persons employed or wishing to be employed from the exercise of these rights. In Massachusetts, as in some other States, it is even made a criminal offence for one by intimidation or force to prevent or seek to prevent a person from entering into or continuing in the employment of a person or corporation. Pub. Sts. c. 74, § 2. Intimidation is not limited to threats of violence or of physical injury to person or property. It has a broader signification, and there also may be a moral intimidation which is illegal. Patrolling or picketing, under the circumstances stated in the report, has elements of intimidation like those which were found to exist in Sherry v. Perkins, 147 Mass. 212. It was declared to be unlawful in Regina v. Druitt, 10 Cox C.C. 592; Regina v. Hibbert, 13 Cox C.C. 82; and Regina v. Bauld, 13 Cox C.C. 282. It was assumed to be unlawful in Trollope v. London Building Trades Federation, 11 T.L.R. 228, though in that case the pickets were withdrawn before the bringing of the bill. The patrol was an unlawful interference both with the plaintiff and with the workmen, within the principle of many cases, and, when instituted for the purpose of interfering with his business, it became a private nuisance. . . .

The defendants contend that these acts were justifiable, because they were only seeking to secure better wages for themselves by compelling the plaintiff to accept their schedule of wages. This motive or purpose does not justify maintaining a patrol in front of the plaintiff's premises, as a means of carrying out their conspiracy. A combination among persons merely to regulate their own conduct is within allowable competition, and is lawful, although others may be indirectly affected thereby. But a combination to do injurious acts expressly directed to another, by way of intimidations or constraint, either of himself or of persons employed or seeking to be employed by him, is outside of allowable competition, and is unlawful. Various decided cases fall within the former class, for example: . . .   Commonwealth v. Hunt, 4 Met. 111. . . .   The present case falls within the latter class.

·   ·   ·

In the opinion of a majority of the court the injunction should be in the form originally issued.

So ordered.

HOLMES, J. [dissenting.]

·   ·   ·   ·

One of the eternal conflicts out of which life is made up is that between the effort of every man to get the most he can for his services, and that of society, disguised under the name of capital, to get his services for the least possible return. Combination on the one side is patent and powerful. Combination on the other is the necessary and desirable counterpart, if the battle is to be carried on in a fair and equal way. . . .

If it be true that workingmen may combine with a view, among other things, to getting as much as they can for their labor, just as capital may combine with a view to getting the greatest possible return, it must be true that when combined they have the same liberty that combined capital has to support their interests by argument, persuasion, and the bestowal or refusal of those advantages which they otherwise lawfully control. I can remember when many people thought that, apart from violence or breach of contract, strikes were wicked, as organized refusals to work. I suppose that intelligent economists and legislators have given up that notion to-day. I feel pretty confident that they equally will abandon the idea that an organized refusal by workmen of social intercourse with a man who shall enter their antagonist's employ is wrong, if it is dissociated from any threat of violence, and is made for the sole object of prevailing if possible in a contest with their employer about the rate of wages. The fact, that the immediate object of the act by which the benefit to themselves is to be gained is to injure their antagonist, does not necessarily make it unlawful, any more than when a great house lowers the price of certain goods for the purpose, and with the effect, of driving a smaller antagonist from the business. Indeed, the question seems to me to have been decided as long ago as 1842 by the good sense of Chief Justice Shaw, in Commonwealth v. Hunt, 4 Met. 111.   .   .   .

LABOR ORGANIZATION AND CONTRACT

HITCHMAN COAL & COKE COMPANY v. MITCHELL
Supreme Court of the United States, 245 U.S. 229 (1917).

[This was a bill in equity brought by the plaintiff Hitchman Coal & Coke Company, a West Virginia mine operator, to enjoin the defendants, officers of the United Mine Workers of America (U.M.W.A. or Union), a labor organization affiliated with the American Federation of Labor, from interfering with the relations between the mine operators and its employees pursuant to the U.M.W.A.'s attempt to "unionize" the Hitchman mine.

Sometime during the year 1906, a striking group of Hitchman's employees called on its president, stated that they could no longer afford to remain on strike, and asked on what terms they could return to work. They were told that they could come back to work on the condition that they cease membership in the U.M.W.A.; that henceforth the mine would be run nonunion; and that the company would deal with each man individually. They assented to these stipulations and returned to work on a nonunion basis. This agreement between Hitchman and its employees, which prohibited the employees from becoming union members, was known as a "yellow-dog" contract. Hitchman operated its mine in this manner until commencement of this suit, except that eventually it required from the miners a written agreement not to join the union.

In September, 1907, the U.M.W.A. sent an organizer by the name of Hughes into the West Virginia panhandle for the purpose of conducting organizing campaigns at the Hitchman and several neighboring mines. Hughes, who was well aware of the "yellow-dog" contracts that existed between the mine operators and their employees, held conferences with the operators during which he attempted to persuade them to unionize their mines. When this tact proved unsuccessful, Hughes proceeded to interview as many working men as possible and to hold public meetings during which he exhorted workers to join the union, notwithstanding the existence of their "yellow-dog" contracts.

The United States District Court granted Hitchman a perpetual injunction against these described U.M.W.A. activities on two grounds. First, the U.M.W.A. was both a common-law conspiracy in unreasonable restraint of trade and also a conspiracy against the nonunion miners in West Virginia. Secondly, the U.M.W.A., although it knew that contracts between Hitchman and its employees expressly prohibited the employees from entering into relations with the union, endeavored by unlawful means to procure a breach of these contracts. Upon appeal, the Circuit Court of Appeals reversed the District Court's issuance of the injunction. The Supreme Court granted certiorari.]

Mr. Justice PITNEY delivered the opinion of the court.

.   .   .   .

What are the legal consequences of the facts that have been detailed?

That the plaintiff was acting within its lawful rights in employing its men only upon terms of continuing nonmembership in the United Mine Workers of America is not open to question. Plaintiff's repeated costly experiences of strikes and other interferences while attempting to "run union" were a sufficient explanation of its resolve to run "non-union," if any were needed. But neither explanation nor justification is needed. Whatever may be the advantages of "collective bargaining," it is not bargaining at all, in any just sense, unless it is voluntary on both sides. The same liberty which enables men to form unions, and through the union to enter into agreements with employers willing to agree, entitles other men to remain independent of the union and other employers to agree with them to employ no man who owes any allegiance or obligation to the union. In the latter case, as in the former, the parties are entitled to be protected by the law in the enjoyment of the benefits of any lawful agreement they may make. This court repeatedly has held that the employer is as free to make nonmembership in a union a condition of employment, as the working man is free to join the union, and that this is a part of the constitutional rights of personal liberty and private property, not to be taken away even by legislation, unless through some proper exercise of the paramount police power. . . .   In the present case, needless to say, there is no act of legislation to which defendants may resort for justification.

Plaintiff, having in the exercise of its undoubted rights established a working agreement between it and its employees, with the free assent of the latter, is entitled to be protected in the enjoyment of the resulting status, as in any other legal right. . . .

[The Supreme Court reversed the decree of the Circuit Court of Appeals, remanded the cause to the District Court, and directed the District Court to modify its decree by eliminating the provisions of its injunction against the U.M.W.A., which prevented picketing and acts of violence, because there was no evidence that either of these forms of interference had been committed or threatened by the U.M.W.A. This decision had the effect of leaving intact the portions of the District Court's injunction that prohibited the U.M.W.A. from attempting to get the miners to join the union and still remain in the employment of Hitchman.

Mr. Justice Brandeis was joined in dissent by Mr. Justice Holmes and Mr. Justice Clarke. The dissenters argued that both the purpose of and the means used by the U.M.W.A. were lawful. In their view the purpose was to get the employer to bargain collectively with the union—a lawful purpose, and the means used were calculated to encourage men who were *lawfully* free to terminate their relationship of employment with Hitchman to join the union (and then presumably to withdraw from employment), a lawful means since it involved no tortious interference with contractual relations.]

SUMMARY OF MAJOR LABOR LEGISLATION 1914–1964*

1914–CLAYTON ACT

Cases such as Vegelahn created demands from labor for curbing the use of the legal process against union activities. Congress made a beginning in the Clayton Act of 1914. Although the major thrust of that act was to make more specific the nature of antitrust and monopoly offenses by corporations and to tighten restraints on business, alert labor procured an exemption of unions from the antitrust laws. The exempting section of the Act contained the now classical declaration that "the labor of a human being is not a commodity or article of commerce."

In addition to the antitrust exempting section, the Clayton Act (Section 20) contained a provision whereby the federal courts were prohibited from issuing an injunction "in any case between an employer and employees, or between employers and employees, or between employees, or between persons employed and persons seeking employment, involving, or growing out of, a dispute concerning terms or conditions of employment, unless necessary to prevent irreparable injury. . . . "

Between 1916 and 1920, in the thirteen reported, lower federal court cases in which labor organizations sought application of the antiinjunction provision of Section 20 of the Clayton Act, it was held in ten of the cases that the statute did not prevent the issuance of an injunction. This result was based on two independent and inconsistent constructions of the Act. The lower federal courts reasoned, first, that Section 20 was merely declaratory of what the law would be without the statute, and secondly, that Section 20 did create new privileges, so limited in scope, however, that the antiinjunction provisions were applicable only in a case in which the union's purpose was the *immediate* betterment of working conditions.[13]

Organized labor's next step came with the Norris-LaGuardia Act of 1932.

1932 — NORRIS-LaGUARDIA ACT

The Norris-LaGuardia Act greatly limited the power of the federal courts to issue injunctions in connection with most labor disputes. The architects of this Act attempted to avoid the pitfalls of Clayton Act Section 20 by broadly defining a "labor dispute" to include "any controversy concerning conditions of employment . . . regardless of whether or not the disputants stand in the proximate relationship of employer and employee."

---

*Excerpts from this legislation appear in the Appendix at the end of this chapter. (p. 337).

[13]Frankfurter, Felix, and Greene, Nathan, *The Labor Injunction,* p. 165, Macmillan, New York, 1930.

Both the Clayton Act and the Norris-LaGuardia Act were negative. It remained for the Wagner Act to affirmatively declare a policy of the United States to encourage the practice and procedure of collective bargaining; to affirm the right to strike upon failure of collective bargaining; and to create a National Labor Relations Board to administer that policy.

1935 — NATIONAL LABOR RELATIONS ACT (WAGNER ACT)

The National Labor Relations Act of 1935 was a significant aspect of New Deal legislation. The American economy had suffered the great collapse of 1929 and the ensuing early 1930's. President Franklin D. Roosevelt urged the elevation of both corporate profits and workers' wages. Senator Robert Wagner of New York called for legislation to clearly legalize unionism and require collective bargaining as a means of improving workers' earnings. By the same token, the antitrust laws were suspended, under an emergency act called National Industrial Recovery Act,[14] so that corporations could create codes of fair trade practices to improve profits. The National Industrial Recovery Act was held unconstitutional,[15] but the Wagner Act was sustained.[16]

The Wagner Act contained three main thrusts: (1) protection of the workers' right to organize and to bargain collectively; (2) provisions for election machinery to determine union representation; and (3) a directive that employers bargain with the duly elected representatives of the employees' union. The proponents of the legislation articulated three basic themes in support of this legislation: (1) industrial peace would result from restraining employers from interfering with the workers' right to organize and to bargain collectively— traditionally a main source of strikes and other work stoppages; (2) collective bargaining tended to democratize the lives of worker-employees; and (3) the economy would be strengthened by viable and independent unions that could raise wages by insisting on a more equitable division of profits, and thus maintain a high level of consumption and spending. The legislative opponents responded to these arguments by contending that the Act was: (1) unconstitutional; (2) unfair in that it placed restrictions upon employers but not upon unions; (3) tended to destroy the American ideal of a classless society; and (4) failed to protect the individual's right of free choice, so long held sacred in the American society.[17]

---

[14]48 Stat. 195, 15 U.S.C. § 703, approved June 13, 1933.

[15]Schechter Poultry Corp. v. United States, 295 U.S. 495 (1935).

[16]National Labor Relations Board v. Jones & Laughlin Steel Corp., 301 U.S. 1 (1937).

[17]Derber, Milton and Young, Edwin, *Labor and the New Deal* (R. W. Fleming, ed.), pp. 129–145, University of Wisconsin Press, Madison, 1957.

1947 — LABOR MANAGEMENT RELATIONS ACT, 1947 (TAFT-HARTLEY ACT)

The 80th Congress in 1947 noted that whereas the experience before 1935 had shown that *employers* had been possessed of inordinate power over labor, the experience between 1935 and 1947 had demonstrated that certain unfair labor practices of *labor organizations*—in particular strikes—had the effect of burdening and impeding commerce by preventing the free flow of goods. As a result, in addition to tightening the prohibitions upon *employer* interference with the right of labor to organize and to bargain collectively set forth in the Wagner Act, the 80th Congress added several new provisions that designated as unfair labor practices certain activities of *organized labor.* These amendments and supplements to the Wagner Act became Title I of the Taft-Hartley Act.

The 80th Congress in addition incorporated several new titles into the Taft-Hartley Act. In Title II it restored the injunction (after the strike, however) in labor disputes in which the acts or practices "imperil or threaten to imperil the national health or safety." In Title III it provided the United States District Courts with jurisdiction over suits for violation of contracts between employers and labor organizations or between any labor organization and any other labor organization.

1959 — THE LABOR MANAGEMENT REPORTING AND DISCLOSURE ACT OF 1959 (THE LANDRUM-GRIFFIN ACT)

The Landrum-Griffin Act was spurred by a growing concern about undemocratic practices within unions and by the demonstrated abuse of the power of some union officials.

Title I of the Act, designated the "Bill of Rights of Members of Labor Organizations," guarantees to union members freedom of speech and assembly and equal participation in union affairs. It also insures the right of workers to sue their unions and union officers. Title II requires disclosure by union officials and by union employees of detailed information about the financial dealings, operations, and general financial conditions of the union, including disclosure of information concerning their personal dealings that are related either to union or to company matters. Title II also imposes like responsibilities upon employers who enter into financial relationships either with the union or with individual employees. Title III regulates the manner in which one labor organization may assume a trusteeship over any subordinate labor organization. Title IV is designed to insure the fairness of union elections and includes provisions concerning the conduct of such elections and provisions by which an unfair election may be challenged or set aside. Title V imposes certain fiduciary obligations and responsibilities upon union officers and representatives, making them personally liable for engaging in unfair financial dealings with union funds or property and criminally liable for conversion of union funds.

1964 — CIVIL RIGHTS ACT OF 1964

The Civil Rights Act of 1964 sought to implement the 14th and 15th Amendments concerning the right to vote and concerning discrimination in public accommodations and federally assisted programs. Title VII of the Act was directed toward equal opportunity of employment and sought to prohibit discrimination in employment practices by both unions and employers. Title VII makes discriminatory acts of either employers or unions illegal when the unjustified discrimination is based on race, color, religion, sex or national origin. In addition, Title VII establishes an Equal Employment Opportunity Commission that has power to implement the rights granted in the Act.

FEDERAL VERSUS STATE JURISDICTION OVER LABOR DISPUTES

FEDERAL POWER—THE COMMERCE CLAUSE

The laws enacted by the Congress of the United States and the decisions of the federal courts in labor-management matters rest fundamentally on the Commerce Clause of the United States Constitution. Article I, Section 8, Clause 3, gives Congress the power, "To regulate Commerce with foreign nations, and among the several States . . . " All of the statutes quoted in part or cited in this portion of Chapter 7 are founded on that power.

The commerce to be regulated by these statutes, as interpreted by the federal courts, must be commerce among the states, commonly called interstate commerce. An elementary example of interstate commerce occurs when goods move across a border from one state to another in a commercial transaction. A less clear example is one in which workers, while not moving across state lines in their work, perform services on materials that have come to the place of work from another state, abroad or, in any case, are destined after the work has been performed to move on in commerce across a state line. In such a case the workers are engaged in interstate commerce and their rights and obligations are subject to federal laws such as the Wagner Act. This is the holding of the Supreme Court in National Labor Relations Board v. Jones & Laughlin Steel Corp., 301 U.S. 1 (1937).

In an advanced industrial economy such as that of the United States it is more than a little difficult to identify an industrial or commercial activity that does not become interstate commerce. A group of workers picking blackberries in a patch wholly within one state and delivering them then and there for a price into the hats or handkerchiefs of buyers would undoubtedly be engaged in intrastate commerce and therefore not subject to federal labor laws. But, if the United States Supreme Court should hold in such a case that because the blackberry bushes had been imported originally from another state and that therefore the picking was interstate commerce, such a holding would make federal labor laws applicable.

Assuming applicability of federal labor-management laws and assuming that a given state has identical laws or, on the other hand, inconsistent laws, which will be controlling? The doctrine of federal preemption applies, and the cases in this subsection illustrate the principles and refinements of the application of that doctrine.

EXAMPLES OF FEDERAL PREEMPTION

GARNER v. TEAMSTERS, CHAUFFEURS AND HELPERS LOCAL UNION NO. 776[18]
Supreme Court of the United States, 346 U.S. 485 (1953).

Mr. Justice JACKSON delivered the opinion of the Court.

.   .   .   .   .

Petitioners were engaged in the trucking business and had twenty-four employees, four of whom were members of respondent union. The trucking operations formed a link to an interstate railroad. No controversy, labor dispute or strike was in progress, and at no time had petitioners objected to their employees joining the union. Respondents, however, placed rotating pickets, two at a time, at petitioners' loading platform. None were employees of petitioners. They carried signs reading "Local 776 Teamsters Union (A.F. of L.) wants Employees of Central Storage & Transfer Co. to join them to gain union wages, hours and working conditions." Picketing was orderly and peaceful, but drivers for other carriers refused to cross this picket line and, as most of petitioners' interchange of freight was with unionized concerns, their business fell off as much as 95%. The courts below found that respondents' purpose in picketing was to coerce petitioners in to compelling or influencing their employees to join the union.

The equity court held that respondents' conduct violated the Pennsylvania Labor Relations Act. The Supreme Court of the Commonwealth held, quite correctly, we think, that petitioners' grievance fell within the jurisdiction of the National Labor Relations Board to prevent unfair labor practices. It therefore inferred that state remedies were precluded. . . .

The national Labor Management Relations Act, as we have before pointed out, leaves much to the states, though Congress has refrained from telling us how much. We must spell out from conflicting indications of congressional will the area in which state action is still permissible.

This is not an instance of injurious conduct which the National Labor Relations

---

[18]The reader may wish to refer to the Labor Management Relations Act, 1947 (Taft-Hartley Act), Appendix, *infra,* p. 339, before reading this case.

Board is without express power to prevent and which therefore either is "governable by the State or it is entirely ungoverned." In such cases we have declined to find an implied exclusion of state powers. International Union v. Wisconsin Board, 336 U.S. 245, 254. Nor is this a case of mass picketing, threatening of employees, obstructing streets and highways, or picketing homes. We have held that the state still may exercise "its historic powers over such traditionally local matters as public safety and order and the use of streets and highways." Allen-Bradley Local v. Wisconsin Board, 315 U.S. 740, 749. Nothing suggests that the activity enjoined threatened a probable breach of the state's peace or would call for extraordinary police measures by state or city authority. Nor is there any suggestion that respondents' plea of federal jurisdiction and pre-emption was frivolous and dilatory, or that the federal Board would decline to exercise its powers once its jurisdiction was invoked.

Congress has taken in hand this particular type of controversy where it affects interstate commerce. In language almost identical to parts of the Pennsylvania statute, it has forbidden labor unions to exert certain types of coercion on employees through the medium of the employer. It is not necessary or appropriate for us to surmise how the National Labor Relations Board might have decided this controversy had petitioners presented it to that body. The power and duty of primary decision lies with the Board, not with us. But it is clear that the Board was vested with power to entertain petitioners' grievance, to issue its own complaint against respondents and, pending final hearing, to seek from the United States District Court an injunction to prevent irreparable injury to petitioners while their case was being considered. The question then is whether the State, through its courts, may adjudge the same controversy and extend its own form of relief.

Congress did not merely lay down a substantive rule of law to be enforced by any tribunal competent to apply law generally to the parties. It went on to confide primary interpretation and application of its rules to a specific and specially constituted tribunal and prescribed a particular procedure for investigation, complaint and notice, and hearing and decision, including judicial relief pending a final administrative order. Congress evidently considered that centralized administration of specially designed procedures was necessary to obtain uniform application of its substantive rules and to avoid these diversities and conflicts likely to result from a variety of local procedures and attitudes toward labor controversies. Indeed, Pennsylvania passed a statute the same year as its labor relations Act reciting abuses of the injunction in labor litigations attributable more to procedure and usage than to substantive rules. A multiplicity of tribunals and a diversity of procedures are quite as apt to produce incompatible or conflicting adjudications as are different rules of substantive law. The same reasoning which prohibits federal courts from intervening in such cases, except by way of review or on application of the federal Board, precludes state courts from doing so. Cf. Myers v. Bethlehem Shipbuilding Corp., 303 U.S. 41; Amalgamated Utility Workers v. Consolidated Edison Co., 309 U.S. 261. And the reasons for excluding state administrative bodies from assuming control of matters expressly placed within the competence of the federal Board also exclude state courts from like action. Cf. Bethlehem Steel Co. v. New York Board, 330 U.S. 767.

.   .   .   .

We conclude that when federal power constitutionally is exerted for the protection of public or private interests, or both, it becomes the supreme law of the land and cannot be curtailed, circumvented or extended by a state procedure merely because it will apply some doctrine of private right. To the extent that the private right may conflict with the public one, the former is superseded. To the extent that public interest is found to require official enforcement instead of private initiative, the latter will ordinarily be excluded. Of course, Congress, in enacting such legislation as we have here, can save alternative or supplemental state remedies by express terms, or by some clear implication, if it sees fit.

On the basis of the allegations, the petitioners could have presented this grievance to the National Labor Relations Board. The respondents were subject to being summoned before that body to justify their conduct. We think the grievance was not subject to litigation in the tribunals of the State.

Judgment affirmed.[19]

. . . . .

RETAIL CLERKS INTERNATIONAL ASSOCIATION, LOCAL 1625 AFL-CIO v. SCHERMERHORN
Supreme Court of the United States, 375 U.S. 96 (1963).

Mr. Justice DOUGLAS delivered the opinion of the Court.

The sole question in the case is the one we set down for reargument in 373 U.S. 746, 747-748: "whether the Florida courts, rather than solely the National Labor Relations Board, are tribunals with jurisdiction to enforce the State's prohibition" against an "agency shop" clause in a collective bargaining agreement.

In this case the union and the employer negotiated a collective bargaining agreement that contained an "agency shop" clause providing that the employees covered by the contract who chose not to join the union were required "to pay as a condition of employment, an initial service fee and monthly service fees" to the union. Non-union employees brought suit in a Florida court to have the agency shop clause declared illegal, for an injunction against enforcement of it, and for an accounting. The Florida Supreme Court held that this negotiated and executed union-security agreement violates the "right to work" provision of the Florida Constitution and that the state courts have jurisdiction to afford a remedy. 141 S.2d 269.

We agree with that view.

While § 8(a)(3) of the Taft-Hartley Act provides[A] that it is not an unfair labor

---

[19]In San Diego Building Trades Council v. Garmon, 359 U.S. 236 (1959), the union picketed the employer to exert pressure on the employer to retain in his employ only people who were already members of the union or who applied for membership in the union within thirty days after being hired. When the employer sought relief, the National Labor Relations Board declined to exercise jurisdiction over the matter; so the employer brought suit against the union in the State courts of California. The California Supreme Court, knowing of the National Labor Relations Board's refusal to hear the employer's cause, granted the employer an injunction and awarded him damages. The United States Supreme Court granted certiorari and reversed the California Court's decision. The United States Supreme Court relied on Garner v. Teamsters, Local No. 776, and held that "when an activity is arguably subject to § 7 or § 8 of the Act [Wagner Act as amended by the Taft-Hartley Act], the States as well as the federal courts must defer to the exclusive competence of the National Labor Relations Board if the danger of state interference with national policy is to be averted." Hence it appears that the ball fell between the players.

[A]Section 8 (a)(3) [which is also found at p. 341, *infra*], reads as follows:
   "It shall be an unfair labor practice for an employer . . . by discrimination in regard

practice for an employer and a union to require membership in a union as a condition of employment provided the specified conditions are met, § 14(b) [of the Taft-Hartley act] (61 Stat. 151, 29 U.S.C. § 164(b) provides:

> "Nothing in this Act shall be construed as authorizing the execution of application of agreements requiring membership in a labor organization as a condition of employment in any State or Territory in which such execution or application is prohibited by State or Territorial law."

We start from the premise that, while Congress could preempt as much or as little of this interstate field as it chose, it would be odd to construe § 14 (b) as permitting a State to prohibit the agency clause but barring it from implementing its own law with sanctions of the kind involved here.

Section 14 (b) came into the law in 1947, some years after the Wagner Act. The latter did not bar as a matter of federal law an agency-shop agreement. Section 8 (a)(3) of the Taft-Hartley Act also allowed it, saying that "nothing in this Act, or in any other Statute of the United States, shall preclude" one.

By the time § 14 (b) was written into the Act, twelve States had statutes or constitutional provisions outlawing or restricting the closed shop and related devices—a state power which we sustained in Lincoln Union v. Northwestern Co., 335 U.S. 525. These laws—about which Congress seems to have been well informed during the 1947 debates—had a wide variety of sanctions, including injunctions, damage suits, and criminal penalties. In 1947 Congress did not outlaw union-security agreements *per se;* but it did add new conditions, which, as presently provided in § 8 (a)(3), require that there be a 30-day waiting period before any employee is forced into a union, that the union in question is the appropriate representative of the employees, and that an employer not discriminate against an employee if he has reasonable grounds for believing that membership in the union was not available to the employee on a nondiscriminatory basis

---

to hire or tenure of employment or any term or condition of employment to encourage or discourage membership in any labor organization: *Provided, That nothing in this Act, or in any other statute of the United States, shall preclude an employer from making an agreement with a labor organization (not established, maintained, or assisted by any action defined in section 8 (a) of this Act as an unfair labor practice) to require as a condition of employment membership therein on or after the thirtieth day following the beginning of such employment or the effective date of such agreement, whichever is the later,* (i) if such labor organization is the representative of the employees as provided in section 9 (a), in the appropriate collective-bargaining unit covered by such agreement when made; and (ii) unless following an election held as provided in section 9 (e) within one year preceding the effective date of such agreement, the Board shall have certified that at least a majority of the employees eligible to vote in such election have voted to rescind the authority of such labor organization to make such an agreement. *Provided further,* That no employer shall justify any discrimination against an employee for nonmembership in a labor organization (A) if he has reasonable grounds for believing that such membership was not available to the employee on the same terms and conditions generally applicable to other members, or (B) if he has reasonable grounds for believing that membership was denied or terminated for reasons other than the failure of the employee to tender the periodic dues and the initiation fees uniformly required as a condition of acquiring or retaining membership." 61 Stat. 140-141, as amended, 65 Stat. 601, 73 Stat. 525, 29 U.S.C. (Supp. IV) § 158 (a)(3). [Italics added for emphasis, ed.]

or that the employee's membership was denied or terminated for reasons other than failure to meet union-shop requirements as to dues and fees. In other words, Congress undertook pervasive regulation of union-security agreements, raising in the minds of many whether it thereby preempted the field under the decision in Hill v. Florida, 325 U.S. 538, and put such agreements beyond state control. That is one reason why a section, which later became § 14 (b), appeared in the House bill—a provision described in the House Report as making clear and unambiguous the purpose of Congress not to preempt the field. That purpose was restated by the House Conference Report in explaining § 14 (b). Senator Taft in the Senate debates stated that § 14 (b) was to continue the policy of the Wagner Act and avoid federal interference with state laws in this field. As to the Wagner Act he stated, "But that did not in any way prohibit *the enforcement of State laws* which already prohibited closed shops." (Italics added.) He went on to say, "That has been the law ever since that time. It was the law of the Senate bill; and in putting in this express provision from the House bill, [§ 14 (b)] we in no way change the bill as passed by the Senate of the United States." 93 Cong. Rec. 6520, 2 Leg. Hist. of the Labor Management Relations Act, 1947, 1597.

In light of the wording of § 14(b) and this legislative history, we conclude that Congress in 1947 did not deprive the States of any and all power to enforce their laws restricting the execution and enforcement of union-security agreements. Since it is plain that Congress left the States free to legislate in that field, we can only assume that it intended to leave unaffected the power to enforce those laws. Otherwise, the reservation which Senator Taft felt to be so critical would become empty and largely meaningless.

As already noted, under § 8 (a)(3) a union-security agreement is permissible, for example, if the union represents the employees as provided in § 9 (a)[20] (subject to rescission of the authority to make the agreement as provided in § 8 (a)(3)). Those are federal standards entrusted by Congress to the Labor Board. Yet even if the union-security agreement clears all federal hurdles, the States by reason of § 14 (b) have the final say and may outlaw it. There is thus conflict between state and federal law; but it is a conflict sanctioned by Congress with directions to give the right of way to state laws barring the execution and enforcement of union-security agreements.   . . .

.   .   .   .

Congress   . . .   [in this area] chose to abandon any search for uniformity in dealing with the problems of state laws barring the execution and application of agreements authorized by § 14 (b) and decided to suffer a medley of attitudes and philosophies on the subject.

As a result of § 14(b), there will arise a wide variety of situations presenting problems of the accommodation of state and federal jurisdiction in the union security field.   . . .

.   .   .   .

[The Supreme Court then affirmed the decision of the Florida Supreme Court that it had the power (1) to declare null and void the agency shop provision of the collective

---

[20]Section 9(a) of the Wagner Act, as amended by the Taft-Hartley Act (Appendix, *infra*, p. 343), sets forth the procedures by which a labor organization can become the exclusive bargaining agent of employees in an appropriate bargaining unit.

bargaining agreement between the employer and its employees and (2) to grant the nonunion employees the money they had been forced to contribute to the union under the agency shop clause of the collective bargaining agreement.]

Mr. Justice GOLDBERG took no part in the consideration or decision of this case.

UNION TACTICS AND FEDERAL-STATE POLICIES

SENN v. TILE LAYERS PROTECTIVE UNION
Supreme Court of the United States, 301 U.S. 468 (1937).

Mr. Justice BRANDEIS delivered the opinion of the Court.

This case presents the question whether the provisions of the Wisconsin Labor Code which authorize giving publicity to labor disputes, declare peaceful picketing and patrolling lawful and prohibit granting of an injunction against such conduct, violate, as here construed and applied, the due process clause or equal protection clause of the Fourteenth Amendment.

The Labor Code occupies sections 103.51 to 103.63 of the Wisconsin Statute, 1935 (Wis. Laws, 1931, c. 376; Laws 1935, c. 551, § 5). But only the following provisions of section 103.53 are directly involved on this appeal:

"(1) The following acts, whether performed singly or in concert, shall be legal: . . .

"(e) Giving publicity to or obtaining or communicating information regarding the existence of, or the facts involved in, any dispute, whether by advertising, speaking, patrolling any public street or any place where any person or persons may lawfully be, without intimidation or coercion, or by any other method not involving fraud, violence, breach of the peace, or threat thereof. . . .

"(1) Peaceful picketing or patrolling, whether engaged in singly or in numbers, shall be legal.

"(2) No court, nor any judge or judges thereof, shall have jurisdiction to issue any restraining order or temporary or permanent injunction which, in specific or general terms, prohibits any person or persons from doing, whether singly or in concert, any of the foregoing acts."

On December 28, 1935, Senn brought this suit in the circuit court of Milwaukee county, against Tile Layers Protective Union, Local No. 5, Tile Layers Helpers Union, Local No. 47, and their business agents, seeking an injunction to restrain picketing, and particularly "publishing, stating or proclaiming that the plaintiff is unfair to organized labor or to the defendant unions"; and also to restrain some other acts which have since been discontinued, and are not now material. The defendants answered; and the case was heard upon extensive evidence. The trial court found the following facts.

The journeymen tile layers at Milwaukee were, to a large extent, members of Tile Layers Protective Union, Local No. 5, and the helpers, members of the Tile Layers Helpers Union, Local No. 47. Senn was engaged at Milwaukee in the tile contracting business under the name of "Paul Senn & Co., Tile Contracting." His business was a small one, conducted, in the main, from his residence, with a show-room elsewhere. He employed one or two journeymen tile layers and one or two helpers, depending upon the amount of work he had contracted to do at the time. But, working with his own hands with tools of the trade, he performed personally on the jobs much work of a character commonly done by a tile layer or a helper. Neither Senn, nor any of his employees, was at the time this suit was begun a member of either union, and neither had any contractual relations with them. Indeed, Senn could not become a member of the tile layers union, since its constitution and rules require, among other things, that a journeyman tile setter shall have acquired his practical experience through an apprenticeship of not less than three years, and Senn had not served such an apprenticeship.

For some years the tile laying industry had been in a demoralized state because of lack of building operations; and members of the union had been in competition with nonunion tile layers and helpers in their effort to secure work. The tile contractors by whom members of the unions were employed had entered into collective bargaining agreements with the unions governing wages, hours, and working conditions. The wages paid by the union contractors had for some time been higher than those paid by Senn to his employees.

Because of the peculiar composition of the industry, which consists of employers with small numbers of employees, the unions had found it necessary for the protection of the individual rights of their members in the prosecution of their trade to require all employees agreeing to conduct a union shop to assent to the following provision:

"Article III. It is definitely understood that no individual, member of a partnership or corporation engaged in the Tile Contracting Business shall work with the tools or act as Helper but that the installation of all materials claimed by the party of the second part as listed under the caption 'Classification of Work' in this agreement, shall be done by journeymen of Tile Layers Protective Union Local #5."

The unions endeavored to induce Senn to become a union contractor; and requested him to execute an agreement in form substantially identical with that entered into by the Milwaukee contractors who employ union men. Senn expressed a willingness to execute the agreement provided article III was eliminated. The union declared that this was impossible; that the inclusion of the provision was essential to the unions' interest in maintaining wage standards and spreading work among their members; and, moreover, that to eliminate article III from the contract with Senn would discriminate against existing union contractors, all of whom had signed agreements containing the article. As the unions declared its elimination impossible, Senn refused to sign the agreement and unionize his shop. Because of his refusal, the unions picketed his place of business. The picketing was peaceful, without violence, and without any unlawful act. The evidence was that the pickets carried one banner with the inscription "P. Senn Tile Company is unfair to the Tile Layers Protective Union," another with the inscription "Let the Union tile layer install your tile work."

The trial court denied the injunction and dismissed the bill. On the findings made, it ruled that the controversy was "a labor dispute" within the meaning of section 103.62; that the picketing, done solely in furtherance of the dispute, was "lawful" under section 103.53; that it was not unlawful for the defendants "to advise, notify or persuade, without fraud, violence or threat thereof, any person or persons, of the existence of said labor dispute; . . .

"That the agreement submitted by the defendants to the plaintiff, setting forth terms and conditions prevailing in that portion of the industry which is unionized, is sought by the defendants for the purpose of promoting their welfare and enhancing their own interests in their trade and craft as workers in the industry.

"That Article III of said agreement is a reasonable and lawful rule adopted by the defendants out of the necessities of employment within the industry and for the protection of themselves as workers and craftsmen in the industry."

Senn appealed to the Supreme Court of the state, which affirmed the judgment of the trial court and denied a motion for rehearing, two judges dissenting. 222 Wis. 383, 268 N.W. 270, 274, 872. The case is here on appeal.

. . . .

. . . The question for our decision is whether the statute, as applied to the facts found, took Senn's liberty or property or denied him equal protection of the laws in violation of the Fourteenth Amendment. Senn does not claim broadly that the Federal Constitution prohibits a state from authorizing publicity and peaceful picketing. His claim of invalidity is rested on the fact that he refused to unionize his shop solely because the union insisted upon the retention of article III. He contends that the right to work in his business with his own hands is a right guaranteed by the Fourteenth Amendment and that the state may not authorize unions to employ publicity and picketing to induce him to refrain from exercising it.

The unions concede that Senn, so long as he conducts a nonunion shop, has the right to work with his hands and tools. He may do so, as freely as he may work his employees longer hours and at lower wages than the union rules permit. He may bid for contracts at a low figure based upon low wages and long hours. But the unions contend that, since Senn's exercise of the right to do so is harmful to the interests of their members, they may seek by legal means to induce him to agree to unionize his shop and to refrain from exercising his right to work with his own hands. The judgment of the highest court of the state establishes that both the means employed and the end sought by the unions are legal under its law. The question for our determination is whether either the means or the end sought is forbidden by the Federal Constitution.

. . . Clearly the means which the statute authorizes—picketing and publicity— are not prohibited by the Fourteenth Amendment. Members of a union might, without special statutory authorization by a state, make known the facts of a labor dispute, for freedom of speech is guaranteed by the Federal Constitution. The state may, in the exercise of its police power, regulate the methods and means of publicity as well as the use of public streets. If the end sought by the unions is not forbidden by the Federal Constitution, the state may authorize working men to seek to attain it by combining as pickets, just as it permits capitalists and employers to combine in other ways to attain their desired economic ends. The Legislature of Wisconsin has declared that "peaceful picketing and patrolling" on the public streets and places shall be permissible "whether engaged in singly or in numbers" provided this is done "without intimidation or coercion" and free from "fraud, violence, breach of the peace, or threat thereof." The statute provides that the picketing must be peaceful; and that term as used implies not only absence of violence, but absence of any unlawful act. It precludes the intimidation of customers. It precludes any form of physical obstruction or interference with the plaintiff's business. It authorizes giving publicity to the existence of the dispute "whether by advertising, patrolling any public streets or places where any person or persons may lawfully be"; but precludes misrepresentation of the facts of the controversy. . . . Inherently, the means authorized are clearly unobjectionable. In declaring such picketing permissible Wisconsin has put this means of publicity on a par with advertisements in the press.

. . . As the Supreme Court of Wisconsin said:

"Each of the contestants is desirous of the advantage of doing the business in the community where he or they operate. He is not obliged to yield to the persuasion exercised upon him by respondents. . . . The respondents do not question that it is appellant's right to run his own business and earn his living in any lawful manner which he chooses to adopt. What they are doing is asserting their rights under the acts of the Legislature for the purpose of enhancing their opportunity to acquire work for themselves and those whom they represent. . . . The respondents' act of peaceful picketing is a lawful form of appeal to the public to turn its patronage from appellant to the concerns in which the welfare of the members of the unions is bound up."

The unions acted, and had the right to act as they did, to protect the interests of their members against the harmful effect upon them of Senn's action. . . . Because his action was harmful, the fact that none of Senn's employees was a union member, or sought the union's aid, is immaterial.

The laws of Wisconsin, as declared by its highest court, permit unions to endeavor to induce an employer, when unionizing his shop, to agree to refrain from working in his business with his own hands—so to endeavor although none of his employees is a member of a union. Whether it was wise for the state to permit the unions to do so is a question of its public policy—not our concern. The Fourteenth Amendment does not prohibit it.

Affirmed.

Mr. Justice BUTLER dissenting.

Plaintiff lives and works in Milwaukee. Since the latter part of 1931, he has been engaged in performing small tile laying jobs. He has personally performed almost half the manual labor required. He usually employs a tile setter and helper; occasionally he has more than one of each. He has never been a member of the tile layers union. Though a competent mechanic in that trade, he is excluded from membership because he takes contracts and because he has not served the apprenticeship required by union rules. In 1935 he had about forty jobs. His net income was $1,500 of which $750 was attributed to his own labor. The balance, constituting his profit as contractor, was not enough to support him and family.

The clauses of the Fourteenth Amendment invoked by plaintiff are: "No State shall . . . deprive any person of life, liberty, or property without due process of law; nor deny to any person within its jurisdiction the equal protection of the laws." Our decisions have made it everywhere known that these provisions forbid state action which would take from the individual the right to engage in common occupations of life, and that they assure equality of opportunity to all under like circumstances. Lest the importance or wisdom of these great declarations be forgotten or neglected, there should be frequent recurrence to decisions of this court that expound and apply them.

. . . .

"Included in the right of personal liberty and the right of private property—partaking of the nature of each—is the right to make contracts for the acquisition of property. Chief among such contracts is that of personal employment by which labor and other services are exchanged for money or other forms of property. If this right be struck down or arbitrarily interfered with, there is a substantial impairment of liberty in the long-established constitutional sense. The right is as essential to the laborer as to the capitalist, to the poor as to the rich; for the vast majority of persons have no other honest way to begin to acquire property, save by working for money." Coppage v. Kansas, 236 U.S. 1, 14.

. . . .

For, the very idea that one man may be compelled to hold his life, or the means of living, or any material right essential to the enjoyment of life, at the mere will of another, seems to be intolerable in any country where freedom prevails, as being the essence of slavery itself." Yick Wo v. Hopkins, 118 U.S. 356, 370.

. . . .

The judgment of the state court, here affirmed, violates a principle of fundamental law: That no man may be compelled to hold his life or the means of living at the mere will of others. . . . The state statute, construed to make lawful the employment of the means here shown to deprive plaintiff of his right to work or to make lawful the picketing carried on in this case, is repugnant to the due process and equal protection clauses of the Fourteenth Amendment. . . .

I am of opinion that the judgment should be reversed.

Mr. Justice VAN DEVANTER, Mr. Justice McREYNOLDS, and Mr. Justice SUTHERLAND join in this dissent.

THORNHILL v. ALABAMA
Supreme Court of the United States, 310 U.S. 88 (1940).

[The petitioner, Thornhill, was convicted in the Circuit Court of Tuscaloosa County, Alabama upon a complaint phrased substantially in the words of Section 3448 of the Alabama Code which provides:

"Loitering or picketing forbidden.—Any person or persons, who, without a just cause or legal excuse therefor, go near to or loiter about the premises or place of business of any other person, firm, corporation, or association of people, engaged in a lawful business, for the purpose, or with the intent of influencing, or inducing other persons not to trade with, buy from, sell to, have business dealings with, or be employed by such persons, firm, corporation, or association, or who picket the works or place of business of such other persons, firms, corporations, or associations of persons, for the purpose of hindering, delaying, or interfering with or injuring any lawful business or enterprise of another, shall be guilty of a misdemeanor; but nothing herein shall prevent any person from soliciting trade or business for a competitive business."

The testimony showed that during a strike the employer, Brown Wood Preserving Company, scheduled the resumption of operations, and, on the day operations were to resume, Thornhill and six or eight others set up a picket line at the plant and told approaching employees that they were on strike and did not want anyone to return to work. The testimony further showed that Thornhill did not threaten or put any of the employees in fear, but that at least one employee, upon being met by Thornhill returned to his house rather than enter the plant.

Thornhill claimed that the Alabama statute violated his rights under the First Amendment to the United States Constitution, but the Alabama courts, relying on two previous Alabama decisions, upheld his conviction. The United States Supreme Court granted certiorari.]

Mr. Justice MURPHY delivered the opinion of the Court.

. . .

The freedom of speech and of the press, which are secured by the First Amendment against abridgment by the United States, are among the fundamental personal rights and liberties which are secured to all persons by the Fourteenth Amendment against abridgment by a State.

The safeguarding of these rights to the ends that men may speak as they think on matters vital to them and that falsehoods may be exposed through the processes of education and discussion is essential to free government. Those who won our independence had confidence in the power of free and fearless reasoning and communication of ideas to discover and spread political and economic truth. Noxious doctrines in those fields may be refuted and their evil averted by the courageous exercise of the right of free discussion. Abridgment of freedom of speech and of the press, however, impairs those opportunities for public education that are essential to effective exercise of the power of correcting error through the processes of popular government. . . . Mere legislative preference for one rather than another means for combatting substantive evils, therefore, may well prove an inadequate foundation on which to rest regulations which are aimed at or in their operation diminish the effective exercise of rights so necessary to the maintenance of democratic institutions. It is imperative that, when the effective exercise of these rights is claimed to be abridged, the courts should "weigh the circumstances" and "appraise the substantiality of the reasons advanced" in support of the challenged regulations. Schneider v. State, 308 U.S. 147, 161, 162.

. . .

We think that § 3448 is invalid on its face.

The freedom of speech and of the press guaranteed by the Constitution embraces at the least the liberty to discuss publicly and truthfully all matters of public concern without previous restraint or fear of subsequent punishment. The exigencies of the colonial period and the efforts to secure freedom from oppressive administration developed a broadened conception of these liberties as adequate to supply the public need for information and education with respect to the significant issues of the times. The Continental Congress in its letter sent to the Inhabitants of Quebec (October 26, 1774) referred to the "five great rights" and said: "The last right we shall mention, regards the freedom of the press. The importance of this consists, besides the advancement of truth, science, morality, and arts in general, in its diffusion of liberal sentiments on the administration of Government, its ready communication of thoughts between subjects, and its consequential promotion of union among them, whereby oppressive officers are ashamed or intimidated, into more honourable and just modes of conducting affairs." Journal of the Continental Congress, 1904 ed., vol. I, pp. 104, 108. Freedom of discussion, if it would fulfill its historic function in this nation, must embrace all issues about which information is needed or appropriate to enable the members of society to cope with the exigencies of their period.

In the circumstances of our times the dissemination of information concerning the facts of a labor dispute must be regarded as within that area of free discussion that is guaranteed by the Constitution. . . . See Senn v. Tile Layers Union, 301 U.S. 468, 478. It is recognized now that satisfactory hours and wages and working conditions in industry and a bargaining position which makes these possible have an importance which is not less than the interests of those in the business or industry directly concerned. The health of the present generation and of those as yet unborn may depend on these matters, and the practices in a single factory may have economic repercussions upon a whole region and affect widespread systems of marketing. The merest glance at state and federal legislation on the subject demonstrates the force of the argument that labor relations are not matters of mere local or private concern. Free discussion concerning the conditions in industry and the causes of labor disputes appears to us indispensable to the effective and intelligent use of the processes of popular government to shape the destiny of modern industrial society. The issues raised by regulations, such as are challenged here, infringing upon the right of employees effectively to inform the public of the facts of a labor dispute are part of this larger problem. We concur in the observation of Mr. Justice Brandeis, speaking for the Court in *Senn's* case (301 U.S. at 478): "Members of a union might, without special statutory authorization by a State, make known the facts of a labor dispute, for freedom of speech is guaranteed by the Federal Constitution."

It is true that the rights of employers and employees to conduct their economic affairs and to compete with others for a share in the products of industry are subject to modification or qualification in the interests of the society in which they exist. This is but an instance of the power of the State to set the limits of permissible contest open to industrial combatants. . . . It does not follow that the State in dealing with the evils arising from industrial disputes may impair the effective exercise of the right to discuss freely industrial relations which are matters of public concern. A contrary conclusion could be used to support abridgment of freedom of speech and of the press concerning almost every matter of importance to society.

The range of activities proscribed by § 3448, whether characterized as picketing or loitering or otherwise, embraces nearly every practicable, effective means whereby those interested—including the employees directly affected—may enlighten the public on the nature and causes of a labor dispute. The safeguarding of these means is essential to the securing of an informed and educated public opinion with respect to a matter which is of public concern. It may be that effective exercise of the means of advancing public knowledge may persuade some of those reached to refrain from entering into advantageous relations with the business establishment which is the scene of the dispute. Every expression of opinion on matters that are important has the potentiality of inducing action in the interests of one rather than another group in society. But the group in power at any moment may not impose penal sanctions on peaceful and truthful discussion of matters of public interest merely on a showing that others may thereby be persuaded to take action inconsistent with its interests. Abridgment of the liberty of such discussion can be justified only where the clear danger of substantive evils arises under circumstances affording no opportunity to test the merits of ideas by competition for acceptance in the market of public opinion. We hold that the danger of injury to an industrial concern is neither so serious nor so imminent as to justify the sweeping proscription of freedom of discussion embodied in § 3448.

. . . . .

Reversed.

Mr. Justice McREYNOLDS is of opinion that the judgment below should be affirmed.

INTERNATIONAL BROTHERHOOD OF TEAMSTERS, ETC., UNION LOCAL 309 v. HANKE
Supreme Court of the United States, 339 U.S. 470 (1950).

Mr. Justice FRANKFURTER announced the judgment of the Court and an opinion in which THE CHIEF JUSTICE, Mr. Justice JACKSON and Mr. Justice BURTON all concurred.

These two cases raise the same issues and are therefore disposed of in a single opinion. The question is this: Does the Fourteenth Amendment of the Constitution bar a State from use of the injunction to prohibit the picketing of a business conducted by the owner himself without employees in order to secure compliance by him with a demand to become a union shop?

In No. 309, respondents A. E. Hanke and his three sons, as copartners, engaged in the business of repairing automobiles, dispensing gasoline and automobile accessories, and selling used automobiles in Seattle. They conducted their entire enterprise themselves, without any employees. At the time the senior Hanke purchased the business in June, 1946, which had theretofore been conducted as a union shop, he became a member of Local 309 of the International Brotherhood of Teamsters, which includes in its membership persons employed and engaged in the gasoline service station business in Seattle. Accordingly, the Hankes continued to display in their show window the union shop card of their predecessor. Local 309 also included the Hankes' business in the list of firms for which it urged patronage in advertisements published in the Washington organ of the International Brotherhood of Teamsters, distributed weekly to members. As a result of the use of the union shop card and these advertisements, the Hankes received union partonage which they otherwise would not have had.

Automobile Drivers and Demonstrators Local 882, closely affiliated with Local 309 and also chartered by the International Brotherhood of Teamsters, includes in its membership persons engaged in the business of selling used cars and used car salesmen in Seattle. This union negotiated an agreement in 1946 with the Independent Automobile Dealers Association of Seattle, to which the Hankes did not belong, providing that used car lots be closed by 6 p. m. on weekdays and all day on Saturdays, Sundays and eight specified holidays. This agreement was intended to be applicable to 115 used car dealers in Seattle, all except ten of which were self-employers with no employees.

It was the practice of the Hankes to remain open nights, weekends and holidays. In January, 1948, representatives of both Locals called upon the Hankes to urge them to respect the limitation on business hours in the agreement or give up their union shop card. The Hankes refused to consent to abide by the agreement, claiming that it would be impossible to continue in business and do so, and surrendered the union shop card.

The name of the Hankes' business was thereafter omitted from the list published by Local 309 in its advertisements.

Soon afterwards the Local sent a single picket to patrol up and down peacefully in front of the Hankes' business between the hours of 8:30 a. m. and 5 p. m., carrying a "sandwich sign" with the words "Union People Look for the Union Shop Card" and a facsimile of the shop card. The picket also wrote down the automobile license numbers of the Hankes' patrons. As a result of the picketing, the Hankes' business fell off heavily and drivers for supply houses refused to deliver parts and other needed materials. The Hankes had to use their own truck to call for the materials necessary to carry on their business.

To restrain this conduct, the Hankes brought suit against Local 309 and its officers. The trial court granted a permanent injunction against the picketing and awarded the Hankes a judgment of $250, the sum stipulated by the parties to be the amount of damage occasioned by the picketing. The Supreme Court of Washington affirmed. 33 Wash. 2d 646, 207 P. 2d 206.

The background in No. 364 [the Cline case, the second of the two cases in this opinion] is similar. . . .

.   .   .   .   .

In both these cases we granted certiorari to consider claims of infringement of the right of freedom of speech as guaranteed by the Due Process Clause of the Fourteenth Amendment. 338 U.S. 903.

Here, as in Hughes v. Superior Court, 339 U.S. 460, we must start with the fact that while picketing has an ingredient of communication it cannot dogmatically be equated with the constitutionally protected freedom of speech. Our decisions reflect recognition that picketing is "indeed a hybrid." Freund, On Understanding the Supreme Court 18 (1949). See also Jaffe, In Defense of the Supreme Court's Picketing Doctrine, 41 Mich. L. Rev. 1037 (1943). The effort in the cases has been to strike a balance between the constitutional protection of the element of communication in picketing and "the power of the State to set the limits of permissible contest open to industrial combatants." Thornhill v. Alabama, 310 U.S. 88, 104. A State's judgment on striking such a balance is of course subject to the limitations of the Fourteenth Amendment. Embracing as such a judgment does, however, a State's social and economic policies, which in turn depend on knowledge and appraisal of local social and economic factors, such judgment on these matters comes to this Court bearing a weighty title of respect.

These two cases emphasize the nature of a problem that is presented by our duty of sitting in judgment on a State's judgment in striking the balance that has to be struck when a State decides not to keep hands off these industrial contests. Here we have a glaring instance of the interplay of competing social-economic interests and viewpoints. Unions obviously are concerned not to have union standards undermined by non-union shops. This interest penetrates into self-employer shops. On the other hand, some of our profoundest thinkers from Jefferson to Brandeis have stressed the importance to a democratic society of encouraging self-employer economic units as a counter-movement to what are deemed to be the dangers inherent in excessive concentration of economic power. "There is a widespread belief . . . that the true prosperity of our past came not from big business, but through the courage, the energy and the resourcefulness of small men . . . and that only through participation by the many in the responsibilities and determinations of business, can Americans secure the moral and intellectual development which is essential to the maintenance of liberty." Mr. Justice Brandeis, dissenting in Liggett Co. v. Lee, 288 U.S. 517, 541, 580.

Whether to prefer the union or a self-employer in such a situation, or to seek partial recognition of both interests, and, if so, by what means to secure such accommodation, obviously presents to a State serious problems. There are no sure answers, and the best available solution is likely to be experimental and tentative, and always subject to the control of the popular will. That the solution of these perplexities is a challenge to wisdom and not a command of the Constitution is the significance of Senn v. Tile Layers Protective Union, 301 U.S. 468. Senn, a self-employed tile layer who occasionally hired other tile layers to assist him, was picketed when he refused to yield to the union demand that he no longer work himself at his trade. The Wisconsin court found the situation to be within the State's anti-injunction statute and denied relief. In rejecting the claim that the restriction upon Senn's freedom was a denial of his liberty under the Fourteenth Amendment, this Court held that it lay in the domain of policy for Wisconsin to permit the picketing: "Whether it was wise for the State to permit the unions to do so is a question of its public policy—not our concern." 301 U.S. at 481.

This conclusion was based on the Court's recognition that it was Wisconsin, not the Fourteenth Amendment, which put such picketing as a "means of publicity on a par with advertisements in the press." 301 U.S. at 479. If Wisconsin could permit such picketing as a matter of policy it must have been equally free as a matter of policy to choose not to permit it and therefore not to "put this means of publicity on a par with advertisements in the press." If Wisconsin could have deemed it wise to withdraw from the union the permission which this Court found outside the ban of the Fourteenth Amendment, such action by Washington cannot be inside that ban.

Washington here concluded that, even though the relief afforded the Hankes and Cline entailed restriction upon communication that the unions sought to convey through picketing, it was more important to safeguard the value which the State placed upon self-employers, leaving all other channels of communication open to the union. The relatively small interest of the unions considerably influenced the balance that was struck. Of 115 used car dealers in Seattle maintaining union standards, all but ten were self-employers with no employees. "From this fact," so we are informed by the Supreme Court of Washington, "the conclusion seems irresistible that the union's interest in the welfare of a mere handful of members (of whose working conditions no complaint at all is made) is far outweighed by the interests of individual proprietors and the people of the community as a whole, to the end that little businessmen and property owners shall be free from dictation as to business policy by an outside group having but a relatively small and indirect interest in such policy." 33 Wash. 2d at 659, 207 P. 2d at 213.

We are, needless to say, fully aware of the contentious nature of these views. It is not our business even remotely to hint at agreement or disagreement with what has commended itself to the State of Washington, or even to intimate that all the relevant considerations are exposed in the conclusions reached by the Washington court. They seldom are in this field, so deceptive and opaque are the elements of these problems. That is precisely what is meant by recognizing that they are within the domain of a State's public policy. Because there is lack of agreement as to the relevant factors and divergent interpretations of their meaning, as well as differences in assessing what is the short and what is the long view, the clash of fact and opinion should be resolved by the democratic process and not by the judicial sword. Invalidation here would mean denial of power to the Congress as well as to the forty-eight States.

It is not for us to pass judgment on cases not now before us. But when one considers that issues not unlike those that are here have been similarly viewed by other States and by the Congress of the United States, we cannot conclude that Washington, in holding the picketing in these cases to be for an unlawful object, has struck a balance so inconsistent with rooted traditions of a free people that it must be found an unconstitutional choice. Mindful as we are that a phase of picketing is communication, we cannot find that Washington has offended the Constitution.

· · · ·

Affirmed.

Mr. Justice CLARK concurs in the result.

Mr. Justice BLACK dissents for substantially the reasons given in his dissent in Carpenters & Joiners Union v. Ritter's Cafe, 315 U.S. 722, 729-32.

Mr. Justice DOUGLAS took no part in the consideration or decision of these cases.

[The dissenting opinion of Mr. Justice Minton (Mr. Justice Reed concurring) is omitted.]

UNIONISM AND THE WHOLE SOCIETY

UNRESOLVED LIMITS ON UNION POWER

NATIONAL WOODWORK MANUFACTURERS ASSOCIATION
v. NATIONAL LABOR RELATIONS BOARD
Supreme Court of the United States, 386 U.S. 612 (1967).

Mr. Justice BRENNAN delivered the opinion of the Court.

· · · ·

Frouge Corporation, a Bridgeport, Connecticut, concern, was the general contractor on a housing project in Philadelphia. Frouge had a collective bargaining agreement with the Carpenters' International Union under which Frouge agreed to be bound by the rules and regulations agreed upon by local unions with contractors in areas in which Frouge had jobs. Frouge was therefore subject to the provisions of a collective bargaining agreement between the Union and an organization of Philadelphia contractors, the General Building Contractors Association, Inc. A sentence in a provision of that agreement entitled Rule 17 provides that " . . . No member of this District Council will handle . . . any doors . . . which have been fitted prior to being furnished on the job . . . " Frouge's Philadelphia project called for 3,600 doors. Customarily, before the doors could be hung on such projects, "blank" or "blind" doors would be mortised for the knob, routed for the hinges, and beveled to make them fit between jambs. These are tasks traditionally performed in the Philadelphia area by the carpenters employed on the jobsite. However, precut and prefitted doors ready to hang may be purchased from door manufacturers. Although Frouge's contract and job specifications did not call for premachined doors, and "blank" or "blind" doors could have been ordered, Frouge contracted for the purchase of premachined doors from a Pennsylvania door manufacturer which is a member of the National Woodwork Manufacturers Association, petitioner in No. 110 and respondent in No. 111. The Union ordered its carpenter members not to hang the doors when they arrived at the jobsite. Frouge thereupon withdrew the prefabricated doors and substituted "blank" doors which were fitted and cut by its carpenters on the jobsite.

The National Woodwork Manufacturers Association and another filed charges with the National Labor Relations Board against the Union alleging that by including the "will not handle" sentence of Rule 17 in the collective bargaining agreement the Union committed the unfair labor practice under § 8(e) of entering into an "agreement . . . whereby [the] employer . . . agrees to cease or refrain from handling . . . any of the products of any other employer . . . ," and alleging further that in enforcing the sentence against Frouge, the Union committed the unfair labor practice under § 8(b)(4)(B) of "forcing or requiring any person to cease using . . . the products of any other . . . manufacturer. . . . "[21] The National Labor Relations Board dismissed the charges, 149 N. L. R. B. 646. The Board adopted the findings of the Trial Examiner that the "will not handle" sentence in Rule 17 was language used by the parties to protect and preserve cutting out and fitting as unit work to be performed by the jobsite carpenters. The Board also adopted the holding of the Trial Examiner that both the sentence of Rule 17 itself and its maintenance against Frouge were therefore "primary" activity outside the prohibitions of §§ 8(e) and 8(b)(4)(B). . . .

The Court of Appeals for the Seventh Circuit reversed the Board in this respect. 354 F. 2d 594, 599. The court held that the "will not handle" agreement violated § 8(e) without regard to any "primary" or "secondary" objective, and remanded to the Board with instructions to enter an order accordingly. In the court's view, the sentence was designed to effect a product boycott . . . and Congress meant, in enacting § 8(e) and § 8(b)(4)(B), to prohibit such agreements and conduct forcing employers to enter into them.

The Court of Appeals sustained, however, the dismissal of the § 8(b)(4)(B) charge. The court agreed with the Board that the Union's conduct as to Frouge involved only a primary dispute with it and held that the conduct was therefore not prohibited by that section but expressly protected by the proviso "[t]hat nothing contained in this clause (B) shall be construed to make unlawful, where not otherwise unlawful, any primary strike or primary picketing. . . . " 354 F. 2d, at 597.

We granted certiorari on the petition of the Woodwork Manufacturers Association in No. 110 and on the petition of the Board in No. 111 . . . . We affirm in No. 110 [the dismissal of the § 8(b)(4)(B) charge], and reverse in No. 111 [the charge brought by the N.L.R.B. against the Union under § 8(e)].

[21]Sections 8(e) and 8(b)(4)(B) of the Labor Management Reporting and Disclosure Act (Landrum-Griffin), which added to and amended the Taft-Hartley Act, are reproduced in full in the Appendix, *infra,* pp. 348-349.

I.

.   .   .   .

The Woodwork Manufacturers Association and *amici* who support its position advance several reasons, grounded in economic and technological factors, why "will not handle" clauses should be invalid in all circumstances. Those arguments are addressed to the wrong branch of government. It may be "that the time has come for a reevaluation of the basic content of collective bargaining as contemplated by the federal legislation. But that is for Congress. Congress has demonstrated its capacity to adjust the Nation's labor legislation to what, in its legislative judgment, constitutes the statutory pattern appropriate to the developing state of labor relations in the country. Major revisions of the basic statute were enacted in 1947 and 1959. To be sure, then, Congress might be of opinion that greater stress should be put on   .   .   .   eliminating more and more economic weapons from the   .   .   .   [Union's] grasp.   .   .   .   But Congress' policy has not yet moved to this point.   .   .   .   " Labor Board v. Insurance Agents' International Union, 361 U.S. 477, 500.

The determination whether the "will not handle" sentence of Rule 17 and its enforcement violated § 8(e) and § 8(b)(4)(B) cannot be made without an inquiry into whether, under all the surrounding circumstances, the Union's objective was preservation of work for Frouge's employees, or whether the agreements and boycott were tactically calculated to satisfy union objectives elsewhere. Were the latter the case, Frouge, the boycotting employer, would be a neutral bystander, and the agreement or boycott would, within the intent of Congress, become secondary. There need not be an actual dispute with the boycotted employer, here the door manufacturer, for the activity to fall within this category, so long as the tactical object of the agreement and its maintenance is that employer, or benefits to other than the boycotting employees or other employees of the primary employer thus making the agreement or boycott secondary in its aim. The touchstone is whether the agreement or its maintenance is addressed to the labor relations of the contracting employer *vis-a-vis* his own employees. This will not always be a simple test to apply. But "[h]owever difficult the drawing of lines more nice than obvious, the statute compels the task." Local 761, Electrical Workers v. Labor Board, 366 U.S. 667, 674.

That the "will not handle" provision was not an unfair labor practice in these cases is clear. The finding of the Trial Examiner, adopted by the Board, was that the objective of the sentence was preservation of work traditionally performed by the jobsite carpenters. This finding is supported by substantial evidence, and therefore the Union's making of the "will not handle" agreement was not a violation of § 8(e).

Similarly, the Union's maintenance of the provision was not a violation of § 8(b)(4)(B). The Union refused to hang prefabricated doors whether or not they bore a union label, and even refused to install prefabricated doors manufactured off the jobsite by members of the Union. This and other substantial evidence supported the finding that the conduct of the Union on the Frouge jobsite related solely to preservation of the traditional tasks of the jobsite carpenters.

The judgment is affirmed in No. 110 [the dismissal of the § 8(b)(4)(B) charge], and reversed in No. 111 [the § 8(e) charge brought by the N.L.R.B. against the Union].

[Mr. Justice Harlan concurred in a memorandum opinion in which he noted that the sole objective of the union's activities in this case was protection of union members from job loss due to changing technology. He argued that because there was essentially no

Congressional legislative history on this precise point, the type of arrangement between the Union and Frouge should not be considered unlawful.

Mr. Justice Stewart was joined in dissent by Mr. Justice Black, Mr. Justice Douglas, and Mr. Justice Clark. The dissenters refuted each of the majority's arguments step by step. They concluded that "the relevant legislative history confirms and reinforces the plain meaning of the statute and establishes that the Union's product boycott in these cases and the agreement authorizing it were both unfair labor practices."]

UNRESOLVED LIMITS ON PUBLIC POWER

The Problem

The last case in the preceding subsection on unresolved limits of union power underscores the title of this entire section on labor—Law of the Cases and Legislation Vie in Social Conflict. We have omitted the vigorous refutation by four dissenting Justices in National Woodwork, knowing that the reader would see, unaided, how far Justice Brennan reached to interpret the provision of the Taft-Hartley Act concerning secondary bocotts. Did Congress really intend to favor jobsite carpenters against factory "prefab" workers? From our positions as observers, however, the point is not one of right, wrong, justice, progress, or retrogression; rather it is to see how easy it is, in a science compounded of words, for cases to vie with legislation. Furthermore, our interest attaches to the warning which a 5 to 4 decision always sounds. Either the majority will gain converts on the Court and consolidate its position, or the minority will become the majority. This is the glory of the law—it can verbalize itself to either of the antipodes but always with reasoned words.

We refer again to National Woodwork for a second reason. The issues in that case and all of this chapter, until now, have involved labor and management in the private sector of our capitalistic society. We have seen unionism pass through the law of crimes, torts, and contracts. We have seen the strike curbed by the courts; then the courts curbed by legislation; and finally, the strike declared a matter of right in Section 13 of the Wagner Act. Yet, none of the law and legislation we have been through controls the area of employer-employee relations that we now approach. When the employer is the government—city, borough, township, county, state, federal or any of the innumerable boards, commissions, or authorities that are creatures of government—and the employees are of the 12.5 million Americans who work for government, the concepts and philosophies, not to say emotions, are those of a more ancient and yet, incongruously, less explored world than the one from which we have been taking samples of law and legislation.

In the completely different world of government and government-workers the legal right to strike does not exist. What the law concedes to workers in a shipbuilding yard of the United States Steel Corporation it denies to the workers in a shipbuilding yard of the United States of America. What the law permits and protects for transit workers where the system is privately owned it denies where the system is publicly owned. The janitors and charwomen of a privately owned building, who collect garbage and trash from within the building, may strike, but the municipal sanitation workers, who collect at the building dock or from the curb, may not. Airplane pilots, mechanics, and hostesses may strike. Public school teachers may not. Why? Before giving the answer, let us concede what everyone knows: transit workers, sanitation men, teachers *do* strike; so *do* policemen, firemen, and other employees of government. These violations of the rule do not, as yet, change the rule. They affirm a proposition enunciated in Chapter 1: the law *can* be violated. Again, why the rule?

Government involves sovereignty (a high command). This is true whether the sovereign is a monarch, a dictator, or the people, as we claim in America. The U.S.S.R. makes a similar but more limited claim in the phrase "dictatorship of the proletariat (the workers)." In any society, of whatever nature, government involves the relationship of ruling and being ruled. Spengler puts it bluntly: men are divided between those who command and those who obey. The concept pervades all forms of organization. In Chapter 1 we mentioned the ancient and ubiquitous oaths of fealty, which may have been models for the Ten Commandments. Jehovah's refrain "Thou shalt keep my commandments" rang in the ears of the "chosen people." So it has been always with government—heavenly or earthly—those who are ruled, whether subjects or citizens, must obey government in those aspects of social stability that government finds essential. The alternatives to obedience are to accept punishment, as Henry David Thoreau did, or to rebel, as Daniel Shays did.

In a modern constitutional democracy the citizen may question at any point the constitutional validity of a given order, as we shall clearly see in the next chapter. Yet, when an order of the government has progressed through the internal procedures for the testing of its validity and has been validated—for Americans, by the Supreme Court—the citizen must obey or suffer the consequences. Does the citizen gain some other option when, perchance, he becomes an employee of government as well as citizen? The prevailing doctrine answers, No! The general rule is that there is no right to strike against the government —against any government, by any citizen, whatever his function—by drafted soldiers or by White House gardeners. However, one distinction must be made. The individual White House gardener may quit his job; the soldier may not. But, neither may act in concert to withhold their services from the government.

This principle is so deeply imbedded in the folkways of the government-citizen-employee relationship that there is no significant theory to the contrary. Even in the Marxist state, which supposedly will wither away, workers, all of whom are employees of the state and its agencies, do not claim, assert, or exercise a right to strike. And a labor government in England puts down a strike in a nationalized industry with the same outraged vigor as Calvin

Coolidge mustered when, as Governor of Massachusetts, he helped put down the Boston police strike, saying, "There is no right to strike against the public safety by anybody, anywhere, at anytime."[22]

The Federal Situation

EXECUTIVE ORDER 10988—EMPLOYEE-MANAGEMENT COOPERATION IN THE FEDERAL SERVICE

There are some three million civilian employees of the United States of America. Under an Executive Order issued by President Kennedy on January 17, 1962, those employees may form unions and carry on certain forms of collective bargaining concerning terms and conditions of employment. However, the right to strike is expressly denied in a provision of the Executive Order that precludes recognition of any organization that asserts the right to strike against the government of the United States. (For detailed excerpts from the Executive Order, see the Appendix, *infra*, p. 352.) So accepted is the concept that federal workers may not strike against the federal government that union constitutions and other formal declarations assert a policy against the strike as a means of achieving union objectives.[23]

Nevertheless, it would be premature to predict immunity of our federal government from strike action by its workers. Strikes of government employees are not unusual in Europe, and in 1968, 24,000 Canadian postal employees struck the mails for 22 days to secure a substantial pay increase. Even in the United States from March 18 to March 26, 1970 there were serious local strikes of employees of the United States Post Office Department. Since centers such as New York City, Pittsburgh, and Chicago were completely closed down for a number of days, the local strikes had national significance although the strikes could not be called nationwide.

The State Situation

By 1970 few states of the Union and few major cities had escaped strikes by such public employees as teachers, sanitation workers, firemen, and policemen. The laws of the states either forbade the right to strike expressly or relied generally on the ancient rule against disobedience of the sovereign. The general rule rested not only on tradition but also on a prestigious pronouncement by O. W. Holmes in 1891, when he was a member of the Supreme Judicial Court of Massachusetts. Concerning a discharged policeman, the Justice said, "The

[22]Spero, Sterling D., *Government as Employer,* p. 280, Remsen Press, New York, 1948. On July 23, 1970, the General Assembly of the Commonwealth of Pennsylvania passed Senate Bill 1333 as amended July 13, 1970 which allows to certain public employees including public school teachers a limited right to strike subject to court injunction if "such a strike creates a clear and present danger or threat to the health, safety or welfare of the public."

[23]Godine, Morton R., *The Labor Problem in the Public Service,* pp. 166–7, Harvard University Press, Cambridge, 1951.

petitioner may have a constitutional right to talk politics, but he has no constitutional right to be a policeman." McAuliffe v. Mayor of New Bedford, 155 Mass. 216 (1891). In Dallas, Texas, the doctrine was invoked to sustain an ordinance forbidding city employees to form a labor organization. Congress of Industrial Organization v. Dallas, 198 S.W.2d 143 (1946). The law forbade not only strikes by employees of government but also any organization. Today, governmental bodies of many American states, such as school boards (an outstanding example), are forbidden by law from recognizing or bargaining with any organization of the employees of government.

We take the recent record of the State of New York and of the City of New York as symptomatic of new developments in the law of the rights of public employees and of the frustrations of government in the development of those rights. The record is as revealing of the unresolved limits of public power as it is redolent of some public workers' sense of unlimited power.

NEW YORK ANTI-STRIKE (CONDON-WADLIN ACT)

On the heels of a Buffalo teachers' strike, the New York Legislature in 1948 enacted the Condon-Wadlin Act, New York Civ. Serv. Law § 108 (McKinney 1959), prohibiting strikes by public employees. Penalties for violation of the Act were automatic dismissal of the strikers, and if rehired, they were barred from any pay increase for three years. The law had a rather uneventful career until December 27, 1965, when 8,000 members of Transit Workers Union voted to strike at 5 a.m. on January 1, 1966.[24] On December 31, 1965, the Supreme Court of New York enjoined this Union and its President Quill and other officers under the Condon-Wadlin Act and under general principles of law against strikes by public employees. The report of the case follows.

NEW YORK CITY TRANSIT AUTHORITY v. QUILL
Supreme Court, Special Term, New York County, 266 N.Y.S. 2d 296, December 31, 1965

TILZER, Justice.

.   .   .   .

This action was instituted to obtain an injunction against the defendants from calling a strike which is to commence at 5 a.m. on January 1, 1966, and from urging and instigating plaintiff's employees to join such strike.   .   .   .

They allege, and have established, that the defendants have called a strike of the plaintiff's employees to commence at or about 5 a.m. on January 1, 1966. This threat hangs ominously over the lifeline of all the citizens of the City of New York, and should a strike be actually called at 5 a.m., as threatened, general paralysis of the activities of the inhabitants of this city will ultimately ensue.

---

[24]All dates and facts appearing in the recitals between the cases in this portion of Chapter 7 may be found by reference to the NEW YORK TIMES INDEX under the appropriate date and subject heading.

The law on this subject has been enunciated and followed beyond peradventure of any doubt. In the leading case of New York City Transit Authority v. Loos et al., 2 Misc.2d 733, 154 N.Y.S.2d 209 (1956), aff'd 3 A.D.2d 740, 161 N.Y.S.2d 564 (1st Dept. 1957), the Court granted a temporary injunction restraining certain employees from striking or instigating a strike or other work stoppage. This case was cited with approval in the Matter of Lerner v. Casey, 2 N.Y.2d 355, at page 367, 161 N.Y.S.2d 7, at page 16, aff'd 357 U.S. 468; reh. den. 358 U.S. 858 (1958) in which Chief Judge Conway reached the conclusion that the Transit Authority had been properly designated a security agency and stated (2 N.Y.2d p. 367, 161 N.Y.S.2d p. 16):

"The Transit Authority performs a function necessary to the security of defense of the nation and the state. This fact was vividly demonstrated recently when certain New York City subway motormen went out on strike. Mr. Justice Lupiano, Special Term, New York County, in issuing an injunction against those motormen, aptly pointed out, New York City Transit Authority v. Loos, 2 Misc.2d 733, 738, 154 N.Y.S.2d 209, 214:

"'It is easy to forget, while the subways are running, that there is room for motor vehicles on the streets only because millions travel by subway; for if all persons had to use surface transportation, the bridges and tunnels and main highways would soon be hopelessly clogged. New York with its immense territory and its five separate boroughs, all protected by unified police and fire departments and having many other integrated services, is dependent for its very life and daily functioning, and for immediate safety of its 8,000,000 inhabitants, on rapid transit facilities which are necessarily used by nearly all persons engaged in all of its governmental and other vital functions. Whatever may be the case elsewhere, and under other conditions, whatever may have been the case in other times, here and now, and for this city, the operation of the rapid transit facilities is a basic governmental service indispensable to the conduct of all other governmental as well as private activities necessary for the public welfare. It is worth re-emphasizing that the subways are the city's arteries upon which its life and daily living depend. * * *'"

.   .   .   .   .

This Court holds that the plaintiff is entitled to a preliminary injunction under the Condon Wadlin Act, and further holds that even if there had never been a Condon Wadlin Act, it would be the duty of this Court to enjoin a strike by plaintiff's employees as unlawful and contrary to the policy of this state.

.   .   .   .   .

.   .   . The staggering effects of a strike at this time on the inhabitants of this city by far outweigh the rights of these defendants. All strikes are ultimately settled, and there is no substantial reason why these defendants should not be compelled to settle their differences with the Authority without such a heavy casualty on the inhabitants of the City of New York.

.   .   . [M]otions for injunctive relief are accordingly granted.

———————————

On December 31, 1965, Quill tore up the injunction papers in the course of a television appearance. On January 2, 1966, contempt proceedings were instituted against Quill, and on January 4, he and five others were sentenced to jail. The next day Quill collapsed and was incarcerated in Bellevue Hospital.

Commerce and industry reported losses at $100 million per day. President Johnson declared that the Federal government would grant low-interest rate loans to injured small business. Bicycle rentals soared.

On January 13, the strike ended with a 15 percent pay increase over a two-year period and fringe adjustments. President Johnson criticized the settlement as violating his Administration's guidelines on wage increases.

On January 14, Quill and the others were released from prison. Quill died suddenly on January 29. Meanwhile, a suit had been filed by a taxpayer, Weinstein, to enjoin the Transit Authority from instituting the wage increases provided by the settlement in contravention of Condon-Wadlin Act.

WEINSTEIN v. NEW YORK CITY TRANSIT AUTHORITY
Supreme Court, Special Term, New York County, 267 N.Y.S.2d 111,
February 9, 1966.

SAYPOL, Justice.

This application . . . was heard by the Court during the recent strike of New York City Transit Authority (Authority) employees. Transportation facilities came to a halt New Year's morning January 1, 1966. Operations resumed after January 13. Petitioner asks for an order restraining, prohibiting and enjoining as illegal the offering or paying by the respondents to the strikers of any amount in excess of their compensation in effect prior to the strike on January 1, 1966, for at least three years after resumption of their reemployments (Civil Service Law, section 108—the Condon-Waldin Law). The respondents . . . cross-moved before answer to dismiss the petition by raising objections in point of law. Counsel for representatives of the striking employees were heard, *amici curiae,* in support of the respondents' cross-motions to dismiss.

The cross-motions are denied, and the respondents may serve and file their answers within ten days of the service of a copy of the order hereon with notice of entry. . . .

There are significant truths to be reminded and remembered here. Important public policy is involved. That public policy is inherent in the common law and written into the Constitution of The State of New York, expressly prescribed in the implementing Civil Service Law and uniformly sustained in judicial decisions and by impressive official opinion against striking the government by public employees. .   .

[Justice Saypol then elaborated upon the human and economic hardships New Yorkers suffered as a result of the strike. He continued:]

The legal relationship and obligations of these respondents under the law are plain. . . .

.   .   .   .

Our highest state court   .   .   .   gave the warning of that great danger which is implicit here in the demonstrated violation of the law. First, the sworn public employees by their strike. Next, compounded by sworn public officers in their compromise yielding and submitting to illegally extorted demands. No personal reasons on their part can justify the ransom extorted from eight million citizens of a government by 30,000 employees, four-tenths of one per centum. If responsible officials cannot stand up in firm resistance, the Court will. Submission today to this unlawful misconduct, under the guise of civil disobedience, grinding into the dirt the civil rights and liberties of the city's millions is craven servility and could lead to disaster for all. And the fear is great that it would come too soon if not bucked abruptly. That opposition could not be too firm, too determined, too stalwart, unyielding and intransigent. The continuing existence of our form of government, the very life, liberty and welfare of the whole citizenry, demands no easier course. It is plain that the respondents are forbidden at their peril from any course which would increase the compensation of the strikers in violation of the Condon-Waldin Law before January 14, 1969.

[Justice Saypol then commented that while the case for the relief sought by Weinstein was clear, the law prevented the court from awarding a summary judgment before the respondents have had an opportunity to answer the petitioners' case. The court then gave the respondents ten days in which to answer.]

AMNESTY ACT FOR TRANSIT WORKERS

Within the 10-day period set by Justice Saypol to allow the respondents to file an answer, the New York Legislature enacted, and on February 16, 1966, Governor Rockefeller signed, Chapter 6 of the Laws of 1966 which gave the striking transit workers amnesty from the penalty provisions of the Condon-Wadlin Act. The law reads as follows.

The People of the State of New York, represented in Senate and Assembly, do enact as follows:

Section 1.   Declaration and findings. The legislature hereby finds that there is imminent danger of a renewal of the transit strike in the city of New York; that a transit strike in January nineteeen hundred sixty-six brought human suffering and severe economic hardships to many and inconvenience to all; that such a strike was a tragedy affecting the lives and livelihood, the safety and well-being of sixteen million people in the world's greatest metropolitan area, and a repetition would be disastrous and intolerable; that such strike was settled after twelve days of chaos, on the basis of the report a mediation panel requested by the mayor of the city of New York; that the parties accepted in good faith the terms contained in such report and the transit workers returned to their jobs; that the present critical situation arises out of a serious question raised in the courts as to the legal capacity of the New York city transit authority and the Manhattan and Bronx surface transit operating authority to approve the terms of the agreement which settled the recent catastrophic strike; that the provisions of this act are necessary in order to protect the health, safety and welfare of the sixteen million people of the New York city metropolitan region against another transit strike and to authorize the approval of the agreement which settled the strike in January.

§ 2.   Notwithstanding any other provisions of law to the contrary the New York city transit authority and Manhattan and Bronx surface transit operating authority are hereby authorized and empowered to continue in employment their hourly-rated operating employees, in the same status as such employees held on December thirty-first, nineteen hundred sixty-five and to pay them the increased compensation contained in the report of a certain mediation panel appointed by the mayor of the city of New York, pursuant to which the employees resumed their duties in the operations of their respective transit facilities.

§ 3.   This act shall take effect immediately.

NEW YORK PUBLIC EMPLOYEES FAIR EMPLOYMENT ACT (TAYLOR LAW)

Meanwhile on January 16, 1966, Governor Rockefeller had appointed a 5-man panel, headed by George W. Taylor, labor advisor to United States Presidents from Roosevelt to Johnson to draft new legislation for the State of New York. The efforts of the panel resulted in the enactment of the New York Public Employees' Fair Employment Act (Taylor Law), which became effective on September 1, 1967, concurrently with the repeal of the Condon-Wadlin Act. N.Y. Civ. Serv. Law §§ 200 et. seq. (McKinney 1967).

In the words of Dr. Taylor, the philosophy and basic premises underlying the Taylor Law are:

(1) There are basic differences between private employment and public employment; many of the policies and practices of the private sector are inapplicable in the public sector.

(2) It is essential to achieve a just balance between the public's right to uninterrupted public service and the right to fair treatment by those who provide those services.

(3) Such a just balance cannot be achieved if a strike by public employees is used as a technique for settling disputes.

(4) It is practically and equitably impossible to permit some public employees to have the right to strike and to deny it to others, according to a supposed distinction based on the essentiality or nonessentiality of the services.

(5) Since a strike cannot be tolerated, effective substitutes must be developed for bringing disputes to a final settlement.

(6) Collective negotiations must involve the effective participation of public employees in determining the conditions of their employment if the substitutes are to be effective.

(7) Certain measures are required to safeguard the equities of public employees in the process of collective negotiations.

(8) The unique nature of government operations dictates that negotiations be concluded in advance of the time that the budget is submitted to the legislative body.

(9) The public interest requires that the impasse procedures include as a last step

one that will lead to a final resolution of the dispute.

(10) Adaptation of the foregoing principles to permit flexibility to accommodate local conditions should be encouraged.

(11) Penalties for violations of the statute prohibiting strikes are necessary for three reasons: (i) to induce compliance with the law, (ii) to avoid preferential treatment, and (iii) to cause all parties to seek fair settlements through responsible means compatible with the public interest. "Governor's Committee on Public Employee Relations, Interim Report," pp. 26-28, New York, June 17, 1968.

The Taylor Law reiterates the ban on strikes by civil servants but attempts to compensate the public employee for the loss of this power by providing impasse procedures. Employee organizations are given recognition as responsible bargaining agents, and provision is made for their acceptance and certification. Commensurate with this status, the union is held answerable for an illegal strike through the imposition of such penalties as fines directed against union funds and a denial of the checkoff privilege for collecting dues.

A three-man public employment relations board (PERB) is created in the state civil service department that, in addition to analytical and informational duties, is empowered to resolve representation disputes, hold hearings and establish panels of qualified persons to act as mediators or fact-finding boards.

In the event of an impasse in negotiations between a public employer and its employees, PERB is empowered to assist in resolving the dispute. If agreement is not reached after mediation, a fact-finding board is appointed. If the dispute persists to within 15 days of the budget submission date, the panel's findings and recommendations are to be transmitted to the chief executive officer of the affected department and to the employee organization. The findings may also be made public.

As a last resort the conclusions of the fact-finding board as well as the arguments and recommendations of the parties to the unsettled dispute are submitted to the legislature for a determination.

Under the penalty provisions of the Law, a striking union can be fined up to $10,000 per day or one week's dues collection whichever is less, and can have its right of checkoff suspended for a period of up to 18 months. An individual striker who violates a court order directing him to return to work may be fined up to $250 or sentenced to jail for up to 30 days.[25]

---

[25]George W. Taylor is Harnwell Professor of Industry, Wharton School of Finance and Commerce at the University of Pennsylvania. Professor Taylor has kindly read the whole of this Chapter 7. He points out that the committee of which he was chairman and which produced the Taylor Law for New York State did not recommend, and the law did not provide for, jail sentences for union leaders. This penalty, he points out, is imposed by a court for violation of its injunction. "In my view," Dr. Taylor continues, "the submission of 'fact-finders' recommendations, etc. to the legislature in an impasse is a distinctive contribution to the question of final determination of the impasse." Unlike E.O. 10988 (*supra* p. 319), the Taylor Law provides for 'pressure' on the legislative body in the form of recommendations by a fact-finding board but not the pressure of strikes or compulsory arbitration.

Concerning penalties, Dr. Taylor believes that the loss of check-off is proving to be an effective

Several months before September 1, 1967, the effective date of the Taylor Law, Albert Shanker, President of the New York City United Federation of Teachers (UFT), advised his union that it could avoid the consequences of the Taylor Law by submitting mass resignations if no contract was reached before the opening of the public schools in the coming fall. Shanker also urged UFT members to borrow several months pay from a bank, using their jobs as collateral, so as to force a possible work stoppage in September.

The New York City School Board carried on negotiations with the UFT throughout the summer of 1967. On occasion, as many as 5000 UFT members picketed City Hall and threatened to strike unless they received pay increases. On August 13, 1967, Mayor Lindsay named a panel of eminent law professors (the Taylor Law not yet being effective) to help settle the contract dispute between the UFT and the School Board. The panel ended its efforts on September 1, 1967 and submitted a report to the Mayor. Shanker reported on September 6, that the UFT negotiating committee had "unanimously" rejected the panel's proposals. The next day, the 2500 UFT delegate assembly rejected the proposed contract and authorized the union to proceed with the mass resignation maneuver.

On September 11, New York City officials, acting under the Taylor Law, secured an injunction against a strike in which some 80 or 90 percent of the teachers were not in school on opening day. The report of this case follows here.

BOARD OF EDUCATION OF THE CITY OF NEW YORK v. SHANKER
Supreme Court, Special Term, New York County, 283 N.Y.S.2d 432,
September 13, 1967.

NUNEZ, Justice.

. . . . .

This brings me now to the application made by the Board of Education for a temporary restraining order and preliminary injunction. It is an undisputed fact that the school year began on Monday of this week, September 11, 1967. It is also a fact that the teachers had an agreement with the Board of Education, which expired June 30, 1967; and that the union officers and the Board of Education have been engaged in an attempt to negotiate a new contract for many months.

It is a conceded fact that while the schools opened on Monday, a very substantial number of teachers did not appear in the schools, and have not been teaching the children.

---

deterrent to the resort to strikes. He points out that the 1969 Amendments to the Taylor Law with respect to penalties conform to the committee's original recommendations. He minimizes the importance of penalties against individual workers, saying "imagine the hearings that would be required to dispose of claims by each individual that he personally didn't strike." He concedes, however, the difficulties when workers will not follow union leaders, observing that "Union leaders cannot be compelled to force individual members to go back to work."

It is claimed, and I will assume it for the purpose of this proceeding, that these teachers have executed their resignations, and that these resignations are now in the hands of the defendant Teachers Union. The fact is that the great majority, said to be around 80 or 90 per cent of the teachers, are not in school, and are not teaching the children.

Mr. Shanker, the President of the Teachers Union, has stated on many occasions that the contract with the Board of Education expired on June 30th, and that the teachers would not go back to work unless they had a new contract.

The proof before me is ample to justify the conclusion, and I find, that the teachers have stayed out as a means of enforcing their demands for a better and improved contract, which encompasses salary, teaching conditions, class sizes, and other disputes between them and the Board of Education, and that they have stayed out and have not returned to work on September 11th because they have been advised to do so by their union officials.

I also find that these resignations were executed and delivered to the union by the teachers at the union's request and as a part of the strategy and plan in dealing with the Board of Education. Of course, every one has the right to resign his position and not return to work, and this includes the teachers. No court, certainly in this country, can compel a teacher to work if he or she did not wish to work. I find, however, that in this case the teachers did not execute these resignations for the purpose of not returning to work and leaving the employ of the Board of Education. They executed these resignations at the union's urging to compel their employer to accede to their demands and as a concerted stoppage of work. It was done in an attempt to evade the provisions of the Civil Service Law, the common law and the decisional law, all of which from time immemorial, forbids and makes illegal a strike on the part of public employees.

The latest statutory enactment defining the term "strike" is contained in Section 201 of the Civil Service Law, which has been referred to by counsel as the Taylor Law. In section 201, subdivision 10, the term "strike" is defined as meaning "any strike or other concerted stoppage of work or slowdown by public employees."

Section 210 of the same law provides as follows: "No public employee or employee organization shall engage in a strike, and no employee organization shall cause, instigate, encourage, or condone a strike."

There have been any number of Court decisions defining strike as "a concerted work stoppage; a combination to obtain higher wages and shorter hours and better working conditions; a cessation of work as a means of enforcing compliance with some demand upon the employer," and similar definitions.

The dictionary, by the way, definition of "strike" is "a concerted stopping of work, or withdrawal of workers' services as to compel an employer to accede to workers' demands, or in protest against terms or conditions imposed by an employer."

I don't think that anyone who has followed the dispute between these two parties, and the actual situation in the public schools of New York City during the last three days, can come to any conclusion other than that the teachers are out on strike, and the Court so finds.

This dispute, of course, has become an emotional issue. My function at this time is limited to deciding the legal issue before me, and that is, whether or not the Board of

Education is entitled to a temporary restraining order and a preliminary injunction because of this illegal strike.

.   .   .   .

I am, therefore, constrained, and I do hereby declare, that the teachers' activities constitute a strike; that they are on strike against the Board of Education; that they are public employees, and a public employee, when he strikes, strikes against government itself. The strike is illegal, and the teachers and the union are engaging in illegal activities in continuing this strike.

The temporary restraining order as outlined in the order of this Court, dated September 10th, and signed by Mr. Justice Gold, is, in all respects, continued as well as the preliminary injunction contained in that temporary order.

On September 20, 1967, the State Public Relations Board (PERB) began hearings to determine whether the UFT's work stoppage had been a strike in violation of the Taylor Law and thus subject to penalty. Finally, on December 1, upon concluding that the UFT's September actions had been a strike, PERB cancelled the union's right of dues checkoff for one year, subject to reinstatement upon the UFT's signing a no-strike pledge.

On September 21, Mayor Lindsay announced a tentative settlement of the dispute, and Shanker asserted that he was certain that the teachers would approve it. However, on September 23, before the vote on the contract was taken, Shanker charged that the School Board had reneged on a portion of the oral agreement. Once again the parties fell into a deadlock.

On September 26, Mayor Lindsay announced a new pact and stated that a "memorandum of understanding" had been signed by both sides. Classes resumed in the New York public schools on September 29, when the UFT voted to accept the contract.

Meanwhile, on September 13, a suit for contempt for violating the no-strike injunction had begun against Shanker and several others, both as individuals and as officers of the UFT. After several delays so that the defendants could participate in negotiations with the School Board, Justice Nunez reached a verdict. The opinion in that case follows.

BOARD OF EDUCATION OF THE CITY OF NEW YORK v. SHANKER
Supreme Court, Special Term, New York County, 283 N.Y.S.2d 548, Oct. 4, 1967.

NUNEZ, Justice.

Plaintiff, the Board of Education of the City of New York, seeks an order adjudging defendant United Federation of Teachers, Local 2, American Federation of Teachers, AFL-CIO (hereinafter referred to as Union), and certain of its officers (the individual defendants), guilty of and punishing them for criminal contempt of court for their failure to obey an order of this Court (Gold, J., Sept. 10, 1967), enjoining them from engaging in any strike in connection with the performance by defendant Union's members of the duties of their employment with plaintiff Board of Education. It is crystal clear from the record before me that the defendant Union herein and its President, the individual defendant Shanker, are guilty of the contempt charged.

.   .   .

In connection with the instant application, numerous and extensive hearings were held by the Court, comprising almost 600 pages of stenographic transcript. The testimony adduced at such hearings demonstrates overwhelmingly and beyond any doubt whatsoever that the defendant Union and its President, Albert Shanker, one of the individual defendants herein, have deliberately, wilfully and contumaciously flouted the clear mandate of the Court which restrained them from engaging in or assisting in any work stoppage against the plaintiff Board of Education. The record, despite its voluminous size, is abysmally barren of a single shred of evidence to indicate, even remotely, anything to the contrary. In fact the testimony offered at the trial indicates that the defendants began preparing for the work stoppage many months ago.

From time immemorial, it has been a fundamental principle that a government employee may not strike. In this sensitive area, neither labor—the public employee—nor management—the governmental agency—in their mutual interdependence can afford the indulgence of arbitrary self-interest at the expense of the public. This principle was reiterated in 1919 by the then Governor of Massachusetts, Calvin Coolidge, when he stated, "There is no right to strike against the public safety by anybody, anywhere, anytime." In his message to the Federation of Federal Employees on August 16, 1937, President Franklin D. Roosevelt stated, "Since their own services have to do with the functioning of government, a strike of public employees manifests nothing less than an intent on their part to prevent or obstruct the operations of government until their demands are satisfied. Such action, looking toward the paralysis of government by those who have sworn to support it, is unthinkable and intolerable."

.   .   .

Defendants, Albert Shanker and United Federation of Teachers, are adjudged guilty of criminal contempt of this Court for their wilful disobedience to its lawful mandate.

.   .   .

After hearing oral argument, the defendant United Federation of Teachers is fined the sum of $150,000.00 for its willful disobedience to the court's lawful mandate. Defendant Albert Shanker is fined the sum of $250.00 and sentenced to jail for a period of 15 days for his willful disobedience of the court's mandate.

———————

On December 15, 1967, the UFT paid its fine. Six days thereafter, Shanker began his jail term. On February 2, 1968, under the leadership of the Uniformed Sanitationmen's Association's President, DeLury, 10,000 sanitation workers struck. The same day the City obtained a temporary order under the Taylor Law restraining the sanitation workers from engaging in the strike.

This order became final on February 5th. On the following day DeLury was found guilty of contempt for disobeying the final order and sentenced to a 15-day jail term.

Meanwhile, on February 7, with 10,000 tons of garbage accumulating daily, the union agreed to service hospitals and other emergency facilities, and Mayor Lindsay set up locations for burning garbage and for distributing 200,000 plastic bags.

On February 10, when the State Board of Health agreed with the City Board's assessment of the gravity of the situation, Governor Rockefeller ended the strike with a plan for the State to temporarily take over the operation of the New York City Sanitation Department. The Health Department immediately arranged with several drug companies to distribute typhoid vaccine, while 1400 sanitationmen began the cleanup with the aid of scores of volunteer residents of the City.

On February 14, in the contempt proceedings against the Uniformed Sanitationmen's Association a fine of $80,000 was levied against the Union and a suspension of its dues checkoff privilege for 18 months was ordered. On February 16, an appeal was taken to overturn DeLury's 15-day jail term. The report of the case follows.

CITY OF NEW YORK v. De LURY

Court of Appeals of New York, 295 N.Y.S. 2d 901 (1968).

FULD, Chief Judge.

We recently decided, in Rankin v. Shanker, 23 N.Y.2d 111, 295 N.Y.S.2d 625, that public employees and labor organizations representing them were not entitled to a trial by jury in a criminal contempt proceeding for the violation of section 210 (subd. 1) of the Taylor Law. In so holding, we concluded that a legislative classification "which differentiates between strikes by public employees and employees in private industry" is reasonable and does not offend against the constitutional guarantee of equal protection of the laws (23 N.Y.2d at p. 118, 295 N.Y.S.2d at p. 631). The case now before us calls upon the court to determine, primarily, whether the Taylor Law's mandate that public employees shall not strike and that labor organizations representing them shall not cause or encourage a strike violates due process requirements of the State or Federal Constitution.

.   .   .   .

We consider, first, the defendants' contention that the Taylor Law is unconstitutional on the ground that, in prohibiting strikes by public employees, it deprives them of due process of law. Manifestly, neither the Fourteenth Amendment to the Federal Constitution nor the Bill of Rights of the State Constitution (art. I) grants to any individual an absolute right to strike. On the contrary, that right is subject to the qualification that, if a strike is for an illegal objective, it is enjoinable at the instance of an aggrieved party. To cull from the opinion of the Supreme Court in International Union, United Auto Workers, A. F. of L., Local 232 v. Wisconsin Employment Relations Bd. (336 U.S. 245, 259–260, 69 S.Ct. 516, 524, 93 L.Ed. 651), " 'the exercise of the unquestioned right to [strike]' * * * did not operate to legalize the sit-down strike, which state law made illegal and state authorities punished. [Case cited.] Nor, for example, did it make legal a strike that ran afoul of federal law [case cited]; nor one in violation of a contract made pursuant thereto [case cited]; nor one creating a national emergency [case cited]."

. . . .

In view of the strong policy considerations which led to the enactment of the Taylor Law, it is our conclusion that the statutory prohibition against strikes by public employees is reasonably designed to effectuate a valid State policy in an area where it has authority to act and that the provisions of subdivision 1 of section 210 do not offend any due process rights of the defendants.

In view of our recent decision in the Shanker case (23 N.Y.2d 111, 295 N.Y.S.2d 625, supra), no extended discussion is required in addressing ourselves to the defendants' point that the prohibition against strikes by public employees (or their representative organizations) violates the equal protection clause of either the United States or the New York State Constitution. . . . As we had occasion to observe in Shanker (23 N.Y.2d, at p. 116, 295 N.Y.S.2d 629),

"Ever since the enactment of the Norris-LaGuardia Act and our State's Little Norris-LaGuardia Act, the view has been uniformly and consistently held that a legitimate distinction between public and private employment is constitutionally permissible. This has been recognized * * * with regard not only to the prohibition against strikes but also to the issue, now confronting us, affecting jury trials."

There are a number of factual differences between employment in the public and private sectors which furnish reasonable justification for disparate treatment vis-a-vis the right to strike. Thus, for instance, the necessity for preventing goods or services being priced out of the market may have a deterrent effect upon collective bargaining negotiations in the private sector, whereas, in the public sector, the market place has no such restraining effect upon the negotiations and the sole constraint in terms of the negotiations is to be found in the budget allocation made by responsible legislators. Again, the orderly functioning of our democratic form of representative government and the preservation of the right of our representatives to make budgetary allocations —free from the compulsions of crippling strikes—require the regulation of strikes by public employees whereas there is no similar countervailing reason for a prohibition of strikes in the private sector. (See Taylor Report, pp. 15–16.) . . .

In view of the basic differences between public and private employment, it may not be said that a classification which prohibits strikes by public employees while failing to legislate against strikes by employees in the private sector is unreasonable, especially when it is considered that strikes by public employees, unlike private employees, have always been subject to injunctions by the courts. Consequently, we conclude here, just as we did in Rankin (p. 119, 295 N.Y.S.2d p. 632), that, "as of the present [time], legislative differentiation between public and private employees, insofar as restrictions on their right to strike and to jury trials are concerned, is reasonable."

. . . .

The order appealed from should be affirmed, with costs, and the question certified answered in the affirmative.

All concur.

De Lury then took an appeal to the United States Supreme Court. The appeal was dismissed. City of New York v. De Lury, 394 U.S. 455 (1969).

On February 17, 1968, both the City and the Sanitation Workers Union agreed to submit the situation in dispute to binding arbitration, although the City doubted the legality of entrusting the expenditure of public funds to non-public, nonelected persons.

AMENDMENTS TO TAYLOR LAW

In the midst of the sanitation workers' strike, the Republican leaders in the New York State Legislature, disheartened by the failure of the Taylor Law to prevent either the teachers' or sanitation workers' strikes, initiated a move to strengthen the Law by exacting stiffer penalties from violators. These efforts culminated with the enactment of certain amendments to the Taylor Law, which became effective on April 1, 1969.

The original Law limited the daily fines that could be imposed on a striking union to $10,000 or one week's dues, which ever was the least. Likewise, under the original Law, the power of the State to suspend the striking union's right to dues checkoff had been limited to a period of 18 months. For a large union like Shanker's United Federation of Teachers, the money penalties amounted to a maximum fine of $.20 per day per member for each day the Union remained on strike. In almost all circumstances, this situation presented the unions with a good bargain.

The 1969 amendments not only removed the financial ceiling from the penalty provisions of the Taylor Law, but they also removed the time constraints on the State's power to revoke the striking union's right of dues checkoff. The greatest change, however, was that under the new amendments, the striking worker would lose two days' pay for each day he remained away from work and upon returning to work must serve one year's probation with loss of job tenure for that year.

LABOR AND MUSICAL CHAIRS

Society is always playing the game. The chairs are always one short of the number of members who would sit when the music stops. For ages labor was left standing. For almost all of man's history physical works have been performed by slaves, who must stand while the social circle sat. Only since the Industrial Revolution and the social surpluses produced by the machine has the worth of the worker's hire escalated. It is the machine—now so helpless unless attended by men—that has created labor power. One may speculate with some reason that technology has done more for labor than the Wagner Act or, to say it another way, the Wagner Act merely validated what technology had already decreed. When the requisite quantity of production depends utterly on the machine and the machine depends utterly on manual tending, then those who tend have power. Unions are a consequence of that circumstance—not the cause. This is not to say that the personal craft unions of carpenters, brick layers, plumbers and hod carriers did not flourish, and they continue to flourish, but the great surge in union power in America has coincided in the second and third quarters of the 20th century with the great increase in mechanization of industry.

Now as automation raises the reasonable prospects of machines making machines, of machines repairing themselves, of machines learning by their mistakes and in consequences teaching themselves how to perform better—as automation frees machines from men, the social music may not stop as often just where labor may take a seat. If one assumes for a moment the whole of the gamut of social functions performed by men-free machines—from teaching, psychiatry and baby-sitting to shoes, ships, and space trains for tours into retrospective infinity—he may correctly predict that the labor conflict, which rightly occupies a sixth of this book, may soon abate.

Let us change the figure of speech from musical chairs to "a seat above the salt." That figure itself belongs to an era of poor technology. Mining technology did not go deep enough; so salt, abundant in nature, was scarce at the medieval table. Hence, a seat at an end of the table where the salt was placed was reserved for the privileged. The privileged of society have always enjoyed legal immunities. The king could do no wrong; nor the members of his court; nor, later, legislators; or diplomats, however illegally parked; or the clergy; nor, at one time, soldiers—the list is long. In the 20th century organized labor has joined the ranks of those who "sit above the salt," who enjoy legal immunities.[26] Injunction seldom lies; violations of law are given amnesty by legislatures; antitrust laws do not apply; torts are excused as legitimate means of furthering the workers' interests; contracts broken are sued upon with difficulty; and only prosecution so zealous that it may go beyond the constitution puts a Hoffa in the penitentiary.[27]

We are in an era (perhaps the end of an era) in which labor can do no wrong. The legislature of the sovereign State of New York moved in disarray to exempt transit workers from the Condon-Wadlin Act, which had been on the books since 1948. Why? The machine, the New York subways, was utterly essential to the mobility of New Yorkers and was utterly dependent on men.

---

[26]Pound, Roscoe, "Legal Immunities of Labor Unions," American Enterprise Association, Inc., Washington, D. C., 1957. There are indications of some erosion in labor's immunities. Even the monumental Norris-LaGuardia Act is coming in for some amelioration by case law. In The Boys Markets, Inc. v. Retail Clerk's Union, Local 770, 398 U.S. 235, decided June 1, 1970, a divided United States Supreme Court held that an injunction would issue to restrain a strike in violation of a union-management agreement to submit to arbitration a dispute under the contract.

[27]See footnote 11 and accompanying text, supra, p. 282.

Today, subways can be activated by electronic controls more exact than human operators. When the subways are automated, the music for musical chairs will be different. However, questions of the justice, equity, virtue, and right or wrong of the transit workers' case do not concern us in this analysis. What does interest us is that a bottleneck in technology at a given time in history made organized transit workers, citizen-employees, more powerful than the sovereign state.

Unlike the transit workers who would not accept the penalties of the Condon-Wadlin Act, the New York City school teachers paid the penalties of the recent Taylor Law, apparently considering 20 cents a day per teacher a good bargain. Shanker served his term of incarceration, and some labor experts said that the Taylor Law would not work. Did they really mean that when enough labor power exists or when any other dominant group power exists, no law will work? The State of New York answered with stiffer penalties.

New York's sanitation workers flouted the Taylor Law, and again in disarray, the sovereign State of New York and the "ungovernable" City of New York temporized with an ad hoc binding arbitration. This brief recital cuts through a welter of politics, charges, countercharges, mountains of garbage, escalating rat populations, and public distress. We are again not concerned with right or wrong but rather with the problems of supervening powers of functional groups, employees of government, when the laws of government are ignored and fail to assure the continuance of the services that government seeks to provide its citizen-taxpayers.

Here are three current theories that could be called, because of the uncertainty that beclouds the issues, pragmatic approaches to the problems of government and its employees:

The Taylor Law in New York State is by far the most consistent with established law and with modern fiscal practices. This most innovative of modern legislative attempts clearly provides government workers the right to organize and to bargain collectively with government. It provides sophisticated procedures for carrying workers' demands right into the legislature, where the ultimate taxing power makes that body the real employer. Yet, if workers are unsatisfied, they have no further recourse. They may not legally strike.

The second theory is both more unconventional and less orderly. The right to strike is denied, consistent with established law, and the right to bargain is allowed. But, if the bargaining goes to an impasse, then the determination of the issue (wages, pensions, working conditions) goes to final and binding arbitration. This solution, unlike the Taylor Law, is seldom of general application; rather it is applied to government employees in critical functions, such as transit, fire and police protection, and, less frequently, to education. There are two points of criticism: (1) can government delegate its power and responsibility to fix the terms of employment of its employees to nongovernmental persons, such as arbitrators; and (2) can government be coerced to exercise the taxing power to satisfy arbitrators' awards? To put the question in a fiscal sense, how can government keep its budgets and its revenues in order if arbitrators' awards can put budgets off balance?

The third theory is sheer opportunism, laissez-faire. One may say of it, as the European philosophers said of William James' pragmatism: it is a way of doing without a philosophy (theory). This third approach assumes that government employees will strike from time to time, law or no law, and that crisis techniques will work as well as any. In other words, government may as well save itself the embarrassment of passing laws only to have them broken by some organization of its employees whose critical function invests it with naked power. Among a people who pride themselves on government by law not by men, such a casual attitude has limited appeal.

Clearly, more thinking is needed about how to reconcile the needs of the public for health, safety, and welfare with the rights of workers (in this conclusion we shall speak of all workers, whether public or private) not to be slaves. The most ardent proponents of collective bargaining contend that the process is futile unless the right to strike exists to break a final impasse—whether the employer is government or private enterprise. Readers of this book will recognize the strike as a form of self-help, casting back to that ancient Roman symbolic procedure in which each contestant grasped a rod to simulate self-help and then obeyed the command of the magistrate: Let go, both of you.

Modern industrial society is not quite ready to emulate the Romans by saying to employers, whether public or private, and to employees: let go, both of you. Yet, modern society is unlikely to tolerate interruptions of the delicately balanced mechanism by which it lives. Margins of health, safety, and welfare are too narrow. Pressures of mouths on food supplies, of bodies on health facilities, of humans on security measures, of the whole infrastructure on protective capabilities are irresistible. As population grows at some rate, however diminished by controls, these pressures will mount to crushing proportions.

Despite the urgencies, gradualism is the key. Without abolishing the strike, a practical impossibility, additional procedural interventions may help to produce more resolutions and thus eliminate the need for the strike. If the parties, whether public or private, are required by law to wait while clarification of positions occurs and all interests are heard—not only those of the disputants but also those of the innocent bystanders, the public—and if more procedures are mandated, self-help may occur less often.

Procedures, however, call for an institution in which they can be carried out. Assume an Industrial Peace Commission at the federal level with counterparts in the states. Assume the strike is not a legal method until the Industrial Peace Commission has heard the case on behalf of all parties, management, whether public or private, labor, and the public. Assume that the IPC is authorized by law to make findings on the merits and recommendations for an agreement.

Assume that management rejects the IPC proposed settlement, then the workers may strike. Assume that the management accepts, then the workers may not strike unless a majority of the organization involved votes in secret ballot to strike.[28]

Technology, economics, sociology are all working to bring a new day in the reconcilation of the workers' needs and rights with the health, safety, and welfare of the whole society.

The old order changeth, yielding place to new;
And God fulfills himself in many ways,
Lest one good custom should corrupt the world.[29]

QUESTIONS

1. Identify the economic and social factors which would explain, as of the year 1806, the decision in Commonwealth v. Pullis.

2. Identify three major branches of law through which the court passed in their opposition to unionism and put into your own words the rationale applicable to each of the three phases.

3. With what legislation did the amelioration of case law on unionism begin? Identify the mountain peaks of labor legislation thereafter and, at the risk of oversimplification, divide that legislation as between pro-labor and anti-labor.

4. Describe the essential features of the three types of shops: closed shop, union shop, agency shop. State which of these shops is now legal, and by virtue of what law, and state whether you agree with the law. Give your reasons.

5. Do you agree with the Congress in its special provision authorizing any given state to illegalize any of the three types of shops? How is this permission to the states to be reconciled with the Doctrine of Preemption? What provisions of what legislation and what case is applicable to this question?

6. Can you reconcile the decision in Senn with the decision in Hanke? If not, why did the Supreme Court of the United States permit both cases to stand? Explain what happened to Thornhill v. Alabama after Hanke. Do you agree with the decision in National Woodwork Manufacturers Association? State why, whether you agree or disagree.

7. Suppose that a manufacturer is fully automated: machines have made the machines which produce the product; machines repair the machines; machines redesign and rebuild the machines; machines take in the raw materials; machines process the raw materials; machines package and direct into the channels of trade the finished product; machines deliver the finished product

---

[28]For a detailed statement of such a plan and a critique, see Sherman, Herbert L., Jr., 28 *University of Pittsburgh Law Review,* 391, March, 1967.

[29]Alfred Lord Tennyson, *Idylls of the King,* Guinevere l. 475.

into the hands of carriers who deliver the product to wholesale and retail establishments not owned or in any way connected with the manufacturer except as purchasers for resale of the product. A labor union which had represented all the employees of the manufacturer, prior to the full automation, pickets the wholesale and retail establishments, protesting that the manufacturer is unfair to organized labor by reason of conversion to full automation in which no employees are required. Does the manufacturer have any rights against the union? If so, what and by reason of what provisions of law does any individual, wholesaler or retailer, have any rights against the union? If so, under what provisions of law? In either case, what are the rights and what legal relief against the picketing, if any, can be obtained?

8.   Do you fully believe that employees of government, for example, sanitation workers, policemen, firemen, teachers, clerks who issue Social Security checks, White House gardeners, or soldiers, should have a right to strike? If you believe that some of these employees should have a right to strike but not others, explain the differentiation. If you believe that none of them should have a right to strike, explain why.

APPENDIX   —   STATUTORY MATERIAL

1914
CLAYTON ACT
Public Law 63–213, 38 Stat. 731, 15 U.S.C. § 17; 38 Stat. 738, 29 U.S.C. § 52, approved October 15, 1914.

Be it enacted by the Senate and House of Representatives of the United States of America in Congress Assembled,

.   .   .   .

Sec. 6.   That the labor of a human being is not a commodity or article of commerce. Nothing contained in the anti-trust laws shall be construed to forbid the existence and operation of labor, agricultural, or horticultural organizations, instituted for the purposes of mutual help, and not having capital stock or conducted for profit, or to forbid or restrain individual members of such organizations from lawfully carrying out the legitimate objects thereof; nor shall such organizations, or the members thereof, be held or construed to be illegal combinations or conspiracies in restraint of trade, under the anti-trust laws.

.   .   .   .

1932
NORRIS-LaGUARDIA ACT
Public Law 72–65, 48 Stat. 70, 29 U.S.C. § 101 et seq., approved March 23, 1932.

AN ACT
To amend the Judicial Code and to define and limit the jurisdiction of courts sitting in equity, and for other purposes.

Be it Enacted by the Senate and House of Representatives of the United States of America in Congress Assembled,

Sec. 1.   That no court of the United States, as herein defined, shall have jurisdiction to issue any restraining order or temporary or permanent injunction in a case involving or growing out of a labor dispute, except in a strict conformity with the provisions of this Act; nor shall any such restraining order or temporary or permanent injunction be issued contrary to the public policy declared in this Act.

Sec. 2.   In the interpretation of this Act and in determining the jurisdiction and authority of the courts of the United States, as such jurisdiction and authority are herein defined and limited, the public policy of the United States is hereby declared as follows:

Whereas under prevailing economic conditions, developed with the aid of governmental authority for owners of property to organize in the corporate and other forms of ownership association, the individual unorganized worker is commonly helpless to exercise actual liberty of contract and to protect his freedom of labor, and thereby to obtain acceptable terms and conditions of employment, wherefore, though he should be free to decline to associate with his fellows, it is necessary that he have full freedom of association, self-organization, and designation of representatives of his own choosing, to negotiate the terms and conditions of his employment, and that he shall be free from the interference, restraint, or coercion of employers of labor, or their agents, in the designation of such representatives or in self-organization or in other concerted activities for the purpose of collective bargaining or other mutual aid or protection; therefore, the following definitions of, and limitations upon, the jurisdiction and authority of the courts of the United States are hereby enacted.

.   .   .

Sec. 7.   No court of the United States shall have jurisdiction to issue a temporary or permanent injunction in any case involving or growing out of a labor dispute, as herein defined, except after hearing testimony of witnesses in open court (with opportunity for cross-examination) in support of the allegations of a complaint made under oath, and testimony in opposition thereto, if offered, and except after findings of fact by the court, to the effect—

(a) That unlawful acts have been threatened and will be committed unless restrained or have been committed and will be continued unless restrained.   .   .   .

.   .   .

Sec. 13.   When used in this Act, and for the purposes of this Act—

(a) A case shall be held to involve or to grow out of a labor dispute when the case involves persons who are engaged in the same industry, trade, craft, or occupation; or have direct or indirect interests therein; or who are employees of the same employer; or who are members of the same or an affiliated organization of employers or employees; whether such dispute is (1) between one or more employers or associations of employers and one or more employees or associations of employees; (2) between one or more employers or associations of employers and one or more employers or associations of employers; or (3) between one or more employees or associations of employees and one or more employees or associations of employees; or when the case involves any conflicting or competing interests in a "labor dispute" (as hereinafter defined) of "persons participating or interested" therein (as hereinafter defined).

(b) A person or association shall be held to be a person participating or interested in a labor dispute if relief is sought against him or it, and if he or it is engaged in the same industry, trade, craft, or occupation in which such dispute occurs, or has a direct or indirect interest therein, or is a member, officer, or agent of any association composed in whole or in part of employers or employees engaged in such industry, trade, craft, or occupation.

(c) The term "labor dispute" includes any controversy concerning terms or conditions of employment, or concerning the association or representation of persons in negotiating, fixing, maintaining, changing, or seeking to arrange terms or conditions of employment, regardless of whether or not the disputants stand in the proximate relation of employer and employee.

.   .   .   .

1935
NATIONAL LABOR RELATIONS ACT (WAGNER ACT)
Public Law 198, 49 Stat. 449, 29 U.S.C. § 151 et seq., approved July 5, 1935.
as amended by

1947
LABOR MANAGEMENT RELATIONS ACT, 1947 (TAFT-HARTLEY ACT)
Public Law 101, 61 Stat. 136, 29 U.S.C. § § 141 et seq., passed by Congress on June 23, 1947 over the veto of President Harry S. Truman.

AN ACT
To amend the National Labor Relations Act, to provide additional facilities for the mediation of labor disputes affecting commerce, to equalize legal responsibilities of labor organizations and employers, and for other purposes.

Be it enacted by the Senate and House of Representatives of the United States of America in Congress assembled,

SHORT TITLE AND DECLARATION OF POLICY
Section 1.   (a) This Act may be cited as the "Labor Management Relations Act, 1947".

(b) Industrial strife which interferes with the normal flow of commerce and with the full production of articles and commodities for commerce, can be avoided or substantially minimized if employers, employees, and labor organizations each recognize under law one another's legitimate rights in their relations with each other, and above all recognize under law that neither party has any right in its relations with any other to engage in acts or practices which jeopardize the public health, safety, or interest.

It is the purpose and policy of this Act, in order to promote the full flow of commerce, to prescribe the legitimate rights of both employees and employers in their relations affecting commerce, to provide orderly and peaceful procedures for preventing the interference by either with the legitimate rights of the other, to protect the rights of individual employees in their relations with labor organizations whose activities affect commerce, to define and prescribe practices on the part of labor and management which affect commerce and are inimical to the general welfare, and to protect the rights of the public in connection with labor disputes affecting commerce.

TITLE I—AMENDMENT OF NATIONAL LABOR RELATIONS ACT

Sec. 101.   The National Labor Relations Act is hereby amended to read as follows:

FINDINGS AND POLICIES

Section 1.   The denial by some employers of the right of employees to organize and the refusal by some employers to accept the procedure of collective bargaining lead to strikes and other forms of industrial strife or unrest, which have the intent or the necessary effect of burdening or obstructing commerce by (a) impairing the efficiency, safety, or operation of the instrumentalities of commerce; (b) occurring in the current of commerce; (c) materially affecting, restraining, or controlling the flow of raw materials or manufactured or processed goods from or into the channels of commerce, or the prices of such materials or goods in commerce; or (d) causing diminution of employment and wages in such volume as substantially to impair or disrupt the market for goods flowing from or into the channels of commerce.

The inequality of bargaining power between employees who do not possess full freedom of association or actual liberty of contract, and employers who are organized in the corporate or other forms of ownership association substantially burdens and affects the flow of commerce, and tends to aggravate recurrent business depressions, by depressing wage rates and the purchasing power of wage earners in industry and by preventing the stabilization of competitive wage rates and working conditions within and between industries.

Experience has proved that protection by law of the right of employees to organize and bargain collectively safeguards commerce from injury, impairment, or interruption, and promotes the flow of commerce by removing certain recognized sources of industrial strife and unrest, by encouraging practices fundamental to the friendly adjustment of industrial disputes arising out of differences as to wages, hours, or other working conditions, and by restoring equality of bargaining power between employers and employees.

Experience has further demonstrated that certain practices by some labor organizations, their officers, and members have the intent or the necessary effect of burdening or obstructing commerce by preventing the free flow of goods in such commerce through strikes and other forms of industrial unrest or through concerted activities which impair the interest of the public in the free flow of such commerce. The elimination of such practices is a necessary condition to the assurance of the rights herein guaranteed.

It is hereby declared to be the policy of the United States to eliminate the causes of certain substantial obstructions to the free flow of commerce and to mitigate and eliminate these obstructions when they have occurred by encouraging the practice and procedure of collective bargaining and by protecting the exercise by workers of full freedom of association, self-organization, and designation of representatives of their own choosing, for the purpose of negotiating the terms and conditions of their employment or other mutual aid or protection.

.   .   .   .

NATIONAL LABOR RELATIONS BOARD

Sec. 3.   (a) The National Labor Relations Board (hereinafter called the 'Board') created by this Act prior to its amendment by the Labor Management Relations Act,

1947, is hereby continued as an agency of the United States, except that the Board shall consist of five instead of three members, appointed by the President by and with the advice and consent of the Senate. Of the two additional members so provided for, one shall be appointed for a term of five years and the other for a term of two years. Their successors, and the successors of the other members, shall be appointed for terms of five years each, excepting that any individual chosen to fill a vacancy shall be appointed only for the unexpired term of the member whom he shall succeed. The President shall designate one member to serve as Chairman of the Board. . . .

. . . . .

Sec. 6.   The Board shall have authority from time to time to make, amend, and rescind, in the manner prescribed by the Administrative Procedure Act, such rules and regulations as may be necessary to carry out the provisions of this Act.

RIGHTS OF EMPLOYEES

Sec. 7.   Employees shall have the right to self-organization, to form, join, or assist labor organizations, to bargain collectively through representatives of their own choosing, and to engage in other connected activities for the purpose of collective bargaining or other mutual aid or protection, and shall also have the right to refrain from any or all of such activities except to the extent that such right may be affected by an agreement requiring membership in a labor organization as a condition of employment as authorized in section 8 (a) (3).

UNFAIR LABOR PRACTICES

Sec. 8.   (a) It shall be an unfair labor practice for an employer—
  (1) to interfere with, restrain, or coerce employees in the exercise of the rights guaranteed in section 7;
  (2) to dominate or interfere with the formation or administration of any labor organization or contribute financial or other support to it: *Provided,* That subject to rules and regulations made and published by the Board pursuant to section 6, an employer shall not be prohibited from permitting employees to confer with him during working hours without loss of time or pay;
  (3) by discrimination in regard to hire or tenure of employment or any term or condition of employment to encourage or discourage membership in any labor organization: *Provided,* That nothing in this Act, or in any other statute of the United States, shall preclude an employer from making an agreement with a labor organization (not established, maintained, or assisted by any action defined in section 8 (a) of this Act as an unfair labor practice) to require as a condition of employment membership therein on or after the thirtieth day following the beginning of such employment or the effective date of such agreement, whichever is the later, (i) if such labor organization is the representative of the employees as provided in section 9 (a), in the appropriate collective-bargaining unit covered by such agreement when made; and (ii) if, following the most recent election held as provided in section 9 (e) the Board shall have certified that at least a majority of the employees eligible to vote in such election have voted to authorize such labor organization to make such an agreement: *Provided further,* That no employer shall justify any discrimination against an employee for nonmembership in a labor organization (A.) if he

has reasonable grounds for believing that such membership was not available to the employee on the same terms and conditions generally applicable to other members, or (B) if he has reasonable grounds for believing that membership was denied or terminated for reasons other than the failure of the employee to tender the periodic dues and the initiation fees uniformly required as a condition of acquiring or retaining membership;

(4) to discharge or otherwise discriminate against an employee because he has filed charges or given testimony under this Act;

(5) to refuse to bargain collectively with the representatives of his employees, subject to the provisions of section 9 (a).

(b) It shall be an unfair labor practice for a labor organization or its agents—

(1) to restrain or coerce (A) employees in the exercise of the rights guaranteed in section 7: *Provided,* That this paragraph shall not impair the right of a labor organization to prescribe its own rules with respect to the acquisition or retention of membership therein; or (B) an employer in the selection of his representatives for the purposes of collective bargaining or the adjustment of grievances;

(2) to cause or attempt to cause an employer to discriminate against an employee in violation of subsection (a) (3) or to discriminate against an employee with respect to whom membership in such organization has been denied or terminated on some ground other than his failure to tender the periodic dues and the initiation fees uniformly required as a condition of acquiring or retaining membership;

(3) to refuse to bargain collectively with an employer, provided it is the representative of his employees subject to the provisions of section 9 (a);

(4) to engage in, or to induce or encourage the employees of any employer to engage in, a strike or a concerted refusal in the course of their employment to use, manufacture, process, transport, or otherwise handle or work on any goods, articles, materials, or commodities or to perform any services, where an object thereof is: (A) forcing or requiring any employer or self-employed person to join any labor or employer organization or any employer or other person to cease using, selling, handling, transporting, or otherwise dealing in the products of any other producer, processor, or manufacturer, or to cease doing business with any other person; (B) forcing or requiring any other employer to recognize or bargain with a labor organization as the representative of his employees unless such labor organization has been certified as the representative of such employees under the provisions of section 9; (C) forcing or requiring any employer to recognize or bargain with a particular labor organization as the representative of his employees if another labor organization has been certified as the representative of such employees under the provisions of section 9; (D) forcing or requiring any employer to assign particular work to employees in a particular labor organization or in a particular trade, craft, or class rather than to employees in another labor organization or in another trade, craft, or class, unless such employer is failing to conform to an order or certification of the Board determining the bargaining representative for employees performing such work: *Provided,* That nothing contained

in this subsection (b) shall be construed to make unlawful a refusal by any person to enter upon the premises of any employer (other than his own employer), if the employees of such employer are engaged in a strike ratified or approved by a representative of such employees whom such employer is required to recognize under this Act;[30]

(5) to require of employees covered by an agreement authorized under subsection (a) (3) the payment, as a condition precedent to becoming a member of such organization, of a fee in an amount which the Board finds excessive or discriminatory under all the circumstances. In making such a finding, the Board shall consider, among other relevant factors, the practices and customs of labor organizations in the particular industry, and the wages currently paid to the employees affected; and

(6) to cause or attempt to cause an employer to pay or deliver or agree to pay or deliver any money or other thing of value, in the nature of an exaction, for services which are not performed or not to be performed.

(c) The expressing of any views, argument, or opinion, or the dissemination thereof, whether in written, printed, graphic, or visual form, shall not constitute or be evidence of an unfair labor practice under any of the provisions of this Act, if such expression contains no threat of reprisal or force or promise of benefit.

.   .   .   .

REPRESENTATIVES AND ELECTIONS

Sec. 9.   (a) Representatives designated or selected for the purposes of collective bargaining by the majority of the employees in a unit appropriate for such purposes, shall be the exclusive representatives of all the employees in such unit for the purposes of collective bargaining in respect to rates of pay, wages, hours of employment, or other conditions of employment. . . .

(b) The Board shall decide in each case whether, in order to assure to employees the fullest freedom in exercising the rights guaranteed by this Act, the unit appropriate for the purposes of collective bargaining shall be the employer unit, craft unit, plant unit, or subdivision thereof. . . .

.   .   .   .

LIMITATIONS

Sec. 13.   Nothing in this Act, except as specifically provided for herein, shall be construed so as either to interfere with or impede or diminish in any way the right to strike, or to affect the limitations or qualifications on that right.

Sec. 14. . . .   (b) Nothing in this Act shall be construed as authorizing the execution or application of agreements requiring membership in a labor organization as a condition of employment in any State or Territory in which such execution or application is prohibited by State or Territorial law.

---

[30]This provision was amended by The Labor Management Reporting and Disclosure Act of 1959 (Landrum-Griffin Act), 73 Stat. 519, 29 U.S.C. §§ 401 et seq. See the amended section and also new Section 8(e), *infra,* p. 349-350.

．　　．　　．　　．

TITLE II—CONCILIATION OF LABOR DISPUTES IN INDUSTRIES AFFECTING COMMERCE; NATIONAL EMERGENCIES

．　　．　　．　　．

NATIONAL EMERGENCIES

Sec. 206.　Whenever in the opinion of the President of the United States, a threatened or actual strike or lock-out affecting an entire industry or a substantial part thereof engaged in trade, commerce, transportation, transmission, or communication among the several States or with foreign nations, or engaged in the production of goods for commerce, will, if permitted to occur or to continue, imperil the national health or safety, he may appoint a board of inquiry to inquire into the issues involved in the dispute and to make a written report to him within such time as he shall prescribe. Such report shall include a statement of the facts with respect to the dispute, including each party's statement of its position but shall not contain any recommendations. The President shall file a copy of such report with the Service and shall make its contents available to the public.

Sec. 207.　(a) A board of inquiry shall be composed of a chairman and such other members as the President shall determine, and shall have power to sit and act in any place within the United States and to conduct such hearings either in public or in private, as it may deem necessary or proper, to ascertain the facts with respect to the causes and circumstances of the dispute. . . .

Sec. 208.　(a) Upon receiving a report from a board of inquiry the President may direct the Attorney General to petition any district court of the United States having jurisdiction of the parties to enjoin such strike or lock-out or the continuing thereof, and if the court finds that such threatened or actual strike or lock-out—

(i) affects an entire industry or a substanital part thereof engaged in trade, commerce, transportation, transmission, or communication among the several States or with foreign nations, or engaged in the production of goods for commerce; and

(ii) if permitted to occur or to continue, will imperil the national health or safety, it shall have jurisdiction to enjoin any such strike or lock-out, or the continuing thereof, and to make such other orders as may be appropriate.

(b) In any case, the provisions of the Act of March 23, 1932 entitled "An Act to amend the Judicial Code and to define and limit the jurisdiction of courts sitting in equity, and for other purposes," shall not be applicable. . . .

Sec. 209.　(a) Whenever a district court has issued an order under section 208 enjoining acts or practices which imperil or threaten to imperil the national health or safety, it shall be the duty of the parties to the labor dispute giving rise to such order to make every effort to adjust and settle their differences, with the assistance of the Service created by this Act.[31] Neither party shall be under any duty to accept, in whole or in part, any proposal of settlement made by the Service.

---

[31]The Service referred to in this section is the Federal Mediation and Conciliation Service which, created by Section 202, proffers its services to parties involved in a labor dispute that disrupts interstate commerce.

Upon the issuance of such order, the President shall reconvene the board of inquiry which has previously reported with respect to the dispute. At the end of a sixty-day period (unless the dispute has been settled by that time), the board of inquiry shall report to the President the current position of the parties and the efforts which have been made for settlement, and shall include a statement by each party of its position and a statement of the employer's last offer of settlement. The President shall make such report available to the public. The National Labor Relations Board, within the succeeding fifteen days, shall take a secret ballot of the employees of each employer involved in the dispute on the question of whether they wish to accept the final offer of settlement made by their employer as stated by him and shall certify the results thereof to the Attorney General within five days thereafter.

Sec. 210.   Upon the certification of the results of such ballot or upon a settlement being reached, whichever happens sooner, the Attorney General shall move the court to discharge the injunction, which motion shall then be granted and the injunction discharged. When such motion is granted, the President shall submit to the Congress a full and comprehensive report of the proceedings, including the findings of the board of inquiry and the ballot taken by the National Labor Relations Board, together with such recommendations as he may see fit to make for consideration and appropriate action.

. . . . .

TITLE III

SUITS BY AND AGAINST LABOR ORGANIZATIONS

Sec. 301.   (a) Suits for violation of contracts between an employer and a labor organization representing employees in an industry affecting commerce as defined in this Act, or between any such labor organizations, may be brought in any district court of the United States having jurisdiction of the parties, without respect to the amount in controversy or without regard to the citizenship of the parties.

(b) Any labor organization which represents employees in an industry affecting commerce as defined in this Act and any employer whose activities affect commerce as defined in this Act shall be bound by the acts of its agents. Any such labor organization may sue or be sued as an entity and in behalf of the employees whom it represents in the courts of the United States. Any money judgment against a labor organization in a district court of the United States shall be enforceable only against the organization as an entity and against its assets, and shall not be enforceable against any individual member or his assets.   . . .

. . . . .

1959

LABOR MANAGEMENT REPORTING AND DISCLOSURE ACT OF 1959
(Landrum-Griffin Act), Public Law 86–257, 73 Stat. 519, 29 U.S.C. §§ 401 et seq., approved September 14, 1959.

Be it enacted by the Senate and House of Representatives of the United States of America in Congress assembled,

. . . . .

DECLARATION OF FINDINGS, PURPOSES, AND POLICY

Sec. 2.   (a) The Congress finds that, in the public interest, it continues to be the responsibility of the Federal Government to protect employees' rights to organize, choose their own representatives, bargain collectively, and otherwise engage in concerted activities for their mutual aid or protection; that the relations between employers and labor organizations and the millions of workers they represent have a substantial impact on the commerce of the Nation; and that in order to accomplish the objective of a free flow of commerce it is essential that labor organizations, employers, and their officials adhere to the highest standards of responsibility and ethical conduct in administering the affairs of their organizations, particularly as they affect labor-management relations.

(b) The Congress further finds, from recent investigations in the labor and management fields, that there have been a number of instances of breach of trust, corruption, disregard of the rights of individual employees, and other failures to observe high standards of responsibility and ethical conduct which require further and supplementary legislation that will afford necessary protection of the rights and interests of employees and the public generally as they relate to the activities of labor organizations, employers, labor relations consultants, and their officers and representatives.

(c) The Congress, therefore, further finds and declares that the enactment of this Act is necessary to eliminate or prevent improper practices on the part of labor organizations, employers, labor relations consultants, and their officers and representatives which distort and defeat the policies of the Labor Management Relations Act, 1947, as amended, and the Railway Labor Act, as amended, and have the tendency or necessary effect of burdening or obstructing commerce by (1) impairing the efficiency, safety, or operation of the instrumentalities of commerce; (2) occurring in the current of commerce; (3) materially affecting, restraining, or controlling the flow of raw materials or manufactured or processed goods into or from the channels of commerce, or the prices of such materials or goods in commerce; or (4) causing diminution of employment and wages in such volume as substantially to impair or disrupt the market for goods flowing into or from the channels of commerce.

.   .   .   .

TITLE I—BILL OF RIGHTS OF MEMBERS OF LABOR ORGANIZATIONS

BILL OF RIGHTS

Sec. 101.   (a)(1) EQUAL RIGHTS.—Every member of a labor organization shall have equal rights and privileges within such organization to nominate candidates, to vote in elections or referendums of the labor organization, to attend membership meetings, and to participate in the deliberations and voting upon the business of such meetings, subject to reasonable rules and regulations in such organization's constitution and bylaws.

(2) FREEDOM OF SPEECH AND ASSEMBLY.—Every member of any labor organization shall have the right to meet and assemble freely with other members; and to express any views, arguments, or opinions; and to express at meetings of the labor organization his views, upon candidates in an election of the labor organization or upon any business properly before the meeting, subject to the organization's established and

reasonable rules pertaining to the conduct of meetings: *Provided,* That nothing herein shall be construed to impair the right of a labor organization to adopt and enforce reasonable rules as to the responsibility of every member toward the organization as an institution and to his refraining from conduct that would interfere with its performance of its legal or contractual obligations.

. . . .

(4) PROTECTION OF THE RIGHT TO SUE.—No labor organization shall limit the right of any member thereof to institute an action in any court, or in a proceeding before any administrative agency, irrespective of whether or not the labor organization or its officers are named as defendants or respondents in such action or proceeding, or the right of any member of a labor organization to appear as a witness in any judicial, administrative, or legislative proceeding, or to petition any legislature or to communicate with any legislator: *Provided,* That any such member may be required to exhaust reasonable hearing procedures (but not to exceed a four-month lapse of time) within such organization, before instituting legal or administrative proceedings against such organizations or any officer thereof: *And provided further,* That no interested employer or employer association shall directly or indirectly finance, encourage, or participate in, except as a party, any such action, proceeding, appearance, or petition.

(5) SAFEGUARDS AGAINST IMPROPER DISCIPLINARY ACTION.—No member of any labor organization may be fined, suspended, expelled, or otherwise disciplined except for nonpayment of dues by such organization or by any officer thereof unless such member has been (A) served with written specific charges; (B) given a reasonable time to prepare his defense; (C) afforded a full and fair hearing.   . . .

CIVIL ENFORCEMENT

Sec. 102.   Any person whose rights secured by the provisions of this title have been infringed by any violation of this title may bring a civil action in a district court of the United States for such relief (including injunctions) as may be appropriate. Any such action against a labor organization shall be brought in the district court of the United States for the district where the alleged violation occurred, or where the principal office of such labor organization is located.[32]

. . . .

TITLE V—SAFEGUARDS FOR LABOR ORGANIZATIONS

FIDUCIARY RESPONSIBILITY OF OFFICERS OF LABOR ORGANIZATIONS

Sec. 501.   (a) The officers, agents, shop stewards, and other representatives of a labor organization occupy positions of trust in relation to such organization and its members

---

[32]An example of the type of suit arising under this section is Grand Lodge, International Assn. of Machinists v. King, 335 F.2d 340 (9th Cir. 1964), *cert. denied,* 379 U.S. 920 (1964), in which the court held that the union could not summarily dismiss plaintiffs, who were appointed officials in the union, for actively supporting a particular candidate for union office by meeting with other members and expressing views favorable to that candidate. The court in this case, in addition to invoking Sections 101(a)(1) and 101(a)(2) in support of its decision, cited and relied upon Section 609 of the Landrum-Griffin Act, which provides: "It shall be unlawful for any labor organization,

as a group. It is, therefore, the duty of each such person, taking into account the special problems and functions of a labor organization, to hold its money and property solely for the benefit of the organization and its members and to manage, invest, and expend the same in accordance with its constitution and bylaws and any resolutions of the governing bodies adopted thereunder, to refrain from dealing with such organization as an adverse party or in behalf of an adverse party in any matter connected with his duties and from holding or acquiring any pecuniary or personal interest which conflicts with the interests of such organization, and to account to the organization for any profit received by him in whatever capacity in connection with transactions conducted by him or under his direction on behalf of the organization. A general exculpatory provision in the constitution and bylaws of such a labor organization or a general exculpatory resolution of a governing body purporting to relieve any such person of liability for breach of the duties declared by this section shall be void as against public policy.

(b) When any officer, agent, shop steward, or representative of any labor organization is alleged to have violated the duties declared in subsection (a) and the labor organization or its governing board or officers refuse or fail to sue or recover damages or secure an accounting or other appropriate relief within a reasonable time after being requested to do so by any member of the labor organization, such member may sue such officer, agent, shop steward, or representative in any district court of the United States or in any State court of competent jurisdiction to recover damages or secure an accounting or other appropriate relief for the benefit of the labor organization.[33]   . . .

(c) Any person who embezzles, steals, or unlawfully and willfully abstracts or converts to his own use, or to the use of another, any of the moneys, funds, securities, property, or other assets of a labor organization of which he is an officer, or by which he is employed, directly or indirectly, shall be fined not more than $10,000 or imprisoned for not more than five years, or both.

[Section 502 requires union officers and agents who handle funds of a trust in which the labor organization is interested to be bonded.]

TITLE VII—AMENDMENTS TO THE LABOR MANAGEMENT RELATIONS ACT, 1947, AS AMENDED

.   .   .   .

BOYCOTTS AND RECOGNITION PICKETING

Sec. 704.   (a) Section 8(b) (4) of the National Labor Relations Act, as amended, is amended to read as follows:

(4)(i) to engage in, or to induce or encourage any individual employed by any

or any officer, agent, shop steward, or other representative of a labor organization, or any employee thereof to fine, suspend, expel, or otherwise discipline any of its members for exercising any right to which he is entitled under the provisions of this Act. The provisions of section 102 shall be applicable in the enforcement of this section."

[33]An example of the type of case arising under this Section is Highway Truck Drivers & Helpers, Local 107 v. Cohen, 334 F.2d 378 (3d Cir. 1964), *cert. denied,* 379 U.S. 921 (1964), in which the Circuit Court of Appeals held that rank and file union members could recover for the union treasury funds spent by the union officers in their legal defense to criminal charges for an alleged conspiracy to cheat and defraud the union of large sums of money.

person engaged in commerce or in an industry affecting commerce to engage in, a strike or a refusal in the course of his employment to use, manufacture, process, transport, or otherwise handle or work on any goods, articles, materials, or commodities or to perform any services; or (ii) to threaten, coerce, or restrain any person engaged in commerce or in an industry affecting commerce, where in either case an object thereof is—

(A) forcing or requiring any employer or self-employed person to join any labor or employer organization or to enter into any agreement which is prohibited by by section 8(e);

(B) forcing or requiring any person to cease using, selling, handling, transporting, or otherwise dealing in the products of any other producer, processor, or manufacturer, or to cease doing business with any other person, or forcing or requiring any other employer to recognize or bargain with a labor organization as the representative of his employees unless such labor organization has been certified as the representative of such employees under the provisions of section 9: *Provided,* That nothing contained in this clause (B) shall be construed to make unlawful, where not otherwise unlawful, any primary strike or primary picketing;

(C) forcing or requiring any employer to recognize or bargain with a particular labor organization as the representative of his employees if another labor organization has been certified as the representative of such employees under the provisions of section 9;

(D) forcing or requiring any employer to assign particular work to employees in a particular labor organization or in a particular trade, craft, or class rather than to employees in another labor organization or in another trade, craft, or class, unless such employer is failing to conform to an order or certification of the Board determining the bargaining representative for employees performing such work:

Provided, That nothing contained in this subsection (b) shall be construed to make unlawful a refusal by any person to enter upon the premises of any employer (other than his own employer), if the employees of such employer are engaged in a strike ratified or approved by a representative of such employees whom such employer is required to recognize under this Act: *Provided further,* That for the purposes of this paragraph (4) only, nothing contained in such paragraph shall be construed to prohibit publicity, other than picketing, for the purpose of truthfully advising the public, including consumers and members of a labor organization, that a product or products are produced by an employer with whom the labor organization has a primary dispute and are distributed by another employer, as long as such publicity does not have an effect of inducing any individual employed by any person other than the primary employer in the course of his employment to refuse to pick up, deliver, or transport any goods, or not to perform any services, at the establishment of the employer engaged in such distribution.

(b) Section 8 of the National Labor Relations Act, as amended, is amended by adding at the end thereof the following new subsection:

(e) It shall be an unfair labor practice for any labor organization and any employer to enter into any contract or agreement, express or implied, whereby such employer ceases or refrains or agrees to cease or refrain from handling, using, selling, transporting or otherwise dealing in any of the products of any other employer, or to cease doing business with any other person, and any contract or agreement entered into heretofore or hereafter containing such an agreement shall be to such extent unenforceable and void: *Provided,* That nothing in this subsection (e) shall apply to an agreement between a labor organization and an employer in the construction industry relating to the contracting or subcontracting of work to be done at the site of the construction, alteration, painting, or repair of a building, structure, or other work: *Provided further,* That for the purposes of this subsection (e) and section 8(b) (4) (B) the terms 'any employer', 'any person engaged in commerce or an industry affecting commerce', and 'any person' when used in relation to the terms 'any other producer, processor, or manufacturer', 'any other employer', or 'any other person' shall not include persons in the relation of a jobber, manufacturer, contractor, or subcontractor working on the goods or premises of the jobber or manufacturer or performing parts of an integrated process of production in the apparel and clothing industry: *Provided further,* That nothing in this Act shall prohibit the enforcement of any agreement which is within the foregoing exception.

(c) Section 8(b) of the National Labor Relations Act, as amended, is amended by striking out the word "and" at the end of paragraph (5), striking out the period at the end of paragraph (6), and inserting in lieu thereof a semicolon and the word "and", and adding a new paragraph as follows:

(7) to picket or cause to be picketed, or threaten to picket or cause to be picketed, any employer where an object thereof is forcing or requiring an employer to recognize or bargain with a labor organization as the representative of his employees, or forcing or requiring the employees of an employer to accept or select such labor organization as their collective bargaining representative, unless such labor organization is currently certified as the representative of such employees:

(A) where the employer has lawfully recognized in accordance with this Act any other labor organization and a question concerning representation may not appropriately be raised under section 9(c) of this Act,

(B) where within the preceding twelve months a valid election under section 9(c) of this Act has been conducted, or

(C) where such picketing has been conducted without a petition under section 9(c) being filed within a reasonable period of time not to exceed thirty days from the commencement of such picketing: *Provided,* That when such a petition has been filed the Board shall forthwith, without regard to the provisions of section 9(c) (1) or the absence of a showing of a substantial interest on the part of the labor organization, direct an election in such unit as the Board finds to be appropriate and shall certify the results thereof: *Provided further,* That nothing in this subparagraph (C) shall be construed to prohibit any picketing or other publicity for the purpose of truthfully advising the public (including consumers) that an employer does not employ members of, or have a contract with, a labor organization, unless an effect of such picketing is to induce any individual employed by any other person in the course of his employment, not to pick up, deliver or transport any goods or not to perform any services.

Nothing in this paragraph (7) shall be construed to permit any act which would otherwise be an unfair labor practice under this section 8(b). . . .

BUILDING AND CONSTRUCTION INDUSTRY

Sec. 705.   (a) Section 8 of the National Labor Relations Act, as amended by section 704 (b) of this Act, is amended by adding at the end thereof the following new subsection:

(f) It shall not be an unfair labor practice under subsections (a) and (b) of this section for an employer engaged primarily in the building and construction industry to make an agreement covering employees engaged (or who, upon their employment, will be engaged) in the building and construction industry with a labor organization of which building and construction employees are members (not established, maintained, or assisted by any action defined in section 8(a) of this Act as an unfair labor practice) because (1) the majority status of such labor organization has not been established under the provisions of section 9 of this Act prior to the making of such agreement, or (2) such agreement requires as a condition of employment, membership in such labor organization after the seventh day following the beginning of such employment or the effective date of the agreement, whichever is later, or (3) such agreement requires the employer to notify such labor organization of opportunities for employment with such employer, or gives such labor organization an opportunity to refer qualified applicants for such employment, or (4) such agreement specifies minimum training or experience qualifications for employment or provides for priority in opportunities for employment based upon length of service with such employer, in the industry or in the particular geographical area: *Provided,* That nothing in this subsection shall set aside the final proviso to section 8(a) (3) of this Act: *Provided further,* That any agreement which would be invalid, but for clause (1) of this subsection, shall not be a bar to a petition filed pursuant to section 9(c) or 9(e).

(b) Nothing contained in the amendment made by subsection (a) shall be construed as authorizing the execution or application of agreements requiring membership in a labor organization as a condition of employment in any State or Territory in which such execution or application is prohibited by State or Territorial law.

· · · ·

1964
CIVIL RIGHTS ACT OF 1964
Public Law 88-352, 78 Stat. 253, 42 U.S.C. § 2000e, approved July 2, 1964.

Be it enacted by the Senate and House of Representatives of the United States of America in Congress assembled, That this Act may be cited as the "Civil Rights Act of 1964."

· · · ·

Title VII—Equal Employment Opportunity
· · · ·

DISCRIMINATION BECAUSE OF RACE, COLOR, RELIGION, SEX, OR NATIONAL ORIGIN

Sec. 703.   (a) It shall be an unlawful employment practice for an employer—

(1) to fail or refuse to hire or to discharge any individual, or otherwise to discriminate against any individual with respect to his compensation, terms, conditions, or privileges of employment, because of such individual's race, color, religion, sex, or national origin; or

(2) to limit, segregate, or classify his employees in any way which would deprive or tend to deprive any individual of employment opportunities or otherwise adversely affect his status as an employee, because of such individual's race, color, religion, sex, or national origin.

(b) It shall be an unlawful employment practice for an employment agency to fail or refuse to refer for employment, or otherwise to discriminate against, any individual because of his race, color, religion, sex, or national origin, or to classify or refer for employment any individual on the basis of his race, color, religion, sex, or national origin.

(c) It shall be an unlawful employment practice for a labor organization—

(1) to exclude or to expel from its membership, or otherwise to discriminate against, any individual because of his race, color, religion, sex, or national origin;

(2) to limit, segregate, or classify its membership, or to classify or fail to refuse to refer for employment any individual, in any way which would deprive or tend to deprive any individual of employment opportunities, or would limit such employment opportunities or otherwise adversely affect his status as an employee or as an applicant for employment, because of such individual's race, color, religion, sex, or national origin; or

(3) to cause or attempt to cause an employer to discriminate against an individual in violation of this section.

(d) It shall be an unlawful employment practice for any employer, labor organization, or joint labor-management committee controlling apprenticeship or other training or retraining, including on-the-job training programs to discriminate against any individual because of his race, color, religion, sex, or national origin in admission to, or employment in, any program established to provide apprenticeship or other training.

· · · · ·

EQUAL EMPLOYMENT OPPORTUNITY COMMISSION

Sec. 705. (a) There is hereby created a Commission to be known as the Equal Employment Opportunity Commission, which shall be composed of five members, not more than three of whom shall be members of the same political party, who shall be appointed by the President by and with the advice and consent of the Senate. [The remainder of Section 705 gives the Commission broad powers to appoint attorneys and agents, to investigate violations of the Act, and to cooperate and aid both public and private agencies and also individuals in exercising their rights under this Act.]

· · · · ·

1962
EMPLOYEE-MANAGEMENT COOPERATION IN THE FEDERAL SERVICE
Executive Order 10988, 27 Fed. Reg. 551 (1962), approved by President Kennedy on January 17, 1962.

WHEREAS participation of employees in the formulation and implementation of personnel policies affecting them contributes to effective conduct of public business; and

WHEREAS the efficient administration of the Government and the well-being of employees require that orderly and constructive relationships be maintained between employee organizations and management officials; and

WHEREAS subject to law and the paramount requirements of the public service, employee-management relations within the Federal service should be improved by providing employees an opportunity for greater participation in the formulation and implementation of policies and procedures affecting the conditions of their employment; and

WHEREAS effective employee-management cooperation in the public service requires a clear statement of the respective rights and obligations of employee organizations and agency management:

NOW, THEREFORE, by virtue of the authority vested in me by the Constitution of the United States, by section 1753 of the Revised Statutes (5 U.S.C. 631), and as President of the United States, I hereby direct the following policies shall govern officers and agencies of the executive branch of the Government in all dealings with Federal employees and organizations representing such employees.

Sec. 1.   (a) Employees of the Federal Government shall have, and shall be protected in the exercise of, the right, freely and without fear of penalty or reprisal, to form, join and assist any employee organization or to refrain from any such activity. Except as hereinafter expressly provided, the freedom of such employees to assist any employee organization shall be recognized as extending to participation in the management of the organization and acting for the organization in the capacity of an organization representative, including presentation of its views to officials of the executive branch, the Congress or other appropriate authority. The head of each executive department and agency (hereinafter referred to as "agency") shall take such action, consistent with law, as may be required in order to assure that employees in the agency are apprised of the rights described in this section, and that no interference, restraint, coercion or discrimination is practiced within such agency to encourage or discourage membership in any employee organization.

Sec. 2.   When used in this order, the term "employee organization" means any lawful association, labor organization, federation, council or brotherhood having as a primary purpose the improvement of working conditions among Federal employees, or any craft, trade or industrial union whose membership includes both Federal employees and employees of private organizations; but such term shall not include any organization (1) which asserts the right to strike against the Government of the United States or any agency thereof, or to assist or participate in any such strike, or which imposes a duty or obligation to conduct, assist or participate in any such strike, or (2) which advocates the overthrow of the constitutional form of Government in the United States, or (3) which discriminates with regard to the terms or conditions of membership because of race, color, creed or national origin.

. . . . .

Sec. 16.   This order . . . shall not apply to the Federal Bureau of Investigation, the Central Intelligence Agency, or any other agency, or to any office, bureau or entity within an agency, primarily performing intelligence, investigative, or security functions if the head of the agency determines that the provisions of this order cannot be applied in a manner consistent with national security requirements and considerations. When he deems it necessary in the national interest, and subject to such conditions as he may prescribe, the head of any agency may suspend any provision of this order . . . with respect to any agency installation or activity which is located outside of the United States.

.   .   .   .

8 Law is Ever and Anon Burdened With Dissent

Introduction. 355
Concerning Speech, Action, and War. 358
    Bond v. Floyd 359
    United States v. O'Brien 361
    Tinker v. Des Moines Independent Community
      School District 365
    United States v. Sisson 371
    Watts v. United States. 377
Law and the World: What Price the Individual?. 380
Questions 385

INTRODUCTION

Congress shall make no law respecting an establishment of religion, or prohibiting the free exercise thereof; or abridging the freedom of speech, or of the press; or the right of the people peaceably to assemble, and to petition the government for a redress of grievances.[1]

Voltaire did not say, "I disapprove of what you *do,* but I will defend to the death your right to *do* it." In fact, he is probably not even the author of the immortal epigram in which the key word is "say," rather than "do."[2] Neither the First Amendment nor Voltaire would abridge speech, but both are silent on action. The distinction between speech and action is so firmly rooted in commonsense that, except for some of the cases in this section, it seems unnecessary to emphasize the point.

Society can, within rather loose bounds, hold talk cheap. For action, how-

---

[1] First Amendment to the Constitution of the United States, ratified by three-fourths of the States on December 15, 1791.

[2] An English writer, S. G. Tallentyre (E. Beatrice Hall), attributed the words to Voltaire in a book *The Friends of Voltaire,* published in 1906. Research by others failed to discover any such saying in Voltaire's writings, and Hall, who may have unwittingly made her own immortality, said 30 years later that the words were a paraphrase of Voltaire's attitude. Stevenson, Burton, *The Home Book of Quotations,* pp. 726:5, 2276:1 (9th ed.), Dodd Mead, New York, 1964.

ever, the bounds must be tighter. Voltaire *did* say in his *Essay on Tolerance,* "Think for yourselves, and let others enjoy the privilege to do so too." This aphorism is akin to freedom of speech, but there is no counterpart in any civilized society that says, "Permit another to strike you so that you may have the privilege of striking him." Such a principle would negate the "domestic tranquillity" that the Preamble to the Constitution of the United States declares to be one of the objectives of the formation of "a more perfect union." The principle of order in society (tranquillity) is prime. (It must have arisen in dim ages past, concurrently with the taboos against incest and the restraints on sexual promiscuity.[3])

The principle of freedom of speech did not arise with the First Amendment to the Constitution—consider the participatory democracy of the Greek cities, particularly Athens, where meetings, discussions, and voting by the assembled citizens were the mode of government. Nor did actions by government *against* speech arise with the domestic tensions of the Vietnam War—witness the death of Socrates for allegedly teaching religious heresies. Rather, the declaration in the Preamble to the Constitution of intent "to form a more perfect union" reflects the learning and sense of history of some of the framers of the Constitution, who had no illusions about perfection in government. They knew the past imperfections in governments and sought only to improve upon the record.

The issue of the will of the state versus the conscience of the individual is ancient. It did not arise with the attempted refusals to be drafted for the Vietnam War. The classical case is that of Sophocles' *Antigone,* 25 centuries ago. The tragic Oedipus had two daughters and two sons. Oedipus, self-blinded in remorse for his unwitting crimes of patricide and incest, was banished from Thebes. One of the sons of Oedipus, Polyneices, treasonously revolted against Creon, successor to Oedipus as Head of State, and in battle slew, and was slain by, his brother Eteocles, who had remained loyal to the State. Creon decreed for the traitor that:[4]

> No one shall bury him, no one mourn for him,
> But his body must lie in the fields, a sweet treasure
> For carrion birds to find as they search for food.

This was a cruel and unusual punishment. Polyneices' sister, Antigone, violated the decree, giving the brother such poor ceremony as she could on the spent battlefield, saying in defense:[5]

---

[3]See Mann, Thomas, footnote 3, Chapter 1; also White, Leslie A., *The Science of Culture,* E-105, p. 305, Grove Press, New York, 1949.

[4]Fitts, Dudley and Robert Fitzgerald, *Sophocles—The Oedipus Cycle,* p.186, Harvest HB 8, Harcourt, New York, 1939, 1941, 1949.

[5]*Id.,* p. 203.

Your edict, King, was strong,
But all your strength is weakness itself against
The immortal unrecorded laws of God.

The conscience of the individual against the will of state—today, this ancient issue is appropriately called the "Antigone question."

War is an unfailing cause of domestic dissent. It is true that many, if not all, religions extol fighting: The sacred Indian Vedas contain accounts of great battles from which enlightenment is drawn; the Old Testament is full of approved fighting "before the Lord;" and New Testament Christianity speaks of hosts and employs the terminology of earthly kingdoms. Islam invented, in its early, spectacular growth, the neatest formulation for warfare: Islam is the realm of peace and it is the duty of Muslims to expand that realm—by the sword.

Pacifism has always pressed hard on war for the dominant role in the affairs of men. Yet, it is pacificism that, through the ages, has been the more verbally violent. Euripides' Trojan Women, produced in 415 B.C., followed close upon the unconscionable siege and capture of the island of Melos by the Athenians, whose patron Athena was a goddess of wisdom and warfare. Euripides' scathing invective about the Trojan War, which he uses as material for his outraged conscience, reads, with better poetry, very much like the anguish of the 1960's about the United States in Santo Domingo or in Vietnam. Euripides depicts the recovery of the foolish, beautiful Helen by her cuckolded husband Menelaus as a bitter dissolutionment, after all the death and devastation in Troy. We may read, according to some, Vietnam for Troy. Pacifism is not new.

Selective pacifism had its precedent in Henry David Thoreau's refusal to pay taxes because he did not approve of the Mexican War. His doctrine of civil disobedience, where individual conscience is invoked, passed full circle from America to the Indian Mohandas K. Gandhi and back to the American Martin Luther King. Although in the 1960's it was the cry of domestic injustice that sounded loudly in America, it was war in Vietnam that pressed the American law relentlessly toward the curbing of presidential and congressional powers in warfare.

The cases in this section are confined to the Antigone question, as it is exemplified in this eighteenth decade of the American Constitution. Although some members of the Supreme Court might go that far, a curbing of war powers is unlikely to take the crude and direct form of a judicial injunction against the chief executive, even in a legal controversy over declared and undeclared wars. (See Mora v. McNamara, Chapter 2, p. 70, *supra.*) It would be unnecessary. If individual American citizens may legally decide not to go to Vietnam, and enough of them do so, then there will be peace at some price. Why not then the Berlin Wall, or Hawaii or Alaska or, again, Bunker Hill? Such are the hard questions raised in this section.

The reader may speculate that the cases in this section will always be distinguishable because they are referable to the highly controversial Vietnam War. But all wars are controversial. Our war of independence was so controversial that New York State furnished more troops to George III than to George Washington. While Washington's troops did not lack ammunition, they *were* lacking in rations to the point of starvation because, among other causes, Americans fled into the wilderness rather than pay taxes.[6] In the War Between the States, President Lincoln exercised powers that made President Johnson seem Mr. Milquetoast. Lincoln called for enlistments not yet sanctioned by Congress, declared a blockade, and suspended the writ of habeas corpus (more ancient and sacred than free speech), with Chief Justice Taney vainly protesting the latter action.[7] We must look deeper than the particular dissension about the Vietnam War for a rationale of the cases in this section. Let us consider them and then indulge a final comment.

CONCERNING SPEECH, ACTION, AND WAR

BOND v. FLOYD
Supreme Court of the United States, 385 U.S. 116 (1966).

MR. CHIEF JUSTICE WARREN delivered the opinion of the Court.

The question presented in this case is whether the Georgia House of Representatives may constitutionally exclude appellant Bond, a duly elected Representative, from membership because of his statements, and statements to which he subscribed, criticizing the policy of the Federal Government in Vietnam and the operation of the Selective Service laws. . . .

Bond, a Negro, was elected on June 15, 1965, as the Representative to the Georgia House of Representatives from the 136th House District. Of the District's 6,500 voters, approximately 6,000 are Negroes. Bond defeated his opponent, Malcolm Dean, Dean of Men at Atlanta University, also a Negro, by a vote of 2,320 to 487.

On January 6, 1966, the Student Nonviolent Coordinating Committee, a civil rights organization of which Bond was then the Communications Director, issued . . . [a] statement on American policy in Vietnam and its relation to the work of civil rights organizations in this country. . . .

. . . . .

On the same day that this statement was issued, Bond was interviewed by telephone by a reporter from a local radio station, and, although Bond had not participated in drafting the statement, he endorsed the statement in these words:

"Why, I endorse it, first, because I like to think of myself as a pacifist and one who opposes that war and any other war and eager and anxious to encourage people not

---

[6]Morrison and Commager, *The Growth of the American Republic.* p. 204, Vol. 1, Oxford University Press, New York, 1953.

[7]*Id.,* Vol. 1, p. 699.

to participate in it for any reason that they choose; and secondly, I agree with this statement because of the reason set forth in it—because I think it is sorta hypocritical for us to maintain that we are fighting for liberty in other places and we are not guaranteeing liberty to citizens inside the continental United States.

"Well, I think that the fact that the United States Government fights a war in Viet Nam, I don't think that I as a second class citizen of the United States have a requirement to support that war. I think my responsibility is to oppose things that I think are wrong if they are in Viet Nam or New York, or Chicago, or Atlanta, or wherever."

. . . . .

The interviewer also asked Bond if he felt he could take the oath of office required by the Georgia Constitution, and Bond responded that he saw nothing inconsistent between his statements and the oath. Bond was also asked whether he would adhere to his statements if war were declared on North Vietnam and if his statements might become treasonous. He replied that he did not know "if I'm strong enough to place myself in a position where I'd be guilty of treason."

[Early in 1966, when the Georgia House of Representatives was scheduled to convene, 75 House members challenged Bond's right to be seated. Bond was given a hearing before a Special Committee to determine exactly what Bond had said and his intent. After the hearing, the Special Committee, in its report to the Georgia House, stated that Bond's endorsement of the SNCC statement and his supplementary remarks showed that "he does not and will not" support the Constitutions of the United States and of Georgia, that he gives aid and comfort to the enemies of the United States, and that his statements "are reprehensible and are such as to tend to bring discredit and disrespect of the House." The House adopted the committee report and voted 184 to 12 not to seat Julian Bond as a member of the Georgia House of Representatives.

Bond then instituted an action in the District Court for the Northern District of Georgia seeking both injunctive relief and a declaratory judgment that the Georgia House action was (1) unauthorized by the Georgia Constitution and (2) violated Bond's rights under the First Amendment. The District Court determined that it had jurisdiction to decide the constitutionality of the Georgia House action but divided on the merits of the case. The majority of the District Court reasoned that Bond's right to dissent as a private citizen was diminished in some unstated degree by his decision to seek membership in the Georgia House. Moreover, the majority concluded that the SNCC statement and Bond's related remarks went beyond permissible criticism of national policy and that therefore Bond could not in good faith take an oath to support the State and Federal Constitutions.]

MR. CHIEF JUSTICE WARREN continued:

We conclude as did the entire court below that this Court has jurisdiction to review the question of whether the action of the Georgia House of Representatives deprived Bond of federal constitutional rights, and we now move to the central question posed in the case—whether Bonds's disqualification because of his statements violated the free speech provisions of the First Amendment as applied to the States through the Fourteenth Amendment.

The State argues that the exclusion does not violate the First Amendment because the State has a right, under Article VI of the United States Constitution, to insist on loyalty to the Constitution as a condition of office. A legislator of course can be required to swear to support the Constitution of the United States as a condition of holding office, but that is not the issue in this case, as the record is uncontradicted that Bond has repeatedly expressed his willingness to swear to the oaths provided for in the State and Federal Constitutions. . . . Thus, we do not quarrel with the State's contention that the oath provisions of the United States and Georgia Constitutions do not violate the First Amendment. But this requirement does not authorize a majority of state legislators to test the sincerity with which another duly elected legislator can swear to uphold the Constitution. Such a power could be utilized to restrict the right of legislators to dissent from national or state policy or that of a majority of their colleagues under the guise of judging their loyalty to the Constitution. Certainly there can be no question but that the First Amendment protects expressions in opposition to national foreign policy in Vietnam and to the Selective Service system. The State does not contend otherwise. But it argues that Bond went beyond expressions of opposition, and counseled violations of the Selective Service laws, and that advocating violation of federal law demonstrates a lack of support for the Constitution. The State declines to argue that Bond's statements would violate any law if made by a private citizen, but it does argue that even though such a citizen might be protected by his First Amendment rights, the State may nonetheless apply a stricter standard to its legislators. We do not agree.

Bond could not have been constitutionally convicted under 50 U.S.C. App. § 462(a), which punishes any person who "counsels, aids, or abets another to refuse or evade registration." Bond's statements were at worst unclear on the question of the means to be adopted to avoid the draft. While the SNCC statement said "We are in sympathy with, and support, the men in this country who are unwilling to respond to a military draft," this statement alone cannot be interpreted as a call to unlawful refusal to be drafted. Moreover, Bond's supplementary statements tend to resolve the opaqueness in favor of legal alternatives to the draft, and there is no evidence to the contrary. On the day the statement was issued, Bond explained that he endorsed it "because I like to think of myself as a pacifist and one who opposes that war and any other war and eager and anxious to encourage people not to participate in it for any reason that they choose." In the same interview, Bond stated categorically that he did not oppose the Vietnam policy because he favored the Communists; that he was a loyal American citizen and supported the Constitution of the United States. He further stated "I oppose the Viet Cong fighting in Viet Nam as much as I oppose the United States fighting in Viet Nam." At the hearing before the Special Committee of the Georgia House, when asked his position on persons who burned their draft cards, Bond replied that he admired the courage of persons who "feel strongly enough about their convictions to take an action like that knowing the consequences that they will face." When pressed as to whether his admiration was based on the violation of federal law, Bond stated:

"I have never suggested or counseled or advocated that any one other person burn their draft card. In fact, I have mine in my pocket and will produce it if you wish. I do not advocate that people should break laws. What I simply try to say was that I admired the courage of someone who could act on his convictions knowing that he faces pretty stiff consequences."

Certainly this clarification does not demonstrate any incitement to violation of law. No useful purpose would be served by discussing the many decisions of this Court which establish that Bond could not have been convicted for these statements consistently with the First Amendment.   . . .

The State attempts to circumvent the protection the First Amendment would afford to these statements if made by a private citizen by arguing that a State is constitutionally justified in exacting a higher standard of loyalty from its legislators than from its citizens. Of course, a State may constitutionally require an oath to support the Constitution from its legislators which it does not require of its private citizens. But this difference in treatment does not support the exclusion of Bond, for while the State has an interest in requiring its legislators to swear to a belief in constitutional processes of government, surely the oath gives it no interest in limiting its legislators' capacity to discuss their views of local or national policy. The manifest function of the First Amendment in a representative government requires that legislators be given the widest latitude to express their views on issues of policy.   . . .

The decision of the District Court is reversed.

UNITED STATES v. O'BRIEN
Supreme Court of the United States, 391 U.S. 367 (1968).

["Any person   . . .   (3) who forges, alters, knowingly destroys, knowingly mutilates, or in any manner changes any such certificate [in this case, "draft cards"] or any notation duly or validly inscribed thereon   . . .   or (6) who knowingly violates or evades any provision of this title or rules and regulations promulgated pursuant thereto relating to the issuance, transfer, or possession, of such certificate, shall, upon conviction, be fined not to exceed $10,000 or be imprisoned for not more than five years or both   . . .   " Universal Military Training and Service Act, 50 U.S.C. § 462(b)(1965).

The rules and regulations spoken of above, provide:

"Every person required to present himself for and submit to registration must, after he is registered, have in his personal possession at all times his Registration Certificate (SSS Form No. 2) ["draft card"] prepared by his local board which has not been altered and on which no notation duly and validly inscribed thereon has been changed in any manner after its preparation by the local board. The failure of any person to have his Registration Certificate (SSS Form No. 2) in his personal possession shall be prima facie evidence of his failure to register.   . . .   " 32 C.F.R. § 1617.1(1962).

Likewise, Section 1623.5 of Volume 32 of the Selective Service Regulations, promulgated in 1955, contains similar provisions concerning the Notice of Classification certificate:

"Every person who has been classified by a local board must have in his personal possession at all times, in addition to his Registration Certificate (SSS Form No. 2), a valid Notice of Classification (SSS Form No. 110) issued to him showing his current classification.   . . .   " 32 C.F.R. § 1623.5(1962).]

MR. CHIEF JUSTICE WARREN delivered the opinion of the Court.

On the morning of March 31, 1966, David Paul O'Brien and three companions burned their Selective Service registration certificates on the steps of the South Boston Courthouse. A sizable crowd, including several agents of the Federal Bureau of Investigation, witnessed the event. Immediately after the burning, members of the crowd began attacking O'Brien and his companions. An FBI agent ushered O'Brien to safety inside the courthouse. After he was advised of his right to counsel and to silence, O'Brien stated to FBI agents that he had burned his registration certificate because of his beliefs, knowing that he was violating federal law. He produced the charred remains of the certificate, which, with his consent, were photographed.

For this act, O'Brien was indicted, tried, convicted, and sentenced in the United States District Court for the District of Massachusetts. He did not contest the fact that he had burned the certificate. He stated in argument to the jury that he burned the certificate publicly to influence others to adopt his antiwar beliefs, as he put it, "so that other people would reevaluate their positions with Selective Service, with the armed forces, and reevalutate their place in the culture of today, to hopefully consider my position."

The indictment upon which he was tried charged that he "wilfully and knowingly did mutilate, destroy, and change by burning   . . .   [his] Registration Certificate (Selective Service System Form No. 2); in violation of Title 50, App., United States Code, Section 462 (b)." Section 462 (b) is part of the Universal Military Training and Service Act of 1948. Section 462 (b)(3), one of six numbered subdivisions of § 462 (b), was amended by Congress in 1965, 79 Stat. 586 (adding the words italicized below), so that at the time O'Brien burned his certificate an offense was commited by any person, "who forges, alters, *knowingly destroys, knowingly mutilates,* or in any manner changes any such certificate   . . .   " (Italics supplied.)

When a male reaches the age of 18, he is required by the Universal Military Training and Service Act to register with a local draft board. He is assigned a Selective Service number, and within five days he is issued a registration certificate (SSS Form No. 2). Subsequently, and based on a questionnaire completed by the registrant, he is assigned a classification denoting his eligibility for induction, and "[a]s soon as practicable" thereafter he is issued a Notice of Classification (SSS Form No. 110). This initial classification is not necessarily permanent, and if in the interim before induction the registrant's status changes in some relevant way, he may be reclassified. After such a reclassification, the local board "as soon as practicable" issues to the registrant a new Notice of Classification.

Both the registration and classification certificates are small white cards, approximately 2 by 3 inches. The registration certificate specifies the name of the registrant, the date of registration, and the number and address of the local board with which he is registered. Also inscribed upon it are the date and place of the registrant's birth, his residence at registration, his physical description, his signature, and his Selective Service number. The Selective Service number itself indicates his State of registration, his local board, his year of birth, and his chronological position in the local board's classification record.

The classification certificate shows the registrant's name, Selective Service number, signature, and eligibility classification. It specifies whether he was so classified by his local board, an appeal board, or the President. It contains the address of his local board and the date the certificate was mailed.

Both the registration and classification certificates bear notices that the registrant must notify his local board in writing of every change in address, physical condition, and occupational, marital, family, dependency, and military status, and of any other fact which might change his classification. Both also contain a notice that the registrant's Selective Service number should appear on all communications to his local board.

.   .   .   .   .

O'Brien . . . argues that the 1965 Amendment [prohibiting the destruction of draft cards] is unconstitutional as applied to him because his act of burning his registration certificate was protected "symbolic speech" within the First Amendment. His argument is that the freedom of expression which the First Amendment guarantees includes all modes of "communication of ideas by conduct," and that his conduct is within this definition because he did it in "demonstration against the war and against the draft."

We cannot accept the view that an apparently limitless variety of conduct can be labelled "speech" whenever the person engaging in the conduct intends thereby to express an idea. However, even on the assumption that the alleged communicative element in O'Brien's conduct is sufficient to bring into play the First Amendment, it does not necessarily follow that the destruction of a registration certificate is constitutionally protected activity. This Court has held that when "speech" and "nonspeech" elements are combined in the same course of conduct, a sufficiently important governmental interest in regulating the nonspeech element can justify incidental limitations on First Amendment freedoms. To characterize the quality of the governmental interest which must appear, the Court has employed a variety of descriptive terms: compelling; substantial; subordinating; paramount; cogent; strong. Whatever imprecision inheres in these terms, we think it clear that a government regulation is sufficiently justified if it is within the constitutional power of the government; if it furthers an important or substantial governmental interest; if the governmental interest is unrelated to the suppression of free expression; and if the incidental restriction on alleged First Amendment freedom is no greater than is essential to the furtherance of that interest. We find that the 1965 Amendment to § 462 (b)(3) of the Universal Military Training and Service Act meets all of these requirements, and consequently that O'Brien can be constitutionally convicted for violating it.

The constitutional power of Congress to raise and support armies and to make all laws necessary and proper to that end is broad and sweeping. Lichter v. United States, 334 U. S. 742, 755-758 (1948); Selective Draft Law Cases, 245 U. S. 366 (1918). . . . The power of Congress to classify and conscript manpower for military service is "beyond question." Lichter v. United States, *supra*, at 756; Selective Draft Law Cases, *supra.* Pursuant to this power, Congress may establish a system of registration for individuals liable for training and service, and may require such individuals within reason to cooperate in the registration system. The issuance of certificates indicating the registration and eligibility classification of individuals is a legitimate and substantial administrative aid in the functioning of this system. And legislation to insure the continuing availability of issued certificates serves a legitimate and substantial purpose in the system's administration.

.   .   .   .   .

We think it apparent that the continuing availability to each registrant of his Selective Service certificates substantially furthers the smooth and proper functioning of the system that Congress has established to raise armies. We think it also apparent that the Nation has a vital interest in having a system for raising armies that functions with maximum efficiency and is capable of easily and quickly responding to continually changing circumstances. For these reasons, the Government has a substantial interest in assuring the continuing availability of issued Selective Service certificates.

It is equally clear that the 1965 Amendment specifically protects this substantial governmental interest. We perceive no alternative means that would more precisely and narrowly assure the continuing availability of issued Selective Service certificates than a law which prohibits their wilful mutilation or destruction. . . . The 1965 Amendment prohibits such conduct and does nothing more. In other words, both the governmental interest and the operation of the 1965 Amendment are limited to the noncommunicative aspect of O'Brien's conduct. The governmental interest and the scope of the 1965 Amendment are limited to preventing a harm to the smooth and efficient functioning of the Selective Service System. When O'Brien deliberately rendered unavailable his registration certificate, he wilfully frustrated this governmental interest. For this noncommunicative impact of his conduct, and for nothing else, he was convicted.

.   .   .   .

In conclusion, we find that because of the Government's substantial interest in assuring the continuing availability of issued Selective Service certificates, because amended § 462 (b) is an appropriately narrow means of protecting this interest and condemns only the independent noncommunicative impact of conduct within its reach, and because the noncommunicative impact of O'Brien's act of burning his registration certificate frustrated the Government's interest, a sufficient governmental interest has been shown to justify O'Brien's conviction.

.   .   .   .

Since the 1965 Amendment to § 12 (b)(3) of the Universal Military Training and Service Act is constitutional as enacted and as applied, the Court of Appeals should have affirmed the judgment of conviction entered by the District Court. Accordingly, we vacate the judgment of the Court of Appeals, and reinstate the judgment and sentence of the District Court. This disposition makes unnecessary consideration of O'Brien's claim that the Court of Appeals erred in affirming his conviction on the basis of the nonpossession regulation.

It is so ordered.

Mr. Justice MARSHALL took no part in the consideration or decision of these cases.

[The concurring opinion of Mr. Justice HARLAN is omitted.]

Mr. Justice DOUGLAS, dissenting.

The Court states that the constitutional power of Congress to raise and support armies is "broad and sweeping" and that Congress' power "to classify and conscript manpower for military service is 'beyond question.'" This is undoubtedly true in times when, by declaration of Congress, the Nation is in a state of war. The underlying and basic problem in this case, however, is whether conscription is permissible in the absence of a declaration of war. That question has not been briefed nor was it presented in oral argument; but it is, I submit, a question upon which the litigants and the country are entitled to a ruling. I have discussed in Holmes v. United States, [391 U.S. 936

(1968)], the nature of the legal issue and it will be seen from my dissenting opinion in that case that this Court has never ruled on the question. It is time that we made a ruling. This case should be put down for reargument and heard with Holmes v. United States and with Hart v. United States, [391 U.S. 956 (1968)], in which the Court today denies certiorari.

The rule that this Court will not consider issues not raised by the parties is not inflexible and yields in "exceptional cases" (Duignan v. United States, 274 U. S. 195, 200), . . . to the need correctly to decide the case before the court. . . .

.   .   .   .

TINKER v. DES MOINES INDEPENDENT COMMUNITY SCHOOL DISTRICT
Supreme Court of the United States, 393 U.S. 503 (1969).

Mr. Justice FORTAS delivered the opinion of the Court.

Petitioner John F. Tinker, 15 years old, and petitioner Christopher Eckhardt, 16 years old, attended high schools in Des Moines. Petitioner Mary Beth Tinker, John's sister, was a 13-year-old student in junior high school.

In December 1965, a group of adults and students in Des Moines, Iowa, held a meeting at the Eckhardt home. The group determined to publicize their objections to the hostilities in Vietnam and their support for a truce by wearing black armbands during the holiday season and by fasting on December 16 and New Year's Eve. Petitioners and their parents had previously engaged in similar activities, and they decided to participate in the program.

The principals of the Des Moines schools became aware of the plan to wear armbands. On December 14, 1965, they met and adopted a policy that any student wearing an armband to school would be asked to remove it, and if he refused he would be suspended until he returned without the armband. Petitioners were aware of the regulation that the school authorities adopted.

On December 16, Mary Beth and Christopher wore black armbands to their schools. John Tinker wore his armband the next day. They were all sent home and suspended from school until they would come back without their armbands. They did not return to school until after the planned period for wearing armbands had expired—that is, until after New Year's Day.

This complaint was filed in the United States District Court by petitioners, through their fathers. . . . It prayed for an injunction restraining the defendant school officials and the defendant members of the board of directors of the school district from disciplining the petitioners, and it sought nominal damages. After an evidentiary hearing the District Court dismissed the complaint. It upheld the constitutionality of the school authorities, action on the ground that it was reasonable in order to prevent disturbance of school discipline. 258 F. Supp. 971 (1966). The court referred to but expressly declined to follow the Fifth Circuit's holding in a similar case that prohibition of the wearing of symbols like the armbands cannot be sustained unless it "materially and substantially interfere[s] with the requirements of appropriate discipline in the operation of the school." Burnside v. Byars, 363 F. 2d 744, 749 (1966).

On appeal, the Court of Appeals for the Eighth Circuit considered the case *en banc.* The court was equally divided, and the District Court's decision was accordingly affirmed, without opinion. 383 F. 2d 988 (1967). We granted certiorari. 390 U.S. 942 (1968).

I.

The District Court recognized that the wearing of an armband for the purpose of expressing certain views is the type of symbolic act that is within the Free Speech Clause of the First Amendment. See West Virginia v. Barnette, 319 U.S. 624 (1943); Stromberg v. California, 283 U.S. 359 (1931). Cf. Thornhill v. Alabama, 310 U.S. 88 (1940). . . . As we shall discuss, the wearing of armbands in the circumstances of this case was entirely divorced from actually or potentially disruptive conduct by those participating in it. It was closely akin to "pure speech" which, we have repeatedly held, is entitled to comprehensive protection under the First Amendment . . .

First Amendment rights, applied in light of the special characteristics of the school environment, are available to teachers and students. It can hardly be argued that either students or teachers shed their constitutional rights to freedom of speech or expression at the schoolhouse gate. This has been the unmistakable holding of this Court for almost 50 years. In Meyer v. Nebraska, 262 U.S. 390 (1923), and Bartels v. Iowa, 262 U.S. 404 (1923), this Court, in opinions by Mr. Justice McReynolds, held that the Due Process Clause of the Fourteenth Amendment prevents States from forbidding the teaching of a foreign language to young students. Statutes to this effect, the Court held, unconstitutionally interfere with the liberty of teacher, student, and parent. . . .

In West Virginia v. Barnette, *supra,* this Court held that under the First Amendment, the student in public school may not be compelled to salute the flag. Speaking through Mr. Justice Jackson, the Court said:

"The Fourteenth Amendment, as now applied to the States, protects the citizen against the State itself and all of its creatures—Boards of Education not excepted. These have, of course, important, delicate, and highly discretionary functions, but none that they may not perform within the limits of the Bill of Rights. That they are educating the young for citizenship is reason for scrupulous protection of Constitutional freedoms of the individual, if we are not to strangle the free mind at its source and teach youth to discount important principles of our government as mere platitudes." 319 U.S., at 637.

On the other hand, the Court has repeatedly emphasized the need for affirming the comprehensive authority of the States and of school authorities, consistent with fundamental constitutional safeguards, to prescribe and control conduct in schools. See Epperson v. Arkansas, [393 U.S. 97 (1968)], at 104; Meyer v. Nebraska, *supra,* at 402. Our problem lies in the area where students in the exercise of First Amendment rights collide with the rules of the school authorities.

II.

The problem presented by the present case . . . does not concern aggressive, disruptive action or even group demonstrations. Our problem involves direct, primary First Amendments rights akin to "pure speech."

The school officials banned and sought to punish petitioners for a silent, passive, expression of opinion, unaccompanied by any disorder or disturbance on the part of petitioners. There is here no evidence whatever of petitioners' interference, actual or nascent, with the school's work or of collision with the rights of other students to be secure and to be let alone. Accordingly, this case does not concern speech or action that intrudes upon the work of the school or the rights of other students.

Only a few of the 18,000 students in the school system wore the black armbands. Only five students were suspended for wearing them. There is no indication that the work of the school or any class was disrupted. Outside the classrooms, a few students made hostile remarks to the children wearing armbands, but there were no threats or acts of violence on school premises.

.   .   .   .

As we have discussed, the record does not demonstrate any facts which might reasonably have led school authorities to forecast substantial disruption of or material interference with school activities, and no disturbances or disorders on the school premises in fact occurred. These petitioners merely went about their ordained rounds in school. Their deviation consisted only in wearing on their sleeve a band of black cloth, not more than two inches wide. They wore it to exhibit their disapproval of the Vietnam hostilities and their advocacy of a truce, to make their views known, and by their example, to influence others to adopt them. They neither interrupted school activities nor sought to intrude in the school affairs or the lives of others. They caused discussion outside of the classrooms, but no interference with work and no disorder. In the circumstances, our Constitution does not permit officials of the State to deny their form of expression.

We express no opinion as to the form of relief which should be granted, this being a matter for the lower courts to determine. We reverse and remand for further proceedings consistent with this opinion.

Reversed and remanded.

[The concurring opinions of Mr. Justice WHITE and Mr. Justice STEWART, and the dissenting opinion of Mr. Justice HARLAN, are omitted.]

Mr. Justice BLACK, dissenting.

The Court's holding in this case ushers in what I deem to be an entirely new era in which the power to control pupils by the elected "officials of the state supported public schools . . . " in the United States is in ultimate effect transferred to the Supreme Court. The Court brought this particular case here on a petition for certiorari urging that the First and Fourteenth Amendments protect the right of schools pupils to express their political views all the way "from kindergarten through high school." Here the constitutional right to "political expression" asserted was a right to wear black armbands during school hours and at classes in order to demonstrate to the other students that the petitioners were mourning because of the death of United States' soldiers in Vietnam and to protest that war which they were against. Ordered to refrain from wearing the armbands in school by the elected school officials and the teachers vested with state authority to do so, apparently only seven out of the school system's 18,000 pupils deliberately refused to obey the order. One defying pupil was Paul Tinker, 8 years old, who was in the second grade; another, Hope Tinker was 11 years old in the fifth grade; a third member of the Tinker family was 13, in the eighth grade; and a fourth member of the same family was John Tinker, 15 years old, an 11th grade high school pupil. Their father, a Methodist minister without a church, is paid a salary by the American Friends Service Committee. Another student who defied the school order and insisted on wearing an armband in school was Chris Eckhardt, an 11th grade pupil and a petitioner in this case. His mother in an official in the Women's International League for Peace and Freedom.

As I read the Court's opinion it relies upon the following grounds for holding unconstitutional the judgment of the Des Moines school officials and the two Courts below. First the Court concludes that the wearing of armbands is "symbolic speech" which is "akin to pure speech" and therefore protected by the First and Fourteenth Amendments. Secondly, the Court decides that the public schools are an appropriate place to exercise "symbolic speech" as long as normal school functions are not "unreasonably" disrupted. Finally, the Court arrogates to itself, rather than to the State's elected officials charged with running the schools, the decision as to which school disciplinary regulations are "reasonable."

Assuming that the Court is correct in holding that the conduct of wearing armbands for the purpose of conveying political ideas is protected by the First Amendment, . . . the crucial remaining questions are whether students and teachers may use the schools at their whim as a platform for the exercise of free speech—"symbolic" or "pure"—and whether the Courts will allocate to themselves the function of deciding how the pupils' school day will be spent. While I have always believed that under the First and Fourteenth Amendments neither the State nor Federal Government has any authority to regulate or censor the content of speech, I have never believed that any person has a right to give speeches or engage in demonstrations where he pleases and when he pleases. This Court has already rejected such a notion. In Cox v. Louisiana, 379 U.S. 536 (1964), for example, the Court clearly stated that the rights of free speech and assembly "do not mean that anyone with opinions or beliefs to express may address a group at any public place and at any time." 379 U.S. 536, 554 (1964).[8]

---

[8]In Cox, a 1965 case, the United States Supreme Court reversed the conviction of the appellant, an ordained minister and a Field Secretary of the Congress on Racial Equality (CORE), who had been arrested while conducting a peaceful protest against racial segregation in Baton Rouge, Louisiana. At the time of appellant's arrest, the civil rights demonstrators were standing on the sidewalk across the street from the courthouse.

Reverend Cox was convicted under a Louisiana statute reading:

"No person shall willfully obstruct the free, convenient and normal use of any public sidewalk, street, . . . or other passageway, or the entrance, corridor or passage of any public building, . . . by impeding, hindering, stifling, retaining or restraining traffic or passage thereon or therein."

The United States Supreme Court found that the statute itself provided no standard for the determination of local officials as to which assemblies to permit or prohibit. Thus, the Court, in overturning Cox's conviction, declared that "it is clearly unconstitutional to enable a public official to determine which expressions of view will be permitted and which will not or to engage in invidious descrimination among persons or groups either by use of a statute providing a system of broad discretionary liscensing power or, as in this case, the equivalent of such a system by selective enforcement of an extremely broad prohibitory statute."

However, the Court held that the First Amendment would not preclude such a statute when properly drawn, saying:

" . . . The rights of free speech and assembly, while fundamental in our democratic society, still do not mean that everyone with opinions or beliefs to express may address a group at any public place and at any time. The constitutional guarantee of liberty implies the existence

While the record does not show that any of these armband students shouted, used profane language or were violent in any manner, a detailed report by some of them shows their armbands caused comments, warnings by other students, the poking of fun at them, and a warning by an older football player that other, non-protesting students had better let them alone. There is also evidence that the professor of mathematics had his lesson period practically "wrecked" chiefly by disputes with Beth Tinker, who wore her armband for her "demonstration." Even a casual reading of the record shows that this armband did divert students' minds from their regular lessons, and that talk, comments, etc., made John Tinker "self-conscious" in attending school with his armband. While the absence of obscene or boisterous and loud disorder perhaps justifies the Court's statement that the few armband students did not actually "disrupt" the classwork, I think the record overwhelmingly shows that the armbands did exactly what the elected school officials and principals foresaw it would, that is, took the students' minds off their classwork and diverted them to thoughts about the highly emotional subject of the Vietnam war. And I repeat that if the time has come when pupils of state-supported schools, kindergarten, grammar school or high school, can defy and flaunt orders of school officials to keep their minds on their own school work, it is the beginning of a new revolutionary era of permissiveness in this country fostered by the judiciary. . . .

. . . Nor does a person carry with him into the United States Senate or House, or to the Supreme Court, or any other court, a complete constitutional right to go into those places contrary to their rules and speak his mind on any subject he pleases. It is a myth to say that any person has a constitutional right to say what he pleases, where he pleases, and when he pleases. Our Court has decided precisely the opposite. See, e.g., Cox v. Louisiana, 379 U.S. 536, 555;[9] Adderley v. Florida, 385 U.S. 39.[10]

of an organized society maintaining public order, without which liberty itself would be lost in the excesses of anarchy. The control of travel on the streets is a clear example of governmental responsibility to insure this necessary order. A restriction in that relation, designed to promote the public convenience in the interest of all, and not susceptible to abuses of discriminatory application, cannot be disregarded by the attempted exercise of some civil right which, in other circumstances, would be entitled to protection. One would not be justified in ignoring the familiar red light because this was thought to be a means of social protest. Nor could one, contrary to traffic regulations, insist upon a street meeting in the middle of Times Square at the rush hour as a form of freedom of speech or assembley. Governmental authorities have the duty and responsibility to keep their streets open and available for movement. A group of demonstrators could not insist upon the right to cordon off a street, or entrance to a public or private building, and allow no one to pass who did not agree to listen to their exhortations. . . .

"We emphatically reject the notion urged by appellant that the First and Fourteenth Amendments afford the same kind of freedom to those who would communicate ideas by conduct such as patrolling, marching, and picketing on streets and highways, as these amendments afford to those who communicate ideas by pure speech. . . . "

[9]See footnote 8, p. 368, *supra.*

[10]In Adderley the petitioners, students at Florida A.&M. University, assembled at the school grounds to form a march to the county jail, where certain of their schoolmates who had been arrested during a civil rights demonstration were incarcerated. Upon their arrival at the jail, the petitioners were met by a deputy sheriff who, asserting that petitioners were blocking the entrance to the jail and fearing that they might attempt to enter it, asked the petitioners to leave the jail grounds. When the petitioners failed to heed this request, they were arrested for trespass and

In my view, teachers in state-controlled public schools are hired to teach there. Although Mr. Justice McReynolds may have intimated to the contrary in Meyers v. Nebraska, certainly a teacher is not paid to go into school and teach subjects the State does not hire him to teach as a part of its selected curriculum. Nor are public school students sent to the schools at public expense to broadcast political or any other views to educate and inform the public. The original idea of schools, which I do not believe is yet abandoned as worthless or out of date, was that children had not yet reached the point of experience and wisdom which enabled them to teach all of their elders. It may be that the Nation has outworn the oldfashioned slogan that "children are to be seen not heard," but one may, I hope, be permitted to harbor the thought that taxpayers send children to school on the premise that at their age they need to learn, not teach.

.   .   .   .

Change has been said to be truly the law of life but sometimes the old and the tried and true are worth holding. The schools of this Nation have undoubtedly contributed to giving us tranquility and to making us a more law-abiding people. Uncontrolled and uncontrollable liberty is an enemy to domestic peace. We cannot close our eyes to the fact that some of the country's greatest problems are crimes committed by the youth, too many of school age. School discipline, like parental discipline, is an integral and important part of training our children to be good citizens—to be better citizens. Here a very small number of students have crisply and summarily refused to obey a school order designed to give pupils who want to learn the opportunity to do so. One does not need to be a prophet or the son of a prophet to know that after the Court's holding today that some students in Iowa schools and indeed in all schools will be ready, able, and willing to defy their teachers on practically all orders. This is the more unfortunate for the schools since groups of students all over the land are already running loose, conducting break-ins, sit-ins, lie-ins, and smash-ins. Many of these student groups, as is all too familiar to all who read the newspapers and watch the television news programs, have already engaged in rioting, property seizures and destruction. They have picketed schools to force students not to cross their picket lines and have too often violently attacked earnest but frightened students who wanted an education that the picketers did not want them to get. Students engaged in such activities are apparently confident that they know far more about how to operate public school systems than do their parents, teachers, and elected school officials. It is no answer to say that the particular students here have not yet reached such high points in their demands to

subsequently convicted. There was no evidence that the sheriff or his deputy objected to what was being said or sung by the demonstrators or that he disagreed with their protest.

The Supreme Court of the United States affirmed the petitioners' convictions, holding that "the State, no less than a private owner of property, has power to preserve the property under its control for the use to which it is lawfully dedicated. For this reason, there is no merit to the petitioners' argument that they had a constitutional right to stay on the property, over the jail custodian's objections, because this 'area chosen for the peaceful civil rights demonstration was not only reasonable but also particularly appropriate. . . . ' " "Such an argument," continued the Court, "has as its major unarticulated premise the assumption that people who want to propagandize protests or views have a constitutional right to do so whenever they please. That concept of constitutional law was vigorously rejected in two of the cases petitioners rely on, Cox v. Louisiana, [379 U.S. 536, 559], at 554–555 and 563–564. We reject it again. The United States Constitution does not forbid a State to control the use of its own property for its own lawful nondiscriminatory purpose."

attend classes in order to exercise their political pressures. Turned loose with law suits for damages and injunctions against their teachers like they are here, it is nothing but wishful thinking to imagine that young, immature students will not soon believe it is their right to control the schools rather than the right of the States that collect the taxes to hire the teachers for the benefit of the pupils. This case, therefore, wholly without constitutional reasons in my judgment, subjects all the public schools in the country to the whims and caprices of their loudest-mouthed, but maybe not their brightest, students. I, for one, am not fully persuaded that school pupils are wise enough, even with this Court's expert help from Washington, to run the 23,390 public school systems in our 50 States. I wish, therefore, wholly to disclaim any purpose on my part, to hold that the Federal Constitution compels the teachers, parents, and elected school officials to surrender control of the American public school system to public school students. I dissent.

UNITED STATES v. SISSON
United States Federal District Court, 297 F.Supp. 902 (D.C. Mass. 1969).

[Section 456(j) of the Universal Military Training and Service Act allows certain persons deferments and exemptions from active military training and service, and in part provides:

"(j) Nothing contained in this title shall be construed to require any person to be subject to combatant training and service in the armed forces of the United States who, by reason of religious training and belief, is conscientiously opposed to participation in war in any form. As used in this subsection, the term "religious training and belief" does not include essentially political, sociological, or philosophical views, or a merely personal moral code. Any person claiming exemption from combatant training and service because of such conscientious objections whose claim is sustained by the local board shall, if he is inducted into the armed forces under this title be assigned to noncombatant service as defined by the President, or shall, if he is found to be conscientiously opposed to participation in such noncombatant service, in lieu of such induction, be ordered by his local board, subject to such regulations as the President may prescribe, to perform for a period equal to the period prescribed in section 4(b).[11] such civilian work contributing to the maintenance of the national health, safety, or interest as the local board pursuant to Presidential regulations may deem appropriate. . . . " 50 U.S.C. § 456(j) (1967).]

WYZANSKI, C.J.

.   .   .

This court in this opinion addresses itself   .   .   .   to a further consideration of the never-abandoned issue whether government can constitutionally require combat service in Vietnam of a person who is conscientiously opposed to American military activities in Vietnam because he believes them immoral and unjust, that belief resting not upon formal religion but upon the deepest convictions and ethical commitments apart from formal religion, of which a man is capable.

.   .   .   .

---

[11] Section 4(b) [Title 50, Section 454(b)] provides that persons inducted into the Armed Forces shall serve on active duty (including training) for a period of twenty-four consecutive months, unless sooner released.

The usual preliminaries having been completed, Local Board No. 114, Middlesex County, Massachusetts, on Form 252, executed and mailed to Sisson March 18, 1968 an order to report for induction on April 17, 1968. Sisson received the order. On the scheduled day he reported to the local board and from there went to the Boston induction center, as required. At the Boston center, Sisson, after the officer in charge had painstakingly warned him of the consequences, deliberately refused to take the step forward which is, as he understood, the symbolic act of accepting induction.

The evidence shows that the proceedings were in every respect regular. Sisson has never made complaint that there was any error with respect to his registration, the chronological order in which he was called, his physical, mental, and moral examinations, or any other procedural step.

Sisson does not now and never did claim that he is or was in the narrow statutory sense a religious conscientious objector.

Sisson graduated in 1963 from the Phillips Exeter Academy and in 1967 from Harvard College. He enlisted in the Peace Corps in July 1967, but after training he was, for reasons that have no moral connotations, "deselected" in September 1967. In January 1968 he went to work as a reporter for The Southern Courier, published in Montgomery, Alabama. That paper assigned him to work in Mississippi, where he was when he received the induction order.

The first formal indication in the record that Sisson had conscientious scruples is a letter of February 29, 1968 in which he notified Local Board No. 114 that "I find myself to be conscientiously opposed to service in the Armed Forces. Would you please send me SSS Form No. 150 so that I might make my claim as a conscientious objector." On receiving the form, Sisson concluded that his objection not being religious, within the administrative and statutory definitions incorporated in that form, he was not entitled to have the benefit of the form. He, therefore, did not execute it.

But, although the record shows no earlier formal indication of conscientious objection, Sisson's attitude as a nonreligious conscientious objector has had a long history. Sisson himself referred to his moral development, his educational training, his extensive reading of reports about and comments on the Vietnam situation, and the degree to which he had familiarized himself with the U.N. Charter, the charter and judgments of the Nuremberg Tribunal, and other domestic and international matters bearing upon the American involvement in Vietnam.

On the stand Sisson was diffident, perhaps beyond the requirements of modesty. But he revealed sensitiveness, not arrogance or obstinacy. His answers lacked the sharpness that someimes reflects a prepared mind. He was entirely without eloquence. No line he spoke remains etched in memory. But he fearlessly used his own words, not mouthing formulae from court cases or manuals for draft avoidance.

There is not the slightest basis for impugning Sisson's courage. His attempt to serve in the Peace Corps, and the assignment he took on a Southern newspaper were not acts of cowardice or evasion. Those actions were assumptions of social obligations. They were in the pattern of many conscientious young men who have recently come of age. From his education Sisson knows that his claim of conscientious objection may cost him dearly. Some will misunderstand his motives. Some will be reluctant to employ him.

Nor was Sisson motivated by purely political considerations. Of course if "political" means that the area of decision involves a judgment as to the conduct of a state, then any decision as to any war is not without some political aspects. But Sisson's table of ultimate values is moral and ethical. It reflects quite as real, pervasive, durable, and commendable a marshalling of priorities as a formal religion. It is just as much a residue of culture, early training, and beliefs shared by companions and family. What another derives from the discipline of a church, Sisson derives from the discipline of conscience.

Thus, Sisson bore the burden of proving by objective evidence that he was sincere. He was as genuinely and profoundly governed by his conscience as would have been a martyr obedient to an orthodox religion.

Sisson's views are not only sincere, but, without necessarily being right, are reasonable. Similar views are held by reasonable men who are qualified experts. The testimony of Professor Richard Falk of Princeton University and Professor Howard Zinn of Boston University is sufficient proof. See also Ralph B. Potter, New Problems for Conscience in War, American Society for Christian Ethics, January 19, 1968; War and Moral Discourse, John Knox Press, 1969.

· · · ·

THE CONSTITUTIONAL POWER OF CONGRESS TO DRAFT CONSCIENTIOUS OBJECTORS FOR COMBAT DUTY IN A DISTANT CONFLICT NOT PURSUANT TO A DECLARED WAR

Indubitably Congress has constitutional power to conscript the generality of persons for military service in time of war. Selective Draft Law Cases, 245 U.S. 366 (1918). . . .

Whether this constitutional power exists in time of peace has been thought by some justices of the Supreme Court to be an open question. See Holmes v. United States, 391 U.S. 936, 938–949 (1968); Hart v. United States, 391 U.S. 956 (1968); McArthur v. Clifford, 393 U.S. 1002 (1968). However, this court, until otherwise authoritatively instructed, assumes that Congressional power to conscript for war embraces Congressional power in time of peace to conscript for later possible war service. . . .

This court's assumption that Congress has the general power to conscript in time of peace is not dispositive of the specific question whether that general power is subject to some exception or immunity available to a draftee because of a constitutional restriction in favor of individual liberty. . . .

· · · ·

The sum of the matter is that a careful scholar would conclude in 1969, as Professor Powell did in 1941, that "Notwithstanding all judicial declarations, it has not been actually decided that a conscientious objector, not within any group exempted by Congress, can be put into the front-line trenches or put into the army where certain refusals to obey orders may be punished by death." [See Powell, "Conscience and the Constitution," in *Democracy and National Unity*, William T. Hutchison, ed., p. 18 (1947).]

Yet, open as the issue may be, *this Court in the following discussion assumes that a conscientious objector, religious or otherwise, may be conscripted for some kinds of service in peace or in war. This court further assumes that in time of declared war or in the defense of the homeland against invasion, all persons may be conscripted even for combat service.*

But the precise inquiry this court cannot avoid is whether now Sisson may be compelled to submit to non-justiciable military orders which may require him to render combat service in Vietnam. . . .

. . . .

This is not an area of constitutional absolutism. It is an area in which competing claims must be explored, examined, and marshalled with reference to the Constitution as a whole.

There are two main categories of conflicting claims. First, there are both public and private interests in the common defense. Second there are both public and private interests in individual liberty.

Every man, not least the conscientious objector, has an interest in the security of the nation. Dissent is possible only in a society strong enough to repel attack. The conscientious will to resist springs from moral principles. It is likely to seek a new order in the same society, not anarchy or submission to a hostile power. Thus conscience rarely wholly disassociates itself from the defense of the ordered society within which it functions and which it seeks to reform not to reduce to rubble.

In parallel fashion, every man shares and society as a whole shares an interest in the liberty of the conscientious objector, religious or not. The freedom of all depends on the freedom of each. Free men exist only in free societies. Society's own stability and growth, its physical and spiritual prosperity are responsive to the liberties of its citizens, to their deepest insights, to their free choices—"That which opposes, also fits."

Those rival categories of claims cannot be mathematically graded. There is no table of weights and measures. Yet there is no insuperable difficulty in distinguishing orders of magnitude.

The sincerely conscientious man, whose principles flow from reflection, education, practice, sensitivity to competing claims, and a search for a meaningful life, always brings impressive credentials. When he honestly believes that he will act wrongly if he kills, his claim obviously has great magnitude. That magnitude is not appreciably lessened if his belief relates not to war in general, but to a particular war or to a particular type of war. Indeed a selective conscientious objector might reflect a more discriminating study of the problem, a more sensitive conscience, and a deeper spiritual understanding.

It is equally plain that when a nation is fighting for its very existence there are public and private interests of great magnitude in conscripting for the common defense all available resources, including manpower for combat.

But a campaign fought with limited forces for limited objects with no likelihood of a battlefront within this country and without a declaration of war is not a claim of comparable magnitude.

Nor is there any suggestion that in present circumstances there is a national need for combat service from Sisson as distinguished from other forms of service by him. The want of magnitude in the national demand for combat service is reflected in the nation's lack of calls for sacrifice in any serious way by civilians.

. . . .

Most important, it does not follow from a judicial decision that Sisson cannot be conscripted to kill in Vietnam that he cannot be conscripted for non-combat service there or elsewhere.

It would be a poor court indeed that could not discern the small constitutional magnitude of the interest that a person has in avoiding all helpful service whatsoever or in avoiding paying all general taxes whatsoever. His objections, of course, may be sincere. But some sincere objections have greater constitutional magnitude than others.

There are many tasks technologically or economically related to the prosecution of a war, to which a religious or conscientious objector might be constitutionally assigned. As Justice Cardozo wrote "Never in our history has the notion been accepted, or even, it is believed, advanced, that acts thus indirectly related to service in the camp or field are so tied to the practice of religion as to be exempt, in law or in morals, from regulation by the state." Hamilton v. Regents of University of California, 293 U.S. 245, 267 (1934).

Sisson's case being limited to a claim of conscientious objection to combat service in a foreign campaign, this court holds that the free exercise of religion clause in the First Amendment and the due process clause of the Fifth Amendment prohibit the application of the 1967 draft act to Sisson to require him to render combat service in Vietnam.

The chief reason for reaching this conclusion after examining the competing interests is the magnitude of Sisson's interest in not killing in the Vietnam conflict as against the want of magnitude in the country's present need for him to be so employed.

The statute as here applied creates a clash between law and morality for which no exigency exists, and before, in Justice Sutherland's words, "the last extremity" or anything close to that dire predicament has been glimpsed, or even predicted, or reasonably feared.

When the state through its laws seeks to override reasonable moral commitments it makes a dangerously uncharacteristic choice. The law grows from the deposits of morality. Law and morality are, in turn, debtors and creditors of each other. The law cannot be adequately enforced by the courts alone, or by courts supported merely by the police and the military. The true secret of legal might lies in the habits of conscientious men disciplining themselves to obey the law they respect without the necessity of judicial and administrative orders. When the law treats a reasonable, conscientious act as a crime it subverts its own power. It invites civil disobedience. It impairs the very habits which nourish and preserve the law.

THE CONSTITUTIONAL POWER OF CONGRESS TO DISCRIMINATE AS IT DID IN THE 1967 DRAFT ACT BETWEEN THE DRAFT STATUS OF SISSON AS A CONSCIENTIOUS OBJECTOR AND THE DRAFT STATUS OF ADHERENTS TO CERTAIN TYPES OF RELIGIONS

The Supreme Court may not address itself to the broad issue just decided. Being a court of last resort, it unlike an inferior court, can confidently rest its judgment upon a narrow issue. . . . [I]t is incumbent on this court to consider the narrow issue, whether the 1967 Act invalidly discriminates against Sisson as a non-religious conscientious objector.

The draft act now limits "exemption from combat training and service" to one "who, by reason of religious training and belief, is conscientiously opposed to participation in war in any form" 50 U.S.C. App. Section 456(j), commonly cited as Section 6(j) of the Act as amended.

A Quaker, for example, is covered if he claims belief in the ultimate implications of William Penn's teaching.

Persons trained in and believing in other religious ways may or may not be covered. A Roman Catholic obedient to the teaching of Thomas Aquinas and Pope John XXIII might distinguish between a just war in which he would fight and an unjust war in which he would not fight. Those who administer the Selective Service System opine that Congress has not allowed exemption to those whose conscientious objection rests on such a distinction. See Lt. Gen. Lewis B. Hershey, Legal Aspects of Selective Service, U.S. Gov. Printing Office, January 1, 1969, pp. 13–14. This court has a more open mind.

However, the administrators and this court both agree that Congress has not provided a conscientious objector status for a person whose claim is admittedly not formally religious.

In this situation Sisson claims that even if the Constitution might not otherwise preclude Congress from drafting him for combat service in Vietnam, the Constitution does preclude Congress from drafting him under the 1967 Act. The reason is that this Act grants conscientious objector status solely to religious conscientious objectors but not to nonreligious objectors.

. . . [I]t is difficult to imagine any ground for a statutory distinction except religious prejudice. In short, in the draft act Congress unconstitutionally discriminated against atheists, agnostics, and men, like Sisson, who, whether they be religious or not, are motivated in their objection to the draft by profound moral beliefs which constitute the central convictions of their beings.

This Court, therefore, concludes that in granting to the religious conscientious objector but not to Sisson a special conscientious objector status, the Act, as applied to Sisson, violates the provision of the First Amendment that "Congress shall make no law respecting an establishment of religion or prohibiting the free exercise thereof." . . .

.   .   .   .

To guard against misunderstanding, this Court has *not* ruled that:

(1) The Government has no right to conduct Vietnam Operations; or

(2) The Government is using unlawful methods in Vietnam; or

(3) The Government has no power to conscript the generality of men for combat service; or

(4) The Government in a defense of the homeland has no power to conscript for combat service anyone it sees fit; or

(5) The Government has no power to conscript conscientious objectors for noncombat service.

Indeed the Court assumes without deciding that each one of those propositions states the exact reverse of the law.

All that this Court decides is that as a sincere conscientious objector Sisson cannot constitutionally be subjected to military orders (not reviewable in a United States constitutional Court) which may require him to kill in the Vietnam conflict.

Enter forthwith this decision and this court's order granting defendant Sisson's motion in arrest of judgment.[12]

---

[12]The United States Supreme Court entertained an appeal in Sisson, but in a 5 to 3 decision dismissed the appeal, June 29, 1970, on procedural grounds so technical as to be "nonsense" according to Mr. Justice White in a dissent in which Mr. Chief Justice Burger and Mr. Justice Douglas concurred. United States v. Sisson, 399 U.S. 267 (1970). Mr. Justice White said, "Admittedly, the issues raised by Sisson are difficult and far-reaching ones, but they should be faced and decided." Nevertheless, students of the history of the United States Supreme Court are seldom surprised to see a majority of the Court defer, for as long as possible, a decision upon so troublesome a question as Sisson's selective (against the Vietnam War) conscientious objection.

WATTS v. UNITED STATES
Supreme Court of the United States, 394 U.S. 705 (1969).

["Whoever knowingly and willfully deposits for conveyance in the mail or for a delivery from any post office or by any letter carrier any letter, paper, writing, print, missive, or document containing any threat to take the life of or to inflict bodily harm upon the President of the United States, the President-elect, the Vice President or other officer next in the order of succession to the office of President of the United States, or the Vice President-elect, or knowingly and willfully otherwise makes any such threat against the President, President-elect, Vice President or other officer next in the order of succession to the office of President, or Vice President-elect, shall be fined not more than $1,000 or imprisoned not more than five years, or both." 18 U.S.C. § 871(A), as amended, (1964).]

PER CURIAM.

After a jury trial in the United States District Court for the District of Columbia, petitioner was convicted of violating a 1917 statute which prohibits any person from "knowingly and willfully . . . [making] any threat to take the life of or to inflict bodily harm upon the President of the United States . . . "[18 U.S.C. § 871 (a).] The incident which led to petitioner's arrest occurred on August 27, 1966, during a public rally on the Washington Monument grounds. The crowd present broke up into small discussion groups and petitioner joined a gathering scheduled to discuss police brutality. Most of those in the group were quite young, either in their teens or early twenties. Petitioner, who himself was 18 years old, entered into the discussion after one member of the group suggested that the young people present should get more education before expressing their views. According to an investigator for the Army Counter Intelligence Corps who was present, petitioner responded: "They always holler at us to get an education. And now I have already received my draft classification as 1—A and I have got to report for my physical this Monday coming. I am not going. If they

As this book goes to press, the United States Supreme Court has decided both issues it left open when it dismissed Sisson's appeal. In Welsh v. United States, 398 U.S. 333 (1970), the Court held that within the terms of the conscientious objector exemption, Section 456(j) of the Universal Military Training and Service Act, quoted p. 371, *supra,* the exemption applied if the beliefs of the objector "are sincerely held and . . . are, *in his own scheme of things, religious."* [Emphasis is the Court's.] The Court, rephrasing its criterion, said, "The test might be stated in these words: 'A sincere and meaningful belief which occupies in the life of its possessor a place parallel to that filled by God of those admittedly qualifying for exemption.' " Hence the nontheistic aspect of Sisson's claim for exemption was approved in Welsh

In United States v. Gillette, 8 Cr.L.Rptr. 3155 (1971), the Supreme Court raced the second issue it left open in Sisson, *viz.,* whether any individual may be exempt from service in the armed forces because of his conscientious objection to a particular war. Gillette claimed exemption because of, in the words of the trial court, "an opinion, a feeling, a belief that the Vietnam War is immoral and unjust." The Court in denying Gillette his claim held that the exemption in Section 456(j) for those who oppose "participation in war in any form," can on a straightforward reading bear but one meaning: "that conscientious scruples relating to war and military service must amount to conscientious opposition to participating personally in any war and all war." Although the Court in its 8 to 1 decision relied primarily on statutory construction grounds, it did note that the Government's limiting exemptions to those objecting to all war allowed the administration of the conscription laws without consideration of the political views of the claimant.

ever make me carry a rifle the first man I want to get in my sights is L. B. J." "They are not going to make me kill my black brothers." On the basis of this statement, the jury found that petitioner had committed a felony by knowingly and willfully threatening the President. The United States Court of Appeals for the District of Columbia Circuit affirmed by a two-to-one vote. . . .

We reverse.

At the close of the Government's case, petitioner's trial counsel moved for a judgment of acquittal. He contended that there was "absolutely no evidence on the basis of which the jury would be entitled to find that [petitioner] made a threat against the life of the President." He stressed the fact that petitioner's statement was made during a political debate, that it was expressly made conditional upon an event—induction into the Armed Forces—which petitioner vowed would never occur, and that both petitioner and the crowd laughed after the statement was made. He concluded, "Now actually what happened here in all this was a kind of very crude offensive method of stating a political opposition to the President. What he was saying, he says, I don't want to shoot black people because I don't consider them my enemy, and if they put a rifle in my hand it is the people that put the rifle in my hand, as symbolized by the President, who are my real enemy." We hold that the trial judge erred in denying this motion.

Certainly the statute under which petitioner was convicted is constitutional on its face. The Nation undoubtedly has a valid, even an overwhelming, interest in protecting the safety of its Chief Executive and in allowing him to perform his duties without interference from threats of physical violence. . . .   Nevertheless, a statute such as this one, which makes criminal a form of pure speech, must be interpreted with the commands of the First Amendment clearly in mind. What is a threat must be distinguished from what is constitutionally protected speech.

. . .   [T]he statute initially requires the Government to prove a true "threat." We do not believe that the kind of political hyperbole indulged in by petitioner fits within that statutory term. For we must interpret the language Congress chose "against the background of a profound national commitment to the principle that debate on public issues should be uninhibited, robust, and wide-open, and that it may well include vehement, caustic, and sometimes unpleasantly sharp attacks on government and public officials." New York Times Co. v. Sullivan, 376 U. S. 254, 270 (1964). The language of the political arena, like the language used in labor disputes . . .   is often vituperative, abusive, and inexact. We agree with petitioner that his only offense here was "a kind of very crude offensive method of stating a political opposition to the President." Taken in context, and regarding the expressly conditional nature of the statement and the reaction of the listeners, we do not see how it could be interpreted otherwise.

The motion for leave to proceed *in forma pauperis* and the petition for a writ of certiorari are granted and the judgment of the Court of Appeals is reversed. The case is remanded with instructions that it be returned to the District Court for entry of a judgment of acquittal.

It is so ordered.

MR. JUSTICE STEWART would deny the petition for certiorari.

MR. JUSTICE WHITE dissents.

[Mr. Justice FORTAS, joined by Mr. Justice HARLAN, dissented to the granting of certiorari and also to the fact that upon granting certiorari the Court made its ruling in this case without a hearing.]

MR. JUSTICE DOUGLAS, concurring.

The charge in this case is of an ancient vintage.

The federal statute under which petitioner was convicted traces its ancestry to the Statute of Treasons (25 Edw. 3) which made it a crime to "compass or imagine [intending or designing] the Death of . . . the King." Note, Threats to Take the Life of the President, 32 Harv. L. Rev. 724, 725 (1919). It is said that one Walter Walker, a 15th century keeper of an inn known as the "Crown," was convicted under the Statute of Treasons for telling his son: "Tom, if thou behavest thyself well, I will make thee heir to the CROWN." He was found guilty of compassing and imagining the death of the King, hanged, drawn, and quartered. 1 J. Campbell, Lives of the Chief Justices of England 151 (1873).

In the time of Edward IV, one Thomas Burdet who predicted that the king would "soon die, with a view to alienate the affections" of the people was indicted for "compassing and imagining of the death of the King," 79 Eng. Rep. 706 (1477)—the crime of constructive treason with which the old reports are filled.

In the time of Charles II, one Edward Brownlow was indicted "for speaking these words, that he wished all the gentry in the land would kill one another, so that the comminalty might live the better." 3 Middlesex County Rec. 326 (1888). In the same year (1662) one Robert Thornell was indicted for saying "that if the Kinge did side with the Bishops, the divell take Kinge and the Bishops too." *Id.,* at 327.

While our Alien and Sedition Laws were in force, John Adams, President of the United States, en route from Philadelphia, Pa., to Quincy, Massachusetts, stopped in Newark, New Jersey, where he was greeted by a crowd and by a committee that saluted him by firing a cannon.

A bystander said, "There goes the President and they are firing at his ass." Luther Baldwin was indicted for replying that he did not care "if they fired through his ass." He was convicted in the federal court for speaking "seditious words tending to defame the President and Government of the United States" and fined, assessed court costs and expenses, and committed to jail until the fine and fees were paid. See J. Smith, Freedom's Fetters 270–274 (1956).

The Alien and Sedition Laws constituted one of our sorriest chapters; and I had thought we had done with them forever.

Yet the present statute has hardly fared better. "Like the Statute of Treasons, section 871 was passed in a 'relatively calm peacetime spring,' but has been construed under circumstances when intolerance for free speech was much greater than it normally might be." Note, Threatening the President: Protected Dissenter or Political Assassin, 57 Geo. L. J. 553, 570 (1969). Convictions under 18 U. S. C. § 871 have been sustained for displaying posters urging passers-by to "hang [President] Roosevelt." United States v. Apel, 44 F. Supp. 592, 593 (D. C. N. D. Ill. 1942); for declaring that "President Wilson ought to be killed. It is a wonder some one has not done it already. If I had an opportunity, I would do it myself." United States v. Stickrath, 242 F. 151, 152 (D. C. S. D. Ohio 1917); for declaring that "Wilson is a wooden-headed son of a bitch. I wish Wilson was in hell, and if I had the power I would put him there," Clark v. United States, 250 F. 449 (C. A. 5th Cir. 1918). In sustaining an indictment under the statute against a man who indicated that he would enjoy shooting President Wilson if he had the chance, the trial court explained the thrust of § 871:

"The purpose of the statute was undoubtedly, not only the protection of the President, but also the prohibition of just such statements as those alleged in this indictment. The expression of such direful intentions and desires, not only indicates a spirit of disloyalty to the nation bordering upon treason, but is, in a very real sense, a menace to the peace and safety of the country. . . . It arouses resentment and concern on the part of patriotic citizens." United States v. Jasick, 252 F. 931, 933 (D. C. E. D. Mich. 1918).

Suppression of speech as an effective police measure is an old, old device, outlawed by our Constitution.

LAW AND THE WORLD: WHAT PRICE THE INDIVIDUAL?

In modern times in democratic societies there are confrontations between the state and the individual citizen that involve both domestic tranquility and external threat. On the domestic front law enforcement agencies are under constitutional scrutiny, as we saw in Chapter 3. Here the pendulum swings between the needs of the state for internal security and the rights of the individual to have his liberties.

On the international front there are no world law enforcement agencies because there is no world government and hence no world law. Absent world government, diplomacy, treaties—more breakable than unbreakable—and war are the modes by which some semblance of world order, without world law, is maintained. There *is* a world court, but seldom is a vital issue submitted to it. There are important world conventions about mail and travel, even about how to conduct war; and there is a body of law, called international, that concerns trade, commerce, and many other controversies that individuals may submit to some court. Nevertheless, among nations there is no counterpart to national government, either totalitarian or democratic, and the time for such government does not seem near.[13]

The fact of no global government and the fact of war as the terminal point of international bargaining (like the strike as the terminal point of collective bargaining) both exist. Few human beings enjoy the fact of war; hence the plans, ancient and contemporary, from Euripides to the Quakers, to abolish or to diminish the role of war in the affairs of man are many. One may believe that institutions and conditions like the European Common Market, the United Nations, the North Atlantic Treaty Organization, or the existence of a bipolar world of Russia and America (even a tripartite world of America, China, and Russia) may minimize the risk of war, even guarantee the nonuse

[13]See generally Katz, Milton, *The Relevance of International Adjudication,* Harvard University Press, Cambridge, Massachusetts, 1968; Hazard, Leland, *Empire Revisited,* Richard D. Irwin, Homewood, Illinois, 1965.

of war. One may believe that even the threat of nuclear incineration will prevent any big war. But no one knows. The wish is father to the thought.

One may hope and believe that modern biologists in the 20th century are teaching man, by scientific studies of animals, more about himself than have all the philosophers and theologians of the past. By using the still doubtful analogies from animals to men, we discover that for ages we have been wrong about the jungles: they are, contrary to folk-thought, areas of relative peace because animals clearly define territories and live in harmony within the species and within that territory, as long as there is an external threat. *Enmity = Amity plus Risk* is Ardrey's at once hopeful and gloomy finding about animals.[14] Whether this finding means anything about man and warfare, we do not know. Animals have exercised self-government much longer than men.

It is the dreary experience of men in recorded history, which Gibbon called "little more than the register of the crimes, follies, and misfortunes of mankind,"[15] that has made some men think and act in desperation against war. But only some men—never the majority of men—otherwise governments, often called the culprits, would be powerless to wage war. It is exactly because, in a democracy, government is presumptively representative of the majority that pains are taken to nurture dissent, in order that the minority may have a fair field and all possible favors to become the new majority. Only in this way can the state avoid what DeTocqueville called, "the tyranny of the majority." How many favors should the state accord the minority, however small, just to assure itself against a possible tyrannical majority? We are in doubt about the proper relationship between the state and the individual when the existence of the state is threatened from abroad. Assume a state in which no citizen is proceeded against for any offense except by the most impeccable procedures. The equable past will be small comfort to the citizens if another state, imbued with harsher concepts, conquers them. Their good state is gone; a bad state has prevailed. Much, not all, of the conquest of history involves the subjection of a superior civilization to an inferior culture, not yet a civilization. (Witness Genghis Khan for a case in point.) Among many of the peoples of Southeast Asia, conquest has been so much the everyday order that the word "conqueror" *is* the word for government. On the other hand, a state that makes itself, like Sparta, into a garrison may not be fit for its citizens. In the words of the king of Siam to Anna, "It's a puzzlement."

One of the problems is the lack of a dominant theory of the state. Rousseau called the state a "moral and collective body," an association of individuals, a "public person." Adler summarizes, "It is called by its members, *state* when passive, *sovereign* when active, and *power* when compared with others like

[14]Ardrey, Robert, *The Territorial Imperative,* Chap. 8, Atheneum, New York, 1966.

[15]Commager, Henry Steele, *The American Mind,* p. 283, Yale University Press, New Haven, Connecticut 1950.

itself." Again Rousseau: the state is "a moral person whose life is in the union of its members." But to Hegel the state "is the organic whole no part of which can have a separate life." He goes beyond that analogy to the physical organism: "The march of God in the world, that is what the state is." We have no problem in identifying Hegel with Creon, the Caesars, the English Stuarts, and Hitler. Although we would have difficulty finding another Western political writer to represent the concepts of Rousseau, he can be identified with Thomas Jefferson. In any case, it is an oversimplification to make Hegel and Rousseau the only characters in the dichotomy. Socrates and Plato might play the same roles. It is, however, sufficient to say that because there is no general agreement among thinkers about the nature of the state, there is an understandable uncertainty about the state's behavior toward the individual when the state feels threatened.

For a rationale of the cases in this section we can select one word—not an earth-shaking word like justice or injustice but a scientific word—*differentiation*. The word could be distinction, or it could be discrimination, except that that word's least preferred meaning, irrational favoritism, has gained currency. The best word, however, is differentiation. It is a word the tragic Creon did not understand:[16]

> I'll have no dealings
> With lawbreakers, critics of the government:

But why? Lawbreakers and critics of government are part of society. They must be dealt with. The only question is, How?

> Whoever is chosen to govern should be obeyed—
> Must be obeyed, in all things, great and small,
> Just and unjust.

How foolish not to differentiate between the great and the small! Of course, the Greece of 2500 years ago did not have a clear concept of the separation and the integrity of legislative, executive, and judicial powers. Nor was the critical role of procedures, which we introduced in Chapter 1 and which we shall shortly dramatize and humanize in our closing Chapter 9, as well understood in Creon's time as in Lyndon Johnson's time.

We apply the concept of differentiation to the cases in this Chapter. Bond had a First Amendment right to criticize the Vietnam War and that right was not diminished by his status as an elected legislator. Bond merely talked, but O'Brien burned a draft card contrary to a law enacted to facilitate the constitutional power of Congress to raise and support armies. The burning was action against not only the Vietnam War but also the power of the state to marshal troops in any war. O'Brien must pay the penalty. There was differentiation between speech and action as between Bond and O'Brien.

[16]See footnotes 4 and 5 and accompanying text, pp. 369, 370, *supra.*

In Tinker, on the other hand, action (wearing black armbands) was equated with speech, but there was differentiation between the great and the small. The draft card was a great and perennial symbol of government embedded deeply, despite its trivial physical worth, into the official complex of administrative necessity. The black armbands were as cheap as talk and represented no part or portion of necessary paraphernalia of government.

We have elected to confine this chapter to some significant cases involving Vietnam. The reader will bear in mind that we do not deal with the whole body of law concerning freedom of speech and religion and the right of assembly and protest. In this summary we point up a pattern of differentiation that the courts are framing to divide the great from the small in war protest cases. The principles laid out for Vietnam will be applicable in comparable situations.

Sisson is a troublesome case. It would seem to probe the outer borders of respect for the subjective feelings of the individual against the declared will of the state. The portion of the opinion which holds that conscientious objection to war need not rest on religious training and belief and the decision in Welsh are in keeping with the times. Some theologians are teaching that God is dead. In any case, as Mr. Justice Harlan pointed out in Welsh, while the state need not respect any conscientious objection, if it does, no discrimination can be made as between deistic and nondeistic motivation. But the portion of the opinion in Sisson which holds that the conscientious objection may be selective calls for discussion and prediction.

The problem with selective conscientious objection is not immediately with the objector. It is quite credible that Sisson may find it against his morality to kill in Vietnam but not in North Korea. The problem is that when an objector establishes a permissible area for which he may be conscripted, he requires the judiciary to pass on a question that belongs to the Congress and the President. Judge Wyzanski says that Vietnam poses "no likelihood of a battlefront within this country." He concludes that "in the present circumstances there is no need for combat service from Sisson." That is a military judgment. It is as if an amateur chess or checker player should make or not make a move that only a master player's experienced judgment could pass upon. It seems probable that the doctrine of separation of powers precludes the judiciary from approving selective consicentious objection on the ground of military expediency. (This rationale was alluded to in United States v. Gillette, *supra* note 12, p. 377). Meanwhile, those with a sense of history may bemuse themselves by imagining a Roman legionnaire's telling Julius Caesar, "I will defend Rome at its gates but I will not fight in Gaul."

Watts demonstrates how little we are disturbed in modern times by talk. Words which do, read literally, make a threat against the life of a President, are nonetheless tolerated—set in the comic drama of the occasion. Justice Douglas' learned concurring opinion shows that in all the tragic and awful business of statecraft and warfare we have not yet lost our sense of humor.

We have noted throughout the book the interaction between law and environment. The reader knows that by environment we do not mean exclusively physical environment in the sense of, for example, climate, although British climate played its role in giving English law its case by case aspect (Chapter 1, p. 21 et seq.). We do not mean by environment exclusively technology or economics, although we saw their dramatic role in the development of what is now probably a mass producer's all but absolute legal liability for personal or property damage caused by a mass-produced product (Chapter 5). We do not mean exclusively sociology, although we have seen how a United States Supreme Court decision, such as Brown v. Board of Education or Baker v. Carr, has made new environments in education and in politics (Chapter 2). We do not mean exclusively growing humanism, but we have seen its role in the hundred years during which organized labor moved from legal castigation as criminality to a seat at the table of the mighty.

Law and environment—the reader will see in the impact, first of one upon the other and then of the other upon one, the ancient question of the chicken and the egg, or is it the egg and the chicken?

Judge Wyzanski's opinion in Sisson was long in the making—almost 25 centuries, beginning when Sophocles opposed a lone, young woman against the state in *Antigone* (p. 356, *supra*). Perhaps 2,000 years have elapsed, during which the Judeo-Christian concept of the dignity and worth of the individual has moved at glacial speed from a myth, such as Androcles and the Lion,[17] to the legal arena in which Sisson and the United States of America are pitted —a lone individual against the mighty state. A tradition, which is old and yet new in the eons of man's time on earth—the tradition of human dignity—may have become an environment that will make law. Sisson was the law, but it was the law in an inferior federal court, however distinguished the judge of that court may be. While this book was in press, the United States Supreme Court decided Gillette on its merits, as it did not decide Sisson on its merits (see note 12, *supra*, p. 377). The law is forever in the making. No book ever has the final word.

QUESTIONS

1. How would you define the "Antigone question"?

2. Do you agree with Mr. Justice Douglas in his dissent in O'Brien that the Supreme Court should decide the question whether conscription is permissible in the absence of a declaration of war?

---

[17]The classical story is of a slave who once removed a thorn from the paw of a lion. Years later the two chanced to be set to mortal combat in the arena where human life and death were the sport of emperors. The lion recognized his benefactor and refrained from attacking. See George Bernard Shaw's play, "Androcles and the Lion."

(a) If so, give your opinions on what would be the international consequences if the Court should hold conscription for military service in Vietnam, an undeclared war, unconstitutional.

(b) Suppose, after the Court rendered a decision as hypothecated in (a), the President of the United States asserting his constitutional powers as Commander-in-Chief of the Army and Navy (Article II, Section 2.1) should continue to order drafted men to Vietnam. How would you resolve the impasse?

3. Do you agree with Mr. Justice Fortas for the majority or with Mr. Justice Black, dissenting, in Tinker? Give your reasons.

4. Assuming that the United States Supreme Court sustains selective conscientious objection, and assuming that you were, thereafter, Director of Selective Service, what criteria would you promulgate to draft boards to guide them in determining the validity of an individual draftee's selective objection to a particular war?

9 Law is Meted Out Through Human Institutions

Introduction 386
  Criminal Procedure. 388
  Civil Procedure 391
The Trial. 395
  The Judge. 395
    A Note on The Trial of William Penn 398
      Bushell's Case. 398
      In re Oliver 400
  The Jury 403
    Duncan v. Louisiana 407
  The Witness. 408
  The Lawyer. 413
    The Art of Cross Examination 413
      A Perjurer Unmasked by Lincoln 413
      A Sham Expert Pilloried by Wellman. 415
    Lying—With or Without Motive. 416
    Substitutes for Human Testimony 417
    Conviction of the Innocent 418
Justice and Professional Discipline 419
  Of the Lawyer 419
    People ex rel. Karlin v. Culkin 422
  Of the Judge 424
  Of the Media 426
    Sheppard v. Maxwell 429
    The Right of Fair Trial and Free Press 434
Questions 436

INTRODUCTION

There is a distinction between substantive law and procedural law. In the preceding eight chapters of this book we have dealt with substantive law. We have traced law back to some of its origins; we have seen some of the limitations on the judging process; and we have watched the pendulum swing between the state's concern for its own security on the one hand and for the liberties of the individual on the other. We have learned that the state takes account of broken promises, and we have analyzed the processes of the judicial mentality in the struggle for consistency in framing a doctrine of manufacturers' liability to users of the product. We have spoken of the expediency that controls law when the case is between two innocent parties—one of whom must suffer from the wrongdoing of a third. We have seen the developing role of law—the rise and decline of both case law and statutory law—in the stresses of conflict between management and labor. Finally, we have examined the "Antigone Question" when an individual opposes his conscience to the will of the state.

All that we have said on these subjects, all of the cases we have adduced, relate to substantive law—to types of conflicts, issues, and questions to which courts will address themselves—either in criminal proceedings, in which the state charges the individual with an offense against society or in civil proceedings in which an individual charges another individual with the violation of a right or the failure to perform a duty that the law accords to the complaining individual.

The distinction between substantive law and procedural law can, risking some oversimplification, be stated quite simply: *Rights are not self-enforcing; obligations are not automatically performed.* These propositions apply to the dictates of the state concerning crimes as well as to tortious conduct or contractual obligations of individuals. What constitutes a crime, tort, or contract; these are matters of substantive law. What the state or an individual may do, and how, after a crime is charged or after a tort has been committed or after a contract has been breached; these are matters of procedural law. The offended state may proceed against the alleged criminal; the injured victim of the tort or the damaged promisee in a contract may proceed against the offending party—state against individual, individual against individual—the formalities of procedure are essential. Only out of such procedures is it determined that a crime *was* committed and what punishment will be assessed or that a tort or contract *existed* and what recompense will be allowed.

It will be well to keep some broad categories of law in mind (and sight) as this chapter on procedure unfolds. A graphic representation should help.

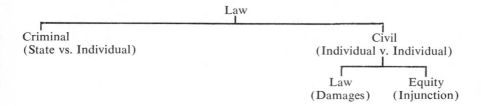

The chart is, however, an oversimplification. The state, for example, may proceed against the individual on the civil side for injunction against conduct, which is also a crime. Antitrust law violations are a usual example. Yet the chart is a good working tool for opening our discussion of procedural law: how does the state proceed when its police force, or citizens for that matter, suspect some crime or offense of some nature against the state; how does an outraged individual proceed against his offender when personal confrontation and discussion have failed?

CRIMINAL PROCEDURE

> On the sidewalk, Sunday morning,
> Lies a body, oozin' life;
> Someone sneak-ed round the corner.
> Is the someone Mack the Knife?
> From a tugboat, by the river,
> A cement bag's droppin' down.
> The cement's just for the weight, dear,
> Bet ya Mackie's back in town.
> Louis Miller disappeared, dear,
> After drawing out his cash,
> And Macheath spends like a sailor.
> Did our boy do something rash?[1]

We have three evidences of possible crime: a bleeding body on the sidewalk; something to be anchored at the bottom of a river; a spending spree. None of the stated facts necessarily constitutes a crime, but all of them suggest the probability of crime. The known facts are worthy of policemanship. The stage just before criminal procedure is about to begin—it is the "Sherlock Holmes" stage, which so intrigued Sir Arthur Conan Doyle, precursor of the contemporary detective story writers.

If there is life in the body, can the victim speak, can he relate what happened, did he see and can he describe his assailant; or is this gang warfare, and the victim chooses not to speak? If the body is dead, what instrument was employed, can it be found, and if some instrument is found in a place in some way related to the body and the killing, can it be matched with the injury to the body—blood type, bits of flesh or fiber, or matching conformations of the instrument and the wound? Also, as to the cement bag, what is in it or attached to it when the river police fish it to the surface? What clues? Who saw the lavish spender? What talk? Marked bills? Detection of crime comes first. Criminals do not usually announce their crimes in advance or report them afterward;

---

[1]Weill, Kurt, "The Threepenny Opera," as recorded by MGM from a production at Theater de Lys, New York, N. Y. (Eng. adaptation of lyrics by Marc Blitzstein; music by Kurt Weill; original lyrics by Berthold Brecht).

they must be ferreted out, with methods consistent with those guidelines illustrated in Chimel, Abel, Berger, Katz, Terry, and Miranda, which we noted in Chapter 3.

A suspected criminal having been identified, the procedures from that point on are established by law for cases under the jurisdiction of the United States and the several states, respectively. These laws are usually known as codes of criminal procedure. There are points of difference among the 51 sets of laws (one for the United States and one for each of the states). Nevertheless, there are more points of identity than of difference: therefore, it will be sufficient to follow as a model the requirements of Rules of Criminal Procedure for the U.S. District Courts.[2]

The first step is a complaint in writing stating the essential facts constituting the offense charged. It must be made by the accusing person under oath before a commissioner or other officer of the United States empowered to commit or detain accused persons.

On the basis of the sworn complaint, a warrant for the arrest of the accused person will issue from the commissioner's office and will be served by an officer of the United States Government upon the accused person, who must then appear before the commissioner. The commissioner will then inform him of the complaint against him, of his right to retain counsel, of his right to have a preliminary examination, and that he is not required to make a statement but any statement made by him may be used against him. The commissioner must allow the defendant reasonable time to consult counsel and must usually allow the accused person his freedom on bail in an amount bearing an appropriate relationship to the gravity of the offense.

The federal district court will now summon a grand jury, if one is not already in session. The grand jury is an institution of great antiquity in Anglo-American law.[3] In modern times in the federal courts it consists of not less than 16 nor more than 23 members.

---

[2] United States Code, Title 18, effective September 16, 1938, as amended, U.S. Government Printing Office, Washington, D.C., 1964 ed.

[3] In England, Henry II (1154–1189) set in motion a procedure which involved the oath of twelve Knights or, failing Knights, twelve good and lawful men. Pollock & Maitland say, "The highly respectable knights or freeholders of the hundred are not likely to know at first hand much about the crimes that have been committed among the peasantry or of the good or ill repute of this or that villein. On the other hand, it is not to be tolerated that free men should be sent to the ordeal merely by the oaths of the unfree, and undoubtedly in the thirteenth century many or most of the representatives of the vills were men whom the lawyers called serfs. This is of some importance when we trace the pedigree of the indictment. From the very first the legal forefathers of our grand jurors are not in the majority of cases supposed to be reporting crimes that they have witnessed, or even to be the originators of the *fama publica*. We should be guilty of an anachronism if we spoke of them as 'endorsing a bill' that is 'preferred' to them; but still they are handing on and 'avowing' as their own a rumour that has been reported to them by others." This machinery was not invented by Henry II. It had been employed by William the Conqueror. Pollock and Maitland, *The History of English Law,* 2nd. ed. Vol. II, p. 643 *et seq.*

The case against the accused person will now be taken before the grand jury where the only persons present are the jurors, the attorneys for the government, the witness under examination, interpreters, when needed, and a stenographer. After the grand jury has heard the evidence, no other person may be present with the jurors in their deliberations. The proceedings in general are secret and may be disclosed only under limited rules and regulations.

The grand jury, once impaneled, must serve until discharged by the court but may not serve longer than eighteen months. The grand jury represents one of the early important procedures for the protection of citizens against the possibility of rash, intemperate, whimsical, or venal institution of prosecutions by law-enforcing agencies of government. Although only attorneys for the government and witnesses called by such attorneys have appeared before the grand jury, although the accused person himself has no right to appear before the grand jury, unless permitted by government attorneys, and although the proceeding is unilateral and *ex parte,* nevertheless, a grand jury will frequently be unimpressed by the government's presentation and will refuse to indict the accused person.

If the grand jury brings an indictment against the accused person, for which purpose twelve of the jurors are a sufficient number, the indictment must be disclosed by the grand jury to a judge in open court. It must be a plain, concise, and definite written statement of the essential facts constituting the alleged offense. The indictment may contain several portions, known as "counts," may charge separate offenses, and may specify the means by which the alleged offenses were committed or may state that the means are unknown.

After an indictment, which may run against one person or several persons, an arraignment then ensues.

The arraignment must be conducted in open court and consists of reading the indictment (sometimes an alternative to the indictment, known as an information, is permitted for lesser offenses) to the accused person who is entitled to a copy of the indictment or information. The accused person may then plead not guilty, guilty, or, with the consent of the court, *nolo contendere.* This third type of plea means that the individual pleads neither guilty nor not guilty and, in effect, throws himself upon the mercy of the court.

After the accused person's plea, there may be a limited number of motions raising defenses and objections; there may be depositions under procedures for taking testimony under oath in advance of the actual trial. Subpoenas for witnesses may issue, and subpoenas requiring production of documentary evidence and of objects may be employed. There are other preliminaries.

We are now ready for the trial, which usually must be held in the court of the district in which the alleged offense was committed. We shall deal with trial procedures subsequently. Meanwhile we proceed to a delineation of preliminary procedures in *civil* cases as distinguished from *criminal* cases. Since the drama of the trial in its fundamentals is the same whether the case is criminal or civil, we shall treat the trial in both types of case in one writing.

CIVIL PROCEDURE

We come now to the civil side of the chart which appears on page 387, *supra*. A person, believing himself aggrieved by another and feeling strongly enough about his grievance to pursue the matter, will first restrain his impulse to punch his offender on the nose. In a civilized society he will sublimate his emotions by talk. In his talks with relatives and friends he will ultimately encounter the advice that he should see a lawyer. He may be reluctant—it is well known that lawyers charge for their services. He may take advantage of the free legal aid services that are available to the indigent in larger communities. He may also avail himself of lawyer referral services that are maintained by many local bar associations for predetermined preliminary and modest fees.

However outraged an individual person may feel by reason of the conduct of another, such a person will often be a poor judge of his own case. For example: *A* appears on a college campus and delivers a lecture in the course of which he says "God is dead." *B*, deeply and personally affronted by such a statement, wishes to bring suit against *A*. *B* does not know exactly for what he would sue, but he has a strongly conscientious impulse to discredit or punish *A* for the statement or to prevent him from making it again. When *B* consults a lawyer he will be quickly told, what the readers of this book will recall from Chapter 2, that *A*'s statement is not actionable; that the question of existence or nonexistence of God is for philosophers and theologians but not for the courts.

On the other hand, suppose that *A* in that same campus address had said that *B had said,* "God is dead." This is a very different situation. When *B* goes to a lawyer, he will be asked at once if *A*'s statement is true. *B* will reply, "Not true." Never would he, a deeply religious man, make so irreverent a statement. Furthermore, *B* will tell his lawyer, "I am a salesman of bibles and religious writings, and *A*'s false statement before a public audience will adversely affect my business." The lawyer will tell *B* that if it can be proved that *A*'s statement was false, then *B* has a cause of action against *A* for slander and that if it can be proved that *B* has suffered damages by reason of the falsehood, *B* should be able to get recompense in money. Furthermore, if there is the probability that *A* will repeat the false statement, *B* may be able to get an injunction against *A* to prevent the repetition. *B* will ask the lawyer how much it will cost. The lawyer will reply that there is a small fee payable to the court for filing the suit, and that there will be lawyer's fees. *B* will ask the lawyer, "How much?" and he will reply, "That depends upon the amount of work involved, but the fee will be reasonable." If *B* decides to bring the suit, then certain rules of civil procedure take hold of the situation.

It having been determined that, in a lawyer's opinion, there is a cause of action, meaning a set of facts of which the court will take cognizance, the procedures from that point on are established by law. As in the case of criminal codes, there are codes of civil procedure. They vary among the several states and as between the several states and federal government. Nevertheless, there are more points of identity than of difference: therefore, it will be sufficient to follow as a model the requirements of Federal Rules of Civil Procedure.[4]

The federal rules govern the procedure in the United States district courts in all suits of a civil nature whether cognizable as cases of law, or in equity, or in admiralty (the last category involving cases of controversy arising over maritime matters).

The reader will recall the discussion on causes of action in Chapter 2 and will be prepared for the federal rule that, "There shall be one form of action to be known as 'civil action.'" The rules provide that a civil action is commenced by filing a complaint in writing with the court. This is done in the office of the clerk of the court, an administrative official, who attends, among many matters, to the maintenance of the docket of pending cases. The clerk will see that a summons is issued to the defendant in the case. The person who initiated the suit is known as the plaintiff or complainant. The summons will be signed by the clerk and will be delivered to the defendant. It will contain requisite information, such as the name of the court, the names of the parties, the name and address of the plaintiff's attorney, and the time within which the rules require the defendant to appear and defend. That time under the federal rules is 20 days. The time may be extended on application to the court. If the defendant does not appear and defend, meaning that if he or his lawyer does not file some appropriate response within the 20 days, a judgment in default may be rendered against him for the relief demanded in the complaint. A plaintiff or defendant may, respectively, lodge his suit or enter a defense without aid of counsel—a risky business unless the individual possesses some unusual charisma or is in some posture especially appealing to the court.

There are precise rules concerning personal service of the summons on the defendant, and there are situations in which the defendant may be served at points outside the territorial limits of the court. There are rules for making a proper record in the office of the federal marshall, or in the office of the sheriff, as that officer is often called in a state jurisdiction.

The complaint filed by the plaintiff and an answer filed by the defendant are called pleas. In some cases, a defendant, once sued, will elect to assert his own claim against the plaintiff. This is called a cross-claim or a counter-claim. These are the pleadings authorized by the federal rules. Nevertheless, under

[4]United States Code, Title 28, effective March 21, 1946, as amended, U.S. Government Printing Office, Washington, D.C., 1964 ed.

certain circumstances and with the approval of the court, motions and other papers may be filed.

One of the most ancient of pleadings is called the demurrer by which a defendant pleads, in effect, that admitting all the facts stated in the plaintiff's petition, there is nevertheless no cause of action. Such would be the plea in the hypothetical case in which *B* wished to sue *A* for saying "God is dead." Pleas in the nature of a demurrer under the federal rules must be set forth in the answer.

The complaint must set forth a claim for relief by (1) a short and plain statement of the grounds upon which the courts jurisdiction depends, (2) a short and plain statement of the claim showing that the pleader is entitled to relief, and (3) a demand for judgment for the relief to which the pleader deems himself entitled. Relief in the alternative or of several different types may be demanded. For example: in our hypothetical case, *B* can demand not only money damages for *A*'s slander but also an injunction to prevent repetition of the slander.

A defendant in his answer must state in short and plain terms his defense to each claim asserted, and he may admit or deny the averments upon which the adverse party relies. It is common practice for the defendant to admit matters (such as, names and addresses, dates, authenticity of documents, signatures, etc.) that could be readily proved, but only at expense of the time of the court, the lawyers, and the parties involved. It is the function of pleadings to narrow and define those issues that justify the attention of the court.

Pleadings must be signed by an attorney of record in the case, and his address must be stated. A party who is not represented by an attorney may sign his pleading and must state his address. These are necessary rules for enabling the clerk of the court or the marshall to serve notice upon the parties, or their attorneys, of various developments in the case, such as, the filing of the pleadings or setting of case for preliminary arguments or for trial. In ordinary practice, lawyers themselves serve upon their opponents notice of all such matters.

There are also rules about counter-claims and cross-claims, about the rights of third parties to intervene, and about amendment and supplementation of pleadings.

In many courts there is a salutory function performed by the judge, called pre-trial procedure. The judge may in his discretion direct the parties to appear for a conference to consider:

(1) the simplification of the issues;

(2) the necessity or desirability of amendments to the pleadings;

(3) the possibility of obtaining admissions of fact and of documents that will avoid unnecessary proof;

(4) the limitation of the number of expert witnesses.

(5) the advisability of presenting preliminary reference of issues to a master (special officer of the court) for findings to be used as evidence when the trial is to be by jury; and

(6) such other matters as may aid in the disposition of the action.

Some judges use the pretrial procedure to induce the parties to compromise and thus to dispose of the case without trial.

There are rules about who is a real party in interest, about the capacity of the party to sue or be sued, and about infants or incompetent persons. There are rules about what claims may be joined and what remedies may be joined in one action; likewise, as to what interested persons may be joined in one action. There are rules about bringing class actions in which one or more members of a class, which is numerous and in which questions law and fact are common, may bring an action on behalf of the whole class.

In addition to the pre-trial conference, there is another procedure which contributes to the efficiency of the administration of justice. A rule provides that any party may take the testimony of any person, including another party, by deposition upon oral examination or written interrogatories for the purpose of discovery or for use as evidence in the action, or for both purposes. The use of such depositions, which may be taken in advance of trial, under oath, and without leave of the court, although the court will supervise the proceedings under certain circumstances, produces a great deal of clarifying information and may substantially lessen the length and burden of the trial.

Another federal rule provides that any party may procure an order of court requiring any other party to produce and permit the inspection, copying, or photographing of any documents, papers, books, accounts, letters, photographs, objects, or tangible things—not privileged—that constitute or contain evidence relating to the action. Furthermore, such an order may permit any party to enter on any designated land or other property in the possession or control of a party to the litigation for the purpose of inspecting, measuring, surveying or photographing the property. Another rule provides that if physical or mental condition is an issue, a party must submit to a physical examination or mental examination by a physician in advance of trial. Another rule provides procedures for gaining expeditious admission of facts or of genuineness of documents.

It will now be obvious to the reader that the concept of trial *by surprise* is not approved in the federal rules; instead it is the reverse. Those rules and the rules of most of the states encourage parties, through their lawyers, to drastically diminish the area of controversy before the case reaches the court for trial.

We have sought to avoid tedium by summarizing only the salient rules of criminal and civil procedure. We come now to that triumph of human restraint that has intrigued all civilized men from the children of Israel at Kadesh, 3000 years ago, to the children of television in the 20th century—the trial.

THE TRIAL

THE JUDGE

Judging is an aspect of rulership whose origins are lost in antiquity. Judging is older than the legislative process, and while it is an aspect of rulership, it is at once commingled with and independent of the executive. Judging even in mythology claimed independence of other aspects of rulership. As related in Chapter 1, the Greeks conceived of the goddess Themis as possessed of an inventory of judgments, preexistent to the cases. Zeus, himself, by whom Themis became mother of the Seasons and of the Fates, must look to her in the hard cases. The chief of the gods was not above the law, as in another clime the Norse god Wotan discovered when he encountered the laws of his wife Frica in the Nibelungenlied legend.[5] Wotan fain would free himself of Frica's laws by breeding to earth's mother, Erda, a hero above law's petty restraints. Yet all mythology and all history attest that neither man nor gods may rule by whimsy alone.

Perhaps, it is useless to consider whether law precedes rulership. This could very well be a metaphysical question, the answer to which would forever elude rationality. Certainly we know that law has no agency for the expression of itself except the human agency. That is the meaning of the title of this final chapter.

In the Greek and Norse mythologies, which made Themis and Frica the custodians of law binding even upon Zeus and Wotan, the modern concept of the separation of powers was forecast. Indeed, with respect to the administration of justice, it took history a long time to catch up with mythology. A paragraph or two will demonstrate the point.

After the successful escape of the children of Israel from Egypt and their military victory at Kadesh, the biblical account says that "Moses sat to judge the people; and the people stood by Moses from the morning until the evening."[6] Now Moses was clearly the ruler and leader (with the help of Yahweh, of course) and had instinctively, for want of a better word, assumed the role of judge. It is significant that the account says that he "sat to judge." Sitting is the posture for thought; standing is the posture for action. Thus it is today that the phrase is "to sit" with respect to the convening of a court. (This is

[5]See Shaw, Bernard, *The Perfect Wagnerite: A Commentary on the Niblung's Ring,* Brentano's, New York, 1909.

[6]Exodus, Chap. 18, *The New Indexed Bible,* John A. Dickson Co., Chicago, Illinois, 1923.

not an invidious comparison between sitting and standing. Rather the point is that the role of leadership and the role of judging are fused in unity.)

We leap now from Moses at Kadesh to the Normans in that part of northwestern France known as Normandy and, ultimately, after William the Conqueror, to England and, within the next 200 years, to southern Europe, Italy, Sicily, and the Mediterranean shores, where the Norman gift not only in architecture but also in rulership flourished. We are indebted to Adolf A. Berle, Jr., for the following account of the same impulse to combine judging with leadership that is exposed in the Book of Exodus.[7]

> William, Conqueror-King of England and Duke of Normandy, had died at Rouen. At a beautiful church at St. Etienne de Caen, a throng of nobles, bishops, soldiers, clerks, and common people assembled to pay their last respects. The funeral offices had been said, and the pallbearers were about to lower the old Duke's body into the tomb prepared for it.
>
> Then an obscure man, Asselin by name, broke from the crowd, with the one clamor that could stop so great a ceremony. He cried, "Haro!"
>
> The proceedings stopped then and there. It was Asselin's right to state his grievance. It was simple: this land, this ground on which the church rose in stately columns, belonged to his father and to him. Duke William had taken it by force and had made no reparation. The very grave was on the site of his family homestead. The bishops consulted and promptly made arrangements. They paid at once sixty sous in token compensation for the few square feet of earth in which the Duke was now to be buried. They promised compensation for the land taken. Then, and only then, was William the Conqueror interred; . . . So the story comes down through the account of Augustin Thierry, and it bears every mark of being substantially true.
>
> The "Haro" cry had long been known in Norman law. It was the recognized means of appeal to the conscience of feudal power. It is said—no one really knows —that William's predecessor, the Northman, Duke Rollo, had had statesmanship enough to see that justice must go with power and he had gone in person from place to place in Normandy directing that all who suffered wrong at the hands of his neighbor, or of the feudal officers, or even from the Duke himself, should cry, "Ha! Rollo!" whereupon the Duke must listen to his cause and decide it according to the law of God and good conscience. In any event, it had become a fixed Norman custom. In somewhat different form a like appeal was the practice in England from and after the Conquest. . . . Even in Normandy, tossed by recurrent feudal storms, it became the basis of a special jurisdiction (there presently emerged Norman judges of "Haro," competent to give extraordinary relief remarkably similar to the relief dispensed by British Chancellors and equity courts). . . . But besides power, there were also conceptions of right, and morality, and justice. From these even the king was not exempt. . . .

Then quickly, as history goes, we pass from that Norman Rollo through

---

[7]Berle, Adolf A., Jr., *The Twentieth Century Capitalist Revolution*, Chap. III, Harcourt, Brace & Jovanovich, New York, 1954.

William the Conqueror to his grandson, Henry II (1154–1189), who learned or knew intuitively what Moses had learned over 2,000 years earlier from his sophisticated father-in-law, Jethro, priest of Midian—the necessity for the decentralization of the administration of justice. Jethro advised Moses to appoint rulers (judges) over 10s, 50s, 100s, 1,000s.[8] According to Thomas Mann,[9] Moses complained to Jethro that if he delegated the function of judging the judges would take bribes and would therefore not do justice. But, according to Thomas Mann, Jethro defended his recommendation on the ground that there would be the right of appeal and that the appeal would go to judges of the longest tenure who had taken the most bribes and had therefore become less subject to bribery and more interested in justice. Even today, there persists a dichotomy between judges appointed for life, and therefore economically secure, as in the federal judiciary system of the United States, and judges elected for terms in the lower courts of most states.

Pollock and Maitland declare that Henry II was truly interested in the work of justice and learned from year to year the lessons that experience taught him. They relate that from the year 1176 the king chose five men, two clerks and three laymen, who were not to depart from the king's court but were to hear all of the complaints of the kingdom; questions that they could not decide were to be reserved for the king and his wise men.[10] So it was that English-Norman administration of justice had progressed in two short centuries from Rollo to Henry II, from a court on horseback to a fixed and established court representing the specialized function of judging. Henry II, whose extensive travels to weld his domain gained in western Europe by his marriage to Eleanor of Aquitaine to the English domain gained by the conquest of his grandfather, perceived the necessity of delegation, and thus out of necessity the judicial function, at least at the lower levels, was divorced from personal rulership.[11]

In the American state of Texas, west of the river Pecos, we have a composite of legend and fact that demonstrates the role of personality in the emergence of law in an embryonic society. The Gold Rush of 1849 brought an influx of population to the barren wastes of the American West, including western Texas. A certain Roy Bean set himself up there in a town called Langtry located along the Southern Pacific Railway. Bean is given encyclopedic dates of about 1825 to 1903. One of his biographers, Everett Lloyd, says that he was an elected justice of the peace in Val Verde County, Texas.

Roy Bean's courtroom was in his saloon, named Jersie Lillie for the English actress, Lillie Langtry. Roy Bean's robing for the court consisted in removal

[8]Exodus, Chapter 18, *The New Indexed Bible,* John A. Dickson Co., Chicago Illinois, 1923.

[9]Mann, Thomas, *The Tables of the Law,* Knopf, New York, 1945.

[10]Pollock & Maitland, *The History of English Law Before the Time of Edward I,* Vol. 1, 2nd ed., Cambridge University Press at Cambridge, 1952, pp. 153, 154.

[11]Kelly, Amy, *Eleanor of Aquitaine,* Vintage Books, New York, 1957.

of his bar apron and the donning of an old alpaca coat. Since there were no accommodations for jailing accused or convicted persons justice was done entirely by fines—immediately pocketed by Judge Bean. One account published by Lloyd has the justice at the site of a dead person in whose clothing he found a gun in the one pocket and $40 in another. "Law West of the Pecos," as Bean invariably described himself, decreed a fine of $40 against the corpse for carrying a concealed weapon, and both the weapon and the $40 were pocketed by the enterprising judge. Ridiculous as this and other accounts of frontier judicial personalities may seem, Bean is an historical character in modern times in a budding society in which, for the most part, issues were disposed by the party with the quickest six-shooter. Bean emerges, as countless figures in all of the past have emerged, claiming the right to do justice by force of personality. The biographers say that Bean possessed a single law book. On an occasion when an Irishman was charged with the killing of a Chinese, the Irishman, a good spender in Bean's saloon, was acquitted on the ground that Bean could find nothing in the book making it a crime to kill a Chinaman.[12]

If the reader is amazed that such antics as those of Judge Roy Bean could occur within our own contemporary century, let him remember that the fee courts, sometimes known as justices of the peace, have existed into this century in such communities as the Commonwealth of Pennsylvania. The difference between the case of Bean and the corpse and a contemporary speed trap is one of degree only. It is true that in the time of Lord Coke, over 300 years ago, a fee court, that is, a court in which the judge has an interest in the financial outcome, was held unconstitutional. This was in Bonham's case.[13] Yet folkways persist.

From Jethro's commonsense cure for lower judges taking bribes to Judge Roy Bean's judicial extraction of $40 from a corpse is a span of almost 3,000 years, but Arnold Toynbee asserts that there is no evidence that man has changed physically or spiritually in a hundred thousand years. Mankind obviously wishes to think of law and justice as pre-existing—over and above him, greater than humanity. The hard fact is that law is administered by human beings through human institutions, both with varying degrees of fallibility. Judges are human beings, and courts are human institutions.[14] It is not a perfect world. Yet if a society exists, in whatever measure of excellence, the courts, particularly the appellate courts, will attain an intellectuality well above the average because judges are for the greater part the products of rigorous cultural training.

[12]Lloyd, Everett, *Law West of the Pecos,* rev. ed., Naylor Company, San Antonio, Texas, 1967. Sonnichsen, C. L., *Roy Bean—Law West of the Pecos.* Macmillan, New York, 1943.

[13]Bowen, Catherine Drinker, *The Lion and the Throne,* Little Brown, Boston, 1956, p. 315. For more on Bonham's case, see, Chapter 1, p. 27, *supra.*

[14]See, generally, Frank, Jerome, *Law and the Modern Mind,* Brentano's New York, 1930.

A NOTE ON THE TRIAL OF WILLIAM PENN AND WILLIAM MEAD
FOR CAUSING A TUMULT

(From the Compleat Collection of State Tryals, first published in 1719.
Republished by Marshall Jones Company, Boston, 1919 in edition by Don C. Seitz.)

Upon his return to London in 1670 from Ireland, where he had been on family business, William Penn, a devout Quaker since his student days at Oxford in the early 1660's, attempted to make his way to the usual Quaker meeting place in Gracechurch Street, only to find the area cordoned-off by soldiers. As a protest to the martial activity, Penn began to preach to the people in the open street. Immediately thereafter he and one William Mead were arrested and indicted for preaching and speaking, thereby causing an unlawful and tumultous assembly to the disturbance of the peace.

The trial of William Penn and William Mead was held in London at the Sessions at Old Bailey on September 1, 3, 4, 5, 1670. The trial is best remembered for the courage and skill with which Penn exposed the illegality of the prosecution. In addition, the trial stands as a landmark because a jury asserted the right to decide in opposition to the directions of the court. The case of the jurors is *Bushell's Case,* 6 How. St. Tr. 999 (C.P. 1670). In Bushell's Case the jurors who had been incarcerated solely because of their refusal to reach a verdict as directed by the trial court in the William Penn case brought a writ of habeas corpus and were released. Chief Justice Vaughan rendered a notable opinion in the case. He distinguished between the ministerial and judicial acts of a jury, and held that a jury's verdict when rendered according to the best of their judgment is a judicial act for which they may not be criminally punished. He reasoned that since the jury are the judges of the facts, if a trial judge can order the jury under pain of punishment to accept his view of the facts there would be no need for a jury.

Bushell's Case had an important impact on freedom of speech in the United States. Alexander Hamilton, in his defense of John Peter Zenger, a colonial publisher who had allegedly libeled the Governor of New York, employed the story of Bushell's Case to curb the efforts of the prosecution to coerce the jury. After delineating the facts of the case, Hamilton declared that Bushell's Case:

" .   .   . established for Law, That the Judges, how great soever they be, have no Right to Fine, imprison, or punish a Jury, for not finding a Verdict according to the Direction of the Court. And this I hope is sufficient to prove, That Jurymen are to see with their own Eyes, to hear with their own Ears, and to make use of their own Consciences and the Understandings, in judging of the Lives, Liberties or Estates of their Fellow Subjects."

William Penn's fine was settled anonymously, and he was released in time to be present at his father's death on September 1, 1670.

IN RE OLIVER
Supreme Court of the United States, 333 U.S. 257 (1948).

Mr. Justice BLACK delivered the opinion of the Court.

A Michigan circuit judge summarily sent the petitioner to jail for contempt of court. We must determine whether he was denied the procedural due process guaranteed by the Fourteenth Amendment.

In obedience to a subpoena the petitioner appeared as a witness before a Michigan circuit judge who was then conducting, in accordance with Michigan law, a "one-man grand jury" investigation into alleged gambling and official corruption. The investigation presumably took place in the judge's chambers, though that is not certain. . . . A prosecutor may have been present. A stenographer was most likely there. The record does not show what other members, if any, of the judge's investigatorial staff participated in the proceedings. It is certain, however, that the public was excluded —the questioning was secret in accordance with the traditional grand jury method.

After petitioner had given certain testimony, the judge-grand jury, still in secret session, told petitioner that neither he nor his advisors believed petitioner's story—that it did not "jell." This belief of the judge-grand jury was not based entirely on what the petitioner had testified. As will later be seen, it rested in part on beliefs or suspicions of the judge-jury derived from the testimony of at least one other witness who had previously given evidence in secret. Petitioner had not been present when that witness testified and so far as appears was not even aware that he had testified. Based on its beliefs thus formed—that petitioner's story did not "jell"—the judge-grand jury immediately sentenced him to sixty days in jail. Under these circumstances of haste and secrecy, petitioner, of course, had no chance to enjoy the benefits of counsel, no chance to prepare his defense, and no opportunity either to cross examine the other grand jury witness or to summon witnesses to refute the charge against him.

Three days later a lawyer filed on petitioner's behalf in the Michigan Supreme Court the petition for habeas corpus now under consideration. It alleged among other things that the petitioner's attorney had no been allowed to confer with him and that, to the best of the attorney's knowledge, the petitioner was not held in jail under any judgment, decree or execution, and was "not confined by virtue of any legal commitment directed to the sheriff as required by law." An order was then entered signed by the circuit judge that he had while "sitting as a One-Man Grand Jury" convicted the petitioner of contempt of court because petitioner had testified "evasively" and had given "contradictory answers" to questions. The order directed that petitioner "be confined in the county jail . . . for a period of sixty days . . . or until such time as he . . . shall appear and answer the questions heretofore propounded to him by this Court . . . ."

The Supreme Court of Michigan . . . rejected petitioner's contention that the summary manner in which he had been sentenced to jail in the secrecy of the grand jury chamber had deprived him of his liberty without affording him the kind of notice, opportunity to defend himself, and trial which the due process clause of the Fourteenth Amendment requires. . . . We granted certiorari to consider these procedural due process questions.

[The United States Supreme Court next made it clear that the petitioner did not challenge the constitutionality of Michigan's unique grand jury system which permits a single judge to appoint prosecutors and to summon witnesses, even though the traditional federal grand jury is composed of 12 to 23 members. Nor did petitioner challenge the fact that the Michigan judge sitting as a one-man grand jury operated with the utmost secrecy, as a grand jury must since it does not try or convict but only investigates and detects crime ending its proceedings with either a report, a no-bill or an indictment. The Supreme Court emphasized that what the petitioner did challenge was the fact that the Michigan law allowed the circuit court judge to turn the one-man grand jury proceedings, without changing its secret character, into a contempt proceeding in which the witness immediately became the defendant.]

Mr. Justice BLACK, speaking for the Supreme Court, continued:

. . . Thus our first question is this: Can an accused be tried and convicted for contempt of court in grand jury secrecy?

First.   Counsel have not cited and we have been unable to find a single instance of a criminal trial conducted in camera in any federal, state, or municipal court during the history of this country. Nor have we found any record of even one such secret criminal trial in England since abolition of the Court of Star Chamber in 1641, and whether that court ever convicted people secretly is in dispute. Summary trials for alleged misconduct called contempt of court have not been regarded as an exception to this universal rule against secret trials, unless some other Michigan one-man grand jury case may represent such an exception.

This nation's accepted practice of guaranteeing a public trial to an accused has its roots in our English common law heritage. The exact date of its origin is obscure, but it likely evolved long before the settlement of our land as an accompaniment of the ancient institution of jury trial. In this country the guarantee to an accused of the right to a public trial first appeared in a state constitution in 1776. Following the ratification in 1791 of the Federal Constitution's Sixth Amendment, which commands that "In all criminal prosecutions, the accused shall enjoy the right to a speedy and public trial . . . " most of the original states and those subsequently admitted to the Union adopted similar constitutional provisions. Today almost without exception every state by constitution, statute, or judicial decision, requires that all criminal trials be open to the public.

The traditional Anglo-American distrust for secret trials has been variously ascribed to the notorious use of this practice by the Spanish Inquisition, to the excesses of the English Court of Star Chamber, and to the French monarchy's abuse of the lettre de cachet. All of these institutions obviously symbolized a menace to liberty. In the hands of despotic groups each of them had become an instrument for the suppression of political and religious heresies in ruthless disregard of the right of an accused to a fair trial. Whatever other benefits the guarantee to an accused that his trial be conducted in public may confer upon our society, the guarantee has always been recognized as a safeguard against any attempt to employ our courts as instruments of persecution. The knowledge that every criminal trial is subject to contemporaneous review in the forum of public opinion is an effective restraint on possible abuse of judicial power. One need not wholly agree with a statement made on the subject by Jeremy Bentham over 120 years ago to appreciate the fear of secret trials felt by him, his predecessors and contemporaries. Bentham said: " . . . suppose the proceedings to be completely secret, and the court, on the occasion to consist of no more than a single judge, —that judge will be at once indolent and arbitrary: how corrupt soever his inclination may be, it will find no check, at any rate no tolerable efficient check, to oppose it. With publicity all other checks are insufficient: in comparison of publicity, all other checks are of small account. Recordation, appeal, whatever other institutions might present themselves in the character of checks, would be found to operate rather as cloaks than checks; as cloaks in reality, as checks only in appearance."[A]

In giving content to the constitutional and statutory commands that an accused be given a public trial, the state and federal courts have differed over what groups of spectators, if any, could properly be excluded from a criminal trial. But, unless in Michigan and in one-man grand jury contempt cases, no court in this country has ever before held, so far as we can find, that an accused can be tried, convicted, and sent to jail, when everybody else is denied entrance to the court, except the judge and his attaches. And without exception all courts have held that an accused is at the very least entitled to have his friends, relatives and counsel present, no matter with what offense he may be charged.   .   .   .

In the case before us, the petitioner was called as a witness to testify in secret before a one-man grand jury conducting a grand jury investigation. In the midst of petitioner's testimony the proceedings abruptly changed. The investigation became a "trial," the grand jury became a judge, and the witness became an accused charged with contempt of court—all in secret. Following a charge, conviction and sentence, the petitioner was led away to prison—still without any break in the secrecy. Even in jail, according to undenied allegations, his lawyer was denied an opportunity to see and confer with him. And that was not the end of secrecy. His lawyer filed in the State Supreme Court this habeas corpus proceeding. Even there, the mantle of secrecy enveloped the transaction and the State Supreme Court ordered him sent back to jail without ever having seen a record of his testimony, and without knowing all that took place in the secrecy of the judge's chambers. In view of this nation's historic distrust of secret proceedings, their inherent dangers to freedom, and the universal requirement of our federal and state governments that criminal trials be public, the Fourteenth Amendment's guarantee that no one shall be deprived of his liberty without due process of law means at least that an accused cannot be thus sentenced to prison.

Second.   We further hold that failure to afford the petitioner a reasonable opportunity to defend himself against the charge of false and evasive swearing was a denial of due process of law. A person's right to reasonable notice of a charge against him, and an opportunity to be heard in his defense—a right to his day in court—are basic in our system of jurisprudence; and these rights include, as a minimum, a right to examine the witnesses against him, to offer testimony, and to be represented by counsel. Michigan, apparently concedes that the summary conviction here would have been a denial of procedural due process but for the nature of the charge, namely, a contempt of court, committed, the State urges, in the court's actual presence.   .   .   .

.   .   .   .   .

It is "the law of the land" that no man's life, liberty or property be forfeited as a punishment until there has been a charge fairly made and fairly tried in a public tribunal.   .   .   .   The petitioner was convicted without that kind of trial.

[A]Bentham, *Rationale of Judicial Evidence* 524 (1827).

The judgment of the Supreme Court of Michigan is reversed and the cause is remanded to it for disposition not inconsistent with this opinion.

Reversed and remanded.

[Mr. Justice Rutledge concurred in the result reached by the majority but asserted that the Court had departed from the Constitution when it permitted selective departure by the States from the scheme of ordered liberty established by the Bill of Rights.

Mr. Justice Jackson and Mr. Justice Frankfurter dissented. Each urged that the case be remanded to the Supreme Court of Michigan in the interest of federal-state relations, since, in their view, that court had not had an opportunity to pass upon the precise issues decided by the majority.]

THE JURY

It is common knowledge that in English-American courts (a) the jury finds the facts, (b) applies the law as the judge has instructed it on the law, (c) reaches a verdict—in criminal cases, of not guilty or guilty, or in civil cases, a verdict of damages, for example, in cases of tort or breach of contract— and (d) assesses the penalty. Juries may of course find that the defendant has not violated any right of the plaintiff or failed to perform an obligation, in which case no damages will be assessed. It is a popular concept that juries will find for the plaintiff in the majority of cases, the only question being how much?

Surprisingly, the origin of the jury system is not in English democracy but rather in Frankish royalty.[15] Pollock and Maitland say that in historical essence the jury was a body of neighbors summoned by some public officer to give upon oath a true answer to some question. Again surprisingly, the jurors were not to give the answer to the question on the basis of evidence they were to hear in a trial but rather out of knowledge that the jurors already possessed. In the 12th century a *trial* still involved in the Frankish *inquisitio,* the prerogative of Frankish kings, procedures like those in the English communal courts —antique modes of proof, such as the ordeal and the oath with oath helpers. Underlying the ordeal was the superstitious belief that the result of the ordeal, whether by combat, fire, or otherwise, disclosed the will of God. For example, the trial of a suspect of witchery, more often than not involving a woman, could be so absurd by modern standards as to involve the tying of her right-hand thumb to her left-foot great toe and the converse. Then when thrown into water if she floated she was guilty and would burn. If she sank she was innocent.

Pollock & Maitland say that the jury was not involved in the trial by ordeal; rather the jury was a group of men, summoned by the Frankish king, "the best and most trustworthy men of a district," to be sworn to declare, for example, what lands, what rights, the king had or ought to have in their district. The

[15]Pollock and Maitland, *The History of English Law,* Vol. 1, 2nd ed., University Press, Cambridge, 1952, p. 138, *et seq.*

king used this privilege of summons to avoid litigation of the crude type just mentioned. The king would rely on the verdict of the neighbors instead of on battle or ordeal. He used the procedure also to detect grave crimes that might threaten the king's peace. The neighbors must say whether they suspected anyone of murders or robberies. The procedure, which the king employed in support of his own rights, was granted by him as a favor to others.

Pollock & Maitland find this procedure in the Frankish empire as early as the 9th century. They conclude, "Such is now the prevailing opinion, and it has triumphed in this country [England] over the natural disinclination of Englishmen to admit that this 'palladium of our liberties' is in its origin not English but Frankish, not popular but royal." One aspect of the origin is filled with some irony. The original jury was composed, as is the modern jury, of trustworthy men (and now women), but it was a precise requirement that they already knew the facts to be reported to the sovereign or would by their own devices discover them. The modern jury must, if at all possible, be ignorant of the facts and issues, saving only such inevitable knowledge as they may have from news media that an alleged crime has occurred or a particular litigation has been instituted. It is understandable that in England, where research into institutional origins has been of longer duration than would have been possible in much younger America, the right of trial by jury has been much curtailed.

In England until 1854 the jury trial was the only form of trial used in any common law court. Since the Act of Judicature of 1883, jury was to be had as a matter of course only in actions of libel, slander, malicious prosecution, false imprisonment, seduction and breach of promise of marriage. In all other actions the jury had to be requested. Subsequently, in 1918, the right to a jury trial was abolished except for the six matters mentioned above and in cases of fraud. In 1933 the law was amended to provide that the right to a jury trial in fraud cases would be granted only to the party charged with the fraud. The trial judge may now, upon application, grant a jury trial in other civil matters; however, his discretion is quite unfettered. In 1956 trials by jury accounted for approximately two to three per cent of all civil trials in English courts.[16]

In the United States the right of trial by jury is deeply embedded in folk thought about what is a fair trial. The VI Amendment to the Constitution of the United States guarantees the jury trial in criminal prosecutions. The VII Amendment provides

> In suits at common law, where the value in controversy shall exceed twenty dollars, the right of trial by jury shall be preserved, and no fact tried by a jury shall be otherwise reexamined in any court of the United States, than according to the rules of the common law.

The word *preserved* implies that the Constitution does not create the right to

---

[16]Joiner, Charles W., *Civil Justice and the Jury*, Prentice-Hall, Englewood Cliffs, New Jersey, 1962, pp. 59–61; quoting Sir Patrick Devlin, *Trial by Jury*, 1956, pp. 130–133.

trial by jury. It is presumed to be embedded in the English common law concept of due process, although, as we have noted, the English legislative enactments do not appear to be bound by or dependent upon such presumption. The Seventh Amendment, of course, is primarily applicable to the federal courts although it will be seen that in Duncan v. Louisiana, *infra,* the Sixth Amendment was held to constitute one of the liberties which the Fourteenth Amendment guarantees to the citizens of the state. That Amendment provides:

> In all criminal prosecutions, the accused shall enjoy the right to a speedy and public trial, by an impartial jury of the State and district wherein the crime shall have been committed, which district shall have been previously ascertained by law, and to be informed of the nature and cause of the accusation; to be confronted with the witnesses against him; to have compulsory process for obtaining witnesses in his favor, and to have the assistance of counsel for his defense.

The constitutions of the fifty states and legislation in those states provide considerable variation in the extent of the right of an individual to a trial by jury.

The State constitutional provisions on juries may be broadly divided into three categories:

(1) The right of trial by jury shall be inviolate.

(2) The right of trial by jury shall remain inviolate.

(3) The right of trial by jury as heretofore used or enjoyed shall remain inviolate.

The constitution of Ohio is an example of the first category; it also permits a verdict by less than an unanimous jury:

> The right of trial by jury shall be inviolate, except that, in civil cases, laws may be passed to authorize the rendering of a verdict by the concurrence of not less than three-fourths of the jury.   (Art. I, § 5, adopted September 3, 1912).

The constitution of California is an example of the second category; it permits a verdict by less than an unanimous jury and permits the jury to consist of less than twelve persons:

> The right of trial by jury shall be secured to all, and remain inviolate; but in civil actions three-fourths of the jury may render a verdict. A trial by jury may be waived in all criminal cases by the consent of both parties, expressed in open court by the defendant and his counsel, and in civil actions by the consent of the parties, signified in such manners as may be prescribed by law. In civil actions and cases of misdemeanor, the jury may consist of 12, or of any number less than 12 upon which the parties may agree in open court.   (Art. I, § 7, as amended November 6, 1928) (prior to the amendment a jury could not be waived in felony cases).

The constitution of Pennsylvania is an example of the third category:

> Trial by jury shall be heretofore, and the right thereof remain inviolate, (Art. I, § 6, adopted November 3, 1874.)

Juries, like judges, are the butt of much sarcastic humor; for example, the foolish outcome of the breach of promise suit in "Trial by Jury."[17] Buffoonery about law, lawyers, judges, and juries, although not so theatrically and musically excellent as that in Gilbert and Sullivan, is commonplace in Anglo-American song, verse, and art. The walls of many lawyers' and judges' chambers are lined with etchings and prints lampooning lawyers, juries, and judges. The works of the French painter and caricaturist Honore Daumier contain satirical representations of courtroom personalities.

On the other hand the jury system has its vigorous supporters. Anyone who samples the opinion of students will encounter an inborn majority impulse to defend the system. Even unschooled persons will quickly reach for words and concepts beyond their vocabularies to identify trial by jury as an inalienable right, frequently expressing a vague and mistaken conviction that the right was gained at a great battle at Runnymede, some even making reference to the Magna Charta.

The jury system has not only its popular defenders but also its intellectually sophisticated supporters, as will be seen in the Duncan case, *infra*. James Gould Cozzens, who in *The Just and the Unjust* takes his place with a few perceptive nonlawyers such as Charles Dickens in *Bleak-House,* offers through Judge Coates an excellent defense of the jury system.[18]

> Judge Coates said, 'A jury has its uses.   .   .   . It's like a—' he paused. 'It's like a cylinder head gasket. Between two things that don't give any, you have to have something that does give a little, something to seal the law to the facts. There isn't any known way to legislate with an allowance for right feeling.'
>
> 'Well, Vredenburgh told Harry this Court wasn't enforcing the Sixth Commandment.'
>
> 'From the bench?'
>
> 'Oh, no. Afterward, in the Attorneys Room. I guess he thought the jury had given a little more than it needed to. He said he was disgusted with it.'
>
> 'He won't feel that way tomorrow. Tom's got better sense than that. In his time, he's had trouble with his temper.'
>
> 'What was that?'
>
> 'It was long ago,' Judge Coates said. 'When he was district attorney, he used to go off the handle now and then. He got over it. It isn't a matter of any interest now. Juries didn't always find what he thought they ought to in those days, either. Justice is an inexact science. As a matter of fact, a judge is so greatly in a jury's debt, he shouldn't begrudge them the little things they help themselves to.'
>
> 'I don't follow,' Abner said.
>
> 'The ancient conflict between liberty and authority. The jury protects the Court. It's a question how long any system of courts could last in a free country if judges found the verdicts. It doesn't matter how wise and experienced the judges may

[17]*A Treasury of Gilbert & Sullivan,* Deems Taylor, ed., Simon and Schuster, New York, 1941.

[18]Cozzens, James Gould, *The Just and the Unjust,* Harbarce Modern Classics (Harcourt), 1942, pp. 427–428.

be. Resentment would build up every time the findings didn't go with current notions or prejudices. Pretty soon half the community would want to lynch the judge. There's no focal point with a jury; the jury is the public itself. That's why a jury can say when a judge couldn't, 'I don't care what the law is, that isn't right and I won't do it.' It's the greatest prerogative of free men. They have to have a way of saying that and making it stand. They may be wrong, they may refuse to do the things they ought to do; but freedom just to be wise and good isn't any freedom. We pay a price for lay participation in the law; but it's a necessary expense.'

'You mean,' said Abner, 'that in order to show he's free, a man shouldn't obey the laws.'

'A free man always has been and always will be the one to decide what he'd better do,' Judge Coates said.

In the United States the jury is a deeply entrenched folk institution. It will give way to a less cumbersome and expensive system for determination of facts, but it will yield only slowly to more technically precise methods.

DUNCAN v. LOUISIANA
Supreme Court of the United States, 391 U.S. 145 (1968).

Mr. Justice WHITE delivered the opinion of the Court.

Appellant, Gary Duncan, was convicted of simple battery in the Twenty-fifth Judicial District Court of Louisiana. Under Louisiana law simple battery is a misdemeanor, punishable by a maximum of two years' imprisonment and a $300 fine. Appellant sought trial by jury, but because the Louisiana Constitution grants jury trials only in cases in which capital punishment or imprisonment at hard labor may be imposed, the trial judge denied the request. Appellant was convicted and sentenced to serve 60 days in the parish prison and pay a fine of $150. Appellant sought review in the Supreme Court of Louisiana, asserting that the denial of jury trial violated rights guaranteed to him by the United States Constitution. The Supreme Court, finding "[n]o error of law in the ruling complained of," denied appellant a writ of certiorari. . . . [A]ppellant sought review in this Court, alleging that the Sixth and Fourteenth Amendments to the United States Constitution secure the right to jury trial in state criminal prosecutions where a sentence as long as two years may be imposed. . . .

Appellant was 19 years of age when tried. While driving on Highway 23 in Plaquemines Parish on October 18, 1966, he saw two younger cousins engaged in a conversation by the side of the road with four white boys. Knowing his cousins, Negroes who had recently transferred to a formerly all-white high school, had reported the occurrence of racial incidents at the school, Duncan stopped the car, got out, and approached the six boys. At trial the white boys and a white onlooker testified, as did appellant and his cousins. The testimony was in dispute on many points, but the witnesses agreed that appellant and the white boys spoke to each other, that appellant encouraged his cousins to break off the encounter and enter his car, and that appellant was about to enter the car himself for the purpose of driving away with his cousins. The whites testified that just before getting in the car appellant slapped Herman Landry, one of the white boys, on the elbow. The Negroes testified that appellant had not slapped Landry, but had merely touched him. The trial judge concluded that the State had proved beyond a reasonable doubt that Duncan had committed simple battery, and found him guilty.

The Fourteenth Amendment denies the States the power to "deprive any person of life, liberty, or property, without due process of law." In resolving conflicting claims concerning the meaning of this spacious language, the Court has looked increasingly to the Bill of Rights for guidance; many of the rights guaranteed by the first eight Amendments to the Constitution have been held to be protected against state action by the Due Process Clause of the Fourteenth Amendment. That clause now protects the right to compensation for property taken by the State; the rights of speech, press, and religion covered by the First Amendment; the Fourth Amendment rights to be free from unreasonable searches and seizures and to have excluded from criminal trials any evidence illegally seized; the right guaranteed by the Fifth Amendment to be free of compelled self-incrimination; and the Sixth Amendment rights to counsel, to a speedy and public trial, to confrontation of opposing witnesses, and to compulsory process for obtaining witnesses.

The test for determining whether a right extended by the Fifth and Sixth Amendments with respect to federal criminal proceedings is also protected against state action by the Fourteenth Amendment has been phrased in a variety of ways in the opinions of this Court. The question has been asked whether a right is among those " 'fundamental principles of liberty and justice which lie at the base of all our civil and political institutions,' " Powell v. Alabama, 287 U.S. 45, 67 (1932); whether it is "basic in our system of jurisprudence," In re Oliver 333 U.S. 257, 273 (1948); and whether it is "a fundamental right, essential to a fair trial," Gideon v. Wainwright, 372 U.S. 335, 343-344 (1963). . . .   The claim before us is that the right to trial by jury guaranteed by the Sixth Amendment meets these tests. The position of Louisiana, on the other hand, is that the Constitution imposes upon the States no duty to give a jury trial in any criminal case, regardless of the seriousness of the crime or the size of the punishment which may be imposed. Because we believe that trial by jury in criminal cases is fundamental to the American scheme of justice, we hold that the Fourteenth Amendment guarantees a right of jury trial in all criminal cases which—were they to be tried in a federal court—would come within the Sixth Amendment's guarantee. Since we consider the appeal before us to be such a case, we hold that the Constitution was violated when appellant's demand for jury trial was refused.

.   .   .   .

The judgment below is reversed and the case is remanded for proceedings not inconsistent with this opinion.[19]

THE WITNESS

The facts to be found by a jury will be evidenced in many ways. If the fact in issue is a will, then the writing, attested by witnesses who observed the statu-

[19]The Supreme Court of the United States is still zealous to protect the right of trial by jury of an accused person even though a statutory invasion may have an administratively laudable purpose. For example, in New York State a statute designed to reduce the backlog of allegedly petty criminal cases by limiting jury trials in the New York City Criminal

tory formalities at the signing of the will, may speak for itself. If, however, the signature is challenged, a handwriting expert may become a witness. If the testator's sanity is questioned by disappointed expectant beneficiaries, an expert psychiatrist may become a witness. One such may be adduced by the proponents of the will; one by the opponents; one by the judge. They may all disagree, each with the other, or they may agree in part and disagree in part —with such nice distinctions that even a judge will be confused. Yet the case must be decided.

The fact in issue may be the speed of an automobile, the color of a traffic light, the volume of a sound or its nature, the proper description of a person (height, weight, physiognomy, dress), the identification of an object (revolver, sawed-off shotgun, switch-knife), the sequence of events (who threw a paving stone first), the time of day or night, the size of a crowd, or the position of an object in a room or on a public street. The examples of fact-inquiries are literally numberless. Few facts are self-proving. There are certainties of course —an identified dead body, for example, although even there mistakes have been made, innocent and otherwise. Uncertainties predominate in court contests about facts, and the conflicting testimony of witnesses is the grist of the judicial mill.

Witnesses may be generally categorized: the nonexperts (the great commonalty of witnesses) and the experts (in every field and branch of human knowledge: economics, engineering, handwriting, psychology, psychiatry, sociology). No realm of human learning is irrelevant at some time or other in a court proceeding. The nonexpert brings to the judge and to the jury his human integrity; he swears to tell the truth. The expert brings to the judge and to the jury his learning, acquired by well-documented experience, by education, or, better still, by education and experience. He also swears to tell the truth.

Nonexpert witnesses may be divided among honest witnesses who are right, honest witnesses who are wrong, and dishonest witnesses—perjurors. By the same token experts may be divided among honest experts who are right, honest experts who are wrong, and dishonest, putative experts who are for sale to any litigant. As to the dishonest witnesses, expert or nonexpert, the techniques of cross-examination are some guarantee or protection for the truth. Examples of those techniques are set forth in the ensuing subsection on lawyers. As to honest witnesses who are wrong, there is a wealth of psychological data that have been accumulated over the past half century but as yet are only partially recognized in trial procedures. Some examples of those data follow.

The human being is usually quite sure that whatever he saw he saw correctly; he is almost equally sure, although he may be shaken somewhat on cross-examination, about what he heard. The proverb has it that "seeing is

Courts was held inapplicable to a case in which the term of imprisonment might have been more than six months. Baldwin v. New York, 399 U.S. 66 (1970).

believing"—not that "hearing is believing." Nevertheless, human beings do see and hear things that leave their fellowmen unconvinced, doubtful, to say the least. Mohammed saw the angel Gabriel as reported by Tor Andrae:[20]

> I went out of the cave, and while I was on the mountain, I heard a voice saying: O Mohammed, thou art Allah's Apostle, and I am Gabriel! I looked up and saw Gabriel in the form of a man with crossed legs at the horizon of heaven. I remained standing and observed him, and moved neither backwards nor forwards. And when I turned my gaze from him, I continued to see him on the horizon, no matter where I turned.' Finally the vision vanished, and Mohammed returned to his family.

To the faithful such experiences are called visions or revelations; to the psychologist these experiences of certain human beings are subjects of scientific interest.

With the birth of modern psychology, in the work of William James at Harvard around the turn of the century, the attention of students to the accuracy of observations of normal persons has been directed. An early investigator in this area was Hugo Munsterberg. His publication was called *On The Witness Stand.* In the following passage Professor Munsterberg discloses the inaccuracy of his own observations:[21]

> Last summer I had to face a jury as witness in a trial. While I was with my family at the seashore my city house had been burglarised and I was called upon to give an account of my findings against the culprit whom they had caught with a part of the booty. I reported under oath that the burglars had entered through a cellar window, and then described what rooms they had visited. To prove, in answer to a direct question, that they had been there at night, I told that I had found drops of candle wax on the second floor. To show that they intended to return, I reported that they had left a large mantel clock, packed in wrapping paper, on the dining-room table. Finally, as to the amount of clothes which they had taken, I asserted that the burglars did not get more than a specified list which I had given the police.
>
> Only a few days later I found that every one of these statements was wrong. They had not entered through the window, but had broken the lock of the cellar door; the clock was not packed by them in wrapping paper, but in a tablecloth; the candle droppings were not on the second floor, but in the attic; the list of lost garments was to be increased by seven more pieces; and while my story under oath spoke always of two burglars, I do not know that there was more than one. How did all those mistakes occur? I have no right to excuse myself on the plea of a bad memory. During the last eighteen years I have delivered about three thousand university lectures. For those three thousand coherent addresses I had not once a single written or printed line or any notes whatever on the platform; and yet

[20]Andrae, Tor, *Mohammed: The Man and His Faith,* Harper, (Harper Torchbooks/The Cloister Library), New York, 1960, p. 44

[21]Munsterberg, Hugo, *On The Witness Stand,* Clark Boardman Co., New York, 1949, pp. 39–41.

there has never been a moment when I have had to stop for a name or for the connection of the thought. My memory serves me therefore rather generously. I stood there, also, without prejudice against the defendant. Inasmuch as he expects to spend the next twelve years at a place of residence where he will have little chance to read my writings, I may confess frankly that I liked the man. I was thus under the most favourable conditions for speaking the whole truth and nothing but the truth, and, as there is probably no need for the assurance of my best intentions, I felt myself somewhat alarmed in seeing how may illusions had come in.

Professor Munsterberg had taken an oath to tell the truth, the whole truth, and nothing but the truth. He had intended so to do. Yet by his own testimony he had perjured himself—not intentionally, although that would have been a question for the jury in a charge of perjury—but by reason of faulty observations. We must assume that the vast majority of witnesses are as honest as the academician Munsterberg—and potentially as mistaken.

In Chapter 4 of this book, which we called, "The Law Makes the Promise Good," we pointed out that a society of liars would be quite impossible by any standards we know. In a society in which division of labor is a key fact we must be able to rely upon the word of most men. The dishonest promisor must be the exception, not the rule. So it is with the administration of justice. If it were the case that all witnesses intended to lie, then court proceedings would be travesties. The fact is to the contrary. A distinguished English judge, Parry, has added his personal testimony to the assumption of honesty in witnesses.[22]

Judge Parry says that he is glad to know himself, and he hopes that he has convinced his fellow citizens, that the crime of perjury is a rare one in our courts and that most of the errors of testimony are due to defective observation, false reminiscences, the deflecting influence of suggestion, and the pleasures of imagination. He says that very often the "wish to believe" is a strong factor in bringing about false testimony. Judge Parry continues to express his faith in scientific investigation, and he concludes that when mankind understands more fully and scientifically the real causes of error in human testimony, which the professors have only in recent years begun to study scientifically, we shall be able to set about amending our ways and checking our bias and imagination, and shunning the perils of undue suggestions.

Acute distortions of perception of physical objects and scenes occur in the case of normal persons, as with Munsterberg. What about the credibility of abnormal persons? One person out of every twenty has some mental problems. Such persons testify as witnesses. Mental illness does not show itself with a brand on the brow of the unfortunate person. Mental illness is sly at concealing itself. Persons appearing quite normal to the inexpert observer might very well be suffering from acute mental problems. Such persons testify; such persons

[22]Parry, Edward Abbot, *What The Judge Thought,* Knopf, New York, 1923, p. 101, *et seq.*

look honest; such persons take an oath to tell the truth, the whole truth, and nothing but the truth; such persons may tell the truth as they see it, but they do not see the truth—they see it darkly through the glass of their own mental abnormalities. In sum, and at the risk of oversimplification, we, all of us, in varying degrees, see things not as they are but as we are.

For an intermediate summary about the nature of the administration of justice by juries and by judges, we now ponder what has always been an obvious human condition. Judges are fallible human beings beset with prejudices, biased by contemporary social norms, arrogant sometimes, as in the case of the trial of William Penn, and other times confused and indiscreet, as in the case of Oliver. But here again the vast majority of judges, like the vast majority of mankind, are honest, hard-working, conscientious, responsible members of society, who are aware of the high responsibilities that they carry, and who are learned and disciplined in the procedures by which they must discharge those responsibilities.

Likewise with juries—they are fallible human beings, with a complex, even among so small a number as 12, of biases prevalent in a pluralistic society. The jury may be as tenacious, brave, and as successful in the assertion of its independence, as in Bushell's case, or as immune to the law and the facts or as benighted and wrong in its decision, as in Cozzen's *The Just and the Unjust.* It may be that juries often use crude methods. It is a widespread tradition among lawyers that in a damage suit, for example, each juror will put down the number of dollars he thinks the plaintiff should have; the total is then divided by twelve, and that is the verdict of the jury, in order to get home by dinner time.

> The hungry judges soon the sentence sign,
> And wretches hang that jurymen may dine.[23]

One may also enjoy the sardonic, as in Finley Peter Dunne on expert testimony.

> Whin the case is all over, the jury'll pitch th' tistimony out iv the window, an' consider three questions: "Did Lootgert look as though he'd kill his wife? Did his wife look as though she ought to be kilt? Isn't it time we wint to supper?"[24]

After the fun and the sarcasm have had their play, we come, at last, to the sober realization that however much we may expect a jury system to yield to more efficient and less cumbersome processes the jury is not a venal institution in our society. It may be that the good the juries do could be done more expeditiously and more economically, but certainly we cannot classify juries as public enemies. We cannot think of them in the same terms as we think of organized crime. The jury institution is a good institution in the moral sense,

---

[23]Pope, Alexander, *Rape of the Lock,* Canto III, 1.21.

[24]Finley Peter Dunne, "On Expert Testimony," cited in Stevenson, Burton, *The Home Book of Quotations,* 9th ed., Dodd, Mead & Co., New York, 1964.

given human frailties. It is not an immoral institution. One proof of that assertion is the rare case in which it is found that a jury was successfully subverted. There are all too many cases of attempts to corrupt the jury, such as the Hoffa case (see p. 282, *supra*). The failure of such attempts attests to the predominant integrity of our society and therefore to the juries drawn from that society.

We have seen, however, that whatever the wisdom of most judges or whatever the integrity of most juries, they are equally dependent upon the testimony of witnesses in the great majority of cases. We have seen that the quality of that testimony leaves much to be desired. Let us come therefore to the role of lawyers in this imperfect world of judical administration.

THE LAWYER

The Art of Cross Examination

The lawyer does that for his client which the client would do for himself if he could.

Samuel Johnson

In the list of great trial lawyers of the 20th century, always a small number in any generation, is the name of Francis L. Wellman. He recorded his own experiences and those of other trial lawyers in *The Art of Cross-Examination*.[25] Two examples: one of a perjurer, unmasked by Abraham Lincoln, and one of a sham expert devastated by Francis L. Wellman will demonstrate some aspects of the art of cross-examination.

A PERJURER UNMASKED BY LINCOLN

A simple but perhaps instructive example of cross-examination, conducted along these lines, is quoted from Judge J. W. Donovan's "Tact in Court." It is mainly interesting in that it is reported to have occurred in Abraham Lincoln's first defence at a murder trial.

'Grayson was charged with shooting Lockwood at a camp-meeting, on the evening of August 9, 18—, and with running away from the scene of the killing, which was witnessed by Sovine. The proof was so strong that, even with an excellent previous character, Grayson came very near being lynched on two occasions soon after his indictment for murder.

'The mother of the accused, after failing to secure older counsel, finally engaged young Abraham Lincoln, as he was then called, and the trial came on to an early hearing. No objection was made to the jury, and no cross-examination of witnesses, save the last and only important one, who swore that he knew the parties, saw the shot fired by Grayson, saw him run away, and picked up the deceased, who died instantly.

[25]Wellman, Francis L., *The Art of Cross-Examination,* Macmillan, New York, 1924, pp. 54 and 99.

'The evidence of guilt and identity was morally certain. The attendence was large, the interest intense. Grayson's mother began to wonder why 'Abraham remained silent so long and why he didn't do something!' The people finally rested. The tall lawyer (Lincoln) stood up and eyed the strong witness in silence, without books or notes, and slowly began his defense by these questions:

Lincoln: And you were with Lockwood just before and saw the shooting?

Witness: Yes.

Lincoln: And you stood very near to them?

Witness: No, about twenty feet away.

Lincoln: May it not have been *ten* feet?

Witness: No, it was twenty feet *or more.*

Lincoln: In the open field?

Witness: No, in the timber.

Lincoln: What kind of timber?

Witness: Beech timber.

Lincoln: Leaves on it are rather thick in August?

Witness: Rather.

Lincoln: And you think *this* pistol was the one used?

Witness: It looks like it.

Lincoln: You could see defendant shoot—see how the barrel hung, and all about it?

Witness: Yes.

Lincoln: How near was this to the meeting place?

Witness: Three-quarters of a mile away.

Lincoln: Where were the lights?

Witness: Up by the minister's stand.

Lincoln: Three-quarters of a mile away?

Witness: Yes, answered ye *twiste.*

Lincoln: Did you not see a candle there, with Lockwood or Grayson?

Witness: No! what would we want a candle for?

Lincoln: How, then, did you see the shooting?

Witness: By moonlight! (defiantly).

Lincoln: You saw this shooting at ten at night—in beech timber, three-quarters of a mile from the light—saw the pistol barrel—saw the man fire—saw it twenty feet away—saw it by moonlight? Saw it nearly a mile from the camp lights?

Witness: Yes, I told you so before.

'The interest was now so intense that men leaned forward to catch the smallest syllable. Then the lawyer drew out a blue covered almanac from his side coat pocket—opened it slowly—offered it in evidence—showed it to the jury and the court—read from a page with careful deliberation that the moon on that night was unseen and only arose at *one* the next morning.

'Following this climax Mr. Lincoln moved the arrest of the perjured witness as the real murderer, saying: 'Nothing but *a motive to clear himself* could have induced him to swear away so falsely the life of one who never did him harm!' With such determined emphasis did Lincoln present his showing that the court ordered Sovine arrested, and under the strain of excitement he broke down and confessed to being the one who fired the fatal shot himself, but denied it was intentional.'

.   .   .   .

A SHAM EXPERT PILLORIED

The professional witness is always partisan, ready and eager to serve the party calling him. This fact should be ever present in the mind of the cross-examiner. Encourage the witness to betray his partisanship; encourage him to volunteer statements and opinions, and to give irresponsive answers. Jurors always look with suspicion upon such testimony. Assume that an expert witness called against you has come prepared to do you all the harm he can, and will avail himself of every opportunity to do so which you may inadvertently give him. Such witnesses are usually shrewd and cunning men, and come into court prepared on the subject concerning which they are to testify.

Some experts, however, are mere shams and pretenders. I remember witnessing some years ago the utter collapse of one of these expert pretenders of the medical type. It was in a damage suit against the city, which I defended. The plaintiff's doctor was a loquacious gentleman of considerable personal presence. He testified to a serious head injury, and proceeded to "lecture" the jury on the subject in a sensational and oracular manner which evidently made a great impression upon the jury. Even the judge seemed to give more than the usual attention. The doctor talked glibly about "vasomotor nerves" and "reflexes" and expressed himself almost entirely in medical terms which the jury did not understand. He polished off his testimony with the prediction that the plaintiff could never recover, and if he lived at all, it would necessarily be within the precincts of an insane asylum. I saw at a glance that this was no ordinary type of witness. Any cross-examination on the medical side of the case would be sure to fail; for the witness, though evidently dishonest, was yet ingenious enough to cover his tracks by the cuttlefish expedient of befogging his answers in a cloud of medical terms. Dr. Allan McLane

Hamilton, who was present as medical advisor in behalf of the city, suggested the following expedient:—

Counsel: 'Doctor, I infer from the number of books that you have brought here to substantiate your position, and from your manner of testifying, that you are very familiar with the literature of your profession, and especially that part relating to head injury.'

Doctor: 'I pride myself that I am—I have not only a large private library, but have spent many months in the libraries of Vienna, Berlin, Paris and London.'

Counsel: 'Then perhaps you are acquainted with Andrew's celebrated work 'On the Recent and Remote Effects of Head Injury'?'

Doctor (smiling superciliously): 'Well, I should say I was. I had occasion to consult it only last week.'

Counsel: 'Have you ever come across 'Charvais on Cerebral Trauma'?'

Doctor: 'Yes, I have read Dr. Charvais's book from cover to cover many times.'

Counsel continued in much the same strain, putting to the witness similar questions relating to many other fictitious medical works, all of which the doctor had either 'studied carefully' or 'had in his library about to read,' until finally, suspecting that the doctor was becoming conscious of the trap into which he was being led, counsel suddenly changed his tactics and demanded in a loud sneering tone if the doctor had ever read Page on 'Injuries of the Spine and Spinal Cord' (a genuine and most learned treatise on the subject). To this inquiry the doctor laughingly replied, 'I never heard of any such book and I guess you never did either!'

The climax had been reached. Dr. Hamilton was immediately sworn for the defence and explained to the jury his participation in preparing the list of bogus medical works with which the learned expert for the plaintiff had sworn such familiarity.

Lying—With or Without Motive

The motivation for untruth is sometimes obvious as in Lincoln's moonlight case in which Sovine had, by his own standards, the best possible motive to lie—the wish to save his own neck. Again, in Wellman's case of the bogus medical expert, a motivation for perjury was abundantly and disgustingly clear. The pompous doctor was for sale.

Criminal investigations and ensuing court preceedings are a constant battle against the lie—conscious, unconscious, motivated, unmotivated. The investigating officer must be suspicious not only of the suspect but also of the complainant. Murders are reported by the murderers themselves to avoid suspicion. Complainants report robberies of large sums of money in order to account for improvident losses or guilty defalcations. Burglaries are charged to cover up financial difficulties and fires are set—in both cases to collect insurance.

A witness may lay the blame on an innocent person out of spite. Persons who yearn for publicity may give wrong information just to see their names in the newspapers. Relatives or friends of an accused person withhold information. Witnesses who fear personal injury, or even death, by the hands of those they might implicate, may testify falsely. A prospective witness may even falsify in order to avoid the inconvenience of attendance in a trial, or witnesses may lie because they are timid and wish to avoid publicity. Hatred of a policeman in particular or of the police in general may induce perjury. Conviction that a particular law is unjust may be a reason for lying. Informers seeking an offered reward may deliberately lie.

In some cases suspects will not tell the truth because the truth might involve innocent persons. The author encountered a case in which the alibi was not offered because it would have disclosed that the accused person, while innocent of the charge, was at the time embarked upon a clandestine adventure with another man's wife. One person may accept the responsibility for the acts of others in order to save a group at his own expense. This appears to have been true in the case of Grover Cleveland who, while running for the presidency of the United States, conceded fatherhood of an illegitimate child although the lady in question was accessible to a number of gentlemen (Cleveland at the time being the only unmarried man among them).[26]

Substitutes for Human Testimony

In general it must be said that there are few substitutes for human witnesses. Yet mankind's efforts to find a road to fact or fiction, guilt or innocence, other than by way of the testimony of human beings, have been persistent—in all times and in many societies. Larson has a summary of examples of such efforts in ancient times. For examples:[27]

Ordeal with red-hot iron.   The trial by red-hot iron *(judicium ferri, juise)* was in use from a very early period and became one of the favorite modes of determining disputed questions. It was administered in two essentially different forms. The one *(vomeres igniti, examen pedale)* consisted in laying on the ground at certain distances 6, 9, or in some cases 12, red-hot plough-shares, among which the accused walked barefooted, sometimes blindfolded, when it became an ordeal of pure chance, and sometimes compelled to press an iron with his naked feet. The other and more usual form obliged the patient to carry in his hand for a certain

---

[26]Nevins, Allan, *Grover Cleveland,* Dodd Mead, New York, 1932, p. 162 *et seq.*

[27]Larson, John A., *Lying and Its Detection,* The University of Chicago Press, Chicago, 1932, p. 75. (See generally Chapter VII.)

distance, usually 9 feet, a piece of red-hot iron, the weight of which was determined by law and varied with the importance of the question at issue or the magnitude of the alleged crime. The hand was then wrapped up and sealed, and three days afterwards the decision was rendered in accordance with its condition *(Laws of Athelstane,* IV, 7). . . . Occasionally, when several criminals were examined together, the same piece of heated iron was borne by them successively, giving a manifest advantage to the last one, who had to endure a temperature considerably less that his companions.

Sophocles and the iron ordeal.   In Sophocles, *Antigone,* the guards protest their innocence to Creon, of any complicity in the burial of Polynices and offer to establish their innocence by ordeal, in the following lines:

'Ready with hands to bear the red-hot iron, To pass the fire, and by the Gods to swear That we not did the deed, nor do we know Who counselled it, or who performed it.'

Some modern techniques are a substantial improvement over ordeals of fire or water. The radar detection of rate of speed of a moving vehicle is generally accepted as definitive testimony not dependent upon human observation. The degree of alcoholic influence is now determined by a variety of techniques accepted as prima facie definitive. The results obtained with a lie detector (polygraph), which depends upon the proposition that a human being cannot tell a lie without an increase in blood pressure, respiration rate, and other physiological manifestations (all measured and integrated by a device that correlates the symptoms and integrates them into a graphic curve), are accepted by the courts to a limited extent—only as a piece of evidence, not as definitive proof. For the greater part, however, we are left with the art of cross-examination for the discovery of perjury and for the uncovery of the honest but mistaken witness.

Conviction of the Innocent

It must by now be obvious that since the techniques for ascertaining truth are as inexact as humanity itself is fallible in its observations and devious in its disclosures, there must be miscarriages of justice. Such is the case. Justice is rough. The ascertainment of truth in court proceedings is not an exact science. Grievous mistakes are made. It is one of the heartbreaking aspects of the administration of justice to the moment of this writing that innocent persons do languish in jails, have been executed, and that recompense, even in those jurisdictions that make provision for recompense for false arrest and erroneous conviction, can never be adequate. Although the contemporary risk of ruin, including death, is perhaps not as great as that in the six-shooter era of Judge Roy Bean, that risk is still substantial.[28] Organized society is not necessarily safer than the jungle.[29]

[28]See generally, Borchard, Edwin M., *Convicting The Innocent,* Garden City Publishing Co., Garden City, New York, 1932; Lofton, John, *Justice and the Press,* Beacon Press, Boston, 1966, p. 212 *et seq.*

[29]See generally, Ardrey, Robert, *The Territorial Imperative,* Atheneum, New York, 1966.

JUSTICE AND PROFESSIONAL DISCIPLINE

OF THE LAWYER

Specialization of biological function is an aspect of life itself.[30]   In human affairs it is the foundation of professionalism.[31]

The steps in the development of professionalism are: delegation of authority by the sovereign or assumption of function by the laity, as in the case of the Hippocratic tradition on the Island of Cos[32] or, as we noted, in Rome in the last days of the Republic. An early aspect of professionalism is the recording and organization of the wisdom of the function—medicine, law, architecture, engineering, for examples; then the teaching on the basis of the organized written materials of the profession. An early organizer of Roman law was Gaius whose work was an important foundation for the master organization of Roman law, known as Corpus Juris (see Chapter 1, p. 18). Bracton was a thirteenth century organizer of English law; Littleton came 200 years later; and then Coke, with his Institutes, in the first half of the seventeenth century.

Hard on the heels of organization, perhaps even concurrently, comes the teaching of the body of professional skill, knowledge, and wisdom. As noted in Chapter 1, the English law schools, called "Inns of Courts," are of such antiquity that scholars have not succeeded in ferreting out their precise beginnings. Teaching is invariably an aspect, and an early aspect, of professionalism.

Standards for admission to the profession, such as the Hippocratic Oath, are an invariable aspect of professionalism; governmental approval of such standards is the next step. At the beginning of the Christian era, Augustus authorized certain jurists to give opinions of law which had the Emperor's authority. Thus the modern practice of licensing by the state of doctors, lawyers, engineers, architects—and, to descend quickly in a long scale, morticians and beauticians—is a universal practice in all advanced societies. This certification by license, or at least by membership in a professional association, is the guarantee of competence. From the earliest times (we must continue to return to the Hippocratic tradition for an example), the license is not only a guarantee to the public of the competence of the professional but also a protection to the educated and the qualified professional against mavericks and charlatans. It is sometimes a complaint that professionals are too zealous in creating high standards for admission. It is charged that there are too few medical schools in the United States, hence a shortage of doctors, or that associations of teachers have been too arbitrary about artificial standards concerning methodology. The complaint is made sarcastically that Einstein could not have qua-

[30]Gray, Peter, *The Encyclopedia of Biological Sciences,* Reinhold Publishing Corporation, New York, 1961, pp. 197–201.

[31]Sarton, George, *A History of Science,* Harvard University Press, Cambridge, Massachusetts, 1952, p. 331, *et seq.*

[32]*Id.,* at p. 331, *et seq.*

lified to teach elementary mathematics in a public school system because he lacked the requisite number of credits in an authenticated school of education.

The converse of the exclusion from the profession of incompetents is the internal discipline of those who have been admitted but have fallen from grace by the standards of the profession. Professional men come by the practice of forming very tight and powerful associations naturally—in the biological sense of specialization of function and also in the culturalogical sense of community of interest, learning, and purpose. In the United States, the American Bar Association is national in its scope, and its committees are working constantly not only upon the dissemination of information among the membership of developments in the fields of substantive and procedural law but also upon standards of ethics for the profession. It is this last activity that interests us now.

Every state in the Union has its own bar association, many of them "integrated," which means that a lawyer's license to practice is ineffective in that state unless he belongs to the bar association and abides by its standards of lawyer's responsibility to the client and to the public. In a number of states the ultimate disciplinary control over members of the bar lies in procedures that occur under the direct auspices of the highest court of the state.

One of the functions of bar associations, particularly of the American Bar Association, is to articulate standards or canons of professional responsibility. This is not to say that all members of any bar association are in complete agreement as to what those canons and standards should be. This is apparent when we note that the original Canons of Professional Ethics of the American Bar Association were adopted in 1908 and there was no major revision until the year 1969. These Canons have now been reduced to generalized statements, nine in number, which follow:[33]

- A lawyer should assist in maintaining the integrity and competence of the legal profession.
- A lawyer should assist the legal profession in fulfilling its duty to make legal counsel available.
- A lawyer should assist in preventing the unauthorized practice of law.
- A lawyer should preserve the confidences and secrets of a client.
- A lawyer should exercise independent professional judgment on behalf of a client.
- A lawyer should represent a client competently.
- A lawyer should represent a client zealously within the bounds of the law.
- A lawyer should assist in improving the legal system.
- A lawyer should avoid even the appearance of professional impropriety.

[33]*Code of Professional Responsibility* adopted by the American Bar Association, August, 1969.

Under each of the nine Canons there are detailed Disciplinary Rules preceded by dissertations, both historical and philosophical, as to the reason for the particular rules. For example, there is a disciplinary rule among several hundred specific injunctions that a lawyer who receives information clearly establishing that his client has, in the course of the representation, perpetrated a fraud upon a person or tribunal (court) shall promptly call upon his client to rectify the same and that if his client refuses or is unable to do so, he shall reveal the fraud to the affected person or tribunal.[34]

We cite one other Disciplinary Rule because any reader who watches television or listens to radio will know that this Rule, if it had been in effect in recent years, would have been repeatedly violated. The new Rule is as follows:[35]

(B) A lawyer or law firm associated with the prosecution or defense of a criminal matter shall not, from the time of the filing of a complaint, information, or indictment, the issuance of an arrest warrant, or arrest until the commencement of the trial or disposition without trial, make or participate in making an extrajudicial statement that a reasonable person would expect to be disseminated by means of public communication and that relates to:

(1) The character, reputation, or prior criminal record (including arrests, indictments, or other charges of crime) of the accused.
(2) The possibility of a plea of guilty to the offense charged or to a lesser offense.
(3) The existence or contents of any confession, admission, or statement given by the accused or his refusal or failure to make a statement.
(4) The performance or results of any examinations or tests or the refusal or failure of the accused to submit to examinations or tests.
(5) The identity, testimony, or credibility of a prospective witness.
(6) Any opinion as to the guilt or innocence of the accused, the evidence, or the merits of the case.

The lawyer is an officer of the court. His first duty is to assist the court in seeing that justice is done. By the same token his role and function as an adversary and a proponent of his client's best interest is fully recognized, as can be seen from the Canons. Nevertheless, he may not pursue that advocacy without regard to the truth or without regard to facts known to him that may have a significant bearing upon the ultimate conclusion in the case. A telling example of this dual role as officer of the court and as advocate for the client is found in one of the new rules requiring that a prosecutor tell the defense of any evidence supporting the innocence of the defendant. It is true that the role of advocacy seems to imply winning the case, but the Canons put a sharp curb on that competitive impulse and compel reverence for truth above urge to victory.

[34] *Id.* at p. 87.
[35] *Id.* at p. 89.

PEOPLE ex rel. KARLIN v. CULKIN
Court of Appeals of New York, 248 N.Y. 465 (1928).

Appeal from Supreme Court, Appellate Division, First Department.

Petition by the People of the State of New York, on the relation of Alexander Karlin, for a writ of habeas corpus to Charles W. Culkin, as Sheriff of the County of New York, for the release of relator from custody under a commitment for contempt in refusing to testify in an investigation on petition of the Association of the Bar of the City of New York and others. From orders of the Appellate Division . . . affirming an order of the Special Term, dismissing the writ and remanding relator to custody, and an order adjudging him in contempt, he appeals. Affirmed.

CARDOZO, C. J. A petition by three leading bar associations, presented to the Appellate Division for the First Judicial Department in January, 1928, gave notice to the court that evil practices were rife among members of the bar. "Ambulance chasing" was spreading to a demoralizing extent. As a consequence, the poor were oppressed and the ignorant overreached. Retainers, often on extravagant terms, were solicited and paid for. Calendars became congested through litigations maintained without probable cause as weapons of extortion. Wrongdoing by lawyers for claimants was accompanied by other wrongdoing, almost as pernicious, by lawyers for defendants. The helpless and the ignorant were made to throw their rights away as the result of inadequate settlements or fraudulent releases. No doubt, the vast majority of actions were legitimate, the vast majority of lawyers honest. The bar as a whole felt the sting of the discredit thus put upon its membership by an unscrupulous minority.

It spoke its mind through its associations, the organs of its common will. The court was asked to inquire into the practices charged in the petition, and any other illegal and improper practices, either through an investigation to be conducted by itself, or through some other appropriate procedure. It was asked upon the conclusion of the investigation to deal with the offenders in accordance with law, and to grant such other remedies as would avoid a recurrence of the evil and maintain the honor of the bar.

The court responded promptly. It held (speaking by its presiding justice) that its disciplinary power is not limited to "cases where specific charges are made against a named attorney." It will act of its own motion, whenever it has reasonable cause to believe that there has been professional misconduct, either by one or by a class. Information may be adequate to define the offense and identify the offender. If so, charges will be preferred, and the offender brought to trial. On the other hand, information may be so indefinite as to make charges impossible or improper without further inquisition. If so, the power of inquisition, it was held, is commensurate with the need. "Only by such means will the court be able to devise appropriate rules to prevent the continuance of such evil practices, and bring the unworthy to judgment, and protect the worthy in the profession from suspicions in the public mind."

The order of the Appellate Division designates a justice of the Supreme Court to conduct the investigation at an appointed term, with full authority "to summon witnesses and to compel the giving of testimony and the production of books, papers, and documentary evidence." The petitioning associations are authorized to furnish counsel in aid of the inquiry. The investigation is to extend into the practices described in the petition and any other practices obstructive or harmful to the administration of justice.

The court conducting the inquiry is to report the proceedings to the court making the order, i.e., the Appellate Division, with its opinion thereon, and upon the coming in of the report there is to be such other and further action as shall seem just and proper.

The investigation proceeded in the form directed by the order. Many witnesses were examined. They were given the privilege at their option of examination in camera. There came a time when the appellant, a member of the bar for 25 years, was served with a subpoena. He appeared in court, but refused to be sworn. His practice had involved the trial of many actions for personal injuries. He was called to testify as to his conduct in the procurement of retainers in these cases and in others. There is no denial that the testimony had relation to the ends of the inquiry. His refusal to testify was a challenge to the inquiry as a whole. Upon his persisting in that challenge, the court adjudged him in contempt, and committed him to jail until he should submit to be sworn and examined. A petition for his release upon habeas corpus was dismissed. Both orders, the one adjudging the contempt and the one dismissing the writ, were affirmed by the Appellate Division. They are now before this court.

The precise question to be determined is whether there is power in the Appellate Division to direct a general inquiry into the conduct of its own officers, the members of the bar, and in the course of that inquiry to compel one of those officers to testify as to his acts in his professional relations.   .   .   .

"Membership in the bar is a privilege burdened with conditions." Matter of Rouss, [221 N.Y. 81, 84]. The appellant was received into that ancient fellowship for something more than private gain. He became an officer of the court, and, like the court itself, an instrument or agency to advance the ends of justice. His co-operation with the court was due, whenever justice would be imperiled if co-operation was withheld. He might be assigned as counsel for the needy, in causes criminal or civil, serving without pay. Code Crim. Proc. § 308; Civil Practice Act, §§ 196, 198. He might be directed by summary order to make restitution to a client of moneys or other property wrongfully withheld. Matter of H., an Attorney, 87 N.Y. 521. He might be censured, suspended, or disbarred for "any conduct prejudicial to the administration of justice." Judiciary Law, § 88, subd. 2. All this is undisputed. We are now asked to hold that, when evil practices are rife to the dishonor of the profession, he may not be compelled by rule or order of the court, whose officer he is, to say what he knows of them, subject to his claim of privilege if the answer will expose him to punishment for crime. Matter of Rouss, supra. Co-operation between court and officer in furtherance of justice is a phrase without reality, if the officer may then be silent in the face of a command to speak. There are precedents of recent date, decisions in Wisconsin and Ohio, upholding the power of the court by a general inquisition to compel disclosure of the truth. .   .   .   Precedents far more ancient, their roots deeply set in the very nature of a lawyer's function, point the same way.

"The Supreme Court shall have power and control over attorneys and counselors at law." Judiciary Law, § 88, subd. 2. The first Constitution of the state declared a like rule in terms not widely different. Provision was there made that "all attorneys, solicitors, and counselors at law hereafter to be appointed, be appointed by the court, and licensed by the first judge of the court in which they shall respectively plead or practice, and be regulated by the rules and orders of the said courts." Constitution of 1777, § 27. What was meant by this provision that lawyers should be "regulated by the rules and orders of the said courts"? Would the men who framed the Constitution of 1777 have been in doubt for a moment that a rule or order might be made whereby lawyers would be under a duty, when so directed by the court, to give aid by their testimony in uncovering abuses?   . . .

. . . More than three centuries ago evils not unlike those revealed in this petition disturbed the English courts. They met the situation in much the same way, by an inquest under oath as to the conduct of their officers.

We conclude that the refusal [by Karlin to answer the investigator's questions] was a contempt (Civil Practice Act, § 406), and that the investigation must proceed. In so holding we place power and responsibility where in reason they should be. No doubt the power can be abused, but that is true of power generally. In discharging a function so responsible and delicate, the courts will refrain, we may be sure, from a surveillance of the profession that would be merely odious or arbitrary. They will act considerately and cautiously, mindful at all times of the dignity of the bar and of the resentment certain to be engendered by any tyrannous intervention. No lack of caution or consideration can be imputed to them here. They did not move of their own prompting, but at the instance of the very bar whose privacy and privilege they are said to have infringed. In the long run the power now conceded will make for the health and honor of the profession and for the protection of the public. If the house is to be cleaned, it is for those who occupy and govern it, rather than for strangers, to do the noisome work.

The orders are affirmed.

POUND, CRANE, ANDREWS, LEHMAN, KELLOGG, and O'BRIEN, concur.

OF THE JUDGE

In the history of judicial integrity money is one of the prime factors. In England, although the judicial institutions established by Henry II were significant innovations in independence of the judiciary, by the 12th century judges did not appear to have regular salaries. In 1268, Robert Brus, the first Chief Justice of the King's Bench, was granted a salary of a hundred marks—quite nominal. In the reign of Henry III, salaries were from 20 pounds to 40 pounds for certain judges. Salaries did increase as the importance of the function was clarified, but the smallness of the salary and, equally important, the irregularity with which it was paid were factors in judicial scandals. Large landowners found it expedient to make grants of pensions, rents, or lands to the King's judges. Additional fees were granted to the judges. During the 16th century, increases in their salaries were made several times.[36] The effort to make judges financially secure has continued throughout the generations.

Holdsworth points out that from earliest times the salaries of the judges had not formed their only sources of income. There were fees for various steps and

[36]Holdsworth, Sir William, *A History of English Law,* Vol. 1, Methuen and Co., London, 1956, p. 252, *et seq.*

actions in the judicial process. Functionaries who performed ancillary administrative court services were appointed by the judges. These appointments were known as "saleable offices" because the fees were important and the sale by judges of the administrative office constituted an emolument of the judicial office. There were long centuries of attempted amelioration of these practices for enhancing the income of judges, but they were not in fact completely eliminated until the English Judicature Acts of 1873.[37]

Let us leap forward now to the 20th century—from the Mosaic times of 1200 B.C. (Chapter 1, p. 7-9, *supra*) to the times of Edward I, when there were widespread judicial scandals, to the time of Mr. Justice Abe Fortas of 1969. No justice of the Supreme Court of the United States has ever been removed from office in the proceedings for impeachment that the United States Constitution provides. Nor had any justice of that Court resigned under fire until Mr. Justice Abe Fortas did so after it was charged by Life Magazine (May 4, 1969) that he had received a payment (later returned) of $20,000 from a private foundation.[38]

In the last analysis the discipline of judges in the highest office is in public opinion. We have pointed out how machinery is provided by lawyers through their bar associations for the discipline of offending brethren. In the case of high court judges, however, it is a matter of public conscience. True, a judge may be indicted and tried for crime, and there are such cases of record. A highly placed federal judge, Martin T. Manton, was convicted of bribery, fined $10,000, and sentenced to 2 years imprisonment.[39] There are a few other such cases. When the ethical standards of a justice of the Supreme Court of the United States become involved, then impeachment can function; as can public outrage, when it required the resignation of Mr. Justice Fortas. The private life of a judge or justice is viewed by people with great tolerance, except the private financial life. In that regard he who wields the ancient power of judging must be free of the least suggestion of an interest which might bias his judgment.[40]

The unfortunate Fortas episode resulted in resolutions of the judges,[41] at a special session of the Judicial Conference of the United States called by then

---

[37] *Id.* at p. 647, *et seq.*

[38] *New York Times,* May 16, 1969, p. 1, col. 8, reports that on May 15, 1969 Mr. Justice Fortas submitted to President Nixon his resignation from the Supreme Court of the United States.

[39] United States v. Manton, 107 F.2d 834 (2d Cir. 1938), *cert. denied,* 309 U.S. 664 (1939).

[40] The United States Senate refused to confirm President Nixon's nomination of Judge Clement Haynsworth to the United States Supreme Court because he had failed to disqualify himself in lower court cases that involved corporations in which he owned stock. *New York Times,* November 22, 1969, p. 1, col. 7.

[41] See *New York Times,* June 11, 1969, p. 17, col. 1.

Chief Justice Earl Warren, forbidding a judge in regular active service to accept compensation of any kind, whether in the form of loans, gifts, gratuities, honoraria, or otherwise for services performed or to be performed by him except that provided by law for the performance of his judicial duties. Exceptions were provided under strict control of the appropriate Judicial Council. Beginning May 15, 1970, federal judges are required to file annually with the Judicial Conference statements of investments and assets.

Curiously, although the Fortas case precipitated those resolutions just noted, they have not been self-imposed upon the Supreme Court. They apply only to the lower and intermediate federal judiciary. The case with the justices of the Supreme Court is still governed only by judicial conscience, impeachment, or public outrage.

The remarkable fact about the rectitude of judges is not that there is occasionally a judge who does not understand the ethics of his office, even when that office is the highest judicial office in the land. The remarkable fact is that there are not more such cases. As with a road in the wilderness, the marvel is not that the road is bad but that it is there at all. Judges are human beings and as human beings they are related to every bit of life that ever existed on earth; they bear the burdens of that evolutionary fact. Judges' ancestors, as were the ancestors of all humanity, were vigorous primates, undisciplined and unguided except by nature. Civilization is itself a negation of animal nature. Judges, like the rest of us, are animals, with all the implicit nobility and all the inescapable doom of that destiny.

OF THE MEDIA

In times of hysteria, the media may be the mob. So stern a judgment will rarely be found among journalists, but there are exceptions such as the distinguished John Lofton. He says, " 'If the public seems to take a harsh view toward a certain type of offense, newspaper reports concerning this offense are likely to reflect the same outlook. (Conversely, an indulgent public attitude toward illegal conduct is also likely to be mirrored in news stories.) The mass media are more effective in reinforcing people's basic attitudes than in converting them to new attitudes.' " Mr. Lofton continues, "If unprovable but probable cases of press publicity which wronged the innocent were to be cited, the list would be endless. In the absence of proof as to where the overall weight of publicity comes to rest on the scales of justice, we can only observe that—given the usual conditions: the unattractiveness of the suspect, the outrage of the community over a wrong, the demands for action, the avenging nature of the public, the customary police-press alliance, and the imitative character of the press—publicity tends to fall on the side of the prosecution." [42]

[42]Lofton, John, *Justice and the Press,* Beacon Press, Boston, 1966, pp. 189, 211 in part quoting from J. Klapper, "Effects of Mass Communication," *Pub. Opin. Quart.* XXI, 458, 1957-1958.

In general, as a court of justice, the press is no better than the public, and the public will be at least as bad as the press. In short, neither is a court of justice. But together they can, and do, subvert judicial procedures—make the court the tool of the mob.

We should pause briefly to consider the hysteria that can unsettle established judicatory procedures. Perhaps before hysteria comes revenge—one of the most elementary of human emotions. "Thou shalt not suffer a sorceress to live." (Ex. 22:18) "Ye shall tread down the wicked; for they shall be ashes under the soles of your feet." (Mal. 4:3) The biblical cases involve vengeance against violators of social norms with respect to which the majority need, for their own support, the sadistic satisfaction of punishment of the offender. Menninger says:[43]

> The inescapable conclusion is that society secretly *wants* crime, *needs* crime, and gains definite satisfactions from the present mishandling of it! We condemn crime; we punish offenders for it; but we need it. The crime and punishment ritual is a part of our lives. We need crimes to wonder at, to enjoy vicariously, to discuss and speculate about, and to publicly deplore. We need criminals to identify ourselves with, to secretly envy, and to stoutly punish. Criminals represent our alter egos —our 'bad' selves—rejected and projected. They do for us the forbidden, illegal things we *wish* to do and, like scapegoats of old, they bear the burdens of our displaced guilt and punishment—'the iniquities of us all.'
>
> Them we can punish! At them we can all cry 'stone her' or 'crucify him.' We can throw mud at the fellow in the stocks; he has been caught; he has been identified; he has been labeled, and he has been proven guilty of the dreadful thing. Now he is eligible for punishment and will be getting only what he deserves.

Revenge is more understandable than pure hysterical seizure of a whole community, as we shall see in the following example from Woodward.[44]

> The Salem witchcraft craze is one of the strangest episodes in Puritan history. It lasted only one summer—in the year 1692. The entire living generation believed implicitly in witches, in imps and devils. A girl who had been a captive among the Indians had actually seen the devil. She told the learned Cotton Mather about it, and he was greatly impressed. "The Divel that visited her," he wrote, "was just of the same Stature, Feature, and complexion with what the Histories of the Witchcrafts beyond-sea ascribe unto him; hee was a wretch no taller than an ordinary Walking Staff; hee was not of a Negro but of a Tawney, or an Indian color; hee wore a high-crowned Hat, with strait Hair; and had one Cloven Foot."
>
> A belief in witches was equally widespread, and in the forty years before the Salem outbreak ten witches had been convicted and hanged in New England. In every case they appear to have been women who, for some reason or other, had become

[43]Karl Menninger, M.D., *The Crime of Punishment,* Viking Press, New York, 1966, pp. 153, 154.

[44]W. E. Woodward, *A New American History,* Farrar & Rinehart, New York, 1936, pp. 95, 98.

unpopular with their neighbors. One of them was a Mrs. Hibbins, a widow who declared that the courts had defrauded her out of her husband's estate. After a while they got tired of hearing her accusations, so they tried her as a witch, found her guilty and hanged her.

The Salem craze started with the antics of two little girls. One of them was a daughter, and the other a niece, of Rev. Samuel Parris, pastor of the Salem church. The little girls began to behave in a peculiar manner. They frothed at the mouth, vomited pins, and held their arms and legs in impossible postures. They claimed that they were pinched and bitten by unseen people. A yellow bird flits in and out of the testimony. Nobody but the children saw the yellow bird; it was invisible to all others. The yellow bird communicated devilish secrets. It was called "a spectral witness" and was accepted as a fact. A doctor was called in; he was apparently unable to diagnose two plain cases of major hysteria.

.   .   .   .   .

One of the curious features of these trials was that anyone could escape punishment by admitting the charge. The court readily turned loose acknowledged witches and hanged those who swore they were not guilty. The theory behind this remarkable procedure was that the devil would not permit a real witch to acknowledge her calling; that was a condition of the fire-and-brimstone contract between the witch and her evil master. Those who confessed and admitted their knowledge of witchcraft were, therefore, either impostors or self-deluded persons.

Governor Phips, who had lately come from England, was away on a trip, and his wife signed a pardon for someone who had been convicted. Thereupon Lady Phips was charged with being a witch herself. They were considering ways and means for bringing her into court, and doubting if it could be done at all, when the governor returned. As soon as he heard what had happened he indignantly dismissed the court, put a stop to all proceedings, and released everybody who was still in jail. That was the end of the Salem witchcraft craze. Nineteen persons had been executed; fifty-five had confessed to being witches and were pardoned, and a hundred and fifty were still awaiting trial.

In the centuries and decades before the speedy and ubiquitous coverage of events by the media—newspapers, radio, and television—mobs were formed by word of mouth, messengers racing through the pointed firs of the north, over the dry sands of the west, and through the murky bayous of the south. Such mobs gained a spirit of hysterical vengeance from personal assemblage.[45] Now, on occasion—not always—the harsh words of an earlier assemblage can be read in the press, the shrill voices can be heard on the radio, and faces of uncontrolled passion can be seen on the television. The mob need not assemble. Indeed, what would seem like a charge against the media must be understood to have the good consequence of preventing the assemblage. On the other hand, the power of the media can work the will of the unassembled mob upon the established institutions for the administration of justice.

---

[45]See generally Caughey, John W., *Their Majesties the Mob*, University of Chicago Press, Chicago, Illinois, 1960.

We come now to the Sheppard case in which the Supreme Court in restrained judicial words of inescapable intent has taken account of what we have said about the media.

SHEPPARD v. MAXWELL
Supreme Court of the United States, 384 U.S. 333 (1966).

[Mr. Justice Clark delivered the opinion of the court and summarized the facts as follows:

"Marilyn Sheppard, petitioner's pregnant wife, was bludgeoned to death in the upstairs bedroom of their lakeshore home in Bay Village, Ohio, a suburb of Cleveland. On the day of the tragedy, July 4, 1954, Sheppard pieced together for several local officials the following story: He and his wife had entertained neighborhood friends, the Aherns, on the previous evening at their home. After dinner they watched television in the living room. Sheppard became drowsy and dozed off to sleep on a couch. Later, Marilyn partially awoke him saying that she was going to bed. The next thing he remembered was hearing his wife cry out in the early morning hours. He hurried upstairs and in the dim light from the hall saw a "form" standing next to his wife's bed. As he struggled with the "form" he was struck on the back of the neck and rendered unconscious. On regaining his senses he found himself on the floor next to his wife's bed. He raised up, looked at her, took her pulse and "felt that she was gone." He then went to his son's room and found him unmolested. Hearing a noise he hurried downstairs. He saw a "form" running out the door and pursued it to the lake shore. He grappled with it on the beach and again lost consciousness. Upon his recovery he was laying face down with the lower portion of his body in the water. He returned to his home, checked the pulse on his wife's neck, and "determined or thought that she was gone." He then went downstairs and called a neighbor, Mayor Houk of Bay Village. The Mayor and his wife came over at once, found Sheppard slumped in an easy chair downstairs and asked, "What happened?" Sheppard replied: "I don't know but somebody ought to try to do something for Marilyn."

In December, 1954, Dr. Sam Sheppard, was sentenced to life in prison for the second degree murder of his wife, Marilyn.

After spending nearly 10 years in prison, early in 1964 Sheppard brought a petition for a writ of habeas corpus in the Federal District Court for the Southern District of Ohio alleging that he had been deprived of a fair trial because of the trial judge's failure to protect him from the massive, pervasive and prejudicial publicity that attended his prosecution. The District Court granted Sheppard the writ subject to the Ohio's right to try him again. The Court of Appeals for the Sixth Circuit reversed the District Court by a divided vote, and the United States Supreme Court granted certiorari. The Supreme Court concluded that Sheppard had not received a fair trial consistent with the "due process" clause of the Fourteenth Amendment, and therefore, reversed his conviction in the case.

The facts of the case showed that the following irregularities among others took place. During the pre-trial investigation of the homicide, local newspapers not only emphasized evidence that tended to incriminate Sheppard but ran front page editorials with titles such as "Why Isn't Sam Sheppard in Jail?" and "Quit Stalling—Bring Him In." Once Sheppard was indicted and preparations for trial had begun, the newspapers published the names and addresses of prospective jurors who thereafter received a number of letters and phone calls concerning the case. At the trial some twenty reporters were seated at a press table located between the counsel table and the bench. These reporters were permitted to overhear and report confidential communications between Sheppard and his counsel. Further, a public radio station was set up in, and allowed to transmit from, a room adjoining that in which the jury held their deliberations. Throughout the trial the jurors were permitted access to both newspapers and television and, while deliberating on the verdict, were permitted to make phone calls. In addition, several prospective witnesses were interviewed by the news media and their testimony disclosed. However, by far the most harmful abuse by the media was their extensive publication of accusations and allegations of events as to which no evidence was ever adduced at trial.

Mr. Justice CLARK, speaking for the Court in reversing Sheppard's 1954 conviction, reasoned:]

The principle that justice cannot survive behind walls of silence has long been reflected in the "Anglo-American distrust for secret trials." In re Oliver, 333 U.S. 257, 268 (1948). A responsible press has always been regarded as the handmaiden of effective judicial administration, especially in the criminal field. Its function in this regard is documented by an impressive record of service over several centuries. The press does not simply publish information about trials but guards against the miscarriage of justice by subjecting the police, prosecutors, and judicial processes to extensive public scrutiny and criticism. This Court has, therefore, been unwilling to place any direct limitations on the freedom traditionally exercised by the news media for "[w]hat transpires in the court room is public property." Craig v. Harney, 331 U.S. 367, 374 (1947). The "unqualified prohibitions laid down by the framers were intended to give to liberty of the press . . . the broadest scope that could be countenanced in an orderly society." Bridges v. California, 314 U.S. 252, 265 (1941). And where there was "no threat or menace to the integrity of the trial," Craig v. Harney, *supra,* at 377, we have consistently required that the press have a free hand, even though we sometimes deplored its sensationalism.

But the Court has also pointed out that "[l]egal trials are not like elections, to be won through the use of the meeting-hall, the radio, and the newspaper." Bridges v. California, *supra,* at 271. And the Court has insisted that no one be punished for a crime without "a charge fairly made and fairly tried in a public tribunal free of prejudice, passion, excitement, and tyrannical power." Chambers v. Florida, 309 U.S. 277, 236-237 (1940). "Freedom of discussion should be given the widest range compatible with the essential requirement of the fair and orderly administration of justice." Pennekamp v. Florida, 328 U.S. 331, 347 (1946). But it must not be allowed to divert the trial from the "very purpose of a court system . . . to adjudicate controversies, both criminal and civil, in the calmness and solemnity of the courtroom according to legal procedures." Cox v. Louisiana, 379 U.S. 559, 583 (1965) (Black, J., dissenting). Among these "legal procedures" is the requirement that the jury's verdict be based on evidence received in open court, not from outside sources. Thus, in Marshall v. United States, 360 U.S. 310 (1959), we set aside a federal conviction where the jurors were exposed "through news accounts" to information that was not admitted at trial. We held that the prejudice from such material "may indeed be greater" than when it is part of the prosecution's evidence "for it is then not tempered by protective procedures." At 313. At the same time, we did not consider dispositive the statement of each juror "that he would not be influenced by the news articles, that he could decide the case only on the evidence of record, and that he felt no prejudice against petitioner as a result of the articles." At 312. Likewise, in Irvin v. Dowd, 366 U.S. 717 (1961), even though each juror indicated that he could render an impartial verdict despite exposure to prejudicial newspaper articles, we set aside the conviction holding: "With his life at stake, it is not requiring too much that petitioner be tried in an atmosphere undisturbed by so huge a wave of public passion. . . . " At 728.

.   .   .

At intervals during the trial, the judge simply repeated his "suggestions" and "requests" that the jury not expose themselves to comment upon the case. Moreover, the jurors were thrust into the role of celebrities by the judge's failure to insulate them from reporters and photographers. . . . The numerous pictures of the jurors, with their addresses, which appeared in the newspapers before and during the trial itself exposed them to expressions of opinion from both cranks and friends. The fact that anonymous letters had been received by prospective jurors should have made the judge aware that this publicity seriously threatened the jurors' privacy.

. . . Sheppard stood indicted for the murder of his wife; the State was demanding the death penalty. For months the virulent publicity about Sheppard and the murder had made the case notorious. Charges and countercharges were aired in the news media besides those for which Sheppard was called to trial. In addition, only three months before trial, Sheppard was examined for more than five hours without counsel during a three-day inquest which ended in a public brawl. The inquest was televised live from a high school gymnasium seating hundreds of people. Furthermore, the trial began two weeks before a hotly contested election at which both Chief Prosecutor Mahon and Judge Blythin were candidates for judgeships.

While we cannot say that Sheppard was denied due process by the judge's refusal to take precautions against the influence of pretrial publicity alone, the court's later rulings must be considered against the setting in which the trial was held. In light of this background, we believe that the arrangements made by the judge with the news media caused Sheppard to be deprived of that "judicial serenity and calm to which [he] was entitled." Estes v. Texas, *supra*, at 536. The fact is that bedlam reigned at the courthouse during the trial and newsmen took over practically the entire courtroom, hounding most of the participants in the trial, especially Sheppard. At a temporary table within a few feet of the jury box and counsel table sat some 20 reporters staring at Sheppard and taking notes. The erection of a press table for reporters inside the bar is unprecedented. The bar of the court is reserved for counsel, providing them a safe place in which to keep papers and exhibits, and to confer privately with client and co-counsel. It is designed to protect the witness and the jury from any distractions, intrusions or influences, and to permit bench discussions of the judge's rulings away from the hearing of the public and the jury. Having assigned almost all of the available seats in the courtroom to the news media the judge lost his ability to supervise that environment. The movement of the reporters in and out of the courtroom caused frequent confusion and disruption of the trial. And the record reveals constant commotion within the bar. Moreover, the judge gave the throng of newsmen gathered in the corridors of the courthouse absolute free rein. Participants in the trial, including the jury, were forced to run a gantlet of reporters and photographers each time they entered or left the courtroom. The total lack of consideration for the privacy of the jury was demonstrated by the assignment to a broadcasting station of space next to the jury room on the floor above the courtroom, as well as the fact that jurors were allowed to make telephone calls during their five-day deliberation.

.   .   .   .

The court's fundamental error is compounded by the holding that it lacked power to control the publicity about the trial. From the very inception of the proceedings the judge announced that neither he nor anyone else could restrict prejudicial news accounts. And he reiterated this view on numerous occasions. Since he viewed the news media as his target, the judge never considered other means that are often utilized to reduce the appearance of prejudicial material and to protect the jury from outside influence. We conclude that these procedures would have been sufficient to guarantee Sheppard a fair trial and so do not consider what sanctions might be available against a recalcitrant press nor the charges of bias now made against the state trial judge.

The carnival atmosphere at trial could easily have been avoided since the courtroom and courthouse premises are subject to the control of the court. As we stressed in Estes, the presence of the press at judicial proceedings must be limited when it is apparent that the accused might otherwise be prejudiced or disadvantaged. Bearing in mind the massive pretrial publicity, the judge should have adopted stricter rules governing the use of the courtroom by newsmen, as Sheppard's counsel requested. The number of reporters in the courtroom itself could have been limited at the first sign that their presence would disrupt the trial. They certainly should not have been placed inside the bar. Furthermore, the judge should have more closely regulated the conduct of newsmen in the courtroom. For instance, the judge belatedly asked them not to handle and photograph trial exhibits laying on the counsel table during recesses.

Secondly, the court should have insulated the witnesses. All of the newspapers and radio stations apparently interviewed prospective witnesses at will, and in many instances disclosed their testimony. A typical example was the publication of numerous statements by Susan Hayes, before her appearance in court, regarding her love affair with Sheppard. Although the witnesses were barred from the courtroom during the trial the full *verbatim* testimony was available to them in the press. This completely nullified the judge's imposition of the rule. .   .   .

Thirdly, the court should have made some effort to control the release of leads, information, and gossip to the press by police officers, witnesses, and the counsel for both sides. Much of the information thus disclosed was inaccurate, leading to groundless rumors and confusion. . . .   Defense counsel immediately brought to the court's attention the tremendous amount of publicity in the Cleveland press that "misrepresented entirely the testimony" in the case. Under such circumstances, the judge should have at least warned the newspapers to check the accuracy of their accounts. And it is obvious that the judge should have further sought to alleviate this problem by imposing control over the statements made to the news media by counsel, witnesses, and especially the Coroner and police officers. The prosecution repeatedly made evidence available to the news media which was never offered in the trial. Much of the "evidence" disseminated in this fashion was clearly inadmissible. The exclusion of such evidence in court is rendered meaningless when a news media makes it available to the public. For example, the publicity about Sheppard's refusal to take a lie detector test came directly from police officers and the Coroner. The story that Sheppard had been called a "Jekyll-Hyde" personality by his wife was attributed to a prosecution witness. No such testimony was given. The further report that there was "a 'bombshell witness' on tap" who would testify as to Sheppard's "fiery temper" could only have emanated from the prosecution. Moreover, the newspapers described in detail clues that had been found by the police, but not put into the record.

The fact that many of the prejudicial news items can be traced to the prosecution, as well as the defense, aggravates the judge's failure to take any action.   . . .
Effective control of these sources—concededly within the court's power—might well have prevented the divulgence of inaccurate information, rumors, and accusations that made up much of the inflammatory publicity, at least after Sheppard's indictment.

More specifically, the trial court might well have proscribed extra-judicial statements by any lawyer, party, witness, or court official which divulged prejudicial matters, such as the refusal of Sheppard to submit to interrogation or take any lie detector tests; any statement made by Sheppard to officials; the identity of prospective witnesses or their probable testimony; any belief in guilt or innocence; or like statements concerning the merits of the case. See State v. Van Duyne, 43 N.J. 369, 389, 204 A. 2d 841, 850 (1964), in which the court interpreted Canon 20 of the American Bar Association's Canons of Professional Ethics to prohibit such statements. Being advised of the great public interest in the case, the mass coverage of the press, and the potential prejudicial impact of publicity, the court could also have requested the appropriate city and county officials to promulgate a regulation with respect to dissemination of information about the case by their employees. In addition, reporters who wrote or broadcasted prejudicial stories, could have been warned as to the impropriety of publishing material not introduced in the proceedings. The judge was put on notice of such events by defense counsel's complaint about the WHK broadcast on the second day of trial. In this manner, Sheppard's right to a trial free from outside interference would have been given added protection without corresponding curtailment of the news media. Had the judge, the other officers of the court, and the police placed the interest of justice first, the news media would have soon learned to be content with the task of reporting the case as it unfolded in the courtroom—not pieced together from extra-judicial statements.

From the cases coming here we note that unfair and prejudicial news comment on pending trials has become increasingly prevalent. Due process requires that the accused receive a trial by an impartial jury free from outside influences. Given the pervasiveness of modern communications and the difficulty of effacing prejudicial publicity from the minds of the jurors, the trial courts must take strong measures to ensure that the balance is never weighed against the accused. And appellate tribunals have the duty to make an independent evaluation of the circumstances. Of course, there is nothing that proscribes the press from reporting events that transpire in the courtroom. But where there is a reasonable likelihood that prejudicial news prior to trial will prevent a fair trial, the judge should continue the case until the threat abates, or transfer it to another county not so permeated with publicity. In addition, sequestration of the jury was something the judge should have raised *sua sponte* with counsel. If publicity during the proceedings threatens the fairness of the trial, a new trial should be ordered. But we must remember that reversals are but palliatives; the cure lies in those remedial measures that will prevent the prejudice at its inception. The courts must take such steps by rule and regulation that will protect their processes from prejudicial outside interferences. Neither prosecutors, counsel for defense, the accused, witnesses, court staff nor enforcement officers coming under the jurisdiction of the court should be permitted to frustrate its function. Collaboration between counsel and the press as to information affecting the fairness of a criminal trial is not only subject to regulation, but is highly censurable and worthy of disciplinary measures.

Since the state trial judge did not fulfill his duty to protect Sheppard from the inherently prejudicial publicity which saturated the community and to control disruptive influences in the courtroom, we must reverse the denial of the habeas petition. The case is remanded to the District Court with instructions to issue the writ and order that Sheppard be released from custody unless the State puts him to its charges again within a reasonable time.

It is so ordered.

Mr. Justice BLACK dissents.[46]

The Right of Fair Trial and Free Press

At long last the American Bar Association has taken account of the prevalence of mob pressures brought to bear upon courts by way of the media. In 1969 the Association published a monograph on *The Rights of Fair Trial and Free Press.*[47] The Manual is a cautious document. The standards proposed are summarized as follows.[48]

- The standards are directed primarily to lawyers, court and law enforcement personnel, and not to the press.
- They specify types of prejudicial information which lawyers participating in a case *should not release,* because such information may not be admissible in court and could influence the outcome of the trial.
- They provide *for the prompt release* from official sources of basic facts about crimes committed and circumstances surrounding them.
- They urge law enforcement agencies to follow the same rules as apply to lawyers with respect to withholding of specified prejudicial information before trials.

[46]In October 1966, Dr. Sam Sheppard was retried for the murder of his wife. Dr. Sheppard did not take the witness stand at the second trial, and the trial judge properly admonished the jury that Sheppard's failure to take the stand was within the defendant's constitutional rights and that the jurors were not to "draw any inference from his failure to testify."

The judge gave the case to the jury at 10:30 a.m. on November 16. The jury returned a verdict of not guilty at 10:15 p.m. the same day. "At the verdict, Mr. Sheppard slammed his hand on the table at which he sat with a resounding blow of exultation, then put his head in his left hand and broke into shoulder-shaking sobs." *New York Times,* November 17, 1966, p. 1, col. 1.

Dr. Sam Sheppard died in Columbus, Ohio, on April 7, 1970, at the age of 46. *New York Times,* April 7, 1970, p. 45, col. 1.

[47] *The Rights of Fair Trial and Free Press,* an Information Manual for the bar, news media, law enforcement officials and courts. Prepared and published by The American Bar Association Legal Advisory Committee on Fair Trial and Free Press, 1155 East Sixtieth Street, Chicago, Illinois 60637.

[48]*Id.* at p. 10.

They do not impose restrictions upon the freedom of the media to publish information they are able to obtain through their own initiative, or to criticize law enforcement or the courts.

The Manual decidedly reflects the reasonable position of the media that they publicize only what the police, the sheriffs, the bailiffs, the court attendants, the lawyers, and the judges do and say—for publication. Therefore, it is understandable that the Manual directs itself to the conduct of law enforcement and judicial officials more than it does toward the conduct of the media.

It is true that a judge has the inherent power to maintain order, decorum, and propriety within the courtroom and within the precincts of the courtroom. A spectator in the courtroom who becomes boisterous, or one who even engages in audible whispers or assumes contemptuous facial expressions, can be controlled by the judge and if necessary can be ejected from the premises. The law with respect to litigants and lawyers who become boisterous in the courtroom is just now in the making.[49]

---

[49]Seven persons were charged with crossing state lines with the intent to incite a riot at the 1968 Democratic National Convention in Chicago. In United States v. Dellinger, in the Federal District Court in Chicago, some of the accused and their defense counsel, William M. Kunstler and Leonard I. Weinglass, were boisterous in the courtroom. They assumed that they could not get justice and therefore were entitled to disrupt the proceedings by referring to Judge Julius J. Hoffman as a racist, fascist pig, a Nazi, and other epithets. There were shoving and shouting matches involving the accused, the marshalls, the spectators, and counsel for both sides.

At the close of the four-and-a-half months of trial, the jury, after 40 hours of deliberation, found Lee Weiner and John Froines not guilty as to all counts and David T. Dellinger, Rennie C. Davis, Thomas E. Hayden, Abbie Hoffman, and Jerry C. Rubin not guilty of conspiracy to cross state lines with intent to incite a riot but guilty of individually crossing state lines with intent to incite a riot and then taking affirmative actions toward that end. Judge Hoffman sentenced the five to five years in prison, $5,000 fine, and all costs of prosecution. Judge Hoffman denied bail on the ground that the five were dangerous men. New York Times, February 19, 1970, p. 1, col. 3; New York Times, February 21, 1970, p. 1, col. 1.

Judge Hoffman also had sentenced the attorneys and three of the seven for contempt. William M. Kunstler received a total of four years, thirteen days, and the others to lesser but severe penalties. New York Times, February 16, 1970, p. 1, col. 4.

The United States Court of Appeals for the Seventh Circuit fixed bail at a total of $155,000. Under the provisions of the 1968 Bail Reform Act, $15,500 was paid into court to satisfy the obligations. This took place shortly after the sentencing and denial of bail by Judge Hoffman occurred. The case is now on appeal to the Seventh Circuit Court of Appeals. New York Times, March 1, 1970, p. 1, col. 5.

Meanwhile, in Illinois v. Allen, 397 U.S. 337 (1970), the United States Supreme Court reaffirmed the power of a judge to remove a boisterous defendant from the courtroom if the defendant's presence would seriously obstruct the trial. In Allen, the defendant was argumentative and boisterous, refused appointed counsel, threatened the life of the judge, kept talking so as to interrupt the trial, and kept up a stream of invectives aimed at the judge, the witnesses, and the attorneys. Allen was excluded from the courtroom during the State's case-in-chief except for a few times when he was brought in for identification. At those times, he began again to assault the judge with vile and abusive language. He was again removed to a separate room, where he was restrained.

The Supreme Court, noting that exclusion of an accused from the courtroom should occur only where absolutely necessary, nonetheless approved of the trial judge's actions. (*continued*)

When a news reporter or a radio reporter with his recording machine or a television reporter with his camera insists upon presence in the courtroom or in the adjacent corridors and rooms in such a way as to disrupt the proceedings, as was clear in the case of Sheppard, then the First Amendment to the Constitution of the United States is immediately involved. Congress shall make no law . . . abridging the freedom of speech, or the press. The Sixth Amendment is also involved. It provides for a *public* trial. But it also provides in criminal cases for trial by an "impartial jury." There's the rub. How to protect the right of the public to know what goes on in the courtroom and at the same time how to protect the accused against the hysteria of the mob. It is a difficult question. It is such a question as does not lend itself to instantaneous ultimate resolution. It is a conflict more likely to be solved as the society matures and as a decent respect for the rights of the accused curbs the excesses of journalistic enterprise.

QUESTIONS

1. What is the difference in function between a grand jury and a jury?

2. What is the authority for the Rules of Criminal Procedure for the U.S. District Courts? For the Federal Rules of Civil Procedure?

3. What is the function of pre-trial procedure?

4. Who are the principal actors in a trial? What are their several and separate roles?

5. Why do you think the jury has been all but abolished in England and is still widely used in the United States of America. With regard to the jury, which system do you prefer? Why?

6. Did your idea of why lawyers in the courtroom act the way they do change after you studied Chapter 9? If so, from what before to what after?

In New York, Justice Murtaugh of the State Supreme Court suspended pretrial hearings for thirteen Black Panthers accused of plotting to bomb public places, possession of illegal weapons, attempted murder, and attempted arson. The defendants had refused to restrain themselves. Justice Murtaugh announced that, until the defendants agreed not to disrupt the proceedings by vile and abusive language and demonstrations, there would be no proceedings. *New York Times,* February 26, 1970, p. 1, col. 2. All thirteen had been incarcerated for over a year because they could not make bail ranging from $50,000 to $100,000. After several meetings, the defendants accepted Justice Murtaugh's conditions and the proceedings continued. *New York Times,* March 31, 1970, p. 1, col. 5.

The American College of Trial Lawyers has issued a report calling upon judges to ban from their courts, for as much as six months, any lawyer who wilfully contributes to disorder in the courtroom. The report says, "Although disruptive tactics have occurred occasionally in the past, they now threaten to become systematized and popularized among small but militant segments of the profession and the general public." The report recommends that judges should cite lawyers for contempt whenever, and as soon as, lawyers misbehave, rather than waiting until the trial ends, as Judge Hoffman had done. *New York Times,* July 23, 1970, p. 27.

7. Do you think that judges should be required to admit television cameras in the courtroom? Whatever your answer, why?

8. Do you approve of our society's leaving the discipline of lawyers and judges largely to their own institutions of bar associations and courts, or do you think that legislatures should prescribe laws and penalties for the conduct and misconduct of lawyers and the judges?

9. What is the difference between substantive law and procedural law?

10. Consider only what you have learned about the trial in Chapter 9 and then decide whether concerning the trial, law has controlled environment more than environment has changed law. Give the reasons for your decision.

Epilogue—A Note on the Unique Tenth Commandment

"It may be law, but it's not justice." Many a defeated litigant has sounded the complaint. It is not only about court decisions but also about legislative enactments that the popular distinction is made between law and justice. Some statutes are said to be just, others unjust; but the crieria for the distinction are elusive. The problem of law versus justice divides not only men and women on the street—surprisingly articulate when interviewed without warning by ambulatory television and radio reporters—but also scholars, ancient and modern. The issue emerges in the expressions of rulers and statesmen of old.

"To resist him that is set in authority is evil." So runs one of the maxims preserved now for more than 4000 years from Ptahhotep, one of Egypt's great administrators.[1] If resistance to authority (law) is evil, then obedience of law is good. Justice is good. Thus, quickly, we have come to a simplistic concept of justice: it consists in conformity to law.

This is the positive law theory, which holds that justice is in those laws which society finds it necessary, expedient, or possible to enforce; justice is what society does to an offender against society; justice is an aspect of society: no society—no justice.[2] Justice, like William James' test of truth, is what works, what gets accepted, in the marketplace of life. Justice and law are one and the same.

This simple equating of justice and law may but beg the question, which is, in this author's view: does justice do some work in society which law does not do? Fuller tentatively offers a definition of law. "A law," he says, "in the most general and comprehensive acceptation in which the term, in its literal meaning, is employed, may be said to be a rule laid down for the guidance of an intelligent being by an intelligent being having power over him."[3] On the other hand, speaking historically, Pound identifies 12 conceptions of law which may be paraphrased and collated by categories.[4].

Deistic: a divinely ordained set of rules for human action or old customs which have proved acceptable to the gods;

Moralistic: a philosophically discovered system of principles ex-
                         pressing the nature of things, to which, therefore, man
                         ought to conform his conduct—an immutable moral
                         code—a reflection of divine reason which determines
                         the "ought";

Sociological: the recorded wisdom of the wise men of old or a
                         body of agreements among men in politically organ-
                         ized society as to their relations with each other, where-
                         by the individual human will may realize the most
                         complete freedom possible consistently with the like
                         freedom of others (such precepts may have been dis-
                         covered philosophically in juristic writing and in judi-
                         cial decisions);

Political-Economic: a body of commands of the sovereign authority or a
                         system of rules imposed on men in society by the
                         dominant class in furtherance, conscious or uncon-
                         scious, of its own interests or the dictates of economic
                         and social rules discovered by observation of what
                         would work and what would not work in administra-
                         tion.

We must lay aside the deistic concept of law since it falls in an area of
belief and therefore eludes analysis. We are reaching, however, for a distinction, if any, between law and justice and may try the moralistic category of
ideas of law with an illustration from the tenth commandment of Moses:
"Thou shalt not covet." Obviously, this commandment is unenforceable by
man against man. Coveting is the unreachable secret of the individual. In
Fuller's terms the commandment could not be law: no being, however intelligent, has power to prevent another being from coveting. And yet there seems
to be something right and proper about not coveting—some element of the
"ought."

Certainly, in a society in which private property is recognized and protected, as in the ancient Hebrew society and in modern western world societies, a rule against covetousness would be useful if a preponderant majority
of the society adhered to the rule, either as voluntary self-discipline or from
fear of divine punishment—no matter which. Coveting is the first step to larceny, to theft, to forceable entry and burglary, to any illegal taking. If the
commandment not to covet were to be universally observed, crimes against
property would not occur. Furthermore, not-to-covet has a practical moral,
as Shakespeare pointed out in "The Rape of Lucrece":

> "Those that much covet are with gain so fond,
> For what they have not, that which they possess
> They scatter and unloose it from their bond,
> And so, by hoping more, they have but less."

Yet the injunction, resting on divine command with the sanction of Moses and of Shakespeare, with all that, is unenforceable. Is it law? No, because it is unenforceable. Is it something else—justice?

The answer may lie in a second theory of justice—the natural right theory. This theory informs us that justice and injustice are not to be equated with law; justice is above law, providing criteria for whether law is good or bad; and—the distinguishing feature of the theory—justice is based on the natural right of each to have his due; justice answers to something more than the needs of law or of society—justice is concern for the needs of man as man.[5] This theory has prestigious proponents: in alphabetical order, Aquinas, Aristotle, Augustine, Blackstone, Cicero, Hegel, Jefferson, Kant, Plato, to name fewer than half of those to whom the meticulous Bird attributes the theory.

Now we put the natural right concept to the test of the tenth commandment. The concept appears to stand up well. The reader will recall from Chapter 1 that there was an earthly model for the Ten Commandments—the ordinary feudal oath, indigenous in the area, by which the earthly lord bound his vassal to him. For Moses to convert it into the foundation for monotheism, the integrity of the family, and the elements of social stability was a stroke of genius. Private property became fundamental in the social order of Old Testament times, legally establishing those who had and those who had not. The tenth commandment supported the ethic of private ownership, but only morally—only in *support* of enforceable law. The tenth commandment was not the only Mosaic protection of private property. There were punishments for the overt offenses which could be observed and proved. The enforcement problem would have been reduced if there had been universal abstention from coveting, but the private-property social order was not dependent upon that abstention. The natural right theory of justice would seem to make justice a good handmaiden of law in a society of the established Hebraic ethic and in modern capitalism, but not a *sine qua non*.

A third concept of justice is the social good theory, which eschews both the equating of justice with law or with man's natural rights. This theory holds that justice derives exclusively from society and consists ultimately in promoting the social good. This theory agrees with positive law in holding justice to be an aspect of society and disagrees with natural right, whose dictum holds that justice is due the individual regardless of law or the social good.[6] Some proponents of this third theory are Bentham, Hume, Mill, Pound, among others. They are not confounded by the question. "How is the social good determined?" The theory accepts the social good as some norm toward which men work together—a good greater than any individual or private good, "achievable only through men acting in common, and one in which individuals can find their own good."

The social good theory is the modern theory. No great ancient name appears among its proponents. It is a theory which arises in the industrial and political turbulence of the eighteenth and nineteenth centuries. Its appeal lies in its political declaration of independence from fatalism, and its danger lies in the threat to the individual from the tyranny of the majority—the democratic state.

The unenforceable tenth commandment would play not even a moral role under the social good theory of justice. Indeed, the tenth commandment might well be considered unjust by the criteria of social good if the society should determine that private ownership of property were not consistent with the social good. Certainly, the tenth commandment would have no place in a society which had determined to be socialistic in the pure form. A rule against coveting would have no place in a social ethic expressed simply, "From each according to his ability, to each according to his need."

When a concept can be buffeted about through the ages, with no abatement of assaults upon its several attributed meanings in modern times, one may properly ask: does the concept of justice earn its salt in the practical affairs of mankind? Is it fair to say, as Falstaff did about honor,

> Well, 'tis no matter; honour pricks me on. Yea, but how if honour prick me off when I come on? how then? Can honour set to a leg? no: or an arm? no: or take away the grief of a wound? no. Honour hath no skill in surgery, then? no. What is honour? a word. What is that word honour? air. A trim reckoning!—Who hath it? he that died o' Wednesday. Doth he feel it? no. Doth he hear it? no. 'Tis insensible, then? yea, to the dead. But will it not live with the living? no. Why? detraction will not suffer it. Therefore I'll none of it: honour is a mere scutcheon:—and so ends my catechism.[7]

The sophistry in Falstaff is disclosed in the opening line: "Well, 'tis no matter; honour pricks me on." Mankind has been pricked on by more than one word which eluded his definition.

Therefore, this author may be pardoned for suggesting that the concept of justice as something beyond and separate from law has long done, and does do, important work in the affairs of men. When Hammurabi caused to be engraved on that stone which now rests in the Louvre, "I established law and justice in the language of the land, thereby promoting the welfare of the people,"[8] he set in stone his intuitive understanding of the social good theory, just as 500 years earlier the Egyptian Ptahhotep with equal certainty espoused the positive law theory. What the great untutored rulers of mankind have known, we articulate slowly in spans of ages.

Modern psychology, not the least that of Sigmund Freud, has taught us the loneliness of the individual.

> ... Against the dreaded outer world one can defend oneself only by turning away in some other direction, if the

difficulty is to be solved single-handed. There is indeed another and better way: that of combining with the rest of the human community and taking up the attack on nature, thus forcing it to obey human will, under the guidance of science. One is working, then, with all for the good of all . . .[9]

Dr. Freud was writing before some of the delusionments which science has brought to us. He was writing before the nihilism and the baffling drive for anarchy in the third quarter of the twentieth century. Obviously, he did subscribe, possibly unwittingly, to the social good theory. But perhaps there is something more poignant in his phrase, "turning away."

Despite man's acquiescence in principles of order,[10] men are coerced by inscrutable law. Men do suffer at the hands of other men. Men do find government as remote and inaccessible as Kafka's *Castle,* and in turning away they must have some place to turn. If the concept of justice is something that every man may claim as his own, as *his* property, as *his* unassailable conviction of what is right, even though he thinks of a right which will come to him some other time in some more blessed future, then who is to say that justice, though it be an illusion to think of it as something other than law, is not useful in the most realistic, pragmatic sense?

REFERENCES

1. Gardiner, Sir Alan, *Egypt of the Pharaohs,* Great Britain, Oxford University Press, 1961, pp. 105-106; Wilson, John A., *The Burden of Egypt,* Chicago, University of Chicago Press, 1951, pp. 91-95.

2. Bird, Otto A., *The Idea of Justice,* New York, Frederick A. Praeger, 1967, pp. 43 *et seq.*

3. Fuller, Lon L., *The Problems of Jurisprudence,* Brooklyn, The Foundation Press, Inc. 1949, p. 122, Temporary Edition.

4. Pound, Roscoe, *An Introduction to the Philosophy of Law,* New Haven, Yale University Press, 1954, Chapter 2 Revised Edition.

5. Bird, *supra,* pp. 118, 119.

6. Bird, *supra,* p. 79 *et seq.*

7. Shakespeare, William, *King Henry IV*—Part I, Act 5, Scene 1.

8. Sarton, George, *A History of Science,* Cambridge, Harvard University Press, 1952.

9. Freud, Sigmund, *Civilization and Its Discontents,* reproduced in Britannica Great Books, Vol. 54, p. 772.

10. Fuller, *supra,* p. 693 *et seq.*

Index

ABORTION
  See Birth Control.
ABSOLUTE LIABILITY
  See also Manufacturer's Liability;
    Torts.
  Case, 230*ff*.
  Commentary, 247.
ADLER, MORTIMER
  on justice, 256.
  on the state, 381-82.
ADMINISTRATIVE LAW
  Generally, 270-83.
  Origins of, 271-72.
ADMIRALTY LAW
  See Maritime Law.
ADVISORY OPINIONS
  See also Case or Controversy;
    Justiciability; Political Questions.
  Cases, 45-49.
  Commentary, 50, 61.
AGENCY SHOP
  See also Labor Law.
  Case, 301.
  Definition of, 279.
AMERICAN BAR ASSOCIATION
  Canons of Professional Ethics, 420-21.
    Reference in case, 433.
  Description of, 420.
  The Right of Fair Trial and Free Press,
    434.
AMERICAN DEMOCRACY
  See also Bonham's Case; Coke, Sir
    Edward.
  Legal foundations of, 25-27.
AMERICAN FEDERATION OF
    LABOR, 273, 281.
AMERICAN LAW INSTITUTE
  See also Restatements.
  Description of, 146.
ANALOGY, REASONING BY
  Cases, 191-96.
  Commentary and explanation, 190-91,
    200-01.

ANDRAE, TOR
  Mohammed: The Man and His Faith
    on evidence, 410.
ANTIGONE (Sophocles' Trilogy, *The
    Oedipus Cycle*), 24, 356.
ANTIGONE QUESTION
  Generally, 355-85.
  Commentary, 380-85.
  Definition of, 357.
ANTITRUST LAWS
  Jurisdiction, and, 39, 388.
  Labor unions, and, 271-82, 295.
APPEALS
  See also Courts; Jurisdiction; Law.
  Generally, 35-36.
  Federal courts, in the, 35.
  Henry II, at the time of, 397.
  Moses, at the time of, 397.
  State courts, in the, 36.
APPORTIONMENT
  Baker v. Carr, 63.
    Aftermath of, 68-69.
  Constitutional Amendment, 77-78.
  Guaranty Clause, 64-65.
  Republican form of government, 64-65.
AQUINAS, THOMAS
  on justice, 256.
ARCHBISHOP OF CANTERBURY
  See Becket, Thomas à; Henry II;
    Lanfranc; Laud.
ARDREY, ROBERT
  The Territorial Imperative, 381, 418.
ARISTOTLE
  on justice, 256.
ARRAIGNMENT, 390.
  See also Criminal Procedure.
ARREST
  See also Criminal Procedure; No
    Knock Law; Search and Seizure;
    Stop and Frisk.
  Administrative, 94-97.
  as a procedural step, 389.

Search incident to, 87.
with a warrant, 87, 114.
without a warrant, 92, 94, 104, 124.

BAR ASSOCIATIONS
See also American Bar Association.
Description of, 420.
BEAN, JUDGE ROY, 397-98.
See also Judging; Justices of the Peace.
BECKET, THOMAS à, 23, 25.
See also Canon Law; Henry II.
BERLE, ADOLF A., JR.
The Twentieth Century Capitalist
Revolution
on judging and leadership, 396.
BILL OF RIGHTS
See also Bonham's Case; Coke, Sir
Edward.
Generally, 81-130.
First Amendment, 30, 111, 304-14,
355-85, 426-36.
Fourth Amendment
See Arrest, Criminal Procedure;
Search and Seizure; Stop and
Frisk.
Fifth Amendment, 111-24.
Sixth Amendment, 111, 404-08, 436.
Seventh Amendment, 111, 404-08.
BIRTH CONTROL
Canon law, and, 17.
Cases and commentary, 56-58.
BONHAM'S CASE, 26, 398.
See also Bean, Judge Roy; Fee Courts;
Justices of the Peace;
Magistrates.
BOWEN, CATHERINE DRINKER
See also Bonham's Case; Fee Courts;
Justices of the Peace.
The Lion and the Throne, 26-27.
BRACTON, 23.
See also English Law.
BREACH OF CONTRACT
See Remedies.
BRYANT, ARTHUR
The Story of England—Makers of the
Realm, 21-22.
BUSHELL'S CASE, 399.

CALVIN, JOHN
Usury, and, 18-19.
CANON LAW (CHRISTIAN LAW)
See also Becket, Thomas à; Henry II;
Law.
Early Christian, 16-17.
Medieval, 17-19.
CANONS OF PROFESSIONAL
ETHICS, 420-21, 433.

CARPENTERS INTERNATIONAL
UNION, 314.
CASE OR CONTROVERSY
See also Advisory Opinions;
Declaratory Judgments.
Generally, 29-31, 49-51.
Criteria, 43-49.
Fictitious suits, 33ff.
Moot cases, 30, 49.
Real disputes, 29-31, 51.
Real party in interest, 29-31, 55.
Ripeness, 29-31, 51.
Standing, 55.
Unripe controversy, 29-31, 49, 51.
CAUSES OF ACTION
See also Case or Controversy; Civil
Procedure; Writ System.
Commentary on and definition of, 53-55,
391-95.
Comparison of contract and tort,
200-05.
CHARLES I, KING OF ENGLAND,
23, 25.
See also Canon Law; English Law;
Roman Law.
CIVIL PROCEDURE
See also Causes of Action; Procedure.
Generally, 391-95.
Discovery (Pre-trial), 393-94.
Federal Rules of Civil Procedure, 392ff.
CIVIL RIGHTS ACT OF 1964
See also Labor Legislation.
Summary, 298.
Text, 351.
CLAYTON ACT
See also Labor Legislation.
Commentary, 276.
Summary, 295.
Text, 337.
CLOSED SHOP
See also Labor Law.
Definition of, 278-79.
CODES
Corpus Juris (Justinian), 18-24, 419.
Hammurabi (Babylonian), 6, 12, 23.
Lex Salica (Germanic), 19-20.
Napoleonic, 20.
XII Tables (Roman), 10-11.
COKE, SIR EDWARD
See also Bonham's Case; Judging;
Justices of Peace.
on acts of Parliament, 25-27.
on fee courts, 398.
Petition of Rights, 112.
COMMON LAW
See Law.
COMMON PLEAS COURT, 35-36.
See also Courts.

COMPLAINT
  See also Procedure; Writ Systems.
  Civil, 392.
  Criminal, 389.
CONDON-WADLIN ACT (NEW
      YORK CIVIL SERVICE LAW
      §108)
  See also Labor Legislation; Taylor
      Law, Transit Workers' Amnesty
      Act.
  Commentary, 333-34.
  Discussion, 320-24.
CONFESSIONS
  See also Bill of Rights; Fifth
      Amendment; Fourteenth
      Amendment.
  Generally, 113-30.
  Omnibus Crime Control and Safe
      Streets Act of 1968, Title II, 127.
CONGRESS OF INDUSTRIAL
      ORGANIZATIONS, 273, 281,
      321.
CONSIDERATION
  See also Contract Formation.
  Cases, 146*ff.*
  Restatement definition, 149.
CONSTITUTION
  See also Bill of Rights; Bonham's Case;
      Coke, Sir Edward.
  Amendments to
    First, 58, 304-14, 355-85, 429-36.
    Fourth
      See Arrest; Criminal Procedure;
          Search and Seizure.
    Fifth, 113-24.
    Sixth, 403-08, 436-37.
    Seventh, 404-05.
    Fourteenth, 111*ff,* 304-14, 330,
        400-03, 407-08, 429-34.
    Fifteenth
      Statute implementing, 298.
  Articles of
    Article I
      Section 2, 72*ff.*
      Section 5, 72*ff.*
      Section 8, Cl. 3 (Commence clause
          and labor disputes), 275*ff.*
      Separation of powers under, 61*ff.*
    Article II
      Separation of powers under, 61*ff.*
    Article III
      Section 2 (Jurisdiction of federal
          courts), 34-41.
      Separation of powers under, 61*ff.*
    Article IV
      Section 4 (Republican form of
          government), 63*ff.*

    Article V
      Convention to amend the
          Constitution, 77-78.
    Full faith and credit clause, 31-33,
        37-39.
    Interpretation of, 79.
    Separation of powers, 61-79.
    Unions and
      Governmental employees strikes,
          317-36.
      Picketing, 304-14.
CONTRACT FORMATION
  See also Contracts; Remedies.
  Generally, 132-60.
  Acceptance, 144.
  Capacity, 136.
  Consideration, 146.
  Identity of Agreement, 152.
  Intent, 138.
  Legality of subject matter, 154.
  Mutual mistake, 153.
  Mutuality of obligation, 150.
  Offer, 142.
  Statute of Frauds, 156.
CONTRACTS
  See also Contract Formation;
      Remedies.
  Generally, 132-197.
  Damages
    See Remedies.
  Executed, 135.
  Executory, 135.
  Freedom of, 135.
  History of, 134-36.
  Planning, and, 133-36.
  Remedies
    See Remedies.
  Restatements of
    See Restatement.
  Social contract, 135.
  Yellow-dog contract, 275-76, 293.
CONTINENTAL CONGRESS, 369.
CONTRACEPTION
  See Birth Control.
COPERNICUS, 4.
COOLIDGE, CALVIN
  on labor law, 318-19, 329.
CORPUS JURIS, 11, 18-24, 419.
COURTS
  See also Appeals; Fee Courts;
          Jurisdiction; Justices of the
          Peace; Magistrates.
  Generally, 29-79.
  Autonomy of, 49.
  Introduction to, 29.
  Fee Courts, 26-27, 398.
  Federal system of, 35-36.

Special system of, 36.
State system of, 35-36.
COZZENS, JAMES GOULD
   The Just and the Unjust
   on the jury, 406.
CREON (Sophocles' Trilogy, *The
   Oedipus Cycle)*, 356-57, 382.
   See also Antigone; Antigone Question;
      Sophocles.
CRIMES
   See also Criminal Law; Criminal
      Procedure; Criminal Statutes.
   Narrowly construed, 86.
   Offenses, 82.
   Strictly defined, 83.
CRIMINAL LAW
   See also Crimes; Criminal Procedure;
      Criminal Statutes.
   Generally, 81-131.
   Confessions, 111-130.
   Enforcement of, 82-83, 388-91.
CRIMINAL PROCEDURE
   See also Arrest; Crimes; Criminal
      Law.
   Generally, 388-91.
   Arraignment, 390.
   Arrest, 389.
      See also Arrest.
   Complaint, 389.
   Discovery, 390.
   Federal Rules of, 388-91.
   Grand jury, 389.
   Indictment, 390.
   Plea, 390.
CRIMINAL STATUTES
   Omnibus Crime Control and Safe
      Streets Act of 1968
      Confessions, 127.
   Wiretapping, 103.
CROMWELL, OLIVER, 23.
CROSS EXAMINATION
   Generally, 408-19.
   Perjurer, of the, 413.
   Sham witness, of the, 415.
   Wellman, Francis L.,
      The Art of Cross Examination, 413.
CRUEL AND UNUSUAL
      PUNISHMENTS, 129.
   See also Raleigh, Sir Walter.
CUSTODY
   Nature of in confession cases, 122-23.

DAMAGES
   See Remedies.
DEBT, WRIT OF, 53.
   See also Causes of Action; Writ System.
DECALOGUE, 7-9.
   See also Ten Commandments.

DECLARATORY JUDGMENT ACT,
   46.
DECLARATORY JUDGMENTS, 46,
   56, 70.
   See also Advisory Opinions; Case or
      Controversy.
DEFAULT JUDGMENTS, 32, 38.
DESEGREGATION
   Generally, 58-62.
   "All deliberate speed," 61-62.
DISCOVERY
   Civil Procedure, 394.
   Criminal Procedure, 390.
DISSENT, RIGHT OF
   Generally, 355-85.
DOMESDAY BOOK, 26.
DOOLEY, MR.
   See Dunne, Finley Peter.
DOYLE, SIR ARTHUR CONAN, 388.
DUE PROCESS OF LAW
   See also Bill of Rights; Constitution.
   Definition of the standards under the
      Fourteenth Amendment, 111-13.
DUNNE, FINLEY PETER
      (Mr. Dooley)
   on juries and expert testimony, 412.

ECONOMICS
   Relation to law, 15-16, 19, 137-38,
      255-68, 332-36.
EDWARD I
   Judicial scandals at the time of, 425.
ELIZABETH I, QUEEN OF
      ENGLAND, 25.
   See also Bonham's Case; Coke, Sir
      Edward; Foundations of
      American Democracy.
EMPIRE
   Relation to law, 3, 5-6, 8, 18, 21, 24-25,
      35, 395-99.
ENGLISH LAW
   See also Canon Law; Coke, Sir
      Edward; Law.
   Early history of, 19-20.
   Judges, and, 424-25.
   Medieval history of, 21-27.
EQUITAS, 15.
EQUITY
   Generally, 14-16.
   Contract remedies in, 183-90.
   Historical development of, 14-16.
EXECUTED CONTRACT, 135.
EXECUTIVE ORDER 10988,
      EMPLOYEE-MANAGEMENT
      COOPERATION IN THE
      FEDERAL SERVICE
   Summary, 319.

Text, 352.
EXECUTORY CONTRACT, 135.
EXPECTATION INTEREST
    See also Remedies.
    Cases, 162-67.
    Discussion, 161.
EVIDENCE
    See Cross examination; Witnesses.
EXPERT WITNESSES, 408.
    Cross-examination of, 415-16.

FEE COURTS, 26, 398.
    See also Bean, Judge Roy; Bonham's
        Case; Justices of the Peace;
        Magistrates.
FICTION
    See also Procedure.
    Amelioration of law by
        in contract, 190-96, 201-06, 227-34,
            243-47.
        in Roman law, 13-14.
        in tort, 201-06.
FICTITIOUS SUITS, 33, 37.
    See also Case or Controversy.
FINGERPRINTS, 124.
FORCE
    Law, and, 6, 128.
FROST, ROBERT
    on boundaries, 30.
FULL FAITH AND CREDIT, 31, 38-39.

GABRIEL
    as seen by Mohammed, 410.
GAIUS, 11, 18, 419.
    See also Codes.
GALILEO, 129-30.
GENERAL AVERAGE, LAW OF, 9-10.
GILBERT AND SULLIVAN
    on jury trials, 406.
GOMPERS, SAMUEL, 272.
GOVERNMENT EMPLOYEES
    Right to strike, and, 317-36.
GRAND JURY, 389-90.
    See also Jury.
GREECE, ANCIENT
    Cities, of, 11, 14.
    Gods and law, in, 12.
    Maritime law, in, 9-10.
    Separation of powers, in, 50.

HAMMURABI
    See Codes; Empire.
HEBREW LAW, 9-12, 50, 125, 395-97.
HEILBRONER, ROBERT
    The Making of Economic Society, 6, 134.

HENRY II
    See also Becket, Thomas à; Canon
        Law; English Law.
    Development of the grand jury system,
        and, 389-90.
    Judicial institutions, and, 424.
    Lanfranc, and, 23.
    Organization of courts, and, 397.
HENRY III
    Judicial institutions at the time of, 424.
HIRING HALLS
    Definition of, 280.
HOFFA, JAMES, 282, 333, 413.
HOLDSWORTH, SIR WILLIAM A.
    A History of English Law
        on judges, 424-25.
HOLMES, OLIVER WENDELL, JR.
    Consistency in law, 252.
    Logic in law, 200.
    on free speech, 30.
    on labor unions, 319-20.
HOMESTEAD STEEL STRIKE, 273-74.
HUGHES, CHARLES EVANS
    on the Constitution, 79.
    on Supreme Court vote-casting—"The
        Man on the Flying Trapeze," 78.

INDICTMENT, 390.
    See also Criminal Procedure.
INDUSTRIAL PEACE COMMISSION,
    335-36.
INDUSTRIAL REVOLUTION
    See also Economics.
    Relation to law, 332-33.
INHERENTLY DANGEROUS
            INSTRUMENTALITY
    See also Absolute Liability;
        Manufacturer's Liability;
        Negligence; Torts.
    Cases, 206-220.
    Commentary, 220-23, 247-53.
INJUNCTIONS
    See also Unions.
    in contract, 188-90.
    in labor law, 275*ff*.
INNS OF COURT, 26, 419.
INTERROGATIONS
    See also Confessions.
    Generally, 113-30.
INTERSTATE COMMERCE
            COMMISSION, 272.
INTERNATIONAL BROTHERHOOD
            OF TEAMSTERS
    See also Hoffa, James; Unions.
    Case, 311.

JACKSON, ANDREW
    on separation of powers, 79.

JAMES, WILLIAM
  on society, 274, 335.
JEFFERSON, THOMAS
  See also Advisory Opinions.
  on separation of powers, 44, 71.
  on the state, 312.
JETTISON, LAW OF, 9-10.
JETHRO
  on judging, 397.
JOHNSON, SAMUEL
  on lawyers, 413.
JUDGES
  See also Courts; Fee Courts; Judging;
    Justices of the Peace; Trials.
  Functions of
    at trial, 395-403.
    at pre-trial, 393-94.
  Names of
    Bean, Judge Roy (Law West of the
      Pecos), 397-98, 418.
    Brus, Robert (First Chief Judge of
      King's Bench), 424.
    Fortas, Abe (First Justice to resign
      from the United States Supreme
      Court), 425-26.
    Haynsworth, Clement F. (Denied
      seat on Supreme Court), 425.
    Hoffman, Julius (Judge at Chicago
      trial), 435.
    Holmes, Oliver Wendell, 30, 200, 252,
      319-20.
    Hughes, Charles Evans, 78, 79.
    Manton, Martin T. (Convicted for
      accepting bribes), 425.
    Marshall, John (First Chief Justice of
      the United States Supreme
      Court), 16, 79.
    Warren, Earl (Chief Justice of the
      United States Supreme Court),
      125, 425-26.
  Power to maintain order and decorum
    in the Courtroom, 432-33.
  Thoughts on judges
    Holdsworth, Sir William A., 424-25.
    Pope, Alexander, 412.
JUDICIAL POWER, 41-44.
  See also Case or Controversy.
JUDGING
  See also Judges.
  Appeals to conscience, 255-57.
  at the time of
    American West, 397-98, 418.
    Ancient Greece, 11-13.
    Augustus Caesar, 11, 419.
    Henry II, 23, 389-90, 397, 424.
    Moses, 7-12, 395-97.
  Functions, 393-95, 403, 432-33.

  on judging
    Berle, Adolph A., 396.
    Process of, 247-51.
JUDGMENTS
  by default
    See Default Judgments.
  Extra-territorial effect of, 39-40.
  in rem, 38.
JURISDICTION
  See also Advisory Opinions; Case or
    Controversy; Courts;
    Declaratory Judgments.
  Generally, 31-41.
  Defacto exceptions to, 38-40.
  Federal
    Diversity of citizenship, 40-41.
    Federal question, 40-41.
  in rem, 38.
  Labor disputes, and, 298.
  Money limits, and, 41.
  Personal, 37-40.
  Substantive, 40-41.
    See also Special Courts.
  Territorial, 34-37.
JURY
  Criticism of, 405-07, 412.
  Function at trial
    Bushell's case, 399.
  History of trial by
    Generally, 403-05.
    Germanic origins, 20, 403.
    Henry II, and, 389, 403.
  State Constitutional guarantees of trial
      by
    California, 405.
    Ohio, 405.
    Pennsylvania, 406.
JUSTICE
  Commentary and quotations, 255-57.
  Epilogue—A Note on the Unique Tenth
      Commandment, 438.
JUSTICES OF THE PEACE, 398.
  See also Bean, Judge Roy; Bonham's
    Case; Coke, Sir Edward; Fee
    Courts; Magistrates.
JUSTICIABILITY
  See also Case or Controversy;
    Jurisdiction.
  Criteria, 41*ff.*
  Growing concepts of, 58*ff.*
JUSTINIAN
  See Codes.

KENNEDY, JOHN F.
  Assassination of, 40.
  Executive order 10988 (Employee-
      Management Cooperation in the
      Federal Service)

Commentary, 319.
Text, 352.
KNIGHTS OF LABOR, 273.

LABOR LAW
See also Labor Legislation; Unions.
Agency shop, 279, 301.
Antitrust laws not applicable to unions,
    276, 295.
Closed shop, 278-79.
Dues picketing, 278.
Executive order on Employee-
    Management Cooperation in the
    Federal Service, 319, 352.
Free-rider, 277.
Government employees
    Generally, 317-36.
    Concerning the right to strike
    in the federal service, 319.
    in New York, 320ff.
    in Pennsylvania, 319.
Hiring halls, 280.
Industrial Peace Commission, 335-36.
Injunctions in 276ff, 295ff.
Jurisdiction over labor disputes, 298.
LaFollette Committee Reports, 274.
McClellan Committee Reports, 282.
National Labor Relations Board, 271,
    272, 296, 298-304, 339ff.
Right to work laws
    Case, 301.
    Commentary, 277-78.
Union Shop, 278-79.
Yellow-dog contract, 275-76, 293.
LABOR LEGISLATION
Federal
    Clayton Act
        Discussion, 276, 295.
        Text, 337.
    Civil Rights Act of 1964
        Discussion, 298.
        Text, 351.
    Labor-Management Relations Act
        (Taft-Hartley Act)
        Discussion, 279-80, 297.
        Text, 339.
    Labor-Management Reporting and
        Disclosure Act of 1959
        (Landrum-Griffin Act)
        Discussion, 281-82, 297.
        Text, 345.
    National Labor Relations Act
        (Wagner Act)
        Discussion, 276-77, 296.
        Text, 339.
    Norris-LaGuardia Act
        Discussion, 276, 295.
        Text, 345.

State
    New York Civil Service Law §108
        (Condon-Wadlin Act), 320.
    New York Public Employees Fair
        Employment Act (Taylor Law)
        Amendments to, 332.
        Discussion, 324ff.
    Pennsylvania Labor Relations Act,
        319.
    Transit Workers Amnesty Act (New
        York), 323.
LANDRUM-GRIFFIN ACT
See Labor Legislation.
LANFRANC, 22-25.
See also Archbishop of Canterbury;
    Canon Law.
LAUD, 23.
See also Archbishop of Canterbury;
    Canon Law.
LAW
    Administrative, 271ff.
    Anglo-American, 53, 62.
    Anglo-Saxon, 21-25.
    Antitrust, 39, 276, 337, 388.
    as a substantive body, 13, 54.
    Chinese law, 2.
    Christian
        See Canon Law.
    Common law, 21, 26, 53-54, 198-200,
        220-23, 247-53.
    Historical references
        See also Mythology.
        Generally, Epilogue—A Note on
        the Unique Tenth
        Commandment, 438.
        Asia Minor, 8-11.
        Athelstane, 418.
        Babylon, 5-7.
        Crete, 9-10.
        England, 20-26, 50, 54, 395-426.
        Greek, 9-12, 23-24.
        India, 6.
        Islam, 17-18.
        Mosaic, 7-9, 50, 395-97.
        Norman, 398-99.
        Pagan antiquity, 8-9.
        Rome, 14-21, 23, 26, 419.
        Solon, 10.
    Labor
        See Labor Law.
    Natural law, 15.
    Procedural, 13, 386ff.
    Soviet, 2.
    Statutory, 16, 54.
    Substantive, 13, 16, 54, 247-53, 386-87.
    Theories of
        Epilogue—A Note on the Unique
        Tenth Commandment, 438.

LAW AND
Agriculture, 2.
Dissent, 82, 355-85.
Empire
  See Empire.
Justice, 255-69.
  Epilogue—A Note on the Unique
    Tenth Commandment, 438.
Liberty, 22, 124-31, 380-84.
Logic, 198-200.
Order, 7-9, 22, 124-31, 380-84.
Organization, 3-11.
Planning, 4, 133-36.
Rulership, 76-79, 317-18, 395.
  See also Empire.
Social Change, 4, 7-9.
Technology, 5, 198-253.
Territory, 23, 34-37.
  See also Empire.
Words, 1-5, 13.
LAWS OF NATIONS, 15.
LAWYERS
on cross examination, 413-18.
Professional responsibilities of, 418-24.
LEGAL FICTION
See Fiction.
LEGISLATION
  See also Labor Legislation.
Amelioration of law by, 16, 127, 131,
  201-04, 227-34, 271-72.
Example of modern, 40, 52, 181-82,
  270-354.
LEWIS, JOHN L., 274.
LEX SALICA
See Codes.
LIBERTY, 22, 124-31, 380-84.
LINCOLN, ABRAHAM
Cross examination of a witness, 413-15.
LIQUIDATED DAMAGES
See Remedies.
LOFTON, JOHN
  Justice and the Press
  on the media and law, 426.

McCLELLAN, SENATOR JOHN
Investigation of labor relations, 282.
MACK THE KNIFE
  See also Criminal Procedure.
Relation to criminal procedure, 388.
MAGISTRATES
  See also Courts; Fee Courts; Judges;
    Justices of the Peace.
Roman times, in, 11, 14-15.
MAGNA CHARTA, 27, 406.
MAINE, SIR HENRY
  Ancient Law
    Equity, 14-16.
    Judging in Greece, 11-12.

Legal fiction, 13-14.
Legislation, 18, 131.
Role of ritual in procedure, 12-13.
MAITLAND, FREDERICK
Roman components in English law,
  22-25.
MANN, THOMAS
  The Tables of the Law
    Law and conduct, 8-9.
    Moses and Hammurabi's Code, 23.
    Moses and judging, 7-12, 395.
    Self-help, 9, 12.
MANUFACTURER'S LIABILITY
  See also Absolute Liability; Inherently
    Dangerous Instrumentality;
    Negligence; Torts.
  Generally, 198-254.
  Analysis of, 220-23.
  Based on negligence, 198-223.
  Commentary and predictions on,
    247-53.
  without fault, 223-53.
MARITIME LAW
Jettison and general average, 9-10.
MARTEL, CHARLES
Defeat of Moslems in 732, 18.
MASS MEDIA
Judicial process and, 426*ff*.
MARSHALL, JOHN, CHIEF JUSTICE,
  16, 79.
MEAD, WILLIAM
Trial of, 399.
MENNINGER, KARL
  The Crime of Punishment
    on revenge, 427.
MOHAMMED
Witnessing a vision, 410.
MITIGATION OF DAMAGES
See Remedies.
MOOT CASES, 30, 49.
  See also Case or Controversy.
MOSAIC LAW
  See also Appeals; Judges; Judging;
    Law; Moses.
  Compared to Canon law, 23.
  Compared to pagan law, 17.
  Compared to sovereign law, 22.
  Concern for individual liberties, 125.
  Self-help, and, 9-12.
  Social change, and, 4, 7-9.
MOSES
Indivisibility of a single god, 8.
Judging, and, 7-12, 395.
Ten Commandments, and (law as a
  molder of society), 4, 7-9.
MUNSTERBERG, HUGO
  On the Witness Stand, 410-11.
MURRAY, PHIL, 274.

See also Lewis, John L.; Unions.
MUTUAL MISTAKE
See Contract formation.
MYTHOLOGY AND LAW
  Erda, 395.
  Frica, 395.
  Greek, 395.
  Homeric legend, 12, 395.
  Norse, 395.
  Themis, 12, 395.
  Wotan, 395.
  Zeus, 12, 395.

NADER, RALPH
  Unsafe at Any Speed, 221.
NAOMI
  A Biblical example of territoriality and
    law, 34.
NAPOLEONIC CODE
  See Codes; *see also* Empire.
NATIONAL LABOR RELATIONS ACT
    (WAGNER ACT)
  See Labor Legislation.
NATIONAL LABOR RELATIONS
    BOARD
  Case law, and, 274*ff,* 298-304.
  See also Labor Law; Labor
    Legislation.
NEGLIGENCE
  See also Absolute Liability;
    Manufacturer's Liability; Torts.
  Comparison to contracts, 198-206.
  Definition of, 199.
NEIBUHR, REINHOLD
  The Structure and Nature of Empires
    on force and government, 6, 128.
NEW YORK EMPLOYEES FAIR
    EMPLOYMENT ACT
    (TAYLOR LAW)
  See Labor Legislation.
NEW YORK SANITATION WORKERS'
    STRIKE, 329-32.
NEW YORK TEACHERS' STRIKE,
    326-29.
NEW YORK TRANSIT WORKERS'
    STRIKE, 320-24.
NEXUM, 134-35.
  See also Contract.
NISI PRIUS, 35-36.
  See also Appeals; Courts.
NO CRIME WITHOUT A LAW, 83-85.
NO KNOCK LAW, 130.
NOLO CONTENDERE, 390.
  See also Criminal Procedure.
NORMAN CONQUEST, 19-22, 396-97.
  See also William the Conqueror.
NORRIS-LaGUARDIA ACT
  See Labor Legislation.

OATHS
  Medieval jury oaths, 19-20.
  Promissory oaths and contract, 134.
OEDIPUS REX (Sophocles' Trilogy,
    The Oedipus Cycle), 24.
  See also Antigone; Creon; Sophocles.
OMNIBUS CRIME CONTROL AND
    SAFE STREETS ACT OF 1968
  Confessions, 127.
  Wiretaps, 103.
ORDER
  Liberty, and, 22, 124-31, 380-84.
ORGANIZATION OF COURTS
  See also Appeals; Courts.
  Federal system, 35-36.
  Henry II, at the time of, 397.
  Moses, at the time of, 7-12, 395.
  State system, 35-36.

PARRY, EDWARD ABBOTT
  See also Judges; Witnesses.
  What the Judge Thought, 411.
PEACHUM, MRS. *(Three Penny Opera*
    by Bertholdt Brecht)
  on the role of law, 3.
PENN, WILLIAM
  See also Judging.
  Trial of, 399.
PLEADINGS
  See also Causes of Action; Procedure;
    Writ System.
  American system, 392-94.
  English system, 53-55, 392.
POLITICAL QUESTIONS
  See also Advisory Opinions; Case or
    Controversy; Separation of
    Powers.
  Generally, 29-79.
  Cases, 33, 44, 63, 70, 72, 76-79.
POLICEMANSHIP, 81-83, 125-26.
POLLOCK AND MAITLAND
  History of English Law
  Early Christian law, 19-24.
  Early English law, 19-24, 26.
  Jury system and its origins, 19, 389-90.
POUND, ROSCOE
  Legal Immunities of Labor Unions, 333.
POWELL, ADAM CLAYTON
  Case concerning, 72.
PRIVITY
  Defined, 205, 221.
PROBABLE CAUSE, 92, 93.
  See also Arrest, with and without a
    warrant; Criminal Procedure;
    Search and Seizure; Stop and
    Frisk.

PROCEDURE
  See also Civil Procedure; Criminal
    Procedure.
  Generally, 12-13, 388-95.
  At the time of
    American West, 397-98, 418.
    Henry II, 23, 389-90, 397, 424.
    Moses, 7-12, 397.
    Rollo (Norman), 396-97.
    William Penn, 399.
  Role of ritual, and, 12-13.
  Self-enforcing, law is not, 11-13, 82,
    387.
  Self-help, 12-13.
PROFESSIONAL RESPONSIBILITY
  American Bar Association Canons of
    Professional Ethics, 420-21, 433.
  American Bar Association Right of Fair
    Trial and Free Press, 434.
  Hippocratic Oath and tradition, 419.
  Judge, of the, 424.
  Lawyer, of the, 419.
  Media, of the, 426.
PROFESSIONALISM
  See also Bar Association.
  History of, 11, 419-20.
PROMISSORY ESTOPPEL, 191-192.
  See also Remedies by Analogy to
    Contract.
PROMISSORY OATHS, 134.
PROSPECTIVITY; PROSPECTIVE
    APPLICATION OF
    CONSTITUTIONAL RIGHTS,
    427-28.

QUILL, MICHAEL, 321-22.

RALEIGH, SIR WALTER
  See also Coke, Sir Edward.
  Sentence of, 25, 129.
RAMSES II, 7.
REAL DISPUTE, 29-31, 51.
  See also Case or Controversy.
REAL PARTY IN INTEREST, 29-31,
    55.
  See also Case or Controversy.
REGULATORY BODIES
  History of, 274-75.
RELIANCE INTEREST
  See Remedies.
REMEDIES
  Generally, 160-96.
  Expectation interest, 161, 162-67.
  Injunctions, 188-90.
  Liquidated damages, 172-77.
  Mitigation of damages, 177-83.
  Reliance interest, 161, 167-70.
  Restitution interest, 161, 170-72.

Specific performance
  Generally, 183-88.
  Personal property, 185.
  Real property, 183.
REMEDIES BY ANALOGY TO
    CONTRACT
  Generally, 190-91.
  Promissory Estoppel, 191-92.
  Quasi Contract, 192-96.
REPLEVIN, 53-54.
  See also Causes of Action; Writ system.
REPUBLICAN FORM OF
    GOVERNMENT
  See Apportionment.
RES IPSA LOQUITUR, 223-27, 247-48.
RESTATEMENT
  Contracts, of
    Consideration, 149.
    Offer and acceptance, 146.
    Undisclosed misunderstanding, 153.
  Torts, of
    Section 402A, 241, 246, 247.
RIGHT OF FAIR TRIAL AND FREE
    PRESS, THE, 434.
RIGHT TO WORK LAWS
  Case, 301.
  Discussion, 277-78.
RIPE CASES, 29-31, 49-51.
  See also Case or Controversy; Moot
    Cases.
RITUAL, ROLE OF, 12-13.
  See also Procedure.
ROLLO, DUKE
  See also Procedure; William the
    Conqueror.
  Development of English procedure from
    Norman law, 396-97.
ROMAN LAW
  Ancient procedures and rituals, 12-13.
  Fictions, in the, 13-14.
  History of, 10-27.
  Professionalism, and, 11, 419-20.
ROOSEVELT, FRANKLIN DELANO
  Labor relations, and, 274, 329.
ROUSSEAU, JEAN JACQUES
  Social contract, 135.
RULERSHIP
  See also Judging.
  Commentary on law, and, 76-79, 395.
RUNNYMEDE, BATTLE OF
  Issuance of the Magna Charta and its
    relation to trial by jury, 406.
RUTH
  A Biblical example of territorialty and
    law, 34.

SALEM WITCHCRAFT TRIALS,
    427-28.

See also Trials.
SCOTT, AUSTIN
on law, 40.
SEARCH AND SEIZURE
   See also Arrest; Criminal Procedure;
      No Knock Law; Stop and Frisk.
   Administrative, 94-97.
   Electronic, 98-103.
   Search incident to arrest, 87.
   without a warrant, 87, 92, 94, 98, 104,
      124.
SELF-HELP
   See also Procedure; Ritual.
   at the time of
      Ancient Rome, 11-13.
      Modern contract theory, 134.
      Moses, 12, 24.
SELF-INCRIMINATION
   See also Confessions; Interrogations.
   Privilege against
      Cases concerning, 113-24.
      Commentary, 124-30.
      Fifth Amendment
         See Bill of Rights; Constitution.
SEPARATON OF POWERS
   See also Advisory Opinions; Case or
      Controversy; Political Questions.
   Cases, 44-46, 63-68, 70-72, 72-76.
   Commentary, 49-50, 76-79.
   Relation to administrative bodies,
      271-72.
SHAYS, DANIEL
   Rebellion and law, 318.
SMITH, ADAM
   See also Economics.
   Wealth of Nations, 7.
SOCIETY AND LAW
   Types of societies
      Command, 6-7.
      Market, 6-7.
      Status, 6-7.
SOPHOCLES
   See also Antigone; Creon.
   The Oedipus Cycle, 24, 356-57, 382.
SPECIAL COURTS, 36.
   See also Courts.
SPECIFIC PERFORMANCE
   See Remedies.
STANDING
   See Case or Controversy.
STARE DECISIS, 200.
   See also Common Law; Law.
STATUTE OF FRAUDS, 159
   Personal property, 157.
   Real property, 156.
STEELWORKERS ORGANIZING
      COMMITTEE, 276-77.

STOP AND FRISK
   See also Arrest; Criminal Procedure;
      Search and Seizure.
   Cases, 104, 111.
   Commentary, 124-30.

TAFT-HARTLEY ACT (LABOR-
      MANAGEMENT
      RELATIONS ACT)
   See Labor Legislation.
TAYLOR LAW (NEW YORK PUBLIC
      EMPLOYEES FAIR
      EMPLOYMENT ACT)
   See Labor Legislation.
TEAMSTERS, INTERNATIONAL
      BROTHERHOOD OF, 282,
      311.
TEN COMMANDMENTS, 7-12, 318.
   See also Hebrew Law; Mosaic Law.
THEMIS, 12, 395.
   See also Judging.
THOREAU, HENRY DAVID
   on civil disobedience, 318.
THREEPENNY OPERA
   Mrs. Peachum concerning law, 3.
   Mack the Knife concerning procedure,
      388.
TORTS
   See also Absolute Liability;
      Manufacturer's Liability;
      Negligence.
   Generally, 198-254.
   Definition of, 199.
   Manufacturer's Liability,
      Negligence, under doctrines of,
      200-01, 206-20.
      without fault, 223-47.
   Relation between contracts, and, 200-07.
TOYNBEE, ARNOLD
   on man and nature, 5, 398.
TRANSIT WORKERS' AMNESTY ACT
   See Labor Legislation.
TRANSIT WORKERS' UNION (NEW
      YORK), 320-25.
TRIALS
   See also Courts; Judges; Judging;
      Lawyers; Witnesses.
   Generally, 395-418.
   Conduct of the
      Judge, 395-403, 424-26.
      Jury, 399, 403-07.
      Lawyer, 204-06, 408-24.
      Media, 429-37.
      Witness, 408-413.
   Public and open
      Cases, 400-03, 429-34.
      Commentary, 434-37.

TRIBONIAN
Corpus Juris, and, 18.
TRUMAN, HARRY S.
Veto of the Taft-Hartley Act, 281.
TWELVE TABLES OF ROMAN LAW,
10-11.
See also Codes.

UNIFORMED SANITATIONMEN'S
ASSOCIATION (NEW
YORK), 329-332.
UNIONS, UNIONISM
See also Labor Law; Labor
Legislation; Names of particular
strikes; Names of particular
unions.
Automation, and, 332-33.
Carnegie, Andrew, and, 274.
Contract, and, 275-76, 293.
Crime, and, 275, 283.
Frick, Henry Clay, and, 274.
History of, 271-83, 332-36.
Legal immunities of, 333.
Tort, and, 275, 290.
Yellow-dog contract, and, 275-76, 293.
UNION SHOP, 278-79.
See also Labor Law.
UNITED FEDERATION OF
TEACHERS, 326-330.
UNITED MINE WORKERS OF
AMERICA, 274, 276.
UNITED STATES SUPREME COURT
See also Bill of Rights; Constitution;
Courts.
Functions of, 35-36, 111-13.
USURY
Changing the law of, 19.

VOLTAIRE, FRANCOIS M.A.
on freedom of speech and action, 355.

WAGNER ACT (NATIONAL LABOR
RELATIONS ACT)
See Labor Legislation.
WAGNER, SENATOR ROBERT, 276.
WARRANT
See Arrest; Search and Seizure; Stop
and Frisk.

WARRANTY, BREACH OF
See also Manufacturer's Liability;
Negligence; Torts.
Cases, 201, 227, 243.
Commentary on tort, and, 204-06.
WARREN, EARL, CHIEF JUSTICE,
125, 425-26.
WELLMAN, FRANCIS L.
The Art of Cross-Examination
a perjurer, 413.
a sham witness, 415.
WILLIAM THE CONQUEROR
Development of grand juries, and, 389.
Development of English procedural law,
and, 396-97.
Development of English substantive
law, and, 21-26.
WILLIAMS, ROGER
Development of American law from
English law, 26.
WIRETAPPING, 98-103.
See also Search and Seizure.
WITNESSES
See also Cross Examination.
Generally, 408-13.
Accuracy of, quotation from Hugo
Münsterberg, On the Witness
Stand, 410-11.
Expert and non-expert, 409.
Lying, 409, 413-15, 416-17.
Sham, 409, 416.
Substitutes for human, 417-18.
WOODWARD, W. E.,
A New American History
on the Salem witchcraft trials, 427-28.
WRIT SYSTEM, 53-55, 392.
See also Causes of Action; Procedure.

YELLOW-DOG CONTRACTS
See Labor Law.

ZOSER
Pyramids—an example of planning and
law, 4, 24.
ZEUS
See also Law; Mythology.
Relation of mythology, God and law,
12, 395.